*Civil War Courts-Martial
of North Carolina
Troops*

Civil War Courts-Martial of North Carolina Troops

ALDO S. PERRY

McFarland & Company, Inc., Publishers
Jefferson, North Carolina, and London

LIBRARY OF CONGRESS CATALOGUING-IN-PUBLICATION DATA

Perry, Aldo S., 1924–
Civil War courts-martial of North Carolina troops / Aldo S. Perry.
    p.   cm.
Includes bibliographical references and index.

ISBN 978-0-7864-6585-9
softcover : acid free paper ∞

1. Courts-martial and courts of inquiry — United States — History —19th century.
2. Courts-martial and courts of inquiry — Confederate States of America.
3. Trials (Military offenses) — United States — History — 19th century.
4. Trials (Military offenses) — Confederate States of America.
5. Soldiers — North Carolina — Biography.
6. Soldiers — Confederate States of America–Biography.   I. Title.
KF7641.P47 2012   973.7'1— dc23   2012003253

BRITISH LIBRARY CATALOGUING DATA ARE AVAILABLE

© 2012 Aldo S. Perry. All rights reserved

*No part of this book may be reproduced or transmitted in any form
or by any means, electronic or mechanical, including photocopying
or recording, or by any information storage and retrieval system,
without permission in writing from the publisher.*

Front cover images © 2012 Shutterstock; cover design by
David K. Landis (Shake It Loose Graphics)

Manufactured in the United States of America

*McFarland & Company, Inc., Publishers
Box 611, Jefferson, North Carolina 28640
www.mcfarlandpub.com*

In memory of Dorothy and in honor of
David, Nathan, Martin and Matthew

Table of Contents

Acknowledgments ix
Abbreviations xi
Preface 1
Introduction: Confederate Duty, Discipline and Death 3

Part I: Army of Northern Virginia

1. History of North Carolina Troops in the Army of Northern Virginia 15
2. Third Corps, Wilcox Division, Branch-Lane-Barry Brigade 20
3. Third Corps, Wilcox Division, Pender-Scales Brigade 42
4. Third Corps, Heth Division, Pettigrew-Kirkland-MacRae Brigade 65
5. Third Corps, Heth Division, Cooke Brigade 88
6. Second Corps, Rodes Division, Daniel-Grimes Brigade 108
7. Second Corps, Rodes Division, Anderson-Ramseur-Cox Brigade 120
8. Second Corps, Early Division, Hoke-Godwin-Lewis Brigade 134
9. Second Corps, Early Division, Garland-Iverson-Johnston-Toon Brigade 149
10. First and Third North Carolina Infantry Regiments 158
11. First Corps 176

Part II: Department of North Carolina

12. History of North Carolina Troops in the
    Department of North Carolina 177
13. Ransom Brigade 180
14. Clingman Brigade 199
15. Martin-Kirkland Brigade 209

Part III: Army of Tennessee

16. History of North Carolina Troops in the Army of Tennessee 243
17. Fifty-Eighth and Sixtieth North Carolina Infantry Regiments 247
18. Twenty-Ninth and Thirty-Ninth North Carolina Infantry Regiments 262
19. Palmer Brigade 268
20. Jackson Brigade 273

Part IV: Attached Units and Local Defense

21. Cavalry 275
22. Artillery 287
23. North Carolina Local Defense Force 307
Epilogue: March Off, Straggle Home 311

Chapter Notes 325
Bibliography 343
Index 349

Acknowledgments

This study has extended over twenty-five rewarding years. Some of the men and women who were so very helpful in the early years have regretfully passed from life and memory, but thankfully most remain in mind. Those still active continue to give gracious guidance to one and all, from the established historian to the beginning genealogist.

Louis Manarin, Hank Jordan, and Matt Brown, compilers and editors of *North Carolina Troops, 1860–1865*, have earned the enduring gratitude of countless researchers for their meticulous effort over many years. Each succeeding volume has surpassed the prior volume in the depth of narrative and accuracy of detail.

Jack Bunch in his *Roster of the Courts-Martial in the Confederate States* has provided a handy reference for Confederate courts-martial which will, no doubt, support further comparative studies on a state by state and unit by unit basis. In addition to saving many hours of searching for a court record, he has untangled the spelling of many a name — no small accomplishment in itself.

Michael Meier, William Lind, and Michael Musick at the National Archives gave invaluable assistance in the search for court-martial records and related material, though at times they cringed a bit when they thought I was intent on going through every box and volume in their care.

Robert Krick, then at the Fredericksburg National Park site, was exceptionally kind while offering encouragement and material for a neophyte thrashing about in the field of Civil War research and Confederate military executions.

All of the staff at the Manuscript Department at Perkins Library, Duke University, were friendly and prompt in locating the over 400 collections that were searched. Mrs. Janie C. Morris deserves special thanks for long ago copying a Confederate Imprint when that violation could lead to a drumhead court and immediate execution at the library entrance. The Perkins librarians were most considerate as they pointed the way through a bewildering complex of wings and floors to the desired stacks.

The Wilson Library at the University of North Carolina at Chapel Hill sheltered many happy hours searching through the Southern Historical Collection, the North Carolina Collection and the Rare Book Department. Though names are no longer recalled the faces and smiles are still before me. Davis Library gave access to published works not otherwise available.

Uncounted afternoons were spent at the University Library, Cambridge, England. This is a copyright library and the shelves are tightly packed with volumes on every aspect of the wars and warfare of the English people.

Weekly visits, over many years, to the State Library of North Carolina, the State

Archives and the Genealogy Department were pleasurable and yielded much detailed material. Larry Odzak and Earl Ijames increased the value and pleasure of each visit.

Special thanks to Dr. Susanna Lee at North Carolina State University and to Dr. Peter Carmichael at West Virginia University for their comment and encouragement. Deepest gratitude to Summerlin Page for her close reading and insightful suggestions of the full text.

And I must certainly mention the immeasurable contributions of my dear friend and research aide Betsy H. Powers and her passion for accuracy.

Abbreviations

AAIG Assistant Adjutant and Inspector General

AAG Assistant Adjutant General

Abs absent

ADC Aide-de-camp

Adj Adjutant

AIG Adjutant and Inspector General

AIGO Office of the Adjutant and Inspector General

AW Articles of War

Awol absent without leave

Co Company

CM Court-martial

Davis Davis Library, UNC Chapel Hill

Ex Executed

GO General Order

GP Governors Papers

HG Home Guard

Inf Infantry

LC Library of Congress

LD Local Defense

NARA National Archive and Records Administration

NCC North Carolina Collection, Wilson Library, UNC Chapel Hill

NCM North Carolina Militia

NCT North Carolina Troops

OR Official Records Union and Confederate Armies

Perkins Manuscript Department, Perkins Library, Duke University

PM Provost Marshal

RG Record Group

Reg Regiment

SHC Southern Historical Collection, Wilson Library UNC Chapel Hill

SHSP Southern Historical Society Papers

SO Special Order

SR Service Record

SS Sharpshooters

TBE To be executed

Vol Volume

Wilson Wilson Library, UNC Chapel Hill

Preface

Life here on earth may be seen as an endless series of chance events. Some are large and significant, often affecting tens of thousands of people; others are small and apparently inconsequential, perhaps not realized by any individual. Large or small, they are often interconnected and bear one upon the other. The vast majority of these happenings usually go unrecorded and unrecognized — but not so in wartime, when a detailed exchange of information and precise record-keeping is vital to reach a victory. The American Civil War was fought when pencil and paper, pen and ink and printer and press were the common means of communicating. Fortunately, many of the documents thus created are available to allow a study of patterns of activity and the trend of wartime events. Supplementing these more or less official records are literally millions of letters written to and from the soldier in the field and friend and family at home. This awesome accumulation of material may be approached by going down a variety of paths, many of which have been trod time and again, while others are barely discernible in the rock and gravel. This study chooses to focus on a subject in the latter group, the military trials and frequent executions of wayward Confederates enrolled in units from the State of North Carolina. The availability of printed service records for these men and the accessibility of extensive manuscript collections greatly aid the entrance to this new path for Civil War study. Still, some men left life and service leaving little more than a spot of bloody ground as their mark in history, so the path is not always clearly posted.

Those who were executed, most often deserters, were among some 450 men enrolled in North Carolina commands who were sentenced to death by a general court-martial or a military court. This study of nearly a half regiment of these men is arranged by army, corps, division and brigade. It opens with the opinions of well-known military leaders on discipline, military courts and execution. This is followed by an outline of Confederate efforts to enroll troops and to take to trial and punishment those who violated their enrollment oath. Regiments within a brigade are presented in numerical order with an analysis of court, absence and casualty activity for selected companies in each regiment. Focus on court activity by company allows for company-to-company comparisons and emphasizes the wide disparity in disciplinary needs within a regiment and brigade. Then follows, in order by court-martial date, the service records for brigade men who were given a death sentence as found in Adjutant and Inspector General records, in General Orders, and correspondence. The name of the soldier, as found in military records, and his unit of service and court-martial date head each section concerning a condemned soldier. For those who were executed, comments on the execution and various comments on the ritual are included. For those who succeeded in avoiding execution, an explanation is provided when known. Supplemental materials that reflect on the discipline, concerns and morale of soldiers in the brigade are placed in chronological order along with the court record. The brigade experience as to absences, courts-martial, deaths and executions is then summarized. North Carolina regiments not assigned to North Carolina brigades are treated by regimental number. For comparative purposes, the experiences of neighboring Confederate states as to enrollments, absences, courts, and executions are listed and comments offered. The study concludes with comment on the potential effect of an earlier resort to the execution stake and on the value to the cause, of the lives that were sacrificed on the execution cross.

In sum, this study provides the foundation for a soldier-to-soldier and unit-to-unit comparison of the effectiveness of military discipline and punishment in the years 1861 to 1865. To aid in the evaluation and to buttress the words, it is often necessary to resort to numbers. A question might be raised: are Confederate records accurate enough to give some degree of credence to numerical comparisons? When an obvious trend is found in the records of an entire company, and that same indication is found in other companies; when sampling supports the same trend; and when letters and anecdotal evidence add further verification, the reply must be affirmative. Granted that when service records note "absent with out Leif," or simply end in the first year or two of the war, a legitimate question can be presented.

Over the course of these many years of research, several thousand copies of manuscript pages have been accumulated along with 35,000 index cards. Somewhere in this material lies hidden the detailed source for a handful of quotes that lack full identification but are included in the text. The quotes could have been easily removed without damage to the main thrust of the work but, they are accurate and do add commentary that offers increased insight and may be useful for some readers, so they are included. In that same light, some quotes contain words that are not presently in accepted usage; they represent the tenor and tone of the times and they are quoted and included as written. Spelling and punctuation in quoted material is printed as found with consideration that writing by firelight, on an uneven surface, with an imperfect instrument may produce a distorted word or letter. When a change is necessary for clarity, the change is indicated. Also keep in mind that a third to a half of the soldiers in some companies were not literate and letters from them were written by others. Files are found that have letters signed with a single name but written in obviously different hands.

Keep in mind three cautionary notes; no distinction is made in men that are listed as deserters, absent without leave or failed to report for duty. All are included in the broad category of absent. If a soldier is absent without leave, returns, and then deserts, it is counted as two absent incidents. Court-martial dates may be the date the court was authorized, convened, or the date when the accused appeared in court. Numbers shown in the died category are for those who died natural deaths, if any death can be considered natural in wartime. Also included are men whose cause of death was not recorded. Accidental deaths are not included. Killed numbers included those killed in battle or dead of battle wounds. Dead counts are the total of dead and killed.

It is hoped that this study provides a foundation for further research into the many factors involved in the disciplining and executing of Confederate troops from North Carolina and from her sister states.

Introduction

Confederate Duty, Discipline and Death

"Follow the strict path of duty"[1]

"Soldiers, like missionaries, must be fanatics," and when either falter or forsake their calling, cause and conviction are seriously weakened.[2] Discipline steadies the wavering and holds the fearful firmly on course. Not all men are suited for the rigors of life in camp and combat. Nor are they able to fully control deliberately inflamed wartime emotions. Discipline controls both fear and passion. The passion to kill for some, the urge to flee for others—each must be restrained. The foundation of that restraint is the certainty that swift punishment awaits all who falter. The execution stake was the wooden linchpin of that certainty in the 1860s. Discipline, buttressed by execution, offered a resource that could lead to an established Confederacy. "In these dark days of the Republic our cause depends solely upon the discipline of the Army and upon the unbroken determination of the men to fight to a successful issue."[3]

As warfare grew more civilized so grew the need for discipline and punishment. Field Marshal Arthur Wellesley, the First Duke of Wellington, explained: "I do not see how you can have an army at all, unless you preserve it in a state of discipline; nor how you can have a state of discipline unless you have some punishment."[4] "The real meaning of punishment, if it means any thing, is the example,— it is to prevent others, by the example of what they see the criminal suffer, from committing that same or a similar offence."[5] There must be some ultimate corporal punishment to support the enforcement of the lesser forms of punishment. Equally, if punishment is not given to the estimated one-fifth of a regiment that requires disciplinary action, a gross injustice is done to the other four-fifths of the men who have obeyed orders and been firm in their duty. That need also held for Confederate North Carolinians; fewer than one-third of all companies required two-thirds of court ordered disciplinary punishment. In November 1813, the Duke commented on the action of a court: "It is very unpleasant to me to be obliged to resist the inclination of the General Court-Martial, to save the life of this soldier; but ... the supposed mercy will turn out to be extreme cruelty, and will occasion the loss of some valuable men to the service."[6] The same comment was made by senior Confederate officers.

The First Counsel of France, Napoleon Bonaparte, was tolerant of a low level of discipline before and after an engagement; but he did execute those who pillaged or plundered. And he was not hesitant in executing ranking army officers and civil administrators who grossly failed in their duties. Killing prisoners of war when they could not be provided for was acceptable.[7] This was not done directly by Confederates, though some would maintain that Confederate prison camps served essentially the same purpose.

Frederick the Great offered his insights into the art of war. After explaining how to select men for his army, "Even if the number [of troops] is attained, however, the men still are worth nothing, if they are undisciplined. Discipline begins with the generals and works down to the drummer boys.... Soldiers can be governed only with sternness and occasionally with severity. Since they greatly outnumber their superiors, they can be held in check only through fear."[8] In a closing admonition, "On no account, however, should there be any relaxation of strict discipline."[9]

The Italian folk hero Giuseppe Garabaldi often fought a larger, better trained and better equipped opponent in his native land. Though his legion was often little more than a partisan band, he demanded obedience and enforced discipline, once ordering that a man be executed for pillaging a chicken from a villager.[10] The skill and aggressive leadership of the flamboyant Italian was recognized by those directing the Federal armies, and he was offered a commission as a major general. This offer was not accepted; apparently Garibaldi insisted on a higher rank.[11]

General George Washington fought near hearth and home with a small number of volunteers and a large number of not-so-willing soldiers, at times on the verge of mutiny. They were drawn from a population about evenly divided on which side they wished to cast their lot. It was essential that desertion be controlled and that citizens not be abused. General Washington was firm in his belief that "discipline is the soul of an army."[12] At times he disagreed with the finding of a court-martial. In a statement that is often repeated verbatim by Confederate generals, he was "unwilling to dissent from judgement [sic] of court martial." But he was "obliged utterly to disapprove these sentences: the punishment being entirely inadequate to the offense."[13]

Colonel Friedrich Wilhelm Ludolf Gerhard Augustin Von Steuben arrived at the encampment at Valley Forge in February 1778, a time of great peril. The well-being of the soldiers and the need for confidence and trust in their officers were paramount in his mind. Men must love those in whose charge they fight. The officers were to gain this affection by treating their men "with every possible kindness."[14] Concern for the welfare of the common soldier, however, did not preclude the need for appropriate punishment. An organizational table for the provost of the army, prepared by Colonel Steuben, includes some sixty men. Among them are four executioners, probably at least one an experienced hangman, though the term may also describe men who would execute all punishment, such as flogging or branding. A mercenary Swiss army made the same provision for an executioner and three helpers some 400 years earlier. Thoughtfully, they also provided for six prostitutes to accompany their men, thereby reducing unrest and aiding in the maintenance of discipline. At least one Federal officer, General Joseph Hooker, also realized the value of that ageless occupation, though less formally structured in his army.

As Confederate soldiers grew accustomed to military service, honor and the fear of bringing humiliation and shame on one's self, one's family, community or state were sufficient to keep them in the fight. The ultimate punishment for blatant deserters was to be drummed out of the service. They were no longer in that better class of men deemed fit to defend the honor of the state. This strong bond of honor, this conviction that Southern soldiers were a better class of men, began to loosen in April 1862 with the passage of the acts authorizing conscription of men into the Confederate army, and extending the service of enrolled volunteers. Not only were many of the conscripts not eager to fight, but some of those whose service was extended lost their initial enthusiasm. The net effect was that the number of men in the army who really did not want to be there increased substantially. A thoughtful comment made soon after passage of the acts proved prophetic: "I do not think Conscript Act will do. Congress has turned up jacks. I fear there will be many deserters."[15]

Two months later, Secretary of War George W. Randolph repeated the alarm: "Our Armies are so much weakened by desertion and by the absence of officers and men without leave, that we are unable to reap the fruit of our victories, and to invade the territory of our enemy. We have reverted to Court Martials & military executions ... but still the evil continues and unless public opinion comes to our aid we shall fail to fill our ranks in time to avail ourselves of the weakness and disorganization of the enemy."[16]

Public opinion was of little aid. Midway through the second year of war an ominous number of men chose to absent themselves from the service. Courts for these men were so burdensome that Special Order #222, Office of the Adjutant and Inspector General, September 1862, released all men awaiting trial for their first desertion. Absences placed a heavy burden on the military, not only in the direct loss from the ranks, but also in guarding men who awaited trial or were being punished. One soldier remarked that in his regiment half of those present were guarding the other half who were in the guardhouse. A corps commander urgently appealed for an additional 50 twenty-pound and 50 twenty-four-pound cannon balls, with chains attached, in order that he might carry out the sentences imposed by courts in his command, a far cry from the intended use of the projectile.[17]

In this analysis no distinction is made between desertion, absence without leave, or failure to report after enrollment. Whatever the description, discipline was challenged, there was a vacant place in the ranks and one less musket aimed at the enemy. Confederate Articles of War stated that a soldier absent from a command, or more than one mile from camp or absent from an assigned post, without proper authority, could be charged as absent without leave. No mention is made of a specific length of time, the absence being sufficient to indicate the intent. As absences increased orders were issued that an absence of more than a week or ten days must be recorded as desertion, and with that went the grave implication of capital punishment.[18] If a similar order had been in place in early 1862, the vast majority of absences would have been recorded as desertion.

On January 23, 1863, amnesty was offered by Major General Gustavus W. Smith, in an attempt to encourage absent men to return to duty. The proffer also included the stern warning that enlisted men who did not return, or were later absent, would be tried by the newly formed Military Court and "if found guilty they will be sentenced to death whether present or absent and commanders will be ordered to execute the sentence whenever the condemned can be arrested."[19] This last warning, that men would be tried *in absentia*, was not often the case for North Carolina troops, one or two possible instances appearing in records.

Governor Zebulon B. Vance could not accept that desertion was greater from North Carolina units than from the other states and so informed the Secretary of War on May 25, 1863.[20] Nor could he understand why he did not have sufficient influence with Confederate authorities to remove "obnoxious" Virginians—officers serving in local offices in North Carolina—when the need arose.[21]

Deserters of a different sort than those who simply wanted to avoid service posed a double-edged threat to the Confederacy. Men who deserted directly to the enemy not only resulted in one less soldier, but they carried with them details on the strength and disposition of their units. Numerous references are found that valuable information was obtained from deserters.[22] Federal forces had orders to immediately send all Confederate deserters forward to headquarters without allowing them to talk with anyone.[23] General Robert E. Lee issued a circular that captured Confederates were to give the enemy only their name, company and regiment, but that was of little import to a deserter.[24]

Soldiers who presented an imminent threat to the order or authority of the Confederate army were subject to immediate, on-the-spot execution. General James Longstreet issued orders to that effect on April 21, 1862, while commanding the Department of Northern Virginia."[25] Brigadier General Roger A. Pryor issued General Order #6, on January 20, 1863, to his command on the Blackwater in Virginia. As desertion had "become scandalously prevelant," persons caught more than two miles from camp without a proper pass and giving evidence of wanting to desert, "shall be shot at once without the formality of a trial to this end persons so caught will be immediately sent to these headquarters with the witnesses in the case."[26]

Wayward soldiers who were not killed in an act of defiance were placed in arrest to await trial. The arresting officer had eight days to prepare and present charges and specifications against the prisoner. That protection was assured in the 79th Article of War; similarly, the 82nd Article required that an officer holding a soldier in arrest report that fact within twenty-four hours. Officers were ordered not to "vent personal resentment" when preparing official charges; no doubt there was great temptation to do so when the man was a known shirker, a trouble maker or a deserter.[27] A broad charge, violation of some Article of War, was supported by a detailed specification of the crime.

When needed, a general court-martial could be convened by the officer in command of an army, corps or district, normally a major general or lieutenant general. A brigadier or a colonel in command of a district could also authorize a court. Thirteen officers was the requisite number for a court-martial, if such a number could be gathered without "manifest injury" to the service, in which case as few as five officers could comprise a legal court. The prisoner at trial had the right to challenge the appointment of any member of the court and to have counsel to assist him in his defense. Appointed members of the court were sworn in individually by the Judge Advocate and he was sworn by the Presiding Judge. Oath taking was repeated for each case that was brought before the court. Courts were under the immediate direction of a Presiding Judge or President, usually a field-grade officer, who scheduled the hours when the court would meet, insured that procedures were followed, and generally handled administrative matters. He had no greater authority on the decisions of the court than did any other member.

At trial, the first requirement of the prosecution was to identify the charged man by name, rank, company and regiment, and to verify that the accused was a duly enrolled soldier in the Confederate service. One threshold of verification was that the prisoner had drawn money from Confederate sources. When that was established the Judge Advocate read the charges and specifications of the alleged offense. Specifications had to include information as to the time and place of the alleged offense, as could be best determined. The article of war, or army regulation, that made the actions of the defendant a military crime was noted. Caution was required; charges citing the wrong article of war could result in the release of a prisoner, and a vague charge of violating some unspecified article of war was also fatal. The accused then entered his plea of guilty or not guilty for each count. In the absence of a plea by a prisoner a plea of not guilty was placed on the record. Witnesses for the prosecution testified and the prosecution was closed. The defense then had the right to present their witnesses or decline to do so.[28] All witnesses could be cross-examined. It was the responsibility of the Judge Advocate to insure that the prisoner had a full and fair opportunity to present all evidence that he and his counsel thought would be useful in his defense. Upon completion of testimony, the court went into closed session to begin their deliberations. When a decision was reached the Presiding Judge and the Judge Advocate signed the court record which was sent to the officer who authorized the court for his approval.[29]

When that review was complete a three part general order was issued, usually printed but occasionally handwritten. Part I identified the court, when and where it had met, and under what authority. Part II listed the essential information contained in the charges and specifications against the accused, his name, rank, unit designation and the legal basis for the trial. The decision of the court, guilty or not guilty, on each charge and on every specification followed. Acquittal for those judged to be not guilty, specific punishment for the guilty, and any other recommendation the court might wish to make ended that part of the general order. Part III included the approval or disapproval of the court's decisions, and quite often comment on those decisions, by the convening officer. Also included were his orders as to the officer who would be responsible for carrying out the approved punishment and when and where it was to be done. The reviewing officer also had the option of suspending execution of a death sentence until the pleasure of the President could be made known. If the work of the court was completed or the convening officer wanted the court dissolved, that was included in a closing statement.

A surge in the number of death sentences sent forward by field commanders to await the pleasure of the President drew the attention of General Samuel Cooper. With reference to the 89th Article of War:

> The intent of this article is not to relieve Commanding Generals of responsibility, but to enable them, in difficult and doubtful cases, to refer the question to higher authority. But it has been observed that in many cases, where the course to be pursued was rendered obvious by the evidence, commanding officers have nevertheless availed themselves of the privilege conferred in the article referred to, by sending on the record to be reviewed by the President. The duties of the executive are sufficiently onerous ... it is proper to remark, that there are cases of capital punishment and dismissal where the duty of the Commanding General is rendered by the court record too plain to be doubted and in which the responsibility "in time of war" being fixed upon him in the first instance by the law, should not be avoided.[30]

Mistakes were often made in matters of form and court procedure, to the consternation of the commanding officer when a hardened deserter was freed on a technicality, to his relief when a youthful soldier who had made a misguided attempt at desertion was released from a death sentence. So many court records with obvious errors were sent forward to the headquarters of General Robert E. Lee and General John B. Hood that they approved circular orders advising on the correct preparation of court-martial documents and the legal pitfalls therein.[31] A book by Major Charles Lee was recommended reading for officers assigned to a court.[32] Four copies of his *Vade Mecum* were sent to the Military Courts of Generals Jackson, Longstreet and Smith on January 24, 1863.[33]

Military Courts were authorized by the Confederate Congress on October 9, 1862, and the Presidential appointees were announced by the AIGO in General Order #109, issued on December 20, 1862. The newly-formed courts were to have three judges. They held the rank of Colonel of Cavalry and were paid $210 a month. The first courts, including a Judge Advocate, were assigned to each of nine army corps. These twenty-seven jurists included three from North Carolina, Colonels Thomas Ruffin, William B. Rodman and David H. Carter. As the war went on, men with a legal background who were not physically able to support the Confederacy in the field continued their contribution within the Military Court system.[34]

Secretary of War James A. Seddon had the opinion that Military Courts improved the morale and efficiency of the army and "generally secured a larger measure of satisfaction to their judgments."[35] From the few existing records, judges sitting on a Military Court were more active in questioning defendants and witnesses than were the officers at a general court-martial. From the onset there was an implication that the newly organized courts would be firm in dealing with convicted deserters. Within the two-thirds concurrence requirement they could put forth a death sentence, and often did. The General Commanding retained approval authority for Military Court decisions. But the men sitting on a Military Court did not intend to be a rubber stamp for an officer of any rank. Colonel David Carter emphatically stated that his court would decide the guilt or innocence of men appearing before it on a strictly legal basis, and they would not willingly make an example of a man just because an officer felt that it was necessary in a particular instance. In a long letter concerning the trial of two deserters from the Fifth Virginia Infantry, dated August 26, 1863, Colonel Carter vigorously emphasized his position:

> The Military Court of this Corps is a separate, distinct, and independent department of it, and it can only be valuable and efficient for the administration of law, and the enforcement of discipline, while it remains so. All its official acts are performed under the solemn sanction of an oath, and whenever it yields to outside pressure from any quarter — whether it be to secure the approval of Major Generals by consulting their prejudices or to escape their petulant censures, it ceases to answer the high purpose for which it was created.[36]

In the case at point, Major General Edward Johnson had specifically endorsed that the soldiers at trial should be made examples of. When this was not done, the General launched a verbal tirade toward the court. This raised the ire of Colonel Carter and he proceeded to attack the specifications of the charges against the men as presented to the court. They were so "unskillfully and bunglingly" drawn that a lawful conviction was impossible, the Colonel responded. He then went on to counter-attack with the statement that any officer who lets such "blunders" pass through his office should be replaced.[37]

Before long, the Military Courts that were formed to relieve officers of court duty and to insure prompt trials for accused soldiers were themselves inundated with cases. Many were trivial, leading corps commanders to issue orders that violations for which the likely punishment was less than a month of hard labor and loss of pay be handled at the company and regimental level rather than sent to a higher court. Not all officers agreed that Military Courts were needed or effective. General Cooper learned of this opinion in a letter from Colonel T. L. Rosser dated February 11, 1865. Among their shortcomings, he noted that the courts were made of men from the same communities of the men at trial, they never had the moral courage to perform their duties in a "fearless and manly way," and the courts were composed of politicians who had seen no service. He closed his missive saying that the service would "never have discipline as long as Military Courts were in existence," particularly in judging charges placed against officers.[38] Earlier misgivings were tersely made known to the AIGO. "It is now difficult to have the sentence of death [and] execution when inflicted. Military Court was appointed for such cases."[39]

For the guilty, courts were given "wide discretion" in awarding punishment, bound only by the "laws and customs" of the service.[40] Some courts ingeniously exercised this latitude as they ordered a series of punishments for a crime they thought particularly egregious. A death sentence was mandatory only upon conviction of violation of the 55th Article of

War, Forcing a Safeguard; death for other specified crimes was a decision for the court. Execution by musketry, "to be shot with leaden bullets until he is dead," or "hanging by his neck betwixt the sky and earth," were sentences intended to immediately end the life of the convicted. Flogging and a lengthy imprisonment, either of which might offer only a slight delay in death, were available when warranted. Flogging, usually thirty-nine lashes but no more that fifty, required a respite of thirty days before a second whipping. Why thirty-nine lashes came to be accepted as a norm may well rest in biblical times. The Apostle Paul said in 2 Corinthians 11:24, "Of the Jews five times received I forty stripes save one." The save one provision was inserted to avoid any chance that a miscount would break Jewish law limiting lashes to forty. Congress prohibited flogging after a sentence of repetitive floggings was given to a man in the Fiftieth North Carolina regiment; they did so in April 1863.[41] Branding with a one- or two-inch letter appropriate to the crime, "D" for deserter, "T" for thief, was a frequent sentence in the early years. "D" was also used to punish drunkenness, which blurred whether a marked man was a detested deserter or a common drunk. The recommended solution was that deserters be branded on the left hip, those convicted of drunkenness on the right hip. Prison sentences of up to five years, or the duration of the war, were frequent. Prison days might be served with an iron ball attached to a leg, at hard labor, or with periods of a bread and water diet. A bread and water sentence was restricted to fourteen days, to be followed by a fourteen day respite; this sequence could not be repeated more than six times a year. A soldier might be sentenced to march before his unit accompanied by an armed escort, or to carry a heavy object, such as a log or a haversack of rocks, for hours a day. He might be suspended by his thumbs with feet barely in contact with the ground, or stand on a barrelhead wearing a placard labeled "deserter," or "thief," as the case might be. He might be pilloried, bucked and gagged, made to sit astride a narrow beam or wear a white feather in his cap to show that he was a coward. Courts were allowed to be lenient if a man before them had a "natural disability to distinguish good from evil." But if those so labeled "idiots and lunatics" were lucid at the time of the crime, they could be punished with consideration for the degree of their disability.[42]

Not all court decisions were well considered. A soldier was dismissed from the service for embezzling or stealing. It was logically pointed out to the court that dismissal was not the proper punishment, or very soon everyone would be stealing something or other merely to leave the service.[43] A reviewing officer had the prerogative of setting aside a court's decision and ordering that they reconvene to reconsider their previous effort. Phrases such as "a simple farce," "totally inadequate," or "Would bring Courts-martial into utter contempt" are found in the remarks of a displeased commander. Some officers, though unhappy with a decision, accepted it; others returned the court to the task to present a result more to their liking. Among the officers who had established reputations as fine disciplinarians, the tendency was to accept and enforce the decision of a court as it was put forth. In commenting on a case then before him, General T. J. Jackson wrote: "One great difficulty in the army results from over lenient Courts and it appears to me that when a Court Martial faithfully discharges its duty that its decisions should be sustained. If this is not done, lax administration of justice and corresponding disregard for law must be the consequence."[44]

The complete court record, according to Army Regulations #871–877, was to be immediately sent forward to the AIGO at Richmond. Judged by posting dates, some commands were very lax in that regard. In the range of 10 percent of such documents were never sent or never reached the proper office, and others were posted many months after the trial date. Once the records reached the AIGO they were reviewed for legality, proper form, authority of the court, and any comment or action by the reviewing officer. The venerable Adjutant General Samuel Cooper and his staff promptly notified field commands when they strayed beyond their proper authority. A death sentence mitigated by a reviewing officer usually brought a rather curt note from General Cooper that only the President had that authority. Field officers frequently asked General Cooper to guide them in resolving issues concerning courts-martial—where they could be held, could they move about, who had authority to convene, who was entitled to court records, and so on. To the very end, General Cooper and his staff were vigilant in insuring that the Confederate armies conducted their affairs in a prescribed legal manner, on occasion citing precedent in the United States and British armies.[45] The first British reference to a military court is found in 1571. "They enter into consultation and call a martiall court."[46]

General orders concerning the findings of a court in the larger armies were normally printed in rather large runs, 400–500 at mid-war and nearly twice that number toward the end.[47] They were usually distributed within a week of the responsible officer's review. The army in Virginia published on average 100 general orders a year. Special orders were forthcoming on a nearly daily basis. Circular orders were also used to instruct and inform on administrative matters and were issued as the need arose, eight or ten times a year. About one-third of army and corps general orders dealt with court-martial results, the remainder with current needs of the service. It was very important in the mind of General R. E. Lee that general orders dealing with courts-martial be promptly published and that delivery to the army be expedited. That would insure that other soldiers would know of the punishment and might be dissuaded from a similar offense, which would "insure the beneficial effect of prompt punishment."[48]

After a decision of a court had been published, appeals, petitions and pleas were often sent forward. The convicted, friends, company and regimental officers, relatives, those who opposed the death penalty, all were apt to appeal. Their efforts were directed to the President, the Secretary of War, and not infrequently to Governor Vance when a soldier from North Carolina was involved. Executions were often delayed for weeks or months while sentences were reviewed and appeals considered, particularly when an influential person was involved. Recommendations were prepared by the AIGO, the Secretary of War and aides to the President when the gravity of a case warranted the President's time and attention. In some cases the decision was that he "would not interfere" when it was desired that the sentence of the court should stand. But more often than not, the President acted favorably for the condemned man and the sentence was either remitted or commuted to a term of imprisonment. Appeals were so frequent that the Secretary of War requested the appointment of an officer to review all such activity and determine the appropriate action. He supported his recommendation saying, "Painful responsibility attaches to all these cases which will not allow them to be lightly treated." The alternative to the appointment was, in the Secretary's opinion, to place approval of court decisions in the hands of the field commander, with no right of further appeal.[49]

Upon the final decision that the death sentence would be carried into effect, the hopes of the prisoner were then reduced to the whim of fate, or to his own ingenuity and rather limited resources. Death from disease might preempt the agonizing steps to the stake, or valiant service in a fortuitous engagement might bring forth a reprieve. Or a prisoner might end his own life before the humiliation of execution. Escape from confinement, aided by the complicity or poor marksmanship of a guard, gave a chance for life when all else failed.

With all but the slightest hope now past, the last days of Confederate service began for the condemned. For those that had committed a treasonous act and were to be hanged, the wait was not long. Short shrift, usually a day or two, was their common allotment. For men who were to be shot, five or seven days after the General Order was received at the command of the condemned was the usual period of grace — time to write friend and relative, dispose of what little he had and to prepare for the beyond.

The General Commanding designated an officer to carry the sentence into effect. That officer selected a site and gave orders as to assembly of the troops, and assigned a regimental officer, or the Provost Marshal General, to arrange and supervise the execution. The men selected for the firing detail, including a reserve detail in case the first volley was not lethal, were brought together for instruction and practice. A crisp volley, as if from a single weapon, was desired to maintain the military precision of the execution. Coffin plank was hammered together, a pole cross implanted, a grave shoveled. The regiments were assembled. If a band was available, they were stationed on the execution field. References note that a band played the "Dead March" from *Saul*, by George Friderick Handel. The order of execution was read. A chaplain often offered a final prayer and a doctor positioned to verify that the executioners' work was done. A final command and the execution was carried into effect. If the condemned was not killed, the reserve detail, or a soldier in the detail, was brought forward to complete the task. Before the disgraced body was hidden in an unnamed grave, the assembled troops were marched past the pierced and bloody remains sagging on the crude cross. The dismal march was to be in slow time (sixty steps a minute) if the execution was by musketry but in common time (ninety steps a minute) by the scaffold.[50] The apparent intent was to remove the slightest respect for a person executed by hanging, most often a traitor to the cause. The common time march by, at least on one — and likely other — executions, may have passed a living person suspended by a strangling noose. "In twenty minutes all signs of life had ceased" suggests that death by hanging did not always arrive in a merciful manner.[51]

The Adjutant and Inspector General's Department was established in February 1861 to maintain such records as necessary to keep the Secretary of War informed on the condition of Confederate forces. Rosters and registers were kept, unit fitness assessed, legal issues weighed. General and special orders were issued for the guidance of the army. Some general orders required wide distribution and a substantial printing effort; 4,640 copies of GO #19, AIGO, dated February 7, 1863, were finally sent off on April 4, 1863.[52] The order dealt with enlistment of men in regiments other than those of their initial enrollment. Orders intended for upper command levels were printed in quantities of 100 or so and distributed within four or five days of origination. GO #49, AIGO, dated April 23, 1863, was released on April 27.[53] The office also included a Judge Advocate's section to review court-martial transcripts to insure that those involved in the process, from General Commanding to the court recorder, precisely followed all rules and regulations. This office kept a ledger of every individual who went to trial before a general court-martial or a Military Court for which it received the trial record. The AIGO reminded all commands in General Order #36, March 21, 1864, AIGO, that trial records, including orders concerning the trial, were to be sent to the War Department "with as much expedition as practicable." There are instances where North Carolina soldiers were legally executed but the trial record was not posted by the AIGO, and others where the posting was delayed for a year or more.

Hand-written trial transcripts of Confederate courts-martial are relatively rare, but a few are found in service records of soldiers who had some involvement with a court. These transcripts are often lengthy, particularly those concerning notorious officers. A handwritten 107 page trial record is found in the service record of Private Thomas Dunphy, 14th Virginia Infantry.[54] At trial, Private Frank Hughes of the Fourteenth was acquitted of assaulting a superior — 9th Article of War; he deserted just three months following his release from arrest.

In August of 1864, General Cooper was asked to give the count of officers who were tried and convicted of drunkenness since the beginning of the war. He replied that 222 were brought to trial on charges of drunkenness, 71 were acquitted and 151 convicted.[55] Strangely, no correspondence has been found that any civil or military authority ever requested or received a count, or state distribution, of executed men.

No record has been found that an officer in a North Carolina Confederate unit ever received a death sentence, though there were cases where commanding officers thought that a death decision was well justified. An officer convicted of cowardliness in combat demanded a death sentence in the view of some commanders. Court records do show that officers enrolled in units from other Confederate states were sentenced to be executed, and at least three executions resulted.[56]

An informative comparison is found in the execution of North Carolina troops in relation to those that took place in the invading army. At least 160 men from North Carolina commands were executed for military crimes, 267 men were executed in the Federal army. Executions of North Carolina troops were primarily for desertion, and the executed were usually natives of North Carolina or a nearby state. Half of the Federal executed were either foreign-born or of color. Nearly 100 Federal troops were executed for rape or murder so the total number of Federal executions for military crimes is approximately the same as that for North Carolina troops.[57] The Federal army exceeded a million men; the executed North Carolinians were taken from an enrollment one-tenth in size. Though Federal executions would have been higher had not President Abraham Lincoln stopped executions for desertion for the last year of war.[58] Looking at two Northern states that were comparable to North Carolina in the number of men available for service, troops attributed to Connecticut suffered 24 executions, 18 of the men were foreign-born. Massachusetts furnished over 150,000 troops; 13 were executed, 3 were of foreign birth.

In our earlier struggle when men from North and South fought together, courts-martial were the point where the civilian — temporarily turned soldier — confronted military justice. For our purpose, an estimated 200,000 men served in the Revolutionary War. Records of 2,666 courts-martial concerning these men are available. About 1 percent of the estimated enrollment went before a military court, half for some form of desertion. These courts returned 173 death sentences, 6 percent of the men at trial.[59] Considering that General Washington was apt to be rather lenient in enforcing the death penalty for mutiny, it seems sensible that he would be sympathetic to appeals for men condemned for simple desertion. An assumption of not more than 50 military executions of Revolutionary soldiers appears realistic.

Confederate and Federal soldiers who fought in the Mexican War had experience with the evil of desertion. About 9,000 men deserted from the invading force of 80,000. Alleged deserters from United States troops enrolled in the Saint Patrick Battalion of the Mexican army were captured, tried and sentenced to be hanged. General Winfield Scott approved 50 death sentences for 70 convicted deserters.[60]

In World War I, the British army, notorious for the rattle of rifle fire at a dawn execution, executed 346 men in all theaters of war; the executed were drawn from a total force of nine million men. Enlisted soldiers were taken before nearly 300,000 courts-martial, the bulk of which were for crimes other than desertion, drunkenness, disobedience and the like. As a result of these courts, 3,080 death sentences were put forth; this was just a shade over 1 percent of the men at trial. Of those so sentenced, 346 were executed—11 percent of the men who were sentenced to death.[61] British soldiers were executed at a rate of 1 for every 26,000 of those in service. One estimate of executions of French soldiers in World War I lists the number as 133; other estimates range as high as 700.[62] For Italian troops there is an indication that 4,000 soldiers were ordered to be executed and that 750 met that end, 19 percent of those condemned.[63] Remarkably, it is found that only 48 German soldiers were executed in World War I.[64] A double handful of American soldiers were executed for military crimes in all of the wars of the twentieth century, 10 in World War I, 1 in World War II, though a significant number were executed during the World Wars for violent civil crimes, murder and rape, most often.[65] One estimate is that World War II German military courts issued 30,000 death sentences and that 22,000 were carried into effect.[66] Another estimate reduces the executed to 12,000, with the suggestion that it might be greater.[67] German executions of 15,000 suggests resort to that extreme punishment far beyond anything experienced by North Carolinians. However on examination, German executions occurred in a range of 1 for every 600 to 700 men in service; North Carolinians were executed at a rate of 1 for every 800 men in service, a small, and thought provoking, difference.[68] Estimates of executions carried out by the Soviets are almost beyond comprehension, being from two to five times greater than those of the Germans.[69] An estimated 10,000 Frenchmen were killed by their countrymen after World War II.[70]

Men and boys of the Old North State were taken to their execution place more often than were soldiers from any other state in our wartime history. When all was said and they were in their grave, a measure of dignity and military bearing was maintained in these rituals. Yet, one must weigh how full that measure. Confederate executioners sighting wobbling muskets under a variety of slouched hats, wearing a collection of worn and soiled clothing, firing a ragged volley at an equally tattered target. Certainly not a scene that would impress onlookers with the majesty of military justice, but rather one more likely to bring forth emotions of futility and needless death. Still, the march past the bloody corpse kept men in the ranks for a time.

Of the North Carolinians who mounted the scaffold or marched to the stake, many accepted their fate with composure, perhaps even with a final show of bravado. Thousands watched as they died; they were the tragic attraction in a ritual they never imagined would one day unfold. Volunteers who rushed to the flag in 1861, conscripts with just days of service, farm laborers, men taken from destitute families, boys caught up in a sudden impulse, discouraged men, unsure soldiers influenced by others, cowardly men, all were sacrificed in view of others little different in appearance or conviction. And there among the fearful and awe-struck onlookers were those who but for official reluctance would have long ago been bound to the execution cross. Their execution thus more firmly grounded the foundation of Confederate discipline and secured the one resource that could bring an early end to the war.

Part I. Army of Northern Virginia

1

History of North Carolina Troops in the Army of Northern Virginia

"Material of which it is composed is the best in the world."[1]

General Robert E. Lee held the opinion that he had the right men to form a victorious army. On September 7, 1862, he gave his assessment to President Jefferson Davis: "I need not say to you that the material of which it is composed is the best in the world, and, if properly disciplined and instructed, would be able successfully to resist any force that could be brought against it." However, a caveat was forthcoming: "But there are individuals who, from their backwardness in duty, tardiness of movement and neglect of orders, do it no credit."[2] These men, including officers, should be identified and disciplined or removed from their responsibilities. Field officers must be stalwart and determined in battle; any men that abandoned the fight must be returned to the ranks, or "our army will melt away." Another difficulty was foreseen, "Owing to the constitution of our courts-martial ... great delay and difficulty in correcting daily evils ... require more promptness and certainty of punishment."[3] "A better way of correcting this great evil" would be the appointment of a military commission, made up of men of known confidence and trust, to accompany the army to judge such matters that might be brought before it.[4] A blending of civil judicial acumen and military expediency was proposed. The suggested commission was to have its own Provost Marshal and a guard unit to promptly execute its decisions. Every outrage on citizens, or on their property, would be promptly and equitably dealt with. In a well-turned phrase, General Lee described the perpetrators to be punished as "stragglers who consume all they can get from the charitable and all they can take from the defenseless."[5] Military Courts for the various armies were appointed within a few months. An independent provost to enforce court decisions was not organized. It does seems incongruous that an army commander dedicated to maintaining discipline would consider abandoning that bedrock of discipline, punishment inflicted by the very officers and men the culprit had betrayed.

Following the return from Gettysburg, General Lee addressed the President: "The number of desertions from the army is so great and still continues to such an extent that unless some cessation of them can be caused I fear success in the field will be seriously endangered." He then explains that an amnesty order which he had previously issued on August 11 was not effective in bringing men back to the ranks. It may have had the opposite effect. Men left their company with the idea that they would take advantage of the amnesty on their return, after a stay at home. He went on:

> In one corps the desertions of North Carolinians and to some extent Virginians has grown to be a very serious matter.... Great dissatisfaction is reported among the good men in the Army at the apparent impunity of deserters.... I would now respectfully submit to your Excellency the opinion that all has been done which forbearance and mercy call for and that nothing will remedy this great evil which so much endangers our cause except the rigid enforcement of the death penalty in future cases of conviction.[6]

General Lee had earlier requested that General Samuel Cooper confirm his authority in death sentence cases. He noted that the 65th and 89th Articles of War "gives me no power to remit or mitigate the sentence of death or cashiering. I can only execute said sentence or refer them to the President."[7] General Lee wanted to know if his interpretation was correct. That being the case he "may have to transmit many cases" for presidential review.

At the end of October 1863, after two months of intense execution activity, General Lee deemed it necessary to again state his position on the enforcement of the death sentence. In commenting on leniency which had been extended in a case involving a man in the Forty-First Virginia Regiment, General Lee wished to "express my sincere apprehension ... the consequence of a relapse to that lenient policy past experience has shown to be so ruinous to the army and in the end cruel to men" was again in effect. After a few executions, a number of men were pardoned leading to a recurrence of desertion to an "alarming extent.... All the blood that has been shed for the maintenance of discipline" was now useless and "will result in the painful necessity of shedding a great deal more." Punishment was "inflicted almost exclusively for the warning of others." Still, for some soldiers the, "slightest prospect of escape [was] embraced," and only the "sternest punishment" and the conviction that such punishment was inevitable was the "only means of avoiding the recurrence of these occasions."[8] The General was resolute in his stand that there should be no negotiation with deserters; they should voluntarily return to the army and stand trial. They should expect some punishment but they would not face a death sentence. He explained to the Secretary of War, "But in fact courts-martial invariably take into account in their decisions the voluntary return of a prisoner, and I have never known one who so returned to be sentenced to death."[9]

When the executions of soldiers accelerated in the early months of 1864, President Davis asked General Lee to comment on the advisability of offering clemency to convicted soldiers. A specific case involving the Fifty-Second Virginia was at issue and served as a vehicle for a broad policy overview. General Lee offered his opinion:

> My views are based upon those considerations of policy which experience has satisfied me to be sound, and which are adverse to leniency, except in cases showing some reason for mitigation. If it were only a matter of the individual soldier involved, then prior good conduct might well offer a basis for mitigation of a sentence. But I am satisfied that it would be impolitic and unjust to the rest of the army to allow previous good conduct alone to atone for an offence most pernicious to the service, and most dangerous as an example.[10]

General Lee explained that it was his practice to give the accused the benefit of all extenuating circumstances that would not injure the service. But a field commander could yield no further:

> It is certain that a relaxation of the sternness of discipline as a mere act of indulgence, unsupported by good reasons, is followed by an increase of the number of offenders. The escape of one criminal by pardon, or a general amnesty, encourages others to leave in the hope they will be given similar consideration. But the effect of the example is the chief thing to be considered, and that it is injurious, I have no doubt. The military executions that took place to such an extent last autumn, had a very beneficial influence, but in my judgment, many of

them would have been avoided had the infliction of punishment in such cases uniformly followed the commission of the offense. But the failure of courts to convict or sentence to death, the cases in which pardon or commutation of punishment had been granted upon my recommendation, and the instances in which the same indulgence was extended by your Excellency upon grounds made known to you by others, had somewhat relaxed discipline in this respect, and the consequences became apparent in the increased number of desertions.[11]

After a short summary of the current state of desertion, General Lee went on: "But the number is sufficiently great to show the necessity of adhering to the only policy that will restrain the evil, and which I am sure will be found to be truly merciful in the end."[12] The closing recommendation to the President was that men should not be released from a sentence, "except for good cause shown." It is worth noting that General Lee accepted his share of the responsibility for the increase in desertion while graciously suggesting that the President was not well advised in his lenient treatment of convicted men, and that courts must also share the responsibility as they were now reluctant to convict deserters or to sentence men to death. These observations were addressed to the President on April 13, 1864, just a year before the final surrender and a week after General Lee had recommended to the President the remission of a death sentence in the cases of ten convicted deserters based on evidence of gallantry in battle, good prior service, or the youthfulness of the offenders.[13]

Desertion continued to seriously weaken the forces in the field, and GO #54, August 10, 1864, Head Qrs. Army Northern VA, "enjoined" all those absent without proper authority to return to their commands.

> The Commanding General deems it only necessary to remind those who have erred through thoughtlessness or negligence, of the shame and disgrace they will bring upon themselves and their families, if they shrink from the manful discharge of duty in the hour of their country's need, and leave their homes to be defended and their independence to be secured by the unaided courage of others.

Voluntary return might "palliate their offence," with some expectation of clemency. "If arrested and brought back, justice to the faithful and true, as well as the interests and safety of the country, requires that they shall suffer the extreme penalty of the law."[14]

Though the view of General Lee on the enforcement of discipline was no doubt well known to General James Longstreet he felt constrained to advise General Lee that over 100 men in General George E. Pickett's command were in the guardhouse for desertion, "and the cause of it may be attributed to the numerous reprieves, no one being executed for two months." Four days later General Lee endorsed the document; "Desertion is increasing in the army, notwithstanding all my efforts to stop it. I think a rigid execution of the law is mercy in the end. The great want in our army is firm discipline."[15] In due course the comments reached the President who rather testily reminded the military men of their proper place: "When deserters are arrested they should be tried, and if the sentences are reviewed and remitted, that is not a proper subject for the criticism of a military commander."[16] This exchange occurred in November 1864. The annoyed President defended his decision, confident that he best appreciated the profound impact of military executions on all of the people of the Confederate states, those in the fight and those at home.

General Cooper wrote to General Lee on February 1, 1865, that he was happy to inform him that his nomination had been confirmed by the Senate and that he was now General-in-Chief of all Confederate armies. Upon being appointed as the highest-ranking Confederate officer, General Lee issued GO #2, February 11, 1865, Head Quarters Armies of the

Confederate States. The order began by stating that the General-in-Chief felt assured that the noble men serving with him would respond to the new call for honor and duty, that they would not barter manhood for peace and the right of self government for life and property. "But justice to them requires a sterner admonition to those who have abandoned their comrades in the hour of peril." Another twenty-day amnesty period was announced for deserters, except for those who had gone over to the enemy or had been once pardoned and again deserted. And as so often before, the repeated refrain — this was to be the last general amnesty and all who desert in the future "shall suffer such punishment as the Courts may impose, and no application for clemency will be entertained."[17] The order also released many men who were imprisoned for just one desertion. GO #3 was directed at an equally vexing problem, men leaving their enrolled unit to join another command. These men were also offered the benefit of amnesty but threatened with a death sentence if they did not return to their proper units. Steps would soon be taken to insure that officers who allowed illegal enrollments would face appropriate charges and punishment.

The desperate nature of the times is then fully revealed in GO #4, February 22, 1865. First, officers who are reported to be "deficient in intelligence, coolness, and capacity" were to be brought before Examining Boards; there an unfavorable result would lead to dismissal from the service. Non-commissioned officers found unable to perform their duties would be returned to the ranks. "File closers" were to be selected from among the "most distinguished for courage, discipline and attention to duty." In action, they were to be positioned "with loaded guns and fixed bayonets" two paces to the rear of every ten men. Their orders were, "If any refuse to advance, disobey orders, or leave the ranks to plunder or retreat, the file closers will promptly cut down or fire upon the delinquents. They will treat in the same manner any man who uses words or actions calculated to produce alarm among the troops."[18] The will to fight is nearly exhausted when it becomes necessary to designate to distinguished and courageous men the task of herding other men into battle. Three days after issuing that stringent order, General Lee felt called upon to adopt a similar stance with General Cooper. After being ordered to suspend the execution of a convicted deserter from the Twenty-Second Georgia, he wrote, "Hundreds of men are deserting nightly, and I cannot keep the army together unless examples are made of such cases," but he suspended the execution "as directed."[19] Shortly before that exchange, General Lee issued a circular order with a more positive tone to all Confederate forces on the strict observance of discipline. "Its effects are visible ... all military history records triumph of discipline and courage far more frequently than those of numbers and resources," indirectly saying that fair and firm discipline was the sole remaining resource of the Confederacy.[20]

Two days after issuing the file closer order and the circular, General-in-Chief Lee wrote to Governor Zebulon B. Vance to state his view that desertion was due, to a large extent, to letters from home and that several hundred men, mostly North Carolinians, had recently deserted from General Hill's corps. They had no fear of being apprehended and had taken their arms with them. General Lee gave his opinion that while the cause was critical but not hopeless for the Confederacy, it was also critical for the Federal side.[21] The same theme was presented to Secretary of War James C. Breckinridge along with the suggestion that it would be helpful if a prominent citizen would speak out to keep men in the ranks.

At months' end, on March 27, 1865, in GO #8, it was ordered that the 23rd Article of War, persuading others to desert, be read daily for one week and then once a week for a month. There would be precious few readings left the Confederacy.[22]

Men could no longer be kept in the ranks. Lawlessness and violence were present throughout the Confederacy—the end was at hand. Widely-varied reasons have been put forth for what led to this desperate state. No sense of nationhood, failure to use the slave resource, poorly conceived conscription policy, and lack of strategic planning all no doubt contributed to the final defeat. But ours is not to dwell on grand strategy; rather we will look to the disciplining and execution of North Carolinians.

2

Third Corps, Wilcox Division, Branch-Lane-Barry Brigade

"eleven more to be shot horible to think of"[1]

Though there was a preponderance of North Carolina infantrymen in the 3rd Corps, led by Lieutenant General Ambrose Powell Hill, their disparity in executions is still noteworthy. The 4 North Carolina brigades that were assigned to the corps in December 1863 had at least 139 soldiers sentenced to death. Of these 64 met that fate—an execution to conviction rate of 46 percent. For 2 brigades of Virginians in the corps, 31 death sentences were put forth, 8 were carried into effect, and 3 are unknown, an execution to conviction rate of 26 percent. Granted, North Carolina records may be more inclusive and were searched in greater depth than those of the Virginians.

A Division Commander in General Hill's Third Corps early on recognized some of the difficulties that would confront his Confederate cohorts. Major General Cadmus Marcellus Wilcox was a North Carolinian by birth and a soldier by profession. While a Brigadier, General Wilcox gave his opinions on the current state of affairs in the Confederate army shortly after the battle at Sharpsburg, Maryland, in September 1862. His comments to his brother were not just family conversation, for John Wilcox was a member of the Confederate Congress and in a position to influence matters brought to his attention. General Wilcox said that there were over 5000 troops useless from want of shoes; a full brigade was temporarily lost at a very critical time in the struggle. All men up to forty-five years of age should be immediately taken into the service without further haggling by Congress. There was a great need to establish military commissions for the administration of justice. Such commissions would not only release badly needed officers from court-martial assignments, but to the mind of General Wilcox, "These commissions would promote discipline, we have no discipline in our army, it is but a little better than an armed mobb, [*sic*] the wanton destruction of private property by our army is a shame and reproach, when our army marches & camps desolation follows, they burn fences, pillage orchards, steal the green corn, killed beef, sheep, hogs & poultry." In Anderson's Division, barely a quarter of the men shown as present were available for duty. "I hope other divisions of the Army are not in quite as bad a fix but I know that they are all more or less demoralized & reduced by stragling [*sic*]."[2] In a more positive tone, General Wilcox recommended that deserving soldiers should be recognized by promotion and that they be allowed to fill vacancies in any company and not be restricted to promotion within their company. This change would aid in removing incompetent officers, as replacements would be readily at hand. General

Wilcox closed his wide ranging and prophetic letter with a rather pedantic reiterating of the main points.

The Wilcox Division was made up of a brigade from South Carolina, led by Brigadier Samuel McGowan, and a brigade from Georgia commanded by General Edward Thomas. Alongside these brigades fought two from North Carolina under the leadership of Generals James Henry Lane and Alfred Moore Scales. Altogether there were 10 regiments of North Carolinians and 9 regiments from the other states. There is no record of an execution in the Georgia brigade and not more than 2 executions in the South Carolina regiments. Nearly 40 executions are found for men in the North Carolina regiments.

No man faced execution during the eighteen months that Brigadier Lawrence O'Bryan Branch led the brigade. In the next twenty-nine months 36 of the men led by Brigadier James Henry Lane were sentenced to be shot to death, and 21 were executed. Men enrolled in 21 companies had direct encounter with a death sentence. Six companies had more than one man executed, 6 companies had 1 executed, and 9 had men spared following a death sentence. Men of Lane's brigade witnessed a variety of punishments.

> I witnessed a sight yesterday I never done before There was a man deserted from this place about six months ago he was courtmarshaled and sentence passed on him to weare a 64 pound ball and chain on his leg for six months and do hard labor besides and at the end of that time to receive 30 lashes on the beare back and be drummed out of the service of the Confederate States. And yesterday he received his 30 lashes on the beare back in front of the whole Batalion he was whipped by a man named Stewart ... you better believe he layed in on well.[3]

In the opening days, it was not only the severity of the punishment that impressed onlookers; it was the public humiliation of the offender. A man was drummed out of the service for stealing a blanket and brandy; an impressed observer noted: "It is a bad looking sight to see a man Marched out With Thief on Boath sids of him and Bair headed and two men walking behind him with there Bayonetts pointing at his back."[4] Southern men did not desert, steal, nor go about without a hat.

Seventh Regiment

Based on the fine absence record of the Seventh, organization and training was well managed. The scope of this achievement is realized when considering the challenges that confronted a company officer: "Sometimes I almost get discouraged in disciplining them. The Captain of a company is like the father of 90 children, all boys, for soldiers are only grown up children after all. When I come home I will give you some [not legible] on the treatment of your juveniles. I believe I have the confidence and esteem of all my men, even those whom necessity compeld me to punish."[5] For the Seventh, 4 conscripts and 3 volunteers were sentenced to be shot. Executions followed for 3 conscripts and 1 volunteer. For the regiment, Company K, Alexander County; Company D, Mecklenburg County; and Company F, Rowan County had 37 men stand before courts-martial; 8 were acquitted. Company D, though attributed to Mecklenburg County, was surely one of the most diverse companies in the Confederate army. During the war 162 men were enrolled, 35 were foreign-born — 21 in Ireland, 20 made their homes in other states — 5 in Northern states, 21 were from a variety of counties in North Carolina and 24 were sent from Camp Holmes. There were 41 absences from the company, all but 5 listed as desertion, and company dead numbered 45.[6] Companies G, H and I had a total of just 5 men go to trial for military crimes; 2 were executed, 3 acquitted. For the regiment there were 67 courts and 13 acquittals. Three of the 4 executions involving men of the Seventh were not recorded in the ledgers of the AIGO at Richmond.

Eighteenth Regiment

In the half-year prior to the first executions of men in the Eighteenth, 61 absences were recorded; in the following half-year just 13 men were willing to accept the risk. At least 1,760 men were enrolled; they compiled a record of 336 absences, 126 of these in the final six months of conflict, overall an absence rate of 19 percent. Execution claimed 7 men of the Eighteenth. The Eighteenth had relatively few men at trial, 28 in total, and 3 were acquitted. Death was the sentence for 7; 8 were given very harsh sentences that might offer only a short reprieve before death. The companies with the most recorded courts-martial, Company D, the Robeson Light Infantry; Company A, the German Volunteers, New Hanover County; and Company C, the Columbus Guards #3, sent forth all of the 7 who were executed. Four in Company A were court-martialed; all were shot to death. Two in Company C were shot. One of 9 defendants from Company D was shot, and 4 were either branded or given 39 stripes. The regiment experienced a modest number of absences during the years of service, with 62 in the last half of 1862 and 79 for the full year of 1863. Though they were willing and loyal when the issue was in doubt, in 1865 90 men gave up the struggle and departed. Two of the companies with many courts-martial, Companies A and D, had in total 89 incidents of absence and 95 deaths. Companies E and F together had 39 recorded absences and 113 deaths. Company E did not have more than 1 absence in any month before 1865. Company F had just 2 instances of more than 2 departures in any month during the war.

Twenty-Eighth Regiment

The Twenty-Eighth had an excellent absence record while suffering heavy loss from death in battle, camp, and hospital. A third of the men faithfully with the brigade at Appomattox were in the Twenty-Eighth. Six men of the regiment heard their death verdicts read, but only 1 was executed. Five of the 6 men so sentenced were volunteers, as was the man who was shot. Charges brought at court were distributed over all companies, much more so than is normally found. The top companies in numbers of courts were Company E, the Montgomery Grays; Company F, the Yadkin Boys; and Company K, the Stanly Guards; together they had a total of 27 trials, 44 percent of the regimental total. The companies with the fewest trials, Company H, Guards of Independence, Orange County; Company A, the Surry Regulators; and Company B, the Gaston Invincibles, experienced 19 percent of the total courts. Five of the 6 men who were sentenced to be shot were in the companies with the most court activity. Company E suffered the death of 75 men, 18 in battle and 57 from disease or cause unknown. Eighteen men absented themselves during the war. As to peer punishment, a letter mentions the "fun" the "boys" had in riding a Lincoln (Federal leaning) man on a rail and then dumping him into a mud hole.[7]

Thirty-Third Regiment

When viewed by company, the Thirty-Third presents a more common pattern of courts-martial than found for the Thirty-Seventh. Nearly 70 percent of 40 courts concerning this regiment were charged to three companies: Company D, the Wilkes Regulators; Company F, the Dixie Invincibles, Hyde County; and Company I, the Confederate Stars, Forsyth County. Eight men were acquitted. The remaining companies of the regiment each had one or two men go before the highest level military court. Two-thirds of all deaths in Company D occurred before the end of 1862. Ninety-Four absences were more evenly balanced, with one-third in each of three years of war.

33-D	1861	1862		1863		1864		1865	no date
Dead		17	19	3	4	5	4	4	
Absent		10	19	16	19	7	14	8	1
Executed				2					

Two executions in September 1863 slowed an increasing tendency to depart. Of the 8 men of the Thirty-Third who avoided execution, 4 deserted a second time, 3 thus ending their service.

Private Syl D. Davis enrolled in Company H of the Thirty-Third on July 15, 1862. On an undated scrap of paper he explained why he was there: "You wanted to know why I went in the 33d well I did not have any choice and if I had it would all been one the conscripts have to fill up companys as they come." On the reverse side, "Some of our Forsyth Boys ran away from here last Sunday night a week [August 1862] they caught Mitt Fieddler [Milton Fiddler] & Alx [Alexander] Spaugh and brought them back & gave them one lick from 3 hundred and fifty men each."[8] Not deterred, Private Spaugh began a second absence which led to a sentence of branding with the letter "D," two inches in height. The men that ran the gauntlet ran to the enemy in the final months of war.

Thirty-Seventh Regiment

The Thirty-Seventh enrolled approximately 1850 men during the struggle, an average of 185 per company. There were at least 590 incidents of absence, a rate of 32 percent. Courts convicted 81 men: 14 were sentenced to death; 6 were executed; 14 at trial were acquitted. Serious desertion activity began in the summer of 1862 and the exodus increased in the summer of 1863. The 6 executions apparently reduced desertion for a half-year, but departures began anew and reached former levels in the final three months of war. Of the 36 soldiers in the brigade who were given death sentences by military courts, 14—39 percent—were men of this regiment. At least 4 men were killed in confrontations with authorities while they were deserters.

Men of Company A, the Beauregard Rifleman, Ashe County; Company E, the Watauga Minutemen; and Company H, the Gaston Blues account for 56 percent of the 81 court-martial convictions recorded for the regiment. Seven of the 14 who were sentenced to be executed were from these same companies. Eleven of the 14 were volunteers. Company E had the most men brought to trial, 21 in all, but nearly half of their trials ended with acquittal of the accused. Regimental officers had a difficult time preventing men absenting themselves from Company A. Eighty-three incidents of absence are found on the records of the company, 19 men with 2 or more violations. Some absentees enrolled in other units; men so doing were treated as deserters under authority of the 22nd Article of War, and officers of those units were ordered to return the men to the Thirty-Seventh.[9] Men of Company C, Mecklenburg County; Company D, Union County; and Company K, Alleghany County, were subject to the fewest courts, with a total of 6. In neatly symmetrical fashion, 14 percent of the men of the regiment who went before courts-martial were sentenced to be shot to death with musketry, 14 percent were acquitted of all charges, and 14 percent were given a severe sentence other than death.

Courts-Martial

(The name, regiment, company and court-martial dates are shown for men given a death sentence by a military court.)

PHILLIP C. GRIFFIN 37-D, (February 23, 1863). A youthful Private Griffin experienced combat, capture, wounds, desertion and a threat of execution during his three and a half years in the army. The desertion attempts began when Private Griffin left his company, the North Carolina Defenders, while near Fredericksburg, Virginia, on December 13, 1862. He returned, only to again desert on December 15, this time with the intention of going to North Carolina. Weeks later Mr. A. L. Meeks arrested the homeward-bound boy, for which he was paid $30 when he delivered the private to General John H. Winder's command at Richmond on January 7, 1863.[10] The prisoner went before a court on February 23 and was likely startled when he learned that he was to be shot; the decision of the court was published on May 6, 1863. On review, the death sentence was set aside and Private Griffin was returned to duty to survive two wounds, a brief absence without leave, and final surrender at Appomattox.

Privates Thornton and Marion Sexton, Company A, Thirty-Seventh, were under guard in late March 1863 following their return from an unauthorized absence. Private Thornton Sexton wrote that he wanted to "avail myself of the opportunity of letting you know" of their condition. He goes on, "They put us in the Guard House and we are there yet my trial was today I proved all I wanted to that I was not able to come back I do not know what will be done with me Marions trial has not come on yet."[11] The brothers from Ashe County were absent once again a few months later, Private Marion Sexton for seven months, after which he was tried and sentenced to a year of hard labor. Brother Thornton urged Marion to return to the regiment. "Marion the col Barber [Barbour] ses if you will come Back now you Shant Bee hert and the cornel Ses for you to not come under guard Sow hery and come Back."[12] No trial or punishment record has been found for either absence of Private Thornton Sexton.

HEZEKIAH C. GRAHAM 7-F (April 4, 1863). Misbehavior before the enemy and desertion were the life threatening charges brought against Private Graham. A death sentence was deemed warranted by a court; however, they were moved to consider an outstanding record of gallantry by Private Graham at the battles of New Bern, Cedar Creek, Second Manassas, Ox Hill, Harpers Ferry, Sharpsburg and Shepherdstown. This impressive record led the court to recommend suspension of sentence until the decision of the President could be known, the reviewing General concurring with their opinion. While awaiting a decision,

Private Graham was absent without leave for a brief period. This absence did not result in any further action by regimental officers, and the President eventually acted favorably, finding that Private Graham was eligible for release under an amnesty act that the President had recently put in place. He returned to duty until the fall of 1864, when his service record ends.

GEORGE W. HIATT 28-A (April 4, 1863). Private Hiatt was first informed that he was to be shot for violation of the 52nd Article of War, misbehavior before the enemy. To his relief he then heard that the execution of sentence was suspended until the decision of the President could be made known. This unanimous recommendation by the court, accepted by the reviewing officer, was based on the conduct of Private Hiatt at the battles of Sharpsburg and Fredericksburg, among others. Private Hiatt was officially released under authority of the presidential proclamation of amnesty issued on August 1, 1863, this decision relayed in SO #212, AIGO, September 7, 1863. A year later, the fortunate private was captured by the enemy, ending his service in the Surry Regulators.

On the night of May 19, 1863, a Thursday, at least 24 and possibly as many as 32 men enrolled in Company A of the Thirty-Seventh deserted, taking their arms and ammunition with them. Some men obtained extra ammunition from men who were not deserting. General Lee, in taking official notice of the affair, noted that the men had just been paid. He alerted army units located in the area where the deserters might attempt a river crossing to be watchful and then emphasized, "I need not enlarge upon the extent to which this evil will grow if not at once stopped."[13] AIGO records reveal that just 3 of the absentees were ever brought to trial at a level where the death penalty might be invoked. One was sentenced to be shot; however, his sentence was later commuted to five years' imprisonment. Two others were initially sentenced to a year in prison; their sentences were remitted. The desertion incident was brought to the attention of Governor Z. B. Vance by Confederate Secretary of War J. A. Sedden.[14] One source referred to the 32 deserters as a squad; that is typical usage of the word in the Civil War period when referring to a group of unknown size and does not indicate a mass defection by an organized army unit.[15] The same usage of squad is found in official orders: "He will send on the discharged prisoners in squads of not over 50 each."[16]

LEWIS ORRANT 37-E (May 27, 1863). Well before the mass desertion from the Thirty-Seventh in May 1863, 26 men of the same regiment attempted to desert in August of 1862; Private Orrant was among them. He had served for nearly a year after volunteering for duty with the Watauga Minute Men. Following his desertion, Private Orrant remained at large until March 1863. Unfortunately he went to trial a week after the group departure from Company A. He was found guilty of desertion and sentenced to be shot. A Chaplain visited Private Orrant and another condemned man just days before their scheduled executions. He recorded his thoughts: "Monday June 1st 63 I was sent for today to visit some men who are condemned to be shot on Wed and Fri respectively. They seem to be perfectly prostrated with distress at the prospect of meeting such an end, yet, both profess to feel that their sins are pardoned."[17] A decision was apparently made that separate executions would be more effective in quelling desertion, or more befitting the occasion. The first execution was suspended, and within a few months Private Orrant was returned to his company. He stayed for another year, but on July 7, 1864, again deserted from camp near Petersburg, Virginia. On this occasion he took a less risky route directly into the lines of the enemy and soon after took the oath. A Private Jacob Orrant also served in Company E of the Thirty-Seventh until captured in April 1865.

ANDREW RUTHERFORD 37-K, (May 27, 1863). Private Rutherford, the condemned man imprisoned with Private Orrant, was conscripted in August 1862. He was not involved in the mass desertion of regimental men; he took his leave from the Alleghany Tigers prior to March 1863. On May 25, he was in arrest and delivered to a military prison and court-martialed just days later. The court found that he was guilty of desertion and delivered a death sentence, which was approved. While awaiting their final hour, he and Private Orrant received a second visit from their Chaplain who recounted, "Tuesday June 2 63 Called again to see the convicts of the 37th Regt. Tried to talk searchingly to them. They seemed more resigned to their fate. Just after I left them an order came from the S-W [Secretary of War] suspending the execution of the sentence and bringing them to Richmond."[18] The action of the Secretary resulted in commutation to imprisonment, or the suspension continued for three months. It mattered little, on September 2, Private Rutherford died at the prison hospital at Richmond. An older brother, Private Thomas Rutherford, served in a different brigade; he deserted in August 1862 and had no further service record.

HENRY SIMPSON BEAM 37-H (August 14, 1863). Private Beam abandoned his company, the Gaston Blues, while at Hamilton's Crossing, Virginia, on June 6, 1863, 1 of 24 who made the same decision that month. For this breach he was tried on two charges: violation of the 52nd Article of War, misbehavior before the enemy, and for desertion. The court found him guilty on each charge but went on to state that their decision was based entirely on the misbehavior charge. No consideration was given to the desertion charge, because punishment for that offense was removed by the amnesty offered in the presidential proclamation of August 1, 1863. General A. P. Hill did not agree with this interpretation and offered his reasoning:

> The proceedings in the foregoing case are approved. The finding is disapproved. According to the evidence, the accused was with his company during the day while in line of battle near Hamilton's Crossing, with the enemy in view, and did not absent himself till after dark, when it was going on picket at Moss Neck, where he would have been farther removed from the presence of the enemy. It would, therefore seem that his strongest motive in leaving was to desert. That he was guilty of desertion, in the most flagrant circumstances, is clearly proved; and, but for the amnesty to such offences granted by the President, richly deserves the extreme sentence pronounced upon him. But as his intention appears to have been desertion, mingled it may be with personal fear, the sentence of the Court cannot be sustained, without infringing upon the proclamation of the President. The sentence is therefore not confirmed, and Private Beam will be released from arrest and restored to duty.[19]

The General would not approve the subterfuge of the misbehavior decision to punish a deserter who would otherwise be released. Notwithstanding the risk and likelihood of a second death sentence, Private Beam was absent without leave twice in 1864. For the first absence in March and April 1864 the conscripted soldier went before a court-martial; their decision is not known. The punishment, if any, was not great, for Private Beam was soon back with his company. No record of a trial for the second incident that began on August 11, 1864, has been located. Private Beam was captured and paroled at war's end. Private David L. Beam deserted from Company H three weeks before his older brother. The younger man was caught and imprisoned for seven months at hard labor. He later deserted to the enemy.

GREEN RICHARDSON MORRIS 28-E (August 22, 1863). Private Morris was an independent, freethinking man who experienced frequent conflict with his officers. His first brush with authority came when he was tried by a general court-martial in March 1862, seven months after going into the ranks. The nature of his offense was not recorded. In August that year, he deserted while at Manassas, VA, in a shameful and cowardly manner when faced with the prospect of an engagement with the enemy. He was returned in arrest from this flight in January 1863. Again, punishment, if any, is not indicated. In April, he refused to obey a lawful order to clean his gun, saying that the Colonel could clean the gun himself.[46] In May, Private Morris once again deserted, this time from near Chancellorsville, VA, in the same shameful and cowardly manner. For this last crime he was tried and convicted, with his death sentence announced in GO #90, September 25, 1863, Army of Northern Virginia. President Davis may have commuted the death sentence and sent the prisoner to Castle Thunder, Richmond, VA. Another reference indicates the sentence was remitted. Release from prison by April 4, 1864, transfer to the Fourteenth Regiment, and parole at war's end then followed for Private Morris.

ALLEN ABSHER 33-D (August 27, 1863). Private Absher volunteered in October 1861 and made his first attempt to desert a year later in the fall of 1862. On his return, he was tried on a lesser charge of absent without leave; he was found guilty and ordered to forfeit three months pay, and to clean the camp area for two hours every day for three months. While undergoing this punishment, he was not to be excused from other duties, nor have leave for six months. This decision was handed down on June 14, 1863. Not content with his condition or thankful for his minimal punishment, Private Absher soon decided to risk a second desertion, which ended in his arrest and return to Camp Holmes at Raleigh on July 31, 1863. Fair fortune followed in his footsteps and he was released from punishment by virtue of the presidential amnesty of August 1. Perhaps thinking that he indeed had a charmed life, Private Absher did not rejoin his regiment after his release, but went to Louisa County, Virginia, where he was arrested. Private Absher went before a Military Court on August 27; when that court's findings were published on September 10, 1863, Private Absher learned that he would be shot.

ESOM FUGIT 33-D (August 27, 1863). After volunteering in March 1862, Private Fugit deserted in the fall and did not return until early 1863. He was restored to duty in time to be wounded at Chancellorsville in May, but then deserted, to be absent until arrested and taken to Camp Holmes, North Carolina, in late July. As in the case of Private Absher, punishment for this foray was avoided by presidential amnesty. Private Fugit was released from Castle Thunder under orders to return to his command. However, he also made his way to Louisa County, Virginia. There he was apprehended and taken to his regiment. Private Fugit was tried on August 27, found guilty, and sentenced to be shot in seven days.

Chaplain Francis M. Kennedy offered his assessment of the spiritual and emotional condition of Private Absher and Fugit: "Friday September 18th 63 Visited two men from the 33 Regt who are condemned to be shot for desertion tomorrow morning. They professed to feel prepared for their change."[20] For the man of faith execution was simply a change. On the execution day, recently appointed Hospital Steward Syl D. Davis, Thirty-Third Regiment, wrote and underlined that he expected to have a "spicy" time with the Yankees before long. Going on:

> I saw 2 men in our Regt shot through with 8 ounce balls [the number of balls] each for desertion. The troops were all assembled on the surrounding hills where they could have far view I was very near them, the way the scene was conducted it was somewhat affecting, more so than one might imagine. Tim Conrad stood by my side all the time and saw the affair.[21]

Later he wrote "Deare and Loving" this day to recount events for his wife: "The men are still deserting and going home last Saturday there was 2 men shot in Lanes brigade for desertion next Saturday there is eleven more to be shot horible to think of."[22] It is not clear if the Chaplain had an official role in the ceremony: "Saturday Sept 19 63 Witnessed the execution this morning of the two men from the 33rd Regt. They met their fate with unflinching fortitude but it was a very revolting sight. They died almost instantly upon the discharge of the guns."[23] Captain James S. Harris, Company B of the Seventh Regiment, gives more detail.

> On the 19th of September we were called to witness for the first time, a military execution for the crime of desertion. The unhappy victims (two in number) were members of Company F [Company D, Thirty-Third Regiment]. They were tried by a Court-Martial, found guilty, and the death penalty imposed. The brigade was drawn up in three sides of a square, and the condemned men, accompanied by their spiritual advisers marched in front of each regiment with their arms tied behind their the backs, and the band meanwhile playing the "dead march," after which they were tied to stakes a few feet apart and blindfolded. The guard — 24 in number, were about fifteen feet distant, and, at the command, Fire, the unfortunate men were instantly killed. The different regiments were then marched by the dead men so that each one might see for himself, the terrible consequences of desertion, which is sadly on the increase, and notably so, from our own state.[24]

Company D enrolled 172 men; 70 made 93 attempts to depart the company. In the year before the double execution, 35 men decided to leave the company. In the year following their march past the bloody remains 13 did so.

SAMPSON COLLINS 37-D (September 1, 1863). Private Collins, Company D, went to trial under the menacing military charge of misconduct in the face of the enemy, "which act occurred when he abandoned his company and regiment then in line of battle near Gettysburg, PA, on July 3, 1863, in a cowardly, shameful and disgraceful manner." The court decision in the case was made known on September 17, GO #88, Army of Northern Virginia; the accused private was to be shot.[25] He left $8 and some clothing behind when he was escorted from the guardhouse to the place of execution on September 26, 1863.[26]

GREEN W. FORD 37-H (September 1, 1863). Private Ford was age eighteen when he volunteered in October 1861. Six months later he was given a $30 bounty for extending his term of service. When his case was heard, testimony was developed similar to that in the case of Private Collins; Private Ford had abandoned his company, "then in line of battle before the enemy and in range of the enemies batteries near Chancellorsville," on May 1, 1863.[27] Private Ford was returned to the command after an absence of five days. For his fearful decision, Private Ford was to be court-martialed. While awaiting his hearing, he was confined for several weeks at the prison hospital with scurvy. The upcoming court would be the second for the young private. In December 1862, he went on trial for violation of the 21st Article of War, absent without leave. Found guilty by that court, he was ordered to forfeit two months' pay and to be reprimanded at the head of his regiment. "The court being lenient, on account of previous good conduct in several battles and particularly in going into the battle of Cold Harbor when complaining and apparently unwell."[28] The decision of the second court, that Private Ford was to be shot to death, gave painful notice that this court was not willing to make an allowance for previous good conduct, or for the age of the volunteer. He was shot on the morning of September 26.

JESSE M. LUTHER 28-E (September 2, 1863). The charges against Private Luther centered on his urging a brother to not come to the army, this in mid–July when the effects of the carnage at Gettysburg were still fresh in mind. The private was found guilty on all counts and was given a death sentence, but execution of sentence was suspended awaiting a decision by the President. While waiting to learn the President's pleasure, the officers of the Twenty-Eighth, and members of Private Luther's family, were active on his behalf. Chaplain Kennedy told of his part in the effort in a diary entry made on September 28.

> Eight more men from our Brigade sentenced to be shot next Saturday — among them Charles McSwain (Brother of M. A. McSwain of our Corp) and J. M. Luther from my Reg't. Luther's case was referred for final decision to President Davis and I go down with him [McSwain] today bearing a Petition from the officers of the Reg't for his pardon.

The next day he continues: "Laid my petition before the President or rather placed it in the hands of one of his aides. Got a letter of introduction from Dr. Minnigerode, but did not see the President. Called and saw Luther."[29] The effort to save the life of Private Luther continued into early November, Chaplain Kennedy was again involved: "Lent my horse to Miss Luther who goes to Gen'l Lee to intercede for her brother who is under sentence of death. The same man for whom I took a petition to the President.[30] Months of anxious waiting followed for the condemned, his family, and his comrades. This delay was due, in part at least, to misplaced records. Finally SO #52, March 3, 1864, AIGO announced; "The sentence of death against Private Jesse M. Luther, Company E, Twenty-Eighth NCT Army of Northern Virginia is commuted, by order of the President to four months hard labor at such place as the commanding general may appoint." If the spared soldier served his full sentence, he was captured soon after his release from confinement and exchanged and paroled in March 1865. Private Godfrey Luther enrolled in Company E of the Twenty-Eighth on the same day as brother Jesse and was also captured by the enemy in the last days of war.

JAMES S. GREER 37-B (September 3, 1863). Three men with the last name of Greer, all from Watauga County, enrolled in the Thirty-Seventh Regiment on September 14, 1861. A year later, Private James S. Greer joined them. At year's end, Private James Greer was listed on company records as a deserter, having left his command while near Fredericksburg, VA. The detail of his return to service is not known, but on March 23, 1863, Private Greer again deserted from Camp Gregg, VA, this time successfully urging Privates Newton and Madison Greer to go with him. The persuasive deserter was arrested while hiding in a cave in North Carolina and taken back to his command on August 28. He went to trial within a week. The court found him guilty of three violations of the Articles of War: the 20th, concerning desertion, the 22rd, persuading others to desert, and the 52nd, misbehavior before the enemy, by abandoning the Watauga Marksmen, then at Hamilton's Crossing, VA, in a disgraceful, cowardly and shameful manner. Their death decision was placed on record. Over the course of the war, Private Greer's company enrolled 177 men; they recorded 87 incidents of absence. These absences began in 1861 and went on at a relatively even pace till the end. Private Madison Greer was tried for desertion in 1864, suffering loss of pay and four hours of hard labor every day for a year. Private Newton Greer was captured by the enemy and exchanged in the final months of the war. Private Vincent Greer was killed at the battle of Gaines' Mill in May 1862. Private James Greer went to a deserter's grave just three days short of a year of service.

ELKANA LANIER 18-C (September 9, 1863); and JACOB E. LANIER 18-C (September 9, 1863). Privates Elkana and Jacob Lanier were conscripted into the army a week apart in August of 1862. They deserted together a year later in August of 1863. They were at large for six days, were arrested and held for trial. A death by musketry sentence was published on September 17. Their executions took place nine days later. One month had elapsed from the day that they left their company in search of food in the minds of friend and kin, deserters as judged by the military. The brothers told their parents of their plight by letter; Private Elkana Lanier also wrote to his wife. In the letters they said that they were simply searching for food when they were arrested and then tried for desertion. Neither mentioned that they were actually absent for nearly a week while on their search. Private Jacob Lanier accepted that he and his brother would be executed and explained why to his father, just two days before his execution: "The officers have determined to have a better disciplined army than heretofore, and so it must be that they make examples of some to check the remainder, it has fell our unhappy lot to be an example."[31] The brothers bore their burden with remarkable composure considering that one or both had witnessed the execution of Privates Absher and Fugate on September 19. "I saw them shoot two men yesterday that lived in Wilkes County, and there are six more to receive it next Saturday, one for only talking about the Confederacy."[32] This stated in a very matter of fact manner, considering that the brothers were among those to be shot. The young men were reconciled to their fate and found great solace in the prospect of everlasting life. But they were also concerned with leaving a clean slate here on earth. Private Jacob Lanier wrote: "Dear Father, dispose of my things that are few and worthless as you see proper to make my debts clear."[33] The young soldier's letters were as precise and accurate as any legal brief could be, and their deaths were to be a warning for others. They were not selected by random lot; they had clearly violated the Articles of War at a time when there was a desperate need to check desertion.

WILLIAM P. LEE 18-C (September 9, 1863). Private Lee was conscripted in September 1862 and executed in September 1863. As a conscript, he was placed in a company of men recruited in Columbus County that maintained a fine absence record. In the year before his death, Private Lee was briefly present for duty in early 1863. All but a few weeks of his forced military obligation were spent as a patient in Confederate hospitals or as a Federal prisoner of war. Private Lee deserted on August 25, from camp near Orange Court House, VA, but was back at camp by September 1 and on trial for his life on September 9. He was shot on September 26.

CHARLES J. MCSWAIN 28-K (September 9, 1863). Private McSwain had an unblemished two-year service record. But the futility of the war must have grown, for on August 23, 1863, he put forth an honest hope: "I wish the Southern Confederacy would go back into the Union for I have nothing to fight for."[34] Three days after making the statement, he deserted and was absent for a week before being arrested and taken to trial. When the decision of the court was published, he learned that he was found guilty of desertion and of conduct prejudicial to the service. He was to be shot. A month after expressing his feelings and then deserting, he was blindfolded awaiting execution. Company K, the Stanly Guards, recorded just 2 unauthorized absences in four years of service. On the day before the scheduled executions of the 7 men Chaplain Kennedy noted: "Our prisoners who were lodged with the Provost Marshal when the Brigade moved, for safe-keeping, were brought down this evening. I called and spent some time with them in prayer and conversation. These are seven of the poor fellows who will die at the stake tomorrow. God have mercy on their souls!"[35] On the execution day the Chaplain commented: "The condemned men were shot this morning about 11 o'clock. I baptized two of them just before the execution. All professed to have obtained peace with God save one poor fellow who did not seem satisfied with his condition ... I don't think I shall ever forget the scene."[36]

The comment by the good Reverend concerning the "one poor fellow" suggests a difficulty understanding why the condemned man would not accept his just punishment, acknowledge his sin, and profess his faith in foregiveness. Private William D. Alexander, Company D, Thirty-Seventh Regiment, simply stated, "Seven men were shot to death with musketry by sentence of Courtmartial." The days preceding and following the executions were "all quiet in camp."[37] In an article published in North Carolina's *Fayetteville Observer* on October 3, gruesome detail is added to the brief accounts offered by the chaplain and the private. After describing the preliminary ceremony the correspondent goes on:

> The prisoners were then pinioned to the stakes, a white-bandage placed over their eyes, the officer commands "Ready," every musket drops to that position; "Aim," and they are leveled at the breasts of the unfortunate men. "Fire," every gun flashes together; six of the condemned are killed instantly, the seventh received five balls in his bowels, but they were aimed too low to cause instant death. He was again bound to the stake, six men were brought forward and immediately ended his sufferings. One of them at the flash of the guns, jumped to his full height, breaking the cord that bound him, and fell forward perfectly dead. The troops were now marched by the corpses and back to camp.... Thus ended this mournful tragedy. It is to be lamented that our authorities are compelled to resort to such extreme measures, but it is absolutely necessary and the result thus far has been very satisfactory.[38]

How the reporter determined that the results were "very satisfactory" would be of interest. The increased emphasis on executions had been in place just over a month before the report.

Major George Sidney Thompson, Quartermaster for Lane's brigade, formally submitted a quarterly report four days after the executions. Along with other supplies, such as horseshoes, coal and axle grease, Major Thompson listed the material that was issued to conduct the execution rite and to properly dispose of the bodies. Two and a quarter yards of cotton cloth was procured to be "used as bandages for the men that were executed."[39] The cloth was white according to a newspaper account. Assuming that each man accepted the proffered blindfold, a strip slightly less than a foot in width, enough for a double fold, was deemed sufficient to mask the muskets pointed at their hearts. For their ignominious burial in the Virginia soil on the property of a Dr. Madison Thomas Newman near Liberty Mills, VA, the dignity of providing coffins was preserved. Two hundred and thirty feet of plank was allocated for coffins.[40] That would provide five boards of pine a bit over six feet in length. The practice was to make coffins of a size to fit the occupant.[41] Private Ford was five feet, nine inches in height, so he was likely placed in an average size coffin: six feet in length, eighteen inches across, and twelve inches on the side. To fasten the whole together, for the brusque move to a common grave, eleven and a half ounces of nails, between thirty-five and forty, were provided for each coffin, five pounds in all. Burial of a body not encased in a coffin was considered inhumane, regardless of the circumstance of the death.[42] Brigadier General Lane and Quartermaster Thompson both signed the report attesting that all stores had been "necessarily expended in the public service." Every disbursement, every debt owed by a soldier, all were accountable for in precise measure in the 1860s.

In the month of September 1863, 22 North Carolinians were shot at the stake in the Army of Northern Virginia.[43] Others were killed in the isolation of their homes. Private Andrew Jackson Lewis, Thirty-Seventh Regiment, Company G, was "shot as deserter and killed at home," this on October 8, 1863, in Alexander County.[44] Five men of the brigade were killed while in desertion; 4 were enrolled in the Thirty-Seventh Regiment. Two other men in the regiment were allegedly "shot after surrender."[45]

JOHN SHOOK 18-A (October 10, 1863). Private Shook deserted his regiment twice during the fifteen months of service that followed his conscription into the German Volunteers, New Hanover County, in August 1862. The first absence began at Fredericksburg, VA, on December 13, 1862, and extended over the next four months. No record of punishment for this desertion has come to light. The second attempt to avoid further service began at Camp Gregg, VA, less than a month after Private Shook had returned to duty from his first absence. This absence began on April 27, 1863, and did lead to a court-martial. The court convicted the prisoner and concurred that he should be shot, the decision being announced in GO #93, October 24, 1863, Department of Northern Virginia.

M. D. SIGMAN 18-A (October 1863). Private Sigman was conscripted, deserted, arrested, and shot on the same days as Private Shook. The record of Private Sigman, however, does not show any attempt at a prior desertion, as was the case with Private Shook. Chaplain Kennedy noted his activity in the days preceding the execution of Privates Sigman and Shook.

> Wednesday, October 28, Somebody stole all our bacon last night. Wednesday, November 4th Called to see two men of the 18th Reg't who are condemned to be shot tomorrow, and were just brought to camp today. They are both members of the Lutheran Church and profess to feel prepared for death. They desire the Sacrament of the Lord's Supper and I rode through the neighborhood trying to get wine, but have failed so far. Thursday, November 5th Succeeded this morning in getting some wine from my friend Capt. Oates. In company with the Rev. A. W. Morris, administered the Sacrament to the two convicts. Held service with them, and then walked with them to the place of execution. At the stake I read the burial service, Bro. Morris prayed, they were tied to the stakes, the word was given, and one of them was killed, but the other had to be shot a second time. A most revolting spectacle. The names were Hook [Shook] and Sigman from Co. A 18 N.C. Reg't. Grand cavalry review by Lee grandest show ever witnessed.[47]

The Chaplain witnessed contrasting events that day, each intended to keep men in the ranks, a double execution and a grand cavalry review.

JAMES HOLMAN 37-F (October 30, 1863). Private Holman volunteered for a year of Confederate service, doing so in September 1861. In April 1862, he was given a $40 bounty for extending his enlistment in the Western Carolina Stars, Wilkes County. Slightly over half of the 191 men who enrolled in the company were absent at some point during the war. In December Private Holman was absent without leave. The next May he abandoned his company at Chancellorsville, VA, and on July 23, 1863, deserted while near Front Royal, VA. The last desertion attempt was successful for four months, but then Private Holman was jailed in Franklin County, VA. A four-day stay cost the Confederacy five dollars, and then Private Holman was escorted back to the army. He went before a court gathered on October 30. The charges against him included the abandonment at Chancellorsville and the most recent desertion. He was judged guilty on both of these charges but not guilty on a charge of persuading Privates B. H. Kilby and J. H. Kilby, both of Wilkes County, to desert with him. The same court that sentenced Private Holman to death heard the case against Private B. H. Kilby. He was treated leniently because he was young, and "the pallitory drift of the evidence," indicated he was "susceptible to persuasion."[48] Despite the "pallitory drift," he was sentenced to three months' confinement with a ball and chain attached to a leg. No record has been found of a trial for Private J. H. Kilby, who was several years younger than Private B. H. Kilby. Chaplain Kennedy movingly wrote on November 14:

> Attended the execution of Private James Holman, Co F. 37th Reg't, Wilkes Co. shot for desertion and misbehavior in the presence of the enemy. Poor fellow! his nerves were terribly

unstrung, and I fear he was not prepared for his change. Just before the guard was ready, he asked that I should request them not to shoot him in the face. His wish was respected and he died from the first volley, pierced with three balls in the heart and one in the thigh.[49]

That Private Holman was not shot in the face was likely a matter of chance more than anything else. At least two in the execution detail missed their target completely, and one shot quite low, possibly wishing to comply with the last pleading of the kneeling soldier. Private William D. Alexander, Company C, tersely stated, "Nov 14 Holdman [sic] of Co. "F" was shot for desertion."[50] An embarrassed Private A. J. Proffit, Company D, wrote home: "I can say to you that I had the mortification of seeing James Holman shot to death on the 14th of this inst. Which was quite a trying scene I have seen 10 men shot for desertion Which is a shocking scene but I have seen so many horrible things that nothing has much affect on me."[51] A second member of the Proffit family wrote to his sister, "We have a fine company and it is increasing all most daily They have stopped desertion in the army by shooting a few I have witnessed the death of 12 by musketry for deserting The last one was James Howlman [sic] he was shot last Saturday I have sean as many men shot as I wish to some haft to be shot the second time and that is quite a sight to see."[52]

Another observer noted the reaction of the man at the stake, "There was one shot to death with musketry in our Brigade yesterday for desertion. He took it more at heart than any I have seen. We have eight prisoners in our Regt all for desertion. Some of them will be shot."[53] Private Phillip Walsh was more emotionally involved when he wrote, "I am sorrey to inform you of the deth of James Holman he was shot yesterday at 11 Clock I cud not bare to see it all though I hope he is beter off he said that he was prepared to die he though I rote his wife a letter an started it to day I am sorry for wife and children I done all I cud to save his life but it was all in vane."[54]

GEORGE W. SHIPWASH 28-F (November 23, 1863). Private Shipwash was a frequent deserter and partially successful in that he was able to avoid the procession to the stake. Within his first two years of duty with the Yadkin Boys, beginning in June 1861, he deserted three times. Brought to trial for the first attempt, Private Shipwash, along with five others of the regiment, was given the relatively light punishment of confinement while wearing a six-pound ball attached to his ankle for fourteen days. The desertion and subsequent punishment was not entered on his service record. Such a light sentence led General Joseph R. Anderson, District of Cape Fear, on December 23, 1861, to prophetically observe that the punishment was very mild and continued attempts to desert would show such leniency's inefficiency. He further urged that the court should insist upon punishment adequate to repress deserters.[55] The truth of this pronouncement grew increasingly evident for Private Shipwash and others in the years ahead. Arrested after a third desertion attempt; Private Shipwash was taken to trial on November 23, 1863. This court, though probably unaware of General Anderson's earlier comment, declined to continue any misguided leniency. Private Shipwash was sentenced to be shot to death in seven days. Within a few days, in some fashion, perhaps escaping from an inattentive guard, the condemned man gained sufficient freedom to be captured by Federal forces on December 5. The following year he took the oath and was released at Philadelphia, PA.

JOHN A. TEAGUE 37-G (November 26, 1863). Private Teague volunteered for a year of service in the Alexander Soldiers in October 1861. When this term of service was legally extended, he began a series of unauthorized absences, each more serious than the last. In his initial effort to leave the service, he deserted from near Gordonsville, VA, on May 17, 1862. For seven months he was able to avoid arrest but was eventually returned to camp in early 1863. No punishment for this extended absence is noted on his record. Private Teague stayed in the ranks until June 20, when he again stole away, this time taking his gun and accouterments with him. Now armed, Private Teague was able to elude pursuers for five months, but was then caught and brought back to his command on November 11. Court-martialed on November 26, Private Teague learned that he was to be shot. The sentence was published on the day after Christmas. While under sentence of death, the elusive private managed to escape from his guard, this time taking the prudent step of going directly to the enemy, near Liberty Mills, VA, on January 6, 1864. Two months after reaching the enemy lines, he signed his oath to the Federal government. Private Teague was the second condemned man in the brigade to escape from the guardhouse in the past month. A soldier in his regiment reported: "That man that was to bee shot he got a way last Wednesday befor he was to bee shot Fryday."[56]

The same court that sentenced Private Teague also heard the case against Private Jordan S. Councill, a resident of Watauga County who had enrolled in the Thirty-Seventh in September of 1861. Private Councill was absent without leave in late 1862. He expressed his views on his trial and subsequent sentence in a letter to his wife written on January 17, 1864.

> Dear Companion I taken haggaman [Sergeant Hamilton D. Hagaman, Company B] for my witness my self I herd him give in his eveidense and I think he gave me justes as near as he could I think I would a come clere if it had not to a bin for barber he had the punishment put one me an if I live to gite oute of this ware he will fare but midlen ... my punishment was red out one dres perad the 6th of this instant to ware a ball and chain 3 months and do polese duty 4 ours each day an foreit all pay that is due me upe to the last of february 1864 well my Deare I donte care a darn for the money for it ant now conte [no count] now how but the other is whate I dred an I donte dred it mch for I donte think it is as as much disone [dishonor] to me as it is to the mane that has it pute one me I donte intend to do any duety while I ware it I will see them in hell first an I tell you if they pute it one me I am done fitin that is shore.[57]

Private Councill did not survive the war to gain his revenge on the man that he blamed for his punishment, "if it had not to a bin for barber." Nor did the man he blamed; Colonel William M. Barbour died in December 1864.[58]

EPHRAIM OSBORNE 37-A (December 1863). Private Osborne was conscripted into the Beauregard Riflemen, Ashe County, in August 1862. There he held to his obligation until May 19, 1863, when he deserted to remain absent for seven months. He was brought back under guard in December. Taken to trial before a Military Court, the initial sentence was that Private Osborne should be shot. But in a very unusual step the court reconsidered their decision and reduced the death sentence to five years' imprisonment and loss of pay. The prisoner served one year of the sentence before he was returned to duty by virtue of GO #2 in early 1865. The amnesty that was offered in that order also applied to men who were imprisoned for one attempt to desert.[59] Private Osborne vindicated the judgment of Confederate authorities by remaining in the ranks till the final surrender.

With the hardships, trials, and executions weighing heavily on him, a mature and thoughtful member of the Seventh reflected on the state of things in a letter of January 22, 1864: "For it is the universal opinion of mankind generally that a soldiers life, in time of war, is the roughest existence possible; and it is an indisputable fact that we, of the army of Northern Virginia experience as great hardships as any soldiers <u>ever</u> did." The writer emphasizes his remark by saying that the army is, "half fed, badly clad and <u>almost entirely</u>

barefooted." With a remarkable degree of foresight: "It is rather discouraging to reflect that while we are suffering all that men can suffer, the people at home are almost ready to backout and give up the business. It is painful for a man to think that he must suffer and die in a cause that <u>may</u> be rendered execrable by a 'reconstruction' at some future day."[60]

How prophetic, and more so year by year as the sacrifice of so many fades in memory.

DILLA MATHESON 7-A (February 1, 1864). Private Matheson volunteered to fight for the Confederacy a few weeks after the people of North Carolina made their commitment. Except for bouts of illness, the volunteer was present for duty for two years until April 3, 1863, when he deserted from Camp Gregg, VA. It was not until year's end that Private Matheson was arrested to be taken back to his regiment. He delayed the trip by breaking arrest, only to be recaptured and warily escorted to his command. Private Matheson stood before a court convened on February 1, 1864. The prisoner was given a death sentence, which then went forward for presidential consideration on March 12, and was immediately returned on March 13. Such a rapid response to a death appeal usually indicated that President Davis declined to take favorable action, but in this case the sentence was commuted and the prisoner was taken to a military prison at Richmond. While confined, he went to the prison hospital and was able to escape from that place on May 14, 1864, to begin his third desertion attempt. Through some unknown combination of errors, a SO #256, October 17, 1864, AIGO, was released stating that the sentence of the court put forth on February 1, was remitted. The circumstances that led to this late order may indicate that the quick return of the presidential appeal in March was due to a clerical or administrative error. There is no service record for Private Matheson after his escape from the prison hospital.

GEORGE W. MURPHY 7-K (February 25, 1864). Private Murphy was absent due to sickness from the day of his conscription in September 1862 until May of 1863, at which time he was formally listed as a deserter. Finally with his company in January 1864, Private Murphy did not long loll about before leaving in that same month. He was apprehended on February 14, and went before a Military Court. The court's decision was that Private Murphy should be shot to death. The prisoner received a visit from Chaplain Kennedy on the morning of his execution day. "Friday March 18, 1864 Called to see Private Murphy of the 7th Regiment who was shot at 11 o'clock this morning for desertion."[61] No comment is made by the Chaplain on Private Murphy's acceptance of his fate; he may have been of a different persuasion. After the execution, Private William D. Alexander, Thirty-Seventh Regiment, wrote in his diary: "March 18 a man in the 7th was shot for desertion all has been quiet in camp since the first of March."[62] Also in the same regiment, a soldier sent news of the execution to those at home and indicated that more such events might follow.

> I will say to you that i saw a man shot today he belongs to the 7 north carolina ridgment in our Brigade I will say to you that five of our company run away on the 14 day of March and on the 17 day of March tha was brong back and put in the gard house I will tell you thare names Jery [Jeremiah] Blackburn and Elich [Alexander] Pendergrass and William Miller and James Holoway [Holloway] and George Black these is the five men wee dont now what tha will doo with them.[63]

More about these men follows anon. Private Peter Peterson, Company H, Twenty-Eighth Regiment, made brief mention of the execution. "It is very cold here now and geting colder every minitt I saw a man shot last Fryday and I don't want to see any other one."[64]

In the week before Private Murphy was shot, a private in the Twenty-Eighth, summarized his view on the current state of morale, writing to his wife in Catawba County.

> The soldiers all say the want go threw another campaign the say there is no use of it and I will soon see if the will doe so or not the all say we are [worn] out and its time to quit fighting but a few big men think otherwise and I reckon as long as the people will obey them the war will go on till the country is ruined and all the poor killed and perished to death.⁶⁵

An early expression of a rich-man's war and a poor-man's fight expressed by one in the latter class.

In a very legible hand befitting a man who wanted to become a Quartermaster-Clerk, a soldier also in the Twenty-Eighth wrote his parents on March 13: "I must tell you that five of our company run a way a bout 2 weeks a go I will tell you their names I guess father you know part of them Alford Peoples Henry Plowman Richmond Hall Zack Melton and eight of company F I am in hopes they will ketch them all."⁶⁶ He later inquired if the Home Guard had been ordered out to take up deserters. His query seems to show a concern that deserters were not being actively pursued rather than that he was considering setting out on that course.

A rather desperate tone is voiced by a soldier in the Thirty-Third, Company I:

> Good news I have none to communicate we have still hard times here [not legible] and much dissatisfaction is prevailing in the army many the soldiers many are deserting some cross the lines and go over to the yankees last night was a week ago 23 twenty three from my company walked away at one time which ruined our company there is only about 18 of us left and all our best and ablest men are goin those that are left are the most of them weakly men.⁶⁷

Within a week men writing home mentioned one large and several small desertions from their brigade. Men who were brought back the day before Private Murphy was shot had little hope.

GEORGE BLACK 37-A (March 23, 1864). Private Black experienced a full measure of military life after volunteering in August 1861. Capture by the enemy, parole, a period of absence without leave, wounding in battle, recovery, desertion and then execution all came to him as events followed one on the other. Before departing with the men of the Thirty-Seventh, mentioned above, Private Black had earlier deserted on May 19, 1863, and was not back with his command until January 18, 1864, an absence of eight months.

JEREMIAH BLACKBURN 37-A (March 23, 1864). The service record of Private Blackburn offers a divergence of evidence as to the strength of his commitment to the Confederacy. He initially volunteered for one year of service and later extended his enlistment. Sometime in the summer of 1862 he was wounded; records show that it was a slight wound, perhaps indicating that it might have been inconsequential for a more robust soldier. Around that same time he was confined in prison and was treated at the prison hospital. Whether he started his unauthorized leave from the prison or from the hospital is not clear, but he was absent and remained so until February 1863. On his return he was found unfit for further field duty and was detailed to the Medical Director at Camp Winder, VA, and was then hospitalized with a wound to his leg. After returning to duty, the troubled man shot off one of his fingers. He was later detailed as a nurse. This latest deliberate maiming suggests that the earlier slight wounds in the extremities were also self inflicted. In any event, at that point Private Blackburn took more direct action and deserted the army on June 1, 1863. He was back with his regiment by December 16, 1863, but then left with Private Black and the three others. From his record it can be gathered that Private Blackburn was a man who suffered more than most men in the emotional horror of combat. His contribution to the cause was to be at the execution cross. Privates Black and Blackburn were shot to death for desertion on Thursday, April 14, 1864. The men who deserted with them were sentenced to two years of hard labor. The effect of the double execution was minimal in the mind of one writer. He first told his sister that he would likely see many "Yankeys" before he would see her and then went on, "You will hear of one of the awfules times that ever has been since this war commence tha ar fixin for it now I was at lanes Brig yesteday I saw to men shot I tell you tha need not kill men for deseren for it dont do any good."[68]

JOHN W. LOOPER 7-K (April 1864). Private Looper deserted from his company on May 16, 1862, several months short of a full year of army service; and for most of that time he was hospitalized. The desertion that began in 1862 continued until March 24, 1864, an absence of twenty-two months. A few days after he was arrested, his wife wrote to Governor Vance.

> Capt. Robert Teague came to my house and has taken my Husband of from me and my poor little children on to the Army again he went of very chearfull and willingly and always has tould me that he intended going back and staying his time out during the War whenever he got so that he thought he could stand it but he always had been weekly and did not leave the Army with the intention of staying but for fear of the punishment of a deserter he was still afraid he would not be able to stand it he has still remained at home with me and has helped me carding spinning and weaving I could not tell hardly the amount of cloth he has wove likewise spinning (etc) he wove 50 od yards for one of my neighbors for bread and meat for his family ... I could get every neighbor I have to sign this petition if I had time but I have neglected writing to you so long owing to the deep snow we have had I could not get out to do any thing of the kind and I had this opertunity of starting you these few lines to pray you to have som pity and compasion on us my husband name is John W. Looper I must come to a conclusion hoping you will be merciful to us and I do pray that God will be the same to you Your humble servant Nancy Looper.[69]

There is no endorsement on the letter to indicate that it was ever sent to Confederate authorities who could take some action on the appeal. Private Looper was shot to death on April 30, 1864. Captain James S. Harris recorded the event more as a stain on the honor of the regiment than with any sense of feeling for the dead man. "On Saturday, April 30th, Private John W. Looper, company K, Seventh Regiment North Carolina troops was shot to death with musketry for desertion, the first and only execution that has occurred in the regiment."[70] Private Looper's service record and the comments of his wife describe a man who was not strong, in good health, or with any desire to be in the army. His long absence no doubt was a factor in leading the court to hand down a death sentence, and return in arrest afforded the court little ground for compassion. Private Looper was not a man who easily adapted to camp life, little different from Private Blackburn, but once in service there was little recourse that would spare their lives; in one manner or another they would serve the Confederacy.

Given his way, Captain James Albert Summers of Company A, Thirty-Third Regiment, would gladly have increased the number of men shot by at least one. Writing to an officer in the Iredell Militia, the Captain informed him that Private Peter C. Stewart of his company had once again deserted. The Captain related that two young women of Iredell had written to the wavering private urging him to come home and spend the summer like he did the last, and that "Gen. Green & Capt Bush would defend him." Unmoved by the poetic allusion, Captain Summers wanted the deserter brought back, not that he thought it would aid the service but that "I may have him shot." After giving more detail on the absence, the Captain warmed to his cause in closing: "If it is less trouble to you to have him shot than to send him back all right that is all the use that I have for him & if he comes back & the court don't shoot him I will."[71] The Captain emphasized his resolve with a vigorous underline. Private Stewart was returned to the army, tried and sentenced to hard labor. His second attempt at desertion does not appear on his record.[72]

LEWIS PRIME 28-F (May 4, 1864). General Order #46, June 25, 1864, 1st Corps, Army of Northern Virginia, stated that Private Prime deserted his regiment on March 2, 1864, while at Liberty Mills, VA, and remained absent until April 19, 1864. He was returned under guard. For this absence Private Prime received a death sentence from a Military Court that convened on May 4, 1864. The sentence, name of the prisoner, and unit in which he served are recorded in AIGO records. Other documents affirm that Private Prime was released from prison on the authority of GO #2. While these records clearly establish Private Prime's service, no other military records have been located to verify that he did indeed serve with North Carolina troops.

JACKSON CHURCH 37-A (May 4, 1864). Private Church deserted from his company while encamped near Richmond in July 1862. He remained a deserter until brought back under guard to the army, then at Liberty Mills, VA, on April 23, 1864. There he was tried and sentenced to death by a Military Court. While the court was in session, Lane's brigade was ordered to action in the Petersburg area, where they were occupied for the next several days. No further service record for Private Church has been found. His service record ends with the passing of the death sentence. The convicted prisoner may have escaped during the preparation for battle. Or he may have been quickly dispatched to lie with other executed men in unmarked graves near Liberty Mills, VA. The likelihood of either is about equal, leaning toward execution. This based on the length of his desertion and the comments of another soldier that he observed 21 executions of men in his brigade.[73] There are 20 known executions for this brigade, and Private Church is the most likely of the condemned to be the 21st.

Private Noah Smith and his brother-in-law, Private Martin V. Willis, enlisted in the Twenty-Eighth on July 30, 1861. Each deserted on more than one occasion to return to Iredell County. In the summer of 1864, Governor Vance was asked to provide some assurance that Private Smith could return to his command without fear of being shot as a deserter.

> He proposes to give himself up & return to his Co. if he could have any assurance that he would not be shot. He is a deserter now for the second time. He also has a brother-in-law Willis who is now a deserter for the third time rather a desperate character whose influence it is believed has caused their Noah Smith to desert. I am not authirised, neith[er] can I ask any favour for Willis who deserves to die.[74]

The writer goes on to describe the father of Private Smith as being one, "who is quite a poor man." Within a month of the appeal, Private Smith returned to his unit. At year's end the deserters were confined in the guardhouse. They were tried on October 22, 1864; each was sentenced to hard labor, Private Smith for twelve months and Private Willis for eighteen months. The sentences were remitted.

DANIEL PATE 18-D (October 7, 1864). Private Pate quickly stepped forward to enroll in the Robeson Rifle Guards, on the decision of North Carolina to go to war. By July 1862, the enthusiastic volunteer had enough of army life and began a series of three desertions that would essentially keep him away from his regiment until a few days preceding his execution. His case was heard at trial on October 7, 1864, and General A. P. Hill approved the resulting death sentence. The execution of Private Pate took place on October 19, 1864. A young man from Robeson County testified against the deserter at his trial:

> After a few days, after returning, I saw two men shot at the stake for desertion in the presence of our brigade. I saw 21 shot this way for desertion during the last and second last winter of the war. One of them being a man of our own company David [sic] Pate, and against whom no witness had to testify before the court martial but myself, as I was Orderly Sergeant and had to keep account of all present and all absent with or without leave — Sad Fate.[75]

Sergeant Augustus Evander Floyd, age twenty, goes on to relate that he had himself flirted with the death penalty when he was found asleep at his post, but he received a gentle reprimand. Sleeping on post violates the 46th Article of War and conviction carries a potential death sentence, as Sergeant Floyd was well aware. Wartime fortune smiled on some but abruptly frowned on others. "Some people is lucky anyhow as for me I am lucky too but mine all turns out to be bad luck."[76]

BARNEY HALL 18-A (November 2, 1864). Private Hall went off to war on June 15, 1861. He deserted from his regiment while near Fredericksburg, VA, on December 14, 1862. Arrest and return did not come about for two years. Finally at trial on January 12, 1865, Private Hall was ordered to be shot and General A. P. Hill approved the court's proceedings. The execution took place on January 21, 1865.

SAMUEL SHUMATE 37-F (February 9, 1865). Private Shumate deserted from the General Hospital at Danville, VA, on September 26, 1862, while being treated for a wound received in action at Manassas, VA. Privates Samuel and Esley Shumate had enrolled together on September 24, 1861, only to desert together after a year of service. The men remained absent for much of the war. Private Samuel Shumate returned to his command, apparently voluntarily, on December 27, 1864, whereupon he was confined in care of the Third Corps Provost Marshal. He was tried for desertion on February 9, 1865, and sentenced to be shot. On review of the sentence, it was determined that his case fell within the conditions of a general amnesty offered to deserters by General J. G. Martin, Department of Western North Carolina, in his GO #4. Private Esley Shumate did not rely on an amnesty order to spare his life; he went directly to Federal units on the first day of 1865. Private Samuel Shumate survived the war and was paroled in April 1865.

JOSEPH HONEYCUTT 7-G (February 1865). Private Honeycutt's age, forty-four, and his trade, shoemaker, may have enabled him to avoid conscription for two years after passage of the law in 1862. But amendments to the original conscription act removed both of these shelters, and another unwilling private was enrolled at Camp Holmes in August 1864 and sent to the Wake Rangers in the Seventh Regiment. Five months after leaving his family, Private Honeycutt wrote home to tell his wife that he was to be executed for desertion. His service records offer no information on the events that led to the letter. No other reference that a trial was held, a death penalty was handed down, or that an execution took place has been found. Private Honeycutt wrote home on March 3, 1865:

> I have to state to you the sad news that tomorrow at 12 o'clock that I have to die. I have to be shot to death for starting home to see my wife and dear children and was arrested and brought back and court-martialed and am to be shot at 12 o'clock. Me and D. M. Furr have to die but thanks be to God I am not afraid to die. I think when I leave this world I will be where Mary and Martha are.... My dear wife Nancy, I have to bid farewell to you. I want you to keep what things you have and pay my debt. And I want Julius and Ephraim to have my shop tools and I want them to take good care of them and remember me ... and I have 25 or 30 dollars and I shall spend 5 of them in the morning before I suffer. Dear Wife that is four

months service. I can't write like if I was not in trouble. I don't mind death like I do to leave my family for I have to suffer so much here that I don't fear.[77]

Private Honeycutt also asked that all of his debts be cleared by his wife, who had little enough to raise the family as it was. Men had real concern for respect in their community, even when bound for a deserter's grave and leaving a destitute family. On the morning of his execution day, Private Honeycutt wrote a final note to Nancy:

> This is the 4th day of March at 9 o'clock. I must soon be in eternity. I don't desire this but I am not afraid to die. I want you to get all of your child's funerals preached that are dead. Nancy, I want to see you one more time if I could be we can't meet any more. I want you and all the children to meet me in heaven.[78]

Private Honeycutt said that he was leaving a portion of four months' pay for his wife, indicating that he started for home in early 1865. He enrolled in August 1864 and was present for duty in the September–October reporting period.

DANIEL M. FURR 7-G (February 1865). The military record of Private Furr is the same as that for Private Honeycutt, and if the Honeycutt letter is accepted as truthful, the similarity continued on to their side by side execution. They were each conscripted on August 20, 1864, and were allegedly shot on March 4, 1865. No other verification has been found.

WINCHESTER C. PALMER 7-D (March 1, 1865). Private Palmer was conscripted into service on August 8, 1864. He had been eligible for service under the conscription laws for at least a year before being sent to Camp Holmes. On March 1, 1865, Private Palmer was court-martialed, found guilty as charged, and ordered to be shot. General Henry Heth's approval of the death sentence was made known on March 22, 1865, and the record was sent to the Secretary of War on March 30. No record of action has been found. Private Palmer survived the war and was back at his home after his eight months of service and a close brush with execution. Brothers Napolean and Pierson Palmer were killed while fighting for the Confederacy two years before Winchester was conscripted.

Summary

Of the 36 soldiers in the Branch-Lane-Barry Brigade who were sentenced to be shot, half lived in Wilkes or a contiguous county. At the time of the 1860 census, 17 of the condemned were married, 12 were single. The average age of those to be shot was twenty-five. Conscripts made up 13 of the condemned, 8 were shot. The lives of 13 of the 23 condemned volunteers ended on the execution field, approximately the same rate of execution for each group. A notable difference, executed volunteers served a little over two years; conscripts served less than a year. Volunteer or conscript, their execution delayed desertion decisions by six to eight months, based on a 21 company sample.

```
                1861    1862      1863      1864     1865   no date
Abs/Co           .3    2.4  6.8   6.7  4.3  2.0 5.2   5.6
To be executed                5    17        7    1    4       2
Executed                           12        4    1    3
```

Just over 700 men of the brigade were present at Appomattox; over 8,500 men were enrolled during the war. Twelve companies that had at least one man executed had an absence rate of 23 percent. Nine companies that had men so threatened but who then avoided execution had an absence rate of 24 percent. Companies that did not experience an execution threat had an absence rate of 17 percent. The total number of known deaths from all causes falls within a range of 52 to 73 per company, based on a sample of 16 companies.[79] In contrast, the number of absences from a company varied from as few as 3, Twenty-Eighth, Company C, to as many as 93, Thirty-Third, Company D, from a sample of 33 companies. Company C had 81 deaths, Company D, 58. Company C had no executions, Company D had 2. A wily Confederate might observe the number of dead, those departing and those executed, and conclude that the prospect for survival for one remaining in the ranks was far less than for one deciding to leave forthwith.

3

Third Corps, Wilcox Division, Pender-Scales Brigade

"They shoot men out hear for lively hand."[1]
"They cant get the pore class of people ciled faste a nof and they must shoot sum of them."[3]

Before the end of the conflict, 50 men of the Pender-Scales Brigade were sentenced to be shot to death; 18 were executed. Brigadier William Dorsey Pender was promoted before the time of intense execution activity. Frequent appearances on the execution field would have been an emotional burden for the young and devout officer. The strain of leadership in the early going was revealed when Colonel Pender wrote to his wife on October 11, 1861, "Yesterday and today I have felt as if I wanted to run and hide myself, and remain alone. God in his mercy sustains me." He goes on to comment on a court-martial then in session, "Putting charges against many that involve death. And then trying of those charges. The continued drag upon our tempers."[2] Although many charges did carry a potential death sentence, courts did not often return death verdicts in the opening days of war. The first execution in the brigade would not take place for sixteen months.

Upon learning of his promotion, Brigadier Alfred Moore Scales wrote his wife that he had been "made a sure enough Brigadier Gen." The letter went on: "We have in this division shot 15 or 20 men for desertion and more will be shot yet but it has had a fine effect in hurrying up those who are absent without leave every train brings large no's."[4] Only one of those executed was from his brigade. He did not keep his wife up to date on executions or suggest that they were burdensome to him as they grew more common. Quite the opposite, two days after an execution he wrote, "My life is very monotonous the duties each day being the same with but little variation save now and then rumour connected with our or the enemys movement in regard to the coming campaign."[5] Another man in his charge would be executed within the week and 8 more would follow by year's end.

The brigade of General Scales had 5 regiments comprising 54 companies. It led all North Carolina brigades in the total number of trials, at least 402, as recorded by the AIGO. Two regiments of the brigade also led all North Carolina regiments in the number of military trials, the Sixteenth with 111 and the Twenty-Second with 106. When the results of the 402 brigade trials were made known, 50 men were sentenced to be shot, and 52 were acquitted. The 3 most trouble prone companies of each regiment accounted for 57 percent of all Brigade trials. The least troublesome 3 companies from each regiment were charged with only 9 percent of the total. Six companies of the 54 in the brigade, accounted for one-third of all brigade courts.[6]

Thirteenth Regiment

During the war, 8 men of the Thirteenth were sentenced to be executed and 3 were shot; all were conscripts who were not long in camp. The Thirteenth had the fewest number of men to go before a court-martial in the brigade, just 52; 10 were acquitted. Company D, the Leasburg Grays, Caswell County; Company I, the Rockingham Rangers; and Company K, the Dixie Boys, Rockingham County had the largest number of recorded courts. From these companies, only one man was given a death sentence.

Sixteenth Regiment

The Sixteenth Regiment witnessed the executions of 4 comrades. Two of these men were conscripts and were likely comrades in name only. Company D, the Rutherford Riflemen; Company F, the Buncombe Guards; and Company K, the Columbus Riflemen were responsible for 54 percent of the 111 courts attributed to the regiment. Company F was a major contributor with 28 courts; but severe punishment was limited to 2 men to be flogged and 1 to be branded. Just under half of the 28 men who were court-martialed for desertion went on to make a second attempt. At the conclusion of the 111 trials of men in the Sixteenth, 7 were acquitted and 7 heard a death verdict.

Twenty-Second Regiment

The first soldier in the Twenty-Second Regiment to be informed that he would be executed heard that stern pronouncement on October 29, 1863, this after 30 months of strife. Within the next year, 10 men in the regiment would know that same dreadful moment, and for 3 their fears would be realized. Court-martial records for the Twenty-Second show that 11 men were sentenced to be executed, and 18 were acquitted. A third group of 16 men was given severe punishment: branding with a "C" for coward or a "D" for deserter, or up to fifty lashes on the bare back and imprisonment.

The militia in Randolph County killed at least 2 deserters from the Twenty-Second. Two of the most punished companies in the regiment were from that county. They were Company I, the Davis Guards; and Company L, the Uwharrie Rifles, adding Company F, the Alleghany True Blues; the three had men charged with 57 courts-martial. That was 54 percent of the regimental total of 106 courts, and these same companies accounted for 9 of the 11 death sentences placed on men of the regiment. Forty years after the war a soldier in the Twenty-Second recalled that he was "very fortunate in having good and kind officers from first to the last of the war."[7]

Thirty-Fourth Regiment

Seven men of the Thirty-Fourth were sentenced by military courts to be shot to death; 3 were executed. Enlisted men of the Thirty-Fourth appeared before courts-martial at 55 trials. Of these, 7 resulted in death sentences and 5 ended with acquittal. There were 15 severe sentences meted out by courts; 40 percent of the men of the regiment who went before a general court-martial were sentenced to either severe punishment or to death. Of the 50 men of the regiment who were convicted by a military court, 19 deserted a second time, 16 of whom reached the desired end of avoiding further service. Two companies that experienced the most court convictions, Company A, the Laurel Spring Guard, Ashe County, with 12; and Company H, the Rough and Readys, Cleveland County, with 7, had the largest number of death sentences, 3 in each case. Company K, the Montgomery Boys, had 5 men convicted at trial; one was given a death sentence. Another of the Montgomery Boys had a strong thirst for coffee and stole a haversack and a half of the beans. Private Willis Hurley was one of eight with that family name in the company so there were many to enjoy each bubbling pot. At trial he was sentenced to hard labor for his term of service.[8] The officers of the company had a taste for more bracing refreshment: "I think a good many of our officers were drunk all the time."[9]

Thirty-Eighth Regiment

Officers sitting on 78 military courts of men of the regiment returned death sentences for 17; 5 were executed, and 12 acquitted. The Thirty-Eighth enrolled 1,380 men; absences were 317, or 23 percent. There was early and ample evidence that desertion would be an ongoing concern for several companies. In October 1862, Adjutant David M. McIntire published a list of 98 men, nearly a full company, who were then absent. A reward of $30 was offered for each man. Two-thirds of them were from companies, B, E and F. Over the next thirty months, men of these companies would be involved in nearly half of all absences affecting the regiment. Of the 24 members of Company B, Men of Yadkin, that were included on Adjutant McIntire's list, 12 were in arrest by January 1863. All were court-martialed; 9 were found guilty of desertion, and 3 were acquitted. Sentences for the guilty ranged from death by musketry to carrying a log about camp. Now, as to the effectiveness of this range of pain, 11 of the 12 went on to a second and successful desertion. The soldier who received a painful sentence of fifty lashes on his bare back returned to the ranks and was later cited for his gallantry in battle. Of the 24 men of Company B absent on October 1, 1862, 18 ended their military commitment by desertion, and 6 remained with the company. In total, 76 absence incidents were recorded for Company B. Contrast that record with Company A of the same regiment. The Spartan Band from Duplin County had just 12 absences from Alpha to Omega. The two companies suffered nearly the same number of deaths, 36 in Company A and 38 in Company B.

The names of 17 men from Company E, the Richmond Boys, appear on the Adjutant's list. Court records do not show that any went to trial. For the war, military courts tried 8 men of the company; 7 were successful in their second desertion.

Company F, the Sulpher Wild Cats, of Catawba County, had 22 men included on the list of deserters. All of these men returned to duty; 5 at trial received sentences of confinement or flogging or branding. Essentially all 22 men went back to the ranks and had no further blemish on their records. In sum, of the 98 men from the Thirty-Eighth who were absent in October 1862, 25 were court-martialed, and 18 — nearly three-fourths — went on to a second and successful desertion. This experience with repetitive absence brings into question the effectiveness of any punishment short of death.

Efforts to control desertion were well directed, if not lastingly effective. Of the 17 men of the Thirty-Eighth sentenced to be shot to death after February 1863, 12 were enrolled in the companies that had absentees on the October 1862 listing. AIGO records show that 78 courts were held for men of the Thirty-Eighth. Companies B and F were the company of record for 43, as they were for 9 of the 17 men sentenced to be shot and for 3 who were executed.

Courts-Martial

WILLIAM A. TOMLIN 38-B (February 1863). Private Tomlin entered the service on April 19, 1862, just days after the Confederate Congress approved the conscription laws. On July 4, after serving less than three months, Private Tomlin asserted his own personal independence and deserted. The October 1862 listing of deserters from Company B has his name as Private W. A. Tomlinson, with a desertion date of June 31. For the next six months Private Tomlin was able to avoid arrest, but on January 3, 1863, he was taken into custody and delivered to Camp Holmes by J. E. Reeves of Surry County. For this act the public-spirited Mr. Reeves received $30 in bounty and $1.75 for travel expense.[10] The prisoner was taken before a general court-martial held in early February. The court agreed on a death sentence. The sentence was approved, and Private Tomlin was executed on Monday, February 23, 1863. One observer stated: "He fell a lifeless corpse pierced by ten Minnie balls two of which went through his head thirty-three years at the time."[11] If the writer's observations are correct, this was an unusual execution. The practice was that those loading the execution weapons, normally officers, would load only half of the weapons with a ball, buck, or a combination of the two. If Private Tomlin was actually hit by ten balls it would be noteworthy that so many weapons were loaded, and even more remarkable that they were aimed so accurately. The reference to "Minnie balls" was likely made to impress the reader rather than based on factual information. One possible explanation for the accuracy of those shooting at Private Tomlin is found in the remarks of a soldier writing to his parents on February 26.

> I can say that on last Monday I saw a man shot for crimes which I suppose deserve death he was shot by eight or ten men all at the same time which would appear to you I suppose rather a horable sight though it did not appear so terable as I had anticipated though if he is as mean as has been represented I do not know that it very much matter.[12]

The writer noted that Private Tomlin had committed "crimes" and that he was a "mean" man. The plural "crimes" may account for the severity of the sentence and "mean" for the accuracy of the shooting. Another observer noted that he had witnessed the execution of Private Tomlin. "I saw one man shot to death this week for desertion. Several have been branded in our regiment for desertion."[13]

A private in the same regiment as Private Tomlin wrote to a former officer of his company on March 30, 1863, a month after the execution. First commenting on his health and that of the company, the writer goes on to say that the men do not like the officers they now have, "The younger Lieutenants feels there keeping about as much as a 12 year old boy feels about his post."[14] An earthy reference to a perceived lack of concern on the part of company officers, as seen by one in their care. From scattered mention, there is an indication of a general lack of confidence in company officers in the Thirty-Eighth. A "rabble" tried to kidnap a company commander.[15] An officer in Company F resigned because he was "wanting in moral courage."[16] Officers failed to attend roll call and yet punished men who did not do so.[17] Noncommissioned officers were also found wanting: "Sergt Benneck acted very cowardly and the Genl thrashed him with his sword on Saturday the 20th [September 1862] and he has not been seen since."[18] Sergeant David J. Benneck was absent without leave on two occasions before being captured by the enemy. The dissatisfied soldier who commented on the young Lieutenants closed his letter with a note: "Our Regt is getting in Conscripts there has about 50 come Co. E. has got none nor dont want them unless they come from Richmond Co there is to be more here how much they look like sheep driven to the Slaughter pen which is it is not much better."[19] Officers with little concern for those in their charge, conscripts to be slaughtered, these are not good omens as the war goes into the third year.

A man in the Thirteenth wrote that two men had died as a result of being flogged.[20] An equally brutal infliction of this punishment is found in AIGO records for a military court that pronounced sentences for four slaves. One was to be hanged, another to receive 25 lashes, a second, 30 and the third, 39, the lashings to be repeated on each of four successive mornings.[21]

WILLIAM EARLE 34-H (May 1, 1863); and MARTIN J. EARLE 34-H (May 27, 1863). Well into their second year of duty, the Earle brothers deserted on April 21, 1863, while camped near Fredericksburg, VA. The absence continued until May 19, when they were taken under guard to their regiment. A second source shows that they were in arrest by April 29, a week after leaving their unit. For their running away, be it for a week or a month, the brothers were sentenced to be shot. General Lee on June 2 advised General A. P. Hill that the death sentence had been confirmed and to notify the prisoners. He went on to say that a general order announcing the decision would go to the printers the next morning.[22] The order for the execution was published on June 3. Two days later a private in the Thirty-Fourth wrote to his brother:

> Well, brother, I have nothing interesting to relate to you at this time more than I am sorry to say to you that there is to be two men in our Regt. shot to death on next Friday for deserting their colors. They got their sentence this morning and was chained together. They are members of Company H and are brothers. Brother, 'tis hard to see men served in this way but I think it just and right. We have ten other prisoners in our Regt. They look very grim today. The reason why they are shooting so many when they run away, they took their arms and intended to fight their way through but was overpowered and brought back. That is the same as rebelling against their Country — so a nuf of that.[23]

Service records do not show any stoppage in pay for the weapons, so presumably they were recovered when the boys were arrested. Execution was scheduled for June 13. On some unknown authority it was delayed or suspended and the death sentences were set aside on August 28, 1863. The brothers returned to duty with Company H and remained faithfully in the ranks until captured in April 1865, justifying the actions on their behalf.

Private E. R. Harris of Company C, Sixteenth Regiment, was in confinement and thought that he would be shot, so he broke his guard and deserted. His June 1863 letter to Governor Vance for aid included the additional gambit that he would bring in other men with him if he could be given assurance of a reprieve.[24] He did return and was sentenced to loss of pay for the time of his absence.

JOHN THOMAS 34-K (September 4, 1863). Private Thomas twice chose to chance desertion from his company. After the first decision, made while he was hospitalized in July

1862, he was absent for eight months. When he returned he was tried, found guilty and sentenced to have the left-half of his head shaved in the presence of his regiment and to forfeit eight months' pay. This was made known on March 17, 1863. On review, the head-shaving portion of the sentence was remitted as Private Thomas had returned in good faith under an amnesty proclamation issued by Governor Vance in January 1863. Those accepting the Governor's offer were assured immunity from punishment other than loss of pay for the time of their absence. Deserters brought "disgrace and infamy" on themselves for failing to resist the "brutal and half savage" invaders. Their act would bring "shame and suffering on heads of innocent" and the "finger of scorn" pointed at their families, intoned the Governor.[25] At least one man enrolled in the Twenty-Second did not agree with the Governor. He regretted that the proclamation prevented "the full reward which conduct deserves."[26] Possibly encouraged by the amnesty offer following the first escapade and likely expecting that another would be forthcoming, Private Thomas deserted in mid–August 1863 while near Orange Court House, VA. On this foray, he was only able to avoid apprehension for about two weeks, for he was under guard by August 29. Tried on September 4, his death sentence was published on September 17 in GO #88, Army of Northern Virginia, and he was shot to death on September 26. A correspondent believed that a meeting held in Montgomery County in support of the Federal cause led to the decision of Private Thomas and several others to desert, apparently feeling that they would be sheltered on their return to the county. The writer laconically noted, "John Thomas of our company will be shot next Saturday."[27]

There were many crimes that did not carry the threat of a death sentence or even require a general court-martial but still had a negative effect on other soldiers and their will to fight. Stealing kettles, frying pans, spiders, or other cooking implements was a serious concern in an army where men often cooked their rations in small groups with few utensils. Basic cooking implements likely rotated about as those that were stolen were replaced in like manner, with perhaps a legitimately obtained pot or pan occasionally added to the mix. One compatriot in Company A went on trial for stealing a bucket and his punishment was that he was to march before the regiment wearing a sign reading "bucket stealer."[28] Another man whose spider had wandered away related in a letter home that he had trudged about the camp, calling "Spider come home," but the cry went unheeded. A spider was a frame, or a pot, with legs, to provide support over the embers of a wood fire. The wagon that carried the cooking utensils was called the spider wagon by North Carolinians.[29]

HENRY D. LOVE 13-K (September 15, 1863). Private Love volunteered to fight for the Confederacy on May 22, 1861, and fight he did for two years. But at the battle at Chancellorsville, VA, which began on May 1, 1863, he was charged with misbehavior before the enemy, "While advancing in line of battle, expecting to be engaged with the enemy ... did shamefully abandon his company and regiment until May 4, 1863 after the battle was over."[30] For this violation, Private Love was court-martialed on September 15, and given a death sentence. Following a communication from the President, General Lee remitted the sentence on October 2, and Private Love returned to duty. He was later wounded and then paroled at war's end.

An officer in the Sixteenth would have been shot for failing to suppress a mutiny, "except for his ignorance and inability to appreciate the serious nature of the offence."[31] This is the first mention that an officer of the brigade was so ignorant that he could not be shot. A second officer received a similar appraisal about a month later.

SAMPSON K. CANNON 16-E (September 18, 1863). Private Cannon volunteered for duty in the Burke Tigers on May 10, 1861. At age twenty-four, he earned promotion to Sergeant, fulfilling that responsibility until deserting while near Culpeper Court House, VA, on July 25, 1863. Five weeks after forsaking his trust, he was in confinement awaiting a court-martial. The court, held on September 18, found the defendant guilty as charged. Their death decision was approved with publication of GO #90, September 25, 1863, Army of Northern Virginia. On October 2, General Lee notified Adjutant General Cooper that he had suspended execution of the sentence until the next Tuesday, October 6. General Lee then indicated his intention by adding the ominous comment, "If I hear nothing to the contrary their execution will take place as ordered."[32] This comment would indicate that General Lee had delayed the execution at the request or suggestion of General Cooper. General Cooper intervened more forcefully, on October 5, when he ordered General Lee to continue the suspension of the execution saying that a letter of explanation was coming. This exchange at the highest level of the Confederate army may have, in part, been brought about by a plea from Lieutenant J. M. Sides, Company E, Sixteenth Regiment to Governor Vance, dated September 24.

> Sir S. K. Cannon a member of Capt. A. S. Clouds Co. E 16th NC Regt is charged with desertion and the court sentens him to be shot to death with musketry next Saturday. Srg S. K. Cannon deserted the 25th July 1863 returned Sept 2 1863. Cannon has been a very good soldier Never has miss a fight that the Reg has been in while he was with the Reg He was wounded Dec 18 1862 and went home that is the only time he has been home duren the war he did not miss many fights by goen home he went threw Maryland and Pennsylvania and fought bravely [not clear] Time is short.[33]

The urgency of the request is emphasized by repeating "Time is short," on the outside of the folded sheet. There is no indication that Governor Vance directed that any action be taken. Enlisted men in Company E directed their own entreaties directly to President Davis. Their requests were granted with the issuance of SO #279, November 23, 1863, AIGO. This action was taken, "on the pledge of the company that no further desertions shall occur therein." The men of Company E honored the pledge. There was just one other desertion before March of 1865. Private Cannon returned to duty and was restored to his former position as 2nd Sergeant on the first day of 1864. He survived the war.

JOHN M. MICHAELS 16-E (September 18, 1863). Though Sergeant Michaels was six years younger than Sergeant Cannon, their service experience was closely entwined. They entered the service on the same day, enrolled in the same company, were returned from desertion, court-martialed, and then sentenced to be shot at the same time. Sergeant Michaels was the first to desert, starting for home some six weeks before Sergeant Cannon. As in the case of Sergeant Cannon, Lieutenant Sides also directed a letter to Governor Vance on behalf of Sergeant Michaels. In this letter he placed more emphasis on the desperate conditions at home that led to the desertion. "The cause of his desertion was this His father and mother is both dead and there was a houseful of little children and no one to take ker of them and he went home."[34] Private Michaels was released from his death sentence in the same order that released Private Cannon, with the same comment on the pledge of Company E. He also regained his rank and survived the war.

WILLIAM CLAPP 16-H (September 18, 1863). Conscript William Clapp was under escort to his designated regiment, the Sixteenth, when he fled on October 10, 1862, while between Staunton and Bunker Hill, VA. Nearly a year later, he was arrested by men of the Sixty-Eighth North Carolina Militia, Guilford County, and delivered to Camp Holmes.

Lieutenant G. L. Greeson (Grason) received $60 for his effort in bringing in his bag of conscripts.[35] Private Clapp went to trial on September 18, and learned that he would be shot when GO #90, September 25, 1863, Army of Northern Virginia was published. The conscript was executed on October 3, never having served a day of duty with the men who shot and buried him. A witness observed that only one ball of the first volley struck Private Clapp. If accurate, the firing detail had little will to kill, or they were terrible marksmen. Two reserve executioners were brought forward to fire at point-blank range. Contrast this marksmanship with that at the execution of Private Tomlin of the Thirty-Eighth, who was allegedly struck with ten balls. This writer noted that he had witnessed the earlier execution of Private Tomlin, but made no mention as to the number of balls that tore his body.[36] On the day after the execution, Private P. H. Warlick, Co F, Thirty-Fourth expressed his thoughts to his wife.

> There was one man shot in the 16 yesterday and [seven] in lanes brig yesterday was a week ago it appears they cant git the pore class of people ciled faste a nof and they must shoot sum of them but thers a time a coming when they will have to account for all this eavelness.[37]

Another soldier in the same company offered his honest opinion of the poor leadership of the company and regiment, and goes on to emphasize the growing disaffection with conscripts coming to the regiment.[38]

Private Noah R. Kelly of Co. E, Thirty-Eighth, also started a letter home on October 4 in which he expanded on his timely return and his fidelity to the colors. The latter statement, while no doubt sincerely offered soon after the death of Private Clapp, leaves a hollow ring when Privates Richmond Kelly and Noah Kelly subsequently desert, adding to the already noteworthy desertion record of their company. Shortly after returning to the camp of the Thirty-Eighth near Orange Court House, VA, after his fourth desertion, Private Noah R. Kelly, Company E, wrote to his cousin:

> My Dear Cousan It is with the greatest love and pleasure I take my pen in hand to inform you that I am not well at present though I as so as to get about My dear cousan I have not much nes [news] to communicate to you at this time though I will give you all I have times are hard [not legible] they are shooting deserters here for their first desertion thanks be to my God that I got to my Reg't when I did if I had not perhaps I should have [not legible] but I am here standing by my colors and [not legible] expect to see any of you any more until this wicked war does come to an end.[39]

Private Kelly was fortunate in that he had taken advantage of a presidential amnesty to return from his latest absence. Once he had enlisted on October 31, 1861, Private Kelly began a consistent pattern of deserting every three or four months, remaining absent for a wary interlude, then returning for a short stay, before beginning the next round. Considering a venture back to his regiment after his latest excursion, the well-experienced deserter had the foresight to see that a clemency request was directed to Governor Vance by officers of the Eightieth Regiment North Carolina Militia.

> Wadesboro [Anson County] NC Sept 19th 63 Gov Vance Dear Sir Noah R. Kelly who has been a deserter has seen the error of his way and has voluntarily renounced his course and now asks pardon at your hands and desires you to stay the punishment that would otherwise [not legible] him in the 38th NCT to which he belongs. Those interpose in his behalf as we the Militia Officers of the 80th NCM believe he will henceforth remain true to his colors.[40]

Three days later, Lieutenant John B. Ingram, Eightieth NCM, was paid $48 for the arrest and delivery of N. R. Kelley and Robert Brooks to Colonel Peter Mallett. No doubt

Private Kelly was convincing when he "renounced his course" and really was committed to "remain true to his colors" at the time, but six months later, in April 1864, he undertook his fifth and last desertion, this time going directly into the lines of the enemy. He survived captivity to take the oath at war's end. Private Richmond Y. Kelly of the same company had a similar record of repetitive desertions and he was sentenced to three months' confinement with a ball and chain attached to his leg in December 1863. He made his last desertion attempt — which was successful — in May 1864.

CYRUS DRUM 38-G (September 29, 1863). Private Drum volunteered on March 7, 1863. Though age thirty-seven, he was still liable for conscription. Just two months later, in early May, he was wounded in the battle at Chancellorsville, VA. When his recuperative furlough ended he did not return to duty and was officially classified as a deserter on August 13. He voluntarily returned to his regiment on September 23 when he was placed under guard to await a court-martial. After hearing his case, the court came down with a death sentence that was made known on October 4, but included in the same order was an unusual observation by the General Commanding:

The execution of the sentence in the case of Private Cyrus Drum is in consideration of the noble and patriotic conduct of his excellent wife, in not desiring to see him as a deserter, and in sending him immediately back to the army, is suspended until the decision of the President is known....The General Commanding cannot pass this case without expressing his sincere admiration for Mrs. Drums conduct, and hopes she will find many imitators. If the women of the Confederacy will do likewise, desertion will cease and it is hoped that her husband will hereafter prove himself worthy of one of the heroines of this struggle.[41]

The death sentence that was first suspended by General Lee was then remitted by the President in SO #54, March 5, 1864, AIGO. Private Drum did not disappoint his wife, Nancy, or the General Commanding; he fought through the war and surrendered at Appomattox.

A second officer in the brigade who avoided execution had risen to the rank of Captain before going absent without leave. His reason for leaving was that he thought he would be dropped as an officer and then conscripted back into the same company. His fears were well grounded, for in commenting on the case, the court said that the accused should be shot but that he was an "ignorant and unintelligent" man, this surprising comment coming after the officer had served two years as a company Captain.[42]

In October 1863 those considering desertion were increasingly aware that their lives were in the balance. An absentee from Company D of the Thirty-Eighth acknowledged his predicament when he explained to Governor Vance that he had left his company and "now they are goin to shoot me when the can come up with me."[43] Private Rufus Strickland returned to camp October 5, 1863, and after a court-martial was sentenced to three months' confinement with a ball and chain attached to his leg.

JOHN N. JONES 16-F (October 26, 1863). Private John N. Jones of Company F, Sixteenth Regiment, was one of five named Jones, all of Buncombe County, to enlist in the same company on the same day, May 7, 1861. After nine months of camp life, Private John N. Jones left kin and companion without grant of leave in February 1862. He was tried for this offense of being absent without leave and knew the humiliation of having the left side of his head shaved and forfeiture of ten months' pay — a very light sentence for a long absence. Six months later, on July 11, 1863, Private Jones again fled from camp, this time while near Hagerstown, MD, and was a fugitive until September 25, 1863. At trial a month later, the court took notice that this was the second offense for the prisoner and handed down a death verdict. The finding of the court was approved with the execution to be carried out seven days after publication of the order on November 4, 1863. Records do not validate that Private Jones was definitely shot on the appointed day. Considering the emphasis placed on executing deserters in the fall of 1863 and lack of any record of intervention, it is likely that the execution took place as scheduled.

Another of the Jones men, Private Montraville M. Jones, had enlisted on the same day as the executed man, and awaited a court-martial for a "frivolous offence" in December 1864. Not as naive as some North Carolinians who went before military courts, Private Jones took the prudent step of writing to Governor Vance to secure a statement as to his standing in Buncombe County, because "the court seems to be very strict respecting a persons former deportment in life." The writer felt that a favorable response by Governor Vance would "tend to be beneficial to me in my case." The Governor instructed that a reply should state, "I know Jones and his family in Buncombe they are accounted both loyal and respectable."[44]

PETER TRAFFENSTEDT 38-F (October 27, 1863). Private Traffenstedt twice left his home in Catawba County to serve with Confederate forces. A voluntary enlistment in Company L, Sixteenth Regiment, began on March 15, 1862, and ended with discharge after four months of duty. A note in his service record indicates that he was age eighteen when discharged. The homebound youngster was in poor health suffering measles, great emaciation, chronic diarrhea, and incipient phthisis pulmonalis. Understandably disillusioned by his initial experience in camp and apparently not willing to again volunteer, the discharged soldier was conscripted in March of 1863 and assigned to Company F, Thirty-Eighth Regiment. Six months in the ranks was enough for Private Traffenstedt and he left his command. He reconsidered this decision and decided to return after an absence of six weeks. The charge of desertion was still pressed before a court on October 27. Not swayed by the prisoner's age and voluntary return, the court concurred that he should be shot to death, but then immediately recommended leniency. General Lee agreed with their recommendation and ordered suspension of the execution until the President could review the case. The death sentence was remitted by Special Order on March 3, 1864. The relieved man was present for duty through October 1864, when his service record ends.

DAVID HOLLAR 38-F (October 28, 1863). Private Hollar was brought back to his regiment, along with other deserters, on October 17, 1863. His desertion began earlier in the year, in May, after nineteen months of duty. He had enrolled on October 31, 1861. Nearly two years after to the day, on October 28, he went before a military court charged with desertion, his life in their hands. The finding of the court was that he was guilty as charged and that he should be shot for his crime. The death sentence was remitted and the charge reduced to absent without leave. Punishment was forfeiture of pay for the period of absence. This was very minimal punishment for an absence of five months, inasmuch as other men were executed after absences measured in days. The grateful private returned to duty and stayed on to the final day at Appomattox, VA.

ALLEN HUFFMAN 38-F (October 28, 1863); and DAVID HUFFMAN 38-F (October 28, 1863). The Huffman brothers had practically identical service experiences from enlistment to the prospect of blindfolding moments before their execution. The young men left their home in Catawba County when they volunteered for service on October 31, 1861. They faithfully kept their place in the ranks until June 17, 1863, when they deserted, while near Stephensburg, VA. They were able to avoid arrest for four months but were then detected and detained to be returned to their command to face trial. This proceeding took place on October 28, and at its conclusion the brothers were told they would be shot. The death sentences were remitted, and both men returned to serve honorably for the rest of the war.

ELIAS LAEL 38-F (October 28, 1863). A second set of brothers, also from Catawba County, enrolled on the same day as did the Huffman brothers in October 1861. Privates Elias and Lawson Lael went into the same company with the Huffman boys. Private Elias Lael deserted on June 18, 1863, while the regiment was near Culpeper, VA, taking his Enfield rifle and accouterments when he left. The well-armed deserter was brought back after an absence of four months, appeared before a court, and later learned that he was to be shot to death. This sentence was apparently set aside, for he again appeared before a court in December. Thereafter he was confined at Castle Thunder and later at Prison Hospital #13, where he died of bronchitis on August 15, 1864. Private Lawson Lael deserted two months after his brother, but they were taken back to their units at the same time. He received a lighter sentence, loss of pay and two months' extra duty, and then served until the end.

NOAH WINEBARGER 38-F (October 28, 1863). About a year after joining the service, Privates Daniel and Noah Winebarger first absented themselves from their unit, this on September 16, 1862. At some point they returned to camp but then, again together, left their company without proper authorization, this on May 25, 1863. Private Noah Winebarger avoided capture for five months. But once arrested, he was tried, convicted and sentenced to be executed, all in short order. No record of punishment for Private Daniel Winebarger has been found. He had returned to duty three months before his brother was brought back. The sentence of the condemned brother was remitted and the brothers were captured by the enemy at Hanover Junction, VA, on May 23, 1864, and imprisoned at Point Lookout, MD.

These three sets of brothers from Catawba County enrolled in Company F, Thirty-Eighth Regiment, and served a year or more. All made decisions to desert; all left families in which the mother was the sole parent in 1860. In the fall of 1863, it was obvious to men of the Thirty-Eighth that men convicted of desertion were apt to be executed. Far fewer men left camp at that time. For the six months following September 1863, only 14 absences were recorded for the regiment, but by the spring of 1864, absences increased and continued to final surrender.

SAMUEL C. ALLRED 22-L (October 29, 1863). A two-year record of attentive duty was abruptly negated when Private Allred deserted on August 1, 1863, while near Culpepper Court House, VA. Within two months he had second thoughts and voluntarily returned to his regiment. Even though he came back unescorted, he was taken under guard to Castle Thunder at Richmond, there to await his trial. On October 29, a court heard his case; he was found guilty of desertion and sentenced to be shot. The court then made the unanimous recommendation to delay the execution of sentence until the President's decision could be known. Private Allred's conspicuous gallantry in battle, his general good conduct and his voluntary surrender to authorities were facts all duly noted in the court's comments in support of their decision. The transmittal that General Lee sent to the President offered the same reasoning. With these favorable endorsements before him, the President remitted Private Allred's death sentence in SO #52, March 3, 1864, AIGO. Within a year, the reprieved man died at Richmond from an unknown cause. His service record has this note:

"He was one of the most attentive soldiers in the company when present."[45] The final qualifying "when present" seemingly refers to his time absent on detail as a teamster, rather than to his brief absence in the fall of 1863.

EDMOND M. BERRY 22-H (October 29, 1863). Private Berry shared in the benevolent grace of the same court that had acted with consideration for Private Allred. The boys were in the same regiment, and their service records were quite similar. Private Berry had served since June 6, 1861, deserting a day or two before Private Allred, but they were both back with their command on the same day. The court for Private Berry convened on October 29, 1863; the decision that he should be shot was announced five days later. However, as in the prior case, the court went on to say that the guilty man was an "obedient and good soldier," one who had shown gallantry in five or more battles. The execution was suspended by General Lee; the sentence was then remitted in SO #53, March 4, 1864, AIGO. General Lee in his statement took note of the long service of Private Berry and mentioned his gallantry at Seven Pines and other engagements. He was present for duty in November 1864.

MILTON LAMB 22-I (November 4, 1863). Enlistment day for Private Lamb was March 1, 1862. Seven months later, he deserted while near Bunker Hill, VA, on October 25. His defection extended for nearly a year, until September 2, 1863, when he was delivered to Camp Holmes by an officer of the Sixty-Eighth North Carolina Militia of Guilford County. After due deliberation by a court Private Lamb was informed that he would be executed. In some manner, or by some authority yet undiscovered, the private avoided execution. He was last reported on a clothing record in March 1864, but this offers scant proof that he was with his company. Company I had a total enrollment of 184 men during the war, they were charged with 65 incidents of unauthorized absence and faced 25 military courts, second highest for the brigade. By war's end 44 company men were dead.

In November 1863, Private John W. M. Abernathy, Company M, Sixteenth Regiment, wrote to ask for the Governor's assistance in ending his absence. His "aged parents" said he should return immediately for "I have brought them to trouble by behaving myself in such an unlawful way."[46] He closed by saying that his father would have him arrested, and sent back if he did not promptly return to his company.

JACKSON IRELAND 38-B (November 1863). Two privates of Company B, Thirty-Eighth, took an active approach to avoiding a death sentence that was announced in GO #101, November 24, 1863, Army of Northern Virginia. A week after learning that they would be shot, the men broke their guard and ran for their lives. One, Private Ireland, had little to lose; the sudden dash was his third desertion. The second attempt, for which he was confined and awaiting execution, began when he deserted at Chancellorsville, VA, on May 3, 1863, and ended in arrest and return under guard on November 7. His escape from the guardhouse preserved his life, for he avoided capture for the remaining fifteen months of war.

JAMES M. MANLEY 38-B (November 1863). The other man who fled from the guard was Corporal Manley. His first excursion as a deserter started when the regiment was at Sharpsburg, MD, on September 17, 1862. He was able to avoid apprehension for fourteen months but was eventually jailed and then taken back to stand trial, which resulted in a death sentence. While absent from his command, he was reduced in rank. After his escape from the guardhouse, he avoided any further confrontations with Confederate forces. In March of 1864, local authorities knew that he was somewhere about in Rutherford County, but he was not arrested.[47] He was present for duty for twelve of his forty-one months of service.

WILLIAM SHAW 13-F (November 1863). Private Shaw, an older man at thirty-six on enlistment, was conscripted but could be kept in the ranks a scant few weeks before he was willing to accept the risk of execution for desertion. Privates William and Augustus Shaw of Davie County were conscripted on March 26, 1863. A little over two weeks later, they deserted from Camp Gregg, Fredericks-burg, VA. Private William Shaw was caught and brought back to Brandy Station, VA, on October 28, after being absent for six months. He was tried and sentenced to be shot, the decision made known on November 24, 1863. Rather than a short, merciful wait of seven days to make his peace with friends, family and God, a first hopeful, then agonizing delay followed the release of his execution order. Initially, a suspension of sentence was granted to allow the accused prisoner the privilege of producing exculpatory evidence. He was unable to develop substantive information sufficient to sway authorities, and an order was issued to proceed with the execution. That decision raised a technical point on the legality of proceeding with an execution that was not carried into effect on the day originally set because the army was in motion. After due consideration, that argument was not considered persuasive by the authorities at the War Department.[48] Private William Shaw was legally dispatched on April 26, 1864. Private Augustus Shaw was never apprehended.

OLIVER H. LOOPER 38-G (November 1863). Private Looper was a lad of eighteen years when he enlisted in Alexander County in November 1861. Many of the days that followed were either in a hospital or bed-ridden in camp. While on an illness furlough, Private Looper decided not to go back to his command and was officially classified as being absent without leave on August 1, 1863. He eventually went back to his company but in early October decided to return home. Once there he "found out that he had done rong," and asked Governor Vance to help him get transportation for the long trip back.

> Alexander County, NC State This November the 7th 1863 Gov..Z..B..Vance I this morning take the opportunity of conversing with you in this way in the first place I had been in regiler service for too years and never had but one furlow and I heard of so many deserting and coming home and so at last I thought I would go too and some persuaded me to go and I went home to my parents and I am here at home at this time and I found out I had done rong and I want to go back and I dont want the gard to take me and I want you to send me a transpatation back to my regiment Will you be so kind as to send me a paper that I can go to my reg and pleas grant my request I left my camp the 3 of October 1863 and got home October 30th 1863 if you will oblige me send to York Inst PO Alexander Co NC I am a Private in Company G.. 38 reg NC Troops. O.. H Looper To Govner Z.. B.. Vance.[49]

By November 19, Private Looper was on his return journey having been sent on his way to Camp Vance, not by the Governor, but by the Fifth Regiment North Carolina Home Guard. The watchful guard was cautioned on the character of the prisoners in their care. "Oliver H. Looper overstayed his furlough surrendered he is of good character will do to trust." In contrast, a man of the Fourth Regiment, "caught and needs much attention will run again if he gets half a chance has jumped from the train near Raleigh."[50] True to his word, Private Looper returned to camp near Richmond. But by November 27, he was at Castle Thunder under sentence of death, sent there by order of Captain Blackford.[51] He was released from the sentence. A wound led to his assignment to the Invalid Corps. Private Looper was present for duty less than six months, though on regimental rolls for three years.

WILEY BARE 34-A (December 12, 1863). Private Wiley Bare was one of five with that surname who enrolled in Ashe County on August 10, 1861. After a year, Private Bare deserted his company and was absent for fifteen months. Safely in hand on December 12, 1863, he was court-martialed and sentenced to be shot. On hearing the decision of the court, the prisoner became "partially deranged" and "insensitive to everything."[52] The President reviewed the case but declined to interfere in the execution.[53] Just two days before the scheduled execution Brigadier Scales wrote to Major J. A. Engelhard, AGM. "Head Qtrs Scales Brigade Jan 7th 1864 Maj. I am informed that Private Wiley Bare of Co A 34 R NCT who is to be executed on Saturday next for [line not legible]. I learn further that he has been for some time past subject to these spells. If he continues so up to the day of execution shall he be executed in this condition."[54] Two days after this request for guidance, Surgeon J. F. Miller of the Thirty-Fourth provided his written professional opinion.

> Med Dept 34 NCT Jany 9th 1864 I certify that I have carefully examined Prvt Wiley Bare Co A 34th NCT now under sentence of death and find him laboring under what appears to be partial derangement of his intellectual faculties. He has presented these symptoms of great nervous excitement, such as spasms, since he has heard of the decision of his case; appears to be insensible of every [not legible] about him. How much of these symptoms may in his case be feigned I am unable to determine. It has been reported to me that he was similarly afflicted before the war but I have no personal knowledge of the fact.[55]

That same day Colonel R. H. Chilton, AAG, Army of Northern Virginia, ordered that the execution of Private Bare be suspended for one week. A second medical opinion was then placed on the record.

> I find him labouring under severe mental cerebral disease produced I think by mental anxiety acting upon a mind naturally weak. I regard his condition as critical and he cannot in my opinion survive but a few days without a change for the better and under the most favourable circumstance I do not think he will recover for a period less than ten or fifteen days. P. W. Young Surgeon 38 NCT.[56]

Whatever the true diagnosis of his condition, Private Bare was at least aware that it would not be wise to risk a third evaluation. In late January 1864, he regained sufficient control of his faculties to escape from confinement, and quickly went into the lines of the enemy on February 4. It was noted that Private Bare arrived with a sprained wrist and frozen feet, but no mention is made of his mental state. The Federal prisoner took the oath and not long thereafter returned to Ashe County, based on the age of his fourth and fifth children.

CALVIN WOODY 34-A (December 14, 1863). Private Calvin Woody enlisted in August of 1861 and deserted for the first time in September of 1862. He avoided those bent on taking up deserters for fourteen months but was finally caught and then court-martialed on December 14, 1863. Not long thereafter, Private Woody was informed that he was to be shot for his military crimes. After the sentence was approved, the record went to the Secretary of War for his review. It was a moot point, for the condemned man took matters into his own hands and escaped from the guardhouse. He went into enemy lines on February 24, 1864, was imprisoned, took the oath and allowed to go to Philadelphia, PA. Unknown to the private, President Davis sent the trial record of his case back to General Lee for review. Another record shows that Private Woody was pardoned by GO #2 in February 1865. This is likely a case of inaccurate reporting, though he may have headed south from Philadelphia and was captured by Confederate forces.

No doubt curious as to who was responsible for the escape of the prisoner, the General commanding the Third Corps queried the Colonel of the Thirty-Fourth. In his three-page reply, the Colonel explained that he had carefully ordered that the guard be vigilant and that the prisoner be tied hand and foot. The prisoner, at night, asked that he be taken to the sinks [latrine]. While there, he ran from the guard, whose weapon misfired, and Private Woody escaped in the darkness. Colonel William Lee Lowrance recommended that the officer in charge of the guard be severely punished for disobedience of orders and neglect of duty.[57]

GEORGE MCSWAIN 34-H (December 14, 1863). Private George McSwain told his enrolling officer that he was thirty-five when signing on the rolls of the Thirty-Fourth on October 1, 1861. He left his company on August 1, 1862 and stayed away until March 1863. In April, he went before a court-martial and was found not guilty of desertion, but was convicted on a lesser absent without leave charge. For this violation, he was punished by fifteen days in the guardhouse with only bread to eat and water to drink and was required to police the camp during that time. No transcript of the court-martial proceeding is available to shed light on the reason for the reduced charge following a relatively long absence. Before the results of the first court were officially published, Private McSwain warily retraced the deserter's path, this time from Guinea Station, VA, on April 20. On this absence he was able to avoid detection until mid–November 1863. The second court for Private McSwain, convened on December 14, was not inclined to minimize the seriousness of an absence of seven months. The prisoner before them was sentenced to be shot when GO #112, December 31, 1863, Army of Northern Virginia, was published. On review, the President "declined to interfere." Private McSwain was one of three who were shot on Saturday, January 9, 1864.

MILTON JOHN HICKS 22-I (December 15, 1863). Privates Hicks of the Twenty-Second was shot to death just a few paces from Private McSwain. He had enlisted at Asheboro, Randolph County, and would die at Orange Court House, VA. Private Hicks first volunteered to serve in June of 1861, but was then discharged in August for an unknown reason, perhaps medical, for the impediment was apparently removed and he again enlisted in the same regiment. Within the month he left his company, this time without the proper authority. His absence continued for seventeen months. On December 15, 1863, Private Hicks, with barely two months of actual duty in thirty months of service, was condemned to death.

ELKANAH H. LAMB 22-I (December 15, 1863). Private Lamb stayed in the ranks with his messmates from enrollment in June 1861 until September 1862, when he was listed as being absent without leave. He avoided arrest for fifteen months but was caught and court-martialed on December 15. This just six weeks after the trial and death sentence of his brother Private Milton Lamb who was enrolled in the same company. Private Elkanah Lamb was found guilty of desertion and sentenced to be shot. The execution followed in due course on the appointed day of January 9, 1864. Six days before the execution, Private James Robinson, Twenty-Second Regiment, mentioned to his father, "Farther they is too men to be shot next Saturday in our regiment they belong to Co. I. one of them is name Lam and the other nam hix."[58] Private Robinson may not have known that a third man — enrolled in a different regiment — was to executed by the side of the men of the Twenty-Second. The day after the executions, Brigadier General Scales notified his superiors;

> I have the honor to report that the prisoners Privates Milton Hix & E. H. Lamb Co "I" 22nd N. C. Regiment and Private George McSwain Co "H" 34th N. C. Regiment condemned to be shot by sentence of Court Martial were duly executed on Saturday the 9th instant seven days after the publication of their sentence and in the presence of the Brigade.[59]

In a less formal fashion one of the executions was reported to a former soldier. Private Felix McEntire, Company C, Thirty-Ninth Georgia, wrote to a man in Rutherford County and included a note for Sam Hoeye (Hoey): "And tell him I saw one of the men that belonged to his company shot his name was George McSwain."[60] Ten months after the execution of Private McSwain, the military aide-de-camp at the executive office contacted Captain Blackford, AAG:

> Private Geo McSwain Co H 34 NC Regt and Private Wiley [interline not legible] to be shot 8 or 10 months ago. Their cases (Ct. Martial Proceedings) have been in this office, but on examination I find no order of reprieve and that the petition for clemency were disapproved by Commandg General. I therefore return the records to you to learn what is the present status of these men and whether they have been shot. Please inform me.[61]

No response has been found.

ANDREW J. EVITT 16-H (February 25, 1864). Private Evitt bravely stepped forward to volunteer for a year of service, on May 14, 1861, days before North Carolina left the Union. The tall, fair, young man also voluntarily reenlisted when called upon to do so in February 1862, for which he was rewarded with a furlough and a $10 bounty. Private Evitt went on to fulfill an additional year of duty before deserting on May 2, 1863. He was not apprehended until February 15, 1864, an absence of over nine months. Ten days after being arrested, he was on trial, and just eleven days after his death decision was announced, he was shot to death, on Friday, March 11, 1864. There are no entries in the records of the executed man that would indicate that he was not a good and faithful soldier. First Lieutenant J. W. Bell of the same company wrote to "Brother Ike" on Monday, March 14, 1864.

> Andrew J. Evitt was executed Friday last by decision of Genl Court-martial. I would have saved him if I could. No person in the army that knew him was willing for him to be shot. He has been in too many battles and done his country too much good to deserve such a death. I think the good that he has done out balances the wrong he did. Apparently like all brave men died without fear. He said he was prepared and did not fear death. He was marched around the line before they tied him to the stake (which is customary before execution) [parentheses in letter]. When he got opposite our company he said goodbye Boys as cool and calm apparently as I ever saw him. I saw three shot at one time this winter for desertion. There has been a good many N Carolinians shot in this army for desertion. Old traitor Holden is responsible for the most of it. He is now a candidate for Govenor. Will your Co vote for him Co "H" is all right for Vance But I cannot say that for all the Cos in the Regt nor in the army. I am afraid he will beat Zeb. If he does I will ask for a transfer to some other state for I will never claim N.C. my native state again. I think the NC soldiers passing through Raleigh [not legible] aught to stop and hang the old son of a bitch. I think about ¾ of the N Carolinians at home are tories through the influence of W. H [sic]. Holden and nearly half of the soldiers. I cant see how he keeps off the gallows or out of Castle Thunder.[62]

The letter closes with the disheartening note that there are only 15 men present for duty in Company H, and half of them are conscripts—a desperate condition for a company that must muster for battle for another full year. This interesting letter offers a fair reflection of the thinking of an officer from North Carolina in March 1864. Military courts did not weigh and balance the full service record of those they condemned. Therefore, many North Carolinians were unfairly executed. Most of the men at home and many of those in the army no longer supported the war. W. W. Holden was the person responsible for this widespread disaffection. Conscripts were of little value to a depleted company. As suggested by

Lieutenant Bell, those that stayed with their company desperately wanted the shirkers and deserters at home to be returned to the army.

Private James Robinson wrote to his father in March 1864.

> Farther Powl Simmons was brought in under guard the other day and they hav got him in under guard now Farther Powell is the worst cowd man I ever saw under guard in my life ... James Hill you wrote to me about ketching Bill lank Ford and Bill Shelton I have seen Shelton he is in the 13 regiment he look very lowdown ... James I wish you all could ketch Furd Ellis and Lawson James they is to be a man shot in our Brigade the 10 of this month he belongs to the 16th Regiment ... John Farther wrote in his letter that I am in the war and he dont want me to never runaway.[63]

Earlier in the month Private Robinson had addressed Mr. J. M. Hill saying in part:

> James you wrote something about ketching deserters you said you was aferd you would hav to do something you didnt want to do ketch some of them boys that has bin laying in the woods so long or shoot them one for they had jest as well be in the army as me ... James they was a man shot last friday he be long to the 16th regiment in our brigade he was shot for deserting his post last June 1863 and was ketched and brout back under guard February 1864.[64]

WILLIAM H. ABSHEAR 34-A (April 5, 1864). Private Abshear enlisted on October 10, 1861. Sixteen months later, he was granted his first furlough, this welcome event coming in February 1863. At the end of his leave Private Abshear did not go back to his company and would not do so until arrested and taken back over a year later. For this betrayal of trust, he was ordered to go before a court-martial in session on April 5, 1864. The prisoner was found guilty as charged, sentenced to death, and shot on Monday April 18, 1864. Twelve days after the execution a soldier made the casual mention, "Shot two in our Brigade a few days ago."[65] The writer was apparently referring to the executions of Privates Abshear and Evitt and was not saying that the men were executed at the same time, as it might be read. A community recollection in Wilkes County is that William was shot in the back during the Civil War, but the remembrance does not offer detail.[66]

MELVIN E. WILLIAMS 22-F (April 20, 1864); OFFA G. WILLIAMS 22-F; (April 20, 1864); S. B. WILLIAMS 22-F (April 20, 1864); W. A. WILLIAMS 22-F (April 20, 1864); and FRANKLIN LAMBERT 22-F (April 20, 1864). Five men of Iredell County deserted from Company F, Twenty-Second Regiment, on April 11, 1864. They left camp near Orange Court House, VA less than a month after they were enrolled. At the end of a week of flight, the five were arrested and shepherded back to their company. The court-martial hearing their case sat on April 30, nineteen days after the flock fled the service. All were judged to be guilty and sentenced to be shot. Four, likely all five, were conscripts. The General officer reviewing the court's decisions approved the death sentences for Privates O. G. and S. B. Williams, while deferring to the pleasure of the President in regard to the life or death of the others. Before the executions could take place, the brigade was involved in the Battle of the Wilderness on May 5 and 6, 1864. Within days, the service of the condemned men was lost to the Confederacy. Privates M. E. and O. G. Williams were wounded, returned to duty but then left their company along with Private Lambert, marking and end to their service. The enemy captured Privates W. A. and S. B. Williams. The latter died in a Federal prisoner of war camp three weeks after his Confederate death sentence. For the record, all of the men were released from their death sentences in SO #285, December 1, 1864, AIGO.

ZACHARIAH FOWLER 13-D (April 28, 1864). Private Fowler, a conscript, was received into Company D, Thirteenth Regiment, on February 28, 1864. He had been taken up for service five months earlier. A week after being placed on the rolls of the company, the recruit deserted while near Orange Court House, VA, on March 7, 1864. In arrest by April 13, he and three others of the Thirteenth were lodged for the night in the Montgomery County, VA, jail. Jailer John W. Snyder was their gracious host. The fee was $2.50 per night, per guest, for minimal accommodations.[67] The next day, the men were on the road to the guardhouse and court-martial. The court hearing the evidence against Private Fowler gathered on April 28. Their decision on a death sentence was published on May 24. On appeal, the Secretary of War commuted the death sentence to a year of hard labor with a ball and chain attached to an ankle. But this was not known on June 15, when Private Fowler was admitted to a military hospital with a gunshot wound suffered in the fighting at Petersburg, VA. Furloughed from the hospital in late July, Private Fowler died at home on August 15, 1864.

ISAAC FRANKLIN 13-G (April 28, 1864). A conscript, Private Franklin was assigned to Company G, Thirteenth Regiment, in August 1863. He deserted on March 7, was tried and sentenced to be shot. On presidential review, his sentence was commuted to a year of hard labor with a ball and chain attached to an ankle and confinement in Castle Thunder. The commutation was made known with the release of SO #206, August 31, 1864, AIGO. Well before this, Private Franklin was wounded in one of the series of engagements that took place around Petersburg, VA. While recovering from the wound, he was furloughed and died at home in the fall of the year.

WILLIAM A. BRADSHAW 13-D (April 28, 1864). Private Bradshaw was conscripted into the Thirteenth on February 1, 1864, and stayed until March 7. His service record list his enrollment as September 13, 1863. It also noted that his wages were improperly drawn through year's end, so he was probably not present for duty from the earlier date. Ten weeks after he was properly signed on, Private Bradshaw was in jail waiting to be taken back to his regiment. The death sentence that was pronounced on him was commuted to hard labor, as was done in the cases of the other men who left with him. Private Bradshaw was transferred to Salisbury Prison in February 1865 and was a Federal prisoner on the tenth of the month. He died while a Federal prisoner at Knoxville, TN, on April 27, 1865.

JAMES RAINS 13-D (April 28, 1864). Private Rains was placed in the Thirteenth Regiment on February 28, 1864, some four months after conscription. Once mustered, Private Rains was present for a week and then deserted while in the vicinity of Orange Court House, VA, along with Privates Bradshaw, Fowler and Franklin. He was arrested and Mr. Wilson Huff, Jailer of Hays County, VA, was paid $1.75 for his overnight stay. Trial began on April 28, a guilty decision followed and he was sentenced to be shot. The sentence was suspended awaiting the decision of the President. In a rather cryptic comment, "For special reasons appearing good to the President," the guilty man was pardoned and released to duty.[68] The "special reasons" found for Private Rains' release are not mentioned. The favorable disposition may have been due to a letter from a J. H. Hyman, addressed to the Secretary of War, asking a pardon for the private.[69] Joseph H. Hyman represented Edgecombe County in the North Carolina House of Commons in 1865 and 1866. The request was prepared on July 4, and Private Rains was released the following month. He returned to duty, survived the next eight months, and took the oath at the conclusion of hostilities, the only survivor of the four conscripts who left the Thirteenth.

ALEXANDER WESTMORELAND 13-H (July 18, 1864). Private Westmoreland went to Camp Holmes for training before being sent to his regiment on February 1, 1864. Just five weeks after arriving in camp, he abruptly left in early March and was absent until July.

The deserter stood before a court on July 18, 1864. In a case similar to that of the conscripts who had deserted earlier in the year, Private Westmoreland might well have expected a prison sentence, but that was not to be. Private Westmoreland was convicted of desertion, ordered to be shot, and was executed on September 9, seven months after being conscripted. His service record notes that he was "killed for desertion," rather than the usual "Executed by sentence of General Court-martial."[70]

A soldier in the Thirty-Fourth may have followed Private Westmoreland to a deserter's grave. "A notorious deserter," left his regiment while in the face of the enemy and was arrested to be dealt with at a later time, but there his service record ends.[71]

That same month, July 1864, a man absent from Company E wrote to Governor Vance requesting a pardon after his second desertion. He was wary of once again returning: "My company has wrote several of them [letters] to me never to go back unless I am pardoned by you. I do not want to bushwhacket therefore I hope you will be kind enough to pardon me for the offences that I have committed."[72] A friend added a note that Private William R. McCaskill was a "good soldier" and that two of his brothers had been killed in battle. A political lure was then cast for the Governor, "I think you will carry this county by a handsome majority."

D. C. F. PENDRY 38-B (August 16, 1864). Daniel Columbus Franklin Pendry became a private in the Thirty-Eighth after enrollment by Captain Columbus L. Cook on October 16, 1861. His father, Private John Pendry of Surry County, was also enrolled on the same day in the same company. Still together, father and son were absent without leave on August 20, 1862. The son returned to duty after an absence of four months. The father returned in the same period and was discharged the next month for being over age; he gave his age as thirty-six on entering the service. After his first relatively minor encounter with military discipline, Private Pendry was involved in more serious trouble in October 1863. He was ordered to appear before a court-martial on charges of beginning and joining in a sedition, and quitting his post to plunder and pillage. Private James S. Angell, who had enlisted on the same day as the Pendrys, faced similar charges as did three others of the Sixteenth Regiment. All of the accused were acquitted as insufficient evidence was produced to warrant their conviction for a "disgraceful" assault on sutlers accompanying the brigade. A furlough was granted to Private Pendry in early 1864. After dutifully returning at the expiration of his leave he decided to desert, taking his armament with him. Four months later he was arrested on August 2, 1864. Two weeks later he was on trial, a determination of guilt was made, and a death sentence was forthcoming. However, the court went on to recommend executive clemency for the guilty soldier. The death sentence was approved by Lieutenant General A. P. Hill, who was not swayed by the clemency statement. Private Pendry was shot to death around August 29, 1864. A week or two after the execution of Private Pendry, Captain C. M. Blackford of the Judge Advocate's Office advised General A. P. Hill that when a court recommends executive clemency, the reviewing General must abide by the court's recommendation.[73] He is required to forward the record for presidential review, even though the recommendation of the court is directed to the General, all of which was of little solace to Private Pendry. In this instance the Judge Advocate's reading of the Articles of War does not appear accurate. The 89th Article states that the responsible General "may" follow the course recommended by a court. Possibly the age and service of Private Pendry influenced the AIGO. He was the youngest and longest serving man of the brigade to be executed.

JOHN W. ALRED 22-E (August 30, 1864). Private Alred served with Confederate forces for a very brief period. Though he volunteered to serve in February 1862, he deserted after being paid in June and was not apprehended until July or August of 1864 after an absence of two years. He went to trial on August 30 and was shot on September 15. He was present for duty for about four of the thirty-one months from enrollment to his death. Private Alred was only twenty or perhaps twenty-one when he knelt before the muzzles of the leveled guns.

RILEY CAGLE 16-D (September 5, 1864). Private Cagle was conscripted into the Sixteenth on March 8, 1863. The next day, Captain E. J. Crowson of the Sixty-Third North Carolina Militia of Randolph County telegraphed Governor Vance: "Beside the acknowledgment of the men Riley Cagle Duncan Woodal and Temple Sprilley we have abundant evidence."[74] What charge or action is alluded to is not known. Regardless, Private Cagle was then a soldier and was wounded at the battle of Chancellorsville, VA, in May. Company rolls carried the wounded man as "absent-wounded" for the next year. During this recuperative period he was able to be up and about for his name is found on a list of open warrants in Moore County, perhaps in connection with the earlier reference to "evidence" in the telegram to the Governor. Matters came to a head in June 1864 when Private Cagle was imprisoned at Richmond, VA, charged with murder and desertion. The accused man admitted that he and Murphy Owens of Montgomery County, and a man named Latham of Moore County, had murdered a wealthy silversmith in Montgomery County. The tradesman had employed Riley Cagle at an earlier time, so the opportunity for enrichment was recognized. The victim of the crime, Pleasant Simmons, held property valued at over $8,000 in 1860. With Private Cagle securely jailed, the option was then presented to Governor Vance as to whether the criminal should be returned to Montgomery County for trial, and likely death by hanging, or be tried by a military court and shot as a deserter. Governor Vance directed an aide to answer: "Inform him that I prefer he should be shot for desertion."[75] The practical Governor was able to avoid the expense and unknown outcome of a county trial while gaining some benefit in suppressing desertion. A week later, Private Cagle was shot to death.

A soldier who was enrolled in Company B of the Sixteenth may well deserve to be included among those executed by Confederate authority, but the record of his case only suggests the fact. Private Abner Brooks enrolled in the regiment in May 1861 and deserted in the same month in 1863. Some four months after leaving the Confederate flag, he enlisted in a Federal regiment only to desert from that regiment just days short of a year later.[76] He was caught, and apparently killed under unknown circumstances in Madison County. At the time, he was classified as a deserter in Federal records, but the United States Congress removed that impediment in 1869. The dead man had deserted from both the Confederate and Federal armies. No doubt there were several men in Madison County quite willing, even anxious, to kill him.

A. T. BEASLEY 38-A (September 5, 1864). Private Beasley, Company A, Thirty-Eighth Regiment, left a scant service record. He was enrolled at Camp Holmes, NC, as a conscript in August 1864. Soon after he deserted, taking his newly issued weapon with him, and was arrested. Private Beasley went to trial on September 5. On September 23, he was shot. All this happening in a five-week period from enrollment to execution. A soldier with the same surname who was enrolled in Company E of the Thirty-Third reportedly deserted and joined another company. The two may be one and the same, which would account for the prompt execution.[77]

M. F. WILLARD 38-H (September 8, 1864). Two weeks after the double execution of Privates Beasley and Walters, Private Willard knelt awaiting the final volley. Private Willard was enrolled at Camp Holmes on July 30, 1864, as a conscript. He deserted on August 17. There is no record that he took a weapon with him. Within two weeks, he was arrested and placed in custody awaiting trial. At trial on September 8, the defendant was convicted and later informed that he would suffer death by musketry. Private Willard was shot on October 12, 1864, less than eleven weeks after being enrolled in the regiment.

In a memoir prepared after the war, a soldier that had served in the Sharpshooters of Scales' brigade commented on the need for the executions in the fall of 1864:

> At this time desertions from the Confederate army had become matters of such common occurrence that it was determined to put a stop to the evil by a summary execution of the law. The sentence was executed with all the formalities suitable to such occasions, and the scene was well calculated to strike terror to the hearts of those who contemplated the commission of this gravest of all military offenses.... These parades were the most disgusting and disagreeable duty encountered during the whole war. One can never forget the looks of the poor fellows moving slowing around to their death. Some were erect and composed; others so nearly dead from terror at the approach of death as to be reduced almost to a state of coma.[78]

The observer closed by saying that there were no deserters from the sharpshooters—"for they were the elite of the army." Sharpshooter units were organized by Act of Congress on April 21, 1862.

JONATHAN BROWN 38-G (September 8, 1864). Private Brown, a conscript, was enrolled at Camp Holmes on July 30, 1864. He deserted his company on August 17, was arrested, and was in the guardhouse by the end of August. After his case was heard on September 8, he was given a death sentence. An appeal then went forward to the President and on September 22, Adjutant General Samuel Cooper notified General A. P. Hill to suspend the execution of Johnson [Jonathan] Brown and M. A. Ussery, while awaiting the decision of the President. The President decided in favor of the convicted men and returned them to duty, this being made known in SO #285, December 16, 1864, AIGO. No further record has been found for Private Brown.

JOHN H. A. WALTERS 38-E (September 13, 1864). Little more is known in the case of Private Walters than was found in the record of Private Beasley who was executed beside him. Randolph County is indicated as his home on enrollment records. He went before a military court on September 13, 1864, and was executed on September 23, 1864.

MARTIN ALFRED USSERY 38-E (September 13, 1864). Private Ussery was conscripted on August 21, 1864, and was at trial twenty-three days later. After release from a death sentence and return to duty in December, he was with his company until March 9, 1865, when he deserted to the enemy.

Why Privates Beasley, Walters and Willard were shot to death and Privates Brown and Ussery were returned to duty by presidential decision is not clear from their nearly identical service records, though the men who were executed may well have had a more extensive absence record than has come to light. Certainly the fact that Privates Beasley and Walters took weapons with them when they departed greatly increased the seriousness of the crime. The willingness to execute Confederate soldiers did not escape notice. "They shoot men out hear for livly hand they have shot two since I cam back to more to be shot next Fryday for desertin," recounted a man in Scales' brigade on September 25, 1864.[79]

THOMAS DANIEL 13-H (October 31, 1864). Private Daniel was a reluctant conscript on June 6, 1864. He did not desert until August 20 and was able to avoid capture until October 18. A court gathered on October 31, heard the case, and the requisite number of members concurred on a death sentence. General A. P. Hill approved the court's decision on November 7. No record of reconsideration or appeal has been found for Private Daniel.

Private John Mansfield, Company K, Thirteenth Regiment, was shot while attempting to desert. The disenchanted volunteer had earlier shot off a finger. When the self-maiming failed to gain his release, he absented himself for a full year but returned for a year before the fatal attempt to flee his company on November 10, 1864.[80]

REUBEN BROWN 16-B (January 14, 1865). Unlike the several conscripts who had preceded him to trial in the fall of the past year, Private Brown had rushed to enlist in the first weeks of war, on April 29, 1861. A brother, Private Jasper Brown, enrolled on the same day. Release from a death sentence for Private Reuben Brown occurred nearly four years later, on March 9, 1865. Private Reuben Brown was in the ranks from enlistment to December 1862, when he deserted from Camp Gregg, VA. For the next two years, he was able to avoid capture, likely while not far from his home in Madison County. Eventually he was found, arrested, and then tried at Asheville in January 1865. The trial resulted in a death sentence for the private. The records of the court were forwarded to the Secretary of War. After his review he approved the sentence, leaving blank the date on which the sentence was to be carried into effect, while assigning the responsibility for the execution to the officer commanding the Western District of North Carolina. Before the day for execution was determined, it was found that Private Brown was eligible for amnesty under the provisions of an order issued by the district commander, Brigadier General J. G. Martin, this finding being announced in SO #57, March 9, 1864, AIGO. Record-wise Private Brown was returned to duty, but his activity for the final month of war is not known. Private Jasper Brown deserted in May 1863 and had no further service record.

Summary

Men who were earlier firm and steady in the ranks left in large numbers in 1865. A man in the Thirty-Fourth Regiment explained his decision in a letter to his wife in early March.

> I can say to you that the times is verry gloomy out heare at this time on our Side the deserting is still going on in our army but the most of them is going to the yankeys now at this time but I think now it is a verry good plan for a man not to desert atall for I think the war will end this Spring anyway and them that Stays with their Company will do the best for them selves for it is better for a man to trust in the Lord then to run a risk to desert for their was a man left our Company last week and he was taken up and brought back and put in the guard house and he may be shot and when they run over to the yankeys our men Shoots at them when they Start a cross the line so I think the best way is to stay with the Company.[81]

The Pender-Scales and Branch-Lane-Barry Brigades offer both similarities and differences in their execution record. One difference centers on the execution of two or more deserters at the same time. In Pender-Scales 15 days were designated to march men to the execution field. On only 2 of these days did multiple executions take place, and 5 men were shot. In total, 18 men were executed before the Brigade, 13 bound to a lonely stake.

In Branch-Lane-Barry executions were ordered on 10 days, 5 individual and 5 multiple executions occurring on these days. Multiple executions ended 15 lives. The brigades experienced about the same number of executions, 18 and 20. Combining them, companies that witnessed a single execution of a company member experienced 3.6 absences per company for the three months after the rite. Companies that viewed multiple executions including one of their company had 1.2 absences in the following three months, an indication that multiple executions were more effective than single executions. Executions in Pender-Scales were evenly distributed over all regiments, each offering 3 to 5 men to the stake. In Branch-Lane-Barry 3 regiments had 7, 5 and 4 men shot, while 2 regiments escaped with just a single execution.

The 50 soldiers given death sentences in Pender-Scales were from homes clustered about Catawba County. Half of these men were married before going into service. Thirty were volunteers who served an average of eighteen months before deserting. The 20 conscripts, were in camp for a little over four months before departing. Condemned volunteers had a slightly better chance of avoiding the execution march; 33 percent were executed, 40 percent of convicted conscripts were shot.

On a company basis, 14 of the 54 that made up the brigade suffered at least one execution. Nine companies had men given a death sentence, but all were spared. The 14 companies that had men executed had an absence rate of 26 percent. Companies with reprieved men had an absence rate of 19 percent. A 10 company sampling of 31 that had no death sentences had an absence rate of 14 percent. There was virtually no difference in the number of deaths in companies with frequent absences to those in companies with far fewer. The first have an absence rate of 41 percent and a death rate of 27 percent.[82] The second have an absence rate of 15 percent and a death rate of 27 percent.[83] The death of another soldier, whether mangled in battle or on a hospital cot, was not a significant factor in driving men to desert.

The Pender-Scales Brigade enrolled approximately 8,000 men; 721 men were present when the Brigade was ordered to put down their weapons. The Thirteenth had the most men in line, 216; they also had the fewest men convicted by military courts. The Sixteenth had the fewest number of men present that day, 95, and they had the most men convicted by military courts. For the brigade, a 16 company sample indicates that desertions in sizable numbers began in the second half of 1862. The first execution followed in early 1863 and increased as absences accelerated in 1864.

	1861	1862	1863		1864		1865	no date
Abs/Co	.8	2.1	10.4	4.3	5.1	5.1	5.3	4.6
To be executed				4	23	12	11	
Executed				1	3	6	8	

A moderating absence experience in the first half of 1863 may have forecast a favorable trend and delayed more decisive measures.

4

Third Corps, Heth Division, Pettigrew-Kirkland-MacRae Brigade

"The axe to be laid to the root of the tree"[1]

Before his appointment as Major General, Henry Heth indicated that he would take a stern stand on desertion when he issued orders that deserters and conscripts who had not reported for duty would be shot wherever they were found. This order was promptly set aside by higher authority.[2] At year's end 1863, the division led by General Heth included the brigades of Kirkland and Cooke, 9 regiments of North Carolina troops. In addition a tenth regiment of North Carolinians was brigaded with regiments of men from Mississippi in the Joseph R. Davis Brigade. A brigade from Virginia, Harry H. Walker's, was assigned to the division at various times. The brigades of men from North Carolina had 53 men sentenced to death for military crimes; the lives of 25 were so ended. The Mississippians in the division had 1 soldier sentenced to be shot, but the sentence was not carried out. The Virginians had 14 men sentenced to be executed, of whom at least 2 were shot. In his memoir, General Heth makes frequent reference to the culture of the American Indian but no reference to executions or the culture of the Confederate enlisted soldier: the realities of wartime duty, desertion, discipline, and camp life are not mentioned.[3]

"Our Reg is attached to Gen. Pettigrews Brigade it is a splendid Brigade."[4] During the course of the war, 32 men of the "splendid Brigade" were told that they would be executed, and 17 met that dismal end. There are three observations to be made about brigade executions. First, the rituals began in late 1862 and continued at a relatively even pace for the next two years. Second, dual executions were common; over half of the men who were shot spent their last living instant alongside another awaiting the same volley. Third, there was no hesitancy to carry out executions on Sunday. Of the execution days for North Carolina troops which can be accurately established, only three took place on Sunday and all three were for men in this brigade. The day before and the day after the Lord's day were most frequently selected for executions, suggesting that the Sabbath was deliberately avoided as a proper day to send souls to eternity, even those of deserters. There is a verified instance where a condemned Confederate was given a reprieve to delay his death from Sunday to the following Monday.[5]

Eleventh Regiment

Men of the Bethel Regiment, also designated as the First Regiment North Carolina Infantry, were reorganized in early 1862 into the Eleventh Regiment. With many of the enrollees having served in the earlier organization, a proud tradition of loyalty and devotion was carried onward with their reconfirmed commitment to the Confederacy. Yet there were some minor disciplinary concerns: Company B, from Burke, Wilkes and Caldwell counties had 5 men convicted by courts-martial; Company G, Orange and Chatham counties, added 4 more; and Company D, Burke County, and Company K, Buncombe County, had 3 each. These 15 incidents accounted for 68 percent of the total court convictions concerning the regiment. Men went before 30 courts, and 8 were acquitted. These few trials brought forth death sentences for two men, and their executions took place in due course. This number might have grown by one but for the intervention of a higher authority. A man enrolled in Company G wrote to his father on January 14, 1863: "Farther I am sory to say that we have the Small Pox in our Regiment thare was two cases last weak and one this morning he belongs to our Company but has bin the gard house for desertion I would not be sory if he would die for I believe theay will shoot him if theay ever try him it is the thrid [*sic*] offence."[6]

Twenty-Sixth Regiment

The Twenty-Sixth had an exceptionally large enrollment, 2022 in all, for a company average of 202 men. Men of the regiment recorded a total of 350 absences, 17 percent of those enrolled. Courts-martial were held for 54 men, and 10 were sentenced to be executed; 5 were so dispatched, and 5 at trial were acquitted. Sporadic desertion began as early as the summer of 1861, increased the next summer, and reached a troublesome level in the winter of the year. A second peak of desertion was reached in June of 1863 and continued at 5 or 6 departures a month until culminating in a final surge in the first months of 1865. Company C, the Wilkes Volunteers; Company D, the Wake Guards; and Company F, the Hilbritten Guards recruited in Caldwell County, accounted for half of all courts for the regiment. Nearly half of the 359 absences recorded by the regiment were charged to these companies. Punishment for men of the Twenty-Sixth was apparently well-centered though infrequent. The Wilkes Volunteers, Company C, with 77 incidents of absence, appropriately had the largest number of life-threatening trials, 12 in total. In the 12 cases, 4 death sentences were forthcoming, with 3 carried into effect. The 77 absence incidents involved 68 men. Only 26 of these men completed their military service in a present-for-duty status. For this company, once a soldier made a decision to desert there was only a 30 percent chance that he would be of lasting aid to the Confederacy. Just over one-third of the 187 men who were enrolled in Company C decided to cut and run between the fall of 1861 and 1865. The lives of 52 men in the company ended while they were in service. Contrast the record of Company C with that of Company E, the Independence Guards, Chatham County. This company enrolled 200 in its ranks; only 17 left without proper authority, while 57 were dead at war's end. In Company B, recruited in Union County, the Waxhaw Jackson Guards, an early twelve-month volunteer struggled with the decision on reenlistment. "Tha air triing to get us to rein list fur two years as soon as we surv this twelv months." The threat of conscription for those not reenlisting was pointedly made by regimental officers. Private William H. Glen was undecided: "I hav never put mi name to none of them papers I think will go home befor I stick mi name to a nother paper if all the res of the bois goes in fur two years if you all is willing and thinks that you can git a long with out me if I lives til our time is out and nothing I maby I mit go."[7] As to discipline in the regiment, Private Glen wrote, "Our Col is very strict and we have to be Regular on duty to avoid punishment." He mentions, by name, that a straggler was threatened with execution but that fact "aught not to get to his family I just write this to tell you what feelings they have here for A wall."[8] Service records of men of the Twenty-Sixth reveal that their regiment suffered far more battle-related deaths than did the other regiments in the brigade. An average of 6 sampled companies shows battle-caused deaths as 32. A sampling of 16 companies of the other brigade regiments indicates battle deaths as 10. As a regiment, the Twenty-Sixth knew many variations of desertion and punishment.

Forty-Fourth Regiment

The Forty-Fourth was the first regiment of Pettigrew's brigade to witness the execution of a soldier from its ranks. That shattering end awaited 4 deserters, while 5 would be spared after hearing their death sentence, though the fate of 1 is not clear. Acquittal for 5 men followed after 79 courts. Company D, the Pitt Regulators, was the company of the first man in the regiment to be executed. Company H, the Montgomery Guards, experienced frequent absences that peaked in a serious outbreak in August of 1863. One of the company was executed shortly thereafter. This company led all others in the brigade with an absence rate approaching 50 percent. Disease or an unknown cause claimed 35 lives, while 3 men were killed in confrontations with the enemy. Company E, the Chatham Turtle Paws, and Company B, formed in Edgecombe County, also had men taken to the place of execution. Overall Companies E, and H, together with Company G, recruited in Orange and Alamance Counties, account for 68 percent of all court convictions for the Forty-Fourth.

Forty-Seventh Regiment

The Forty-Seventh had limited exposure to the death sentence, only 2 cases being noted in regimental records, each concerning desertions that occurred in 1863. Though in the opinion of one, company grade officers were not overly energetic: "I begin to thing [sic] that we have got some very lazy officers [sic] in our regiment. They are inclined to play possum."[9] Nor did rank preclude comment: "General Martin is totally unfit to command. I thank God that I have not been with him."[10] A low rate of absence is characteristic of the Forty-Seventh. Company B, Franklin County, was exemplary in that it had no recorded absences.[11] Company E, formed in Wake County, had 9 courts-martial, but no man faced the ordeal of a death sentence. Of the 9 who were convicted of desertion, 7 were given severe sentences ranging from fifty lashes and hard labor for the rest of the war to a year of hard labor. Company C, Wake County, followed with 7 convictions. One man of Company C did learn that he would be shot to death, but overall this company received rather mild sentences for what were somewhat shorter periods of absence. Company F, the Sons of Liberty, Franklin County, had 7 men convicted after trial and 1 was executed. For the regiment, 50 court appearances ended with 8 acquittals.

Fifty-Second Regiment

The Fifty-Second tested the effectiveness of army discipline under a variety of circumstances. Friendship, family ties, and religious beliefs all intrude in the pattern of desertion for the regiment. The desertion-prone companies of the Fifty-Second experienced peaks of desertion in the months of June and July in each of three years of the war; relatively few men were left to desert in 1865. The regiment lost 5 men to execution while 4 were reprieved after being condemned. Forces searching out deserters killed 3 men. One of these deaths was graphically described. The deserter died after "having his brains shot out while in the woods."[12] Only 17 men of the Fifty-Second were convicted by military courts; 5 others were acquitted, but 9 of the guilty learned that their lives would end with a burst of musketry. Soldiers of 3 companies were the recipients of 15 of the 17 convictions issued by courts-martial, 88 percent of the total number. Company F, the Wilkes Grays; Company B, the Randolph Guards; and Company D, McCullochs Avengers of Stokes County, enrolled all of the men who were given death sentences. Half of the companies of the regiment had no recorded courts; 2 companies had 1 each. Company F, Wilkes County, experienced the largest number of absences, 60, but no executions from a wartime enrollment of 212 men. A two-time deserter was given a death sentence; it was approved but was not carried into effect. Six others went before a military court; sentences ranged from a year of hard labor to marching around camp carrying a knapsack full of rocks. Company D, not half the size with just 93 enrolled men, had 2 men executed; desertion was just one of the charges placed against these men.

Courts-Martial

Pettigrew Brigade

JOHN H. PARTIN 26-D (April 25, 1862). Private Partin may never have fully realized his good luck in surviving the war to apply for a North Carolina pension in 1905. While a young man, he fled from the battlefield at New Bern, NC, and failed to obey direct orders to return in early 1862. He was court-martialed on April 25, found guilty on the charges, and sentenced to be shot. The court, in recording the decision, failed to note that two-thirds of the members had concurred in that decision. The reviewing officer, General T. H. Holmes, quickly spotted the error and released the prisoner. In a perhaps sardonic aside in GO #24, April 30, 1862, Department of North Carolina, General Holmes commented that the error was "no doubt clerical."[13] After release and return to duty, Private Partin transferred to the Forty-Seventh Regiment, still in the Pettigrew Brigade. A year later the transferee again deserted on August 23, 1863, to remain absent until the following April. Good luck remained with him however, for there is no record of a second court-martial. In September, the two-time deserter was captured by the enemy where fair fortune continued to smile as he survived Federal imprisonment to take the oath in May 1865.

Sergeant Franklin Scarborough, Company H, offered his view of life in the Confederate army on August 10, 1862:

> I am glad the conscripts have come out I hear they are in Richmond to day I hope they will learn something of a soldiers life for those that have never experienced it can draw no idea If it were not for the love of liberty no man would stay in camp satisfied again today you are brave tomorrow a coward men in camp do not study about the danger they are in, its every man for himself.[14]

JAMES CAIN, BRANCH'S LT. ART. (September 10, 1862). Private Cain, executed alongside Private Bowers, offers an equally puzzling enigma as to who he was and why he was shot. Captain Branch's Light Artillery was operating with Colonel Singletary's command when the double execution took place; this was before the battery was assigned to a larger North Carolina artillery unit. In Virginia, the *Petersburg Express* gave a description of the executions the day following the event. The *Hillsborough Recorder* reprinted the account a week later for the benefit of North Carolina readers.

> Deserters Shot.—James Cain, of Capt. Jas. K. Branch's Artillery, and John Bowers of Company D, 44th regiment NC. troops, were shot, in obedience to the sentence of the Court Martial, at the encampment of Col. Singletary's command, at 1¼ o'clock, yesterday afternoon. They were taken out of jail an hour or two before, and conveyed to the spot of execution, (a short distance southeast of the city,) in an ambulance wagon, their arms pinioned, and their persons well guarded. Cain bore his fate with apparent indifference, and laughed and conversed, as though he were going to a wedding feast. He considered the sentence that had been passed upon him, a just one, and said that had the Confederate government been so strict twelve months ago, the army would have been saved the loss of many valuable soldiers, and he for one, would have still been in the ranks. Bowers, on the other hand, exhibited a vastly different spirit from that of Cain. He wept profusely when brought out of jail and while being taken to the place of execution, but subsequently bore up better. They were shot at 1¼ o'clock, and both fell dead at the first fire, pierced by several balls. It is earnestly to be hoped that the execution of these men may have a beneficial effect upon the army, especially that portion of it encamped in this and adjacent vicinities.[15]

The inference from the closing statement is that absentees from the army were causing mischief about Petersburg.

JOHN BOWERS 44-D (September 11, 1862). Private Bowers was shot to death on Tuesday November 4, 1862, at a field southeast of Petersburg, VA. Private Bowers joined the Forty-Fourth on August 20, 1862, as a substitute for an unnamed soldier. The substitute was of conscription age but was not a resident of North Carolina. Three weeks later he stood before a court-martial. After the case was presented, the prisoner was judged guilty and given a death sentence, likely indicating that this was not his first entanglement with the Confederate Articles of War. He may have been one of those who offered themselves as substitutes, then immediately departed to seek another opportunity for profit.

ANDREW WYATT 26-B (Prior to January 26, 1863). Sergeant Wyatt was one of a small number of Confederate soldiers who were spared moments before execution. No indication has been found that his dramatic reprieve was deliberately staged to heighten the effect on the assembled troops. The events that led Sergeant Wyatt to his harrowing experience at Magnolia, Duplin County, began with his conscription from his home in Ashe County in September 1862. Three others with the same surname went into service that day. Eleven weeks later, Sergeant Wyatt deserted from Garysburg, NC, where a camp of instruction was located. He was arrested ten days after departing from Garysburg while attempting to cross the Roanoke River and was hospitalized after his arrest. A court-martial, a guilty judgment and a death sentence to be carried into effect on January 26, 1863, followed. A contemporaneous diary entry clearly sets the day of the Sergeant's heart stopping brush with death: "Monday January 26th 1863-Remained all day in camp of the 26th Regiment North Carolina Infantry. Saw the brigade (Pettigrew's) march out to witness the execution of a deserter (Sergeant Wyatt) 26th North Carolina Infantry but he was reprieved by the solicitation of the colonels of the brigade. Weather fair but clouded up at night but no rain."[16] A soldier of Pettigrew's Brigade describes a more intense experience:

> Farther I must tel you about a horiable sight that I had to witness yester thare was a man belonging to the 26Reg of this Brigade tride for desertion and comdemed to be shot yesterday

> in the presence of the Brigade at the appointed time the troops was drawn up for the awful sight the man was brought out for executian with a file of men to do the work of death the criminal was posted for the work and the proceedings of the Court Marchel waar read out to the great astonisishment [*sic*] of all General French repreived him by the solistation of the diferent Carnals of the Brigade Father I never was so sory for a man in my life as he came to the place of execution he came out criing but when he found he was repreived I never saw such an alteration in any man.[17]

Slightly different versions of the proceedings are found in other correspondence. Private J. A. Bush, also a member of Sergeant Wyatt's regiment, recalls the happenings in the final minutes before the planned execution: "And there was a man by the name of Wyatt was set on his box to be shot. The regiment was formed in a hollow square and a courier came dashing up to Col. Burgwyn with a reprieve for him."[18] Colonel Henry King Burgwyn, age twenty-one, was then the youthful leader of the Twenty-Sixth. Another writer adds more detail to the climactic moment, together with some information on the desertion.

> Arrested at a crossing of the Roanoke river ... he was taken out in a wagon to the place of his execution, where the brigade was drawn up in a three-quarter square to witness the shooting. The prisoner was blindfolded, ordered to kneel down by the freshly dug grave, the firing squad stood with their guns at "ready" and the officer was reading the sentence, when an orderly rode up with an order from General French ... granting a pardon.[19]

From the several accounts the condemned man was either "posted," "set on his box," or "kneeling" by his grave when he was repreived, the second most likely accurate. After his dramatic pardon, Sergeant Wyatt returned to duty and death at Gettysburg, PA, his life extended by five months. There was not a great outpouring of sympathy offered for Sergeant Wyatt. "To-morrow our brigade (Pettigrew's) will be ordered out to witness the execution by shooting of a member of the 26th N.C. for desertion. I understand there has been about fifty desertions in that regiment perhaps by shooting one now and then it will put a stop to their leaving."[20] The observations of the writer are quite accurate; regimental records show at least 38 absences in the preceding three months.

JOHN VINSON 26-G (March 1863). Private Vinson was the second of three substitutes enrolled in Pettigrew's brigade that faced death by musketry. He began active service by agreeing to replace an enrolled soldier on March 6, 1862, before passage of the conscription acts. Substitute Vinson deserted on September 8, 1862. A court-martial sentenced him to receive thirty lashes on his bare back and then to be confined on a bread and water ration. The sentence was reduced or remitted. Not dismayed by the threatened punishment, Private Vinson again deserted his command in March 1863 was arrested, tried and then ordered to be shot. For reason unknown, he was released from the death sentence and returned to duty in time to carry the regimental colors at Gettysburg. This honor, if that be the case, following an earlier wound at Malvern Hill, suggests his soldierly qualities and may account for his earlier lenient treatment. He died of wounds in August of 1864. Some residents of Chatham apparently knew John Vinson. An eighteen-year-old soldier enrolled in Company G wrote to his parents on April 13, 1863.

> I suppose you have heard of George Briggs Alford Way John Pike John Vinson & Anderson Way running a way five of them left within a few day of each other furlows has stopped in our company on account of their leving if we dont get more to eat and give us furlows one half of the Regt will leave as soon as General Green puts forth for I cant stand it much longer the way we are treeted and I dont think we would be blamed for leaving the way we have to faire I dont wish to disterbe your feelings in your old day for we are getting louszy and almost naked i had as leave die in one place as another.[21]

The young man would not have long to stand the rigors; he died at Gettysburg, PA, to be forever sheltered by General Green.

JOSEPH H. HALEY 47-C (March 4, 1863). The specifications on the charges brought against Private Haley on March 4, 1863, emphasize his little regard for army order and discipline. He was enrolled in the regiment on April 29, 1862. GO #32, June 18, 1863, Department of North Carolina and Southern Virginia, summarizes his escapades.

> Specification #1 Leave Company and regiment on January 8, 1863 until January 21, 1863 when he returned to his company. Specification #2 Did leave while on picket at City Point with W. L. Davis and others but was arrested at or near Camp French — he being drunk and unable to proceed further, confined guard house November 15, 1863 [1862]. Specification #3 Deserted at Goldsboro while enroute North Carolina to Virginia did leave company and regiment July 8, 1862 until brought to regiment at Camp Campbell, Virginia.[22]

At trial in Goldsboro, the prisoner pled guilty to the first charge but not guilty to the others. The court found him guilty on all counts and went on to observe: "Court considers an aggravated case such as contemplated by Circular from Headquarters Department North Carolina, January 29, 1863 which excepts cases of men deserting their posts or in the face of the enemy or other aggravated circumstances."[23] A death sentence followed and was promptly approved. A drunken picket who left an assigned post imperiled the entire command. The convicted prisoner was to be shot to death on the seventh day following issuance of GO #32, June 18, 1863, Department of North Carolina, the execution to be at a time and place to be determined by the Brigade Commander. Despite the finality of approval, Private Haley was released and restored to duty at the end of June. Soon thereafter he was captured and exchanged, only to be captured toward war's end.

BENJAMIN F. THREAT 52-D (April 14, 1863). Private Threat was enrolled at Camp French, Petersburg, VA, on October 21, 1862. His brief service record shows that he was present for duty through March 1, 1863, and that he was shot for desertion. A North Carolina "Roll of Honor" entry indicates that Pri-vate Threat was a conscript credited to Union County. He was in the service for seven months.

DULIN STARNES 52-D (April 15, 1863). Private Starnes was a restless man, as evidenced by his encounters in several regiments. He first enrolled in Company F of the Thirty-Fifth on October 4, 1861, but seventeen days thereafter he reconsidered his decision and enrolled in Company I of the Thirty-Seventh on October 21. An unauthorized change of regiments violated the 22nd Article of War and carried a possible death penalty. Eight months after this change of heart, Private Starnes decided to forsake the service. On July 5, 1862, he deserted the Thirty-Seventh. If correctly recorded, he was conscripted into the Fifty-Second in October; capture by Federal troops soon followed, as did a parole in December. In March of 1863, the peripatetic private was back with the Fifty-Second but once again made the decision to move on. He deserted around April 1, with a youthful companion, Private Benjamin Threat of the same company. A cautionary note in the service record of Private Starnes states that there is no clear evidence that the material therein is for the same soldier. When they deserted the Fifty-Second, Private Starnes was thirty-one, and Private Threat was eighteen. The two were not long at liberty, within two weeks they were standing before a court-martial, Private Threat on April 14, and Private Starnes on April 15, 1863. The man and boy were found guilty and sentenced to be shot. The specifications against the prisoners may have involved more than their short-lived desertion. Private Ivan Boyles, Fifty-Third Regiment, told his parents in a letter home that "They runaway and went home and done some mean mischief and killed a militia Colonel in Union County they belonged to the 52nd Regt NC Troops."²⁴ This would explain the death sentence for Private Threat, for a two-week absence was usually considered as absent without leave. In an unnumbered General Order issued on May 2, 1863, at Kinston, NC, Major General D. H. Hill directed: "In consequence of movement of the Brigade Brig. Gen. Pettigrew is relieved from the duty of supervising the execution of Pvt Berry Threat and Dulin Starnes Co D 52nd NC Reg. These privates will be shot to death with musketry on the 11th May 1863 in accordance with the sentence of the court published in General Orders #9 Headquarters Dept. NC April 28, 1863 under the direction of Brig. Gen Daniel in the presence of his Brigade."²⁵ In the evening of the chosen day, the executions were carried into effect. They were well attended; the change in brigade responsibility may have made more men willing to witness the execution of unknown soldiers. One of those affected by the change in arrangements was a member of a regiment then assigned to the Daniel brigade. He wrote to those at home:

> On Monday last I went out and witnessed the execussione of two poor fellows that deserted us at Washington, it was rather an imposing and impressive scene ... and after the chaplins had talked to them some half hour (they looked very badly and was quite penitent) ... the guard took their positions remained there some 10 minutes and the order was given very slowly ... Fire' and at the announce of the last fatal word the two poor fellows that was kneeling side by side fell one to the right and the other to the left pierced through breast and head with the deadly musket ball — so thus ended the life of two deserters from the army. I never care to see any one else shot in a cooled time — but the great majority of the soldiers did not care for the example that was made of these two unfortunate wretches.²⁶

It is not clear whether the writer is referring to the execution as the example that was not cared for, or if he is commenting on the cruelly drawn out ministration by a Chaplain, the delay in the positioning of the guard, or the agonizing wait for the final command. All "in a cooled time," could mean at a slow, deliberate pace, or it might be read as indicating a passionless, emotionless killing, or a death not in the heat of battle. The sensitive General Pettigrew might have had his men more humanely dispose of the criminals. Private Boyles had further information for the folks at home. He wrote:

> I have some more news this time than I ever have before this was an awful site there was two men shot to day in presents of about 8 thousand men I could not see both of the men when they was shot but I saw one of them fall there was 24 loaded guns shot at the men and only 3 ball hit one and 5 hit the other I tell you it was an awful site to see I never want to see any more such as I saw this day it awful to think of.²⁷

Two accounts mention the number of balls that hit the dead men; it would be informative to know if it was the older man that was most often hit. Not knowing how many weapons were actually loaded the accuracy was either reasonably good or quite bad. Other men were less affected by the double execution. Private James E. Green, Company I, Fifty-Third, simply noted in his diary, "& on the 11th there was 2 men shot for desertion by Daniel's Brigade the men belonged to the 52d Regt NC Troops."²⁸ Lieutenant L. L. Polk, Forty-Third Regiment was equally brief: "Yesterday I had to witness the execution of 2 deserters." He felt "wrong and sad and bad," and needed a visit home to restore himself. In a remarkably prescient moment, he writes "I see no chance for the war to stop before March 1865."²⁹ The immediate effect of desertion on the lives of soldiers who remain loyally in the ranks is clearly put forward by Sergeant Anderson C. Myers, Company D, Fifty-Second Regiment, in a letter to his wife a few days before the trials of Privates Starnes and Threat. The Sergeant sorrowfully explained:

I have no doubt but it will be a good many months before I get home I know I want to see you all as bad as any person ever did but the chance is bad for a furlough now in this company for 8 days ago two men did desert from the company Dulin Starns & Benj Threat both conscripts from Union County & where a man does desert from a company it stops furloughs in the company.[30]

The fact that furloughs would be stopped would not be a deterrent for a deserter who left with no intention of returning. It might deter those considering going home for a month or two with some thought of an eventual return. They would face the prospect of a trial and formal punishment and possibly the cudgels in a gauntlet line of the boys they had deprived of leave. Writing to his mother, a soldier in the execution brigade did not give any detail of the affair: "Two men were shot yesterday for deserting. They were shot in the presents [sic] of the Brigade."[31] Soldiers writing to their mothers did not often mention executions, that news was usually for fathers, brothers or male friends. Understandably, young men did not want to add to the many worries of their mothers. Private Louis Leon, Fifty-Third Regiment, gives a fuller, though more matter-of-fact, account of the executions when he notes:

> We moved our camp to the north side of town. Then we marched to an open field this afternoon, and drawn up in line to see two men shot for desertion. After they were shot, we marched by them and saw one was hit six times and the other four. Their coffins were by their sides, right close to their graves, so that they could see it all.[32]

Private Leon gives the impression that seeing the open grave and awaiting coffins intensified the agony of the men at their stakes. Executions carried out by a brigade other than that of the executed would have little value except that of well-deserved punishment. Though horrified, the men in the executing brigade did not see the affair as a warning to them. At point, the Daniel brigade experienced a surge in absences in the same month that they executed the Pettigrew men. Companies G and K of the Fifty-Third had a total of 32 men leave the ranks in the May and June reporting period, by far the most absence activity in any like period.[33]

Within a fortnight of the interment of Privates Threat and Starnes, Brigadier General Pettigrew prepared a long letter to Governor Vance on the subject of desertion by North Carolinians. In the General's opinion, had General J. E. Johnston and General P. T. Beauregard been better disciplinarians, much of the current concern would have been prevented. "Unfortunately they were not," he went on to say, which then formed a base for the present situation in which men were deserting with impunity, encouraged by letters from home, certain in-state newspapers and other active groups within the state. Only the Governor could correct this evil, for "I feel the thing has gone to such an extent that requires the axe to be laid to the root of the tree."[34] In his brigade, the General vouchsafed, the regiments would shoot a deserter as "quickly as they would a snake."

The impact of the recent executions was not lost on Private E. R. Harris of Company C, Twenty-Sixth Regiment, who was court-martialed in April and then heard, unofficially, that he was to be shot. With this warning, he broke his guard and returned to his home in Iredell County. From there he wrote the Governor for his assistance in returning without punishment. He also wanted authority to arrest a neighbor and take him back with him. Governor Vance instructed an aide to reply that Private Harris should "report himself immediately."[35]

Governor Vance emphasized conditions in North Carolina when he recounted an incident in Yadkin County to President Davis. While attempting to arrest deserters, two militiamen were killed; the slayers were arrested but released by a judge who ruled that the State of North Carolina did not have any legal right to arrest deserters, as this right rested solely with the Confederate government. The Governor then explained that soldiers from his state thought the law conscripting men into the army was unconstitutional and that civil authorities would therefore protect them once they reached home. In closing, Governor Vance pointed out that the furloughs promised when the conscription act was passed had not materialized, adding discontent to a vexing condition.[36]

Amnesty was offered to deserters by Governor Vance on May 11, 1863. It was hoped that this would cause men to return to the colors without fear of punishment. An unintended effect of this proclamation is noted in correspondence sent to Governor Vance by Mrs. Martha J. Hogan on behalf of her husband. Private Alexander Hogan deserted from Company H of the Forty-Fourth in the spring of 1863. Martha was in contact with the Governor in early July to request that her husband not be punished for simply returning home. In a very well-organized letter, she first emphasized, "He did not come home with the intention of lying out he said when he got home he wanted Governor Vance to make another proclamation so he could return unpunished." Obviously the first proclamation had created the impression that soldiers might return home for a spell and then, from time to time, the Governor would offer amnesty allowing their return without suffering any serious punishment. Martha goes on: "His brother was under you when you was Colonel if all the poor soldiers had good officers they would not run away as the do ... then when they return be punished it is too hard."[37] Neither Martha nor Alexander could read nor write, so they must have had some help in addressing the Governor. There is no record that her husband returned to his company.

Some men with multiple desertions escaped severe punishment, and some men were given very complex sentences. Private James Church, Twenty-Sixth Company B, on March 25, 1863, was sentenced

> to be marched bareheaded in a barrel shirt at the point of a bayonet in front of his regiment on six successive dress parades. He shall wear a ball and chain twice the weight of a soldier's gun and accouterments continuously for thirty days, to be carried on shoulder on all marches with the regiment. He shall be kept bucked and gagged at all times when not on a march sixteen of each twenty-four hours, unless commanding officer and surgeon [determine] life is in danger in which case he will be tied to a post or a tree or [put to] hard labor. He may be put in ranks on engagement. If he conduct himself in manner becoming a patriotic North Carolina soldier he shall be released from further punishment and returned to duty. If sickness delays, must still undergo full measure [of sentence]. He is to be kept a prisoner until execution of sentence.[38]

This sentence followed a five-month absence that began in November 1862; Private Church had no further record after his third desertion in May 1864.

ASA ADAMS 44-E (June 4, 1863). Private Adams went into the army as a substitute on March 10, 1862. After two weeks with Company E of Chatham County, the substitute deserted, returned and then deserted once again, all within the first month of service. He returned from the second desertion and remained with the Forty-Fourth until April 15, 1863, when he deserted for the third time while his regiment was camped near Greenville, NC. The deserter was arrested in Alamance County, his home county, and returned to Camp Holmes by Captain W. V. Montgomery of the Forty-Eighth North Carolina Militia on May 4. A month later, on June 4, Private Adams, now with a record of multiple desertions, went before a court-martial and was found guilty. It was ordered that he be shot within ten days of publication of GO #78, July 20, 1863, Army of Northern Virginia. The execution was to take place under the direction of the officer commanding the regiment, a rather unusual assignment, for normally that grim responsibility was assigned to an officer at the brigade or division level. The Forty-Fourth was located in the vicinity of Hanover Junction, VA, at the time of the execution order. The commanding officer of the Forty-Fourth, Colonel George B. Singletary, was no doubt relieved when General Lee interceded on behalf of the condemned substitute. Eight months earlier, the Colonel had the duty of sending Privates Bowers and Cain to their graves. On August 7, 1863, General Lee directed General Hill to suspend the execution of Private Adams until the decision of the President was known. The order noted that Private Adams was to be shot "this day," allowing little time for any unforeseen delay in getting the order to the regimental commander. General Lee then presented a summarization of the case to the President; "He has been in the woods or in arrest eighteen months except on trains from Goldsboro, Newbern and back to Gordonsville." Then he asked if the disclaimer in the Presidential Amnesty that removed those "twice convicted" of desertion from amnesty consideration, applied to Private Adams. Apparently the decision was that the prisoner was indeed eligible for the amnesty, for he was released and transferred to the Fifth Regiment, from whence he promptly deserted until returned on December 14, 1864. No record of a trial for this desertion has been located. Shortly after the last return, Private Adams was captured by Federal troops. From his previous activity, it was not likely to have been a hard-fought capture. The restless private headed for home in the spring of each year that he was in service.

While other soldiers were willing to accept the dishonor and risk of desertion, Private John A. Jackson of the Twenty-Sixth entertained a notion of leaving but wrote home in May of 1863 that "I think I can stand it at least I intend to try it a while longer before I do like B. Stutts."[39] Private Jackson was in the ranks at the last surrender, Private Benjamin W. Stutts deserted in March 1863 and had no further service record.

JAMES H. WAGGONER 44-G (June 13, 1863). Four with the family name of Waggoner reluctantly signed on for Confederate service on October 14, 1862. Within two weeks, three of the conscripts, Privates William, James and Henry Waggoner, deserted; the fourth, Private Moses Waggoner, remained in camp. Private James Waggoner was absent until February 1863, when he went back to his company. The returning private was present for three months before again having second thoughts on army life, whereupon he again deserted on May 16. This time he avoided arrest for only a few weeks. He was court-martialed on June 13, and when the decision of the court was published in GO #78, July 20, 1863, Army of Northern Virginia, the prisoner was informed that he would be shot for twice deserting. The reviewing officer made the decision to suspend the execution until the pleasure of the President was known, offering some hope to the threatened man. On August 7, General Lee was advised to continue the suspension of Private Waggoner's execution while awaiting the President's decision. And on that note, so ends the military record of Private James Waggoner. Private Moses Waggoner died in a military hospital in September 1863; his possessions included a Bible, a pocketknife, and an empty pocketbook, with a total value of $11.50. Private Henry Waggoner returned to his company and then began his second desertion in April 1864. Private William M. Waggoner had no service recorded after his desertion in 1862. A likely assumption would be that Private James Waggoner died while imprisoned, awaiting the President's pleasure.

The firmly Confederate wife of a faltering soldier is found in correspondence concerning Private J. Harvey L. Lafevers of Company F in the Twenty-Sixth. He and a fellow soldier, Private Sidney Hood, deserted and returned home in June of 1863. According to a supplicant to the Governor, Private Lafevers received a cool reception. "The truth is this Lafevers has a fine wife and she has told him plainly that he could not live with her if he did not go back to his Co." The news of their departure reached Caldwell County before the deserters had made their way there. Their jaunt home took over three weeks. On hearing that her husband was on his way home, "His wife was very much hurt and said she would not give him anything to eat no I will not give him a drink of water."[40] The properly chastened, and thirsty, spouse returned to be captured at Bristoe Station, VA, in October 1863. Private Sidney Hood returned to camp, was also captured at Bristoe Station and died while a Federal prisoner. Private Lafevers survived his imprisonment and took the oath.

JOHN M. HARRISON 44-B (August 22, 1863). The 23rd Article of War authorizes the death penalty when a soldier is convicted of persuading others to desert. Private Harrison was charged with using mutinous language to persuade others to desert. Apparently he never followed his own advice, for a desertion charge is not mentioned in the court record. While in camp near Orange Court House, Virginia, on August 14, 1863, the outspoken private attempted to persuade soldiers to leave the service. He was tried on that charge on August 22. A sentence of death was announced in GO #88, September 10, 1863, Army of Northern Virginia. Private Harrison was shot to death with musketry for his use of mutinous language; he was killed on Sunday September 20, 1863, the first North Carolinian to be executed on that day of the week. Private Harrison was conscripted from Yadkin County in November 1862 and put into a company of men from a more loyal section centered about Edgecombe County. Either he was not very persuasive, or he chose the wrong audience; his company was among the very best in terms of fewest absences in the brigade. Neither the proceeding, the relative seriousness of the offense, nor the execution elicited much comment from those who were aware of the events. Whether or not the execution would take place at all was an open question in the opinion of one soldier: "There is a man in camp is to be shot today the order was made out last Sunday. I cannot tell whither they will shoot him or not."[41] Another man tersely noted, "A deserter from the 44th reg was shot for desertion. I did not witness it."[42]

Kirkland Brigade

"I prayed that it might be my last."[43]

General William Wheedbee Kirkland was ordered to take command of Pettigrew's brigade on September 7, 1863. Two weeks before that day Captain Henry Clay Albright of Company G, Twenty-Sixth, wrote to his brother:

> Everything continues to grow more gloomy every day I have no doubt desertion will ruin our army taking place every day or two at an alarming rate. I can now put little or no confidence in any of the so-called Chatham Boys. They all speak favorably of desertion (with few exceptions) and I fear they will endeavor to get home after they draw their pay.[44]

Captain Albright's fears were misplaced. There was no surge of desertion in the fall of 1863, either in his company or in his regiment. This favorable trend may have been brought about by the execution of 3 deserters in September and October. A soldier in the Twenty-Sixth told those at home; "We have got a new General now one in the place of J. J. Pettigrew his name is W W Cerkland [sic] of N Carolina he is a very good general."[45] Not all men shared that same high regard. At a change of regimental command, "Then we have old Bill Kirkland for our Col again he has not taken command yet and I do hope he will break his accursed neck before he gets here God save us from tyranny and oppression of such men."[46] A quite different insight put forth by a soldier in a regiment where some saw strict discipline as an absolute necessity while others saw oppressive tyranny.

WILLIAM K. FREEMAN 44-H (September 8, 1863). Private Freeman enrolled in the Forty-Fourth on March 1, 1862, at Troy, Montgomery County. In October, he deserted for the first time but was present for duty by May 1863, when he was granted a thirty-day medical furlough. A month after returning from his furlough, Private Freeman began a second absence of fourteen days. This led to his arrest at Orange Court House, VA; he had made little homeward progress. On the September 8, a court-martial heard the facts in his case, determined that he was guilty as charged, and two-thirds of the court concurred on a death sentence. Ten days later, on Monday October 5, Private Freeman was shot to death. In 1885 William's widow filed a claim for a pension, but it was set aside awaiting further proof of the circumstances of her husband's death.[47] How, or even if, widows, parents or relatives were informed of an execution is not clear from existing records. No indication of an official procedure has come to hand. Private Freeman's company, The Montgomery Guards, did not have a large enrollment, with only 128 enrolled men during the time in service. At least 15 men absented themselves in the month of August prior to the execution of Private Freeman; none chose to do so in the two months after he was shot, but departures then began anew.

JORDAN HARRIS 47-F (September 22, 1863). Private Harris, at an age somewhere between forty-eight and fifty-two, was among the older volunteers when he enlisted on February 22, 1862. His chosen companions were The Sons of Liberty, Franklin County. Before year's end he had a change of heart and left his company. At trial, his punishment was fifty lashes on his bare back, and then to be imprisoned at hard labor for the rest of the war. Avoiding all, or at least the latter portion of his sentence, Private Harris again deserted his regiment while camped at Orange Court House, VA, on August 24, 1863. This desertion lasted just a week; the deserter went before a second court on September 22. A death sentence came down and was published in GO #92, October 4, 1863, Army of Northern Virginia. Private Harris was shot to death on November 1, 1863, the second man of the brigade to be executed on Sunday. Company F had experienced an outbreak of desertion in July and August of 1862 but only 5 men departed in the fourteen months prior to the execution of Private Harris, just 2 left after his death. The prospect of regular pay may have been compelling to Jordan, or perhaps the soldier's life had always been his fancy; a son was named General. A musician in the Twenty-Sixth Regimental Band described the execution and the effect it had on him:

> If ever my heart went out in sorrow and sympathy for a man, it was then, as the poor prisoner stood there, blindfolded, his hands tied behind him, having spoken his last word to any human being, looking his last upon God's beautiful earth, and the consciousness that in a very few minutes he would be face to face with his maker. It was my first time to look upon such a scene, and I prayed that it might be my last.... The impact of the balls seemed to raise the man off of his feet, and he fell backward, and was dead almost instantly. The troops were then marched past the prostrate form, and back to camp in quick time.[48]

From this account the prisoner was shot while he was standing, and not bound to a cross or seated on his coffin. That would mark an unusual execution, for a standing man might flinch, or collapse, and not present a steady target. The musician may have taken a bit of poetic license when he described the blindfolded man as "looking his last upon God's beautiful earth." Private Harris was absent only seven days on his second foray. Unfortunately, those days were a few weeks after General Lee issued a stern warning on the strict imposition of the death penalty for desertion.

SETH T. DULA 26-I (Prior to October 14, 1863). Corporal Dula, was promoted a month after his enlistment in July 1861. He then faithfully campaigned with his comrades for two years and was distinguished for gallantry at the Battle of Gettysburg. Not long thereafter he learned that he was father to a new-born daughter, whereupon he proudly asserted that he was going home to see her, with or without an approved leave. Forced to take the latter alternative, he was arrested and returned to his regiment; after trial he was sentenced to be shot to death. The sentence was promptly remitted. The proud father was killed several months later while leading a charge at Bristoe Station, VA.

THOMAS W. HADDOCK 52-B (January 9, 1864). Private Haddock was conscripted into The Randolph Guards on October 21, 1862, and was with his company six months before deserting at Hookerton, Greene County, NC. After an absence of seven months, forces under the command of General Hoke arrested him on November 18, 1863. Seven weeks later, on January 9, he was court-martialed for desertion, found guilty, and sentenced to be shot. The order for his execution was published in GO #5, January 19, 1864, Army of Northern Virginia. The day of execution was set for the first day of February. A final appeal to the President was turned aside on January 29, and Private Haddock was shot on the appointed day. Private Benjamin F. Haddock, an older brother, was enrolled in the same company. He died of disease six months before the execution of his brother.

WILLIAM STUTTS 52-B (January 9, 1864). Private Stutts, a conscript placed on company rolls on October 10, 1862, deserted his company while at Magnolia, Duplin County, after serving less than four months. He managed to avoid arrest until early November 1863. Held in the guardhouse for two months, he was then court-martialed, found guilty of desertion, and given a death sentence. An appeal for clemency for Private Stutts was rejected. Company B experienced a significant rate of desertion in 1862 and the first half of 1863, but very few men absented themselves in early 1864. Privates Haddock and Stutts were executed minutes apart on February 1, 1864. They were to be killed on the same command "Fire," but it was a gruesomely bungled affair. An officer in the Forty-Seventh describes the happenings in a letter written in two colors of ink to allow easier reading of the both horizontal and perpendicular writing, one over the other:

> Our brigade was drawn up this morning to witness the execution of two men. It was the most touching scene I ever witnessed. The unhappy men under a strong guard was marched around the whole brigade followed by their coffins and a brass band discoursing the most melancholy tune I ever heard they were then marched to their stakes, tied down and the command fire was given. It was very badly done. They were not killed, and such screams I never heard before. The reserve came up promptly and put an end to their existence. I hope I may never again be called upon to witness such a scene. I hope the men will take warning from the unhappy fate of those who were executed to day.[49]

A bungled execution may have been a more effective deterrent than a properly conducted affair. On face value, those who viewed the botched execution did heed the warning. Men in the company of the mangled dead recorded 46 absences in the two years prior to their fate, and only 8 in the year thereafter. Other companies also saw a reduction in desertion for a month or two after the event but then renewed that activity in the summer of 1864. A private, also a witness to the events, told his father of his reaction:

> I have just witnessed a scene that I never want to again ... after the command was given to fire one of the prisoners hollowed a few times the guard was ordered to fire the second time and a third before he was killed the other was fired at twice the guard was about five paces from the prisoner ... as they were tied to the stakes it was an awful sight to behold a terror to all deserters or ought to be I do not think I will ever bring disgrace on my family and relations it is true camp life is a hard one but to die the death of a deserter is a worse one.[50]

Two months later the young man wrote of his faith and his reaction to recent executions:

> Though I feel my unworthiness and sinfulness so plain it appears like that nothing I can do is done as it should be but hoping he will answer my petitions I try to serve him and trust in him. I have seen and went through a great deal of painful duty since I left home the most of it has been with men who was condemned to be shot I wrote about part of it in Roberts letter I have been at the execution of 7 men since I left home last December all of them shot at the stake. The troubles of war are coming in its plain colors.[51]

Corporal B. H. Freeman of Company F, Forty-Fourth, did not give any detail on the bloody execution, nor did he know the names of the executed men: "Pa I saw two men shot Mondy the second [first] of February for desertion from the 52nd Regt in our brigade the was one shot at the same place on Saturday before from the 55th Regt NCT his name was Smith I did not learn the name of them from the 52nd."[52]

When Privates Haddock and Stutts of the Fifty-Second were officially put to death for their crimes, other soldiers were hunting down and killing deserters under less formal circumstances, but even then it was necessary to maintain a legal veneer over the whole affair. The death of two "desperate characters" is related by an officer in the Home Guard in Moore County.

> Brewer & Davis were shot by a squad of Capt Ramsays men (detailed from the 52nd Regt I believe to arrest deserters in this County) while going from their camp in the wood to Ramsays camp near Deep River. They were desperate characters both deserters and [not legible] leaders of the worst band of robbers & plunderers that ever infested any community. It has been said, by their friends and relatives exclusively I think, that they were wantonly murdered. But this I do not believe. A jury of inquest was held over Davis & their verdict was that 'the dec'd came to his death by being shot through the head,' by whom & under what circumstances does not appear.[53]

The service record of Private Joseph Brewer, Company A, Fifth Regiment, indicates he was "killed in woods by troops hunting deserters."[54] The report continues at some length on the prospects of further legal activity in regard to this incident and also relates the killing of another deserter. Thus in early 1864, the struggle to control desertion went on in the wood, on the battlefield and in the courtroom.

HOSEA WATTS 11-B (February 5, 1864). Private Watts deserted from his company while in camp near Kinston, NC, five short weeks after being conscripted on March 5, 1863. The conscript-deserter managed to avoid arrest until early 1864. He appeared before a court-martial on February 5, and after the case was presented, the prisoner was found guilty, death the punishment.

LEMUEL M. SMITH 44-E (February 5, 1864). Private Smith, unlike Private Watts, was a volunteer who had enrolled on March 11, 1862. He had fought with his regiment for eighteen months before being absent without leave for just over two months. Private Smith's trial was on the same day as Private Watts,' and he heard the same dreadful words. Privates Watts and Smith were to be executed side by side on Thursday, February 18, 1864. Private Alfred Smith, enrolled in Company E, Forty-Fourth Regiment, several days before his brother; he was hospitalized, deserted and had no further service record. Two adults in the Smith family were identified as "idiotic" in census records. It was legally permissible for courts and reviewing officers to spare soldiers of limited mental capacity. That factor, if presented to the court, was not sufficient to spare Private Lemuel Smith. The lives that ended on the execution field were different than those often found in multiple executions. The men were not related, were not from the same county, had not enrolled in the same company nor had they enlisted or deserted at the same time. They were just young men with minimal desertion records whose lives were to end at the same instant, but even then a painful difference crept in. The last days and moments of the condemned are described with different degrees of vividness and detail by observers. A Chaplain wrote to his mother five days before the planned execution:

> The object of my visit was to see some poor condemned prisoners that are to be executed next Wednesday.... A petition for a reprieve has been sent up for both the prisoners. Poor fellows neither one of them can read.... I hardly ever felt more the presence of God, than this evening when describing the humiliation of Christ to these unfortunate creatures, contrasting his arrest and condemnation with theirs. They justly perhaps, and he unjustly. One of the condemned ones professed religion while I was there yesterday. I never want to hear my saviour say to me in the last morning I was in prison and you visited me not.... I saw two deserters executed Monday it was a week ago.[55]

Private John Wright of the Twenty-Sixth kept his family up to date on the happenings in his brigade.

> I can inform you that I have again witnessed the execution to day of two more men in this Brigade one from the 11th and the other from the 44th Regt they were tied to stakes and shot to death the whole Brigade was marched out and formed like they was on the first of the month charge against them desertion thus I have witnessed the execution of four deserters when I get home I can tell you more about it.[56]

Chaplain William Pressly Webb explained his duties to a cousin at home:

I have followed four men to the stake, and prayed with them, just before they were shot for desertion. I hope my labours with condemned prisoners has not been in vain, three out of the four embraced religion, and seemed to meet death with Christian fortitude. The two that were executed last Thursday, when following their coffins borne by four men right in front of them, up to the stake which was right at the mouth of their open graves said to their comrades as they passed them, Farewell boys, meet me in a better world.... It was melting to ones heart to hear their earnest prayers, but at the same time a comfort to be able to offer them a Saviour, who saved a dying thief.[57]

Corporal B. H. Freeman of the Forty-Fourth adds detail not found in other descriptions:

> Pa there was two men shot here yesterday the 18th from our Brigade one was from our Regiment and one was from the 11th Reg. the one from ours was named Limuel Smith and the one from the 11th was Joseph Watts they both was shot dead at a steak Limuel Smith was not killed on the first fire then Mr Stark [Rufus H.] had to step out and kill him he hated to do it but had to do it the blood would rush from the holes where the bullets entered them they was shot for desertion Running away from the army is not fine work.[58]

This is the only known instance of an officer ending an execution by a pistol-shot to the head. There are executions that end with a reserve soldier firing his musket close by the head, or the heart, of the condemned. Company B of the Eleventh and Company E of the Forty-Fourth each had a bare handful of deserters after witnessing the deaths of Private Smith and Private Watts.

DAVID DANNER 26-F (March 10, 1864). Private Danner voluntarily went into service on March 20, 1862, and deserted while near Culpeper, VA, on June 16, 1863. The precise length of absence is not recorded but it was likely on the order of eight months, for Private Danner went to trial on March 10, 1864, and a death sentence was forthcoming. A period of hospitalization occurred prior to his desertion, but no other absence or desertion attempt is found in his records while he was in the ranks of the Hilbritten Guards from Caldwell County.

GEORGE WASHINGTON OWENS 26-C (March 12, 1864). Private Owens mustered with the Twenty-Sixth Regiment on June 12, 1861. A year later, he deserted on June 19, 1862, while at New Bern, NC. He was absent until early 1864. After his arrest and trial on March 12, he learned that he would be shot. On March 20 1864, a private in the same regiment rather matter-of-factly informed the folks at home, "Two men in our Regt is to be shot next Thursday one in my Co. Washington Owens and one in Co F Danner."[59] At that time the writer did not know that he would soon be closely involved, physically and emotionally, with the men he mentioned in his letter. Privates Danner and Owens were shot to death on Thursday March 24, near Orange Court House, VA. The field still had the whiteness of a recent heavy snow; snow and life would soon blend in the moist earth. After the executions, Private Wright of the Twenty-Sixth described his part in the final hours of the dead men.

> I can tell you that I have again witnessed the execution of two more men to day they belonged to this Regt. I was detailed on yesterday morning to help guard them I had charge of four men and had to stand 16 hours out of 24 the poor fellows was confined with a ball and chain we had to stand with loaded guns and was ordered to keep them safe with 7 others O Fanny you dont know how bad I felt to see them in that condition and having to guard them the last night that they had t o live I looked at them eat dry bread by itself and felt so bad I gave them some roasted potatoes and butter it done me good to see them eat it One of them (Owens) talked very calm and talked to me about his future state he did not fear being shot he appeared to give satisfaction to all that talked with him. he is old man Cheeks son in law I expect there will be two more in my company shot before long.[60]

Over two weeks after the two privates were killed and buried, Corporal Freeman of the Forty-Fourth wrote, "Farther there is a man in the 11th Regt they say to be shot in a few days 7 days from the 8th day of April. The last letter that I wrote to you one [of] them I wrote his name I put G W his name is Owens I forgot to put Owens."[61] No other reference to a pending execution of a man in the Eleventh Regiment has been found, so the writer likely was mistaken as to the regiment of the condemned soldier. Camp rumors and misinformation about death sentences may have been nearly as effective in slowing borderline deserters as watching an execution. There are several instances where men took life-threatening action when they had heard that they might be shot and did not choose to idle about to see if the rumors were true. Resisting arrest, breaking from a guardhouse, and not returning voluntarily from a fairly short desertion are all examples of how some men reacted to the misleading information that they would be shot if they went back to their regiment. Another writer briefly noted the execution of Privates Danner and Owens: "Two men were shot for desertion." In a lighter note he went on; "At night we took our innocent Charley out hunting Elba dritches it was not very successful for either side."[62] Boyish pranks on not very sophisticated recruits are embedded in the memories of soldiers of many wars, at least one on a solemn day of execution.

WAYNE GALLINGTON LEE 26-D (March 14, 1864); and CHARLES W. LEE 26-C (March 31, 1864). Private Wayne Lee continued his service for fifteen months after being conscripted in August 1862. On the last day of 1863, he was court-martialed for some unknown infraction, possibly a brief period of absence without leave, for which extra duty was the punishment. Not long after this punishment, he began a full-fledged desertion that ended in his arrest and a second court on March 14, 1864. Under sentence of death, Private Wayne Lee was transferred to Prison Hospital #13 at Richmond while suffering from diarrhea. He died there on July 31. His death sentence was remitted by SO #26, October 27, 1864, AIGO, some four months after his death. Private Charles W. Lee voluntarily enrolled in the army only a few weeks after North Carolina had agreed to become a Confederate state. He fulfilled his duty for eighteen months before deserting. Once absent, he was away from his unit for eleven months. For this absence he went before a court-martial on March 31, 1864, was found guilty of the charge of desertion, and given a death sentence. Sent to Castle Thunder to await his fate, he later learned that he was to be pardoned. On October 12, 1864, he died while hospitalized. The Lee boys did not enter the service together, serve in the same company, or desert at the same time. Apparently each made his own decision to desert. Later they were court-martialed by the same court and were imprisoned together at Castle Thunder.

BRAXTON LAWS 26-C (March 26, 1864). Private Laws deserted on July 5, 1863, after being conscripted in September 1862. He was court-martialed on March 26, 1864, and was shot by musketry on a Thursday, twelve days after the trial. Company C had the largest number of men to absent themselves from the Twenty-Sixth. It also led all others in the number of men that went before courts-martial. There was a reduction in desertion from Company C for several months after the execution of Private Laws but those so inclined continued to leave other companies of the Twenty-Sixth. The imminent execution of Private Laws did not elicit sympathy from a member of the same regiment. After commenting on the weather over the last four days he went on to say: "Brackston Laws of Capt Jarratts Co C 26th N.C. T. will be shot tomorrow between the hours of 11 and 2 o'clock for desertion. It is hard but he brought it on himself, therefore he does not get much sympathy." The writer continued with a further note of bitterness: "How does the principles [*sic*] of substitutes and the Malitia officers flourish these days? Do you think there is any chance to get them out?"[63] Deserters, and those who stayed at home by providing substitutes or serving in the militia, met the same disdain from a soldier in the field. Another writer simply mentioned the execution, "On day before yesterday they shot another man his name was Brackson Laws of the 26th Reg NC Troops shot for desertion." He went on to say, "We kept fast day yesterday for the benifit of the country."[64] With a note of irony, another who fasted that day remarked, "I never saw a day more observed in my life."[65] Many were the days of little or no food for the Confederate soldier, whether officially proclaimed or not.

THOMAS L. DURHAM 44-B (April 30, 1864). Private Durham was conscripted on November 18, 1862. Hospitalization at Raleigh followed in February of the next year. By February 9, Private Durham recovered sufficient strength to desert. This absence extended over a full year until he was returned to his regiment then at Orange Court House, VA. On April 30, he was tried for his crime and heard that he would be shot in seven days according to GO #45, May 24, 1864, Department of Northern Virginia. On the day that the order for his execution was published, the life of Private Durham ended, death coming as a result of an infected gunshot wound. Details of the wounding are not provided. Whether he was wounded in a skirmish or shot in an attempt to escape is not known. The conscript was in the ranks less than three months in his eighteen months on company rolls.

JAMES PHILLIPS 52-B (May 3, 1864). After volunteering in March 1862, Private Phillips stayed just two months before deserting from Camp Mangum at Raleigh. He avoided arrest for nearly two years until April of 1864, probably finding a haven in Moore County. Private Phillips was brought before a court on charges of desertion on May 3. The court's decision in his case was published in GO #45, May 24, 1864, Department of Northern Virginia; he would be shot in seven days. Ten days later, whether due to his own ingenuity, the vagaries of war, the laxness of his guard or a quick remission of sentence, the condemned man was captured at Cold Harbor, VA, by Federal forces. Less than three weeks later the former Confederate enrolled in the First United States Volunteer Infantry Regiment.

CLARKSON L. ROBBINS 52-B (May 3, 1864). Private Robbins was a young recruit in April 1862. He served until January 17, 1863, when he deserted, taking his Enfield rifle and ammunition with him. Private Robbins was not arrested until April of 1864 and was court-martialed on May 3. Death was the judgment of the court, but they then recommended leniency. Private Robbins' age, 15 years in 1860, may have influenced their recommendation. The reviewing General suspended the execution of sentence until the decision of the President could be made known. This decision was announced in SO #206, August 31, 1864, AIGO; the life of the private would be spared but his pay up to that point would be forfeited. A month later the pardoned private was wounded, but this did not hinder his desertion to the enemy toward the end of the war.

ELIAS ROBBINS 52-B (May 3, 1864). Just sixteen days after being conscripted on November 11, 1862, Private Robbins deserted while his unit was near the Blackwater River, VA. The fleeing conscript avoided apprehension until April 18, 1864. His name was dropped from the rolls of the company on March 1, 1863. Counting his time in the guardhouse, the conscript had been with his command for about a month before going before a court sitting on May 3. As announced in GO #45, May 24, 1864, Department of Northern Virginia, the conscript was to be shot to death in seven days. Between the publication of that order and June 12, Private Robbins was able to make his way into Federal lines, as had Private Phillips over a week earlier, though the former was supposedly captured. It was noted in Federal records that the prisoner "wishes to take the oath. Will go to the state of Indiana and remain there until the war is over."[66] But that wish was not to be; the prisoner died six months later while still confined at Elmira, NY.

MacRae Brigade

"I aimed a bullet at his heart."[67]

Colonel William MacRae of the Fifteenth Regiment received a temporary appointment as Brigadier General on June 22, 1864, and took his place at the head of his brigade. A contemporary review indicated, "General McRae [*sic*] is a strict disciplinarian — but has secured in an eminent degree the confidence of his men."[68] A private soldier in the Twenty-Sixth offered the opinion that the regiment always performed honorably, resisting any impulse to go home. "If I new as much as I no now when I was at hoam John I would hav ben thair yet ... but the men hate to run a way in the face of them John honor is a grate thing but I am afraid we have pad vary dear for all we will get John thair is not a man in the company but said if they was at hoam they would stay."[69] Once a soldier was legally home, simply staying there was seen as a less serious violation than beginning a desertion from camp and certainly carried less risk.

DAVID W. WELLS 26-C (August 11, 1864). Private Wells quickly volunteered for duty with North Carolina troops once the choice had been made that his state would become a part of the Confederacy. He stood by that decision a full eighteen months, whereupon he deserted. With that option selected and implemented, Private Wells remained a deserter at large until the summer of 1864. He was in arrest and at trial on August 11, 1864, after an absence of twenty months. Found guilty by the court, a death sentence was approved by the General Commanding. Twelve days later, he was shot to death, this on Tuesday, August 23, 1864.

LITEL HOOPERAS 26-F (August 16, 1864). Private Hooperas deserted from his company while at Orange Court House, VA on April 12, 1864, five months after enrolling at Raleigh on November 30, 1863. On August 16, 1864, he was court-martialed. Within two weeks, he was executed. Little more is known about Private Hooperas. The AIGO record of his court-martial has his name as Litel Cooperas. Private Thomas W. Setser, of the same company, for one, was glad that deserters were punished: "I am glad that tha hav Caught R E Fleming and if tha fetch him he is as good as a dead man for tha Shot Happeras he that runaway the Same time that Fleming did and tha hav got too more in the guard house that lefte the Same time Clark and Hicks."[70] Private Hooperas was the only one of the deserters that did not survive the war. Private Setser had a different thought when he too decided to desert, going directly to the enemy. The month after the execution of Private Hooperas, Corporal Freeman neatly summarized the fall of 1864: "They have shot a good many deserters for the last month some more expect to be shot."[71]

MASTON GREENE 44-H (September 7, 1864). Private Greene deliberately left his command while near Orange Court House, VA, after eight months in the army. He enrolled on March 1, 1863. He avoided those searching out wayward Confederates for eight months but was then arrested and brought to trial on September 7, 1864. Found guilty of desertion, his execution was scheduled for September 21. The day before that, General Cooper ordered General Hill to "Suspend execution of Pvt Maston Green 4-H [44-H] condemned to be shot tomorrow."[72] Private Greene waited under the threat of execution for six months before he was pardoned and restored to duty, this on February 11, 1865.[73] He was captured by the enemy on April 2, and died while their prisoner.

JOSHUA STAMEY 11-D (November 23, 1864). The life of Private Stamey, and his time as a Confederate soldier, ended after just eighty days of service. He enrolled, deserted and was arrested all in the September-October reporting period in 1864. A court-martial gathered on November 23, found that the deserter was guilty as charged and a sufficient number agreed that he should be shot. Lieutenant General A. P. Hill approved the decision of the court and the order was carried to conclusion on December 4. Private Stamey was the third man of his brigade to be shot on a Sunday. Company D was raised in Burke County and had a good desertion record with just 15 of 128 enrolled men making that decision. In a 1901 letter of reminiscence, a private of the Eleventh Regiment recalled, "I believe we had only one man shot for desertion in our Reg. he was a Co D man named Stamey it was my sad lot to help shoot him. I aimed a bullet at his heart. Lieut Hoyle was officer of the squad that did the shooting."[74] The writer, Private John C. Warlick, was a young but twice wounded veteran soldier, only twenty-three years old when he aimed at Private Stamey's heart. Comments by a soldier in an execution detail are rare. Private Warlick was either unaware, or had forgotten, that Private Hosea Watts of his regiment had been executed early in 1864. That is understandable, Private Watts was a conscript who was with the Eleventh for only five weeks.

HAMPTON CROUSE 52-F (February 1, 1865). Private Crouse enlisted in the Fifty-Second as a volunteer; however, he was late in reporting for duty. On February 1, 1864, he appeared before a court-martial for having committed some unknown infraction of regulations. For this violation he was ordered to forfeit pay and to be confined for twelve months at hard labor, so the infraction was likely desertion. Even more serious trouble began for the tardy private when he deserted on July 20, a portion of the earlier sentence apparently having been remitted. After arrest and a night in the Montgomery County jail, he was brought back to his regiment on December 20. On February 1, 1865, a year to the day after his first appearance before a court, he stood before another; this court issued a death sentence. General Hill approved the findings of the court on February 9. In the confusion of the final days at Petersburg, VA, Private Crouse was captured by Federal soldiers and sent to Point Lookout, MD, where he took the oath and was eventually released.

ALPHEUS GALLAHORN 52-B (March 22, 1865, Drumhead). Private Gallahorn became Corporal Gallahorn not long after being mustered with the Fifty-Second, in early March 1862. Corporal Gallahorn abandoned his regiment in August of 1863 and persisted in his desertion for the next nineteen months. When Alpheus went from his home to the army an older brother, Aaron, had already given his life in the service. A second brother, Zebedee, followed Aaron in death. Lieutenant Colonel A. C. McAllister of the Forty-Sixth Regiment was ordered to proceed with a force of men to the area of Randolph, Chatham and Moore counties to break up and disperse bands of deserters. Specifically he was ordered: "Should you come in contact with deserters who resist your authority, or who have resisted the authority of the Government, you will shoot them down taking no prisoners."[75] The Lieutenant Colonel received the following message from Captain D. E. Green, an officer under his command, on March 22, 1865:

> I sent a detachment under Lt. Hart yesterday to the neighborhood of old Gollyhorne. They succeeded in catching Alpheus Golleyhorn and Walters (the Yankee) Milton Gollyhorn made good his escape. Alpheus Gollyhorn fired upon our men and according to our orders I disposed of him this evening at 4 P.M. he died at the stake. I concluded that I could not shoot the Yankee. I send him to you for to dispose.[76]

One man in the pursuing party was killed and another wounded in this incident at Bear Creek, Randolph County. Within a few days Captain Green was asked to forward to his commanding officer the "evidence and proceedings" in the case. This order must have caused some slight chagrin for the Captain, as there was no mention of legal niceties in the earlier "shoot them down taking no prisoners" instruction to him. The Captain replied that the deserters had fired upon his men with the intent of killing them and then went on:

> If I had been present when he was first taken he would not have been brought to camp. I gave him the benefit of a drum head court martial which condemned him to be shot to death with musketry. I believed that more good to the service would arise from his being shot here or near where he was caught. I believed that by shooting him (one of the most desperate characters in the county) would be a check upon the actions of his comrades. They will begin to believe that we are in earnest and that we are determined to put an end to those men who have been committing those robberies and deppredations in the community.[77]

Governor Vance was asked for his assistance in securing proper authority for those on the ground to make an immediate life or death decision for such men: "Alive, as I believe you to be, to the necessity of summarily disposing of the desperadoes infesting this community that may fall into my hands as the only cure for the alarming evils existing here I am confident that your endeavors will be used to have me clothed with all lawful powers necessary to that end."[78] Colonel McAllister requested authority to order a general court-martial, or be assigned a military court, or to proceed with drumhead courts.

The Yankee mentioned by Captain Green as being captured along with Private Gallahorn was the subject of an urgent inquiry to Governor Vance.

> I hold an escaped prisoner Yankee who, but for the misinterpretation of my orders would not have been taken alive. He is recognized as an officer of an armed band of deserters, is a notoriously audacious robber, is suspected of having participated in two murders recently committed in the County, & is one of a party that fired upon my men. Is a drumhead Court allowable in his case? Please answer the last question by telegram.[79]

No reply has been located, but a formal Military Court made up of a Major and two Captains was appointed to hear the case against Private Walters, the court to sit on March 28, 1865. A partial transcript of the trial shows that the prosecution put forth one witness in an attempt to associate the prisoner with the Gallahorns. Besides the robbing and associated charges, he was guilty of being "a leader and councellor of such armed bands of deserters and robbers."[80] Charges also included the murder of a John Vanderford. Soldiers with the same name as the victim are found in Confederate military records, but it is not clear whether the deceased was a soldier or a civilian. Walters was tried and his death sentence, unanimous in court records, was published in GO #3, Head Qtrs Detach Cooke's & Lane's Brg. March 30, 1865. The fact that the court's decision was stated as "unanimous" rather than following the nicety of a "two-thirds concurring" statement was not deemed sufficient to set aside the verdict in this affront to the Confederacy. Private William F. Walters, Third Indiana Cavalry, was shot to death, not hanged, as he might have been if a Confederate deserter fighting with the enemy.

Governor Vance was not alone in his concern that a civil war would destroy the frail mountain society. John A. Burnette, a citizen soldier, writing to a soldier in Kirkland's brigade, expressed his feelings:

> I have been engaged for the last week in getting up the conscripts & deserters from the army.... It is a very disagreeable business to go around and hunt them up & I expect to have some very hot work to do the coming week for there is some who say they will die at home rather than go & the order is to take them dead or alive & I assure you that it is a very unpleasant business to have to treat neighbors in that way.[81]

Seven absentees from the brigade were killed by the Home Guard.

Summary

Governor Z. B. Vance began the war confidently leading an eager company of North Carolinians, The Rough and Ready Guards, Company F, Fourteenth Regiment, against a common enemy. Four years later, he desperately struggled to preserve some semblance of order amid the chaos of civil war. Over 2,000 men served in the Twenty-Sixth, the regiment once led by the Governor. Just 131 men of that regiment were present to put down their arms at Appomattox. The company of men that he led as Captain Vance had just 5 men present on the day of surrender.

When all were assembled, the 5 regiments of the Pettigrew-Kirkland-MacRae brigade presented a meager 430 men at their final muster. None of the 32 soldiers of the brigade who were sentenced to be shot to death were there among them, though 7 survived the war. At least 20 of the 32 condemned were married. All of those whose place of residence is known came from Wake or counties to the west. Nearly one-quarter of the condemned, 7, were from Wilkes County. The 13 conscripts in the brigade who were condemned to death served an average of five and a half months before fleeing. Condemned volunteers were in the ranks nearly fourteen months before deserting. Eleven companies that had 453 absences, and 100 courts-martial, had 49 deaths per company. Eleven companies with 183 absences and 16 courts had 47 deaths per company. Buried at their place of execution, were 17 soldiers of the brigade: 8 were volunteers; 8 were conscripts; 1 was a substitute.

	1861	1862	1863	1864	1865	no date
Abs/Co	.1	2.0	5.8	7.2 4.8	3.4 4.0	2.2
To be executed		1	2	6 4	12 4	1	2
Executed			1	2 3	7 3	1	

The lives of 10 of the 17 executed ended in 5 double executions. The benefit of double executions was muted for this brigade because companies of the executed had good to moderate desertion records before their sacrifice; some executions were not directly desertion related; half the executed were conscripts. A more beneficial outcome may have resulted had the executed been from companies that experienced a much higher rate of desertion. The 12 companies that had men marched to the stake had an absence rate of 20 percent; 12 companies that had no men so sacrificed had an absence rate of 17 percent. A sample of 11 companies with a high number of absences, 41 per company, had 9 military courts per company, and a company average of 49 deaths with 12 executions in total.[82] Eleven companies with fewer absences, 17 per company, had 2 courts per company, they averaged 47 deaths and had a total of 5 executions.[83] Deaths in combat for the high absence companies were 15 per company, and 16 for the low absence companies. There were execution spectacles on eleven separate days over a period of two years. It is not known how many people witnessed the summary execution of Private Alpheus Gallahorn at the Springs near Pages toll house on the old plank road.[84] The other executed men paid their toll in a less scenic setting.

5

Third Corps, Heth Division, Cooke Brigade

"It was the saddest sight I ever witnessed"[1]

A few months after John Rogers Cooke took brigade command, the Colonel of the Forty-Eighth objected to his appointment on the basis that Cooke was a Virginian leading men from North Carolina. Colonel R. C. Hill, did not object to Cooke simply because he was a Virginian, but he was a junior officer and "he is intensely Virginian in feeling.... His whole staff is Virginian — only orderlies excepted because he could not procure Virginians." The proud North Carolinian concluded: "Now if I am to play second fiddle to the end of the war I don't wish the first to be played by a Virginian."[2] Another soldier shared that thought: "I am in Petersburg among Virginians to rule over me."[3] The ruling "Virginians" had a different view: "And we are gradually getting the North Carolinians straight. A great many have been shot for desertion. There was no other way to put a stop to it."[4] The latter view was expressed by Colonel Powhatan B. Whittle, Thirty-Eighth Virginia Infantry. That regiment had 12 men sentenced to be shot during the conflict; 1 execution has been verified.

Fifteenth Regiment

Twenty North Carolina regiments were assigned to the Third Corps, Army of Northern Virginia, the Fifteenth the only one with no recorded execution. Nor did the regiment have a large number of men go before military courts, 44 in all, and 6 trials ended with an acquittal. Twenty-three of the 38 convicted men were from Company D, the Chatham Cossacks; Company E, recruited in Franklin and Granville counties; and Company C, the Ellis Guards, Cleveland County. Seven of 10 death sentences went to these same companies. Virtually all of these decisions followed a mutiny attempt by men enrolled in Company E in late 1864. Two men avoided execution by deserting to the enemy; a third died while awaiting the stake. Less threatening, an officer in Company D was taken before a court on the charge: "Did bed and cohabit with a free woman of color in an open and notorious manner."[5] He was dismissed from the service.

The first Colonel of the Fifteenth, Robert M. McKinney, was a Virginian by birth. A company officer in March 1862 gave the opinion, "The Col is not much liked by the men he is too good an officer for that."[6] Whether the dislike was due to his being a Virginian, his youthfulness or his strict command is not mentioned.

Twenty-Seventh Regiment

Over 60 percent of the 43 men that were court-martialed in the regiment were brought up on charges resulting from an absence incident in early May 1862; it was essentially confined to men from Company H, the Pitt County Volunteers. Punishment for these men varied from standing bareheaded on parade, standing on a barrel, and forfeiture of pay. Company K, the Saulston Volunteers of Wayne County, and Company E, the Marlboro Guards of Pitt County, each had 4 men go before a general court-martial. These companies and Company H accounted for 35 of 42 court convictions; there was 1 acquittal. Even in the exemplary companies, men would go to extremes to avoid the battlefield; a man enrolled in Company A allegedly cut off his own hand while on leave to avoid a return to combat.[7]

The Twenty-Seventh had only 5 men court-martialed in the final year of war, but there are several caveats when viewing that record. First, the Twenty-Seventh was a relatively small regiment, one that was fairly stable and did not have a large infusion of reluctant enrollees, conscripts who might soon leave camp and thus bring about another cycle of enrollment and desertion. Still, the regiment suffered the attrition found for most regiments. Only 26 men were available for duty in Company G in June of 1864, this dishearteningly falling to 11 a month later.[8] Overall, there were slightly fewer than 1,400 men enrolled in the Twenty-Seventh throughout the regiment's service; in February 1863, 450 men were present for duty. Second, very few men deserted or were absent without leave in the early going; thus, no pattern of lightly punished unauthorized absence was established. Two-thirds of all absences took place after August 1864, and two-thirds of these men joined the exodus into the Federal lines. Third, the regiment was not heavily engaged in the carnage at Chancellorsville or Gettysburg, the horror of which might have brought on more attempts at desertion, though they did gallantly participate at Sharpsburg and at Bristoe Station, also bloody affairs. For the regiment there were 144 incidents of absence, a rate slightly over 10 percent.

Forty-Sixth Regiment

Deserters from the Forty-Sixth were dealt with in a prompt and effective manner; 5 privates were convicted of desertion and given death sentences, and 4 were shot to death on two execution days. Three of the executed were from a company that presented relatively few disciplinary problems. Other men from the same company were tried several months after the executions; they were given rather light sentences after much longer absences. For the entire regiment, the men of the three companies with the greatest number of courts were Company I, the Coharie Guards, Sampson County; Company F, from Randolph County; and Company K, the Catawba Braves. These companies accounted for over half of the 73 courts concerning the regiment; there were 3 acquittals. While Company I led all others, the majority of their offenses took place in either the second year of war or in the final months 1865. The first man of the regiment to be shot was from Company I. One deserter from the Forty-Sixth was killed while resisting arrest.

Forty-Eighth Regiment

The first execution of a soldier from the Forty-Eighth did not happen until January 1864. Within the year, 3 such rites would follow; 2 other men would be threatened, but spared. Men who were taken before courts were evenly distributed over 9 of the companies of the regiment, none having more than 5 men at trial. The tenth, Company K, the Confederate Guards, Forsyth County, had 8 men convicted after their hearing and 2 were shot. Company K had 174 men enrolled during their time of service. There were 49 incidents of absence: 20 of these men returned or were brought back in arrest; 6 returnees later deserted directly to the enemy; 11 others left for parts unknown. Including death sentences, 22 of the 38 courts hearing cases concerning the Forty-Eighth handed down severe sentences; two at trial were acquitted. Desertion was a recognized problem and was dealt with in a firm manner. Though courts-martial were more or less evenly distributed over all companies, absences were not. Company C, Iredell County, had 11 recorded absences. Company D, Moore County, had 59 absences. Company C lost 78 dead from 166 enrolled men, and Company D had 52 dead from an enrollment of 147. Company C established a noteworthy absence record for a company that left the remains of nearly half their men in a grave or scattered about a battlefield.

Colonel Samuel Hoey Walkup was a competent leader of the Forty-Eighth when in combat. However, when in camp, self-centered best describes his demeanor. Even when those in his charge were but a few days from execution, he appeared to lack any understanding of or empathy for the condemned and their families. Brigadier Cooke's vigorous leadership of his brigade was likewise found suspect by the Colonel: "General Lee asks for Cook's Brigade, so says Cook, no doubt Cook's ambition has thrust his Brig. forward hoping to push himself forward by the blood of his Brigade. Ambition will wade through slaughter to a throne and shut the gates of mercy on mankind."[9] As noted in other instances, Colonel Walkup has difficulty with the spelling of family names, in this case his commanding officer.

Fifty-Fifth Regiment

Brigadier Joseph R. Davis, kin to the President of the Confederacy, led the brigade where the Fifty-Fifth fought much of the war. The other regiments in that brigade were the Second, Eleventh, Twenty-Sixth and Forty-Second Mississippi. AIGO records list only 1 man sentenced to be executed from the 4 regiments. However, 10 North Carolinians were so threatened, and 4 were likely executed. The regiment was transferred to the Heth division in mid–1864 and to the Cooke brigade later that year. Men of the Fifty-Fifth went before 38 courts; three trials ended with acquittals. Company B, formed in Wilkes County; Company F, the South Mountain Rangers, Cleveland County; and Company H, recruited in Alexander and Onslow counties, were the companies with the most courts-martial. Of the 10 men who were ordered to be shot, 9 were from these companies, as were 9 of the 11 men that received severe sentences. Company H had 102 enrolled men, including 10 substitutes. The company had 18 recorded absences and 5 men were given death sentences. Men who were tardy in returning from furloughs to harvest their wheat made up the bulk of the absentees.

A sensitive issue for some men of the Fifty-Fifth was expressed at an early date.

> For poor old Nth Carolina, she has sent her noblest and bravest forth to battle for the right; now on Virginias soil arrayed in defence & protection; are thousands of her troops, who get nothing more than the abusive insulting insults, of Virginians, who claim for themselves, all the honor of protecting or defending their own borders; while we are left even without force sufficient to repell the enemy, from our home firesides; our troops are scattered abroad, to protect the hearthstones of those who mock us with their boasted heroism.[10]

The writer continued in the same vein for several pages. The wife of a soldier expressed another common sentiment, one attributed to many Confederate women: "Phillop is advirtest [as a deserter] in the papers I dont want you to come away as bad as i want to see you with out leafe."[11] A apparent incident of self-maiming was frankly confronted when Private George Washington Woodard wrote to his twin brother who was at home, "Bunyan I want to know whether it was you who shot your finger or not."[12] No service record for Bunyan has been found, so the referenced incident may have been preventative to avoid a call to service. The writer died within three months of the query.

Courts-Martial

JOHN HINCHEY 55-B (December 2, 1862). Private Hinchey was absent without leave about three months after he enrolled in April 1862. By December the initial charge was replaced by the more serious charge of desertion. Early in December of 1862, Private Hinchey was tried by general court-martial, found guilty as charged, and sentenced to be shot in two weeks. On December 16, a soldier in the regiment wrote to his parents.

> A young man in Co B 55 Regt was condemned to be shot tomorrow evening the 17th inst but thank god his life is perlonged till January and I hope for good. I hope he will get clear he deserted at Camp Mangum and went home and Sergeant Webb [W. P.] brought him back ten men out of our Co was detailed to shoot him to morrow. They have been drilling several days to shoot to gether. Twelve in all. They did noting but drill an practes shooting and one more is to be whiped in the presence of the Regt an several more to be purnice [punished].... I will tell you the boys was detailed to shoot that young man R. B. E. [Robert B. Elixson] Henry C [Henry C. Adcock] S R Puckett uncle Rob T. B. Daniel two Currins Zack Daniel & I dont recerlect who the other two is they are on gard to day they have got to drill off an on till the time.[13]

The "uncle Rob" is Private Robert D. Wilkerson; he would have a second detail as an executioner later in the war. The death sentence for Private Hinchey was commuted in late January 1863. When Governor Vance inquired as to the presence of several men then under sentence of death and supposedly confined at Petersburg, VA, he was informed by the Provost Marshal at that place,

> I have no man under my charge condemned to be shot. John Hinchy of 55th NC Troops was recently under sentence to be shot, but the same has been commuted to hard work in Fort Caswell, to which place he was sent last Monday by his Colonel.... No case of enforcement of sentence of death under findings of Court Martial has taken place here for some time & I know not of any one at this time under said sentence.[14]

The prisoner was moved on February 9, 1863. Following his forced hard labor at Fort Caswell Private Hinchey returned to active duty with his regiment and served until surrender.

RANSOM HINKLE 15-K (February 26, 1863). Private Ransom Hinkle was one of four brothers conscripted on July 15, 1862. Private Alexander Hinkle was the oldest, followed in age by Emanuel and then Ransom and Christian, who were twin brothers. Just over a month after enrolling, the four decided to leave the company and proceeded to do so on August 20, 1862. Within a week, they were all arrested in Cumberland County, VA, west of Richmond and over 150 miles from their home in North Carolina. Still acting together, the brothers broke arrest to remain deserters for varying periods of time. Private Ransom

Hinkle was the only brother tried for desertion; he was given a death sentence, his trial occurring on March 26, 1863. An appeal for executive clemency was granted in early September; a few weeks later, such an appeal might well have been turned aside and the sentence carried into effect. Private Ransom Hinkle returned to duty and was captured in the last weeks of fighting and took the oath. Alexander never returned; Emanuel did return and was later given a medical discharge. Christian went back and served till the end.

RICHARD TEW 46-I (May 11, 1863). Private Tew stood before a court-martial charged with four counts of desertion.

> 1) Deserted from the hospital at Goldsboro on June 7, 1862; voluntarily returned to camp near Petersburg on July 25th. 2) Deserted near Poolsville, Maryland while in line of battle September 10th; voluntarily rejoined at Fredericksburg on December 6th. 3) Deserted January 18, 1863 until February 10th when returned to camp near Holly Shelter Swamp, NC. 4) Deserted April 25th until May 8th when arrested and brought back to camp near Magnolia, NC, under guard.[15]

Private Tew was found guilty of the last three charges and was sentenced to be shot to death. The sentence was reviewed and approved on June 1. A brother, Private Lewis Tew, also enrolled in the Coharie Guards, was killed at Fredericksburg, VA, on December 13, 1862, a week after Private Richard Tew returned from his second desertion.

PHILLIP HENRY HONEYCUTT 46-I (May 12, 1863). Private Honeycutt volunteered on March 12, 1862; however, he was not mustered into service until April 16. He might better have not reported. After waiting five weeks to begin his army life, he stayed just nine days before beginning a series of short desertions. An account of his activity was developed at a court convened on May 12, 1863. Five charges were drawn:

> 1) Deserted April 25, 1862 from Camp Mangum; arrested and brought back on May 4th. 2) Deserted June 10th from Drewry's Bluff, Virginia; arrested and brought back June 17th. 3) Deserted January 18, 1863; arrested and confined Sampson County, North Carolina, January 28th. 4) Escaped arrest Sampson County; voluntarily returned March 4th. 5) Deserted April 25th Topsail, North Carolina; brought back to Magnolia, North Carolina.[16]

A death sentence for Private Honeycutt was reviewed and approved by Lieutenant General A. P. Hill and published on June 1. The sentence was to be carried out in the presence of Cooke's brigade on June 8, 1863, "wherever they may be." They were in the vicinity of Petersburg, VA, on the designated day, and there Private Honeycutt was executed. But what of Private Tew, his companion in desertion and destined to be in death? A journal recollection by Captain O.W. Carr of the Forty-Sixth sheds some light on why Private Honeycutt made a solitary march to the execution place. The former college professor recalls:

> Went thence to Goldsboro, remaining about a week — during which time I was on Court Martial for the Brigade. Two men were sentenced to be shot for deserting. One subsequently made his escape, the other was executed. I talked and prayed with him more than once — but he seemed to have but a fair idea of his condition and the plan of salvation. I tried to point him to the cross, as best I could.[17]

In another entry he says, "We left Kinston for Va. about the 7th of June — stopping at Petersburg only long enough to witness the execution of the deserter previously mentioned."[18] How Private Tew managed his escape is not known, nor has he been located in subsequent years. In the year before the execution of Private Honeycutt, 9 men absented themselves from Company I; in the year thereafter only 2 took their leave.

Letters from home, and persuasion while at home, influenced deserters in both a positive and negative fashion. Private Isaac Smith, Forty-Sixth, Company K, received a letter from his brother in mid–January 1863: "I wouldd advise you if you want to leave the war go to the other side whear you can get plenty and not stay in this one horse barefooted naked and famine stricken Southern Confederacy."[19] In some fashion Private Smith apparently acted on the counsel, for he was dropped from the rolls of the company in August 1863.

JOHN C. LONG 15-B (September 18, 1863). Private Long was court-martialed for violation of the 46th Article of War, sleeping on post. This infraction took place on August 12, 1863; he was arrested when found with his "accouterments off and asleep while on post at an advanced picket." This serious charge was made even more damaging when it was noted that the sleepy picket had been cautioned that the enemy was in the vicinity. For such an obvious violation, the weary private received a death sentence. The court's action was approved but then set aside, with the comment that the President of the court and the Judge Advocate had each failed to sign the court record. The reviewing officer, General Lee, observed, "A court-martial cannot be too careful in the preparation of its records."[20] Even after nearly 150 years the sigh of relief in not having to approve this death sentence is still nearly audible. Not that the decision was not justified, but so many other men were being shot that September that the death of a tired young soldier would add little to the discipline of the army and might well have a negative effect. Private Long was paroled at Charlotte, NC, in May 1865.

A stint in the guardhouse was not always seen in the same light: "Tha have put me in the gard-haus bute i dont now yet how long tha ame to ceape mee here thare is some severals in here for the same crimes I had a leave stiy in the gard house as not I am not afraid that will herte me bad."[21] A returned absentee wrote to his wife to describe his dislike of being under guard on September 25, 1863.

> I will say to you that we got to the ridgment yesterday and we are garded yet and I dont no how long we will be garded yet we hant had nothing sed to us about running away yet so I cant say to you what tha will doo with us yet but I dont want you to be un easy about me I dont think tha will hurt us but I dont want to be garded much longer no how for I am tired of being garded.[22]

Three months later his wife expressed her anxiety that he would be executed after she was told that execution was likely after a long confinement. "Sorry to hair you was in the gard hous yet but I hope and pray tha wunt cill you for coming home to see us sum thinks tha will cill youns yet because tha cepe youns so long in the gard house."[23] A relatively mild sentence to carry a log about camp was not overly stressful for the private: "It dont tirer me much I can kerry it mitey eassey I can carrey it as essey as again."[24] In early August Private Daniel Setzer wrote his wife that he had heard men at home were saying they would die before going to war. "And that is the way that I would doo if I was back agane I never would leave mi home no more to go to such a war like this whar."[25] And then, three weeks before he was captured, "I wontt fite no more if I can help it."[26]

Not all families encouraged their men to desert. Private Isaac Thompson of Company H was in arrest for desertion and confined under guard. In January 1863, his wife Catharine wrote to Governor Vance on behalf of her "poor" husband. She first explained that her husband was treated badly by his company officers and then said that he was "persuaded by professed friends though in reality enemies he was induced to desert."

As a "distressed" and "destitute" wife, she appealed for a pardon for her husband.

> I would a thousand times rather he were in the service fighting for his country than to be at home as a deserter. But should he be executed for a crime for which others are more to blame than he it will bring me to the grave in sorrow and cast an everlasting stigma upon his innocent children. Do see to this for me and relieve the distress of his wife.[27]

In his endorsement the Governor instructed that the response should say that he had no power in the case. Ten months after the exchange, Private Thompson prepared a personal appeal to Governor Vance. A second desertion had started after he had learned that his family was destitute. Quite sensibly, he reasoned that he volunteered to protect his family; if they were to perish because of his absence, what had he gained? His wife, still loyal to the Confederacy, urged him to return to duty, he told the Governor.[28] Private Thompson returned to the army and survived the war.

The Lieutenant Colonel of the Randolph County Home Guard asked Governor Vance to intercede in the case of Private Zebedee F. Conner, Company F, Forty-Sixth: "I am satisfied that he was influenced to desert by others & kept away longer than he desired to stay by the same influence. He is easily influenced as you can perceive in five minutes conversation with him." Governor Vance noted: "He shall not be shot. They will punish him some but not severely."[29] The deserter voluntarily returned to his command, whereupon he was arrested and placed in the guardhouse. This led to a second appeal to the Governor. He was "persuaded by a bad man a Tory of his county to take the course he did ... and will probably be punished — shot for aught I know."[30] The petitioners on behalf of Private Conner were only partially rewarded for their trust. He was not sentenced to be shot for his second desertion, but within the year he deserted to the enemy.

J. F. HAVNER 46-B (December 16, 1863); JOSIAH RICH 46-B (December 16, 1863); and ROBERT RICH 46-B (December 16, 1863). Two families, joined by marriage, also shared in the sorrow of execution. Three of their men were found guilty of desertion after an absence of four months. Each was given a death sentence. The youngest of the three, Private Robert Rich, was first to enlist, in May 1862. Musician J. Franklin Havner and Private Joseph Rich enlisted on February 18, 1863. The three deserted on July 18, while near Taylorsville, VA. Musician Havner was returned to Brandy Station, VA, on November 7, and the brothers were in arrest twelve days later. At trial in mid–December, they were found guilty as charged. Their death sentences were published on January 19, 1864, in GO #5, Army of Northern Virginia. An immediate appeal was made to the President, but notification that he would not interfere in the case was returned on January 29. That same day, Brigadier General Joseph R. Davis, temporarily commanding Heth's Division, notified General Lee's Chief of Staff: "I have the honor to state for the information of the Genl Commdg that the day for the execution of capital sentences in the cases of...."[31] Following are the names of the men of the Forty-Sixth, together with the names of 3 men of the division who were to be shot. The executions took place on January 30, 1864. Fourteen men chose to leave the ranks of Company B in the year prior to the executions; 4 did so in the following year, none leaving within five months following the affair. On February 1, Lieutenant James A. Graham, Twenty-Seventh Regiment, wrote to his mother:

> One of the 48th Regt was executed last Monday for desertion and 3 of the 46th Regt on Saturday. It was the saddest sight I ever witnessed and I hope I may never see the like again. I

hear they were caused to desert by letters from home. Many a poor soldier has met with the same disgraceful death from the same cause. I wish the people at home would keep in as good spirits as the soldiers in the army do. The 3 men that were shot Saturday said that they were prepared to die. One of them was sprinkled two or three days before and the other two wanted to be baptized but I don't know whether they were or not. The whole army is in as good spirits and as good condition as I ever saw them.[32]

The comments on the baptizing of the condemned men would seem suspect, at least in the case of the Rich brothers as their father was a clergyman according to census records. Then again, a second baptism may have been desired and appropriate with death so near at hand.

Sergeant Henry C. Clegg of the Forty-Eighth also witnessed the execution.

While here I witnessed a tragic scene. Three soldiers were shot to death for desertion. I think they belonged to the 46th N.C. regiment. The brigade was formed in columns in a field about three acres. The doomed men just in the rear of their coffins, and were marched around the field followed by the Chaplain, Rev. C. C. Dodson, doctors and guard. Then came the entire brigade with muffled drums. The men were made to kneel in front of stakes with their hands tied behind them. The guard was ordered to "ready, aim, fire." The guns (about twenty-five) were fired as one. The doctors soon pronounced them dead. Many of the guns were loaded with blank cartridges, so none of the guard knew who fired the fatal balls that sent these poor men into eternity.[33]

Sergeant Clegg later relates that he only used the word "damn" as an imprecation one time during the war, and then only after being forced to do so. A private in the Twenty-Seventh simply noted; "Three men of the 46 NC Regt were shot for desertion."[34] Another soldier was also thankful that he did not have to see the men killed: "Ellen, there were three men shot in our Brigade yesterday for desertion. I was on picket and did not see them shot, and I was glad of it, for that is a sight I do not want to see. All of them belonged to the 46th N.C."[35]

JOHN SMITH 55-H (January 8, 1864). Private John Smith was conscripted into the army and assigned to the Alexander Boys. Seven months later, when marching north toward Pennsylvania on June 15, 1863, he deserted and remained absent until brought back under guard in November. On January 8, 1864, Private Smith was tried for desertion and sentenced to be shot. This was made known in GO #4, January 19, 1864, Army of Northern Virginia. The decision of the court, approved by the General Commanding, was sent to the President for review but he declined to interfere. Private John Smith was shot on the day set for his execution, Saturday, January 30, 1864.[36] On January 29, 1864, Brigadier Davis notified headquarters that correspondence: "States days on which certain men sentenced to be shot in Heth's Division, will be executed. Davis, J. R. Brig Gen."[37] The executions of the men mentioned in addition to Private Smith took place on the days indicated by General Davis. Private Robert F. Smith, also of Company H and very likely brother of Private John Smith, had earlier appealed to Governor Vance for help in obtaining relief from punishment while in arrest for attempted desertion. In a letter dated November 11, 1863, he explained that he had not deserted but had simply gone home to be with his family who were sick, as had many others, he added. When confronted by the Home Guard, he offered no resistance. Other men in very similar circumstances had been released in a "wink" on their return to camp. Private Robert F. Smith then continued:

My brother John Smith is under arrest for the same cause so he wishes you to assist him also if you please. This affair which I have stated in this letter to you is nothing but the plain truth. I never deserted but the one time neither has John. I wish you to write to me or at least to my commander as soon as you can and fail not and you will oblige your friend very much.[38]

Governor Vance initialed the letter for filing. Private Robert Smith's concern was well placed; the court that heard his case gave him a sentence of three years imprisonment. For the first two years he was to have a twelve-pound ball attached to his leg by a chain. This court convened about a month before the court that handed down the death sentence for Private John Smith.

AUGUSTIN W. CROUCH 48-K (January 13, 1864). Private Crouch mustered into service in April 1862 and deserted after one year in the Confederate Guards of Forsyth County, this on May 5, 1863. Arrest and court-martial followed on January 13, 1864. He was found guilty of desertion and sentenced to be shot. The execution of Private Crouch followed on January 25. The remains went to ground near Orange Court House, VA. The trial for Private Crouch began after that of the Rich brothers, but an appeal did not go forward in his case, and he was shot five days before they were dispatched. The brother of Private Crouch, Private John Crouch, also of Company K, deserted twice; the second time he went over to the enemy and then took the oath.

While in the vicinity of Orange Court House, VA, on the day before the scheduled execution of Private Crouch, First Lieutenant J. A. Graham, Company G, Twenty-Seventh Regiment, told his mother of his feelings about this and other executions that were planned for the next few days:

> One of the men in the 48th, in our Brigade is to be shot tomorrow morning for desertion and four more in the Brigade in a few days. The whole Brigade will be called out to witness it, but I would gladly be spared such a sight. I am glad that there are none of them from our Regt our Company has never had a single deserter yet and I hope we never may.[39]

Service records support this statement of a loyal Confederate; Company G, the Orange Guards, enrolled 177 men during the war years and just 6 absented themselves. In the final weeks of war, Captain Graham wrote to his mother that men had departed from his company. He went on, "I had prided myself a good deal on never having had a deserter and hoped that I would never have one. I can't see how any man in his senses can desert if he will only think of it for a moment. Most of the desertions lately have been caused by letters from home."[40] The day following the execution of Private Crouch, First Lieutenant Kenneth Rayner Jones simply recorded, "Nothing of interest on the 26 a man of the 48th was shot to death by musketry for desertion."[41] Private Theophilus Frank of Company B, Forty-Eighth Regiment informed his wife, "A. Swing had to help shoot a man in Co K 48 R [regiment] last monday for deserting."[42] Private Alfred Swing, Company B, was a man of thirty-four years and a steady soldier; he was present for duty for over three years of the struggle. Days after the death of Private Crouch, a soldier in the Forty-Sixth wrote his wife.

> Times very hard here we have but litle to eat I saw a man shot last Monday he was tyed to a stake and twelve guns was shot at him which killed him dead he was in the fortyeight regt in our brigade There is three more men to bee shot next saturday in my redgment it all for deserting sentance was past against eligaky [Elizah] Luck this morning for him to ware a ball and chain three years do hard labor on the fortyfication all the time there several in the gardhouse now waring balls and chains and toting logs of wood and then have to live on nothing but bred and water it two much for men to have undergon we pore soldiers have to think this cruel ware will stop this spring.[43]

Private Luck's sentence was remitted.

Colonel Walkup tried to spare the life of Private Crouch on the technicality that the court's proceedings did not state that two-thirds of the court concurred on the death decision. That error often led to release of a condemned soldier. General A. P. Hill apparently did not agree in the case of Private Crouch. Colonel Walkup returned to the solace of his diary on the day of the execution.

> This day also our Regt witnessed the execution by shooting of Augustine [sic] Crouch from Davidson Co. NC for desertion, sentence of Court-martial. I tried to have it set aside as sentence did not state ⅔ of court concurring. He was unprepared and much concerned. Being busy in leaving for board of examination when he was sent to provost I did not tell him his fate & [he] knew nothing till Sat 23.[44]

That neglect led General Hill to bring charges against Colonel Walkup which resulted in another written tirade. "Accused of gross neglect by Lt. Gen. Hill for not informing Couch of sentence of death against him. He kills 1000 by carelessness vz Bristow [Bristoe Station] & because I do not inform him [Private Crouch] his [General Hill] minions murdered court-martial he blames me."[45] Colonel Walkup defended his delay in informing Private Crouch by reasoning that Private Crouch was "murdered" by the illegal sentence put forth by the court and approved by General Hill. According to Colonel Walkup, Private Crouch learned that he was going to be shot two days before his death. The Colonel dismisses this as a minor oversight readily understandable considering the pressure of official duties. An argument can be made as to the most humane course; is it of consequence if a soldier learns that he is to be shot in seven days, or that he has five days of uncertainty and then learns that he is to be shot in two days? The mores and values of the 1860s placed due significance on allowing time to prepare for death — a time for the condemned to accept the justness of the sentence, to acknowledge his responsibility, and bid farewell to family and friends. On January 28, Colonel Walkup wrote: "Was arrested by Col MacRae under orders from Lt. Gen. A. P. Hill for not informing Couch [sic] of his fate, I had no orders to do so & am to be court-martialled for gross neglect."[46] The Colonel was released from arrest to take charge of his regiment on January 31, then arrested on February 1, and tried before a military court on February 2. He was sentenced to one month in arrest and to be reprimanded. Several days after being placed in arrest, Colonel Walkup briefly noted in his diary: "Three deserters from the 46 NC shot Sat 30 I did not go to see."[47] The Colonel implied that he chose not to witness the executions, but gave no reason why he did so.

On the day that Private Crouch appeared in court, Sergeant Will U. Steiner, Company B, Twenty-Seventh, commented on his assignment as court recorder and on the North Carolinians appearing before them.

> I dare not divulge anything, yet in a general way I CAN TELL you that the Court is quite lenient, only condemning four or five in fifty cases of desertion, to be shot with musketry. As a general thing the N. C. Captains do not assist and instruct their men, how to appear and answer in a Court Martial, as the men from other states. This is readily seen in their manner.[48]

On first look, it would seem unlikely that the captains of North Carolina companies were significantly different from those of the other states. Examination boards established to determine the competency of officers found that 24 percent of officers from Virginia regiments were not competent. For North Carolina regiments the finding was 29 percent, after removal of one regiment that had nearly all officers judged to be incompetent.[49] Company officers from North Carolina may have agreed on the guilt of their men and accepted the need for punishment. Officers of other states, and even those in North Carolina companies with less exposure to desertion, may have felt that it was their responsibility to defend their men with every resource available to them. The comment by Sergeant Steiner that the court to which he was assigned was "quite lenient" suggests that he thought more death sentences should have been forthcoming. A death sentence return of 10 percent, 5 of 50 trials, is well within the range of that experienced by North Carolina troops, and well above that of the other Confederate states.

The Twenty-Seventh was well-trained. Private Lemuel B. Ward, Company F, wrote to his father on April 25, 1863,

> Nothing new to rite only hard times we have hard drilling to do Co. drill in the morning battalion in the evening hardly time to cook vuituals ... we eat any thing here i eat a mes of wild onions yesterday sot wel so fare ... this is the place to harden mens haearts ... but it is disheartning to think of thing.[50]

In October, he followed up with:

> i want you to enqire a bout for a substitute for i cant stand this it aint worth while for me to tell you the fare we have here ... my mind is Pestered at this time my duty is something that i never thought of before i want you to tel some of the Baptis to pray for me.[51]

A close observer of those who served beside him, Lieutenant Thomas Jackson Strayhorn, Company G, Twenty-Seventh Regiment, classified soldiers into three broad groups. First, there were honorable men serving with great conviction who had gallantly stepped forward to defend their state. Then, men whose worst side was brought to the surface by the strain of military duty. Last were the "swells," those who presented a facade of patriotism but would readily abandon the cause when the going was rough.[52] "I am not all surprised at John Webb's getting out of the war or any other of the swells—they are very patriotic to hear them talk and would not be out of the service for anything, but let an opportunity present itself for their escape and see how soon they take advantage of it."[53] Lieutenant Strayhorn indicated that he did not want to serve under a "shade" Captain but wanted a company officer that "risks his life equally with mine."[54] In a more general observation, Lieutenant Strayhorn wrote: "If a man wants to find out about a fellow man let them go through a campaign like this one and I will venture to say his wants will be entirely satisfied."[55] In a personal revelation he notes, "I hope I will not have to go into another fight as long as I live, for the more I go into the more I dread them."[56] His fears quickly came to pass; the Lieutenant died at Richmond, VA, a few weeks after voicing his dread. A soldier in the regiment gave his opinion of those who led them: "But all of our officers are very wicked men, or most all of them."[57] Just days after enrolling: "Mother, you have no thought how they go on down here. I have heard more cursing and swearing since I left home than I ever heard in my life before. Sometimes they get hold of liquour and they get drunk and rip and dance and curse makes me scringe to hear it." He continues, "I can start at one end of the street and find three or four packs of cards and sometimes they get into a row about them gambling is a bad practice let who will follow it."[58] "I feel that I am a lost sinner if I do not find the favor of God. I have been trying to find my Saviour now for a week but have not found him yet but by the Grace of God I am going to press on until I find my Saviour."[59] The devout young man went to the arms of his Saviour in August 1864.

JOSEPH BROCK 27-C (February 7, 1864). Private Brock joined the North Carolina Guards on May 6, 1862, and was present for duty through June 1863. At some point thereafter, he left his regiment. While a Confederate deserter he agreed to join the Second Regiment of North Carolina Union Volunteers on December 4, 1863, and mustered with that regiment on December 26. For this, he was eligible for the first $25 payment of a $100 enrollment bounty. On February 2, 1864, Private Brock was captured by Confederate troops while wearing the uniform of the enemy. Five days later he went before a court-martial, was convicted and was hanged on February 15, along with a dozen others at Kinston, NC.

JAMES A. SMITH 55-B (February 16, 1864). Private James Smith volunteered for service before passage of the conscription laws. Soon after enrollment he was given permission to return home to Wilkes County to bring in his wheat crop. Whether he enrolled in another regiment or deserted is not clear in his brief service record. Private Smith was tried by a court-martial on February 16, 1864, and sentenced to be shot. Twenty-one years later when his widow filed a claim for a pension, she stated that he had died of wounds in February 1864. Considering the court-martial date, this would suggest that Private Smith was executed toward the end of February 1864. Her pension claim was held pending proof of when, where, and how her husband died. No other record has been found.

MASON M. WHITE 15-E (February 19, 1864). Private White first volunteered for duty in the Thirtieth Regiment in August 1861. He was discharged for medical reasons in December 1861. Service in the Forty-Seventh Regiment in February 1862 was followed by an absence without leave and removal from company rolls. He enlisted as a substitute in the Fifteenth in May 1863 and deserted in August while near Fredericksburg, VA. He was in arrest at Castle Thunder in Richmond by early September but was able to gain sufficient freedom to again desert in the November or December period. Along with Private Sampson Hobgood he was arrested in December and returned to the army. Private White went to trial on February 16, 1864, was found guilty of desertion and sentenced to be shot. While imprisoned awaiting execution the condemned man died of disease. A month after his death, his sentence was remitted by SO #58, April 15, 1864, AIGO.

Lieutenant Kenneth Rayner Jones observed, "I found that the spirit of the Lord had visited my camp and great many souls had turned to Christ, and a great many more were seeking mercy at his feet."[60] Another man of faith wrote, "We hav prayer meeting in the brigade every day preaching every night and preaching of Sundays it is a great privilege we hav."[61] His faith did not waver in the winter of war: "I finde it quite a hard task to live as it becometh us by useing every exertion I can to leave off sin and to cleave to our Blest saviour in whom I have to trust."[62] Men of Cooke's brigade often expressed their faith and desire to "seek mercy at his feet." Their faith must be a consideration when evaluating the excellent performance of the brigade.

BENJAMIN ESQUIRE BENTLEY 55-H (February 25, 1864). In early March Private Bentley was informed that he was to be shot to death for attempting to desert. The *Greensboro Patriot*, March 10, 1864, reprinted an item from the *Richmond Enquirer*, "Under Sentence of Death On yesterday morning Benjamin E. Bentley a private in Co. H 55NCI, was placed in Castle Thunder to await his execution of the sentence of death, for desertion. Proper time has been accorded him to communicate with his friends and make his peace with God."[63] A few days after he was confined, Private Bentley took his own life, apparently convinced that no relief would be forthcoming and that death by his own decision was better for him and his family than the ignominy of a military execution. The day of suicide was between March 15 and 17, shortly before his scheduled execution. The effects that Private

Bentley left behind were valued at $4. Hospital records show that a B. E. Bentley died at General Hospital #13, Richmond, between March 12, and March 19. This hospital was known as the Prison Hospital. Private Bentley enrolled in September 1863; he was in the service slightly over five months.

ESQUIRE BENTLEY 55-H (February 25, 1864). There is reasonable evidence that Private Esquire Bentley was sentenced to be executed by a military court. Surviving records, however, do not verify that a soldier with that name served in the Fifty-Fifth. Pension records filed by Fannie Bentley are based on the fact that her husband, Esquire, served in the regiment. Service entry dates are shown as September 1862 and September 1863, dates of death as March 1863, and March 1865. A Private E. Bentley was issued a .58 caliber small arm on February 29, four days after the court-martial of Private Benjamin E. Bentley. SO #216, September 12, 1864, AIGO released Private E. Bentley from his death sentence and returned him to duty. Pension documents for both Benjamin Esquire Bentley and for Esquire Bentley were witnessed by the same former soldier, one who had also served in the Fifty-Fifth. Two different widows submitted the applications. This would indicate that each Bentley served with the pension witness and were presumably known to him. There are two individual AIGO listings for the courts concerning the two men; the same trial date is found on each record. With such closely related names the likelihood of record error is obvious.

THOMAS WILSON DIAL 48-K (March 12, 1864). Private Dial was officially listed as a deserter on September 2, 1862, some six months after volunteering for duty in March 1862. Two years after enrollment, he was in arrest and at trial on March 12, 1864. An extended absence of such length, eighteen months, usually brought forth a death sentence when a prisoner answered to a court. That was the decision for Private Dial; five days after the court heard his case, he was informed that he would be executed. He was to die in seven days, on March 24, as stated in the approval statement of the General Commanding. Still deeply involved in his own concerns, the leader of the regiment, Colonel Walkup, offered his candid opinion of Private Dial. "March 17, 1864 Thos W. Dial of Co K sentence read to be shot next Thursday, seems stupid, indifferent, young, fat, half dead, thoughtless ignorant — I leave today for nomination for Senate N.C."[64] Colonel Walkup's caustic comment as to the soldier's awareness as the hour of death drew near may have been misconceived and far too broadly drawn. Wilson Dial, a day laborer, headed a household of seven people before entering the service. This would suggest a significant acceptance of responsibility and indicate a degree of care and common sense not found in the remarks of his Colonel. Colonel Walkup continued his candid comment in a diary entry on March 24.

> On this day private Thos W. Deal [sic] a condemned deserter from Co K in this regiment was shot by sentence of Court-martial & order of Lt. Gen A. P. Hill and 2 from Kirklands Brigade. Deal [sic] met death quietly and stolidly professing to be changed and willing to die of which evidence was quite feeble. He died like a sick man takes medicine, by nerving himself to the act. I doubt his capacity to know what death meant he seems so indifferent.[65]

Once more, Colonel Walkup has difficulty with spelling the name of a man in his care. On the morning chosen for the execution of Private Dial, Private Theophilis Frank, Forty-Eighth Regiment, included more detail in a letter to his wife: "But I will tel you that thear will bee a man shot to day in company K 48 for deserting John D. Swing and John Rin [Wrenn] are detailed in our Co. to shoot him he will be shot at 11 o'clock."[66] The Swing family must have raised reliable soldiers; Private John Swing and his brother Private Alfred

Swing were each detailed to take an active role in an execution. Private John Swing may not have been as reliable in another instance. When returning from a leave, he was asked to deliver a letter, a book and some butter to a man in his company. The recipient said that he got the book and the letter — but that no mention was made of any butter. Generously, he concluded that the butter probably would not have kept. The Swing brothers that were ordered to kill other soldiers survived the war; it was reported that they looked well, just days before the end.[67] Lieutenant K. R. Jones of the Twenty-Seventh merely states the facts in his comment on March 25. "A member of the 48th shot to death by musketry for desertion in the presence of the Brigade."[68] By underlining "for desertion," the Lieutenant apparently wished to emphasize that the punishment was well deserved.

WILLIAM LINDSEY 55-C (March 14, 1864). Private Lindsey was conscripted into the Fifty-Fifth in late 1862 and served, to the extent that his physical capabilities would allow, through the next year. Sometime before April 1864 the ailing soldier deserted, was arrested, tried and sentenced to be shot to death. Fellow soldiers of the regiment petitioned for a pardon for the condemned man, evidence that he had earned their respect during his sixteen months of service. The AIGO did not reject the petition out of hand but requested the complete record in the case. After review, the appeal for a full pardon was rejected, but the death sentence was commuted to imprisonment and put forth in SO #256, October 27, 1864, AIGO. For much of Private Lindsey's twenty-eight months of service, he was in the guardhouse or in hospitals for scurvy, headaches and rheumatism. Private Lindsey was captured in April 1865 and taken to Point Lookout, MD. A record entry shows that he was released from that place in June 1865; however when asking for a widow's pension in 1908 his wife stated that her husband had died of consumption at the Federal prison camp.

WILLIAM JASPER SHANNON 48-F (April 13, 1864). Private Shannon was condemned to be shot to death following a court-martial sitting to hear charges preferred against him by Colonel Walkup. On March 30, 1864, the Colonel recorded in his diary: "Sent charges and specifications against Wm Shannon for desertion and advising and persuading others to desert."[69] A brother of the charged private was among those that the accused had allegedly persuaded to leave with him. A trial on the charges came about in two weeks, and a week later a diary entry by Colonel Walkup noted on April 20, "W. J. Shannon sent to Richmond under sentence to be shot."[70] Within a month of his arrival at Castle Thunder the condemned man was admitted to Prison Hospital #13 with measles; in June he died of typhoid. An erroneous entry in his service record states that he was released by GO #2 in early 1865. After preferring charges against Private Shannon, Colonel Walkup was willing to support an appeal for clemency on behalf of the conscript but was then persuaded not to take that course. "Preferred to President Davis & his vol surrender wife in tears & he stubborn and pragmatic. I prepared statement but abandoned at Col Hill's suggestion."[71] Why Colonel Hill did not want to bring the voluntary surrender of the prisoner to the attention of the President is not known. Voluntary return of an absentee was normally a mitigating consideration in their favor. As noted, General Lee observed that he never knew of an instance when a soldier who returned voluntarily was executed.[72] Again the choice of words by the Colonel offers insight into his feelings. Despite the tearful intercession of Private Shannon's wife, in her direct appeal to him, the Colonel still finds the prisoner "stubborn and pragmatic." Pragmatic to Lawyer Walkup may have been seen as dogmatic to Colonel Walkup. Private Shannon would not yield and ask the Colonel for help or beg for the clemency that was recommended by the court. Colonel Walkup went on to reveal his displeasure that the distraught wife of the condemned man had the temerity to approach him early in the morning to appeal for her husband's life, while he was coatless, blackening his boots, with his hair uncombed.[73]

JOSEPH MEDLIN 48-A (April 14, 1864). Private Medlin remained with his regiment for over a year. He joined up on March 12, 1862, and deserted in mid-1863. Colonel Walkup noted on April 6, 1864, "Priv Joe Medlin of Co A brought by courier this evening and sent to guard house." A court-martial convened on April 14, found that he was guilty of desertion and concurred on a death sentence. On that same date Colonel Walkup wrote in his diary: "Joe Medlin whipped hard."[74] If taken literally, the returned man was whipped on the day that he went on trial for his life. This may have been an unofficial impromptu whipping by other soldiers, or a semi-official affair arranged by company officers. The verdict of the court had not yet been published, so it is not likely that this punishment was part of the court decision. The prisoner was sent to Castle Thunder and was in the prison hospital when his death sentence was commuted to a year of hard labor, this on September 13. Private Medlin was imprisoned until the closing days of the war when he returned to the ranks only to be captured and then to take the oath.

JOSEPH BRITT 48-D (Prior to May 2, 1864). Private Britt enrolled as a volunteer in March 1862, but he never did get around to joining his regiment in the field. He stayed at home, carried on company records as sick, until December of that year when he was formally classified as a deserter. An entry in his service record for September and October reads, "Absent at home never in camp should be deserter." Private Britt remained at home for two years, until March or April 1864. During that time he chose not to take advantage of any of the several amnesties that were offered to men absent from their commands, if he ever knew of them. In any event, in 1864 Private Britt was at long last with the army, not as a respected volunteer, but as a prisoner to be court-martialed. He was informed on May 2, 1864, that he had been found guilty of desertion as charged and that he would be shot in seven days, with the publication of GO #37, Army of Northern Virginia. The order stipulating the death sentence was never recorded by the AIGO at Richmond. For lack of any other indication it is likely that the approved sentence was carried into effect on or about the chosen day. Company D of the Forty-Eighth had an outbreak of absences beginning in August of 1862 and into the first half of 1863 but few in the months surrounding the time of Private Britt's trial in 1864, adding some support to the notion that he was executed.

THOMAS N. FAULKNER 15-F (Prior to May 2, 1864). The case of Private Faulkner forced intense scrutiny of the delicate balance when weighing life or death for a convicted deserter. While present for duty, Private Faulkner was a brave and obedient soldier, once receiving special recognition for killing a notorious Federal "house-burner."[75] On the other hand, he was also twice convicted of desertion, one of the specifications including the serious act of taking his arms and accouterments with him when he fled. Private Faulkner first deserted while near Richmond on August 12, 1862, and was absent for eight months. He enrolled in May of 1861. Two months after returning, and being subjected to humiliating and painful punishment for that offense, he again deserted, this time taking his weapons with him. This second absence extended over the next ten months as is noted in an abstract of the court proceedings:

> Charge Desertion Specification 1st He deserted the 12th August, 1862 near Richmond and was brought back the 18th April 1863 — absent 8 months & 6 days. Specification II On 8th June while his regiment was on a train passing from Goldsboro to Weldon N.C. he deserted and was brought back 7th April 1864 — absent 10 months less a day. Plea not guilty. Proven except

the charge being brought back the first time. Witness then did not see him until the day after his return, at which time he was under guard. When lodged in the guardhouse for the second offense, accused stated he had started back to deliver himself up when arrested. For his first offense he was punished by being bucked once in front of his regiment and by being tied up by his thumbs three times before dress parade and then put to hard labor in camp. While the accused was with his regiment he was a very obedient and dutiful soldier and as brave a man as there is in the Army. [Capt. Cutts] saw him in one engagement when he attracted attention by his gallantry. I think he killed the Yankee Col Jones when on the march to Newbern. Finding Guilty Sentence — Death. Respectfully Submitted H. E. Young A Adj Genl.[76]

As the court-martial proceedings were being published in GO #37, May 2, 1864, Army of Northern Virginia, General Lee directed that any favorable information concerning Private Faulkner be sent to him.

Hdqtrs Dept NoVa 2d May 1864 General Private Thomas N. Faulkner Co F 15th NC Regt has been tried for desertion and sentenced to be shot to death. The evidence indicates that he has been a good soldier. The General Commanding directs me to say that he will be glad to learn anything special in his favour if any such can be adduced. Very Resply Yr Obt Servt H. E. Young.[77]

The crossout of the word "any" begs speculation. Did Captain Young want to remove the inference that General Lee was anxious to act favorably in the case at hand, the "any" imploring for the slightest good word? Or the exact opposite, did Captain Young want to avoid giving the impression that General Lee felt the sentence equitable and that it was unlikely that any mitigating factors would be found? Most likely the former, but in either case the precise Captain Young would have likely rewritten the short request if he had considered the cross out as revealing of the desire of General Lee. As in the case of Private Britt, court-martial records for Private Faulkner were not posted by the AIGO. The continued interest of the General Commanding was again present in mid–June when Captain Young inquired as to whether Private Faulkner had been executed. On June 23, Brigadier General Cooke telegraphed, "Private Faulkner has not been executed."[78] The next day a petition for pardon was sent to the President on behalf of the condemned soldier. The matter was still under consideration some three months later when Major C. M. Blackford notified General Lee that the record that was said to have been forwarded could not be found.[79] Whether the document in question was found or not, on the following day General Lee recommended a pardon.[80] Five days later, on September 29, Private Faulkner was pardoned of his crimes. An enclosure in the service record of Private Faulkner notes that he expressed his determination to retrieve his character, provided gallantry on the battlefield could effect this.[81] The determination sufficiently subsided some five months after his pledge of gallantry to allow Private Faulkner to again desert. On this occasion he decided not to trust his life to the continued good grace of Confederate authority and deserted directly to the enemy. There he took the oath a few days after reaching the safety of their lines. He was provided transportation to Springfield, IL. Record-wise, Private Faulkner served nearly four years in the Confederate Army, forty-six months from enlistment to final desertion. During that time he was either absent as a deserter or imprisoned as a result of his desertion for two years.

A little over a month after the trial of Private Faulkner there were 14 armed men present for duty in the Company G and just 190 in the Fifteenth Regiment.[82] Remarkably, though nearly 120 men were no longer present in the company only one was absent without leave prior to that point. Even as the number of men in Cooke's brigade dwindled, drill and training went on apace. A soldier wrote to his father; "We are not done drilling yet Cook loves to drill his brigade." To his mother and sister he took a more somber stance, "Life is so un certain and death is shure ... so let us live each day as if we expected it to be the last."[83] He credited daily preaching with adding greatly to his strength.

JAMES BUFF 55-F (August 13, 1864). Four men with the family name of Buff were accepted into the South Mountain Rangers, in early February 1863; there they joined two others named Buff, who had already served some ten months. Private James Buff, the oldest of the lot, deserted not long after receiving his $50 North Carolina enrollment bonus. He was returned from this first desertion attempt in July 1863. A year later in June 1864, Private Buff again deserted the service and was brought back to stand trial on August 13. The court found the prisoner guilty of desertion and sentenced him to be shot. Said sentence was approved and execution occurred in late August or early September 1864. On August 23, 1864, Private James Wilkerson, Company K, remarked on the pending execution of Private Buff but did not comment thereafter.

> We are going to have a man shot do ricklery [directly] his grave is done dug and coffin sitting heare he went home 3 out of our company is got to help shoot him G. S. West and Wash Thomas and Bob Wilkerson is the 3 men Oh the hard times [not legible] poor fellow see now we are near to death night and day.[84]

As mentioned, this was the second assignment to an execution detail for Private Robert D. Wilkerson. A company officer, Captain Peter M. Mull recalled after the war that Private Buff "was shot for desertion in 64 at Petersburg."[85]

WILLIAM B. SMITH 48-E (September 10, 1864). Once conscripted into the army, Private Smith was on duty for just two months before deserting. He was enrolled on August 23, 1862, four months after passage of the conscription laws. As a deserter he remained at large for at least eighteen months, more likely closer to two years, before going before a court-martial on September 10, 1864. A death sentence was approved on September 12, and he was shot to death just five days later.[86] This prompt trial and execution of a deserter was rather unusual; such instances normally found when Confederates switched sides and fought with the enemy before being captured. Not so for Private Smith; his body was in a Confederate grave a week after he stood before a military court. There was a bit of confusion on the very day of Private Smith's execution. President Davis contacted General Lee:

> An entry in our books show that a petition for executive clemency in behalf of W. B. Smith Co. E 48NC was ref to Genl R. E. Lee September 17, 1864 [not legible] Respty returned by direction of the President to Adj Gen for inquiry the President knows nothing of this case or of Gen Lee's purpose in sending his telegram there is no record in this office of this [not legible] name or affairs and no one here knows anything about him.[87]

General Lee's telegraphed response gave the regiment of the condemned man as the Fourth Regiment, which was assigned to a different command. A rather common name and the missing "8" in the regiment of enrollment may account for the confusion.[88] In due course, General Cooper informed General Lee on September 22; "I am directed by the President to inform you that he has examined the record in the case of W. B. Smith 48 E and declined to take any action in the premises."[89] This was no doubt reassuring to General Lee but of little moment to the dead conscript.

In the fall of 1864, executions were not as noteworthy in letters home as were the general conditions in the Confederacy. One writer described the pervasive discouragement, "Mother I am sorry to tell you but it is surtenly so to my opinon that we are a ruined set of people and we are aledy whip I am truely sorry for our men You aught to hear the men talk ait would make you shead tears."[90]

THOMAS G. GREGORY 55-B (October 1864). Private Gregory volunteered to fight for the Confederacy in March 1862. When the harvesting of his wheat became urgent, he was allowed a furlough to gather the crop. On return to the regiment, Private Gregory was assigned to work as a teamster, for which he was paid an extra twenty-five cents a day, a nice increase for a thirty-seven cent a day private. The soldier-teamster was wounded at Gettysburg. A year later, he was charged with misbehavior before the enemy. This violation carried a death penalty, and Private Gregory was ordered to be shot. The death sentence was commuted. He was present with the regiment in the September–October 1864 reporting period but had no further record. Privates John Gregory and George A. Gregory, younger brothers of the condemned man, served in the same company. Private John Gregory was at the final parole. The service record for Private George Gregory ends in October 1864.

DAVID N. WHITE 15-C (November 25, 1864). Private White avoided the distinction of being included in that small group of older men that were executed for desertion; he was fifty-eight on enrollment. The North Carolina Roll of Honor shows that Private White entered Confederate service as a substitute in Company C on August 2, 1862. The service record for the substitute suggests that he may have enrolled as early as May 27, 1862, and that he was absent without leave in the January and February 1863 period. In March 1863, he transferred to Company D of the Fifteenth, and from that company deserted on the last day of July. He was absent fifteen months before being arrested and taken to Castle Thunder in October 1864. At trial on November 25, 1864, he was found guilty of desertion and sentenced to be shot. The next week, General Cooper directed General A. P. Hill to suspend the execution of sentence. The now sixty-year-old soldier was confined until restored to duty by GO #2 in March 1865. He was captured soon thereafter and took the oath after the war ended.

In the bleak days of late 1864, five men of Company E, Fifteenth Regiment, were informed that they were to be shot for exciting and joining a mutiny. Two of these men had faithfully served since May 1861 and the other three since February 1862. A Military Court heard the facts of the mutiny incident in early December 1864, and in their judgment death sentences were warranted, this decision made known in GO #40, December 31, 1864, 3rd Corps, Army of Northern Virginia. The men were from Franklin County; the mutiny charge was the only blemish on the record of four of the five. When word of the imminent executions reached Franklin County there was a flurry of petitioning to gain executive clemency for them. Spiritual leaders and well-respected community members all took part. One petition read:

> We respectfully and earnestly request that your Excellency will extend to these unfortunate young soldiers your clemency. They have as we learn been brave and true soldiers. They have descended from respectable ancestors. Their reputations are dear to us as their countrymen and several of them have aged and dependent parents in some degree dependent upon their future efforts. Some of them have respectable wives and children whose hopes would be crushed by their execution. They are all of highly respectable connexions and we are confident

that their execution would sadden the hearts of our whole community. We therefore humbly pray for Executive clemency.[91]

There were twenty-six signatures on the petition; none appear to be those of people in the immediate families of the condemned. The President, perhaps influenced by the entreaty, remitted the sentences of all of the men involved in what was a "sudden and momentary" affair, as described in another petition.[92] All five were restored to duty upon release of SO #23, January 28, 1865, AIGO.

JOHN P. STROTHER 15-E (December 5, 1864). Private Strother went off to war in February 1862. An absent without leave charge was lodged against him in early 1864. In 1865, he deserted to the enemy, took the oath, and was sent to Springfield, IL.

WILLIAM C. HART 15-E (December 5, 1864). Sergeant Hart immediately agreed to defend his state when North Carolina joined the Confederacy. He enrolled on May 16, 1861, was promoted to Corporal in February 1862, and to Sergeant in December 1863. Corporal Hart was captured by the enemy in September 1862, and exchanged two months later. Though wounded in battle in May 1864, he was present at the surrender of the regiment that he had served for four years.

ALEXANDER MOORE 15-E (December 5, 1864); and ROBERT MOORE 15-E (December 5, 1864). Private Alexander Moore joined the Fifteenth on May 16, 1861, was captured while fighting in Maryland, and was later exchanged to return to duty for the remainder of the war. Private Robert Moore went into Confederate ranks in February 1862. His health was such that he was hospitalized several times while in the service. Confederate pay for the January and February 1864 period was docked for $2.57 because Private Robert Moore lost his bayonet, scabbard and frog. A frog was a holding device to secure a bayonet to a musket. The Privates Moore were paroled at Appomattox, VA.

WILLIS THARRINGTON 15-E (December 5, 1864). Private Tharrington was a dutiful soldier in the ranks of the Confederate army. He joined up in February 1862, was wounded in the battle at Fredericksburg, VA, in December 1862, and returned to duty after his wound healed. He remained with his company to the end.

Two other soldiers of the Fifteenth Regiment may have taken some part in the thwarted mutiny, as indicated by another soldier:

> I don't reckon that you herd that Jack Shorter Nick Strickland and one of the Mores was about to be tied to a stake and shot for some misconduct that they done in the regiment. I could tell you how it come on if I could see you and talk with you but there Colonel Yarbrough worked until he got them off. They were sentence to be shot to death with musketry.[93]

No soldier named Shorter is found on the rolls of the regiment, though several named Short are listed. N. Strickland is in the same company as the mutineers. No other record has been found that implicates either soldier in the affair, though the comment seems quite specific.

WILLIAM F. BENTLEY 55-H (January 31, 1865). A third Bentley of Alexander County was to endure a court-martial and a sentence of death for desertion. The evidence presented to support the desertion charge is not specific as to whether he was tried for one long desertion or for the second of two short desertion attempts. If the former, Private Bentley was a deserter for twenty-seven months. He was in arrest on January 21, 1865, and went before a court ten days later. A death sentence was apparently remitted, for he left the regiment on a medical furlough on March 9, and there his service record ends.

RICHARD KERLY 55-H (January 31, 1865). Private Kerly volunteered to serve in the army in late May 1862 and not long thereafter was granted a furlough to return home to "save" his wheat crop. Whether he returned from this furlough and then deserted is not stated in his record. In any case, he was officially declared a deserter within that period. On January 21, 1865, he was in custody. Private Kerly was court-martialed on January 31, and sentenced to be shot. General A. P. Hill approved the sentence on February 9, and the execution may have been carried into effect within a week or so, though no additional verification has been found.

Summary

Including the Fifty-Fifth, there were 554 men in Cooke's brigade at Appomattox; 471 were from the regiments that made up the brigade in the fall of 1862. Based on a sampling of 27 companies, there was a total enrollment of 5,710 men in these regiments. AIGO records show that they had men appear before 198 courts, 73 of these for men of the Forty-Sixth. A total of 21 men were sentenced to be executed. Musketry killed 8; one was hanged. Acquittals came after 12 of the 198 trials. Of the 1,230 men that served in the ranks of the Fifty-Fifth, 38 appeared before military courts; 3 were acquitted. For the five-regiment brigade, 9 companies had 13 men executed; these companies had an absence rate of 23 percent. Seven companies had men sentenced to death but they were relieved of the sentence; the absence rate for these companies was 11 percent. The same absence rate, 11 percent, is found for 15 sampled companies that had no men so sentenced. Death came to 10 men of the brigade in the form of various accidents that befall armies in the field. Forces searching for deserters killed 4 men of the brigade. Based on an 11 company sample, 9 of 13 executions apparently had an immediate effect on reducing the number of absences from the brigade.

	1861	1862	1863		1864		1865	no date
Abs/Co	2.3	7.7	4.4	2.7	1.2	3.2	6.7	1
To be executed		1	3		3	14	6	3	2
Executed			1			9	2	1

Eleven of the 13 men who were executed were volunteers, as were 26 of the 32 men given a death sentence, 2 of the 26 were substitutes. Fewer than one-fifth of the men sentenced to death were conscripts, half that found for the other North Carolina brigades in the Third Corps. Eighteen of the 32 men sentenced to be executed did not survive the war. Execution claimed 13, 1 took his own life, and 4 died after trial.

Companies with fewer absences lost more men to death than did companies with a larger number. Eleven companies with a high number of absences, 34 per company, averaged 44 deaths. Nine companies with a low number of absences, 16 per company, averaged 49 deaths. The same relationship is found for those who were killed in action or died of wounds. Low absence companies lost 17 men on average, high absence companies had fewer losses at 15.[94] High absence companies enrolled an average of 141 men; low absence companies enrolled an average of 148 men. The numbers balanced by the greater number of dead in the low absence companies. Absences in General Cooke's command were effectively contained in the second half of 1863 and into the first half of 1864, his forceful leaderhsp most certainly a factor.

6

Second Corps, Rodes Division, Daniel-Grimes Brigade

"Thar penalty was death nothing else would do"[1]

After the tragic loss of General T. J. Jackson in early May 1863, Major General Richard Stoddert Ewell was promoted to Lieutenant General with responsibility for the 2nd Corps of the Army of Northern Virginia. War was still a few months in the offing when he wrote: "Officers generally are very much averse to anything like civil war, though some of the younger ones are a little warlike. The truth is in the army there are no sectional feelings and many from extreme ends of the Union are the most intimate friends."[2] It was his opinion that the "Yankee" forces were made up of immigrants, "low foreigners" who were fighting the "best of our people," sturdy agrarian stock, the men from the Confederate states. Utilization of "Negro" troops would, in his mind, pit equals against equals.[3]

All in all, General Ewell was willing to confront desertion with strong measures but not to the extent of his predecessor, the dogmatic General Jackson. For the war, from existing AIGO records, the Second Corps had 165 men sentenced to be executed, and at least 38 were so killed. Half of those sentenced to death were men from North Carolina units, as were three-quarters of those finally executed. Men sentenced to death in the Third Corps of General A. P. Hill had an even chance of avoiding execution; in the Second Corps of General R. S. Ewell, the odds improved to three out of four.

The Second Corps was organized with 3 infantry divisions, 1 of which was led by Major General Robert Emmett Rodes. The Division had 21 regiments in August 1863; 12 were attributed to North Carolina. In the Division 46 men were sentenced to be executed. At least 12 of the convicted were put to death; 11 of the 12 were enrolled in the North Carolina regiments.

A brigade of 4 regiments and a battalion of infantry was organized, trained and led for eighteen months by Brigadier Junius Daniel. While General Daniel was in command, 6 men were given death sentences: 4 were executed. The brigade was unusual in that 3 of the 4 regiments had just 1 man sentenced to death, and in each instance that soldier was executed. In contrast, the fourth regiment had 11 men sentenced to be shot, but 8 avoided that end. Regarding the overall distribution of punishment, the 3 companies of each regiment that had the most enlisted men appear before general courts-martial accounted for 65 percent of Brigade courts. The companies recording the fewest courts contributed just 5 percent of the total.

Thirty-Second Regiment

One man in the Thirty-Second was sentenced to be shot by a court-martial, and the execution was duly carried into effect. The executed man was enrolled in Company I, the Chatham Rifles; that company along with Company F, Catawba County, and Company A, Tyrrell County, accounted for 70 percent of the 25 court convictions attributed to the regiment; 9 at trial were acquitted. Companies B, Pasquotank and D, Northampton Counties had no court record. A young soldier in Company F of the Thirty-Second was described as a Methodist: "And I believe, a pious and consistent man, and therefore, of course, a good soldier."[4] Private Jacob Gamewell Hill who was "naturally weak" died after three months of service.

Forty-Third Regiment

The Forty-Third also had only one man hear his death sentence read, and he was executed three days later. The unfortunate man was enrolled in Company D, one of the best companies in the Forty-Third in terms of having the fewest men go before military courts. Company A, the Duplin Rifles; Company D, from Halifax and Cumberland counties; and Company E, the Edgecombe Boys, in total had only 2 men taken to trial. Company K, the Anson Independents; Company H, the Fisher Light Infantry, Anson County; and Company I, the Anson Regulators, in total had 24 soldiers face charges. These last three companies accounting for 73 percent of all regimental convictions were recruited in Anson County. An officer of the Forty-Third made the accurate observation that the Anson County companies "were more trouble than all the rest."[5] Of the 30 men of this regiment convicted by courts-martial, just 2 ended their service in desertion. At trial, 4 men were acquitted. In general, the regiment did not suffer overly harsh punishment for desertion. Company K had 8 men absent for one to six months and they were punished with two to four months of hard labor. Lesser infractions also required the attention of company officers. Two men were punished for using gunpowder to remove dents in their canteens.[6]

Forty-Fifth Regiment

The Forty-Fifth also had one recorded death sentence, and the convicted man was promptly executed. However, the Forty-Fifth experienced nearly twice the court convictions than did the Forty-Third. The variance between the best and worst companies is much less for the Forty-Fifth than was found for the Forty-Third. In the Forty-Fifth, the worst companies, Company A, the Rockingham Zollicoffers; Company B, from Guilford County; and Company D, the Madison Greys, Rockingham County, accounted for 47 percent of 62 courts, while those with the fewest, Company H, the Rockingham Guards; Company E, the Troublesome Boys, Rockingham County, and Company I, The Border Rangers from Rockingham and Caswell counties, make up 14 percent. At trial, 5 men were acquitted. Company E, the Troublesome Boys, was not really very troublesome. The company chose the name of a nearby creek, not one meant to indicate their intentions. Only 8 of 168 enrolled men took it upon themselves to leave the ranks: 4 were court-martialed. For the company 44 men died while in service and 20 were killed in battle.[7]

Fifty-Third Regiment

Men of this regiment were given severe punishment in more than half of 73 trials that ended with a conviction; 16 trials ended in acquittal. Punishment included death, lashing, branding or lengthy imprisonment. The companies that were most often punished were Company C, the Lexington Guards, Johnston County; Company F, recruited in Alamance and Chatham counties; and Company E, the Farmer Boys, Surry County; they account for 62 percent of all convictions. Companies A, B and I left no court-martial record. A different pattern of absence is found from company to company; some men left when victory was at hand, while others held on until defeat was obvious.

Absent	1861	1862	1863	1864	1865	no date
Co C		4	1	1 14	4	
Co F		9 6	19 9	4 3		
Executed				1		

In the Fifty-Third, 11 men were sentenced to death: 3 were shot, and 2 died while under a death sentence. Of the 11 condemned men 5 did not survive the war, but 6 did, a survival rate of 54 percent. Now, considering the 25 men who were given severe sentences, 13 survived the war; a 52 percent survival rate. Stake or severe sentence, it made little survival difference in this regiment.

One group of men from the Fifty-Third, those who were acquitted after trial, subsequently compiled fine service records; 15 of 16 completed their service with no further blemish on their records. Generally these men were deserters who returned under the assurance of an amnesty offer. Two deserters from the Fifty-Third were killed by the Home Guard, one in Wilkes County and one in Union County. Two men died in the guardhouse shortly after being arrested. Of the 11 soldiers in the Fifty-Third who were sentenced to be shot to death, 6 were enrolled in Company C, the Lexington Guards, and all were from Johnston County. Throughout the war there were 157 men enrolled in the company; 47 had in arrest or court-martial incidents on their service records. A provision in the conscription law allowed men over thirty-five years old to leave the service. Nine men of the company, all in their mid-to-late thirties, took advantage of the opportunity.

Second Battalion

The Second Infantry Battalion enrolled men from three states, but the companies of men who were not North Carolinians were later transferred to regiments of men from their native states, Georgia and Virginia. Company F, Randolph County; Company A, the Brown Mountain Boys, Stokes County; and Company H, the Madison Guards, were responsible for 27 of 31 court-martial convictions concerning the battalion, 87 percent in all. Company B, Surry County, and Company G, Forsyth County, each had 2 men to go before general courts-martial. Severe sentences were issued in about one-third of all court-martial convictions concerning the battalion; 3 at trial were acquitted. Though none of their men were condemned to death, men in the battalion thought such sentences were well deserved. Forces taking up deserters quickly dispatched 3 men of the battalion. Killing deserters was not only justified, but desired: "Two of our men deserted while there One was a man who lives in [not clear] with a wife and several children I do sincerely trust he may be shot. As many as three have been shot for desertion since I have been with this Brigade and several a few days before I came to it."[8]

Courts-Martial

Daniel Brigade

THOMAS BIRD 53-C (July 17, 1862). Private Bird enrolled, as a substitute, in Company C, Fifty-Third Regiment, on April 28, 1862. After honoring his obligation for a short time, he deserted but was soon in arrest to appear before a court-martial held on July 17. The court found that he was guilty on all charges and the requisite number agreed that he should be shot. However, General D. H. Hill disapproved the sentence on September 30, returning the substitute to his company. Private Bird went on to serve another year before succumbing to illness at Raleigh on September 23, 1864.

A private in a regiment temporarily assigned to the brigade gave his opinion on conditions in May of 1863: "We are having a very trying time of it just now. There is much dissatisfaction in Army now about our rations, but the most of the trouble and complaint arises from the Conscripts and not from the regulars there has been a great many desertions for the last three weeks.... There has been some over three hundred desertions in the last three weeks from Gen Daniel's Brigade the one that we are with at present—I wish that I was out of this Brigade, for I do not think Daniel's much of a Gen, and he is as coarse as a [s]andstone, has no polish, he nor his staff, they are a grub worm set as I have ever been with—there is all the difference in the world in this and Pettigrew's Brigade they were all very good officers and gentleman."[9] The term "grub worm set" brings to mind men of little character, grubbing about in their own self-interest. The reference to "over three hundred desertions" in May of 1863 is not far off the mark. Companies E, F, G and K of the Fifty-Third alone had 63 recorded absences during the May–June 1863 reporting period. One company had just three cooking-pots and less than a dozen blankets for the 76 boys that were then present.[10] A soldier reported home that there was "considerable demoralization of our troops," and he feared that there was going to be an "a bon-dance of dissertion."[11] Another thought, "Croakers and deserters ought to be hung from the same scaffold."[12]

Along with their other disciplinary woes, Company F, of the Thirty-Second, had two men involved in an attempt to "ravish a Negro woman." While so bent, they threatened to shoot her husband. It was suggested that one of the perpetrators be subjected to "public castration"; the comment brought forth the following tirade from General D. H. Hill: "The wretch who so disgraces the character of a soldier does not deserve to live.... But to such a licentious animal as—it is supposed the punishment suggested would be worse than death."[13] In any case, castration is not a punishment available to a court-martial. At trial one of the accused men was acquitted while the other was given fifteen days in prison, bread and water his only nourishment, and then he was to be pilloried.

Whatever the cause, the next man to face death by musketry, while led by the "grub worm set," was a conscript. A month before he was tied to his stake, General D. H. Hill had vigorously chastised a court for not invoking a death sentence on a cowardly deserter from Company H, Forty-Third Regiment, the Fisher Light Infantry.[14] The tirade may have influenced the court to put forth a death sentence that led to a prompt execution.

GOVAN HARVELL 43-D (May 5, 1863). Private Harvell was a conscript from Rutherford County who was enrolled in December 1862. His military service is tersely described in three brief entries. For the January–February period of 1863 — absent without leave — AWOL, March–April — absent in arrest, May–June — "Shot by sentence of court-martial." Company D of the Forty-Third was organized with men from Halifax County. Private Harvell and 3 other conscripts from Rutherford went into the company in December 1862. Within nine months, 3 were dead and 1 was absent.[15] After Private Harvell's court-martial on May 5, 1863, the decision of the court, together with the approval of the General Commanding, was formally made known in a General Order issued on May 17. Two days later the Post Commander, Colonel Clark, issued specific orders for the execution scheduled for the next day, May 20. Why there was such an urgency to shoot the conscript is not obvious from surviving records, but events quickly proceeded.

> HeadQtrs Kinston NC May 19, 1863 GO I Pursuant to Gen Order #15 dated Hdqtrs Dept N. C. May 17, 1863 Private Govan Harvell Co D 43rd Reg will be executed tomorrow 20 inst at 12 Mr [Meridian] on the south side of the river near the bridge. II All troops not on duty required to attend. The commanding officers 24 and 49 will cause at least five companies to be present. III Commdg Off 35 Reg will be detailed one subaltern 2 Sgts and 24 men to execute the order.[16]

Private Harvell was dispatched as scheduled. The execution had little effect on desertion from his company; 13 men departed before he was shot and 14 thereafter. The death of an unknown conscript held little import; those forced into service were not often held in high esteem. The ending of Private Harvell's life was not accomplished with the solemn precision so vital in a military execution. Captain W. H. S. Burgwyn wrote in his diary:

> Tuesday 19th Remained in camp all day. An order for the execution of a man for desertion in the 43 NCR to take place at 12 M tomorrow was published [at] Dress Parade & our Regt was detailed to command the executing party. Weather fair & warm. May Wednesday 20th Went out with the Regiment and Brigade and Cooks [sic] Brigade to witness the execution of a man of the 43 NC condemned to be shot for desertion. It was a most painful sight & when after having prayed with his clergyman the front rank did not kill him & the rear rank then had to march up & shoot & they loaded again but it was unnecessary.[17]

First Lieutenant Henry W. Humphrey, the subaltern in command of the execution detail, was promoted a month after the grisly spectacle.

Orders were also issued that men were forbidden to go more than 300 yards from camp without written permission.[18] Would-be absentees were not allowed to roam about to scout out likely routes or to get a head start on their pursuers.

In May 1863, severe sentences were given to Privates Joseph and James Nanny of Rutherford County. While enrolled in Company F of the Forty-Third, the men left their company, were arrested, and went before a court-martial. They were to be bucked and gagged in a public place every alternate two hours between reveille and retreat for five days. Then they were to wear a barrel shirt eight hours a day for ten days. Following this each was to have half of his head shaved, and then marched by every regiment of the brigade. Following that humiliation they were to be confined in a penitentiary for a period of five years.[19] The brothers died of disease in Rutherford within eighteen months of their sentencing.

As many did, a man in the Forty-Fifth expressed his thoughts on the times. Men were "fighting to keep from under Northern bondage" while serving under Southern masters who kept men bound more than the "masters of Africans."[20] The conscription laws certainly added to that feeling of bondage. Another effect of the law is found in the experience of Private John Vernon, Company F of the Forty-Fifth. When he was conscripted in September 1862, he went without a "murmer" according to his wife, when she later asked Governor Vance for aid. He may have departed with a sigh of relief, as he left behind a sizable extended family of twenty-nine members including his wife and children, sisters and their children, a mother, brothers' wives and their children — all of these people at least partially dependent on him for their sustenance. After serving a few months, Private Vernon came home without leave to get warm clothes. He was sick for a spell and just as he was ready to go back, he was arrested and shackled to be taken forcibly to his command. He was driven to escape from his captors according to his wife, "he sayed if he could not go like a man he would not go like a dog."[21] Following this escapade, he was again preparing to return to the army when he was arrested and hand-cuffed; this time under more vigilant guard he was taken to his regiment. After these events, his wife wrote the Governor for a pardon for her husband. The Governor replied that he could not intercede for a three-time deserter. At trial in January 1864, Private Vernon was sentenced to a year of hard labor. He survived the war to return to the many that eagerly awaited him.

A mother in Anson County wrote to Governor Vance in October 1863 to save her son from execution: "I drope you a few lines to inform you that my sone William Lury is in Raleigh in jaile for deserting Sir I hope that you will try to have him not shot as he has not got very good since I am very sery that he deserted and I hope that he never will do so any more please to try to have his life spared I am a pore widow woman."[22] Her son was not shot. He was sentenced to hard labor for one year with a twenty-pound ball attached to his leg by a three-foot chain. At war-end he was on a sick furlough.

JOHN SCARCE 45-E (December 13, 1863). Private Scarce enrolled as a substitute on December 12, 1862. The month after he was paid to take a musket, he deserted and remained absent for four months. Service records for this period offer conflicting evidence as to whether he was hospitalized or in desertion during this entire time. In any case, upon his return the substitute served another month and then decided to again break his obligation. He did so while in the vicinity of Martinsburg, VA, on the march that would lead to Gettysburg, PA. Three months later, the substitute-deserter was arrested in his home county of Pittsylvania, VA, and carried to Orange Court House, VA, under guard. At the completion of his court-martial on December 13, he was judged guilty and sentenced to be shot in seven days after publication of the court's findings on January 8, 1864. The execution was actually carried into effect on January 19, near Orange Court House.

ZENO CURTNER 53-F (December 19, 1863). Military service for another hesitant soldier began when Private Zeno Curtner was conscripted into Company F of the Fifty-Third on October 8, 1862. A month later, on November 10, he deserted to remain absent for a year. The conscript was the only soldier to absent himself from the company that month. That was unusual as those leaving often left with at least one other, but the newly enrolled conscript had little time to gain an accomplice. On December 19, 1863, he was in arrest and standing before a court-martial that found him guilty as charged and concurred that he should be shot. He was one of two men of the brigade executed on January 8, 1864.

JOSHUA PRUITT 53-G (December 19, 1863). The first volunteer to be executed in Daniel's brigade enrolled in Company G, Fifty-Third Regiment, on March 20, 1862. At some point, Private Pruitt apparently regretted his decision, for six months later Privates Joshua and Isham Pruitt were arrested and placed in the jail at Charlotte Court House, VA, this on September 16, 1862. No record of punishment following their arrest has been located for either man. In October 1862, Private Joshua Pruitt again deserted and was absent for several months before returning to his company. Apparently still dissatisfied, or perhaps swept along with others, a third attempt at desertion began on May 20, 1863. As already noted, many desertions from the brigade began in that month. This final, and fatal, attempt to flee the ranks ended prior to December 19, when a court-martial heard the details of his frequent comings and goings, after which they sentenced him to death by musketry. Private Pruitt was executed beside Private Curtner on January 8, 1864. There were 36 absences from Company G prior to the execution of Private Pruitt, but just 6 over the final fifteen months of the struggle. Private Isham Pruitt enrolled in the same company on the same day as had his executed older brother. The younger soldier also deserted but was back in the ranks by December 1862. No court-martial record has been found for him. From existing records, he was present for duty on the execution day of Private Joshua Pruitt. Interspersed with comments on W. W. Holden, the Confederate Congress and desertion in general, Dr. John F. Shaffner notes the progress of events on the day of execution for Private Curtner and Pruitt.

> Today two deserters belonging to Daniel's Brigade of this Division are to be executed with musketry — I have not their names from what Regiment or county — I shall not witness the execution. The poor fellows should be pitied by every one as probably their crime has been committed at the instigation of the teachings of Holden and Co. — My steward has gone over to witness the execution & if he returns before I close this letter I will give you whatever he reports of interest connected with it. Just saw the criminals above alluded to passed here in an ambulance en route to be shot. — They were sitting upon their coffins, and looked miserable indeed. — A Chaplain attended them. — All the prisoners belonging to the Division about 160 in number accompanied the ambulance under guard. — Many of them are to be tried for similar offenses the spectacle will prove a sad and terrible warning one to many. P.S. My steward reports that the two men who were shot belonged to the 45 NC and are from Surry County. — Their bodies were riddled with bullets.[23]

A week later the Doctor asked Colonel David M. Carter to defend him before a court-martial before which he was to appear for disobedience of orders.[24] Such were the twists and turns of army life.

Private J. F. Coghill, writing from the camp of the Twenty-Third to his brother:

> I will tell you something concerning the times, on last friday I was called upon to witness the execution of two soldiers who ware natives of the good old state of N.C, but they had deserted thare post of duty and thare penalty was death nothing else would do so they said but death but it was a heart rending seen to see two men brought up to received thare doom but they seem like that they did not regard it at all but as soon as they ware dead we marched back to camp the weather being considerable cool wee ware very glad to get back the snow is not gone yet and wee have not had a snow ball since it fell but if it had not ben so cold I guess that wee would have had a lively time.[25]

Another soldier placed the executions in a rather low key, "It has been snowing, and is very cold Some of the boys have formed a dramatic company, and I went to see them play Toodles. There were two men shot in our brigade for desertion today."[26]

Private Stephen Frazier, Company K of the Forty-Fifth, writing to his wife a few days after it was announced that an execution was pending, made no mention of the fact. Quite sensibly so, as Stephen repeatedly urged his brothers and his brothers-in-law to volunteer for service in the regiment. Success would have earned a furlough for Stephen. As an additional inducement to the boys at home Stephen went on to say: "Tel the boys that I think they had better come for there is as good a chance to keep out of the war here as there is there for if it gets too hot here we can cross the branch and keep out of it here better than we can there."[27] Learning that Private Scarce would be executed for desertion did not negate the alternative plan for Private Frazier to "cross the branch" to desert to the enemy, if the need arose. That eventuality never came about; Stephen died of typhoid fever within a month of the letter to his wife. At least one other soldier in the Forty-Fifth also planned to flee to Federal lines, saying, "I intend to make the trip at the first opportunity that offers itself."[28] He indicated that other men were in the "club" with him and that their best chance for leaving would be while on picket. Their coming "voyage" was to be led by a soldier named "Bob."

ALVIS PICKARD 53-F (February 9, 1864). Private Pickard volunteered for service in Company F, Fifty-Third Regiment, on April 5, 1862, this just a month after a man of the same name and county had enlisted but never reported for duty in Company B, Forty-Ninth Regiment. Within the next month, the recently enrolled private was absent from his company. Still absent fourteen months later, he was officially listed as a deserter. During this fourteen-month period, in January of 1863, the man who had never reported to the Forty-Ninth was ostensibly transferred to Company D, Fifteenth Regiment, but again never reported for duty. Private Pickard remained at large until February 9, 1864, when he was arrested and returned to the Fifty-Third. A court-martial in session on February 26 found the deserter guilty as charged and concurred on a death sentence. A review by the Secretary of War three months after the conviction led to a suspension of the sentence. For seven months Private Pickard remained in confinement waiting to learn when, or if, he would be shot. Perhaps the most favorable decision that could be hoped for was forthcoming on December 1, when the death sentence was commuted to imprisonment at hard labor for the remainder of the war. Private John Pickard, an older brother of the condemned, enrolled in a different company of the Fifty-Third Regiment and was court-martialed for some violation in April 1863.

The number of men executed from the Fifty-Third might have grown by one except for the compassion shown a young soldier from Company F. He was told that but for his extreme youth — he was seventeen or eighteen years old — he would have been shot for his prolonged desertion; instead he was ordered to labor on public works for three years. A brother, older by a year or two, deserted on the same day and had no further service record. Each gave an age of eighteen when enrolling; they survived the war.[29]

Grimes Brigade

"but a poor privates life is soon forgotten"[30]

In May 1864, after the death of Brigadier General Daniel at Spotsylvania Court House, Brigadier Bryan Grimes assumed command. He understood the need for discipline at all levels of command. Lack of success in General J. A. Early's campaign in the Shenandoah Valley was due to "simply want of discipline," in the mind of General Grimes — a view shared, and expressed, by Confederate officers in other commands.[31] While leading the

Fourth Regiment, Colonel Grimes was critical of the manner in which deserters were punished. The example should be set by punishment administered by officers in direct contact with the men in the ranks. Authorities often assigned imprisonment and labor at some site far distant from the battle line. This was exactly what the deserter desired — to avoid the dangers of the battlefield. His recommendation was that men should be punished in camp and then made to fight. Pointedly he noted that the risk of capital punishment after desertion "was no greater than that encountered in any one pitched battle."[32] A deserter imprisoned far from camp did little to serve as a deadly warning for those with an impulse to flee the ranks, even though the life of the prisoner was in as great jeopardy as if he had been sentenced to death.

General Grimes returned to Pitt County at the ending of hostilities. Five years later, he was shot and killed by a hidden assassin. The murderer was unknown for eight years, at which time a drunken man boasted that he was the assailant. Jailed for drunkenness, within hours he was taken from the jail by a group of men and lynched from a nearby bridge, certainly an application of the swift, direct and local punishment that had earlier been envisioned by the Confederate Brigadier. Anecdotal evidence offered that the assassin was a wartime deserter from the Fourth Regiment.[33]

J. J. JOYCE 53-G (June 8, 1864). The service record for Private Joyce offers a confusion of detail, little of which is verified by other sources. The Roll of Honor for Stokes County shows that Private Joyce went into service in November 1862, at age fifty-two. Other records indicate an entry date of March 1862, at age forty-six. The later record is more likely correct. A furlough was granted to Private Joyce after two or three months of service and a second furlough, approved by General Lee, was forthcoming about a year later. On return from this furlough, he was assigned to duty as a hospital guard. Two months later it was determined that he was now fit for field duty and was so assigned. Weeks later, he was paid off and discharged from the army. Suddenly, unexplainably, an entry in Private Joyce's record states, "Shot to death with musketry on June 8, 1864." No other record of an execution of a soldier in a North Carolina regiment on that date, or in that month, has been located. Records of other states do not reveal that any man named Joyce was executed on the stated date. If correct, the record for Private Joyce shows that he was executed five months after Private Pruitt of the same company. The scant records in the case of Private Joyce are best summarized by a private in the Forty-Fifth: "But a poor privates life is soon forgotten, a great Genls name can go a great ways."[34]

GEORGE W. GOINGS (53-E June 1864). Private Goings joined the Fifty-Third in Surry County on March 27, 1862. Within days he was absent without leave and remained so for two years. He was finally arrested in the March–April 1864 period. No record of the court-martial that heard the case of Private Goings is entered in his service record, but he was tried for his prolonged absence and sentenced to be shot. In June 1864, Mr. J. T. Leach of Johnston County contacted the administration at Richmond in an effort to secure clemency for the condemned man. While the appeal was being processed, Private Goings was admitted to Prison Hospital #13 at Richmond where he died on July 27, 1864. Confederate congressman Leach was a talented, benevolent man who frequently took positions that were critical of the Confederate administration. There were 6 men with the family name Goings enrolled in Company E: 2 died in confinement, 3 ended their service in desertion, and 1 in sickness.

A foreshadowing of the neighborhood-wrenching vendettas in western North Carolina began in 1862. Captain A. M. Church of the Ninety-Third North Carolina Militia, Wilkes

County, was arrested on charges that he had failed to arrest and conscript Harrison Church and his brothers, Jesse and James, and that he had failed to arrest known deserters in the county.[35] Of the 6 men bearing the Church name that were eventually enrolled in the Fifty-Third, 5 deserted by the spring and summer of 1863. Private Harrison Church deserted the regiment that he had voluntarily joined on February 10, 1863, after serving a few days less than three months. He was subsequently dropped from the rolls of his company. The volunteer had been liable for conscription for ten months before going into the service. The deserting private returned to Wilkes County where, at some point, he accepted, or seized, leadership of a band of deserters and Tories who went about the county assaulting and stealing from neighbors, often wantonly destroying their property. In one of the undercurrents of the flow of bitterness, at least one member of the assaulted families may have had some part in denying food to the Church clan. In any event, there was a skirmish, an exchange of gunfire between the Church-led band and official Confederate forces. The leader of the band, Harrison Church, was wounded and captured while concealed in a cave. One source states that he was wearing a Yankee uniform and carrying a Yankee commission when captured.[36] The captured deserter, robber, and accused traitor was taken to Castle Thunder at Richmond to await his fate. He was fortunate in that his captors did not immediately dispatch him. The military status of the captured man, a prisoner of war or a traitor, is not clear in view of the fact that he had been dropped from the rolls of his company. No court-martial record has been located that would help resolve his status. Harrison Church survived the war. In at least one memory, he should not have had that privilege: "I think if we had executed a Lt Col of the Tories in Wilkes Co., (Harrison Church) [name in text] it would have had a good effect. I learn that a deserter from our Reg't who had been returned to duty, put a ladder to a window and ran off with him, although then on post as a sentinel."[37] Governor Vance was kept well informed of the troubles in Wilkes County. Two correspondents advised him of the capture of the "notorious" Harrison Church and his younger brother William. In an incident just preceding their capture, William allegedly used a chain-shot to smash furniture, windows and crockery in a home being vandalized. Cabins and furnishings were set afire, weapons discharged, a "Negro" kidnapped and usable items stolen.[38] The Governor was requested to send troops to break up the bands of vandals; the use of "infiltrators" was suggested.

CALVIN BILLINGS 32-I (November 21, 1864). Private Billings was twenty-one years old when he was conscripted into the Confederate army on October 1, 1862. While encamped at Drewry's Bluff, on the James River ten miles below Richmond, he deserted. Private Billings was not the only member of the company to make that choice; at least a dozen others chose a similar exit during that second winter of war. In the winter of 1864, Private Billings was starkly alone when he knelt at the execution stake. A court-martial held on November 21, 1864, found the deserter guilty; the resulting death sentence was approved by Lieutenant General J. A. Early on December 10, and the execution took place three days later near New Market, VA, just before the regiment was ordered to move east. Private Billings went to trial at a time when Confederate commanders routinely approved prompt execution for deserters. The aforementioned Doctor Shaffner noted in his diary, "December 13 — This evening at 2 o'clock was executed an enlisted man belonging to the 32nd N.C. Regt. Grimes Brigade. About 4 o'clock orders were received to be ready to move at 8 o'clock in the morning."[39] On December 18, Doctor Shaffner expanded on his views:

The troops were rejoiced to get away from Gen'l Early, and I sympathize with them, as I have no confidence in him. He is a bad, old man in many ways. I trust that our men will do better fighting with Gen'l Lee in command, and that desertions, which have been frequent, will now cease. The day before we left the Valley, there was an execution, in the person of a deserter.[40]

HARDY HATCHER 53-C (January 25, 1865). Private Hatcher, now eighteen years old, went into the Fifty-Third in the final months of 1864. What role the conscription laws had in his decision is not known, but not long thereafter he deserted. He was in arrest by January 25, 1865, when he was taken before a court-martial. Guilt was established, he was sentenced to be shot. General Lee approved the sentence of the court, but after further review it was discovered that the presidential amnesty announced in GO # 2 was applicable to Private Hatcher, and he was returned to his post. A few weeks later he was captured by Federal forces at Petersburg, VA.

ELBERT J. HOWINGTON 53-C (January 25, 1865). Private Howington joined Company C, Fifty-Third Regiment, as a recruit from Johnston County on April 17, 1862. He served faithfully until his desertion decision in late 1864, at the same time as Private Hatcher. From that point on, the service experiences of the two men are identical. Private Howington was court-martialed, sentenced to be executed, granted amnesty, returned to duty and was captured by the enemy, as was Private Hatcher. The older of the two, Private Howington, was a seasoned volunteer. Veteran and recruit nearly knelt side by side on the execution field.

JOHN W. TALTON 53-C (January 25, 1865). Corporal Talton held that rank for five months from enrollment to demotion by order of a court in September 1862. He regained the rank in April 1863. Considering his experience, he may have been looked to for leadership by the men who were considering deserting the company. Beginning on January 25, 1865, Private Talton and the other deserters, stood before courts and later learned that they would be shot to death. The sentences were approved by General Lee and then remitted by order of the President under terms of a general amnesty that he had issued earlier in the year. Capture in March 1865 ended his service.

GEORGE D. PITTMAN 53-C (January 26, 1865). Private Pittman enlisted in Company C of the Fifty-Third on May 6, 1864, at age seventeen. For much of what would be his year in the army, he was sick at home or in military hospitals. Between periods of illness he deserted, was court-martialed, and sentenced to be shot. As with the other Johnston County men, his death sentence was approved by General Lee and then remitted under presidential amnesty. Private Pittman was captured at Richmond on April 3.

B. D. PARRISH 53-C (February 2, 1865). Private Parrish enlisted on April Fools' Day in 1864 while a resident of Johnston County. A week and a year later he was ordered to surrender his arms at Appomattox. Except for his brief brush with military discipline, he had always obeyed his orders, and his record bears no other blemish. But for his one misstep, Private Parrish was court-martialed on February 2, 1865, found guilty, and sentenced to be shot. His sentence was remitted under presidential amnesty. Private Parrish was with his company at the final surrender. Private Elizah Parrish enrolled in Company C in October 1862 and ended his service by deserting in December 1864. Private Stephenson Parrish joined the same company as a substitute in March 1862; he died while hospitalized that same year.

Summary

Approximately 6,500 men served in the 45 companies in the brigade led by Generals Daniel and Grimes; about 520 of them were in line at Appomattox Court House. Eighteen companies were studied for enrollment, 142 per company, and absences, deaths and courts-martial. Eight companies with the highest number of courts, 11 per company, suffered 34 deaths and 46 absences per company.[41] Ten companies with the fewest courts, 2 per company, suffered 41 deaths and 19 absences per company.[42] Slightly less than one-third of the dead in the 18 companies died in battle or from battle wounds. Missing when the final roll was called were the 6 men who were executed. Also missing were 7 of the 8 men who had been condemned to death but then spared. These men were either in arrest or had been captured by the enemy. Five of the 6 executed men were bound to the stake in 1864. Conscripts or substitutes were 4 of the 6. The period from July 1862 to December 1863 was a time of intense absence activity. The brigade was in the top third of all North Carolina brigades in terms of the number of courts-martial of enrolled men, but toward the low end as to the number of men sentenced to be executed.

7

Second Corps, Rodes Division, Anderson-Ramseur-Cox Brigade

"we understand we are to be shot for an example to skair others"[1]

Brigadier George Burgwyn Anderson first led the brigade "whose combat record would be equaled by few others,"[2] No executions took place while General Anderson was in command. Brigadier Stephen Dodson Ramseur continued the aggressive leadership of the brigade. He was described as "impetuous, impatient, aggressive and by some regarded as foolhardy."[3] Brigade executions all took place while General Ramseur was in command. Only one man was threatened with execution after General William Ruffin Cox took command in June 1864.

Second Regiment

The only deserter from the Second Regiment to die at the execution stake was also the first soldier of Ramseur's brigade to be sentenced to death. As might be expected under that circumstance, the event was noted by many observers, yet none made mention, if they knew, that the executed soldier was absent from his company for less than a week. The young man who suffered the extreme penalty was a member of Company E, the Guilford Guards, one of the three companies that led the regiment with 17 of 38 court appearances. Five men at trial were acquitted. Companies D, and H, with many men from Wayne County, were the others. The only other man of the regiment sentenced to be shot, was from Company D. That company led all others of the regiment in the number of men that anxiously awaited the decision of a court-martial. In general, men serving in the Second experienced moderate punishment, and it was distributed over all companies.

Fourth Regiment

AIGO records concerning the Fourth list the names of only 3 men who were sentenced to be shot by courts-martial. Other sources add to this number to show that a total of 8 men were given death sentences; 4, all from E Company, were executed. The Fourth led the brigade in the number of men appearing before a court with 58 trials; one-fourth of the trials were for incidents that occurred in the first year of war. Following their trials 7 men were acquitted.

Each company of the Fourth had 3 to 7 men convicted by courts, similar in scope but more even in distribution than was found for the Second Regiment. In the Fourth, the worst companies were Company E, the Southern Guards of Beaufort County, and Companies A and H of Iredell County; with a total of 22 courts, that was 38 percent of all courts for the regiment. It is worth noting that each of these companies suffered a large number of deaths and a modest number of absences. Company H, for example, had 88 deaths and 21 absences; about one-third of the deaths were battle related.

Co H	1861	1862		1863		1864		1865	no date
Dead	8	35	18	13	7	6	1		
Absent		1	3	10	3	2	2		

The least punished units, Company F, the Wilson Light Infantry; Company K, from Rowan County; and Company C, recruited in Iredell County; with a total of 13 courts, accounted for 22 percent of the regimental total. Companies of the Fourth have a more even balance in court appearances than that usually found for North Carolina regiments. Notwithstanding, the Fourth was accountable for over 40 percent of all brigade general court-martial convictions and for nearly three-fourths of the death sentences.

A Lieutenant describes his introduction to command responsibility: "The next 4 or 5 weeks will be the most important to me as the officers are drilling every day and reciting in tactics. It is all new to me and I wish to make myself competent for the position I hold. We have a drill at about 5. O.Clock in the morning and at 8. O.Clock for the Company. Officers drill from 9½ to 10½ and recitation from 11 to 12. Then drill and dress parade in afternoon. Between these intervals I have to read about thirty pages."[4] "It seems hard that a Regiment as well drilled as ours should be kept in Virginia when North Carolina needs our services so much. But we cant help it without resigning and this I do not wish to do."[5]

Fourteenth Regiment

Wartime records for the Fourteenth do not show the name of a single man who was given a death sentence, though they witnessed the executions of men in other regiments. Captain Preston Lafayette Ledford, Company B, recalled his emotion on these occasions: "On two occasions the Fourteenth was called out to witness the execution of some poor soldiers belonging to the army pay the penalty of desertion. It is heartrending to see a comrade shot down in the heat of battle, but it is a more distressing scene to see a soldier shot at the stake."[6] The Fourteenth had 2 accidental deaths, and 1 from an altercation. As might be expected, the Fourteenth had very minimal court activity with just 20 courts and 16 convictions. The most active companies of the regiment, Company D, the Cleveland Blues; Company K, the Raleigh Rifles, Wake County; and Company B, the Thomasville Rifles, Davidson County, accounted for 12 of 16 guilty findings. The Fourteenth had 4 companies with no recorded courts; no company had more than 5, but the devil is found in the detail. One of the companies with no record of a court, Company F, the Rough and Ready Guards of Buncombe County, had 23 desertions from their ranks from the fall of 1862 to March 1865. Captain Z. B. Vance first led the company in May 1861. Of the deserters from the company, 14 thus ended their service—9 went to the enemy. Just 4 of the absentees from Company F had any further military record and no trial record has been found for them.

Thirtieth Regiment

Early on the Colonel of the Thirtieth observed: "I am proud of my Reg: I have never had a single case before a General Court Martial. I always manage them myself. It is certainly as well disciplined a body of troops as I know of."[7] One man of the Regiment was under a sentence of death, and severe sentences were handed down in half of the 25 cases that went to trial; 3 trials ended with an acquittal. Of 11 severe sentences, 8 went to men in the 3 companies that had the most courts-martial. Company E, the Duplin Turpentine Boys; Company I, from Nash County; and Company C, the Brunswick Double Quicks, led all others with 14 court convictions. Company A, the Sampson Rangers; Company F, the Sparta-Band, Edgecombe County; and Company H, from Moore County, had no recorded courts. The bulk of the severe sentences were given after trials held in 1863, as was the single death sentence, which may have drawn the notice of any considering desertion.

Courts-Martial

JAMES FOULKES 2-E (August 28, 1863). Private James Foulkes was not a big man, nor was he very old. Due perhaps to these or other equally unlikely factors, he survived many battles, including the one at Gettysburg, PA, only to be shot to death by Confederate musketry a short ten weeks later. Until his first and only recorded absence on August 13, 1863, while near Orange Court House, VA, the private had an uneventful service record with two periods of hospitalization following his enrollment on July 24, 1861. Five days after he left his regiment, he was arrested near Charlottesville, VA, on August 18, having made his way some twenty-five miles toward North Carolina. A court-martial on August 28, conviction by the court, publishing of the death sentence and execution on September 16, 1863, all followed in rapid order. Unfortunately, Private Foulkes was arrested the day after General R. E. Lee took the decisive stand that desertion must be controlled and that nothing would serve that purpose "except the rigid enforcement of the death penalty in future cases of conviction."[8] There was little hope for compassion from Confederate leaders days later when the life of Private Foulkes was in their hands. A series of military orders to bring about the execution of Private Foulkes began when Lieutenant General Ewell approved his death sentence. Major General Rodes, Division Commander, was assigned the responsibility for carrying the sentence into effect. On September 12, 1863, he issued General Order #40:

> I In accordance with GO no. [blank] Headqtrs 2nd Army Corp a copy of which is annexed Private James Foulkes Co E. 2nd NC Reg will be shot to death with musketry at 12 o'clock on Tuesday, September 15, in the presence of the whole Division by a detail of twelve men from the Provost Guard under command of Lt. Groff [Goff]. The place of execution will be the parade ground where the Brigade was recently reviewed. II Lt. Groff Provost Marshal of the Division will make all the necessary arrangements for the proper carrying out of this order. III Brigade Commanders will have their respective commands in position on the grounds at 11½ o'clock A.M.[9]

The life of Private Foulkes was prolonged one day past the day initially set. Lieutenant Goff, an officer in the Fifth Alabama before being assigned as Division Provost Marshal, carried out his duty without inflicting unnecessary pain or suffering on the condemned. Several witnesses commented on the execution.

September 16, 1863 Today there was a man shot for desertion Eight balls passed through him. The way this is conducted is this: the brigade that he belongs to, or sometimes even the division, is drawn up in full sight of the doomed man. He is tied to a stake in front of his grave, which is already dug, and his coffin is at his side. There is a squad of 12 men and one officer detailed to do the shooting. Eleven of the guns are loaded. The guns are given to them by the officers, so that no man knows which gun is loaded. The order is then given to fire. Thus ends the deserters life. The brigade or division then marches around him; so that every man can see his, the deserters end.[10]

The aiming accuracy of the Provost Guard is noteworthy; various accounts mention that eight to ten balls struck the bound man. In a diary entry: "September 16 — 63 Summerville Ford We shall remain here today Their was a man shot to death today for desertion, the man shot belonged to the 2nd N. C. Regt. We remained here all night a gan."[11] Lieutenant Leonidas Polk, Forty-Third Regiment, wrote to Sally from Raccoon Ford on September 16, "Another deluded wretch of the 2nd N. C. Regt, was shot to day in presence of our Division for desertion. The troops are in excellent health & fine spirits though the conduct of our people at home is depressing our boys considerably."[12] The use of "another" was likely a broad reference to all "deluded "deserters. An officer in an Alabama regiment recorded,

Sept. 15 and 16 Am officer of the guard. Rode's Division, composed of Daniel's and Ramseur's North Carolina brigades, Dole's Georgia, and Battle's Alabama brigades, were marched out to witness a melancholy sight, the public shooting of one of Ramseur's brigade, who was convicted of desertion by a court martial and sentenced to be shot to death by musketry. It was a sad sight, but his death was necessary as a warning and lesson to his comrades. Each regiment was marched in front of the dead body, and his breast was pierced by several balls.[13]

A more compassionate tone:

Our division was called out to witness the execution of a young man, whom it was said was from Casewell County & belonged to the 2nd NC Regiment. It was said that he had fought twenty-one battles and that his desertion was owing to the influence of a widowed & afflicted mother, and of course the sympathies of the troops were touched by the story.[14]

Another spectator wrote:

I see a great sight yesterday I see one of our men shot belonging to the 2 Regiment the division march out to see him shot he was shot for desertion the said they shot nine ball through him he died instantly. There was ten shot last week but I did not go to see them we had a great revival in the camp before we left a good many profest religion and was baptize.[15]

The Colonel of the Forty-Third was impressed by the solemnity of the military execution.

I witnessed yesterday the most solemn scene, that ever appeared before my eyes. A military execution according to the forms of war. The entire Division drawn up in the shape of an amphitheatre & in the centre a stake to which the prisoner was to be bound to be shot. At the appointed time the provost guard with the prisoner approached, with a brass band playing the most solemn funeral dirge that ever came to my ears [not clear]. The prisoner knelt at the stake & a chaplain prayed for him his last prayer on earth & advised him to make peace with his God. As soon as the prayer was over the fatal shots were fired; and then the whole Division marched by the place of execution to witness the remains of the prisoner. It was a most solemn and impressive scene.[16]

Officers found an execution "solemn and impressive," a needed warning, an example for those in the ranks. Enlisted soldiers saw a brutal and terrible sight, and expressed a sympathetic understanding of the plight of the deserter. Within a week of the execution, Private Christopher Hackett, Forty-Fifth, wrote home: "Daniels Brigade Rhodes Division September 21, 1863 There is not quite as much deserting as has been there was a man shot last Wed for desertion his name was James Fulk he belonged to Ramseurs Brigade he was not 18 years of age they tied him to a stake and shot ten holes through him it was a terrible sight."[17] At this timely juncture, General Ramseur presented a "Plan to [General] Lee ... to stop desertion for which he complimented me highly."[18] The plan has not been located.

Men who left the Fourth without proper authority were relentlessly pursued. In August 1863, Captain Charles Gallagher, Company E, Beaufort, was ordered to proceed to North Carolina and there to obtain a force of men to assist in capturing deserters from his own company, "or from other portions of this army." The diligent Captain was also authorized to take action against an officer who had been "tampering with deserters from your company." Apparently the accused officer was encouraging men from Company E to join a local defense unit. Captain Gallagher was provided with twelve men to "go with him within the enemy's lines for the purpose of arresting deserters."[19] The results of this dangerous incursion are not known; however, Captain Gallagher resigned his commission two months after being ordered to take on the formidable task; nearly 70 men were absent from his company in the months preceding his assignment. The seriousness of the defections is best seen from an enrollment listing for Company E that has the names of 52 men conscripted into the company. For these men, 40 are listed as "deserted," 4 are present for duty and 8 are absent for legitimate reasons. Company I, also recruited in Beaufort County, experienced just 6 absences during the same reporting period.[20] One member of the company who did attempt to stray went before a court on January 19, 1863. The court agreed that he should forfeit his pay for the time of absence, have half of his head shaved, ride a wooden horse—a pole six inches in diameter some six feet above the ground—four hours a day for thirty days, his feet to be tied together during the ride, and he was to wear a placard labeled "Deserter." If he had any appetite after these excursions he was to be fed bread and water on alternate days.[21] A soldier in Company C told those at home that some one stole his oil-cloth and blanket: "I guess if I find him out it will be a dear blanket to him we will do him like we did an old deserter a few weeks past take him out and give him thirty-nine on his bare back without leave or license that is the way we did a deserter sometime ago we will not wait for Court Marshal or anything else."[22]

Threats of desertion and lack of support for the war are found in a letter written on April Fools' Day 1863: "Mother there is a soldier deserting every day I hope they will continue to desert until this war is ended." The young man saw no point in deserting, "for theigh would catch you before you could get home." Yet, he says, "I do hope you will git some person to take my place for I want to get out of this place."[23]

In common with many other companies and regiments, deserters left Company E of the Fourth in groups, often with friends or kin. The surnames of Clark, Ross, Lewis and King are found among those with three or more men deserting from the company. Company E experienced a minimum of 68 absences during the war; 90 percent of them, 61, took place in March through June of 1863. Deaths, 56, were more evenly distributed; there were 23 deaths in 1862, and 12 were combat related.

JAMES KING 4-E (December 3, 1863). Three conscripted brothers, Privates Howell,

James and Johnson Jr. King, deserted from camp near Fredericksburg, VA, within a month of their forced enlistment on February 26, 1863. Private Howell King returned from his absence and was later captured by the enemy and died while their prisoner. Private Johnson King avoided arrest and further service. Private James King was apprehended before December 1863 and returned under guard to be court-martialed. The court found that the accused was guilty and that he should be shot. The sentence was put forth on January 19; the execution of Private James King was scheduled for Saturday, January 30, 1864. On Wednesday January 26, Major General Rodes had the honor to notify General Lee's headquarters that the execution would take place on the following Saturday. The soldiers detailed to carry out the sentence were, as in the earlier execution of Private Foulkes, commanded by 1st Lieutenant J. H. Goff of the Fifth Alabama Infantry Regiment, who was the Division Provost Marshal.[24] The Lieutenant discharged his duty as planned and scheduled. Nine days after the event, Lieutenant Goff recounted the last moments of Private King in a letter to the Colonel of the Fourth Regiment:

> Pro Marshals office Rodes Division Feby 9th 1864 Col. Bryan Grimes Comdg 4th NC Regt Colonel I deem it my duty to make known to you the last words of Private James King Co. E of your Regt who was executed for desertion on the 30th of January ult. After bandaging his eyes I told him that he had but two minutes more to live, and asked if he had any message. I only wish that my body may be sent to my friends but I want to say to you, Lieutenant, though others persuaded me to do what I did. The reading of Holden's Paper has brought me to this, but thank God I shall soon be at peace. As it may be the wish of his relatives to know in what spirit he died, I make this statement that if you think proper you may convey it to them. Very respectfully Colonel Yr. Obt Sevt J. H. Goff 1st Lieut Co I 5th Ala Regt. & Pro Marshal Rodes Division.[25]

Colonel Grimes sent the letter up the command chain and within the week General Lee endorsed the remarks to Governor Vance. "Respectfully direct to his Excellency the Governor of North Carolina that he may have it in his power if he thinks proper to communicate to the friends of Private King the state of mind in which he died."[26]

At one of those periods when desertion was being dealt with in a very severe manner, all involved were willing, even anxious, to place much of the blame on William Woods Holden, editor of the *Raleigh Standard*. That a deserter was persuaded by an influential person to do as he did is a common theme in appeals and supplications for mercy. Editor Holden certainly received a large share of the notoriety in that regard. Private King may well have made some comment as Lieutenant Goff tied the blindfold over his eyes but it is unlikely that he offered the well-organized, thoughtful quote recounted to Colonel Grimes. Particularly the reference to the reading of the newspaper published by Mr. Holden, at least if taken literally, for Private James King could not read or write according to census records. Due to mixed service records, probably those of his brother Private Howell King, Private James King is recorded as having taken the oath while a prisoner of war. This error might cause some question as to whether Private King was actually shot. Twenty years after the war men of the Fourth Regiment, S. B. Whitley and E. Tripp, vouched that they were present at the execution of a Private King, though they could not recall which one it was.[27] One other record has been found that erroneously states that both Privates Howell and James King were executed.[28] As to the wish of Private King that his body be sent home to his friends, no evidence has been found that the wish was considered, nor is there any evidence that the remains of any soldier shot to death by musketry was returned to family or friend. There is one instance where a coffin observed on a railroad car was spoken of as holding the body of a deserter, but this remark may be also read as a comment on the fate of deserters in a general way, with no specific knowledge of the occupant of the coffin.[29] In another reference, a family in Guilford County supposedly received the body of a man that was sentenced to be executed.[30] Whether this soldier was executed, died in prison or died in some other circumstance is not absolutely clear. The request of Private King does bring to mind the possible effect of returning riddled bodies of dishonored soldiers to their homes. Might this have greatly increased the resolve to remain in the ranks for a soldier not willing to so dishonor and disgrace his family? Could this have been part of the plan of General Ramseur for controlling desertion? Would it have been seen as a humane family reuniting, or horribly cruel? Families did claim the bodies of some of the men that were hanged at Kinston, NC, in February 1864. These men were executed within a few miles of their homes, but even then it was difficult for many of the grieving families to find the wherewithal to retrieve and bury the remains. The expense of preparing and transporting a corpse over any considerable distance was well beyond the means of most of the families of executed Confederates. Even though death was no stranger when entering a household in the 1860s, whether wife or kin had the emotional strength to withstand the sight of the ball-torn blackened remains is another matter. And deeper their anguish if they had urged the dead man to remain home, or to forsake his duty. Better that more comforting memories of the dead remain undisturbed. Still, one can appreciate the final wish of Private King that his body be returned to rest forever with his family, rather than buried in an unmarked grave in a distant field.

NATHAN MCDANIEL 4-G (December 13, 1863). Private Nathan McDaniel enlisted on June 15, 1861. He served just short of two years, until May 21, 1863, when he deserted from the Fredericksburg, VA, area to head for Davie County. Until August he was at large in the county but was then arrested by the local militia. They were unable to deliver their prisoner to the army; he escaped and avoided arrest for another month, until September 24, 1863. This time he was arrested with "arms in his hands" and a more watchful and vigilant guard escorted him back to his command. Private McDaniel was court-martialed on Sunday, December 13, and found guilty. He was sentenced to be shot for desertion and for breaking arrest. Either crime carried a potential death sentence at the discretion of the court. Major General Rodes notified Chief of Staff Colonel R. H. Chilton on February 3, 1864, that Tuesday, February 9, was set as the day for the execution of the condemned man.[31] Before that day, the sentence was commuted. Private McDaniel was taken to the Military Prison at Richmond on April 10, where he stayed until volunteering to fight in the Winder Legion. On July 9, he deserted to the enemy, lived through ten months in a prison camp, and then returned to North Carolina.

Private W. R. Carpenter was conscripted into Company E, Fourth Regiment, in March 1863; like Private McDaniel, he was also in his twentieth year. Two months after Private Carpenter was taken into the ranks, he deserted, was arrested, and was taken before a court-martial on June 3, 1863. The court found that he was guilty but then stated that they would "decline to pass sentence on account of his youth, inexperience and mental imbecility as shown by evidence and by his general appearance."[32] Following that decision, they quite sensibly recommended that he be discharged from the service. Private Carpenter was not released; he was examined by a Medical Board and found fit for duty. A pardon by virtue of a Presidential Amnesty was granted. Private Carpenter returned to his company for the remaining days of war.

BENNETT CRUMPLER 30-I (December 15, 1863). Private Bennett Crumpler gave his age as thirty-five when he volunteered to join the Thirtieth on May 1, 1862. After volunteering, Private Crumpler was not anxious to continue army life. He was absent without leave when Confederate troops marched into Maryland in the fall of 1862. After returning from this absence, Private Crumpler deserted on March 23, 1863. Seven months later, Captain Taylor of the Thirty-Second Militia, Nash County, received $30 for delivering Private Crumpler to Camp Holmes in Wake County. The deserter was brought to trial on December 15, 1863, found guilty of the charge and sentenced to be shot to death. Before the sentence could be officially published on January 8, 1864, Private Crumpler escaped on December 22, to return to wood and byway. Evidently tiring of this furtive and dangerous life, the fugitive decided that he had best return to his regiment. Toward that safe end, his father appealed to Governor Vance through a very well-to-do intermediary, Mr. Joshua Barnes, a resident of Wilson County.

> Wilson Sept 14th 1864 Gov. Vance My Dear Sir I write to you in behalf of a deserter for information. A deserter by the name of Crumpler was sentenced to wear a Ball & Chain for a length of time while undergoing the punishment made his escape he is now in the woods his friends inform me that he is penitent & anxious to return to service. But he is informed that he has been sentenced by a court-martial to be shot if so he says he knows nothing of it but is afraid to return on that account he has been guilty of no murder or house breaking. In the event that he has been sentenced to be shot for desertion if he returns to the army will he be pardoned. His Father who is an old man & a good citizen & is anxious for his return makes this plea through me. Please let me hear from you. Yours truly & very respectfully Joshua Barnes[33]

Governor Vance noted on the letter: "I have no power to claim his pardon from whatever sentence assessed him." Private Crumpler was likely aware that a death sentence was on record. His fear of returning was certainly sound, as was his decision to remain in the woods for the rest of the war.

Another soldier in the Thirtieth informed his kinfolk at home that if he was ever on the south side of the James River, he would desert and head their way, giving some indication that the strong guards posted at river crossings were a real deterrent to those who considered fleeing from the army. A river crossing posed a greater risk than hiding in the woods and being shot by the Home Guard, at least in this soldier's plan of action.[34]

JAMES F. HONEYCUTT 4-A (March 7, 1864). Private Honeycutt was the first to enlist and the closest to boyhood of the men in his brigade who were sentenced to be shot. He was sixteen years old on enlistment on May 5, 1861, though enrollment records give his age as eighteen. The eager adolescent served in the ranks for two years before deserting to return to Iredell County, doing so in April 1863. While he was there, he did not prudently hide in cave and cranny, but openly moved about the area, obviously wary and alert to avoid capture. After five months of deadly hide and seek, the notorious deserter was finally arrested by the local militia. They may have treated him rather roughly once they had him securely in tow. A local militia officer, Lieutenant Fish, Seventy-Ninth NCM, Iredell County, felt constrained to defend the treatment of the prisoner, which he did by saying that they were justified in doing what they did. Private Honeycutt allegedly threatened to burn the barns of some of the militiamen and to kill some of the others at his first opportunity.[35] Whatever the provocation, there was little the young man could do but bluster and threaten retaliation on his captors. For his part, Lieutenant Fish asked the Colonel of the Fourth Regiment to keep the returning deserter far away from Iredell County and never let him come there again.[36] Following this escapade, and an absence of five months, Private Honeycutt rejoined his company. There was little time for consideration of punishment, as within a few hours Private Honeycutt again deserted, perhaps with the intention of returning to Iredell County to settle with his captors. He was not able to make his way to North Carolina, but he did remain at large in the Danville, VA, area for six weeks before being apprehended. After this arrest, the boyish prisoner was taken before a court-martial on March 7, 1864, found guilty of desertion, and sentenced to death.

However, a sympathetic spirit stood by his side when the court recommended that the execution of sentence be suspended pending review by the President. Their recommendation for leniency was essentially based on the age of the prisoner and mitigating circumstances. While awaiting the President's decision, a member of the Confederate States House of Representatives, Congressman B. S. Gaither of Burke County, requested that President Davis review the case for a possible pardon. He included a letter from Private Honeycutt's company commander, Captain W. F. McRorie, Company A; he was only a year or two older than the condemned prisoner. The officer said that Private Honeycutt was a good soldier and that he was respected by his comrades. He suggested that the leniency shown after the first absence may have led Private Honeycutt to believe he would fare as well on a second desertion and he also mentioned the "ignorance" of Private Honeycutt.[37] While Mr. Gaither continued to press the matter, General R. E. Lee concurred with the recommendation of the court and sent his request for early consideration of this case, and others, to the President on April 7, 1864. The President accepted the favorable recommendation concerning Private Honeycutt. His sentence was commuted to imprisonment at Castle Thunder in Richmond, VA. There he stayed until he volunteered to join the Winder Legion when it was formed to defend the city from attack in August 1864. Within a few days of his leaving the prison, he was captured by the Federals. Upon being interrogated, Confederate Private Honeycutt indicated a desire to be paroled that he might travel to Illinois to live with relatives. His westward journey may have been delayed, as one record shows that he took the oath at Elmira, NY, in 1865.

A deserter from Company A, Fourth Regiment, also from Iredell County, was given more considerate treatment by the Home Guard than was given Private Honeycutt. Private W. C. Hobbs was court-martialed under a charge of desertion in January 1863. He was convicted of a lesser charge of absent without leave for which he received a sentence of confinement in the guardhouse, hard labor, forfeiture of pay and wearing a placard announcing his crime. The behavior of Private Hobbs was not altered by this attempt to shame him into faithful service, for he continued in his desertion attempt. In August 1864 he was taken up by the Home Guard but later claimed that he had come in under an amnesty offered by Governor Vance. The militiamen and his regimental officers each recommended that the clemency plea be accepted. The Militia officer, Captain W. J. Brawley, Seventy-Ninth NCM, Iredell County, advised the Governor: "He is naturally a coward and there is no doubt of his being a man of very little and quite weak mind and would recommend him to executive clemency."[38] The recommendation of the regimental officers followed the same tone. The service record for Private Hobbs has a notation that he deserted twice after being court-martialed in 1863, evidently having a mind sufficient to devise his departures.

One-third of the executions of North Carolinians in the Second Corps were inflicted on men of the Fourth, and all were from Company E. This company was initially formed by men of Beaufort County who proudly chose the name Southern Guards. Half of the nearly 200 men that enrolled in Company E were from Beaufort County. The other half were men who resided in or enlisted in thirty-five other counties of the state. Additionally, there were at least six foreign-born enrollees. About one-third of the total enrollment absented themselves at some point during the war. Virtually all of the Beaufort men that volunteered in the first year of war were faithful in their commitment; there were only 5 desertions among these men. Regimental losses in late 1862 and early 1863 forced companies to add a large number of recruits. Eighty men were enrolled in Company E in the first quarter of 1863, most of them coming from distant counties. The count of those dead from battle and disease continued at an even pace over the war years. In the first half of 1863, 61 men left the company, nearly all of whom had entered the service earlier that same year. Very few of these men were ever arrested to answer for their act, but the bare handful that were arrested and brought back to the regiment soon realized that they would do as sacrificial examples.

JOHN F. OWENS 4-E (April 20, 1864). Private Owens was enrolled as a conscript at Camp Holmes, Wake County, on April 28, 1863. His service record notes, "Has deserted twice."

ROBERT SPARKS 4-E (April 20, 1864). Private Sparks was a conscript from Wilkes County when he enrolled at Camp Holmes, Wake County, on April 28, 1863. His service record mentions two attempts at desertion.

WILLIAM W. WYATT 4-E (April 20, 1864). Private Wyatt was enrolled as a conscript at Camp Holmes on April 28, 1863. Two desertion attempts are noted on his record.

Privates Owens, Sparks and Wyatt were shot to death a year to the day after they were conscripted. They first deserted within a few days of being assigned to the Fourth Regiment. Evidently, they managed to return to their homes and elude those attempting to arrest them until late December 1863, when they were back with their company. There is an indication that they returned under an amnesty offered by General Robert F. Hoke. On March 25, 1864, the three again headed home but were arrested while still in Virginia at Warren's Ferry on the James River. The prisoners went to trial about April 20, 1864, and later learned that they had all been found guilty of desertion and would be shot in seven days. Realizing their time was short, the day after hearing their sentences they prepared a petition for clemency to Governor Vance. Only Private Wyatt could read and write so the petition may have been in his hand.

> To Z. B. Vance Govener of North Carolina April the 21st 1864 Dear Sir This note will inform you that we have been so unfortunate as to have the sentence of death passed on us we started home and was arrested near warren ferry on James River the 25th of March 1864 and brought back and court marchaled there was noting but desertion charged against us we did not take any arm nor nothing of that sort and we was influenced [ink blot] as we would not have started but we did not make this appear at the tryal as we did not know it was necessary and our sentence was to be shot to death with musketry within seven days from the publication of the sentence which was read to us yesterday we understand that we are to be shot for an example to skair others and not principally for crime & we privates J. F. Owens, Wm. W. Wyatt and R. Sparks of Wilkes County NC belonging to the 4th Redgement NC troops do hereby most humbly beseach your highness to hear this our petition and interceed for us and grant us a reprieve if it is possible for the sake of our dear wifes and tender little children and for the sake of our own soles we do most humbly pray you to this our petition and if you cannot get us a repreive we most humbly pray to have our time prolonged till we can prove

the above named fact about our being persuaded to go and till we can prove our caracter & other facts relative to the same — for which we will most sincerely promise and pledge all our honor and our lives and all that is dear to us that we will never — no never- adhere to any counsell that is contrary to Southern rights any more and if our lives can be spared we are willing to fight lik men and die like soldiers — you must excuse this our petition we would have sent it throud our officers but they was gone of on picket and we had not time to wait for them to come back please hear this our petition we most humbly pray your most humble penitents J. F. Owens Wm. W. Wyatt Robert Sparks[39]

Governor Vance received the letter but did not note any action that he wanted taken. The Governor understood the situations where he might be of some help; on others he wrote "file." The three condemned men had a realistic assessment of their situation, "to be shot for an example to skair others and not principally for crime." A comment by Sergeant R. O. Linster, Company C, Fourth Regiment, supports the notion that a deliberate decision was made to make an example of them. "There was 8 men deserted last week some the 2nd time they got a far as the James River was caught and brot back to camp they were from Wilk [sic] County three of them will be shot. One from Co. H Bunfield, is his name, no body seems to simpithis with them. My hands is getting so cold that I will quit."[40] Sergeant Linster had a close association with the headquarters of General Hill and was apparently aware that the decision to shoot three of the prisoners had been made nearly three weeks before the deserters learned the outcome of their trial. The court-martial proceedings would have been forwarded for the General's review and approval before being officially published, and his decision may have been common knowledge well before the actual publication date. The Private Bunfield mentioned by Sergeant Linster was Private Philo Benefield; he was not sentenced to be shot but to serve a prison term at Salisbury, NC, where he was held until December 1864.

When the announcement of the pending ritual was made, it raised grave foreboding. A private wrote, "There will be three men of the 4th NC troops of this Brigade shot on Thursday for desertion I hate very much to have to witness the scene but every man in this Brigade that is not excused by the Dr. will have to go well I have no camp news to communicate to you."[41] The private and his commander, General Ramseur, shared the same feeling, "A most disagreeable duty awaits me. I have to march my Brigade out to witness the execution of three miserable deserters. Oh! Why will these poor miserable men commit this crime and folly."[42] The need for firm, unflinching punishment always concerned this particular officer and gave him considerable anguish, though he recognized his duty. A Chaplain did not express similar misgivings though he had contact with the condemned four days before they were to die: "April 24 — Preach in the A.M. and night. Visit five men condemned to be shot. They are deeply penitent. April 25 — Preach to prisoners and guard. April 28 — See three men, from Wilkes County, shot for desertion."[43] On the day of the executions, Doctor Shaffner noted in his diary, "April 28 Cool & clear morning.— Took choloroform and had a tooth extracted.— Witnessed the execution of Private Owens, Sparks & Wyatt, all of Co. E.— convicted of desertion.— Weather is very cool." Five days later on May 3, "Steve came without the meat — Had him well whipped, and in consequence he has deserted me."[44] Doctor Shaffner of the Fourth Regiment further amplified his remarks in a letter written two days after witnessing the executions.

> On last Thursday I witnessed a very painful scene. Three members of this Regiment, conscripts from Wilkes County, were "shot to death with musketry" agreeable to the findings and sentence of a Court Martial, the one of the 2nd Corps. All had previously deserted, and been

apprehended, but were pardoned. Of course their cases were of an aggravated nature, and could not be passed over a second time with leniency. The poor fellows stated that they had been led to believe that N. C. would return to the Union, and that in leaving the Army and going home they would be sustained by the people. The one said his wife had influenced him to desert, promising him the protection of the neighborhood if he would come home, and taunting him with his want of nerve, as exhibited by fear of risking the consequences! What a miserable woman she now must be! herself and her nine children disgraced and dishonored by an act of the husband and father, which he says he was induced to do by his wife's influence! Each one expressed a hope for eternity, and all met death firmly and bravely. Twelve muskets were aimed at each one, three with blank cartridges, nine loaded with balls. The platoon was only distant ten steps. Each body was pierced with nine holes, and death was almost instantaneous. The entire division was called out, and many others were present as spectators. I earnestly hope I must never witness another spectacle of this character.[45]

The accuracy of the execution "Platoon" in aiming their muskets is mentioned by the Doctor: "Each body was pierced with nine holes." In Ramseur's brigade, execution details are notably accurate in their aim, if the various accounts are equally accurate. Some of those who recorded their impression of the execution would have as soon been spared the experience. One witness in the Fourteenth: "They was tied to stakes and shot to death that way, all three shot one at a time. All three men of family, they were from the eastern part of N.C. I was close by when th[ey] were shot and I never want to see the like again. They was put to death for starting home and taken up on the way."[46] There are three questionable phrases in this reference. "All three shot one at a time" is very likely a simple misstatement of "at one," time. "All three men of family" often suggested that families had a degree of status in their community; the writer apparently intended to say the executed men were married "with" families. "They were from the eastern part of N.C.," the men who first formed Company E, were from the Beaufort County area, which led to the assumption that these men were from the eastern part of the state. A soldier in the Thirtieth Regiment told those at home about his experience.

> I must say something a bout what I saw the other day I saw men Co. E 4th NC regiment marched out into a cold field an tyed to stakes and 36 men shot them I wish I could tel you how I felt I never felt so bad in my life the guns fiered that trimbliled and the blud run down their sids tha were berried their in the cold field I must tel you we have to eat we eat of creceses wild ground hog crters.[47]

A final corroboration is found in a statement made nearly twenty years after the event: "Oct 4th 1883 ... Owen, Sparks and Wyatt were shot for desertion at another time during 1863 — all of Company E 4th NC. Ed Tripp corroborates the writer as to the executions."[48]

The year of execution is misplaced by one. The statement was made by men in the company of the executed men.

ISHAM HARVELL 2-H (April 30, 1864). Private Isham Harvell enlisted in Company H, Second Regiment, on May 27, 1861, while in his twentieth year. After one year of service he was in confinement for some infraction of army rules, whereupon he broke his guard and began his first absence. This on June 14, at Dudley's Depot, NC, just ten miles south of his point of enlistment. Seven months later, on January 19, 1863, the deserter was returned, under guard, to Fredericksburg, VA. After three weeks in confinement, the resourceful young man again had an opportunity to escape the guardhouse, which he promptly seized, this time while in Caroline County, VA. On this absence, arrest was avoided until September 5, when Private Harvell was once more brought back under guard. Two weeks after being confined, the opportunistic and elusive private again fled from his guards and remained absent until January 21, 1864. After this arrest, his guards were obviously more wary and Private Harvell was finally present at court on April 30, 1864. Not too surprisingly, he was found guilty by the court and sentenced to be shot, with the sentence to be carried into effect in seven days by order of the General Commanding. The sentence was published on May 24, but a month later Private Harvell managed his fourth escape, closing a remarkable period of sustained determination to avoid Confederate service.

A. L. Speaks 4-A (Prior to June 7, 1864). Private Speaks was a mature farmer living in Iredell County before conscription in September 1863. After a few weeks of forced service he left his company, returned and departed again in early 1864. He went to trial for his desertion attempts and was sentenced to be shot to death. A petition for a pardon in June 1864 was favorably received, and he returned to duty. There his service record ends.

Isaac S. Swindell 4-E (September 1864). Private Swindell was the last man in the brigade to face a death sentence. He had served from his voluntary enrollment on June 3, 1861, stayed through sickness and wound, but then finally yielded to the lure of desertion in April 1864. The length of his absence has not been discovered but he was tried and sentenced to be shot for his only known violation of military law. On September 20, 1864, the day before Private Swindell was to be shot, General Cooper's office notified General Lee to "Suspend the execution of Private I. S. Swindell sentenced to be shot tomorrow and forward record."[49] Apparently not sure where the Fourth Regiment was at that time, General Cooper also sent the same word to General Early. The subsequent review apparently found cause to either remit or commute the sentence, for Private Swindell survived the war. Agreeing to serve the Confederacy with a simple mark was legal and common. Slightly over one-half of the men that volunteered to join Company E, Fourth Regiment, including Isaac Swindell, could not write their name; 25 of 49 enrolled with an "X," and 4 of the 24 who signed their name did so with obvious labored concentration.[50]

A tragic moment for a soldier is that when his brother, father, or son is killed or fatally wounded while fighting alongside of him. Private Jesse Newsom of Company A, Fourteenth Regiment, expressed his feelings on the day before Christmas 1864.

> I am glad that the rest of my brothers dont belong to the same Company that I do for I never want to belong to a Company that I have a brother in any more, for it is very hard to have a Brother Shot down by my side.... He got wounded in the morning and were carried to the field hospital when I got wounded I was carried to the same hospital when I got there he was dead but I did not want to see him after he was dead.[51]

Private James W. Newsom was killed in October 1864. Private Jesse Newsom survived the war.

Summary

When the Anderson-Ramseur-Cox Brigade stacked their weapons at Appomattox, there were 432 men present, with 153 from the Thirtieth and 55 from the Second at the extremes of most and fewest present. Close to 6,500 men were enrolled in the brigade at one time or another. Of those not present, 5 were executed; 4 were conscripts. For the brigade, 5 of the 11 who were given death sentences were conscripts. These 5 served only a matter of days before leaving; the 6 volunteers who were given death sentences were faithfully in the ranks in the range of two years. The volunteers so sentenced were just past their twentieth year, the conscripts were in their mid-thirties. At least 6 of those ordered to be shot were married men. The western half of North Carolina was home for 9 of the 11 condemned. Though the total is relatively small, nearly half of all condemned soldiers were executed, a record akin to that of brigades on the Virginia front. Six companies with a modest number of absences, 23 per company, experienced 70 deaths per company.[52] Six companies with few absences, 7 per company, lost 60 dead per company.[53] At least 1 man of the brigade was killed by the Home Guard while resisting arrest. Various accidents, exploding shells, guns discharging, drowning or railroad accidents claimed 12 lives. The record of the brigade adds a balanced perspective of the events that brought North Carolinians to the execution stake, though they were not often assembled for that purpose.

8

Second Corps, Early Division, Hoke-Godwin-Lewis Brigade

"The work of discipline is going on"[1]

In the fall of 1863, a Division of the Second Corps was led by Major General Jubal Anderson Early, "Old Bald Head." That old and bald head led a division that included troops representing 4 Confederate states — 8 regiments from North Carolina, 5 from Louisiana, 5 from Virginia, and 6 from Georgia. Over the course of the war, the North Carolina regiments learned that 22 of their men were sentenced to be executed. The other 16 regiments heard similar sentences for 30 men. In the North Carolina regiments 5 were executed, but service records do not show that any men from other states were executed, though several records are not decisive.

A short two months after assuming leadership, Brigadier Robert Frederick Hoke assembled his men to witness the execution of a soldier in the Sixth Regiment. The Sixth and the Twenty-First often required formal disciplinary attention. These regiments were responsible for 80 percent of the 119 recorded courts-martial affecting the Brigade. The Fifty-Fourth and the Fifty-Seventh Regiments accounted for the other 20 percent, but they had a significantly higher rate of men absenting themselves. Looking at the brigade, one-third of the men who went before a military court were either sentenced to be shot or given severe punishment; 108 convictions resulted in 37 life-threatening sentences.

Sixth Regiment

"If you don't want to see the monkey in ten days after you join don't come to the 6th," was advice given to men at home by a soldier of the Sixth.[2] To "see the monkey," or sometimes "see the elephant," meant to experience the raw reality of civil war. Once exposed to that reality, some men were driven to flee, and some made that decision more than once. Others offered armed resistance to those sent to arrest them and were killed far from the field of honor. Some scavenged the dead. Others refused to do so, though they were in desperate need."[3] A few were accused of killing "Negro" prisoners that had been taken in battle.[4] Allegedly they were taken in the woods and hanged; others were shot on a riverbank, or were killed when their brains were beaten out with rifle butts. Private John Rowland killed Private Patrick Murray of Company A with a knife; the assailant committed suicide. Men of the Sixth Regiment saw the monkey in many a light.

Though the Sixth had just 38 enlisted men tried by court-martial, 11 of them, 29 percent, faced death by execution. The majority of these trials, 9, were held in January and February 1865, in the closing months of the war when the regiment was well under authorized strength. In addition to the death sentences, there were severe sentences in 4 other proceedings. In sum, 15 of 38 courts resulted in severe punishment. Men accused of cowardice were sentenced to be forced into future battles, "at the point of a bayonet, if necessary."[5] Of the 11 death sentences, 10 involved just 4 companies, Company E, recruited in Burke County; Company G, Rowan County; Company A, Mecklenburg County; and Company K, Alamance County; these same companies were charged with nearly 70 percent of all courts-martial. Though men of Company K were given 3 death sentences the company had an excellent absence record, 8, while suffering a large number of deaths, 67.

Co K	1861	1862		1863		1864		1865	no date
Absent	2	2	1	3					
Dead	6	16	13	4	8	5	10	4	1

Companies F, I and B had only 3 men at trial and no death sentences. These companies were formed in Alamance, Chatham, Orange and Wake counties. Balanced against the regiment's 11 death sentences; 4 men at trial were acquitted. No record has been located that an officer of the regiment ever went before a military court.

Twenty-First Regiment

Seven men of the Twenty-First were informed that they would be shot to death. All save one were spared. In the fall of 1863, an enrollee wrote that some portion of the regiment had stacked their arms and refused to fight until they were paid and were better fed.[6] No death sentences resulted from this affair, which was perilously close to outright mutiny. Company A, the Davidson Guards; Company G, from Stokes County; and Company K, Forsyth County, were charged with slightly over half of the documented courts involving the Twenty-First, 31 of 59 courts; 4 at trial were acquitted. Of the 7 men who were informed of their imminent execution, 3 were members of Company A, as were 9 who were sentenced to ride a wooden horse, be branded or be confined at hard labor.

Fifty-Fourth Regiment

Men serving in the Fifty-Fourth had little direct experience with the death sentence. In fact, they had little contact with military courts in general. It was not until the very last weeks of conflict that an execution directly affecting the Fifty-Fourth was ordered. And even then, the matter was not of widespread concern, for the condemned man had been with the regiment for only a few months. The regiment was organized in May of 1862 and recruits began to die or depart at that time. Serious acts of multiple desertions did not receive prompt attention in late 1863, when beneficial results might have been realized. In March through June, 22 men deserted from Company G, the Wilkes Guards. Most of these men returned to duty in October 1863. Recordwise, they suffered little or no punishment, or they returned under the shelter of an amnesty offer. Four of the deserters did not return, and the same number later deserted for a second time. Eight men of Company G willingly went into Federal units. One of the difficulties confronting those responsible for taking prompt action to curb desertion is illustrated by the experience of Company E. This company, the Highland Guards, was recruited in Iredell and Wilkes counties. A total of 116 men enrolled in the company. These men had 57 absences charged to their record; 4 made a second attempt to leave the company. Among the 57 absences, 17 were for men that enlisted and deserted on the same day, or within two days in 1862, never again to appear on company rolls. Many of these men had a name or alias of Irish origin. Court-martial records show only the names of 5 men of the Fifty-Fourth who were tried at a general court-martial level during the three years of the regiment's service. At least 1 other was court-martialed, but his record was not posted by the AIGO. Two men were acquitted, another was pardoned, and a fourth was freed after it was determined that he had returned under an amnesty. The sum total of the records for the regiment show that 2 men were actually punished by a court; 1 was sentenced to tramp about camp carrying a log, this following a five-months absence. The other was sentenced to be shot.

Fifty-Seventh Regiment

In the early days, companies of the regiment served as prison guards at the Salisbury site in Rowan County. At the time, the newly recruited Private James C. Zimmerman, Company D, related a very unusual incident to his wife. "One of our company got his fingr cut off one night in his sleep and he or nobody els knows what or who done it it never waked him when it was done."[7] Was it an instance of self-maiming or retribution for some affront with fear of more severe injury if the attacker was revealed? Toward year's end, Private Zimmerman was unhappy with the daily six hours of drill: "If we dont obey we are punished severley and have to do wors than a negro under a mean master."[8] The men alongside Private Zimmerman left a court record that is essentially confined to men of Company B recruited in Rowan County. Men from that company went before 8 courts, nearly half of the recorded regimental total of 17; one trial ended with an acquittal. Desertion difficulties in the company were intermittent throughout the year of 1864. Punishment ranged from two months' confinement while on bread and water rations for alternate two-week periods up to a year's confinement at hard labor. Though the absence record is sparse, there are indicators that the urge to desert was present throughout the regiment. A soldier in Company E from Catawba County told those at home that men were "a runing a way nearley every night."[9] Morale was not helped when a rumor was circulated that General T. J. Jackson did not want either the Fifty-Fourth or the Fifty-Seventh in his corps because there were too many old and too many sick men in the regiments.[10] Six weeks later, one soldier's thoughts turned to the end of war and a pleasurable and busy homecoming, "Not enough men to supply the young widows when the war ends as they will beat the young girl all hollows."[11]

Courts-Martial

Hoke Brigade

THOMAS L. RAY 6-K (January 17, 1863). Though twice the age of most of those he fought beside, Private Ray withstood the strain of army life from enrollment in June

1861 until reaching the field at Sharpsburg, MD, on September 15, 1862. During that engagement, he broke from his company and deserted while they were in the face of enemy, taking with him his rifle and accouterments valued at $41.15. Once absent, he remained a deserter until early January 1863. A court-martial was convened on January 17, when the prisoner heard the charges lodged against him. The court's preliminary ruling was a finding of guilt and a sentence of death, but the majority of the court then recommended mercy for the condemned. Mitigating circumstances were mentioned but not detailed. Consideration of mitigating factors was not a part of a court's purview, but courts sometimes ventured into that area, which was reserved for higher authority.[12] In any event, the circumstances in his case led to the release of Private Ray and his return to duty. His service record ends in December 1864. A second source indicates that he was present when the Sixth put down their weapons at Appomattox, VA.

PORTLAND BAILEY 6-D (January 19, 1863). Private Portland Bailey was the first of three brothers to enlist in the Sixth Regiment; he made his decision on May 28, 1861. In his first year of service, Private Bailey was hospitalized or sick nearly half of the time; the bouts of illness spread over the year. Details of his second year of service were brought forth when he stood before a court-martial held on January 19, 1863. It was charged that on May 31, 1862, while in the presence of the enemy at the engagement at Seven Pines, VA, Private Bailey deserted and remained absent until brought back some three months later. Within weeks of his forced return, Private Bailey again deserted on September 14, 1862, this time while near Boonsboro, MD, and remained absent until January 11, 1863. The hapless private was also charged with shamefully abandoning his company when he deserted at Seven Pines.[13] Officers sitting in judgment found Private Bailey guilty of all charges and specifications. General Lee approved the sentence of death, and the execution was ordered to take place ten days after the publication of GO #13, February 2, 1863, Department of Northern Virginia. Normally that would have set the execution for a day or two following February 12. For some reason, perhaps a delay in printing of the order, Private Bailey gained two weeks of hope. But on February 28, Private A. J. Spease of the Fifty-Seventh Regiment wrote his sister, "I must close my letter as we have to go to see an man shot belongin to the Sixth Regt this evening at one o clock."[14] On the same day, the Sergeant Major of the First Battalion of Sharp-shooters laconically noted, "There is a man to be shot this evening in our Brigade."[15] Private Bailey was shot to death on Saturday, February 28, 1863, at two o'clock in the afternoon. His brothers, Private Sidney J. Bailey, Company B, and Private William A. Bailey, Company D, were present with the Sixth on the day of execution. In a letter written to his sister the day after the execution, Private James Wilson Overcash, Company G, Sixth Regiment gave more details.

> I wrote to you sometime ago that their was a man to be shot in Co D he was shot yesterday at too oclock he did not seem to mind it much. I hope it will be the last one that I ever will have to see their was six blank loaded guns and six ball loads there was two men out of our company S Nance and A. J. Gullet Gullets [musket] did not fire it had a ball in there was five holes threw his breast.[16]

Privates Andrew J. Gullet and Shadrack Nance enlisted on the day after the man they were detailed to kill. Private Overcash and Private Gullet survived the war; Private Nance went to a grave in a Federal prison camp. Another member of the Sixth noted in his diary: "And the 27 was warm and cloudy and our Bass Ban got back from Richmond." "And the 28 which was the last day of February was coal and cloudy. And Mr. Portland Bailey of Company D. 6th Regiment N. C. Troops was shot to death at 2 oclock with musketry." "Now the dark days of winter is gon And the bright days of Spring is come."[17] Private Bailey's march to his grave was likely accompanied by a dirge played by the renowned band of the Sixth Regiment made up of musicians from the present Winston-Salem area. On March 1, Topographical Engineer Jedediah Hotchkiss wrote to his wife, "Yesterday a deserter was shot in the Brigade encamped quite near to us — he wept bitterly, wishing too his family — he fell dead, pierced by five balls — poor fellow — it seems hard, but in no other way can the discipline of the army be maintained."[18] Lieutenant Hotchkiss observed that Private Bailey "wept bitterly, wishing too his family," Private Overcash said the executed man "did not seem to mind it much," quite different impressions by a staff officer and a private. A week after the example made by the execution of Private Bailey, Doctor Shaffner observed:

> The crime of desertion has been severely punished of late, and frequently with death. Several have been shot during the past week, and some are held condemned. In Gen'l Hoke's Brigade, there was an execution of this kind last Saturday. By the same mail with this letter I send several pamphlets to your Father's address, containing proceedings of several Court Martials recently convened in this Department. The sentences generally have been very mild.[19]

Lieutenant Hotchkiss followed his impressions of the execution of Private Bailey with a broader view of discipline.

> One fellow was shot who had been contented in the army until his wife wrote to him with constant complaints until the poor fellow could stand it no longer and as he could get no furlough he deserted & went home, was caught and suffered the penalty of death. The work of discipline is going on — a good many have been shot, some whipped, some drummed out of camp and then put to labor with a ball and chain, some branded on the backsides with letters D. or C. for desertion or cowardice, &c&c. When will wars cease and the necessity no longer exist for such brutal punishments, though necessary. One man escaped, though fired on by three sentinels, the day before he was to be shot.[20]

The writer does not identify the escapee or his unit. Several condemned North Carolinians placed greater confidence on the elusive dash than on the appeal process. Still, the threat of execution loomed large, "They have got us poor soldiers so we have to fight or took up and shot if we desert we have to be shot so we had better fight and risk being killed than to be shot like dogs."[21]

The Twenty-First Regiment was sent to the area around Forsyth County to arrest deserters. Private Zimmerman cautiously mentioned to his wife, "I thought I would wait and see if the diserters was in any danger you wrote to me they wer in no danger but if the 21st goes through and do not arest them I think there is some chance to stay if one gets there."[22]

SAMUEL STONE 57-K (January 1863). Very little is known of either the civil or military activity of Private Stone. Documents show that he entered Confederate service on July 8, 1862, and departed same on November 22, while "in the face of the enemy at Fredericksburg." By December he was in custody and in confinement awaiting trial, which began in January 1863. The court's decision was that he was guilty of the charged crime, and his execution was ordered by the General Commanding to take place ten days after publication of the sentence in GO #19, February 14, Army of Northern Virginia.[23] Clemency for the prisoner was not forthcoming and further orders to proceed with the execution were issued in SO #45, March 3, 1863, Headquarters Early's Division, which stated that the execution of Private Stone should take place on March 16, at 2PM, in the vicinity of the camp. The execution was carried out as directed. There was only one recorded desertion from Private Stone's company in the year after his execution. The death of Private Stone did not elicit much comment. A fellow Confederate simply noted, "Another soldier Private Stone of Company F 57 NC was executed on March 16."[24] One other took the time to make a brief diary entry, "The 16 day of March was cloudy and coal And Mr. Stons in Co F 57 N.C. Regiment was shot to death with musketry."[25] Casual reference to the executions of Privates Bailey and Stone and the ongoing absences was made to Governor Vance, "Two men shot month or two ago ... many others left since."[26]

Private Joseph Overcash suggests that men were weary of war: "All getting very tired of it their is a great many running away their was not any of our regiment goin only out of company G They are from the mountains....There is a man to be shot tomorrow in the 49 Va."[27] Company G, Fifty-Fourth Regiment; the Wilkes Guards, was experiencing a serious outbreak of desertion at the time. On May 25, the Captain of the company wrote that 17 of his men had recently deserted. A member of the brigade observed on May 19, 1863, that 19 men had left the Fifty-Fourth two days earlier, and 7 had fled from the Fifty-Seventh the night before. Arrest and confinement was looked on as a safe haven by some deserters. "If I keep my health I can stand my punishment very well and while I am there I will keep out of danger of the musket balls and grape and shell."[28]

The mother of a soldier in the Sixth Regiment from Alamance County asked for the governor's help in returning her son to the army. She said that she "had rather seen her son dead than to have forsaken the flag of his country."[29] The young lad was only seventeen; he had come home with other deserters and was the only one that wanted to go back. A year later, through an intermediary, the mother of a member of the Fifty-Seventh interceded for her son. His absence had extended over twenty months and the Captain of her son's company said that if he ever returned he would have him shot. The mother said that her son was tired of living in the bushes and now wanted to return if he would be safe from the penalty of death.[30] There is no record that Governor Vance took any action or that her son returned to duty.

An earlier appeal written by Sarah Cox for her husband, William, enrolled in Company D, Fifty-Seventh Regiment, was successful.[31] Private Cox avoided a court-martial after an absence of at least six months. In September 1864, a sister of brothers that enrolled in the Sixth Regiment and then deserted wrote to Governor Vance, "I have two brothers who have bin influenced to disgrace themselfs by deserting their comrades and post of duty."[32] Though she was in humble circumstance, she said she would try to influence her brothers to return. In mid-1863 the beleaguered governor was addressed from Madison County: "Those wicked trash you have sent back to take deserters ... the trash at liberty to go where they please to do what they please ... they must stop or the war will stop."[33] Men from a company of the Twenty-First Regiment were accused of plundering the homes of alleged deserters. The writer then observed that seizing a horse until the deserter presented himself was very effective in bringing them in, thus placing a relative value on horse and man in mid-century North Carolina.[34] Rather than horses, another unit seized fathers or wives until the deserter surrendered.[35] Private Cyrus West, Company C, Fifty-Seventh, a man of "low instincts" and suspected of many offenses, was shot by the Home Guard in Rowan County.[36]

A young soldier was apparently murdered; his killer, if known, was not punished. The boy's mother, when told that her son was accidentally shot, asked the editor of a local paper to set the record straight. "Dear Sir It is with an aking hart i rite those lines to you the awful news of the death of my dear son Ellmore he was shot 2 weeks ago with out any couse at all as you have here to fore treated boath me and him with respect I ask one favor of you that is to have his death published in the patriot rite such a peace as you think he is worthy of he was 20 years of age the 20 of July."[37] A few weeks later an article in the *Greensboro Patriot* noted that Private Elmore Watson Dobson was killed by "a reckless profligate midnight assassin." Private Dobson's service record indicates that his death was accidental.[38]

There was an execution affecting the Fifty-Fourth in 1863, but it was allegedly ordered by Federal authorities and not by Confederates. The regiment was assigned to General Early's command when the incident took place.

> The Yankees are meaner and commit more depredations every time they come in the Valley ... they robbed the citizens of everything they could get hands on and then burned <u>mills</u> and <u>grainaries</u>; they also took up, a man, who was left behind as a nurse (dressed in a Confederate uniform too) tried him & hung him as a spy, I understand Gen'l Early was very mad when he found it out and will I think no doubt retaliate, he is certainly the wrong man to fool with and they will find him so, the man belonged to the 54th N.C. Regt.[39]

In his memoirs, General Early said that he seriously considered executing captured Federal officers in retaliation, but was persuaded that further Federal retaliation on his captured officers would follow.[40]

At least one man in the Twenty-First desperately wanted to get out of the army. He wrote to his former Captain, who was also his cousin. "I am broken down and kneed some rest I will be very much obliged to you to get me off please try and get me off as quick as you can please write to me how you suckseeded I hop you will suckseed in getting me off as I have been in your company and come out with it I hope you will get me off."[41] The plea was sent off in May 1863; the writer was wounded and captured at Gettysburg in July. As General Lee made his way into Pennsylvania on June 29, 1863, Private Marcus Hefner wrote there were 300 deserters in the Division Guardhouse where he was confined, 2000 more at Castle Thunder in Richmond, and 3000 in the Richmond area.[42] Very likely these numbers are inflated, but even reduced by half they represent a serious loss of fighting men at a decisive time.

A trend of desertion from an "unholy" war was noted in the spring of 1863, "for our men are deserting more or less every day, and our leading men are having them shot to death with muskets as fast as they get them back again, 6 men deserted the 6th Regt in one night last week and 11 from the 54th Regt al of our Brigade and they carried their guns with them and they say they intend to fight their way through."[43] The writer concluded that these deadly determined deserters were moved to act because furloughs were no longer given and many men had not been home since enrolling.

THOMAS H. TIPPETT 21-L (April 7, 1864). Private Tippett was conscripted after the law was extended to include men thirty-five- to forty-five-years-old. Three months later, Private Tippett deserted on January 29, 1864, while near Kinston, NC. He was not able to travel very far, for two days later he was returned under guard and put in the guardhouse. The desire to leave the army did not lessen; the next week, he eluded his guard and took to the woods to remain absent until March 29, when he was again brought back under guard. After trial, GO #53, August 8, 1864, Army of Northern Virginia, was printed; it read that Private Tippett was to be shot, but the approving officer directed that the execution be suspended until the pleasure of the President was known. In SO #256, October 27, 1864, AIGO, it was made known that the President had remitted the death sentence and returned Private Tippett to duty. If the record dates are accurate, Private Tippett never knew of his death sentence and the subsequent remittance. Records indicate that he died of wounds received at Spotsylvania, VA, in July 1864, apparently after his court-martial but before publication of the sentence. Prisoners were often given the opportunity to regain their place in the ranks by volunteering to participate in an engagement. Others were ordered to take part in all engagements, at the point of a bayonet, if need be, while undergoing their punishment.[44]

LEONARD HICKS 21-F (April 12, 1864). Private Hicks was conscripted into Company F, Twenty-First Regiment, and there he stayed for at least a year. His first attempt to leave the regiment began at Orange Court House, VA, on August 10, 1863, and ended when he had second thoughts and voluntarily returned on October 18. Within a month he had yet another change of heart and again decided to leave his company. This time he did not reconsider his decision, and four months later he was forcibly returned under guard. After his appearance at a court-martial on April 12, 1864, Private Hicks learned that he had been found guilty of desertion and that he was to be shot to death. The reviewing officer, General Lee, did suspend the execution of sentence until the President could review the case. The decision was pending for six months. After what must have seemed to be an interminable delay for a soldier awaiting execution, a Special Order announced that the death sentence was remitted. Private Hicks then absented himself or was already absent on a medical furlough. He died of disease at home in May 1865. Private Peter Hicks served in the same company and was wounded and captured in July 1863. An experienced Sergeant offered his experience with conscripts in April 1864. He wanted "to see how the conscripts would act ... most of them turned right white ... some wanted a few days leave of absence to go home to join the church, but it was too late to pray when the devil was at hand for all had to go out with us in line of battle."[45]

Godwin-Lewis Brigade

"Poor unfortunate wretches."[46]

Brigadier Archibald Campbell Godwin, a Virginian, was killed by a shell burst six weeks after taking brigade leadership. Command of the brigade was returned to a North Carolinian with the appointment of Brigadier William Gaston Lewis in June 1864. The force available to him was about equal that of one full-strength regiment.

NATHAN YANCY CRUTCHFIELD 21-G (January 2, 1865). Private Crutchfield was likely conscripted into the Twenty-First, or he was a quickly disillusioned volunteer, for he managed just fourteen days in camp before deserting on November 28, 1863. Service records indicate that he was back on duty four months later, but no detail is given. Now better able to accommodate himself to army routine, he remained in camp for eleven weeks before departing once again. For this absence he was ordered to carry a seventy-five-pound log for one hour, followed by two hours confined in the guardhouse; this sequence repeated night and day for one month. In addition, half of his head was shaved and he was denied all indulgences "allowed good soldiers." The guardhouse was not to be a protective shelter; it was ordered that the prisoner be taken into every action. Not too surprisingly, a short time after this weighty experience, Private Crutchfield began a third attempt to leave his regiment. This foray ended with a court-martial convened on January 2, 1865. The charges were theft and desertion. Not guilty was the decision on the theft count, but the desertion charge was sustained, and Private Crutchfield was condemned to death, the execution to take place seven days after publication of GO #1, January 17, 1865, Army of Northern Virginia.[47] At that point his service record ends. The company clerk was instructed to remove his name from the rolls of the company.[48] No explanation is provided. Men were often removed from company rolls, though this was usually due to some form of legal discharge, not while under sentence of death. All placed on the balance, it is likely that Private Crutchfield was executed.

With court-martial proceedings underway in January 1865, a soldier in the Twenty-First expressed his view of the current state of affairs:

> we are whiped un less we will git rein forsment Dear Father I can in form you that I think that we ar about gone up I dont now what will become of uss for our men is all whiped th cant stand to fight any more th wod betr make peas on som tarms or en uther befor spring for the army is boun to to up for if th will qit feeding me I want stay hear that well mak me desert qickery then anything else you can cep this to you selves if you pleas.[49]

This soldier was driven to consider desertion not from fear of being maimed or killed, or for lessened attachment to land and cause, but because he was hungry.

MILAS SHERRILL 6-A (January 6, 1865). Stints of commissary service and hospitalization interspersed with short periods of duty mark Private Sherrill's first two years in the army. On November 10, 1864, while in the area of Woodstock, VA, Private Sherrill deserted the Sixth and was able to avoid detection for five weeks. He was then brought back under guard. When court-martialed on January 6, 1865, he was found guilty and concurrence on a death sentence was reached. General Lee agreed with the decision. There the record for Private Sherrill comes to an end. Considering that he was brought back to the army under guard and that General Lee approved his sentence, it is most probable that Private Sherrill was shot alongside Private Crutchfield.

HARRIS BRITTAIN HAWKINS 6-A (January 7, 1865). Private Hawkins was an older and likely very unwilling conscript when he was ordered to the Confederate army. He deserted in the first summer after his enrollment, at about the time of his hospitalization in August 1864. After further consideration, he voluntarily went back to his regiment on October 1. Still not content with his situation, Private Hawkins again deserted just ten days after returning. Arrest and return under guard on December 16 then followed. A reasoned defense was presented to the court on January 7, 1864. Ten days later Private Hawkins learned that he was guilty as charged and that he would be shot. However, his pleading was not completely in vain, for the court did note mitigating circumstances and the good character of the accused, while unanimously recommending that the sentence be suspended until the President reviewed the case. General Lee recommended three years in prison at hard labor with a ball and chain attached to his leg as an appropriate punishment. The next month, General Order #2 released Private Hawkins and many other convicted deserters. He was captured at Petersburg, VA, in late March and released from Federal prison in June 1865.

KENNETH HENDERSON WARLICK 6-E (January 9, 1865). Unlike many of the other men in the brigade who were court-martialed in early 1865, Private Warlick was an eager volunteer. He went into Confederate service in 1861 and completed a year of duty without notable incident. This changed when he commenced a series of hospitalizations, desertions and arrests that would continue for the next two years. Evidence of this activity was placed on record before a Military Court on January 9, 1865. Past violations of the Articles of War dealing with desertion and misbehavior before the enemy were detailed. On May 2, 1863, he abandoned his company until May 7, this act taking place near Fredericksburg, VA. After returning to camp, he was there two weeks before leaving, his unit still in the vicinity of Fredericksburg. On this occasion, he managed to avoid arrest until December 1. Though obviously not firmly committed to his place in the ranks, Private Warlick lingered with his company until April 1, 1864, when he again left his command, this time while near Kinston, NC. Nearly six months after his departure, he was returned under guard to his brigade then at Staunton, VA, this on October 16. Two days later he abandoned his company while in the face of the enemy at Bell's Grove, VA, and again remained absent until brought back under guard on December 18, 1864. The court heard all of the testimony of his many comings and goings and in a decision announced in GO #1, January 17, 1865, Army of Northern Virginia, Private Warlick was guilty of the multiple charges and sentenced to be shot. The sentence was approved and direction given that it should be carried into effect seven days after publication of the order.

Surprisingly, considering the many escapades of the private, General Cooper notified General Lee to suspend the execution of sentence for ten days, and to acknowledge that he had received the order; General Cooper apparently did not want any mistakes in this case.[50] His caution may have heightened when Congressman B. S. Gaither of North Carolina made an inquiry to the President concerning Private Warlick.[51] Recordwise nothing changed as a result of the query, for on February 22, 1865, it was noted that the time of suspension of sentence had duly elapsed, and with no appeal or further evidence presented, the suspending order was filed. Presumably, at that point, orders were reissued to proceed with the execution, but no verification has been found. Certainly on his record there was little ground for clemency. Still, the futility and overhanging resignation present during the final months of war offered little reason for staging an execution before the pitifully small remnants of a once powerful brigade. One more useless death would have little effect on a small assembly of discouraged soldiers, and would only emphasize how few their number. The death sentences for 4 of the 5 men just discussed, Privates Crutchfield, Sherrill, Hawkins and Warlick were published in GO #1, January 17, 1865, Army of Northern Virginia. Private Hawkins received a favorable recommendation by the court and his sentence was commuted by the President.

Just days before the executions of the condemned soldiers, 5 men assigned to Company A, Fifty-Seventh Regiment, broke their guard and deserted to the enemy. They were in arrest for engaging in a brawl, or a near mutiny, and were not willing to chance a trial. The act of these men from Company A did little to increase the likelihood of leniency for men then under sentence of death. In a letter home on January 30, 1865, a private in the Twenty-First wrote, "I can inform you that thr was too men shot out of our brigade last friday [January 27, 1865] for desurtion I have nothing strang to write at this time."[52] But which of the men were shot? On face value the letter suggests that Privates Sherrill and Warlick of the Sixth were executed. The assumption is made on the basis that the writer would have made more specific mention if Private Crutchfield of his regiment was shot. On the other hand, in the case of Private Warlick, General Cooper had ordered a ten day suspension of the execution; this order was dated February 2, some five days after reference to the two executions. The earliest possible day of Private Warlick's execution was sometime after February 12, and well after the executions that took place on January 27. The third man awaiting execution, Private Sherrill, had a single desertion on his record, that for just over a month's absence. The other men had much more extensive desertion records, but the execution of Private Sherrill was approved by General Lee and no record of appeal or delay in execution of sentence has been found. Unfortunately, none of the men in question are found in 1860, 1870, or 1880 census records. On balance of the available information, it is likely that Privates Crutchfield and Sherrill were the men that were executed on January 27, 1865, and that the execution of Private Warlick followed at a later date.

WILLIAM L. DAVIS 21-A (January 16, 1865). Private Davis was a conscript when he went off to the army on January 27, 1864. Just how he avoided conscription for nearly two years is not known, but subsequent events offer a possible explanation. After six months of duty, Private Davis deserted and remained a deserter until early 1865. He was in confinement by January 16, when he appeared before a court-martial. Soon thereafter it was announced that the court had found him guilty and that he would be shot. Before the execution could be arranged, General Order #2, offering amnesty to all deserters not previously pardoned for a similar crime, was issued. Upon inquiry by Representative James Thomas Leach, Wake County, General Cooper determined that the order also applied to those convicted of one desertion and were then receiving, or awaiting punishment.[53] As a result of this decision, General Lee was directed to suspend the execution of Private Davis, who survived the war. The decision by the Adjutant General immediately raised the question if the same ruling would be made in other cases; the response was affirmative by General Cooper, and as will be seen, this would affect the lives of other soldiers from North Carolina.[54] The inquiry by Representative Leach may suggest that he was instrumental in obtaining an exemption from conscription for William Davis at an earlier time. The Congressman was a strong supporter of the right of state authorities to determine which of their citizens would be exempt from conscription.

GASTON B. WOLF 6-K (January 17, 1865); and JOHN W. WOLF 6-K (January 17, 1865). The younger of the Wolf brothers, Private Gaston Wolf, was the first to volunteer for duty in the Sixth, this on June 20, 1861. Eight months later on March 1, 1862, the older brother, Private John Wolf was accepted into the same company. The younger brother was not there to ease the transition to army life. He was absent in arrest as a result of an unauthorized absence that began at Manassas, VA, within a month of his volunteering. Once the younger man was released from detention, the reunited brothers deserted together on May 3, 1862. They remained in hiding until February of the next year. At that time, they took advantage of an amnesty proclamation made by Governor Vance.

> State of North Carolina — Executive Department, Raleigh, Feby 6th, 1863. Col. I. E. Avery, Comdg 6th N.C.T. Dr Sir, The bearers here of, John A. Wolfe and Gaston Wolfe, privates in Co K. in your regiment, who have been absent without leave, go on to report to you under my proclamation promising them a pardon except forfeiture of pay &c. I should be glad to hear if they report promptly, Very Respectfully, Yr. obt Svt Z. B. Vance.[55]

Having avoided the more serious punishment that might be expected after an absence of eight months, the brothers returned to duty. This time they served six months before they once again deserted, together, while on a march from Culpeper to Winchester, VA, on June 11, 1863. As on their earlier absence, they were able to avoid arrest for a prolonged period. They were not brought to trial until January 1865, when they were found guilty of their second desertion and sentenced to be shot. General Lee approved the death sentences on February 3, 1865. No further information on the whereabouts of the brothers during the last two months of the war has been found. Gaston survived the war. What happened to John is less clear. An entry in his service record states that he died in a Confederate hospital on December 3, 1864. However this record is headed with the name W. A. Wolfe, and is dated a full month before John went before a court-martial in January 1864. It is not likely that John was executed; Gaston had a more extensive desertion record than John, and he is known to have made it through the war. An equally interesting question might be posed as to why John volunteered at a time when his brother was in arrest as a deserter in the shadow of execution. The conscription laws had not yet been enacted, so John was not forced to enroll. Perhaps he went to help a troubled brother adapt to the army, or perhaps he went to bring him home, for neither had a strong attachment to the military.

WILLIAM D. WATTS 6-E (January 17, 1865). Some thirteen months after voluntarily joining the Sixth on March 17, 1862, Private Watts set out on his first attempt at desertion, this on April 11, 1863. For seven months he was successful but on November 10, 1863, he was confined, awaiting return to his regiment. No record of punishment has been found. About a year after the trip back, he began a second desertion that led to a court-martial. On February 3, 1865, General Lee approved his execution. With no prior conviction for desertion on his record, Private Watts would have been eligible for release under General Order #2. Included in the service packet of Private Watts is an entry to the effect that a Private A. W. Watts was paroled at Appomattox on April 9, 1865. No soldier named Watts with those initials is found in the Sixth Regiment. It is not clear if Private Watts was executed, returned to duty or simply disappeared in the confusion of the last months of war.

FRANCIS W. FORD 21-A (January 20, 1865). Corporal Ford served the Confederacy without notable incident for forty-one months; then he deserted on October 4, 1864. This decision came just a month after an unexplained gunshot wound led to his hospitalization. The wound may have been legitimate in battle, or accidental, or it may have been self-inflicted. Wounds on fingers or toes have a correlation for soldiers with desertion records. References to an unusual number of minor wounds supports the observation that some soldiers would use the cover of a skirmish to shoot off a finger or a toe to avoid further service. As early as the summer of 1862 a soldier observed, "Thare is the most hands & fingers Shot off I ever saw."[56] Some form of bodily mutilation has been a resort to avoid conflict since unwilling men have been forced to fight.[57] Whatever the case for Corporal Ford, he deserted just three days after leaving the hospital. A month later, the Corporal was reduced in rank, court-martialed on January 20, 1865, and given a death sentence. General Lee approved the sentence of the court but execution of sentence was suspended awaiting the decision of the President. General Order # 2 was deemed applicable for Private Ford; restoration to duty and parole in April 1865 then followed.

JOHN A. STYERS 21-A (January 20, 1865). Private Styers deserted on October 1, 1864, after more than forty months of duty; he signed up in May 1861. Experience in positions of responsibility, first as a company Sergeant and later as a Brigade Wagon Master, give evidence that the young man knew his own mind and made a deliberate decision on desertion. Full details of his desertion and subsequent court-martial are lacking, but it is known that by February 2, 1865, a court had issued a death sentence for Private Styers. General Lee approved the sentence but then went on to recommend clemency for the condemned.[58] On February 19, the President notified General Lee to suspend the execution.

Later notification came that General Order # 2 was effective in the case of Private Styers, and he was released.[59] Capture by the enemy ended his service in April and oath taking followed in June 1865.

FELIX POOL 6-E (January 25, 1865). Private Pool went on the rolls of the Sixth on December 1, 1864. Two months later, he was taken before a court charged with desertion. Contrast his record of two months' service with that of men of the brigade tried just a few days earlier. These men had served through three grueling years before yielding to the urge to flee and most certainly would have been executed save for an amnesty order. The court, sitting on January 25, 1865, initially found that Private Pool was guilty of the charge and stipulated a death sentence. After rendering their verdict, they were directed by the reviewing officer to reconsider their decision. Following due reconsideration, the court then reduced the sentence to one year of hard labor.[60] Reconsideration of the sentence did not allow introduction of new evidence, but simply allowed further consideration of the record established at the initial trial.[61] Two months after the courts' second deliberation, Private Pool was captured and survived the war.

JAMES P. PARTIN 6-G (January 25, 1865). Private Partin was present with the Sixth for the month of December 1864, an apparent conscript. For some unknown trespass on the Articles of War, most likely desertion, he was condemned to death and the sentence was confirmed on February 4. There is no record that he was released by General Order #2, but that may have been the case. He was captured by the enemy in March and released by them in May 1865.

Men of Private Partin's company may have been influenced in their desertion decisions by letters from Rowan County that voiced discontent with the war as early as the summer of 1863. One reads, "If this war dont soon stop there will be the worst times that ever was the soldiers are deserting as fast as they can." Then the writer mentions a rumor that 60 men had deserted the Sixth Regiment in one night."[62] A soldier wrote home urging the killing of Union men: "He had better thought that then to have wrote it for he knows that his family is dependant on the neighbors."[63] Another writer saw an equally threatening division between the "rich" and the "poor." "But there is to much speculation and to many poor fighting for the rich and the rich trying to get all the poor has after they do all the hard fighting for them just look at the rich bigbugs whare they are and look where the poor man is that is enough to change the tide of battle."[64]

JEFFERSON N. NICHOLS 57-K (January 1865). After joining his regiment in April 1864 at Kinston, NC, Private Nichols served without recorded incident until the fall of the year when he was in arrest. By February 2, of the next year, he had learned that the court that weighed the charges against him had handed down a death sentence, but thankfully they then recommended clemency and General Lee had agreed. Acting very quickly, the AIGO was able to issue SO #47, February 19, 1865, suspending the execution, and Private Nichols was soon released under provisions of General Order #2. Private Nichols was paroled at Appomattox on April 9, validating the confidence shown by the court, and by General Lee.

WILLIAM EARNHART 57-F (February 2, 1865). Private Earnhart enrolled in Company C, Thirty-Third Regiment, and served there for nineteen months before transferring to the Fifty-Seventh in an exchange with Private James C. Corzine. In the September–October period of 1863, Private Earnhart was in arrest and in confinement. He was released or otherwise gained his freedom, to desert while his unit was in the area of Woodstock, VA. A full year elapsed before he was apprehended and taken before a military court on February 2, 1865. For this second violation he was given a death sentence, but was spared by General Order #2, only to be captured by the enemy on March 28.

EMANUEL M. OVERMAN 6-G (February 4, 1865). The year of service of Private Overman is not well detailed in his service record. From other sources it is possible to gather a glimpse of his activity beginning with his entry into the army in May of 1864. A period of hospitalization in December was followed by an attempted desertion. Not much over a month later, he was before a court, on February 4, 1865, and sentenced to be shot. General Lee approved the sentence but was later informed that Private Overman had been among those released by authority of General Order #2. He survived the war.

While these men who had been tried and convicted were in the guardhouse awaiting word on what would happen to them, they were visited by Chaplain John Paris. On Thursday, February 16, 1865, he entered into his diary, "Clear weather. Roads severely muddy. This morning I visited the guard house and held religious services. Returned to it again in the afternoon and distributed religious tracts. Here are about fifty prisoners; and seven of them under sentence of death for desertion. How sad the spectacle." The next day he returned. "Cloudy and rainy weather. I visited the Division Guard House and preached to the prisoners. Poor unfortunate wretches! Seven of them are condemned to be shot on Tuesday 22nd Inst." On February 18, "Beautiful weather I visited the prisoners and held religious services for them." The day before the scheduled executions, "News came that all the prisoners in the Guard House have been pardoned. This is glad news to them indeed."[65]

WILLIAM JONES 54-I (February 15, 1865). Very little information is available on Private Jones and his encounter with military justice. Sometime between his enlistment on the last day of October 1864 and February 15, 1865, the private violated at least one of the Articles of War. He was tried, found guilty, and told that he would be shot. While he awaited execution, General Order #2 was published, and Private Jones was released under its provisions. His Confederate service ended with his capture by the enemy in April.

WILLIAM H. STEWART 21-M (February 28, 1865). There were ten men with the Stewart family name enrolled at various times in the Twenty-First. The commitments of some were measured in days; others were steadfast from beginning to near the end. One of the latter, Private William Stewart, a volunteer from Guilford County in June of 1861, was court-martialed for misbehavior before the enemy. For this violation he went to trial on February 28, 1865. A death sentence was approved by General Lee on March 11, but within two weeks the President remitted the sentence and returned the private to duty. He was captured by the enemy on April 6, 1865, and took the oath in late June.

Summary

When the remnants of the Hoke-Godwin-Lewis Brigade were assembled at Appomattox, there were 447 officers and men present. Over two-thirds were from the Sixth and Twenty-First. These regiments bore much of the Brigade's torment. A sampling reveals that on average they enrolled 183 men per company, of these; 23 absented themselves, 45 died, and 18 were killed in battle or died of wounds.[66] The Fifty-Fourth and the Fifty-seventy enrolled an average of 121 men; 36 left of their own will, 26 died and 7 were dead in combat.[67] In brief, the Sixth and the Twenty-First had one-third fewer absences and twice as many deaths as their brigade brothers.

In the brigade, 22 men were sentenced to death and 5 were executed in slightly over two years of war, commencing in January 1863 and ending in February 1865. Six death sentences were written in 1863 and 1864, and 16 in a brief two months in 1865. For the 16 condemned, 8 were in the fray for three years or more, and 8 averaged less than six months of service. At least 7 of the 22 condemned left a wife at home when they went to the army. Volunteers, 12, were in their mid-twenties, the 10 conscripts were four years older. Men began to leave the brigade in numbers of concern in mid-1862; these departures continued to the end. A sample of 9 companies with a high number of absences, 41 per company, contrasts with 6 companies with far fewer absentees, 13 per company. The high absence companies had 41 deaths, 10 were battle related.[68] The low absence companies suffered 44 deaths, 17 battle related.[69]

An estimated 6,100 men enrolled in the brigade during the war, the Sixth having the most men pass through, on average nearly 200 for each company. The ranking officer in command on the day of surrender wore the three bars of a Captain on his collar. Officers and men were lost in many desperate encounters. Untrained replacements arrived; some died, some were killed, and some fled, again reducing the depleted companies. Amnesty was offered to absent and imprisoned deserters in a desperate effort to add a few men to the ranks. The cycle of combating desertion by execution, followed by the leniency of amnesty, went on to the very end.

9

Second Corps, Early Division, Garland-Iverson-Johnston-Toon Brigade

"There was 4 men runn the gantlett"[1]

Four regiments recruited in North Carolina, the Fifth, Twelfth, Twentieth and Twenty-Third Regiments, were first under the command of an officer who was not a North Carolinian, Brigadier Samuel Garland Jr. of Virginia. No soldier was given a death sentence while in his care. Brigadier Alfred Iverson Jr. was in command for virtually all of the time of court activity that resulted in death sentences for men of the brigade. But the uniqueness of brigade history is that so few men were threatened, and that none were in a doleful procession to the stake or to the gallows.

Fifth Regiment

One infantryman in the Fifth Regiment faced death by execution. The Home Guard killed 2, without benefit of trial. Another soldier was charged with murder of a man serving in the Home Guard, and another was killed while on guard duty. "Accidental discharge of muskets took 3 lives in Company A. A distraught man took his own life. The regiment experienced a limited number of absences; a sampling of 5 companies indicates an average of 19 per company. These same companies had an average enrollment of 168 men, and 69 were dead when the fighting stopped. Of the 69, 20 were killed in battle or died of wounds. For Company B, death came most often at the Peninsula in 1862 and at Gettysburg in July 1863; these heavy casualties did not bring on an increase in absences. The Fifth Regiment maintained a fine absence record throughout the war.

Co B	1861	1862		1863		1864		1865		no date
Absent		1	6	2	1	2	6			
Dead	8	24	19	6	17	3	5	2	1	

Regarding courts, the regiment divides into two groups. The smaller, Companies B, I and K organized in Gates, Caswell and Rowan counties, had no listed courts. The larger group of 7 companies each had at least 1 court of an enrolled man. Company G, formed in Wilson County, was the only company with as many as 4 men to go before military courts. For the regiment, 7 of the 21 men who went to trial eventually ended their Confederate service as deserters. Four at trial were acquitted. One of the 7 deserters was the first soldier in the brigade to be given a death sentence.

Twelfth Regiment

Much like the Fifth, the Twelfth lost more men to accidental death and murder, 7 in all, than were threatened by military execution. Unlike the even distribution of military courts found for the Fifth, the Twelfth had the bulk of their court exposure centered in 2 companies, Company A, the Catawba Rifles, and Company H, the Nash Boys. Their trials, primarily for desertion attempts, were held in December 1863 and accounted for 13 of the 18 courts charged to the regiment. Three trials ended in acquittals. For the regiment as a whole, 6 companies had no listed courts, and 2 companies had 2 or fewer.

A lieutenant in Company F of the Twelfth, one of the companies with no recorded courts, reminisced many years later that the Confederate soldier was never disciplined to army life, and consequently never developed the confidence that comes with being part of a trained, well disciplined unit. Men did not want to drill in the many intricate movements required of companies, regiments and brigades that would build a foundation of confidence and send them shoulder to shoulder to victory. It was the opinion of the writer that officers were not willing to enforce strict discipline because of the possible political effect it might have on their careers after the war. There were many men of the "better class" in his regiment and they freely mingled with their officers, which made the maintenance of discipline much more difficult.[2] The reflections of this mature and thoughtful man, though made many years after the events, was that passage of the conscription acts and the defeat at Sharpsburg, MD, both occurring in 1862, led directly to the inevitable surrender of the cause. In his view, this could be in part attributed to the loss of dedication by the "better class" after enactment of the conscription laws brought less committed men into their ranks. In the same vein, "The truth is we have very few field or company officers worth anything ... impossible to preserve discipline without good field and company officers."[3] A Chaplain who wanted to be a soldier in the army of God was thought to be "a d — d long way from headquarters."[4]

Twentieth Regiment

With a total of 46 attributed courts-martial, the Twentieth accounted for nearly half of those charged to the entire brigade. Company B, the Cabarrus Black Boys, was the only company in the regiment with an unblemished court-martial record. Company G, the Brunswick Guards, with 9 recorded courts; Company F, the Holmes Riflemen of Sampson County, at 7 courts; and Company D, the Columbus Guards, with 6 trials led the other companies. Eight trials ended with acquittal.

Twenty-Third Regiment

As found for other regiments in the brigade, the Twenty-Third had several companies with no recorded courts-martial; these were Company A, the Anson Ellis Rifles; Company B, the Hog Hill Guards; and Company K, the Beatties Ford Rifleman; the last two were from Lincoln County. The 14 courts that the regiment did experience were distributed over the other 7 companies, Company F, the Catawba Guards; Company I, the Granville Stars;

and Company C, the Montgomery Volunteers, were charged with 8 of the 14; 1 man at trial was acquitted.

Courts-Martial

Garland-Iverson Brigade

MICHAEL L. KENNEY 5-E (January 1863). Private Kenney enlisted in Company E on June 8, 1861, as the Fifth was being organized. Within the year he was wounded at Williamsburg, VA, and in the summer of the next year deserted. Private Kenney was court-martialed in January 1863 and was given a death sentence. The sentence was not sustained on review; however, the reviewing General found that there was an "informality in proceedings," causing the verdict to be set aside and the prisoner to be released. Private Kenney returned to his company and served until Saturday, February 25, 1865, when he again deserted. Not willing to risk another court-martial that might be more formal in their proceedings, he went directly to the enemy. Within a week of taking that step, he took the oath and departed for the Indian Territory in the West.

A month after Private Kenney ended his Confederate service, Private L. Torrence of the Twenty-Third described incidents affecting men that served with him. "A man by the name of [Marcus] Benfield in Co F left on Thursday night. I suppose he went to the yanks. There was 4 men runn the gantlett in the 5th N. C. Regt the Saturday before L. C. Torrence started Home for going Home with out lief one of them died the 8th day after he was whiped the Dr said it was the whipping killed him. 3 of the conscripts of our Company are in the gard house for going home with [out] lief I do not know what will be done with them yet there is [blurred] of this Regt in the guard house for the same crime."[5] It is not clear if the whipping was during the gauntlet run, or if the flogging, was inflicted after the man had suffered the pain of the gauntlet. The semi-official gauntlet may have been as effective as the more deliberate court-martial in limiting desertion, judged by the record of the regiment. A soldier in the Twenty-Third North Carolina wrote of a deadly flogging. "Well Pappy those men that you saw whiped heare they are dead and the Col are under arrest and Genel R. E. Lee says if any other man haves any more men whiped in that manner he will have him shot."[6] Just weeks later, flogging was removed as legal military punishment by the Confederate Congress, and this decision was made known to the armies on April 16, 1863. While some men were running the gauntlet, the mother of the young soldier who wrote of the whipping encouraged her son to keep writing: "We can read your letter tolerable well. You must keep writing for practice."[7]

Support for the opinion on the harmful effect of conscription and substitution is found in the records of 7 men that were accepted into Company B of the Twelfth as substitutes late in 1862. Five of these men deserted within days of joining the company. Two, Privates John Murphy and James Riley, purportedly residents of Virginia, enrolled and then deserted on the same day. One was arrested and brought to trial.

JAMES RILEY 12-B (January 1863). Private Riley went into Company B, Twelfth Regiment, on December 7, 1862, as a substitute. He departed the company that same day while camped near Rappahannock Academy, VA. A month later, on January 12, 1863, Private Riley was arrested by three men from his regiment and taken back to the army. He was promptly tried for desertion. The decision of the court was published in General Order #6, January 23, 1863, 2nd Corps, Army of Northern Virginia, and stated that Private Riley was found guilty, and that he would be executed on January 31. Not one to idle away his last week in the hope of more favorable developments, Private Riley, if that be his name, took matters in hand, escaped his guard and fled for other parts.

A corporal and 11 privates left 3 companies of the Twentieth on Sunday, May 17, 1863. They began their trek home two weeks after the battle at Chancellorsville. Ten of the 12 deserters took their arms and accouterments with them. One other private, in arrest for skulking at the recent engagement, broke his guard and went with them. Lieutenant Oliver Williams, Company C, quickly organized a pursuing party and arrested the homeward bound men a short distance from the camp. Though the actual distance covered by the departing men was very short, the consequence was great, little different than if they were deserters of long standing, far from their assigned command. Beginning on May 27, 1863, the men were individually tried by a court-martial held in Rodes' Division, 2nd Corps, Army of Northern Virginia. Working through the week, recessing for Sunday, the court heard the last case, the man who broke his guard, on Monday the first of June.

Before the men were at trial, a man of the Twelfth expressed a view that may have had some bearing on the desertion attempt. "Gen. Daniel's North Carolina Brigade has been put in our division and Gen. Colquitt's Brigade of Georgians, which was in our division has been sent to North Carolina. We were disappointed at not going ourselves. We think too that there are enough North Carolinians in this army now and enough in this division as it has to do most of the fighting in the East. We do not think it fair that too large a proportion should be from any one state."[8] Colquitt's brigade went to North Carolina because of a concern that moving more North Carolinians closer to their homes would exacerbate the desertion problem, already considered as very serious.

ELI BOSWELL 20-D (May 27, 1863). Private Boswell was the first of the 13 would-be deserters to go to trial and he was among the 4 whose death sentences were approved by General Lee. Private Boswell had a period of absence without leave not long after his enrollment in March 1862. After some delay the death sentences for Private Boswell and two others were remitted. SO #173, July 10, 1863, Army of Northern Virginia, noted, "The sentences of Private E. Boswell, Company D, Wm L. Hardee, Company D, W. M. Raymond Company G, are remitted on the recommendation of their Commanding Officer." The recommendation was based on their "good conduct" on the march to South Mountain and the fact that they did not "avail themselves of the opportunity to escape afforded them by the attack of the enemy."[9] Private Boswell received a second wound after his return to duty and the war ended while he was on medical furlough.

WILLIAM LOFTIN HARDEE (20-D May 27, 1863). Private Hardee was the second soldier whose death sentence was approved by General Lee. Why he was included among those to be shot is not obvious from his service record. After enlistment in 1861, he was captured in Maryland in September of 1862 and dutifully returned to his company after his parole. As seen in SO #173, his death sentence was remitted and he returned to duty and was faithful to the final surrender.

WILLIAM B. CARTER 20-D (May 28, 1863). The service record of Private Carter shows that he served just a few days short of three years in the Confederate army. His service began on March 21, 1862. Except for the abortive desertion attempt, there is no other mark to mar his record. After his death sentence was remitted, he was with his company until captured by the enemy in May 1864. He was exchanged a month before surrender, probably in poor health at the time.

JOHN L. HEWETT 20-G (May 28, 1863). A very brief service record for Private Hewett reports that he was with his company from enrollment in October 1861, until his first and only attempt at desertion along with the dozen others. After his reprieve and return to duty, he was detailed as an attendant in a hospital. Later on, he was hospitalized with rheumatism, which eventually led to his being furloughed in January 1865, ending his military days.

WILLIAM SIMMONS 20-G (May 28, 1863). Private Simmons was killed in a skirmish at Liberty, VA, on June 19, 1864. He had recovered from a wound suffered at Gaines Mill, VA, in 1862 and an earlier hospitalization for illness following enrollment on June 19, 1861. Private Simmons was one of the 9 deserters who gained quick release from the threat of execution. A brother, Private Moses Simmons, enrolled in the same company on the same day as Private William Simmons but apparently chose not to leave the company with his brother. Private Moses Simmons was wounded, later captured and died while a Federal prisoner.

JOHN A. BATCHELOR 20-K (May 30, 1863). After his release from the court-ordered death sentence in June of 1863, Private Batchelor had a second brush with military justice when he was absent without leave for over a month beginning in April 1864. Private Batchelor returned to his company after this absence and stayed on to Appomattox. When he enrolled in March 1862, he was forty-two years old, the oldest man among those who headed for home. He and another older man did not take their weapons with them, a very prudent decision; as General Lee duly noted this fact in his favorable comments on their behalf.

ARMIZA F. CUMBEE 20-G (May 30, 1863). Private Cumbee was hospitalized shortly after enrolling in May 1861, and again after his return to duty following his involvement in the short-lived desertion escapade. He later was detailed as a hospital steward before returning to the ranks. A year after he was freed from his death sentence, he began a four-month absence without leave. Two days after returning from this very serious second offense, in view of his earlier conviction, he was captured by the enemy and confined at Harpers Ferry, WV. He remained a Federal prisoner until taking the oath in May 1865.

STEPHEN ELKINS 20-K (May 30, 1863). Private Elkins enrolled at Fort Caswell, NC, in July 1861; a year later he agreed to extend his commitment by two years for which he accepted a $50 bounty. A year after this early affirmation to the cause, the private deserted along with the other men. Once reprieved, he returned to duty and there remained until September or October 1864 when he was absent without leave, ending his Confederate duty. Private Elkins, age thirty, did not take his musket with him when he left his company, as mentioned favorably by General Lee. Private Jonathan Elkins, also of Company K, was hospitalized before his brother was involved in the desertion attempt, and had no further service record in the company.

WESLEY P. GORE 20-G (May 30, 1863); and WILLIAM GORE 20-G (May 30, 1863). Not unexpectedly for two brothers with the same first initial, service records are mixed and interchanged, but some detail may be gleaned on careful search. The brothers enrolled in Company G of the Twentieth, though about a month apart, with Private William Gore enrolling first on May 25, 1861, and Private Wesley Gore following on June 29, 1861. Each joined the abortive desertion attempt. Private Wesley Gore was later promoted to Corporal and then to Sergeant after his return to duty. The brothers were captured at Spottsylvania in 1864 and were exchanged together, in March 1865. A third brother, Private Edward Gore died in November 1861, six months after enrolling and some six months before his brothers took leave of their company.

SAMUEL HICKMAN 20-G (May 30, 1863). Two soldiers above the rank of private joined the brief attempt at desertion, Corporal Hickman was demoted the day the attempt was thwarted. Roughly a year after his desertion, demotion and death sentence, he regained the rank of Corporal. The newly restored corporal was captured a few days after his promotion and was confined in Federal prison at war's end. His service records states that he was "a good soldier."

WILLIAM M. RAYMOND 20-G (May 30, 1863). Private Raymond was the third soldier whose death sentence was approved by General Lee. The sentence was remitted for the same reason as put forward in the other cases; he did not escape during the confusion of battle when he had an opportunity to do so. Private Raymond was wounded both before and after the desertion incident. On May 12, 1864, he was captured by the enemy and died of pneumonia while in their care. The effects he left on earth were his shoes, a jacket and a hat; other clothing was apparently left on his body, or not worth the taking.

JAMES B. WATTS 20-D (June 1, 1863). Private Watts was the fourth man selected by General Lee to be executed as a warning on the evil of desertion, even when begun as a lark. He was the last of the 13 to go before the court, and the most likely man to be executed, if it came down to just one sacrificial example. Private Watts had skulked at the battles of the Wilderness and Chancellorsville. More damning, he had broken his guard to go with the men who were deserting. Whether or not General Lee or the President would have relented and spared Private Watts the execution stake will never be known. Characteristically, the young man eluded his guard for the second time, and went directly to the enemy on July 5, 1863. A few months after reaching the enemy, he took the oath and then volunteered for the Third Maryland Cavalry Regiment, a Federal unit, giving the name Gymsey Watts.

For the group of 12 deserters, the charges and proceedings were identical; the thirteenth man faced the added charge of breaking arrest. In every case, the court repeated the sentence ending with the ominous words "to be shot to death with musketry." The court felt compelled to comment on their decision, "The total indifference manifested by the prisoners, viz: [the names of the twelve deserters followed] on their trials, and in several cases the behavior of the witnesses, approaching even to levity, induces the Court to believe that the gravity of the offence of desertion is not duly appreciated by the prisoners themselves, or by their companions. A course of negligence, indifference and injudicious leniency on the part of those in authority, may often entail the most serious consequences upon those who naturally look to them for example, guidance and instruction."[10] General Lee reviewed the findings of the court and although he confirmed the decisions regarding all of the men, he suspended execution of sentence until the decision of the President was known for 9 of the 13. No such consideration was granted 4 prisoners; their death sentences were approved and their executions scheduled to take place in ten days. Not one to let the verbal thrust by the court pass his front without an attacking sally, General Lee, perhaps stung by the reference to "indifference and injudicious leniency" responded: "The leniency heretofore extended to soldiers guilty of the detestable crime of desertion, instead of suppressing, seems to have encouraged it; and while exercising clemency in some of the above cases, the General Commanding warns all from being misled thereby. Hereafter the sentences of the Courts will be rigidly enforced; and the Courts are reminded, that under their oath they can never inflict a less punishment than that prescribed by the recent act of Congress abolishing flogging in the army, as the mildest penalty for this infamous offence, viz: one year's hard labor in a penitentiary."[11] Before the General Order was printed for distribution, General Lee expanded on his decision in a letter to General Cooper. First he pointed out that the men were captured about a half-mile from their camp on their way home, and that they were taken without resistance. Two of the band, Privates Bachelor and Elkins were not armed; the muskets of the other men were not loaded. There were few cases of desertion in the Twentieth Regiment and all had received slight punishment. Still, some example was needed to check the evil which earlier clemency had encouraged. "I have ordered the execution of four in whose favor nothing was said — which appear to be the worst cases."[12] For the others, the General recommended hard labor with ball and chain attached to a leg for the rest of the war, then discharge and forfeiture of all pay.

All of the 13 deserters that set out on that day in May 1863 were volunteers; 9 had been in the service for two years, more or less. They were enrolled in companies that had experienced very little desertion but had suffered severely in battle. Ten of the departing men were from Brunswick and Columbus counties. Four were married when they went into the army. The notion that some of the men looked on their court-martial as something of a lark gains foundation in that 5 of the men either had, or were members of families that had, property valued at over $1,000, with an average of over $3,000. Five others of the group either had, or were from families with an average of $228 in property.

Johnston-Toon Brigade

"I come right upt to him after he was shot"[13]

There was only one death sentence involving a man of the brigade after Brigadier Robert Daniel Johnston took command. That number might have grown by one but for the laxness of the guards at Castle Thunder. Private Noah Bowman, Company A, Twelfth Regiment, wrote to Governor Vance on November 6, 1863. He was in Prison Hospital #13 at Richmond, VA, at the time. First he explained that he had been granted only one furlough of ten days during his twenty months of duty. He took it upon himself to go home to see his folks, and "staid a good while." Within a day or two of his planned return he was "taken up."[14] His service record shows that he deserted in April 1863, was arrested and imprisoned at Castle Thunder, Richmond, VA, from which place he escaped, only to be recaptured in October. A few weeks after his first plea to Governor Vance, a second appeal stressed that he was praying to be relieved of any punishment. The supplicant decided not to await the result of plea or prayer, and again escaped from Castle Thunder; he went directly to the enemy and took the oath a few months later.

Private William H. Brotherton, Company K, wrote of witnessing an execution: "I saw a man shot for desertion they tied him to a stake and shot in the brest just nine balls in him I was about 150 yards from him I come right upt to him after he was shot."[15] Mention that he "come right upt to him" after the execution, suggests that the private went of his own will, and walked closer to clearly see corpse and cross. He also wrote that he was serving in an honorable manner, despite reports to the contrary circulating at home. These reports were of concern to his family and their unease led the young man to ask members of his company to sign a statement that he did not have to wear a "white badge" denoting that he acted in a cowardly manner during the Battle at Chancellorsville. Nine men signed the statement, which Private Brotherton then sent to his father.[16] A few days earlier, he had asked his father if he should come home to clear his name.[17] Perhaps inclined toward gossip,

Private Brotherton assured those at home that he had not accused a member of his company with deliberately shooting himself to avoid further service.[18] In August 1863 he offered the opinion that, "our armmy is mighly confuse at the present they are still desertin but I think I will hold on awhile longer till times gets worse."[19] As to to desertion he was "attempted some times for it looks like they dont try to meke peace I tell you it take a man with goods spirits to make a warior but still I enjoy myself."[20] "Goods spirits," won the day; the warrior remained with his company until his September 1864 capture by the enemy.

Two men of the Twenty-Third did face the reality of execution, one ordered by a Confederate court and one by order of Federal authorities. The latter was a captured officer of the Twenty-Third, Major Charles Blacknall, who drew the fatal lot in a drawing ordered in reprisal for the alleged execution of a Federal officer.[21] The Major survived that experience but not the war.

CHARLES H. WEST 23-I (December 12, 1863). Private West was wounded at Gettysburg, PA, two years after he enrolled on June 17, 1861. After recovery, he deserted his command while marching from Fredericksburg to Culpepper, VA. Private West appeared before a court-martial held on December 12, 1863. After deliberation, they concurred on a death sentence which General Lee duly confirmed. The execution was set for early 1864, as announced in General Order #109 December 26, 1863, Army of Northern Virginia. The next we learn of Private West is that he was paroled at Greensboro in May of 1865. Unfortunately, there is no record of what took place between the confirmed death sentence and the parole. His brother, Private Elisha B. West, deserted and left no record of return to his regiment.

In late 1863 a soldier in the Twelfth Regiment was ordered to march before his regiment, on dress parade, with a white feather in his cap, his head half-shaved of hair, denoting that he had acted in a cowardly manner in battle. After this humiliation, he was to walk in a circle while carrying a log, this every alternate two hours for twenty days.[22] In the same company, a discontented man was sentenced to hard labor for the rest of the war, and then to be drummed out of the regiment, for attempting to maim himself by firing his musket at his left hand.[23] Sentences that included an after the war provision assumed that there would be a victorious regiment to carry out the ceremony.

Summary

Of the 16 brigade men that were threatened with execution, 14 apparently survived the war. Though none of the 16 were executed, 20 men met accidental or violent non-battle deaths. Four were murdered, 1 committed suicide, 4 were killed by militia taking up deserters, 6 were killed in accidents, most involving discharge of a weapon, and 6 others were killed by falling trees or in railroad accidents. Three men of the brigade were charged with murder. A private in the Twenty-Third refused to obey an order given by a sergeant; he was so enraged that he struck the sergeant with a wooden club, killing him.[24] The assailant was sentenced to five years in prison. A man serving in Company B, Twelfth Regiment, was killed by a man of his own company.[25] Another of the regiment "disappeared mysteriously" in December 1862.[26] Two men were charged with murder of civilians; 1 was whipped and 1 was hanged. Civil authorities wanted the whipped man returned to his regiment to face execution. The military did not want him.²⁷ In the case of the murderer who was hanged, Governor Vance received letters from men who purported to be officers seeking his reprieve. One signed by a James B. Campbell, Lt, Co B 46 NCT began, "Imposing implicit confidence in your humanity to your fellow man," went on to ask for leniency for Joe Carpenter. The writer said that he had visited with Genl R E Lee and that he had "procured (very willingly) from him his approval for your reprieve of said Carpenter."²⁸ Samuel Jamision, Capt. Cmdg B 47th NCT, first emphasized that the condemned man was a faithful soldier and that he would never take any action that would cause the Governor to regret his aid, and closed with, "Trusting that your kind and uninterested benevolence be shown on his behalf thereby putting in the field another faithful soldier to defend our homes."²⁹ Governor Vance simply endorsed the letters, "File away." Neither "officer" who wrote on behalf of Private Carpenter is found on the rolls of the regiments indicated in their letters. The Governor from Buncombe County apparently recognized bunk when he read it.

The Garland-Iverson-Johnston-Toon Brigade had 380 present at Appomattox. At least 99 men had appeared before military courts; 16 were given death sentences—16 were acquitted—none were executed, though several might have marched onto the execution field except for their own ingenuity. Thirteen of the 16 condemned were enrolled in Companies D, G and K of the Twentieth Regiment. Fifteen were volunteers who had enrolled in 1861 or 1862; their average enrollment age was twenty-two. The sixteenth was a forty-six-year-old substitute. Only 4 are known to have been married. The brigade earned a fine record of keeping men in the ranks; those absences that did occur were fairly distributed over three years of war. A sampling of 18 companies shows that the average company enrolled 152 men, 12 absented themselves during their service.³⁰ On average these companies lost 23 men to battle related deaths while 30 died from disease or unknown cause. This brigade was one of two North Carolina infantry brigades that had more men killed in battle than absented themselves. Total deaths ranged from a high of 85 for Company B, Fifth Regiment, to 33 for Company G, Twelfth Regiment. Approximately 6,200 men were enrolled in the brigade. The bulk of these men made their homes in the eastern third of the state. Of 200 sampled companies, only 18 companies lost more men to enemy action than to disease. Eight of the 18 companies are from the brigade first formed by the gallant Garland.³¹

10

First and Third North Carolina Infantry Regiments

First Regiment

"Men inexperienced and totally ignorant of war and its ways"[1]

Early on there was a concern as to the competency of many of the officers of the First. Though this did not portend well for the regiment, it did not lead to widespread desertion. "Camp near Richmond Va. August 14th 1861 No one has drilled the Regt at-all but myself and the officers (subalterns & Captains) are so incompetent (with one or two exceptions) that we will be in bad condition or order for and engagement. Our Lt. Col and Major know comparatively nothing of Military affairs Col Stokes is away and if we get into a fight I trouble to think of the consequences, for myself I do not think, but the lives of others, men inexperienced and totally ignorant or war and its ways, hanging upon the balance as it were, to be sacrificed by incompetent men is terrible to think of. Of one thing I am sure that I shall do my duty and act the part of a man regardless of my life."[2]

The First Regiment ended the war with a record of 37 court convictions posted by the AIGO. Trials were held for 40 soldiers; 3 were acquitted. In the First, Company D, Lincoln and Orange counties; Company C, the Lillington Rifle Guards, Harnett County; and Company E, formed in New Hanover County, were responsible for 65 percent of court convictions. Of the 27 men of the First Regiment whose trial results are known, 5 received death sentences. These men were enrolled in 4 companies. Company E was the company of record of the first man from a North Carolina unit to be executed.

Third Regiment

"We feare veary bad here in Virginia"[3]

The Third Regiment was organized in May 1861. Individual service records for over 1,700 men who served in the regiment show that they were involved in more than 200 absence incidents, some few men making more than one bid to leave the service. AIGO court-martial postings for the regiment list 53 trials; less than one-quarter of the men who absented themselves ever appeared before a court authorized to put forth a death sentence.

Acquittal followed for 4 who went to trial. Company H, the Bladen Volunteers; Company F, recruited in New Hanover County; and Company K, the Holly Shelter Volunteers, New Hanover County, were the companies that had the most men to appear before a court, 61 percent of the total courts for the regiment. Company G, formed in Onslow County; Company A, the Greene County Riflemen, and Company I, the Jeff Davis Rifles, Beaufort County, were the companies with the fewest courts at 8 percent in total. One oddity, Company G, in both the First and Third regiments, had no recorded court appearances. On closer inspection, service records show that 18 men enrolled in Company G, First Regiment, recruited in Washington County, have an absence record. Of these 18, 6 went directly to the enemy, and 11 ended their service, so only 1 man was ever in arrest. Company G, Third Regiment, formed in Onslow County, had much the same experience. Of 12 men listed in unauthorized absence, 4 went over to the enemy and 5 had no further record. No court record has been found for 3 men that did return. The companies that led all others in appearances before courts-martial also led the way in regimental desertions, with just over half of all deserters leaving from these companies. The Third was not immune to soldiers fleeing to the enemy; 35 men chose that course, some by simply bolting while on picket duty, and others by wading into a waterway to make a dripping departure from the Confederacy. At least 2 men of the regiment were drowned in these attempts. Other men resorted to maiming themselves by a well-directed shot at a finger or a toe, a less obvious and a less risky means of avoiding the battlefield. "The medical director reports a very large proportion of slightly wounded men," attesting to the prevalence of such acts throughout the war.[4] An older man, enrolled in the Third, tried both maiming and the river, and he drowned in his effort.[5] The first man of the regiment to face military execution escaped that fate but was later drummed out of the service, only to become involved in a series of events that ranged from bizarre to poignant.

Courts-Martial

GEORGE A. JOHNSON 3-B (April 21, 1862). Private Johnson either volunteered for service in Company B, Third Regiment, on June 8, 1861, or he joined as a substitute for a John Beasly. Private Johnson deserted on April 4, 1862, and was in custody on April 16. Compounding his crime, he had deserted with the intention of going to the enemy, according to the trial record. The court before which he appeared agreed that Private Johnson was guilty as charged and that he should suffer death by musketry. But someone neglected to put in the record that two-thirds of the members of the court had concurred in the decision. For this failure, General T. H. Holmes set aside the verdict and released the prisoner, but not before saying, "There can be no doubt that the sentence is just and would be executed but for the omission."[6] Private Johnson's service record indicates that he deserted on May 1, 1862, three days after release from the death sentence.

Sixteen months later a Private George Johnson was confined in Military Prison at Wilmington, NC. When questioned, he offered a deposition that seems to shed light on portions of his record, but then proceeds to shadow other areas.

> 29 Augt 1863 George Johnson Duplin County Co B 3 Regt NC late Capt Thurston Deserted in May 1862 in company with two others Jas Hanchy & Obed Hanchy. Has been a greater part of the time about town working in government st[not legible] a part of the time working at Gvmnnt salt works 53 year old born in England in 1810 Substitute for Mr. John Beasly of

the county says he has been tried for desertion & sentenced to be shot, but was reprieved and drummed out of his Regiment Asked his Capt for a furlough who declined giving it & went to see his family expecting to return next day but was too much fatigued. Drummond Tilly states in company with Hillton and Tom Sanders at Sally M[not legible] house near Camp Lamb about [blank] June & heard George Johnston boasting of the manner in which he got away from the 3 Regt & how he has remaining from the Regt & stole a locomotive engine at Richmond & went to Weldon where the engine was taken away from him & [not legible] said that the road had been straight that he could have gone direct to New Bern and the Yankees that the confederate states had impressed him & he would not fight for them any more that they had arranged to arrest him but he had a suspicion of it & broke out of house [not legible].[7]

Portions of the above statement are verifiable. The Hanchy (Hanchey) men, of Duplin County, were soldiers in Company B, Third Regiment, and were in arrest for being absent without leave in March and April 1862, as was Private Johnson, who was then court-martialed and given the death sentence. No court record has been found for the two other men. The Roll of Honor for Duplin County indicates that a Private Johnson was drummed out of the Third Regiment, but that record supposedly is for a thirty-year-old resident of the county.

On November 22, 1863, three months after his initial interrogation, George W. Johnson, still imprisoned at Wilmington Military Prison, prepared a memorial to Governor Vance.

Military Prison Wilmington N.C. 22 Nov 1863 to His Excellency, Gov Z. B. Vance Honored Sir: I seat myself to drop a few lines to you on a subject of deep interest to myself, and one that will I have no doubt call forth your tender sympathy and commiseration for suffering and injured humanity. In order to enlighten you on the merits of my case, it is necessary for me to enter into a detail of the particulars. On the 29th of last August I was arrested and thrown into close confinement in the Jail: the cause of this was on account of the false representations of two unknown men to Major Sparrow, to the effect, that I had boasted in their presence of having carried off with out leave or license a R. R. Engine from Richmond Va. and run it to Goldsboro N. C. This you will necessarily perceive is an unnatural and unreasonable conclusion; for how is it supposed that I, or any person, could, without the Knowledge of the Directors and Managers of the respective R. Roads, take from any or either of their Depots or Workshops and Engine, or any other article of such unwieldly proportions — therefore, the falsity of the accusation and the injustice of my present imprisonment. Of the aforesaid crime, I am charged with, I assure you I am totally innocent; and to substantiate the assertion, my previous remarks on the unnaturalness and unreasonablness of the accusation are all that are required. Honored Governor, today I have languished in prison 91 days — and all to satisfy the malignant hatred of two unknown enemies. Here have I been suffering myself, and prevented from rending assistance and support to a destitute family. In consequence, those destitute ones have died of starvation and now sleep their last sleep beneath the cold sod of the mother Earth. Within I enclose you a Scrip for your information taken from the Daily Paper of this City — but I was married legally to her, the child is mine by lawful marriage. Governor, I am according to law exempt, being 54 years old. I have been in the Service and discharged therefrom by the proper military Authoritites. I desire you to oblige me by investigating the case and having me discharged from durance vile. At the time I was arrested I was working on Government Works. Hoping you will attend to the matter for me, I beg leave to subscribe myself your humble and obedient servant. [signed] George W. Johnson Copy of Memorial George W. Johnson to Gov. Vance.[8]

The request to Governor Vance is prepared in a reasoned and objective manner though formal and legal in tone, suggesting that Private Johnson was aided by a person with legal training; or possibly he was so blest. "Durance vile" has a fine English tone. Had he known, the writer might have included a full sentence written in 1794: "In durance vile here must I wake and weep."[9] A week before the appeal was written, on November 14, the wife and child mentioned by the supplicant were found dead in an outhouse near the city of Wilmington.[10] The tone of the memorial and the language therein seem strangely removed from the stark deaths of the destitute family. Governor Vance apparently accepted the truthfulness of the appeal and directed the request into the proper legal channel. Within a week, Mr. Ralph P. Buxton, Solicitor of the Fifth Judicial District at Fayetteville, wrote to General W. H. C. Whiting to secure the release of the prisoner, or at least to turn him over to civil authority in order that he could be brought to trial. "As Law Officer of the State in this Circuit, I ask that Johnson may be released — or if there are grounds to suppose that he has violated the law, that he be turned over to the Civil Authorities to the end that he may be tried."[11] There ends the record of Private George W. Johnson.

MARTIN HOGAN 1-E (July 18, 1862). On the morning of June 6, 1862, Private Hogan was on picket duty near Chickahominy Swamp, VA, when he put down his musket and ran toward the enemy line. Overtaken by swifter and more loyal Confederates, he was taken to the guardhouse to await a court-martial. At trial on July 18, the court found that Private Hogan was guilty of desertion with intent to join the enemy. A death sentence was approved by General R. E. Lee, who directed that the sentence be carried into effect on August 5. Special Order #172, August 4, 1862, Department of Northern Virginia, suspended the execution of Private Hogan, and that of a soldier in a Virginia regiment, because it was "at later period than was contemplated by Commanding General."[12] The respite ended at 10 A.M. on August 12, 1862, when Private Hogan was shot to death by musketry at a time more convenient for the Commanding General and the executioners.

Private Calvin Leach, Company B, First Regiment, mentions the execution.

> July 30, 1862 Wed. 30th Received 35 dollars bounty. Read out on dress parade that Private Wm Hogans [sic] C[o] E 1st NC Reg had been sentenced to be shot to death with the musket for trying to desert. Time next tuesday evening. Tues 12th Finished our part of the breast works, and was assigned to another place on the line. Private William Hogans Co E of this Reg was shot today at 10 o, clock for trying to desert. The Reg was present, I did not see the sight.[13]

The writer was killed in battle in May of '64. Though slightly confusing, the first reference to "tuesday evening" is for Tuesday, August 5, and is consistent with dates on the orders issued by General Lee. Private Edgar Allen Jackson of Company F adds detail.

> A man by the name of Hogan was shot before our Brigade last Tuesday. Jim Darden put one ball in him. He was struck by 8 balls and two buck shot, killing him instantly. Lewis Lawrence was Sergeant of the shooting squad. George Beale of our company put a ball and two buck shot in him, six balls went through his heart.[14]

Private Jackson was killed in May of '63. Privates Darden and Beale and Sergeant Lawrence survived the war. All were enrolled in Company F, First Regiment. The emotional impact of the execution on Private Jackson was not substantially different than that expected after the annual hog killing. There is little, if any, empathy for the dead man and all seemed quite willing to take part in dispatching him, an unknown Irishman. Nearly thirty-eight years after the event, the regimental Colonel recalled that it was during a slack time while awaiting marching orders that an "execution on the person of an Irishman" took place.

Private Hogan was executed by a firing party from his own company and they "did their sad duty like true soldiers."[15] If memory was correct, Captain Guilford E. Dudley, Field and Staff, Assistant Quartermaster, was the officer in charge of the firing party. He had earlier served as a line officer in Company E of the First Regiment, the company of the man whose execution he directed.

WESLEY F. WATSON 1-D (February 15, 1863). Private Watson was spared the somber procession to the execution stake because of the careless handling of his court records, which were extensive. Perhaps his age — he was just seventeen — or that he had promptly stepped forward for service in the gathering Confederate army inclined reviewing authorities to search for any error that could be used to void his death sentence. Their reasoning was legally sound, but certainly the willingness of senior officers to execute very young soldiers varied by command and by situation. Private Watson served in Company G, Twenty-Seventh Regiment, for several weeks early in the struggle. He was discharged in May 1861, likely because he was underage. Some six weeks later he went back into service, now as a Sergeant in the First Regiment. Within eight months he was reduced in rank and soon started a series of desertions that eventually led to the decision that he should be shot. His unauthorized absence was noted in the North Carolina Adjutant General's Letterbook in November 1862. "PS Wesley Watson of Co D 1 Reg NCT is also a deserter, with several others supposed to be in Orange County."[16] Detail on his return to the regiment is not found in service records. The court hearing the case of Private Watson found no evidence that would support a recommendation for clemency. They did note that he was there before them after his third attempt at desertion. General Lee, however, would not approve the death sentence because the "former conviction of desertion not legally approved. As evidence of a prior conviction either the record of the former trial, or at least the General Order announcing the finding and sentence in the case should have been produced."[17] Private Watson was released by pardon of the President on August 3, 1863. This was just a month before the first significant surge in Confederate executions. Within that fateful month, Private Watson was once again absent, this his fourth attempt to desert. On November 13, 1864, the evasive private was again in the control of the military and on his way to Castle Thunder at Richmond, apparently to end his army experience, no further record having been located. The young man was a determined, but not very adept, deserter. He may have been driven by conditions in camp: "Hard times here shore nothing to eat or drink."[18]

Brigadier General George H. Steuart took command of the brigade that included the First and Third Regiments on May 28, 1863. The Thirtieth Virginia Infantry had recently joined the Tenth, Twenty-Third and Thirty-Seventh Virginia regiments serving under General Steuart. The Virginia regiments experienced a total of 6 executions during the war. General Steuart's command was assigned to the division of Major General Edward Johnson, "Old Allegheny," in the Second Corps of the Army of Northern Virginia as preparations began for a thrust into Federal territory. General Johnson's division was largely Virginian, with 13 regiments from that state, 5 from Louisiana and 2 from North Carolina. The Virginia regiments had 70 men sentenced to be shot or hanged, and at least 12 were executed. The men from the Crescent State had 11 men sentenced to death and 1 was executed. The regiments of soldiers from North Carolina had 19 men sentenced to death; 12 were shot.

The near disaster for the Army of Northern Virginia at the July engagement in Pennsylvania led to a determined effort to control desertion. On the first day of August 1863, President Davis put forth a General Amnesty for soldiers of the Confederacy who were absent from their commands.[19] Thus began a series of orders and correspondence that had an immediate and severe effect on men of the Third Regiment. The day following the amnesty offer, President Davis addressed General Lee with the pointed comment, "It is painful to contemplate our weakness when you ask for reinforcements."[20] Desertion was a serious threat to the future of the Confederacy. On the eighth of the month, General Lee, after making observations on the state of affairs, offered to resign or accept a significant demotion.[21] When the offer was not accepted the obviously distraught officer responded: "The lower the position, the more suitable to my ability and the more agreeable to my feelings."[22] President Davis had earlier replied that if a better man was available, "I would not hesitate to avail of his services."[23] On Tuesday, August 11, 1863, the AIGO issued a General Order allowing all officers and men in all commands who were then absent, to return to their commands without punishment, the amnesty extending for a period of twenty days after publication of the order. Just six days later, General Lee again wrote to President Davis urging a resolute and firm stand on severely punishing all deserters, including their prompt execution when so sentenced, except where mitigating circumstances were clearly present. The General supported his stand by offering examples of how desertion was impacting his ability to carry on the war. On August 17, 1863, he wrote:

> Great desertion continues ... N. C. desertions very serious matter ... "Remove all palliation from offense of desertion ... I would now respectfully submit to your Excellency the opinion that all has been done that mercy & forbearance call for, and that nothing will remedy this great evil which so much endangers our cause excepting the rigid enforcement of the death penalty in future cases of conviction.[24]

With such a blunt statement in hand, it was unlikely that even the strong-willed President would offer clemency to deserters, certainly not in the next several weeks, and certainly not to North Carolinians. On August 20, General Lee ordered all corps commanders to send "armed parties in pursuit of deserters."[25] In the time between these statements by General Lee, President Davis proclaimed that Friday, August 21, was to be a day of "fasting, humiliation and prayer."[26]

The deadly impact of these orders and pronouncements then began to unfold for men of the Third Regiment. They would have known that a General Amnesty had been granted by the Commanding General and that all but essential military duties were to be suspended on the fasting day proclaimed by the President. They may not have known that General Lee was aware that soldiers were taking advantage of his amnesty order and leaving their units, apparently intending to return within the grace period. More to the point, privates in the Third certainly did not know that General Lee was now determined to execute convicted deserters, or that he had emphasized that desertion of North Carolina troops was a very serious matter. Some inkling of this sentiment may well have caused men in the ranks to reconsider any impulse to leave.

On Thursday, August 20, the day before the proclaimed day of fasting and humiliation, 13 men of the Third Regiment left their company and headed south. Company K lost 8 and 5 were from Company H. The destination of the small band was southeastern North Carolina. Some took their weapons with them; Confederate and Federal forces were active in the area of their homes and weapons might be needed. And they may have been emboldened by the notion that the area is "full of deserters no effort to arrest them, but they are more highly respected than a soldier who is toiling and fighting to redeem their country from chains and slavery."[27] This little band, these 13 men, had rather normal service records with perhaps a susceptibility to illness and hospitalization, for by and large they were not sturdy men. At least 1 was deemed a good soldier: 4 were wounded in battle; 2 had experienced the rigors of capture and exchange; 3 were conscripts. A minor absence marred the record of 1; they were all novices in the deadly art of desertion. They began their stealthy venture while encamped near Orange Court House, VA, about 20 miles northeast of Charlottesville. A furtive 300 mile trek lay ahead. The route on foot through unknown counties, and along isolated roads and trails, was not without threat or challenge. Organized Confederate and local authorities were intent on arresting absentees. Other bands of deserters, thieves and robbers were equally intent on taking anything of value that they might have — money, weapons, clothing. Simply reaching the James River, 30 wary miles to the south, was the first challenge. Crossing the river was an even greater hazard. The river fords were well guarded by regular Confederate troops, aided by the local militia. They were instructed to use any force necessary to arrest deserters and return them to the fight.

As a wartime die is often cast, near Scottsville, VA, on the James River, the deserters did not encounter men guarding the river but were confronted by a a detail of men from the Forty-Sixth North Carolina who were in search of deserters from their regiment. An attempt to halt and arrest the men of the Third was made, and weapons were fired. In the melee, Lieutenant Richardson Mallett Jr., Regimental Adjutant of the Forty-Sixth, was mortally wounded. As he was dying, the young officer, just twenty-three, is reported to have said, "Tell Colonel Hall I was doing my duty God's will be done."[28] An unidentified deserter was killed and 1 was wounded. Ten of the deserters were arrested and taken under guard to Richmond. The wounded man was left behind for treatment and his arrest followed in several days. One of the deserters was not arrested, either because he was lagging behind or he escaped in the confusion of the melee. The date of the confrontation on the James is not clear from existing records. Considering that the deserters had made their way some 30 miles since leaving camp, it was likely on August 23. The service record for Adjutant Mallett gives his date of death as on or about August 28. The first of the deserters went to trial on August 27. A soldier in the regiment of the Adjutant wrote:

> 46th Regt N.C. Troops Cooks Brigade Camp near Taylorsville, Virginia August 30th 1863 Mrs. Catherine Lefevers & children Dear Wife I must tell you what has taken place Since our men Ranaway our Capt and our Agitient foloward [one line on fold] Selves to take these deserters they did not come acraws our men but met up with Some 12 or 15 others and our agitent ordered them to Surrender and the men Refused dowing saw and at that they booth commensed fireing own booth sides the deserters kiled the agitent or wounded him sow he dide shortly after wordes their was one of the Deserters kiled own on the ground and another wounded that he died shortly afterwordes The balance of the deserters was all taken prisoners But one they are now all confined in Richmond it is thoat they will all be hung or shot But I cant tell for Serten.[29]

The Chaplain of the First Regiment wrote in his diary on August 25, "The militia took up deserters other deserters pursued to waylay and kill and free deserters — Taylorsville — Mr Burke greatly excited."[30] It is not clear if this reference is to the deserters from the Third. It does give an indication of conditions in that James River neighborhood.

After interrogation by Captain J. C. Alexander, AAG, and Major Elias Griswold, AAG, the men were confined at Castle Thunder. Prompt and cursory individual trials began on Thursday, August 27, just a week after the men left their camp, and ended on Saturday the 29. The actual charges and specifications brought against the men are not found in surviving records, no trial transcript or general order has been located. An order that may have had a bearing on the lives of the deserters was issued on August 11; the Judge Advocate General for the Army of Northern Virginia released a circular order detailing the forms and procedures to be followed by a court-martial. That order, just two weeks before trial, significantly reduced the possibility that a procedural error would allow any of the prisoners to avoid their death march, though the mindset of Confederate leadership was such that there was little likelihood of any quibbling over detail.

With the death decisions of the court before him, on Friday, September 4, Major General Edward Johnson ordered Brigadier General George H. Steuart to execute the 10 condemned men on the next day, September 5.

> 1863 Sept 4 Hd Qr Johnson Div R. W. Hunter AAG by order Maj Gen Edward Johnson to Brigadier Gen Geo H. Steuart Maj Gen Comdg direction the execution to-morrow at 4 PM of the enclosed proceedings of Gen C-M condemning 10 men of the 3rd NC to be shot — proceedings and sentence are not to be read to them until daylight — take all precautions to secure them — keep the matter secret until the proceedings are read — select good men for the firing-parties from other regiments — enclose a plat of the formation — send Chaplains to the men — instruct guard-officers to allow no one else to communicate with them — Maj E. L. Moore AAG will report to assist you.[31]

Major Edwin L. Moore, a Virginia banker, had served with the Second Virginia infantry regiment before his current assignment. Why his assistance was deemed necessary is not explained; perhaps it was to add another stern and watchful organizational eye to insure against any disruption of the proceedings. The wording and tone of the order obviously indicates that Major General Johnson was gravely concerned that a mass execution might bring on a general mutiny, particularly by troops from North Carolina, or that there might be a flat refusal by those in the ranks to carry out the execution order. The condemned men were to be informed of their fate only hours before they were to be shot to death; there was to be no time for appeal to higher authority, though it was unlikely that the President would interfere. The prisoners were not to have contact with any person other than Chaplains — no emotion arousing farewell for them. Only "good men" from other regiments were to be assigned to the "firing-parties," indicating a real concern that the men aiming the loaded weapons would deliberately miss the men bound to the stakes. "Take all precautions to secure them" the General ordered, likely fearing that men from North Carolina might storm the guardhouse and free the prisoners.

One can only speculate as to what extent the order of General Johnson reflects the fears and concerns of General Lee. Execution within hours of the reading of the death sentence was normally reserved for only the vilest traitor or spy. Condemned Confederate soldiers were usually given seven days to make their peace with the Almighty, to have some form of contact with friend or family, or to prepare an appeal. In fact, at times Confederate officers were chastised when they did not allow for that consideration. Events surrounding this desertion, at a precarious juncture for the Confederacy, forced aside more humane concerns.

At the appointed time, 4 P.M., Saturday, September 5, 1863, Major General Johnson's entire division assembled to witness the execution of the North Carolinians. Before the brigades were marched on to the field, pioneers were at work setting stout posts, each extending about three feet above the ground. Every post had a hole bored to accept a smaller crosspiece to which the arms of the kneeling soldiers would be firmly bound. A single grave to shelter the coffins was opened at the edge of a nearby wood. There is anecdotal evidence that the execution field was on the former property of President James Madison, though the exact location has not been identified.[32] As the full company of executioners —120 men in the firing parties and those in reserve — marched onto the field, muffled drums beat the cadence of a funeral dirge. The doomed men, living soldiers still, made an effort to march in step to the beat of the drum. They may have believed, perhaps led to believe, that they were acting out a ritual for the benefit of the assembled troops and that a graveside reprieve would be forthcoming. Reading of the death sentences, a prayer by a Chaplain, blindfolding and binding each man to his rude stake took only a short time of shuffling silence. The first shattering volley killed 8 of the kneeling men; attending surgeons found 2 still alive. A portion of the reserve was hurriedly ordered forward to kill them at close range. The entire division marched past the dead, held upright on their cross. Coffins were brought up, the bodies stuffed into place and covers nailed closed as the division marched off.[33] The coffins were taken by wagon to the gravesite. An Episcopal burial service was read. The grave was filled, excess earth mounded above, patiently awaiting return to its former level. No record has been found of a visit to the site by family, friend or mourner. One soldier, who did not witness the executions, recounted the happenings of his day.

> Saturday Sept. 5 1863 I arose reluctantly this morning about 8½ o'clock as lying in bed longer would have cost me my breakfast. We were visited today by a storm of rations — beef, flour, corn, vinegar, peas, salt, soap &c. The ten men under sentence of Court Martial were shot this evening at the camp of Stuart's Brigade in the presence of the division. Several of them were shot 3 times before they were killed. Being engaged about other things I didn't go to witness the scene which is said to have been horrible.[34]

Was the "storm of rations" just another of the chance happenings surrounding the executions? Or were they a calculated offering to reduce the risk of a violent reaction in the ranks by temporarily distracting one source of discontent? A Chaplain who witnessed the executions did not offer any indication of general unrest, as he was otherwise occupied. "1NC Sept 5 Spent most of the day in preparation for the Sabbath. Went out on drill ground late in evening (7) saw ten deserters shot. It was a solemn scene."[35] Another soldier chose not to witness the executions. "Camp near orange Court House Sept 6th Dear Pa. Ten deserters were shot in Johnson's brigade yesterday about 2 miles from us I did not wish to see it."[36] The same distaste was expressed by a man in the brigade.

> Camp Inspection, near Orange C. H. Va. Sept 7th 1863 Dear Friend I suppose you have heard of the execution of 10 men of our Brigade on last Saturday of the 3rd NC They were shot to death by musketry in presence of the whole division. The Surgeons of the brigade were required to be present. Nothing short of a positive order would have induced me to witness that sad scene. The men were accused of desertion, since the presidents proclamation, & murder of an officer who was endeavoring to arrest them. Doubtless it will deter many others from committing a similar offense.[37]

A different opinion was put forth by an officer who did witness the executions:

> Camp near Orange C. H. Va. September 8th 1863 Last Saturday our Div was called out to witness an <u>awful awful</u> scene. Ten men tied to a stake and shot to death. They were Carolinians, North those that were taken near Scottsdale [not legible]. They were good looking men all young. We formed a square so that all could see and after they were shot we then were marched by them. <u>This</u> was done to have a good affect on the men <u>but</u> I doubt its doing much good for our soldiers are hardened to such scenes. And they all say that they ought to have been imprisoned and there work for the government — I think this would have been better myself.[38]

Though this writer was skeptical of the good to be gained, punishment of men enrolled in North Carolina regiments had an indirect effect on other troops. One writes, "It is a right hard matter for us to get permission to leave camp. I suppose it is on account of being in a division with North Carolina troops. With them they are very strict."[39] Three days after the executions, a man of the Third Regiment gave his father a detailed account of the happenings involving men known to them.

> Sept 8th 1863 Dear Pa On returning from Picket on Saturday we were soon called out to our usual drill ground to witness the execution of ten of the men who deserted some weeks since. Our division was formed in Square one side open. The prisoners were marched in charge of the detachment of 120 men who were detailed to perform the executions. The music playing the dead march they marched down. The Prisoners were then made to stand facing the detachment while the sentence was read, by the officer of the day. Prayers were then offered and each Prisoner was then marched to his stake. The Bandages were bound over their faces. The command was given and soon they were hurled into eternity. They were all baptized by Mr. Paterson on Saturday morning and were praying when they were shot. One was a son of Mr. John Futch of Rocky Point and another was named Rainier from Holly Shelter. 5 men from Company K and the others from H. It was a terrible sight and God grant I may not be called to see anything of the kind again. Most the men were good soldiers and brave men. This being their first act of disobedience. Horrel of Bladen is said to have my Pistol, he has not yet been arrested. Harrison Futch one of the party was so badly wounded when taken that he has not yet stood his trial.[40]

Thirteen days after the fateful Saturday the impact of the event began to wane, and a soldier simply informed his sister, "There was ten shot last week but I did not go to see them."[41] Sixteen days after the executions the affair was likened to murder. A soldier in another brigade of North Carolina troops first described another execution of a single soldier and then went on, "Last Saturday was two weeks ago they shot ten at one time in Johnston division they belonged to the 3rd NC I saw some that saw them shot and they said that they murdered them up for they had to call in a reserve before they killed them that must be an awful business."[42]

Newspapers in their reporting of the mass execution were apt to embellish their account as was their wont and inclination. One looked on the event as a warning to others; that anguish in the heart would be carried home, family names were disgraced forever, a "dark stain" was placed thereon. Cries were heard from those bound to the stake, "Oh my poor mother."[43] A second newspaper indicated that the ceremony was impressive, sorrowful and handled with great solemnity. In a sardonic choice of words, it wrote that the volley poured in on the "unhappy" men. It also supported the observation that not all of the men were killed on the first volley, though their report said that 5 men had to be shot a second time, and that the second fire terminated the existence of the "wretched." The dead had "imbrued their hands" in the blood of a gallant officer.[44] A staff officer gave his recollection of the happenings in the Third Regiment as viewed from a command perspective.

> It was to these mountains that a large body of deserters from a North Carolina regiment in Virginia was making a little time back. A whole company had broken away, but was overtaken at a crossing of the James above Richmond. They showed fight and killed several of the pursuers, but were taken back and the leaders tried by court martial. Ten were convicted and sentenced to be shot. There had been too much leniency, and General Lee had the sentence executed. The unfortunates were tied to small sunken crosses in line about ten feet apart, with a firing party in front of each. Their division, Major-General Edward Johnson's, was drawn up in three sides of a hollow square, the deserters being on the fourth. At the word the firing was accurately executed and the men sank dead or dying at the stakes. The division was then marched by, close to their bodies, and it was hoped the lesson would be salutary.[45]

The points of emphasis in the reflections of the staff officer provide a vivid contrast to the impressions of men in the ranks. From a leadership perspective, the men involved were in a "large body" of blatant deserters heading for the mountains to join other bands of deserters; not that 13 average soldiers were heading for home and family. A "whole company" had broken away; not that 5 and 8 men from 2 companies had departed. Only the "leaders" were taken to trial; not that all of those still living were tried, convicted and given death sentences. "Several" of the pursuers were killed; not that a man was killed in each party. The firing at the kneeling men was "accurately executed"; not that the reserve was called up to dispatch wounded men still writhing, bound to their stakes. The ceremony was "salutary," not "awful." The statement "there had been too much leniency" was likely an opinion shared by most of the officers, and many of the men, who were present.

Did the death of the 10 men benefit General Lee's army? A man in the ranks thought it offered very little, "For I believe the more they shot the more deserted, and when they did desert they would go to the enemy, where they knew they would not be found."[46] Another soldier felt, "Doubtless it will deter many others from committing a similar offense."[47] Most all who witnessed the events of the execution day, or those who had the scene related to them, agreed that it was a "terrible," "sad" and "solemn" scene. The reality of death was accepted by those in the service and at home. Death brought an end to earthly pain and suffering. One of the men who was executed, told of the death of his brother, "He was wounded in the head by a mini ball he suffered greatly before dying but sense he is deed I believe he is haply and no doubt far better off than en of us."[48] Death brought relief from the terror and indignity of war.

Other than the desertions in August 1863, Company K had a fine absence record despite a large number of deaths.

Co K	1861		1862		1863		1864		1865	no date
Abs			1	3	2	11	2	2	1	
Dead	1	1	5	36	11	6		1	2	
Executed						5				

The 13 deserters from the Third were from 4 North Carolina counties. There were 3 each from Bladen, Columbus and Wake counties; 4 were from New Hanover. The county affiliation suggests that small groups of men joined to begin their hazardous travels; each may have had a natural leader. The conspirators did some preliminary planning. One wrote that he expected to see those at home in a short time, others added to their available ammunition, another stole a pistol. The decision to leave was not a spur-of-the-moment impulse. A factor in their decision may have been the heavy casualties the regiment suffered in the battles at Chancellorsville and at Gettysburg. The Third lost 67 dead, and 4 times that number were wounded. The Third experienced the most severe losses of the regiments in their brigade, nearly half of the casualties for the entire division.[49]

JAMES ELLIS 3-H (August 27, 1863). Private James Ellis was the oldest of the men who deserted on August 20, and he was the first to be court-martialed. His service record indicates a trial date of August 22, but this may be a recording error. The court record for Private Ellis was not entered into AIGO ledgers until November 11, 1864, fifteen months after his trial. Private Ellis was wounded at Sharpsburg, MD, on September 17, 1862, seven months after voluntarily enrolling in the Third on February 10, 1862. After a recuperative furlough he returned to duty in early 1863 and was continually present thereafter until agreeing to go along in the desertion attempt. Inasmuch as he was the oldest of the men who left that day, and the first to be tried, he may have been thought more influential than the others.

FRANCIS BENSON 3-H (August 27, 1863). Private Francis Benson volunteered to defend his state in May 1861, two days before North Carolina officially seceded from the United States. Having done this, he was then present for duty for one-month or two-month periods usually followed by an absence for sickness requiring hospitalization or a recuperative stay at home. This alternating pattern continued until he deserted on August 20, 1863. A Private Archibald T. Benson enlisted ten days after Private Francis Benson in the same company. He was killed at Gettysburg. Also in the company, Private Thomas Benson was confined in the brigade guardhouse for desertion when the other Benson men were killed. Private William W. Benson of Bladen County, and Company H, Third Regiment, deserted a few months earlier in the year. Men with the Benson family name had tragic experiences with the Third Regiment.

WILLIAM H. KELLY 3-H (AUGUST 27, 1863). Private William H. Kelly enrolled in Company H, Third Regiment, just a day or two after the regiment was mustered into Confederate service in June 1861. Except for a short period of hospitalization and a brief furlough of four days, he was present for duty until deserting on August 20. Had they been able to reach Bladen County Private Benson and Private Kelly might have enjoyed a short stay. "They are still raking the deserters, and I think have got nearly all of them in our County."[50]

DALLAS BUNN 3-K (August 27, 1863). Private Dallas Bunn was conscripted into the army on July 15, 1862. Slightly over a month later he was "sent to the rear" while his unit was engaged near Orange Court House, VA. At the same time, he received his prorated pay of $16.86 and a $50 bounty. After this, Private Bunn was absent for six months, returned to duty for a like period, and then deserted on August 20. When deserting, he took with him his government-owned ordnance valued at $33.98. Testimony in the trials for 4 of the deserters was complete at the end of the first day of court on Thursday, August 27.

DUNCAN R. CLARKE 3-H (August 28, 1863). Private Duncan Clarke enrolled for duty on May 15, 1861, a month after the beginning of war and was present when the Third was first formed. The young soldier, fighting alongside his comrades, was among the 147 regimental wounded at Chancellorsville in May 1863. He was later hospitalized while being treated for some unidentified ailment. Private Clarke was not charged with taking his musket with him when he deserted.

JOHN FUTCH 3-K (August 28, 1863). Private John Futch voluntarily enlisted in Company K, Third Regiment, on February 1, 1862. An older brother, Private Charles F. Futch, and a cousin, Private Hanson M. Futch, were then completing their eighth month of service in the regiment. Private Wily Futch, who enrolled on the same day as Private John Futch, was killed at Malvern Hill in 1862. Private Charles Futch was killed at Gettysburg in 1863. None of the four Futch men who enrolled in the Third survived the war. A Private John Futch was briefly enrolled in the Forty-First Regiment. He entered the service on October 1, 1861, only to be absent without leave on October 18; he never returned to the regiment. Though there are other men named John Futch in New Hanover County, the man who enrolled in the Third is most likely the man who left the Forty-First, based on existing letters that Private Futch wrote to his wife. He indicated that he was in service and that he had few liberties in November 1861, well before he enrolled in the Third Regiment, though there is a two-week disparity in the date of the letter and the record date of his leaving the Forty-First. Two months after Private Futch joined the Third Regiment, he was sick and sent to the hospital at Goldsboro, NC. At mid-year, a company officer of Company K requested that a Wilmington physician determine if Private Futch would ever be fit for further duty or should he be discharged from the army. A favorable prognosis was apparently returned, though the private was absent for the remainder of the year, not returning to camp until early February 1863. He survived the campaigns in the spring and summer of 1863 and then deserted on August 20. Private Futch corresponded regularly with those at home, though most, if not all, of his archived letters were actually written by other soldiers. John had difficulty writing a legible letter, his attempts to do so being a source of family humor. Brother Charles once wrote that he had taken one of John's letters to two different regiments and not one person could read them.[51] On the day that Private Futch deserted his company, he posted a letter home. No direct mention is made that he planned to leave for home that night. However, hints that he might soon see them, that he wanted to eat some watermelon when he got home, and that he also wanted to eat fish with his father-in-law are made in the letter.[52] More directly in the days preceding August 20, John wanted to know if an alleged deserter from the regiment had arrived home, and still more pointedly twice inquired if his wife had drawn any money, apparently referring to funds that were set aside to help the families of Confederate soldiers. There is a note of urgency in the question, indicating that he wanted to be sure she had received all the money that she could get while still eligible for the aid.[53] Some of his comments written in the months before his desertion suggest that he might be receptive to any talk of leaving the army. "I want to see you very bad the worst I ever did in my life."[54] July 12, "We are living the worst life man ever lived rations are short and our duty hard." A week later on July 19, "sick all the time and half crazy." Finally just before deserting, "hard times hard duty."[55]

JOHN N. RAINER 3-K (August 28, 1863). Private John Rainer was wounded in battle at Malvern Hill, VA, on July 1, 1862, thirteen months after enrolling in the Third Regiment at Dogwood Grove, New Hanover County, on June 1, 1861. A few days after being wounded, he was sent to the rear and then spent the next four months in various hospitals before recovering enough to return to duty. Private Rainer took his weapon with him when he deserted. As with several others of the thirteen who deserted from the Third that day, the record of his court-martial was not posted at Richmond until November 25, 1864. His name is given as Rains in that posting. A Private Stephen D. Rainer was also enrolled in the same company; he was discharged from the service a few days after enrolling. The charges against 3 deserters were presented for the consideration of the court on the second day of trials, Friday, August 28, There was to be no weekend delay in marching the prisoners to the stake.

KEARNEY PRIVETT 3-K (August 29, 1863). Private Kearney Privett was a conscript. Two months after conscription, in July 1862, he was sick, abandoned in battle, captured by the enemy and then paroled, all this in the vicinity of Sharpsburg, MD. Following his parole, in October 1862 he was hospitalized at Richmond. He remained there until he took his musket in hand and deserted.

JAMES DAWSON BUNN 3-K (August 29, 1863). Private James Dawson Bunn was conscripted into the Confederate army on July 15, 1862. Nearly a year later, he was captured by the enemy at Chancellorsville in May, and then paroled or exchanged. In between his enrollment and capture, he was sent to the rear on August 23, 1862, while suffering some unstated sickness. When he deserted he carried his ordnance with him. An older brother, Private Wesley Bunn, was also conscripted, and he signed his request that he not be exchanged after his capture by Federal forces in 1862. Another soldier with that family name, Private George A. Bunn, was a conscript on July 15, 1862. He was at home recovering from an illness when the Bunn men made their decisions to desert; otherwise there may have been 3 men with that name bound to their stakes on September 5.

JOHN R. BEDSOLE 3-H (August 29, 1863). Private Bedsole suffered several stays in medical facilities after volunteering for service in February 1862. Wounded at Malvern Hill in July 1862, he was treated for the lingering effects of the wound in November and was then hospitalized with an illness in December and again in May and June 1863 with another illness. After eighteen months of intermittent duty Private Bedsole deserted. The courts-martial for the final 3 of the 10 deserters who were shot on September 5, were completed on Saturday, August 29.

HANSON M. FUTCH (3-K September 1863). Private Hanson Futch volunteered for the army at Dogwood Grove, NC, on June 1, 1861, agreeing to serve the military forces of the state, this within two weeks of North Carolina's act of secession. Except for one brief stay at home in early 1862, he served faithfully; in fact, his service record contains a notation, "He acted well in several engagements." Still, for some reason, he willingly placed his fine record and his life in jeopardy when he went with the deserting men in August, taking his ordnance with him. In the confusion of the arrest at Scottsville, VA, Private Futch was wounded, detained and then formally arrested on September 1. Thereafter he was tried and convicted. His death sentence was known by September 28, with the day of execution set for October 2. A query was directed to President Davis by Colonel William Preston Johnson, ADC, on September 28, 1863.

> Mr. President Hanson Futch 3rd NC Regt & J. M. Luther 28 NC Regt sentenced to death and to be shot Thursday have appealed to your clemency. The proceedings of the courts martial have not yet arrived. Futch is quite a boy. Luthers father is a volunteer in the service.[56] He is the 11th deserter ten having been shot of the party tried for the killing of Lt. Mallett it is stated that he had no gun and is simply a deserter. Shall they be respited for examination of the papers.[57]

Consideration is due one of the more perplexing statements found in clemency correspondence: "Futch is quite a boy." Did Colonel Johnson want to say that the condemned "boy," who was in his early twenties, was really a good soldier? There was certainly an indication that Private Futch was in fact a brave soldier. Or was the Colonel trying to say that he was an active, impulsive lad, perhaps one who did not easily accept army rules and regulations, but was still fine material for the Confederate army? The President, perhaps equally puzzled, requested the full record in the cases at hand on September 26, 1863. Colonel Johnson also noted that "it is stated" that Private Hanson Futch did not have a weapon in his possession in the confrontation at the river crossing. His service record shows that he took ordnance with him, and a lifesaving appeal might hinge on that vital point. The tone of the Colonel's remarks suggests that in his mind there had been enough killing and Private Hanson Futch should be spared. Additional time was needed for the record review and on October 1, the day before the scheduled execution, Adjutant General Cooper suspended the execution of sentence of Private Futch and Private Luther. The President wished to further review the record in each case, noting that Private Futch was "the latter one of the soldiers tried for shooting Adj Mallet." Private Futch was fortunate that the ordered delay actually came about. Garbled orders directing the suspension of sentence were released for a "Private Harreson Fitch of the 2nd NC," and might easily have gone astray and the execution taken place as scheduled.[58] In any event, the suspension continued for several months. While the stay of execution was in effect, Private Futch was confined at Castle Thunder. There, he was infected with smallpox and died of the disease on December 17, 1863, sparing the President further concern.

AMERICUS V. HORRELL 3-K (Prior to January 25, 1864). Private Harrell, a conscript, served thirteen months in the Third before deserting along with the other 12 deserters; he took his government-owned ordnance with him. Allegedly, he also carried a pistol stolen from a man in the regiment. Private Horrell either separated himself from the other deserting men before the river crossing encounter, or he avoided capture during the confusion of the arrest, for he was not in custody until arrested and delivered to authorities at Wilmington, NC, nearly a full month later, on September 25, 1863.[59] A court convened in late 1863, or in early 1864, agreed on a death sentence for him, just as other courts had agreed for the other 12 deserters. The sentence was suspended and the full record in the case was requested by the AIGO, this on January 25, 1864. In some manner, Private Horrell gained sufficient freedom to be captured by Federal troops on October 6. He was confined in Federal prison camp and took the oath in May of the next year, the only survivor of the 13 deserters.

Private William Barefoot, Company H, Third Regiment, is not included in the above account of the deserters who were tried by court-martial and sentenced to be executed. He volunteered for service in February 1862 and served four months before being hospitalized. After returning to duty, he was captured at South Mountain, MD, in August and did not rejoin his command after being exchanged that same month, for he was listed as being absent without leave until January of 1863. Private Barefoot was present for duty during the Chancellorsville and Gettysburg battles and then deserted on August 20, 1863. He was the only deserter with an earlier unauthorized absence charge on his record. Various reports of the confrontation at Scottsville state that at least 1 deserter was killed and 1 was wounded. The wounded man was clearly identified, but the man who was killed is not named in surviving accounts. There are persuasive references that Private Barefoot was that man. He deserted on August 20, along with the other men, but no trial record has been found. Records for all of the others are posted in AIGO records, albeit after a long delay. A North Carolina Roll of Honor entry for Private Barefoot indicates that he "deserted and was shot in arresting him."[60] Although the service record for Private Barefoot does show that he was among the men executed on September 5, it is erroneous. There is no record that he took his weapon when deserting and may have been unarmed when killed.

The deserters from the Third Regiment were in general young men but not mere boys, at least to the extent that age might favorably influence a court or a reviewing officer. On enlistment, the oldest was thirty-two and the youngest eighteen. At least 2 of the 13 lost brothers at Gettysburg, 4 were wounded in earlier engagements, and 9 were hospitalized at various times. Service began for 5 men in 1861, and 8 followed in1862.

Three weeks after the mass execution, a soldier from the Third applied what he had learned from the experience; he fled directly to the enemy. Company H lost 6 deserters on the same day, November 15, 1863. A soldier in Company I, on November 30, 1864, reminded those at home, "Remember that I am coming home if I ha to runaway."[61] This a few days after he was wounded by a shot to a finger.

Eight weeks after the men of the Third were at their final rest, on October 30, 1863, General Lee expressed a concern to the Secretary of War saying that he had "serious apprehension as to relapse to leniency ... ruinous to army ... cruel to men." Pardons granted after a few executions increased desertions to an alarming extent. Men would seize upon the slightest hope to escape the consequence of their acts. "Leniency will not only make all the blood that has been shed for the maintenance of discipline useless but will result in the painful necessity of shedding a great deal more."[62] He might have added that 22 North

Carolinians were executed in September and 3 more in October 1863. Were those the deaths the General now deemed useless?

JAMES R. POWELL 1-F (January 9, 1864). Private James R. Powell of Bertie County enlisted on July 5, 1861, in Murfreesboro, Hertford County, at age nineteen. He abandoned the Hertford Greys at Germanna Ford on the Rapidan River, VA, on November 27, 1864, while his company was engaged with the enemy. Private Powell apparently had second thoughts soon after fleeing his command, for he returned the next morning missing only his cartridge box. For this momentary lapse he was arrested and taken to trial on January 9, 1864, and was sentenced to be shot to death when the proceedings of the court were published in GO #4, January 19, 1864, Army of Northern Virginia. Four days after publication of the order for execution, Captain Thomas D. Boone, Private Powell's company commander, submitted a request to General Lee's headquarters.

> Camp 1st Regt No Ca Troops Jan 23, 1864 Col. In Behalf of James R. Powell, Company F. 1st No Ca Troops condemned to be shot for "misbehaviour in the face of the enemy," I would respectfully request if it be not deterimental to the service that the time for his execution be postponed a few days to allow his mother — his only parent, time to see him. She has been written for and cannot get here under 10 or 12 days — He earnestly prays that he may be allowed to live long enough to see her.[63]

The request was directed to Colonel R. H. Chilton, AAG. The request was approved on the day written by the regimental commander and on the next day by the brigade commander. On January 26, the request proceeded up the chain of command and the Division and Corps commanders added their endorsement. A "respite till Friday week" was granted, providing a scant twelve-day delay as requested, this done by SO #24, January 26, 1864, Army of Northern Virginia. The day before the expiration of this order, SO #33, February 4, 1864, Army of Northern Virginia, granted a further indefinite suspension. Chaplain William R. Gwaltney, First Regiment, had frequent contact with the condemned man from the time of his court-martial until the end of January. The state of mind of the prisoner is suggested in a diary kept by the Chaplain:

> January 21, 1864 Spent forenoon reading & in aft went to Brigade Guard House to converse with a man of my reg who was condemned to be shot for cowardice. He is unprepared to die. He cries and prays most lamentably. His mind is very much confused. January 23, 1864 Went in the morning to see the convict again. Found his mind somewhat more composed. January 24, 1864 aft went to Brigade Guard House to see the criminal after conversing awhile with him I went to Ramseur's Brigade. January 25, 1864 Was introduced to Ramseur & wife ... I then came back to guard house to see the prisoner. January 28, 1864 engaged plank for chapel came back by the guard house and saw prisoner. Trust he has obtained a [not legible]. He has a respite of another week. January 30, 1864 Late in the afternoon went to see the condemned prisoner. January 31, 1864 Was reading & went to guard house to see prisoner Hope he has experienced a change.[64]

No further direct mention of the prisoner is made by Chaplain Gwaltney, but he did visit a prisoner on February 24, 1864, so he may have had some contact with Private Powell that day. While the respite was in effect, the complete trial record was sent to the Secretary of War on February 8. General Lee twice suspended execution of sentence while the review was in progress. On May 19, 1864, Private Powell was pardoned by the President. A full pardon was authorized because Private Powell had voluntarily joined a hastily formed battalion of imprisoned Confederates to defend Richmond, during the week around February 29. In the wording of SO #116, May 19, 1864, AIGO, the released prisoners were to return to their respective commands "without further investigation of, or punishment for, the offenses with which they are individually charged."⁶⁵ Private Powell survived the war.

HILLARY HARVEY JOYNER 1-F (January 22, 1864). Private H. H. Joyner was enrolled in Company F, First Regiment, on April 28, 1862. In his initial year of camp life, he was admitted to a military hospital on two occasions and was granted a thirty-day recuperative leave. On November 27, 1863, while his company was engaged in a skirmish at Germanna Ford on the Rapidan River in Orange County, VA, Private Joyner fled from his assigned place, as had Private Powell of the same company. Once in custody, Private Joyner was charged with misbehavior before the enemy. At trial on January 22, 1864, he was found guilty as charged and sentenced to be shot on or about the seventh day of the next month. Private Joyner was shot to death on February 11, 1864. No mention of his imprisonment or execution is found in the diary of Chaplain Gwaltney who did note that he studied, or wrote, on the days surrounding the execution. Perhaps this indicates that Private Joyner was confined in the division guardhouse rather than in the same location as Private Powell. Private Joyner was tried two weeks after the trial of Private Powell. He was also five years older, and no record has been found that anyone spoke in his behalf. Nine months earlier, his older brother, Private John E. Joyner of the same company, was killed in battle at Chancellorsville, VA.

JOHN JONES 1-C (Prior to February 23, 1864). Private John Jones was an early volunteer in May 1861, and a year later he earned a $50 bounty for extending his enlistment. A year after that, on April 1, 1863, he indicated he wanted to end his enlistment, first by being absent without leave, and then in outright desertion. Private Jones avoided arrest for eight months, but was securely in custody on January 3, 1864. At a court convened in mid–February he was tried, found guilty, and sentenced to be shot. The death sentence was commuted to a month of hard labor by SO #52, March 3, 1864, AIGO, a very substantial reduction in sentence for a soldier absent for an extended period and under a death sentence. Following his lenient treatment, Private Jones returned to duty, was wounded, detailed to detached duty and finally deserted to the enemy on March 14, 1865.

JAMES R. PHILLIPS 3-F (March 4, 1864). Six men with the last name of Phillips were conscripted into Confederate service from Moore County on the same day, July 15, 1862. Of the 6, 1 was killed and 3 were wounded at Sharpsburg, MD, just two months after going into the army. Private J. R. Phillips was among the wounded. Two months after he was sent to the rear to recover, he deserted. A year later he was arrested. At trial, he was found guilty of desertion and, not unexpectedly after such a long absence, sentenced to be shot. On review the sentence was remitted by the Secretary of War, "on order of the President," this order on March 28. News of the pending pardon must have reached the regiment several days earlier and led a company officer to comment, "J. R. Phillips has been pardoned and will I think make a good soldier in future."⁶⁶ The prediction may, or may not, have been borne out. Private Phillips was captured by units of the Federal army on May 6, about five weeks after receiving his pardon. When questioned as a prisoner of war, he stated that he did not wish to be exchanged but wanted to live north of the battle lines. He survived the prison experience and took the oath at High Point, NC, in May 1865.

Summary

There were 72 men from the First Regiment and 58 from the Third Regiment in line on the day of surrender at Appomattox. These 130 men were all who remained from over

3,500 men who were enrolled in the regiments. From the Third, 10 were forever in line in their grave, 2 from the First were in solitary graves, and all found their final rest on Virginia soil. The First and Third were essentially from eastern North Carolina; a single company was from Wilkes County. Military courts concurred on 19 death sentences, 3 conscripts were executed of 5 so sentenced. Married men made up 8 of the 19 sentenced to death. A sampling of 4 companies of each regiment gives an average company enrollment of 176 men for the First and 172 men for the Third. In the First Regiment an average of 62 men were dead by war's end, a 35 percent death rate, and 27 of the deaths were battle related.[67] The Third suffered greater casualties; on average, 71 men in each sampled company did not survive their service, a 41 percent death rate; 32 deaths were combat related.[68] Despite these heavy losses, both regiments had fine absence records, the Third at 11 percent and a sampling of 7 companies of the First indicating a rate of 9 percent.[69] Desertion of a serious nature was pretty much confined to 1863. Few men left in the final year of war, but of course the number of men then present was also far fewer. After that one dreadful September evening in 1863, the Third Regiment was not again assembled to witness the execution of a soldier from their regiment.

11

First Corps

Toward the end of August 1863, a time when the military execution of Confederate soldiers began in earnest, the First Corps of the Army of Northern Virginia did not include any regiments of North Carolina troops. This corps, commanded by Lieutenant General James A. Longstreet, was made up of 4 brigades of men from the state of Virginia, 4 brigades of men from Georgia, and 4 brigades of men from 4 other states. Though surviving records likely do not present a full accounting they do show that 126 men were sentenced to be executed in the units that were assigned to the corps. Of those so sentenced, 11 were executed. Even after a soldier in the First Corps was given a death sentence, he had an excellent chance of surviving the stake. Just one brigade in the First Corps approached the execution experience of the eight North Carolina brigades in the Second and Third Corps of General Lee's army. That was the Virginia brigade of Brigadier General L. A. Armistead assigned to General George E. Pickett's division. This brigade had 45 men ordered to be executed; the lives of 6 soldiers ended in the prescribed manner. The execution rate of those sentenced to death for the brigade was 13 percent. This rate was exceeded by 10 of 11 North Carolina brigades that had men sentenced to be executed. Execution rates of convicted men in the Second and Third Corps of the Army of Northern Virginia exceeded 50 percent for 2 North Carolina brigades. The other brigades from the state fell along a scale down to the teens, all greater than that found for the Virginia brigade.

Part II. Department of North Carolina

12

History of North Carolina Troops in the Department of North Carolina

"Impatient of drill and discipline"[1]

Early on, Brigadier General Richard C. Gatlin led in the defense of the seaward side of North Carolina; he was not competent to do so in the opinion of Governor Henry T. Clark. The Governor questioned the qualification of General Gatlin and other officers: "It seems to me there is manifest want of attention to the proper requisite for an officer." In view of the numbers needed, "there must be many that are not qualified.... Some means of ascertaining fitness of at least commanding officers of companies regiments and brigades" must be found. General Gatlin had shown "entire neglect and inattention to the coast defense of his command."[2] The concern for the fitness of Confederate officers was echoed by a soldier: "From Capt and Lieut that are not fit to make privates. They will turn up Jacks whenever go to fight."[3]

Among the 17 Confederate Generals and Lieutenant Generals who were most often directly involved in decisions regarding capital punishment for troops from North Carolina, only 2 were attributed to North Carolina. Lieutenant General Theophilus Hunter Holmes lacked the decisive aggressiveness sought by his superiors. In the opening stage of Confederate organization he commented, "Close observation of volunteers has convinced they can not be successfully lead by men in whom they have not full confidence and for whose superior intelligence they have not a high respect."[4] A rather ironic comment made by an officer with little confidence in his own ability. General Holmes wrote of his shortcoming soon after being promoted to Lieutenant General: "I would to heaven I had a prompt decisive mind that would determine when and where great risks should be run. Judge of my humility when under these circumstances I find myself made a Lieutenant General."[5] General Holmes released General Order #7, Department of North Carolina, March 25, 1862. He emphasized that with a Federal occupation, "North Carolina will be under his [Federal] worse than vandals despotism to this effect the strictest discipline must be preserved and the commanders of companies, regiments, and brigades are required to enforce the most exact obedience to all orders and regulations."[6] Three days later he closed a report to General Lee: "I am oppressed with the responsibility upon me. The tremendous issue involved make it necessary that a more able brain than mine should direct. Please, therefore, my dear General, come and straighten out this tangled yarn."[7] A fortnight later: "Confidence you so blindly repose in me, and can only pray that God will give me strength to justify it."[8] But doubt overcame confidence: "Do not ascribe this to a want of ambition or to a diffidence, but rather believe that I know myself and have the honesty to sacrifice my vanity to the interest of my country. I can execute but I cannot originate."[9] After four months of soul searching and self doubt General Holmes was transferred.

Next entrusted with the defense of North Carolina was Lieutenat General Daniel Harvey Hill. He was very expressive in his opinion as to why the battle of Sharpsburg in Maryland was not a rousing victory. "Enormous straggling" was the reason why the Federal army was not, "crushed and annihilated.... Thousands of thieving poltroons had kept away from sheer cowardice. The straggler is generally a thief and always a coward, lost to all sense of shame, he can only be kept in ranks by a strict and sanguinary discipline."[10] General Hill urged formation of counter-guerrilla groups in counties of North Carolina and Virginia, "or wherever the infernal Yankees and their rascally Dutch allies can be found." Their duty would be to "kill the murderers and plunderers wherever they show their villainous faces."[11] An April 1863 letter to Governor Vance offered this foreboding: "If conquered by the Yankees our doom will be the most miserable known in history. There is no insult and no indignity these infernal wretches will not inflict upon us."[12] In early May 1863, General Hill implored Governor Vance: "The desertion of our troops is still continuing to increase. In heavens name can we do nothing to stop this fearful evil."[13] Amnesty offers were not an effective option: "Recent deserters have been chiefly those who came in under first amnesty." The alarmed General also expressed his deep concern to the Secretary of War. Desertion was "alarming on the increase," "powerful factions were poisoning public sentiment," and a North Carolina newspaper was "highly treasonable." The General thought that severe punishment, including the execution stake, would be effective in quelling desertion.[14] A few days later in another case in which a deserter was given five years at hard labor, General Hill tersely stated that he "should have been shot."[15] In regard to the Confederate soldier: "He was self-reliant always, obedient when he chose to be, impatient of drill and discipline, critical of great movements and small movements, the conduct of the highest and lowest officers from Mars [sic] Robert down to the new-fledged lieutenant.... Of the shoulder-to-shoulder courage, born of drill and discipline; he knows nothing and cared less.... His disregard of discipline and independence of character made him often a straggler, and the fruit of many a victory was lost by straggling."[16] General Hill did not mention the frequent military execution of North Carolinians in his reminiscing.

Major General William Henry Chase Whiting often made very stern statements when reviewing a court decision, but he wavered when the moment for the deadly volley drew near. His comments on what should be done with all who resisted Confederate authority were equally fierce. In a brief reply to a request from General D. H. Hill, General Whiting explained that he had a party in Bladen County engaged in breaking up a gang of "deserters and freebooters": "I had directed them to be exterminated."[17] Four days later, the bellicose General requested advice on how to legally try a man who was attempting to carry slaves to blockading ships off of Wilmington, concluding with the remark, "Had the pickets put him to death in the act, it would have saved trouble."[18] In the same tone on the arrest of accused spies, "They will be dealt with."[19] When he set aside the findings of one court: "Especial attention is called to the numerous irregularities which mark the proceedings of this Court. There is no more solemn or important military duty than that devolving upon a court martial, sitting to determine the guilt or innocence of their fellow-soldiers — their responsibility extending to life or death, to honor or disgrace of officers.... Want of familiarity with precedent or practice may in some degree palliate irregularity, but for carelessness in either the proceedings or the record, the Commanding General knows no excuse."[20] General Whiting equated the punishment of death for those in the ranks with the odium of disgrace for those who led them. The General also pointed out that the effectiveness of courts-martial in curtailing desertion was reduced because there was no readily accessible procedure to correct court errors that had no bearing on the guilt or innocence of the man at trial.[21] Return of guilty but unpunished men to their company certainly was disheartening for men who remained firmly in line, besides giving a wiser deserter a second opportunity to steal away. Though inclined to waver on death decisions, General Whiting served loyally and with distinction from the beginning to his death when Fort Fisher fell in 1865.

In 1864, General Pierre Gustave Toutant Beauregard was given command in Southern Virginia and North Carolina. He understood the need for discipline at every level of army command. All officers must give "prompt and zealous heed and obedience to all orders emanating from superior authority.... Implicit obedience to the orders of our superior is the soul of discipline.... With it an army becomes disciplined, a perfect, yet simple machine.... Without it an army is soon converted into an armed mob."[22] The General also expected military courts to confine their decisions to the guilt or innocence of the soldier before them. In early 1863, a court indicated that they had taken extenuating circumstances into consideration during their deliberation of the case before them. General Beauregard pointed out that such decisions were his responsibility, adding that he was always pleased to follow the recommendation of a court.[23] Courts continued to consider extenuating factors in their decision-making and the General continued to caution them.[24] He urged all officers assigned to courts to read Lee's *Vade Mecum,* which clearly explained most of the legal and military matters that a court might encounter.[25] General Beauregard did insist, as did most high-ranking officers, that courts follow specific rules in conducting a court and in issuing their ruling. Not to be overly lenient in their decisions was an added caution.[26] In an earlier command, General Beauregard said that he would not approve such "trivial punishment" as having half of a deserter's head shaved along with a sentence of thirty days chained to a thirty-pound weight.[27] This a month after pointing out that "maiming, robbery, rape or destruction of property could properly be punished with a sentence of death."[28] A day earlier, he had approved a sentence of nine and thirty lashes, head to be shaved, and the offender to be drummed from the service for plundering and pillaging a barrel of whiskey.[29]

At year's end 1863, there were 4 brigades of infantry, 18 regiments, assigned to defend eastern North Carolina. Brigadier Seth M. Barton led a brigade of Virginians. Brigadiers Clingman and Ransom directed their North Carolinians; General Martin's brigade was stationed to defend Wilmington. For 3 of the infantry brigades 85 men were tried, convicted and sentenced to death — 11 were executed, an execution rate of 13 percent. The brigade of General Martin had 59 men given death sentences and 21 executed, a rate of 36 percent, this approaches the 46 percent execution rate suffered by North Carolina troops in the Third Corps, Army of Northern Virginia. Sadly, the executions in General Martin's brigade were not evenly distributed. All save one were inflicted on men of the Sixty-Sixth North Carolina.

13

Ransom Brigade

Ransom Brigade

"Very stern and harsh with men under him officers and privates."[1]

The brigade commanded by the Ransom brothers, Brigadiers Robert and Matthew, was notable for the large variance between men who were sentenced to be executed and men who were acquitted following 111 military courts. Acquittals were 2; death sentences were 28. Commonly these categories, at the extremes of military sentencing, are approximately equal. Brigade officers were acquitted more often, nearly 4 of every 10 that went to trial. Officers were held to high standards of conduct and competency, though not always agreed to by a court. The observation is supported by a July 1862 comment of one who served in the Twenty-Fourth: "Genl Ransom is very stern and harsh with the men under him officers and privates yet I think apart from that he is a good officer."[2] Also commenting on discipline, a soldier in the Thirty-Fifth wrote in his diary in February 1863, "Men punished almost every day for some offense or other. One man stood on a stump 3 days for stealing bacon."[3]

Twenty-Fourth Regiment

Johnston County was home for the 2 men of the Twenty-Fourth Regiment who were given death sentences by a military court. Neither man was executed, but neither survived the war. The relatively few men subject to severe punishment in this regiment is entirely consistent with the court record for the regiment but inconsistent with the alleged desertion activity. At one point it was reported through the chain of command that 200 soldiers had deserted from the Twenty-Fourth within the last thirty days, this for a period prior to April 1863. It was one opinion that these desertions were attributable to a recent ruling by a judge in North Carolina that conscription was unconstitutional and could not be enforced. Prophetically, the writer advised a member of General Lee's staff, "Unless something be done, and quickly, serious will be the result."[4] The reported desertion of the 200 men is partially supported by the record of Company E, the Lone Star Boys, from Johnston County. For the two months February and March 1863, 13 men left the company without authorization; 6 returned and later began a second desertion. For the war there were 56 absence incidents, 19 in 1863, 11 in each of the other three years of conflict, and 4 with dates unknown. Total enrollment for the company was 150 men. With all of these comings and goings, an extensive court-martial history might be expected, but only 1 court record has been located for Company E; a death verdict was issued in that case. The record of absences for Company I is similar to that of Company E. It supports that prisoners were not made to answer at court. In Company I, 21 men left of their own will, 8 doing so at least twice, yet only 1 man ever went before a court recorded by the AIGO. Company I enrolled 157 men. With few men appearing before military courts, 9 from the regiment, and one was acquitted, it is not unexpected to find that 5 companies had no record of men being court-martialed.

Twenty-Fifth Regiment

The Twenty-Fifth was recruited in a region where not all families were firmly committed to the Confederacy. Men who did sign on were reasonably sure they would find safe shelter if they decided to flee the army and return to their mountain homes. Desertion attempts by these men often resulted in success. For example, Company I, the Pisgah Guards, Buncombe County, had 168 men enrolled; at least 39 absence attempts were made by enrolled men, yet AIGO records at Richmond list only 3 trials. Desertion was a real embarrassment to a company Sergeant who appealed to Governor Vance for his aid in securing a transfer because he was "ashamed" of his company.[5] Governor Vance may have shared the "shame"; Buncombe was his home county. As was the experience of most regiments, the Twenty-Fifth had men killed in confrontations between deserters and men determined to arrest them. In the minds of the families that lived in the area, there was oftentimes little to separate one set from the other. One letter urged that the mountains of North Carolina be kept clear of deserters but then went on to say that there were 50 men of the Twenty-Fifth searching for deserters, but that they themselves were nothing but an organized band bent on plundering.[6] Men of the Twenty-Fifth went before courts for 35 violations of the Articles of War. Not one was acquitted. Company B, the Jackson Guards, accounted for 8 of these courts. The service records for nearly half of the 35 regimental men who were charged give no indication of the specific offense; however, the punishment suggests that absent without leave was the predominate charge. Frequently the punishment was for a period of hard labor varying from twenty days to six months. Those guilty of a shorter duration absence often wore a flour-barrel shirt, usually labeled befitting the crime, while they stood or marched before their fellow soldiers.

Thirty-Fifth Regiment

While a significant number of men of the Thirty-Fifth were ordered to be executed, 9 in total, existing records do not clearly state that any were shot. The records for 3 of these men ominously end with the soldier under sentence of death. No mention is made that the sentences are under appeal or that records were forwarded for presidential consideration. From the best indication, 1 of the 3 was executed. General D. H. Hill would have increased that number. "Regret that court did not inflict some sharp summary punishment upon the cowardly deserters ... wretches want to be confined in safe place. They are almost as mean as the skulking exempt at home, and are nearly as much deserving of death."[7] Rather than face a Confederate execution, Private Talton Turner was to be placed on the parapet at Fort

Caswell to face enemy fire in any attack on the fort.[8] One reason that more men were not given death sentences and ultimately shot is that they were adept at desertion. Company B, the Marion Men, McDowell County, enrolled 128 men from formation in September 1861 to surrender; 43 were absent at some point, nearly half of them in 1863. Of these known absentees, 20 had no further service record. Five absentees returned but then made another attempt to flee the company. Other men in the company were more anxious to serve. Privates Arrister and Richard Isbell enrolled in Company B on September 11, 1862. Two months later the cousins were discharged, one was underage; his 1860 census age was twelve. The other was overage; his 1860 age was forty-five.

The Thirty-Fifth Regiment offers good evidence of the marked disparity from company to company of the distribution of crime and punishment within a regiment. Over three-fourths of the 38 men of the Thirty-Fifth that were taken before military courts were from three companies: Company K, recruited in Burke, Catawba and Sampson counties; Company G, the Henderson Rifles; and Company B, the Marion Men, McDowell County. None were acquitted. In contrast, the companies that suffered no recorded courts were made up of men from Onslow, Chatham and Mecklenburg counties, Companies A, D and H respectively. All of the 9 men that were sentenced to death were enrolled in Companies B and K. Company B experienced an absence rate of just under 40 percent, Company K under 10 percent. A soldier in Company C wrote to his sister on December 28, 1861, as the first year of passion and violence came to a close.

> There was an old man and a his wife beat nearly to death last Wedensday knight by a part of our regiment it took place about one oclock the alarm came in to the camp an the role was called to see whoe was missing ... the major and part of the men went to house and found three of them there a quarlin they had broke all the dishes and one glass window ... they have been under guard ever since there trial has not come off yet the punishment will be bad I think the balance they was accused of doing is not feten for me to write to you you [*sic*] may no it was tolerable bad if so but there is so many things said here that is not so we do not now when we hear the truth.[9]

Apparently the rumors of the affair alluded to some kind of sexual assault; crimes often go hand in hand, one with another. No court-martial record has been found.

Forty-Ninth Regiment

The Forty-Ninth was the first regiment in the brigade to hear that a man from their ranks would be executed, this introduction to the reality of military discipline occurring in December 1862. In the years ahead, 10 others in the regiment would share that experience. In only 1 of the 11 instances has execution of sentence been fully confirmed; the military service of 3 end on an ambiguous note, but with indications that 2 were executed.

While the Forty-Ninth did not have a large number of men go before military courts, only 28, with one acquittal, those who were brought to trial usually received severe punishment. Nearly three-quarters of those tried were either ordered to be shot or were given harsh punishment. In terms of courts-martial, the worst offending company in the regiment, Company A, from Rutherford and McDowell counties, had 8 courts; 7 resulted in severe sentences, and 1 man was acquitted. Of 143 enrolled men, 58 absented themselves, 15 making more than one attempt to do so. These departures took place at a fairly consistent rate throughout the war. Absences, 21, from Company H, 168 enrollment, were fairly contained after year's end 1862.

Absent	1861	1862	1863	1864	1865	no date
Co A		20	15 13	7 7	11	
Co H	2	12	2 1	1 2	1	

In Company A, 3 men from Rutherford County, Alfred, John and Jonathan Walker, were each subjected to thirty-nine lashes for desertion. Company H, the Gaston Rangers, sent 3 men before courts, as did 3 other companies of the regiment. A private in Company D wrote that 7 men had deserted in early April 1863. Of the 7, 6 were successful in their desertion, in that only 1 was ever arrested.[10] Only 2 recorded courts have been found for Company D. An officer in Company K was determined that a deserter be caught. "I want you to tell Pa to watch out for him I want him to be caught — I got him in as a drummer — so he cannot blame me for disappointing him."[11] The deserter was captured and confined and a year later killed while on picket duty. But the first soldiers with desertion records sufficient to warrant a death penalty were not from Company A or Company D, but were members of Company G, the Kings Mountain Tigers. Two weeks before the men deserted, the resignation of their company captain was accepted because he was "wanting in discipline and capacity."[12]

An officer of the Forty-Ninth felt it necessary to instruct his men to not walk like they were "between plow handles" but to march as if they were "with our sweethearts."[13] After hungry men of the regiment bought some pies that may have been made with dog meat, other regiments barked at them when they were nearby.[14]

Fifty-Sixth Regiment

Companies of the Fifty-Sixth that had no courts-martial listed in AIGO records were: Company A, the North Carolina Defenders, Camden County; Company E, the Moore Guards, Moore and Northampton counties; Company F, the Cleveland Rifleman, Cleveland County; and Company H, the Pettigrew Guards, Alexander and Caswell counties. But on closer look at Company E, the Moore Guards, for example, there were 21 recorded absences from among 114 total enrollees. Of these men, 16 had no further service record after their absence. A similar experience is found for Company A, Camden County. The North Carolina Defenders had 112 enrollment and 19 recorded absences. Only 4 of the absentees were ever again present with their company. In Company B, the Cape Fear Guards, 2 men were absent without leave for a week in April 1863, and on their return were punished by being ordered to march through camp wearing a barrel shirt with the label "AWOL" attached. Following that humiliation they were to be tied by their thumbs to a beam at arm's length above their heads. This painful punishment, suspended by the thumbs, the toes just touching the ground, was for two hours on each of six days.[15] In contrast, 3 men from Company G, were absent for a three-week period in August 1864. They were punished with a year of hard labor while wearing a ball and chain, a much harsher sentence for only two weeks additional absence.[16] Absentees from Company B might well have expected that they would serve as prime examples for severe punishment if they were caught. There were 133 men listed on company rolls. These men made at least 69 attempts to absent themselves, 17 doing so more than once. Absent without leave was the charge against 13 of the 69. All of these men returned to their company; 6 saw and seized a second opportunity to stray and did so successfully. Overall 32 absentees were back in camp to be punished yet only 4 court records are found in AIGO postings. For the regiment there were 11 courts with no acquittals.

Courts-Martial

Robert Ransom Brigade

DANIEL GARDNER 49-G (December 1, 1862). Six months after voluntarily enrolling in March 1862, Private Gardner left his regiment on September 17, 1862, and did not return for five weeks. For this fairly short absence, he was tried and then sentenced to be shot. However, at his trial on December 1, 1862, sufficient exculpatory evidence was introduced to lead the court to recommend unanimously that their just agreed upon death decision be remitted; the recommendation was made known with the publishing of GO #137, December 28, 1862, Headquarters, West Virginia. The court's initial decision may have been influenced by a surge in absences from Company G just prior to the trial. In his review of the proceedings, General Lee agreed with the court's recommendation, remitted the sentence, and restored Private Gardner to duty. He served faithfully thereafter until the final days of war when he was captured. Private Gardner died in a Federal prison camp.

DAVID MCDANIEL 49-G (December 1, 1862). Some six months after enrolling, Private McDaniel felt he had good reason to head for home, which he did on September 16, 1862. As confirmed at trial on December 1, he was absent for two months before being brought back in arrest and under guard. On December 28, his death sentence was published. On review, the sentence was commuted to hard labor with a twelve-pound ball and chain attached to his left leg for the duration of the war; this decision was made known on February 3, 1863. Governor Vance was informed of the decision.[17] The prisoner was escorted to Fort Fisher, Wilmington, NC, to work on the fortifications. The spared, but now imprisoned, man addressed Governor Vance on April 25, 1863.

> Sir I respectfully ask your kind indulgence to consider my case I volunteered in April 10, 1862 in Capt A Roberts of Col Mcafees 49th Regt NCT for three years or during the war in cleveland so I have been in the melvin [Malvern] hill fight I also in the battle around richmond I am forty seven years of age and unable to proform the duties of a soldier my family at home are suffering very badly & I am in the guard house at fort fisher for during the war & I have been here since Feb 7 my crime that I was put here for was being persuaded by an other soldier to leve my command & go home I was gone six days and had started back to my command & had got as fer as Raleigh whare I was arrested by the guard this is all my [not legible] & I sincerely hope you will consider all things & get me released for which you will all ways have the prayers of my suffering family & I will never cease to feel great ful to you With [not legible] Respect David McDaniels to his Excellency Gov Vance.[18]

Governor Vance sent the request to the military and General D. H. Hill reviewed the record. The prisoner was released by virtue of the Presidential Amnesty of August 22, 1863. He returned to duty and was freed from further service by death on February 23, 1864. Several points of emphasis made by Private McDaniel are often found in letters of supplication to State and Confederate authorities. They were persuaded to desert by others. Their family was suffering because of their absence. The petitioner was either on his way back, or just about to start back, when authorities seized him. Privates Gardner and McDaniel were older men, natives of South Carolina, who enrolled in the same company, and made their home in the same general area. One was returned to duty and the other imprisoned for the war.

That decision evidently rested on the fact that Private Gardner returned voluntarily while Private McDaniel was brought back in arrest.

SAMPSON JORDAN 56-K (May 20, 1863). But for the intervention of the relentless natural executioner — disease — Private Jordan may well have been the only man of the regiment to be executed. Private Jordan attempted to depart Confederate service on three occasions, thus becoming a good prospect for the execution stake. Unfortunately for him, he was enrolled in the Confederate Boys of Mecklenburg County, a company with a fine absence record. An account of his disloyalty was developed at a court-martial convened on May 20, only three months after he was enrolled on February 20, 1863. First, he induced soldiers to abandon their post and desert their command, this on April 25. Second, four days later he again persuaded certain members of his company to leave the ranks. Third, the next day Private Jordan followed the advice so freely given and deserted. At trial he was found guilty on all charges and a death sentence was announced on June 7.[19] The day of execution was set for June 19, in the presence of his regiment and if practicable, his brigade, "where ever the regiment or brigade may be at the time." The regiment was preempted of the duty when the condemned man died of typhoid the day before the planned execution. His final effects amounted to $12.

In the opinion of General D. H. Hill, an officer of Company C of the Forty-Ninth well deserved to be added to the list of those executed. GO #19, May 26, 1863, Department of North Carolina, "The sentence in case of Lieutenant Giles Bowers is disapproved being too supremely absurd. It is inconceivable that a court can find a commissioned officer guilty of misbehaviour before the enemy and not sentence him to be shot."[20] If General Hill had his way, Lieutenant Bowers would have been the only officer in a North Carolina regiment to be so threatened. Officers from other states were given death sentences and at least 2 were executed.[21] General Hill did not limit his ire to leniency for officers. A hospital steward who threatened to kill and then struck a superior was fined $200. The General observed: "But it is wonderful that a court could be found with such mistaken views of mercy as to impose a paltry fine upon a man who so richly deserved to be shot to death."[22]

Matthew Ransom Brigade

"The melancholy ceremony was soon over."[23]

Brigadier General Robert Ransom was promoted to Major General in May 1863. Brigade command passed to older brother, Brigadier General Matthew Whitaker Ransom, a lawyer and former Attorney General of North Carolina. His experience with the intricacies of legal proceedings may account for the few trial acquittals for the brigade.

Brigade loyalty may have been reinforced by the realization that there were men in the several regiments who had no qualms over shooting those who refused to fight. Private James Elliott, Company F, recalled that in September 1863, companies of the Fifty-Sixth were sent to the western counties of North Carolina where they "arrested and sent two thousand men to the front that the militia were unable to manage, killing and wounding thirty-five in making these arrests."[24] The account may be overstated. Colonel P. F. Faison notified the colonel of the Wilkes Home Guard, "I have this day sent off about one hundred and eighteen prisoners making in all over five hundred that I have sent from this county. At this rate we can soon leave the county in such a condition that with you as Commander of the Home Guards there will be no fear of the past state of affairs in the future."[25] Considering that Wilkes enrolled just over 1,200 Confederate soldiers, the scope and the seriousness of the "past state of affairs" can be appreciated, though obviously not all of those returned were residents of the county. A month later, men of the Fifty-Sixth were engaged in arresting deserters in Davidson County where conditions were still precarious. The Home Guard dared not move about the area except in goodly number or with a contingent of regular troops.[26] "My home guard are poorly armed inefficient and rendered timid by fear of recent vengeance from the deserters."[27] "When one of us goes out we boath go, when one of us stand gard we both stand. Thare is a heap of deserters about here."[28] A second man in the regiment recalled that nearly all of the people in Randolph and Davidson counties were Union in their leanings and that about half of them were deserters. Conditions did not improve, and in mid–1864, the Fifty-Fourth Battalion Home Guard in Alexander County was informed, "Nothing can be done at this time against the deserters further than to defend yourselves in the best way you can."[29] They apparently responded with a vengeance: "You said the gard was killing everybody they could."[30] Whether it was a Confederate decision or personal revenge that drove the "gard" to kill, the time of reasoned judgment and considerate compassion was long past. A deserter named Northcutt suffered for his misdeeds. "He was tried by a little drumhead court marshal and shot on short notice one mile north of Ashboro as we were leaving that section for Wilkes County, where there was strong Union sentiment hard to hold down."[31] The executed man was not further identified; families with the name Northcott and Northcote lived in the general area of the incident.

CRATON MANORS 49-A (October 10, 1863). Privates Craton and James B. Manors deserted from Company A, Forty-Ninth Regiment, on August 15, 1862. That month marked the beginning of a period of intense absence activity by men of the company. Half of all enrolled men had absences on their record. Private Craton Manors joined up on February 26, 1862; brother Private James Manors followed a few days into March. Six weeks after his departure, Private James Manors was hospitalized with dysentery; the ailment caused his death on September 25. Details surrounding his return are not known. Private Craton Manors likely returned at the same time. He was then present for seven months, whereupon he again departed on April 3, 1863. Six months after this excursion, he stood before a court-martial. On October 10, the court decided that a death sentence for Private Manors was warranted, the sentence being published on December 12, 1863. While under sentence of death, Private Manors was able to elude his guard and set off on a third desertion attempt. On September 24, 1864, a second death sentence was published. Private Manors was one of the select Confederates with the distinction of receiving two death sentences. To the relief of Private Manors, General P. T. Beauregard did not approve the second sentence because evidence of his earlier conviction and subsequent escape was not properly introduced into the proceedings. Furthermore, no reason was given as to why the most recent trial was conducted by a 7 officer court rather than the stipulated number of 13. Finally, the General noted that the statement by the court that the death decision was unanimous was improper and negated the whole proceeding.[32] The unanimous statement may have been deliberately inserted to show that a full court would have reached the two-third concurrence threshold required for a death sentence and that their decision was not determined by just 4 or 5 officers. In any event, all of these errors led to the following directive to the Secretary of War, James A. Seddon, on November 28, 1864. "The President directs me to state to you that the enclosed proceedings of a court-martial in the case of Pvt Craton Manus Co. A 49th N.C. Regt. submitted to him by you, with the information that the record is defective. Very Respectfully Your ObSvt Wm Preston Johnson Col ADC."[33] In endorsing the order, General Beauregard said in his comments that "Manus" should be retained until further orders. On March 5, 1865, General Lee was advised that Private Manors was restored to duty by issuance of General Order #2, February 11, 1865, Head Quarters Armies of the Confederate States.

The Twenty-Fourth was not marched out to witness the execution of one of their regiment, but they were not denied the experience. A literate member of Company E relates:

> We were twelve months volunteers at first, and before time was out all were conscripted of certain ages, and finally nearly all from the cradle to the grave. Many were forced in who were utterly opposed to the war and would have never volunteered, consequently we had a duty-shirking element injected among us unwillingly. Then the suffering and privations of the families at home created great unrest, and wet-blanketed the little spark of patriotism remaining. Letters from their families describing their sufferings and want could not and would not be tolerated. Their mean poor fare and poor pay could hardly be endured and when the letters came from home telling of greater suffering there, many could not endure it and went home and were called deserters. My understanding of a deserter is when a man deserts the colors and joins the enemy. It was from the first class described that I saw two so called deserters executed. They were arrested, brought back, tried by court-martial, proved guilty of desertion, and accordingly shot. They were poor illiterates from the wire grass region of Harnett County and were never imbued with much patriotism. They viewed the wealthy slave owners and possessors of all the rich land and fish and game preserves, with silent disdain. A few barrels of turpentine and tar and a little cleared patch round his log hut was all he had at home. They were conscripts and felt no interest in the war. On the day of execution all the troops were assembled on the beach in a hollow square, with the sea side open. In this square two stakes were driven. Twelve men with loaded muskets stood ten paces away. The prisoners, bound and blinded were tied to the stakes and knelt facing their executioners. The officer in charge called, "Ready! Aim! Fire!" A volley and they fell over dead, without groan or struggle, and their blood soaked in the sand far from their loved ones at home. A horrible example set before a none too patriotic soldiery. Among the guns in the hand of the firing squad were two with blank cartridges. It was the most ghastly scene of all my life, and impressed itself on my memory as nothing else has ever done.[34]

Unfortunately the writer, some forty years after the event, does not offer sufficient detail to identify the executed men.

A polite introduction into the service is found for an officer of the Twenty-Fourth. "Saw Gen Ransom and after he found who I was he was very polite indeed ... and told me he would be happy to see me at any time." Several days later he continued, "Gen Ransom since finding out <u>who I am</u> has been remarkably polite to me."[35] Not all officers were so welcomed. The Colonel of the regiment gave a frank opinion on one of his officers, "Quite young ... very boyish ... possessing few of the qualities of a commanding officer," as he recommended acceptance of his resignation.[36]

HENRY C. GAINES 24-E (October 14, 1863).
Private Gaines deserted twice in 1863, this after his decision to defend his state on May 31, 1861. He remained faithfully in the ranks of an absence-prone company for two years. The first absence began on February 22, 1863, and ended in the March–April period when he was again present for duty. The second absence was also a rather short affair, beginning on August 24, and ending in the

reporting period of September–October. Private Gaines, now with two desertion attempts on his record, was confined in the guardhouse at Weldon, NC. He went from guardhouse to trial on October 14, and the ensuing death sentence was reviewed by General Pickett and approved. Execution of sentence was suspended while the case went forward for review by the Secretary of War. Three months later, the death sentence was commuted by SO #75, March 30, 1864, AIGO. The spared soldier was sent to Castle Thunder, arriving in time to voluntarily take part in the defense of Richmond, then threatened by General Philip H. Sheridan's cavalry. A reward for his renewed commitment was release from the sentence earlier imposed. Unfortunately Private Gaines never knew of this, as he died in a hospital on July 12, 1864. Private Reuben K. Gaines was a member of the same company, perhaps enrolling a few days before his brother. He was discharged in May 1862 because he was overage and deaf. Private Simon Gaines enrolled in Company E in November 1863 and served ten months before deserting. There is no record of his return.

SYLVANUS DEAL 35-K (October 17, 1863). Private Deal was conscripted into the Thirty-Fifth in June 1863, and deserted on a day unknown. The death sentence that followed his court appearance on October 17 was not unexpected. The fall of 1863 was a time when a first desertion, even when measured in days, drew a death sentence. Still, it was not a time for drumhead vengeance. Orderly review procedures were in place for responsible officers to follow when they decided that course appropriate. In the case of Private Deal, the record was sent forward and the sentence suspended until the review was completed. In SO #71, March 25, 1864, AIGO, Private Deal was relieved of punishment and returned to duty by authority of an earlier presidential amnesty. Clothing records show that he was still confined at Castle Thunder in May. Later released, he was wounded in June and thereafter absent.

W. D. MICHAELS 35-K (October 17, 1863). Not long after voluntarily enrolling in the Thirty-Fifth and accepting a $50 bounty for so doing, Private Michaels deserted. He enrolled on March 3, 1862. Eighteen months later, he was before a court-martial. When a decision was made known, it was for the extreme penalty of death, but within days the sentence was suspended and Private Michaels was sent to Castle Thunder to await the result of an appeal. Months later, he was released by authority of SO #71, March 25, 1864, AIGO. The private served the Confederacy for over three years; he was present for duty a small part of that time.

ISHAM CLONTZ 35-B (October–November 1863). Private Clontz deserted twice, first in August 1862 and again in August 1863. He had indicated his willingness to serve in September 1861, so he stayed with his regiment a year before setting forth on each desertion. No record of punishment for the first desertion has been located, but for the second attempt he was court-martialed. With the publishing of the court's findings on December 15, Private Clontz learned that he would be shot. The responsible General approved this finding, but execution of sentence was suspended while the trial record was sent to the Secretary of War for review. After a delay of four months, the decision to commute the sentence to a year at hard labor at Weldon, NC, was made known in SO #88, April 15, 1864, AIGO. The spared private was captured by Federal units in April 1865 and took the oath in June.

MILES HUFFMAN 35-B (October–November 1863). Another conscript who deserted soon after being taken into service was Private Miles Huffman. He was enrolled on May 1, and deserted on July 19, 1863, after just ten weeks of service. Some fourteen weeks later a death sentence was forthcoming following a court's deliberations. On December 15, the full record in the case went to the Secretary of War for review, and in July of the next year the prisoner was released to return to duty. In the final weeks of the struggle,

Private Huffman was captured, confined in a Federal prison, and freed after taking the oath in June 1865. The widowed mother of the Huffman family sent 5 sons to war; 2 did not return. Military courts issued death sentences to 3 of the brothers.[37]

Private M. J. McSween, Thirty-Fifth, C Company, wrote to Governor Vance after his court and sentence of twelve months at hard labor: "This sentence must be regarded as most cruel outrageous and unmerited and the result purely of malice prejudice and tyranny."[38] The point must have been well taken for the sentence was remitted and the soldier later promoted to Sergeant Major. An initial solicitation was mailed to the Governor shortly after his arrest. A third appeal centered on the wish to avoid serving the sentence in Castle Thunder.[39]

CHARLES WASHINGTON SHULL 49-K (October–November 1863). Private Shull was not present for duty for much of the three-year period he was assigned to the Forty-Ninth Regiment. First a brief stint of absence without leave, then sickness, later hospitalization, detail as a nurse, desertion, imprisonment, a wound and finally capture by the enemy fairly sum up his service. The first contact with military justice after an absence in late 1862 did not deter Private Shull from again chancing that course in May and June 1863. The deserter went before a court-martial around October 13. A soldier in the same company writing home on October 13, mentioned that "S Adams will be tried today also Geo Hafner & W. C. [sic] Shull I think they will both be shot as they shoot almost every one they try for deserting. I feel so sorry for their wives and themself."[40] As the writer predicted, Private Shull was indeed found guilty and sentenced to be shot on Friday, December 4. The man who foretold his fate again wrote, "I suppose you know that Shull of our company is to be shot on Friday next and five others belonging to the brigade. Hafner is to be branded with the letter D."[41] The branding sentence for Private Hafner was remitted, and no sentence for Private Adams has been found. Private Shull's record was referred to the Secretary of War on December 15. No action was forthcoming until July 1864 when the death sentence was remitted, and Private Shull received a pardon for aiding in the defense of Richmond.

The scheduled execution of these six men of Ransom's brigade did not take place. The several references establish that their death sentences were published by early December 1863. Lieutenant J. W. Lineberger found time to write on December 5, "They are som six men to be [shot] to Death next wednesday for desertion, they be long to our Brigade they are nary one from our company."[42] And on December 7, "There is six or eight men from our Brigade to be shot to death with musketry in a few days for desertion none from our regiment."[43] Four days later, on December 9, a man in the Forty-Ninth observed, "Some men of our brigade were sentenced to be shot today on account of desertion but for some reason or other their execution has been postponed ten days."[44]

JOSEPH H. TRAFINSTEAD 25-H (October–November 1863). After shouldering a musket following his enlistment on July 15, 1861, Private Trafinstead was then detailed as a hospital nurse for a brief time in 1862. Later he was confined to a Richmond hospital suffering some unknown illness. In what was apparently his first venture into desertion, he departed from his company on August 20, 1863. Within weeks he was confined and awaiting trial. With the publication of GO #4, January 22, 1864, Petersburg, VA, he was very likely startled to learn that he would be shot, probably not reasoning that he simply had the bad fortune to be tried at a time when severe punishment was once again being meted out for desertion. The death sentence was approved by the responsible General, and on that note the service record of Private Trafinstead ends. A brief absence and a record of illness make it likely that death came in some manner other than execution.

SAMUEL SMITH 35-K (October–November 1863). Private Smith voluntarily joined the Thirty-Fifth on October 15, 1861, agreeing to serve for twelve months. The period of service was extended in June 1862, for which the private received a $50 bounty. On April 27, 1863, he left his company to remain absent until the fall of the year when he was in arrest and before a court-martial. The result of the trial, made known with the publishing of GO #4, Department of North Carolina, January 22, 1864, was that Private Smith was to be executed. This decision was approved, and there his service records end. With a longer absence than Private Trafinstead, and no record of illness, it is more likely Private Smith was shot, but there is no evidence to support that notion.

JOSEPH H. VAUGHN 25-D (October–November 1863). In the winter of 1861, on December 28, Private Vaughn voluntarily went into the Twenty-Fifth. He abandoned cause and comrade when he fled on August 15, 1863, after serving twenty months. An absence of about six weeks ended in arrest and trial. With publication of the court's decision he learned that he would be shot. While under threat of execution, Private Vaughn managed to elude his guard and escape, ending his service.

ZIMRI COSTNER 49-H (October–November 1863). Five Costner men volunteered for duty in Company H, Forty-Ninth Regiment, on the same day, March 22, 1862. Six months later, Private Zimri Costner deserted. Once safely home, he was able to avoid authorities for a full year before being arrested and taken back to his command. A court-martial at Weldon, NC, followed in due course. Writing to an absent officer, Captain C. Q. Pettey, on October 19, 1863, mentions, "Zimri Costner has not had his trial yet he is waiting for you to return you are one of his witnesses."[45] Either before or after trial, Private Costner managed to regain sufficient freedom to again desert and return to Gaston County. An officer in the same company as the private warned his kin, "Zimri Costner's doom is death if they ever get him if he is a bout home he would better look sharp."[46] Lieutenant James Wellington Lineberger was a member of a family that had intermarried with the deserter's family, leading a Confederate officer to advise a deserter that he had better "look sharp." There are many conflicting loyalties in a civil war. The warning served no useful purpose, for by the time it reached home, Private Costner was again in shackles and delivered to Camp Holmes, a deserter's grave in the offing.[47] On April 28, Lieutenant Lineberger, writing to his wife, told her that "Zimri Costner will be shot tomorrow if not this evening it looks bad but it seems as there is no other way to do with deserters he never has done any good in the Army."[48] A diary entry dated May 2, tersely states that "Zimri Costner, deserter from Co. 'H' shot."[49] The writer continues, "Zimri Costner of Co. 'H' was shot this morning, in accordance with the sentence of the late Court Martial at Weldon, as the penalty for desertion. We then proceeded on our way towards Greenville, and camped within seven mile of that place."[50] A soldier in Company I of Private Costner's regiment describes how he avoided the execution detail. His company was waiting to rejoin their regiment in Martin County.

> When it came it had a deserter along under sentence of death, and he was to be shot next morning at sunrise. He belonged to our Regiment. Orders came to the Captains of each company to send a man to headquarters who was a good shot with an Enfield rifle. Captain Conner told me to go, I knew very well what I would have to do and begged the Captain to excuse me. I told him it was not my time on detail and if it was I would go without a word. The Captain answered, very well, and called the Sergeant and ordered him to send the next

man on detail, which fell on T. J. Fisher. The poor fellow was shot and buried and we were soon on the march.[51]

This account may to some degree explain the poor marksmanship evidenced in many executions. The Captain was ordered to send a soldier who was "a good shot with an Enfield rifle," yet he wavered and sent the next man on detail. As a final note on Private Costner, a historian of Gaston County commented, "It is sad to record that two were shot for desertion. Colonel Morris a just man says there were extenuating circumstances and these [men] should not have been executed."[52] The reference apparently to Private Costner and Private Green W. Ford of Company H, Thirty-Seventh Regiment. It is difficult to find an "extenuating circumstance" in the record of Private Costner other than family needs or conditions at home. A son, Zimri, was born and named in the year his father was executed.

If correctly recalled, the reference to a sunrise execution is perhaps the only instance where a North Carolinian was dispatched at daybreak. A little daylight was needed to get the regiment roused, fed and assembled. It was probably a brief affair, more likely experienced as an irritant than as a warning for any considering desertion.

WILLIAM L. REECE 25-F (October–November 1863). Private Reece was an early volunteer with the Twenty-Fifth; he joined on June 29, 1861. At the end of his first year of active duty, he was sick and hospitalized. Instead of returning to duty on his release from the hospital, he deserted. The details of his return are not known. The circumstances were such that he was willing to chance a second desertion on March 27, 1863. As expected, he fled to his native county of Haywood, there to remain until challenged by men from his own regiment sent to arrest deserters. In the arresting scuffle, Private George W. Chambers was killed by Private Reece. The young men were cousins who had enlisted together nearly two years earlier. Whether Private Reece made good his escape after this encounter is not clear, but he was in custody by July or August and went before a court-martial in October. Having heard the detail of the desertions of Private Reece and the murder of Private Chambers, the court sentenced the prisoner to death. Their decision and the Commanding General's approval were announced on February 13, 1864. Private Reece was to be shot to death on February 18, 1864. On that day, a diarist noted that the condemned man marched onto the field with six of his executioners marching before him and six more marching closely behind him. Private Reece was accompanied by the Reverend Mr. Deane. The writer, Private Henry A. Chambers, no known relationship to the murdered man, described the event.

> The cold and wind continued throughout the day.... At four o'clock, the regiment was marched out in a field near the rail-road bridge where the whole brigade was assembled to see a man from the 25th regiment shot. The melancholy ceremony was soon over and we returned to camp.... He had twice deserted and had killed one of his own company who, with some others were attempting to arrest him.[53]

A second writer from the Forty-Ninth added more detail: "I have no new to write of much importance The 18th I think it was our Brigade was all marched out in a field to see a man shot there was twelve men shot at him he was tied to a stake I was told four balls hit him he deserted and killed his cousin he belonged to the 25th regt."[54] An officer in another regiment in the brigade described the demeanor of the condemned: "I saw one man exicuted that had bin sentensed by the court they was twelve men shot at him he looked as if he did not care and did not mind it there is more to be shot."[55] A soldier in the Fifty-Sixth wrote home the day after the execution to say, "Thare was a man shot yesterday at Weldon there was 4 Regt marched up to look at it he had runaway he belonged to the 25 Regt I am sory to say that we dont get enough to eat."[56] The impact of the execution on a soldier in the Forty-Ninth was quite different! "We had a splendid time there playing ball and other games until they shot a deserter on our play grounds, which broke up our games at that place."[57] It is not stated whether the games were stopped by order or by the players. Bad feelings, uncontrolled tempers, or a disregard for family honor, all could be offered as solace for the families of the young cousins.

A man in Company B, Twenty-Fifth Regiment, was among 10 prisoners at Weldon, NC, who petitioned Governor Vance for some relief from the conditions of their confinement. They complained that they were not given sufficient food, water or clothing. The Governor promptly replied, "I cannot do anything for them unless I know something of the facts."[58] Apparently lacking persuasive facts to bolster his case, the soldier from Company B abandoned that avenue of appeal, escaped from the guard, and was not heard from again.

JAMES C. FOWLER 25-C (August 26, 1864). Private Fowler went to the Twenty-Fifth on March 22, 1862, and deserted on October 6 of the next year. One record states that he was in arrest by year's end 1863, but he did not appear before a court-martial until August 26, 1864, suggesting that his arrest may have occurred at a later date, or that he returned and there was a second absence. Whatever the circumstance, he presented a defense that was at least partially effective; though the court handed down a death sentence, it recommended clemency by the President. At that point, Private Fowler probably did not feel that he was under any immediate threat of kneeling at the execution stake. Very likely he knew that efforts to secure some respite were being made on his behalf. Captain Wesley N. Freeman, of Company C, prepared a petition which was submitted to the AIGO.[59] His name was also included on an appeal, compiled by John D. Keiley, that requested authorities to delay the executions for additional investigation. The list of condemned men included 8 from North Carolina regiments—7 from Ransom's brigade—2 from Alabama and 1 each from Georgia, South Carolina and Virginia. In a passionate appeal prepared on October 5, 1864:

> General Cooper If you will give me a little respite I pledge my life to show you that some of these poor fellows ought not to be shot. I have but just visited these men & have not had time to ascertain the particulars in each case give them a little more time and I think it more than probable—almost nearly certain that the president & yourself will see sufficient cause to commute the punishment or pardon these men. Your time is too precious to allow special pleading my heart is too honest to indulge it. Please respite these men or ask Gen Lee to respite them to give me a chance of ascertaining the facts in each case. God Bless and prosper you & our cause Jno D Keiley.[60]

In his endorsement on the request Captain Blackford indicated, "No Action by command of Gen Cooper." John Keiley may have had a principled objection to all executions. Or it may be that the man of honest heart opposed war and needless death in any form. The appeal is rather informal, which suggests that Keiley held some civil post in the Adjutant General's Office, or was at least known to General Cooper, hence the "No Action," direction, and no need for the courtesy of a response. The cases that were considered to have merit were processed through regular channels.

No doubt giving due weight to all of the effort on behalf of Private Fowler, the President commuted the sentence of death to twelve months at hard labor. Within a few months the private was restored to duty, captured by Federal troops, and signed the Oath of Allegiance to the Federal government. Before he decided to leave his company, Private Fowler made a written plea to Governor Vance asking for aid for his family, and for other families in Haywood County. The first letter dated March 27, 1863, written after a year of service, pointed out that his family could not live on the monthly pay of a private soldier. He went on to say that local relief distributors were not aiding those in need. He asked that he be appointed "Comosary" for either Haywood or Madison County where he could be of more help to his country than he could in the army where he was often absent due to sickness.[61] The Governor replied that county agents were appointed by county courts. A second letter on October 6, 1864, was sent to the Governor after Private Fowler knew that he had been sentenced to death. He explained, "I received a letter from my wife stating there condition and my two children were both at the point of death and I made every effort to get permission to go home honorably but failed in every effort."[62] The Private described himself as "penitent" and acknowledged "it is through my own disobedience and transgression of the law that has placed me in this condition." Governor Vance made no comment or instruction for a reply on the letter.

WILLIAM HOGAN 49-A (September 1, 1864). The first desertion for Private Hogan commenced on May 15, 1863, fifteen months after he had joined the Forty-Ninth. Upon his own decision, or yielding to the urging of family or friend, he voluntarily went back to his company on August 29, after an absence of three and a half months. Though the date of his next desertion is not recorded, it led to a court-martial and a death sentence published in GO #24, September 24, 1864, Department of North Carolina and Southern Virginia. Three specifications supported the desertion charge and the death sentence was approved by General Beuregard, to be carried into effect seven days after publication of the order. At this point the service record of Private Hogan abruptly ends. Private Hogan's name was not on Keiley's list of condemned men and not on the list that was submitted to the President for his consideration. As this was the second desertion of some length for Private Hogan, it is likely that the execution was carried into effect.

ELKANAH POPE 49-A (September 1, 1864). Another soldier from the Forty-Ninth Regiment, Company A, was included on the appeal to General Cooper.[63] Listed as A. K. Polk, he was in fact Private Elkanah Pope who had joined the regiment on February 2, 1862. In view of the urgency of the request, the error is easily understood. Civil War records are replete with such examples. Still, the effort might better have been concentrated on cases other than that of Private Pope. Within six months of his enrollment, Private Pope began his first attempt at desertion. Initially he was dropped from the rolls of his company, but subsequently he was caught and court-martialed. The sentence of the court was thirty-nine lashes immediately, thirty-nine to follow in two months, as announced in GO #137, December 28, 1862, Army of Northern Virginia. A six-month interval elapsed, and Private Pope once again departed. The next court did not end with a flogging sentence; he was to be shot. A court headed by Colonel J. V. Jordan, Thirty-First Regiment, judged the case and presented the verdict. General Beauregard approved the sentence and ordered that the execution take place seven days following publication of GO #24, September 24, 1864, Army of Northern Virginia. The pleading of John Keiley was prepared just three days before the scheduled execution. Private Pope's name was not included among the names sent forward for Presidential review by the AIGO. No further detail has been found but Private Pope's record suggests that his execution took place as ordered. In the company there were 3 other men with that family name; no desertion attempt marred their records.

ADEN CARVER 35-B (September 6, 1864); and THOMAS CARVER 35-B (September 6, 1864). Two brothers, Privates Aden and Thomas Carver, went into the Confederate army on the same day, December 4, 1861. Private Aden Carver was the first to forsake the flag; he deserted on May 19, 1863, after serving eighteen months. Private Thomas Carver, along with two other Carvers also enrolled in Company B, deserted on September 23. The other two Carvers had no further service record, but about a year later Privates Aden and Thomas Carver were in detention and standing before a court-martial in session on September 6, 1864. When the decision of the court was published on September 24, a death sentence for Private Aden Carver was approved, while the same sentence for Private Thomas Carver, together with that for other soldiers, was suspended awaiting the decision of the President. The names of Privates Aden and Thomas Carver were on the appeal submitted by Keiley. In regard to the plea, Captain Blackford, AAG, advised that records in seven of the cases had been submitted to the President for his consideration. The name of Private Aden Carver was not included. In fact, Captain Blackford carefully included the first name for Private Thomas Carver but only the last names of the other six men, indicating that Private Aden Carver was knowingly excluded from further consideration; it was not an oversight.[64] No other reference concerning the fate of Private Aden Carver has been located in military or post war records. The best indication is that Private Aden Carver was put to death as ordered by the court. The life of Private Thomas Carver was spared with the publication of SO #206, November 1, 1864, AIGO. His sentence was commuted to twelve months at hard labor, that sentence was remitted and Private Carver returned to duty and capture by the enemy.

JOSEPH TARPLEY MCKINNEY 35-B (September 6, 1864). Private McKinney was an early volunteer when he joined the Thirty-Fifth in September 1861. After eight months of service he deserted, not to reappear on company records until his court-martial held on September 6, 1864. Though ordered to be shot, the sentence was suspended awaiting presidential consideration. The name J. T. McKenny [sic] was on the list that Keiley sent to the General Cooper. The decision of the court had been made known in late September. On November 1, the President commuted the death sentence to twelve months of hard labor. Some portion of that sentence was remitted. Private McKinney was captured and signed the oath in mid–1865.

LAWSON GOBLE 49-I (September 13, 1864); and WILLIAM D. L. GOBLE 49-I (September 13, 1864). Father and son were conscripted into the same company on the same day, October 13, 1863. Father and son deserted on the same day, July 15, 1864, two months after the son was wounded. Two weeks later, they were arrested by A. L. Jenkins, for which he received $60 upon their delivery to the Confederate army. They were court-martialed on the same day and were given the same sentence, death, for a first desertion of two weeks. The death sentences were remitted, and father and son returned to duty. Three months later, the father was killed in battle. The son survived capture and a brief time in a prisoner of war camp. Court-martial records for both father and son have the erroneous note, "Shot." They were included on the Keiley list. This is the only known instance where a father and his son were confronted with the march to side-by-side execution stakes. The father was just two years short of exemption from conscription. On enrollment the son gave his age as twenty-five; more likely he was sixteen or seventeen. In 1880, his age was listed as thirty-five. William misstated his age, perhaps to help his father survive a deadly war.

JOHN A. ROCKETT 35-K (September 13, 1864). Private Rockett had a very brief service record after conscription on August 14, 1862. The only entry is that he received a clothing allotment in March 1864. Though not included in the service record, AIGO records show that he definitely went before a court-martial in September 1864. On September 13, a court heard his case and determined his guilt, punishment was to be death by musketry. Five weeks later, receipt of the trial transcript was posted by the AIGO at Richmond, VA. There ends the service record of Private Rockett. His name was not included on the Keiley list. All considered, he likely escaped the execution march.

After the intense trial and execution activity in Ransom's brigade some men appealed to higher authority. A soldier in the Forty-Ninth wrote to his mother that he was invited to a "secret prayer meeting" at a "secret place." He accepted and took part in a "very nice prayer," led by the man who extended the invitation. "But he who giveth life saw fit to call him away the next day."[65]

HAMILTON EVERHART 49-B (October 1, 1864). Six weeks after Private Everhart left his home as a conscript, he left his regiment as a deserter. On July 12, 1862, he enrolled in the Fifteenth Regiment. While absent from that regiment, his company was transferred to the Forty-Ninth. This was of little moment for Private Everhart, for his absence extended over two years, until his arrest around August 31, 1864. He went before a court on October 1. A death sentence for such a prolonged absence was not unexpected; once forthcoming, it was approved. Before the sentence could be carried into effect, Private Everhart escaped his guard and went directly to the enemy while in the vicinity of Hanover Junction, VA. He took the oath and was allowed to travel to New Orleans, LA. In the three years of his obligation to serve the Confederacy, Private Everhart was available to them only four months, and over half of that time was spent in confinement.

WILLIAM DANNER 49-A (Prior to October 5, 1864). The military record of Private Danner offers very few specifics. What is known is that his name, with the correct regimental designation, was included on the Keiley list of names submitted to the AIGO, and that the record in his case went forward to the President. The result was that Captain Blackford informed the petitioner, "The case of Wm Danner has been submitted and returned the President declining to interfere," this on October 11, 1864.[66] No service records for Private Danner have been located. While this is somewhat unusual, there are other instances where only a punishment reference has come to light. The indication that the record went to the President, and that Captain Blackford addressed the case specifically, suggests that a service record did exist. There is the possibility that the reference to Private Danner is in error in regard to name, unit or state. There were other soldiers named Danner in the Forty-Ninth, but their whereabouts are verified. The surname Danner is not found in a search of the records of men that faced execution in other states. The case of Private James Danner, Company F, Forty-Second Regiment, also under sentence of death, was being processed by the AIGO in this same time frame, and confusion in name or unit is certainly a possibility.

While the Fifty-Sixth was mired in the trenches surrounding Petersburg, VA, at the end of November 1864 a soldier wrote to his mother to say that men were deserting from the regiments that were located on each side of his regiment. He went on, "The 24th has lately received over 150 conscripts which has caused the trouble, in some cases old soldiers joining them. The men who have stayed at home, since the beginning of the war are for the most part, either miserable cowards or impugnated with Holdenism ... that is very doubtful whether the efficiency of the army is increased by bringing them into service."[67]

NEEDHAM PRICE 24-C (December 3, 1864). The war was nearly into the third year before Private Price decided to take an active part, perhaps because conscription was imminent. Whatever his reason for enrolling on April 15, 1863, by September he had a change of heart and began a desertion that went into winter of the next year. A military court heard his case on December 3, 1864, and brought forth a death judgment. Within a week the death sentence was approved, but when General Cooper reviewed the case he commented, "It will be perceived that this man was tried by a Mil Ct composed of only 2 members & that ct recommends ... clemency."[68] After the comment by General Cooper, and the recommendation of the court, the death sentence was remitted and Private Price was confined in prison. In early 1865 he was released by General Order #2, soon captured by Federal troops, and died while a prisoner of war at Camp Lookout, MD.

Through the fall and winter of 1864 men continued to desert. A positive view was taken by a loyal soldier who observed that their departure "seems to have taken all the discontent with them."[69] This thought may not have been completely shared by men of the Twenty-Fifth who were in a sharp skirmish with "Tories" at Warm Springs, Madison County, in December. People on each side were killed; there were many discontented in the Confederacy. With so many men skulking about in Western North Carolina, there were inevitable confrontations between the Home Guard, aided by regular army troops, and the deserters. These encounters often led to fatalities for hunter and hunted. In Henderson County, 2 deserters from Company G of the Thirty-Fifth were killed in such an affray, as was an officer in the same company who was bent on arresting those who were fleeing.[70] Later, a Home Guard officer was killed under similar circumstances.[71]

EZEKIEL KUYKENDALL 25-H (January 1865). Private Kuykendall was present for duty for a full year before deserting in July 1862. The circumstance of his return was not recorded. Whatever the fact, by September 24, he had regained sufficient liberty to again depart from his company. This time he was able to avoid arrest for over two years, until December 16, 1864. His trial took place in January 1865. For a second and prolonged desertion, the death sentence was nearly mandatory, and that was the decision of the court. Private Kuykendall was shot to death on February 14, 1865, just two months before the surrender that might have returned him safely to his home. A cousin, Private George W. Kirkendoll, joined the Fifty-Sixth, and deserted four times in his two years in the army, the last time successfully. Private John L. Stuart made casual mention of the execution of Private Kuykendall on the day of execution, "To day one of our Brigade was shot to death for desertion."[72]

Of greater concern, men were not returning from furloughs, thereby stopping furloughs for more deserving men of the company. Other men were deserting, often going directly to the Yankees. Nine days after the execution of Private Kuykendall, a mother wrote to her son. "We was sury to here that man being shot but we was glad to here you dident have it to do God only knows what is to become of us all."[73] A mother offers compassion and concern — compassion for the man at the stake and for the men who were ordered to kill him, concern for the future of her family.

Forty years after the event, a soldier of the Forty-Ninth Regiment recounted his impression of a brigade execution:

We were marched out one Sunday morning to see a deserter shot. We were formed into a hollow square. The unfortunate man was marched out to the place of execution, blindfolded and made to kneel down with his back against a stake. His arms were pinioned, the firing party consisting of twelve men, took their places ten paces in front, in two ranks, and at the command ready, aim, fire, the front rank fired and the poor fellow was dead. It was hard indeed, but then it was the rules of war and had to be carried out. We were then marched back to camp.[74]

Just who the "poor fellow" was is difficult to determine from the reminiscence. Chronologically the placement in the memoir would indicate it was probably Private Costner, but he was put to death on a Monday, not on a Sunday morning as is recalled. The other two verified executions of men in the Ransom brigade occurred on Tuesday and Thursday. As discussed, Sunday was not a day for execution. Two men in the brigade were condemned to death in the time frame of the memoir, April and May 1864; their fate is unknown.

Summary

The brigade of the Ransom brothers has a perplexing history in that only 3 brigade executions are verified. Twice that number have minimal evidence as to their fate. Over 7,000 men served in the brigade; 28 were informed that they would be executed. Privates Reece, Costner and Kuykendall are known to have met that end, and 18 are known to have survived the sentence. How and when the lives of the remaining 7 came to an end is not clear. In the fall of 1863, 2 were told that they would be executed. The other 5 heard their pronouncement in the fall of 1864. For the men sentenced in 1863, it would seem that with eighteen months of war still to be fought there would be some indication of their status in service records. For the second group, the lack of records is more understandable, what with the confusion in the final months of conflict. Still, records do exist for a man in the brigade who was tried and shot at a later point in the war. Of the 5 men in the second group, 2 attempted a second desertion; another deserted with other men; it is likely that these men — Privates Pope, Aden Carver, and Hogan — were executed.

While men were suffering through trials and judgments in 1864, the effective strength of the brigade fell to just over 1,300 soldiers, slightly more than one regiment. Six months later, there were 425 men at Appomattox. At least 10 of those not present were killed in confrontations with deserters or Tories. Accidents claimed the lives of 16 others. The brigade suffered a moderate number of deaths in camp and in battle. From an average enrollment of 150 per company, 23 died from disease or an unstated cause. Those killed outright or who died of battle wounds numbered 12 per company. Those choosing to absent themselves averaged 36 attempts from each of 16 sampled companies.[75] Based on a sample of 10 companies, the peak absence period was the last half of 1862. Absences were reduced by half and remained relatively stable thereafter, despite the rapidly falling number of men present for duty. This trend went on even with an increase in those threatened with execution, and the occasional reality of an execution. March and April and September and October were the reporting periods of concentrated absence activity in each of the three full years of war.

	1861	1862	1863	1864	1865	no date
Absent/Company		.6 10.7	4.7 5.1	3.4 5.8	4.9	
To be executed	2	2	10	12		2
Executed			2	3	1	

Among the 28 men sentenced to execution, 21 were volunteers. Those conscripted were 6, the enrollment status of 1 is not known. The conscripts were in service for less than five months before deserting, while the volunteers remained in camp slightly over a year. Married men accounted for at least 13 of the 28 condemned men, while the marital status of 12 is not known. All but 2 of the threatened men lived or enrolled in western counties of North Carolina.

In terms of executions being centered on companies of disciplinary concern, they were well-directed. The 5 companies of the brigade that likely had men executed had an absence rate of 32 percent. The same number of companies had men sentenced to be executed but were later reprieved, had an absence rate of 17 percent. Companies that had no record of a death sentence had an absence rate of 17 percent. This is not to say that every company with a high rate of absence had men threatened with execution. But it does suggest that the Ransom brothers understood where the ritual might deter onlookers considering their departure.

14

Clingman Brigade

"The most of our boys went to see him shot."[1]

Brigadier Thomas Lanier Clingman led a brigade in which 15 men were sentenced to death; 7 were in the Sixty-First, as were 2 that were likely executed. Another soldier was killed without the legal niceties of a trial and the military trappings of an execution.

Eighth Regiment

The Eighth Regiment had a minimal number of men go before the highest level of military courts. Only 12 records of convictions have been found; 3 at trial were acquitted. Of those tried, 10 were from Companies D and C, recruited in Granville and New Hanover counties, and Company E, the Manchester Guards, Cumberland County, while four companies B, F, H, and K had no record of men going before a general court-martial. For the regiment only 4 men were sentenced to be executed in the course of the war. The same number of men, 4, died either by accidental death or purposely by their own hand. Other men, perhaps more deserving of harsh punishment, were able to prolong their lives by deserting to the enemy. Company B, the Shaw Guards, Currituck County lost 28 of their 133 enrolled men by desertion. Of these, 21 had no record of further service with the company; 3 others went directly to the enemy, so of the 28 men of the company who departed, some as early as 1862, only 3 were ever in custody to be punished. Death displaced absence in taking men from Company B in 1864.

Co B	1861	1862	1863	1864	1865	no date
Absent		14	5 6	1 2		
Dead		5	2 2	14	6	4

In the early going, adding a company to a regiment was pretty much a seat-of-the-pants decision by the officer forming the regiment. "Col Shaw ... spoke to me about Billy Walkers Company and I hinted to him that he would find them a hard set if he took them, so he says he wont bother himself about them unless he cant fill the regiment without them."[2] Even with cautious selection, training a company was still a challenging task. "My company begin to drill very well but we have some awfully hard eggs in it. Baron brought the very scrapings of Edgecombe with him and a more stupid set I never saw but by hard work and strict discipline we are beginning to lick them into shape."[3]

Thirty-First Regiment

Military courts sentenced a soldier from the Thirty-First to death; he was later freed on a procedural technicality. Altogether, existing records indicate that 24 men went to trial for various military crimes; 4 were acquitted and 20 convicted. The 24 trials involved 14 men from Company D, Wake County; Company A, Robeson County; and Company G, Hertford County. Overall, men of the regiment did not unduly suffer by the hand of a military court. A man was sentenced to be branded, this to be followed by confinement and hard labor. Court activity was concentrated in 1864; 19 of 20 convictions were in that period; 1 issued a death sentence. The condemned man was in Company A, one of the companies that accounted for two-thirds of the courts attributed to the regiment. At the other extreme, Companies B, Anson; C, Harnett and Wake; and K, Craven had no posted court-martial activity. This does not indicate an unwavering attachment to the cause, however. Company K records show that at least 48 of 139 enrolled men were absent at some point, many within enemy lines and relatively secure from arrest, at 35 percent the company had the highest percentage of absences, for any of 16 sampled companies of the brigade. A soldier in the Eleventh commented on the Thirty-First Regiment: "The 31 is close by heare about two hundred yards John is at our Camp now he is well and harty he was not in the fite I carried him some Meat and Bread theay had nothing to eat he is very tired of his Reg he is triing to get to our Company I would be more than glad he could it is a pitty for such men as Capt Allison has to be in such a Reg as that is Carnal Jordan is not looked upon with much respect I am sorry that John is in it"[4] Captain Julius F. Allison led Company E of the Thirty-First.

The reaction of General Beauregard to a court-martial decision concerning the Thirty-First was published on May 28, 1863: "The conduct of Lt. Gardner is so loathsome that the Cmdg General regrets that the court did not require the proceedings to be published in the principal papers of his state." The Lieutenant in Company K was dismissed from the service for allowing two soldiers to "pollute themselves in his presence by committing masturbation this in his own quarters."[5] The two soldiers involved in the act, which is rarely mentioned in correspondence and even more rarely the concern of a general court-martial, were ages eighteen and sixteen on enrollment. The older of the two deserted in the fall of 1864; the younger boy was present on company rolls through 1864.

Fifty-First Regiment

Though AIGO court-martial postings for the Fifty-First are incomplete, a pattern of punishment emerges. Company K, the Confederate Stars, Sampson County, had the most men of the regiment to go before a general court-martial, followed by Company G, raised in Columbus, Duplin and Brunswick counties; and Company I, formed in Cumberland and Sampson counties. Together, these companies account for 60 percent of the 27 total courts for the Fifty-First. There were no court acquittals. Companies D, F and H formed in Columbus and Robeson counties had a total of just 2 men listed as appearing before courts. Military courts condemned 3 soldiers of the regiment to death, the first in the summer of 1863.

Sixty-First Regiment

Records kept by the AIGO list only 13 men of the Sixty-First as appearing before general courts-martial. Court appearances started in August 1863 and there were no acquittals.

Company B, the Beaufort Plowboys; Company C, the Neuse Guards, Craven County; and Company G, organized in New Hanover County, were charged with 8 of the 10 counts. Company D, the Vance Guards, a company with no recorded courts, was sent to Chatham, their home county, in July 1864. While there, they forcibly returned 100 men to the army. They allegedly killed 2 of the leaders of the deserters who were active in the county; whether in a skirmish or by summary execution is not stated.[6] In February of 1863, there were 143 men of the regiment absent without leave, deserted, or listed as not having returned to their command after being exchanged.[7]

The Military District issued a circular instructing commanding officers to promptly execute sentences for men convicted by court-martial: "The habit of allowing men to remain in jail after their sentences are published meets with the disapprobation of the Brig. General Commanding."[8] Just, firm, and swift punishment was the keystone of discipline. This was forcefully impressed on the regiment in the case of a deserter from the Sixty-First, Company B; his execution was ordered to take place five days after the publication of his sentence. Company B, the Beaufort Plowboys, was a very small company with a wartime enrollment of 61

Courts-Martial

THOMAS EDWARDS 61-B (Prior to August 17, 1863). Brothers Thomas, Emanuel and Eliall Edwards, deserted the ranks of their regiment some time before May 1, 1863, for on that day they were returned in arrest to face charges. Appearing before a court-martial in July or August 1863, Private Thomas Edwards was found guilty of desertion and sentenced to be shot to death, said sentence to be carried into effect five days after the brigade commander received the order of execution, which was issued on August 17, 1863.[9] The name of Private Emanuel Edwards was not on a similar order by the narrowest of margin. A complex sentence of hard labor with a twenty-four-pound ball attached to his ankle with a chain, solitary confinement, head shaving, and hours standing on a barrel was his punishment.[10] No court-martial record for the third brother, Private Eliall Edwards, has been located. His first name is shown as Rial in some records. The convicted brothers were pardoned and returned to duty by authority of a presidential amnesty proclamation. Private Emanuel Edwards was killed at Drewry's Bluff, VA, in May 1864. Private Thomas Edwards survived the war, as did Private Eliall Edwards.

ALEXANDER MCDANIEL 61-D (Prior to August 17, 1863). Private McDaniel was enrolled in September 1862 and was court-martialed a year later in August 1863. His company, the Vance Guards, Chatham County, had 191 enrolled men. Private McDaniel was tried on a charge of "conduct to the prejudice of good order and military discipline," a catchall charge that could be brought when a more specific charge might not be sustainable. The court hearing his case found that the prisoner was guilty of the charges, and the necessary two-thirds concurred on a death sentence. It was immediately determined that the newly announced presidential amnesty applied to the case of Private McDaniel, and he was released to return to duty. Within the fortnight, he was captured by the enemy and died of a gunshot wound while imprisoned in their care. Whether the shot was deliberate or accidental is not stated.

DAVIDSON EVANS 51-F (Prior to August 17, 1863). Privates Davidson and Michael Evans joined Company F, the Ashpole True Boys, Robeson County, on May 1, 1862. Three months later they deserted, 2 of 15 men who left the company in the last half of 1862. Private Michael Evans was apprehended after just three days. Determined to leave the service, he was successful on a second attempt to do so six weeks after his first arrest. He was officially dropped from the rolls of the company in early 1863 and had no further service record with the regiment. Private Davidson Evans was also dropped from the company rolls while he was evading authorities for some nine months but was then arrested and taken before a court-martial. When the decision of the court was published Private Evans might have heard that he had been convicted by the court and would be shot to death in five days. Or he may never have known of the court's action. Under some unknown authority, possibly the recently announced amnesty offered by the President or a mistaken order, Private Evans was returned to duty on August 10, while under sentence of death. Recognizing that his opportunity might be brief, Private Evans deserted the very next day, on August 11. No further military record has come to light. He survived the conflict. GO #11, August 17, 1863, Department of North Carolina, issued death sentences for Privates Edwards, McDaniel and Evans; it was not posted by the AIGO.

Shortly after Private Evans departed a soldier summarized his thoughts. "They are making a heepe of fuss about Holdens paper i think it is cary a heepe of harm in the armey i under stand that you all are wiped [whipped] at home all wont to go back in the union under Linken i will say to you that we in the armey will never submit as long as we can fight."[11]

One deserter from the Eighth, who seemingly was destined to be shot if he was ever taken back to his regiment, sought the aid of a friend in pleading his case to Governor Vance. In November of 1863 the plea reached the Governor:

> The object of these few lines is in behalf of a deserter who we learn is anxious to return to the service in case he can have a guarantee that he will not be shot or that he can get a pardon from death he as any other person would be is horrified at the idea of being shot as he says like a dog and he has deserted three times but says he never will again if his life can be spared this time.[12]

The absent soldier wanted a transfer to another regiment but would still return if the request was not granted, "as he is very tired of staying in the woods." The soldier named in the appeal did return to his regiment, but two months later deserted to the enemy, overcoming the risk and horror of being shot like a dog.

Another deserter from the Eighth adopted a different line of reasoning for his defense when court-martialed for forging an approval on a request for a leave. The soldier said that he wanted a furlough to go and get some "horizontal refreshments."[13] He carefully phrased his intentions to not offend the gentlemen of the court. The court was not swayed by his well-mannered defense and ordered that he forfeit three months' pay, be held in close confinement for three months, and subsist on bread and water for seven days once in each of the three months of his confinement. The court, with equal delicacy, refrained from specifying that the bread and water refreshment be taken in a horizontal position. Good manners prevailed throughout the day.

In mid–January 1864, some men of the brigade took the opportunity to witness an execution. "I am sorry to inform you that theare was a man shot on the eight of the present month in one mile of our camp But I did not go to see him shot. The most of our boys went to see him shot."[14] There were no men in the brigade under a death sentence at that time, but that would soon change.

MONROE CLAYTON 8-D (January 21, 1864). Private Clayton volunteered for service and remained with his regiment for two years before deserting from Sullivan's Island, SC, on August 15, 1863. Four months later, toward the end of December, John W. Jacobs of a Home Guard unit arrested the deserter and took him to Camp Holmes, for which Mr. Jacobs was paid $9.[15] The money was well spent, for earlier that year, in September, members of Private Clayton's own company went to his home to arrest him but were unable to do so.[16] After his detention at Camp Holmes, he was among a batch of prisoners taken under guard on January 13, to Petersburg, VA, to stand trial for their crimes.[17] Lieutenant A. H. Gregory and Sergeant A. P. Tharrington of Private Clayton's company were ordered to appear before the court to testify at the trial on January 21, 1864.[18] The testimony of the men was not helpful for the prisoner, and after due deliberation the twelve-member court found Private Clayton guilty as charged and the requisite number concurred that he should be shot to death. Brigadier Clingman issued the order on March 21, 1864.

> The execution of Private M. Clayton Co D 8th Reg NC Troops sentenced to death for desertion, will take place in the presence of the 8 and 51 NC Regts at 11 A.M. on Wednesday the 23rd instant in the open ground lying east of the camp of the 51 Regt. The commanding officer of the 8 Regt is charged with the detail connected with the execution.[19]

While the formal scheduling of the execution was in progress, Austin A. Smith addressed the Confederate military on behalf of several condemned men, including Private Clayton. The thrust of his appeal was a general protest against the death penalty, rather than offering specific facts in defense of the men facing execution.[20] Following a preliminary review, President Davis suspended the execution. On close examination of the court's proceedings, General Cooper advised on June 17, 1864, that the sentence of Private Clayton, along with 4 others, should be voided because of a violation of the 64th Article of War by the convicting court.[21] This article states that a court-martial must consist of 13 members unless it is specifically stated in the court record that gathering that number of officers would cause manifest injury to the service. This notation was not made in the records of the case at hand, and therefore the action of the court was voided. This legal turn of events had no immediate effect on Private Clayton; he was a Federal prisoner after his capture on June 1. Likewise, SO #216 September 12, 1864, AIGO, commuting the death sentence to one of hard labor for the war was probably never known to Private Clayton. Death came while he was a Federal prisoner at Elmira, NY, on October 6, 1864.

AMOS NEAL 61-B (Prior to March 1864). There is evidence that a young man enrolled in the Sixty-First was among the Confederate soldiers who were captured in the service of the enemy. Private Neal began his enlistment in November 1861 with the Beaufort Plow Boys. The height of the recruit was listed as five feet, two inches, and his last date of recorded service was July 1862.[22] His age was seventeen. An undated Roll of Honor states that he deserted to the enemy, was arrested, and "hung" at Kinston, NC.[23] The record shows that he volunteered in Beaufort County. Federal records show that a Private Ivey Neal was enrolled in the Second Regiment, North Carolina Union Troops, on January 18, 1864. The enrollee was eligible to receive a $300 bounty, in installments. The record for this soldier states that he was captured and hanged. A conflicting entry in the Federal record states that the soldier in question was at Annapolis, MD, in 1865. The physical description is given as age sixteen, five feet in height and fair complexion. An anonymous officer of the Federal regiment in which Private Neal was enrolled wrote a long statement in March 1864, placing the men who enrolled in Federal units in the most favorable patriotic light, while showing the brutality and barbarity of their Confederate neighbors. In part he said: "One of the victims was a little drummer-boy, named Joey Neal, only fourteen years of age, a fair complexioned, blue-eyed child, an orphan, enlisted in Beaufort by the writer of these lines, out of pure compassion for his destitute state."[24] As can be seen, there are similarities in the Federal and Confederate files that indicate that Private Amos Neal was hanged at an unknown time and place.

FREDERICK BASS 51-F (April 3, 1864). Private Bass enrolled in the Ashpole True Boys, Robeson County, in March 1862 and promptly began the first of 3 absences that eventually led to a charge of desertion, court-martial and a death sentence. The private defended his absences before a court held on April 13, 1864. Five days later when the findings of the court were published in GO #14, April 18, 1864, Department of North Carolina, he was informed that he was to be shot to death in five days in the presence of Clingman's brigade, by order of General Pickett. Although the sentence was initially confirmed, General Pickett either relented sufficiently to await a further review or higher authority ordered a remission of sentence. In any case, Private Bass was restored to duty and remained on company records till the end of 1864.

WILLIAM SWAIN 8-D (April 14, 1864). Private Swain volunteered in July 1861, a full year before passage of the amended conscription laws that would call men of his age, over thirty-five years, to the colors. Enrollment records give his age as forty years and his residence as Terrell [sic] County; they were signed by mark. Service records show extensive periods of sickness or absence; he was rarely present for duty. An unauthorized absence ultimately led to a court-martial on April 4, 1864, which was followed by publication of an order sentencing Private Swain to be shot. General Pickett confirmed the sentence and set the time of execution in five days. The death sentence was suspended, and Private Swain was absent sick at Kittrell, NC through August 1864. After return to duty he was captured by the enemy in late September and taken to Elmira, NY, where he died in January of 1865.

Private Calvin Forrest, Eighth Regiment, Company G, made 2 desertion attempts. He was absent for eight months following the first desertion beginning in November 1862 and for three months after a second attempt that began in December 1863. It is reasonable to gather that these desertions for a relatively long period of time in the spring of 1864 would result in a death sentence, particularly so in the command of General Pickett, even for a very young private; he was sixteen on enrollment. People in his neighborhood in Pitt County apparently came to that same conclusion, or a rumor to that effect reached those who knew the young man. In response, a certified petition asking to spare his life was signed by 24 residents of Greene County and was sent to President Davis. General Pickett replied that Private Forrest had not yet been tried, this as of April 27, 1864. One section of the petition noted that the "party referred to is a mere youth." Another reference was made that his desertions began as a result of "instigation by injudicious friends."[25] The precise nature of any action taken as a result of the petition is not known, but Private Forrest was returned to duty. In the fighting at Cold Harbor, VA, he was shot in the head, blinded in both eyes, and captured by the enemy on June 1, 1864. He was exchanged and guided to his home.

LORENZO D. MANNING 61-B (April 28, 1864). Private Lorenzo Manning enrolled at Washington, Beaufort County, on November 6, 1861, and was present for duty until July 1, 1862. Some time after that, he deserted his company to remain absent until April 28, 1864. A trial and resulting capital sentence would suggest that he was absent for most of that time. The general order announcing that he would be shot to death was published on July 27, 1864, with execution of sentence to take place on August 5.[26] On August 3, the execution was suspended until further orders were forthcoming.[27] On August 16, General Beauregard was informed "Re — L. D. Manning 61-B to be shot on 5 instant. Forwarded on 9 — received yesterday Sent to Sec War as soon as decision of President known will be forwarded."[28] The next record concerning Private Manning was that he was released from confinement as a result of General Order #2, in January 1865. He survived the last several months of war.[29]

WILLIAM A. MANNING 61-B (April 28, 1864). Private William Manning was present with his company from enrollment on November 6, 1861, until July 1, 1862. Hospital records indicate that Private William Manning suffered with catarrh during late 1862 and early into the next year. He gave his age as thirty-seven when enrolling. The next record is that of the court that sentenced Privates Lorenzo Manning and William Manning to death. The execution of the two men was scheduled for the same day. But this was of no consequence to Private William Manning, as he was killed at Cold Harbor, VA, on June 6.

HENRY C. BRITT 31-A (May 2, 1864). There were 5 soldiers with the surname Britt enrolled in Company A, Thirty-First Regiment; 3 of them deserted on July 6, 1864. For one, this was a very serious undertaking; just two months earlier, in May 1864, Private Henry C. Britt was taken before a court-martial charged with desertion. That absence began on February 15, 1863, and he was imprisoned by March or April 1864. For attempting to desert, he received a death sentence. The reviewing officer, General Beauregard, in his official comment, noted that the records of the court failed to state that two-thirds of the members had concurred in approving the death sentence.[30] This mistake was fatal, negating the entire proceedings, and Private Britt was returned to duty. On July 6, 1864, Private Britt again deserted, this time with an older brother, Private Alexander S. Britt, and likely a cousin, Private Giles Britt. No record of further service has been found for any of the three.

D. A. EDWARDS 8-D (August 10, 1864). Privates D. A. and Lucius L. Edwards were very reluctant volunteers, for they deserted the ranks on May 31, 1863, less than four months after being enrolled. The absence for Private D. A. Edwards extended over the next fifteen months until he was arrested and taken back to face a court-martial on August 10, 1864. After being informed that he would be shot for his prolonged absence, Private Edwards without further ado found some means to escape from his guard and head for home. Private D. A. Edwards arrived home on September 8, 1864, and was immediately urged by his family to return to the army, which advice he took and set out to return the very next day. He hoped to avail himself of Governor Vance's Amnesty Proclamation. The Military Aide to Governor Vance summed up the situation in a letter to General Lee, dated October 22, 1864.

> He deserted was arrested, court-martialed & condemned to be shot made his excape & returned home on the 8th Sept.— and was advised by his family to surrender himself under the pardon of Governor Vance ... gave himself up on the 9th ... he of course cannot claim protection under the Governors Proclamation, but under the circumstances His excellency would respectfully recommend him to your mercy — and hopes that the sentence of death will not be executed.[31]

The appeal by the Governor apparently was effective in sparing the life of Private Edwards, and he was sent to Castle Thunder in late January 1865 and then returned to duty under authority of General Order #2. His brother, Private Lucius Edwards, also escaped shortly after being escorted back to his regiment. He was captured or prudently went to the enemy to end his Confederate service.

HENRY W. SILLS 51-K (August 25, 1864). Private Sills was present for duty from enlistment in May 1862 until year's end 1863 without notable incident. In January or February 1864 there was a brief arrest. For the next six months he was present, but then began a summer desertion. Though the specifications on the charges placed against him are not known, he did go before a court on August 25, 1864, was found guilty of the charged desertion and sentenced to be shot. The sentence as published on September 24, 1864, in GO #24, Department of North Carolina and Southern Virginia, was approved, to be carried into effect in seven days after receipt of the order from the General Commanding. The planned execution did not take place. SO #287, November 28, 1864, Army of Northern Virginia, remitted the sentence based on the good conduct and gallantry of Private Sills subsequent to his trial. He was returned to duty by a second order issued by the AIGO. Confederate service for Private Sills ended when he was captured by the enemy in Sampson County in March 1865.

Governor Vance was confronted with a variety of appeals in cases involving desertion in the fall of 1864. In one instance a soldier enrolled in the Fifty-First was convicted of manslaughter in a civil trial. The Governor asked Colonel Hector McKethan of the Fifty-First if he would take the soldier back into his command if the Governor pardoned him of the civil crime. The Colonel said that he did not want the man returned to his command and that the convicted man would likely be shot for desertion if he was sent back.[32]

JAMES SIMMONS 61-G (November 18, 1864). In the spring of 1862, Private Simmons carried his fifty-three years with sprightly step when enrolling at Wilmington, NC. Within weeks, however, the older soldier was hospitalized at Tarboro. Transferred to a hospital at Goldsboro, he deserted from that facility in January 1863. After returning to his company some time before June, he again deserted on July 8. Having gained his freedom, Private Simmons chose to remain absent for a year and four months, He was then arrested and taken to trial on November 18, 1864. A death sentence for Private Simmons was approved five days later. The temporary brigade commander, Colonel Hector McKethan, was directed to carry out the sentence. An order from General Hoke's headquarters dated November 23, 1864:

> The Maj Gen Cmdg desires you to see that the sentences in the foregoing cases are carried out. The execution of Pvt. Simmons will take place at 12 m. on the 26' inst. He is now in solitary confinement in the Div. guard house & will be delivered to you on the morning of that day. The execution will take place in the presence of your Brigade & all necessary arrangements will be made by your order.[33]

No verification has been found that Private Simmons was shot on the appointed day, nor is there any evidence that he was spared. His service record ends with an entry in September–October 1863 stating that he was in desertion from July 1863.

BENJAMIN C. GIBSON 61-H (November 28, 1864). Private Gibson was a faithful soldier in the Hill Guards, Martin County, from November 1861 until November 1862 when he impulsively left camp. The events that brought about that decision began when Private Gibson was refused permission to visit his wife and family for a few hours when his regiment was only a mile and a half from his home. Private Gibson then decided to make the visit without official permission. When he returned the next morning he was placed in arrest. Perhaps he had intended to get back before roll call but was delayed. His reaction to his arrest was as impulsive as his reaction to being denied permission for the short visit home; he broke arrest and deserted, apparently with no intention of returning. A year after deserting the Sixty-First, Private Gibson agreed to join the Federal army, enrolling in Company E, First North Carolina Union Volunteers on October 29, 1863. He served the Federal flag for six months until his capture by Confederates in his Federal uniform at Plymouth, NC, in April 1864. He was taken under guard to Richmond where he was imprisoned awaiting trial. This did not come about until November 28, 1864. There was obviously no vengeful urge for a drumhead court and swift death for the traitor. After trial, a death sentence was handed down and General James Longstreet approved the action of the court. On January 8, 1865, the AAG for General Longstreet was advised:

> I have the honor to inform you that GO #28 Hd Qtrs 1st Army Corp publishing the proceedings of the Military Court appointed for the Corp in the case of Pvt B. C. Gibson Co H 61 NC Regt who is sentenced to death and ordered to be executed 7 days after the publication of this order, was published to this Brigade on the 6th instant and the execution will take place on the 13th.[34]

An officer who was stationed at Fort Fisher, Captain John D. Biggs, Company H, Sixty-First Regiment, said that Private Gibson was at that place awaiting execution when the assault began on January 13. On his own request, the condemned man was released to take part in the defense of the fort. An entry in General Hoke's letter book dated January 10, 1865 states: "Col McKetchen [sic] reports execution of B. C. Gibson."[35] This was a simple recording error, the correct entry being — Col McKethan reports the day set for the execution of B. C. Gibson. Such notification to an officer who ordered an execution was common practice. Another error notes that Private Gibson was released from imprisonment under authority of General Order #2. A third inconsistency is that Private Gibson was sentenced to be shot rather than to be hanged, that being the usual punishment for those caught fighting in the uniform of the enemy. A Private in the Sixty-First named Major Uzzle wrote to his mother in January 1865 and included this mention, "Their is [not legible] a man to be shot here fryday for dezerting I have no more news to write now."[36] The execution of Private Gibson was set for the Wednesday before the Friday mentioned in the letter.

As noted in the cases of Privates Simmons and Gibson, Colonel McKethan was temporarily in command of the brigade while Brigadier Clingman was absent in November and December 1864. This absence had serious repercussions within the brigade. Captain N. A. Ramsey Company D, Sixty-First, informed General Clingman, "Some 10 to 15 of yr Brigade have gone to the enemy. If you do not return, I give it as my private opinion, that at least One Hundred (100) will go to the enemy in less than thirty (30) days."[37] The prophetic Captain was probably accurate in his forecast of imminent desertions, though the precise figure is not known. On November 25, 1864, the Lieutenant Colonel commanding the Thirty-First Regiment reported that 55 men, including 8 sergeants, were not present for the second roll call that day.[38] The situation was succinctly summed when a soldier of the Thirty-First stated that nearly half of those present for duty were guarding the other half who were prisoners.[39] Another soldier had earlier expressed much the same thought: "It seems that it is hard times when it takes one half of the men to keep the other half from running a way."[40]

Summary

The men in the brigade present at the final surrender was in the range of 300. As noted, court-martial records for Clingman's brigade as found in AIGO documents are incomplete. Considering that the brigade was frequently assigned to various commands in the southeast portion of the Confederacy, and that regiments also operated independently, these omissions are understandable. Records of only 10 of the 15 men of the brigade that were threatened with a death sentence are found in AIGO ledgers. Other records indicate a total of 79 courts with 7 acquittals. All of the men who were condemned to death were volunteers. At least half of the volunteers left a wife at home.

The 2 companies that are considered the most likely to have had men executed had an absence rate of 25 percent.[41] Other companies of the brigade had men sentenced to death but were later spared; these 7 companies experienced an absence rate of 21 percent.[42] Sampled companies, 7, that had no death sentences had an absence rate of 19 percent.[43] Men absented themselves from Clingman's brigade at a moderate but steady pace from mid–1862 onward. Absences increased significantly in the final months of 1864. A sampling of 12 companies gives an average enrollment of 135 enlisted men, 27 were absent at some point, 20 died of disease or unknown cause, 10 were killed in battle or died of wounds — rather modest numbers when comparison is made to other brigades.[44]

15

Martin-Kirkland Brigade

"They had to shoot one man twice before they killed him."[1]

Brigadier James Green Martin formed and led a brigade that maintained a reputation as being well disciplined from organization to surrender.[2] A native of North Carolina, the Brigadier was in command from May 1862 to August 1864, a time when 48 men were given a death sentence and 19 were executed.

Seventeenth Regiment

Fully three and half years of the struggle passed before the Seventeenth was assembled to witness the execution of one of their own. In the years of conflict, 9 men of the regiment faced death by musketry; all but 2 survived the ordeal. The Seventeenth experienced significant desertion in the early years, but that was before death sentences replaced shame and humiliation as punishment for that crime. Men of the regiment went before 29 courts, and only 1 was acquitted. Company L was the primary company of desertion activity for the Seventeenth, slightly less than half of the non-commissioned men were from Cabarrus County. Men from this company went before military courts at least 10 times, after which ordeal 6 men were ordered to be shot; 3 were given severe sentences. One escaped with a relatively mild sentence of thirty days at hard labor. For the company, 34 men were entangled in 42 incidents of unauthorized absence. The bulk of these, 38, were classified as outright desertion, and 4 were considered as absent without leave. Total company enrollment was 121, the loss of men was significant. In comparison, Company K, Pitt County, had an enrollment of 117, no record of a general court-martial, and just a single deserter, who departed on two occasions. Of the 6 men of Company L who were ordered to be shot, 4 lived in Cabarrus County. As will be seen, these men did not carry sterling reputations when they marched off to the army, at least in the opinion of one who knew them, but they did elicit sympathetic aid from others.

Forty-Second Regiment

Formed as a battalion to serve as guards at the Military Prison at Salisbury, the men of the Forty-Second often found that they were prisoners being guarded. Desertion was a serious concern in the late spring of 1863. Attention was centered on Company D, formed in Rowan, Davie and Iredell counties, and Companies A and H, recruited in Davidson and Stanly counties. Over 100 men departed these companies. In an effort to maintain company strength they enrolled a total of 603 men. Company D had 17 men go before military courts, Company H had 12 and Company A had 9, 38 in total — well over half of the 66 courts, of which 3 ended in acquittal, involved the Forty-Second. Company H recorded 55 absences from a total enrollment of 150 men, two-thirds of these occurring in August of each of the middle war years. Disease or no stated cause accounted for 20 deaths, and 6 were killed in combat or died of combat wounds.

Co H	1861	1862	1863		1864		1865	no date
Absent		13	6	11	24			1
Dead		3	5	3	4	5	6	

In marked contrast, Company G had 153 enrolled, no recorded courts, and just 2 desertions, these in late 1862. For the Forty-Second, 24 men were sentenced to be shot. Companies D and H sent forth 15, but of the 24 no more than 3 were executed. Of those condemned, 15 were volunteers, 1 a substitute, and 8 were likely conscripts. The substitute was executed but the conscripts were not. At least 18 others were given severe punishment; about half of those in the second year of war. Combining death and severe sentences, 6 of every 10 men of the regiment who went before a court received life-threatening punishment. Absences were not for days, but for months; men did not return of their own will, but resisted arrest. A deserter from the regiment was killed by the Home Guard.

Fiftieth Regiment

An idea of the daunting difficulty of training a Confederate regiment is gained from a recollection that the Fiftieth was initially armed with ten-foot halberd-like weapons, much like a Roman legion. The Confederate weapon was improvised with a pole and two dirks, one tied for stabbing and the other at an angle for hooking or chopping the enemy.[3] Compounding the absence of more lethal weapons, training was impaired by a scarcity of trained officers. The regimental Colonel appealed to Governor Clark for permission to appoint experienced officers to replace 4 that had resigned. In support of his request he observed: "The material of these companies is such that in my opinion, they cannot fill them acceptably from the ranks."[4] A total of 39 trial decisions, with 3 acquittals, have been located for the Fiftieth. Three-quarters of these are for men enrolled in Companies B and D, recruited in Robeson and Johnston counties; Company G, the Rutherford Farmers; and Company H, Harnett County. Company D had 121 enrolled men; they had 34 incidents of absence on record. In contrast to these companies with high court activity, Company A, Person County; Company K, the Green River Rifles, Rutherford County; and Company F, the Moore Sharpshooters, together had only 1 court conviction. Company A enrolled 129 men during the war; the convicted man among them. A deserter from the Fiftieth was killed by the Home Guard. Several others may have suffered a similar fate, but the cause of death is not recorded. Of the 10 men of the Fiftieth ordered to be shot, 7 were reprieved. Records suggest 1 was executed, and 2 records are inconclusive.

Private L. B. Seymour, Company E, Fiftieth Regiment, was convicted of desertion by a court-martial and sentenced to have thirty-nine lashes laid on his bare back once every three months for the duration of the war. In addition, he was to be branded with the letter "D" on his left hand and to have a ball and chain attached to his leg while imprisoned and working at hard labor.[5] The case was brought to the attention of the Confederate Congress in 1863 by Congressman John Perkins of Louisiana who inquired as to the legality of such a sentence; was it in accordance with the law? "If there is any law to justify it, then I say such a law is a disgrace to us and outrages the commonest sentiments of human nature."[6] A bill to prohibit flogging in the Confederate army was introduced. A resolution was passed leading to the abolishment of legal flogging in April 1863.

Sixty-Sixth Regiment

When the Sixty-Sixth Regiment was organized under authority of SO #234, October 2, 1863, AIGO, it brought together two battalions, the Eighth and the Thirteenth, that had formerly operated as partisan rangers or as railroad guards in eastern North Carolina. Perhaps in ominous foreboding, on October 23, 1863, General Whiting expressed his concern to Governor Vance that discipline in Nethercutt's battalion, the Eighth, was "very bad," the General attributing some of this discontent to a particular man who was spreading bad words for his own benefit; he wanted a promotion.[7] Some Confederate dissatisfaction was more ethnic in origin. "There is a great deal of dissatifaction [sic] here among the Jews about what Congress is doing in the conscript bill — they are all going to run away or at least that is what they say. I wish that they were hung."[8] A member of the Eighth Battalion wrote to Governor Vance on October 28, to express his concerns. He, and others, had joined the battalion "with the express understanding that we were to remain in and operate in the Eastern portion of NC." The question was then posed — how could the status of a battalion raised for a special service be changed without the "sanction or authorization" of the Confederate Congress? "My reason for asking such questions is because they are trying to change, or rather force, the 8th Batt. into the 66th NC Regt against the wishes of all of the men of the Batt. In fact some two (200) hundred of the men being now absent without leave, with a fair prospect of numbers of others following without a change of affairs."[9] Service records support the accuracy of the remarks. The writer closes by saying that he thought all of the men would go back to duty if they were returned to the area which was originally promised. No reply has been located.

The consolidation of the Eighth and Thirteenth battalions led directly to the tragic events that would soon follow at Kinston, NC. There were 14 men enrolled in J. H. Nethercutt's battalion and 1 from C. G. Wright's battalion among 22 who were executed by hanging in February 1864, this for serving in Federal ranks while legally enrolled in the Confederate army. Living in a contested area, men in these units were accustomed to the personal conflicts and shifting loyalties found when a war is fought at a hamlet level. Changing allegiance to stand alongside friend or relative was not seen as a traitorous act. It was necessary to protect their families, and in their minds they had never agreed to the consolidation of their units for a purpose different from that for which they had volunteered. Some referred to this as fluttering, a descriptive word but one far from conveying the deadly consequence of the act. From a Confederate view this was merely quibbling over a technical detail. If the men enrolled in the local service battalions did not want to accept the transfer to a line regiment, then many of them would be immediately conscripted into the same regiment.

Courts-Martial

Martin Brigade

DAVID S. CRISCO 42-H (May 5, 1863); and JACOB A. CRISCO 42-H (May 5, 1863). Two Crisco boys volunteered as privates in the Forty-Second on the same day, March 25, 1862. They also deserted and were then arrested together. As brought out at trial, the brothers had deserted from camp near Black Creek Church in southeast Virginia on December 19, 1862, nine months after enrolling. They were confined at Weldon, NC, on February 1, 1863. Their appearance before a court took place on May 5, 1863, three months after their arrest. After their trial, but before the findings of the court were published, Governor Vance inquired as to the charges against them. He was informed by a telegram sent from Goldsboro on May 17 that "D. S. Crisco & J. A. Crisco and Wm. P. Whitley Co H 42nd NCT left camp without permission some time in December last they were arrested the 2nd or 3rd day after they left camp and have been confined ever since."[10] This brief summary certainly did not indicate the seriousness of the offense to the Governor, for the young men were absent for six weeks and had resisted their captors. No record of other action or inquiry by the Governor has been located. When the decision of the court was published in GO #19, May 26, 1863, Headquarters Department of North Carolina, the privates learned that they were found guilty and that they would be executed at Greenville, NC, or at such place as General J. G. Martin might select, in the presence of their regiment on June 5, 1863. The full record was sent to the Secretary of War on June 2; on June 14, the sentences were remitted. Private David Crisco was killed in the first assault on Fort Fisher on December 26, 1864. Service for Private Jacob Crisco ended when he was granted a sickness furlough in October 1864. The third soldier mentioned in the telegram, Private William P. Whitley, enrolled in the same company at the same time as the condemned men and was tried by the same court. In his case the court found that Private Whitley was of weak mind, almost an idiot, and sentenced him to imprisonment for the duration of the war. He was released to duty in the fall of 1863 and regained sufficient mind to devise another desertion about a year later. A man in the regiment wrote home that 2 Whitley men were to be executed and another man had been sentenced to life imprisonment.[11] The writer apparently heard camp gossip that transposed the names of the men to be shot and the man to be imprisoned.

GEORGE W. HINSON 42-C (June 13, 1863). Three months after being mustered on March 24, 1862, and serving on detached service at Salisbury, Private Hinson deserted. He was absent for the next eleven months until in arrest in April 1863. A court heard his case on June 13. A sufficient number concurred that he should be shot. An unknown authority promptly remitted the sentence, and the next month Private Hinson was back on duty. After one additional year of service, he was captured by the enemy and was their prisoner until released in June 1865.

WILLIS P. BARNES 50-B (June 15, 1863). Sergeant Barnes was a Lieutenant in a militia regiment before going into Confederate service. That experience gained his promotion to Sergeant two months after he had enrolled in May 1862. It did not sustain a resolve in battle, as described in records of a court held on June 15, 1863: "Charge: Violation of the 52 Article of War — Misbehavior before the enemy — On April 16, 1863 Leave company and regiment when ordered to front to meet enemy at Grice's Farm, near Washington, North Carolina, and did go back to wagons one mile or more to the rear." Found guilty on this charge by the court, the Sergeant was given a death sentence. General D. H. Hill did not approve the court's action, replying: "The 52 Article of War does not prohibit any act — but prescribes punishment. Its violation does not involve any crime for which a private soldier can be tried. The sentence is disapproved and void. Private Barnes is restored to duty — Nothing but a technical error in draft indictment saves his life which he justly forfeited."[12] This reading of that Article of War appears correct, though it is not consistent with other cases where charges under that article were approved. No record has been found that the ever-vigilant Adjutant General Samuel Cooper offered any comment on General Hill's interpretation. There were 12 men with the Barnes name in Company B. An order for the arrest of Private W. H. Barnes was issued to officials in the Fourth Congressional District in North Carolina. An endorsement on that order, made in January 1865, emphasizes the difficulty in arresting deserters in Robeson County: "This party from what I can learn has been out for a long time, and is still out. I have made many efforts by means of the Home Guard to have him arrested but being in a section of country where there are many hiding places, and most of the inhabitants favorable to desertion every effort has proved of no avail."[13]

CANADA BARNES 50-B (June 17, 1863). Private Barnes deserted from Drewry's Bluff, on the James River some 10 miles below Richmond, on October 15, 1862, six months after joining his regiment on April 21, 1862. He was able to avoid detection as he made his way down from Virginia and then south across North Carolina to return to Robeson County. In the early summer of 1863, he was apprehended and taken to Kinston, NC, to stand trial. A court-martial gathered on June 17 found him guilty of desertion and concurred on a death sentence. After publication of the findings of the court, the Secretary of War was advised of the pending execution. That led to an inquiry as to the location of the records in the case by the AIGO.[14] A few days later SO #180, July 30, 1863, AIGO, was issued ordering a suspension of the execution. Not long thereafter, Private Barnes was returned to duty, there to serve until mid-1864 when his military record ends. He survived the war.

EPHRAIM O. BEASLEY 50-D (June 18, 1863). Sergeant Beasley was appointed to that rank, on a temporary basis, immediately upon his enrollment in the regiment in March 1862. He returned to the ranks in July and deserted from camp near Drewry's Bluff, VA, on December 13, 1862. The absence of Private Beasley extended over the next six months but came to an end prior to June 18, 1863, when he was on trial. A guilty finding and a death sentence followed. Some unknown authority remitted the sentence, and Private Beasley was once again on duty in October. The confidence was rewarded, for he served for the remainder of the war.

WILEY STRICKLAND 50-D (June 20, 1863). Private Strickland willingly joined the Fiftieth in March 1862 and as willingly deserted in November. Seven months later, on June 20, 1863, he appeared before a court-martial that found him guilty of desertion and made the decision that he should be shot. This sentence was remitted and Private Strickland stayed with his unit until the final months of fighting, when he was hospitalized at Greensboro, NC. With a stated enrollment age of forty-seven, Wiley was the oldest man of his regiment to face a death sentence.

ASHLEY BLACKMAN 50-D (June 22, 1863). Private Blackman deserted November 18, 1862, from camp near Drewry's Bluff, VA, eight months after enrolling in March. Seven months after Private Blackman departed, he was brought to trial on June 22, 1863, found guilty, and sentenced to be shot. The sentence was remitted, and Private Blackman served for the rest of the war.

WILLIAM LEGGETT 50-B (June 24, 1863). While marching with his regiment between the towns of Greenville and Washington, NC, Private Leggett left the column, taking his arms and accouterments with him, this on April 20, 1863. His service in the regiment began a year earlier on May 5, 1862. A month after he left his command, he was in arrest and escorted to Greenville. The journey to judgment and justice began when he boarded a railroad car at Lumberton, NC, on May 25. A court convened on June 24, heard the case of Private Leggett; thereafter, two-thirds concurred on a death sentence. Their decision was approved by the General Commanding, the sentence to be carried into effect in seven days. The AIGO asked to be informed on the facts of the case against Private Leggett and on July 25, were told, "Your communication of the 20th reviewed. Proceedings of court-martial in cases of William Leggett and Canada Barnes, 50-B not here — supposed at Petersburg — last HdQtrs — Gen. Hill."[15] SO #180, AIGO, suspending the execution was forthcoming on July 30. Private Leggett returned to the ranks, but his service record ends sometime between July and September 1864. A brother, Private Wright Leggett, served in the same company from September 1863 to September 1864 without notable incident.

WILLIAM D. EXUM 50-C (Prior to July 30, 1863). Private Exum deserted his company on December 10, 1862. Although some records indicate that he was captured within three weeks, they are apparently in error. Another record states that he was arrested and delivered at Camp Holmes by Captain Jonathan S. Pike of the Forty-First North Carolina Militia, Johnston County, on May 28, 1863, suggesting that his absence was closer to six months.[16] He went before a court in July 1863. The court found Private Exum guilty and handed down a death sentence.[17] General Whiting approved the sentence of the court and then went to some length to express his pain in having to sign such "death warrants." In his opinion, this action was necessary in part due to the "mistaken leniency" shown by some earlier courts. A "severe example" was now necessary. The hope of the General was that this would be the last occasion that a soldier would be put to death, for this was a "terrible duty" for the court, for the approving authority, and for the soldiers and companions who witnessed the execution. Not withstanding all of this, the sentence must be executed. But then characteristically equivocating, "Men should have every chance for life however." The President might, if it should please him, stay the proceedings or pardon the soldier or he, the resolute general, would be obliged carry out the execution.[18] As in other cases, the death sentence for Private Exum, so agonizingly approved, was remitted and the private was restored to duty. Federal forces captured him within a few weeks of surrender.

JOHN W. HOLMES 50-D (Prior to July 30, 1863). After enrolling in March 1862, Private Holmes was present for duty for three months before being absent without leave. By September he was back with the company but again departed, this time in a group of 7 men who left Company D on December 13, 1862. On May 29, 1863, he was in arrest and delivered to authorities by Lieutenant S. H. Hood of the 117th North Carolina Militia, Johnston County. For his offense he was tried and sentenced to be shot; the day selected for execution was August 15, 1863.[19] The earlier conviction on the absent without leave charge excepted him from the provisions of a recent presidential amnesty. General Whiting interposed his authority, however, and revoked the order of execution on the scheduled day, this after earlier informing the President that there were no mitigating circumstances in the case of Private Holmes.[20] The freed man served in the ranks for another year and then began his third desertion, this departure from Plymouth, NC, on August 18, 1864. Private Holmes availed himself of an opportunity to go into Federal lines where he would not have to await the last minute vacillation of General Whiting. A younger brother, Private Brazil

[Braswell] Holmes enlisted in Company D in August 1864 and was absent without leave at year's end.

MATTHEW M. BAKER 50-D (Prior to July 30, 1863). Privates Matthew M., Allen R. and Jonathan Baker all deserted Company D, Fiftieth Regiment on December 13, 1862, while the company was encamped near Drewry's Bluff on the James River in VA. They were apprehended in separate confrontations during the ensuing year. Private Jonathan Baker was the first to be caught. Four months after deserting, he was arrested at his home on April 10, 1863. For his crime he was tried and given the rather mild sentence of being bucked and gagged for eight hours. Private Allen Baker was not treated as leniently. The decision in his case was published on August 20, 1863; he was to be branded with the letter "D" 1¼ inch in height and wear a twenty-four-pound ball attached to his left leg while kept at hard labor for the duration of the war. In between the trials of Privates Allan and Jonathan Baker, Private Matthew Baker was given a death sentence, the court decision made known on July 30, 1863. An earlier absent without leave conviction may have contributed to that decision. General Whiting approved the sentence and then, typically, four days later wrote a long letter to President Davis practically appealing for his intervention, while appearing resolute in his command responsibility. General Whiting said that he had reviewed the court proceedings after taking command from General Hill. There were 4 cases at hand involving the crime of desertion. As in the other cases, there were no mitigating circumstances and the General was "with great reluctance compelled to sign their death warrants." He went on to say that the prevalence of the crime, the mistaken leniency of courts-martial heretofore, and the good of the cause all required that action. Still, "men should have every chance for life," if it should please the President to stay the proceedings or pardon the convicted. Since he, General Whiting, had set August 15, for the day of execution, he was "obliged to go through with it." A Special Order scheduling the day of execution for Privates Baker and Holmes for August 22, was revoked immediately after issuance.[21] Private Matthew Baker rejoined his company and served through December 1864.

DENNIS P. WARREN 42-D (Prior to August 20, 1863). Private Warren, a conscript, deserted on May 27, 1863, seven months after he was forced into service. He made a poor choice of day and companions. Others that deserted that day were captured and shot for their crime. Of course, it was the second desertion for those men, and they remained at large for several months longer than did Private Warren. Nonetheless, the court that heard the case of Private Warren determined that death was a just punishment. His execution was scheduled for September 10, to be conducted under the direction of General Martin, as was announced in GO #13, Department of North Carolina, August 20, 1863. The sentence was remitted; Private Warren returned to duty and within a year was transferred to a Confederate engineering regiment. Upon reaching that unit, the transferee deserted to the enemy. Federal authorities sent the deserter to Philadelphia, PA.

J. F. CAMPBELL 42-D (November 11, 1863). Private Campbell was with his assigned regiment for nearly a year after his conscription in October 1862. On September 9, 1863, he deserted from camp near Kinston, NC. Two weeks later he was under guard and on his way back to his regiment to face a court-martial. The court sat in session on November 11; a resulting death sentence was approved, with execution to take place on January 20, 1864. Well before that day, perhaps in the spirit of the season, on the day after Christmas Captain Jacob M. Hartsell wrote to Lieutenant Colonel John Edmunds Brown, his regimental commander, asking that a condemned soldier in the Captain's company be released from a death sentence because: "I think effect of shooting two men in this reg would probably be as good as if four were shot and under circumstances request to commute the sentence."[22] The Lieutenant Colonel in his endorsement named Private Campbell as one of the men to be considered for commutation, though no reason is given. Two of the soldiers that were also under death sentences, and not included in the plea, had records of prior desertion attempts. At various times in the war, the second desertion was an unofficial threshold for awarding a death sentence. Brigadier General James G. Martin endorsed the request and sent it on to the AIGO. A soldier in the Sixty-Sixth kept his wife informed on the status of the convicted men when on January 24, he wrote, "Those men that I wrote you that would [be] shot on the 20th was postponed until the 29th of the present."[23] The complete record of the case was delivered to the Secretary of War on January 29, 1864. The request that originated with the officers of the Forty-Second was found persuasive and in due course SO #107, May 7, 1864, AIGO went beyond the requested commutation and remitted the sentence and returned the deserter to duty. The reason given for the order was, "Special reasons in communication from Captain of Company."[24] Although the Special Order restored the private to duty, the final entry in his records indicates that he remained in prison at least through October 1864.

As noted in the case of Private Campbell, appeals for only 2 of the 4 men that were then under sentence of death were sent forward by regimental officers. The second prisoner so favored was Private Hatley of Company H, Forty-Second Regiment, whose trial would follows in two weeks. The officers may have reasoned that their chance for success was enhanced if they limited their appeal, thus tacitly agreeing that the other death judgments were fully justified.

WILLIAM A. BARKER 42-D (November 17 or 18, 1863). Private Barker was willing to accept the risks of war when he became a substitute for William Hatchett of Iredell County. His service record gives conflicting dates of entry into service; one is in April 1862, two weeks before passage of the conscription laws. In the winter of that year the substitute was absent without leave for a brief period. A more serious desertion attempt began on May 27, 1863, while his company was near Greenville, NC. Four months later, the substitute and deserter was in confinement awaiting trial, which came to pass in mid–November. Private Barker was found guilty of desertion and sentenced to be shot, this made known in GO #7, January 23, 1864, Department of North Carolina.[25] The day set for execution was January 29, 1864, and the order was carried into effect on that day. Though regimental officers made no appeal, a petition for pardon for Private Barker was sent to Confederate authorities by a citizen of Iredell County.[26] Unbeknownst to either party, this was well past the point where relief could be afforded. The petition was duly processed, and on February 16, the AIGO requested the full record in the case. Six weeks later, receipt of the documents was acknowledged and the direction given, "If sentence not executed postpone and submit [record]."[27] General Whiting replied on May 5: "Communication of 28 reference William Barker 40-D sentenced to death by court-martial. It appears that the sentence was executed on the day appointed."[28] Why General Whiting thought it necessary to say "It appears" is not obvious. The words may have been chosen to lessen his role in the execution, or suggest that it took place when he was occupied with matters of greater concern for the Confederacy. Around the time Private Barker left the company, 17 others did likewise. Just 1 left the ranks in the five months after he was shot, but then absences rapidly increased in both the company and the regiment.

GOODIN HINSON 42-C (November 18, 1863). Four months after volunteering to serve in a company formed about Stanly County in March 1862, Private Hinson left his company and avoided arrest until sometime before November when he was court-martialed. For the three-month absence, Private Hinson was sentenced to six months of hard labor and to suffer the shame of being carried down the lines of his regiment astride a wooden rail. That humiliation was not a lasting deterrent for Private Hinson. Willing to risk more deadly punishment, he again deserted, this time with Private Barker of Company D, on May 27, 1863. The men were arrested at the same time. Private Hinson appeared before a court-martial on November 18. His death sentence was announced in the same general order as was that of his accomplice, Private Barker. No record of an appeal of any sort for the life of Private Hinson has been found. The men were executed together on January 29, 1864. Unlike Company D, Company C had a fine absence record for the entire war. Privates Barker and Hinson were shot after each made two attempts to leave the struggle. January 1864 was a time of renewed resolve on the part Confederate leaders to execute those convicted of multiple desertion attempts. Similar firmness throughout the war might have been well centered on companies more deserving than Company D or C of the Forty-Second.

A soldier of the same regiment described the execution of the men: "January 31, 1864 Dear Uncle I will tell you that there was too of our reg shot last Friday did not see it am glad I didn't for they had to shoot one man twice before they killed him they first place they shot him in the legs."[29] The young writer, who survived the war, goes on to say that two men were drowned in a river, one carrying brandy, the other carrying $2,000 in gold and silver. Confederates executing fellow soldiers, botched executions, greedy men fleeing the cause — this was a trying time for a man wanting to stand steady with his company. A second member of the Forty-Second was more interested with the miles of march than details of the executions. "Left Wilmington Jan 17th went 24 miles [not legible] to throw up brest works staid their until the 29 we shot two of our men an started for Shepards town 25 miles South East of Newbern."[30]

WILLIAM F. CASH 42-D (November 23, 1863). Private Cash was a conscript in the Confederate army in October 1862. After being mustered, Private Cash was sick, at home or in military hospitals about half of the time. Illness may have influenced his decision to desert while in the area of Kinston, NC on September 9, 1863. Two weeks after leaving his regiment, the deserter was arrested and held for trial, which came about on November 23. A month later, Private Cash learned that two-thirds of the officers sitting on the court concurred that he was guilty of desertion and that he should be shot. General Whiting reviewed the decision of the court; his keen eye quickly noted that the plea of the defendant, as to his guilt or innocence, was not shown on the record of the court. Also missing was a statement that the court had been properly sworn to perform their duties. For these errors, the entire proceeding was "vitiated," and the private was released and restored to duty.[31] For Private Cash, there were a few months of duty, sickness, and death on September 1, 1864.

EPHRAIM HATLEY 42-H (November 25, 1863). Private Hatley was the second of the two soldiers who were freed from a death sentence after the appeal by Captain J. M. Hartsell. The young private had volunteered for service in February 1862, and upheld his commitment until beginning a brief absence on August 17, 1863. The absence ended just three days later, the entire incident taking place in the vicinity of Kenansville, Duplin County. A court-martial convened on November 25, 1863, decided that his absence, even though it could be measured in hours, warranted a death sentence. As in several other cases General Whiting quickly suspended execution of sentence. After some delay, SO #108, May

9, 1864, AIGO was issued releasing the condemned man "upon petition of officers." Private Hatley was given a $50 bounty on volunteering and was charged $30 for the expense of his arrest. A younger brother, Private Israel Hatley, died four months after enrolling in Company H, in March 1864. Three other privates in the same company as Private Hatley deserted on the same day, August 17. They were captured together three days later and were court-martialed on the same day. All were sentenced to be shot.

LEONARD G. TUCKER 42-H (November 25, 1863). Private Tucker enrolled on March 25, 1862, and was in line at the battle at Bentonville, NC, in March 1865. A short desertion occurred about halfway through his three years of service. After his trial on November 25, 1863, Private Tucker was relieved to learn that General Whiting had not approved his sentence of death because the trial record did not specifically state how the defendant had pled to the charge brought against him. This error, probably clerical, was still sufficient to nullify the proceedings of the court and return Private Tucker to duty.[32] His pay was stopped for the $30 expense of his arrest. Private Tucker was captured at Bentonville on March 14, 1865, and took the oath two months later. An older brother, Private John O. Tucker, was enrolled in the same company for two years that were marked by frequent absences due to illness.

JOSHUA OSBORNE 42-H (November 25, 1863). Private Osborne enlisted on the same day as Private Tucker. He also deserted, was captured and then tried on the same days as his companion from Stanly County. The same error, not stating the defendant's plea, was made in the case of Private Osborne and he returned to the fray until February 1865. His pay was stopped for the $30 arresting fee. Younger brother Private James Osborne went into Company H in July 1863. He was paroled when the conflict ended.

WILSON M. CARTER 42-H (November 25, 1863). Private Carter went into service in April 1863. Less than a year later, he left his company along with Privates Hatley, Tucker and Osborne. The court was attentive to detail in the case of Private Carter, and the trial proceedings contained no irregularity that would release him from the court-imposed death sentence. But members of the court asked that General Whiting consider clemency for the man they had just condemned. Members of his company also submitted a petition on his behalf.[33] General Whiting did act to suspend execution of the sentence, and SO #75, which was issued on March 30, 1864, AIGO remitted the sentence. While the suspension of sentence was in effect, Private Carter was sent to work on fortifications in the vicinity of Wilmington, NC. General Whiting took this step because he was of the opinion that none of the men who were under death sentences would ever be executed. Private Carter was last reported on the rolls of his company in October 1864.

BART B. KNIGHT 42-D (January 23, 1864). Private Knight was in the ranks without noteworthy incident for a full year before deserting on September 9, 1863. His arrest, along with two other deserters, took place near Kinston, NC, later in that same month. A court-martial held before January 23, 1864, issued a death decision for the ten-day absence, the only recorded absence on Private Knight's record. Quite characteristically, General Whiting suspended execution of the sentence while the trial transcript was sent to the Secretary of War. A petition prepared by company officers was placed on the record.[34] Nearly a full year later, SO #294, December 12, 1864, AIGO officially released the prisoner. That was some three months after Private Knight died at Fort Caswell, Wilmington, NC, though a letter of General Whiting's letters erroneously indicates that the private was still at work on November 31, 1864.

JOHN H. GOODNIGHT 17-L (Prior to January 26, 1864). Three of the men from Cabarrus County who faced execution had similar experiences from muster to the threat of death. Corporal Goodnight, the first to desert, left his command on August 27, 1863. His enrollment was on record as of April 1863, and he was in arrest by January 17, 1864. The journey to the guardhouse may have been hastened by a newspaper notice concerning 6 deserters who left the Seventeenth; Corporal Goodnight was among those listed. The ad cost $182 for twelve printings in a local paper.[35] The money was not well spent as just 2 of the 6 deserters were ever brought to trial. Corporal Goodnight was one of them, and he was given a death sentence. Release and return to duty quickly followed in the January–February 1864 reporting period. Private Goodnight was killed in battle at Petersburg, VA, in June 1864.

JESSE M. BARNHART 17-L (Prior to January 26, 1864). Private Barnhart deserted on September 18, 1863; he enrolled on the same day as Corporal Goodnight in April, was in arrest on October 2, and taken back to his command by November 17. Private Barnhart was charged $30 for the expense of his arrest and $4 for loss of a haversack and a knapsack, along with the loss of pay for the period of his absence. His death sentence was commuted, and he was sent to work on the forts defending Wilmington. He survived the war.

DANIEL M. ISENHOUR 17-L (Prior to January 26, 1864). Private Isenhour had a service record identical to that of Private Barnhart. The finding of the court that heard their cases was announced in GO #9, January 26, 1864, Department of North Carolina. Privates Barnhart and Icehour [sic] were to be shot to death on February 5. The death sentence for Private Isenhour was commuted to hard labor, and he gained release from that sentence in 1865. The death sentences for the 3 men of Cabarrus County set off a burst of correspondence and official orders, one writer urging that the men be promptly executed, others urging clemency. On February 6, 1864, the execution of the sentence in the case of Private Icehour [sic] was suspended; on February 10, a like suspension came down for Private Barnhart. Some time would be needed to sort out all of the conflicting comments and observations. No record of suspension of sentence has been found for Private Goodnight. Major Victor C. Barringer of the Home Guard in Cabarrus County was a prosperous lawyer from a wealthy family. On February 11, he urged General Whiting to consider the disastrous effect that leniency toward these men, especially Private Barnhart and Corporal Goodnight, would have on encouraging supporters of deserters in the section of Cabarrus County where the men lived. He first gave his view: "Now I do not hesitate to say that the interest of the Army, especially here at home, requires that some or all of these men should be shot: and if they are regularly convicted I hope no consideration of mercy would be allowed to save them from punishment."[36] In support of his remarks, he went on to point out that the neighborhood where the men lived was the only disloyal section in the county and that lenient treatment would only emphasize that the government was too "timid" to deal with desertion, and further encourage traitors in that area. Private Barnhart was labeled a bad man with only "ruffians" as friends; Corporal Goodnight was also a bad man, a "busy body" and a "mischief maker." General Whiting prepared a letter of transmittal on February 14, to accompany court documents being sent to an aide to President Davis.

> General, I transmit the accompanying letter relative to these men condemned to be shot — I wish it to be understood that I had confirmed the sentences & ordered the executions & by no means am inclined to either shift the responsibility in these cases or to put the Executive Dept to the trouble of reviewing the proceedings — the latter are regular. These cases therefore are simply in which the President may or may not exercise his prerogative of pardon or

clemency irrespective of the guilt of the prisoners — at least I so understand it — In suspending execution in these cases I was governed by two considerations the first that I had executed among a large number of cases a number in my judgment sufficient to produce a salutary effect & the other that for some of these cases urgent petitions for mercy were handed me from the officers of their regiments. One also (not referred to in the accompanying letter) because the culprit was evidently but half witted. I am bound to say that had I received the accompanying letter sooner two at least of these men Barnhardt and Gdnight [sic] would have long ago suffered the extreme penalty of the law.[37]

This letter is a typical reaction of General Whiting in regard to executing deserters. He is resolute and determined in his comments — witness the last line of his letter — but vacillating when the time approaches for execution. What was a perplexed President Davis to do? Here he is presented with a letter from General Whiting first suggesting clemency, and then a forceful statement saying that he would have had the men shot had he received the Barringer letter a few days earlier, which letter the President has before him as he weighs his decision. General Samuel Cooper was also the recipient of one of General Whiting's letters, it was written in much the same tone as that directed to the President. General Whiting explained that he had first confirmed the death sentences for these men and then ordered suspension of the order on "executive clemency." There was no error in the proceedings. He would cause the execution of Barnhart to be carried out, referring to the Barringer letter, but "in the case of Icehour [sic] he was indifferent."[38] The death sentences were commuted to hard labor, leading General Whiting to inquire of General Cooper whether a number of men that were pardoned, Privates Isenhour and Barnhart among them, were given full pardons or if their sentences were commuted to hard labor. In any event he had assigned the men to work on local fortifications as it was unlikely that their execution would ever take place.[39]

Federal recruiters were active in eastern North Carolina in the fall and winter of 1863 and 1864. Between September 1863 and February 1864 some 500 men enrolled in the Second Regiment North Carolina Union Volunteers (hereafter Second NCUV); nearly half made that decision before the end of 1863.[40] For so doing they were eligible for a $100 bounty to be paid in installments of $25. They were also assured that their families would be protected from any retribution and if need be brought within Federal lines.[41] In January 1864 the total enrollment bounty for Federal service was raised to $300. The first installment of the bounty was for $60, the second was for $40. Payment did not begin until completion of three months of service. Absences from the Federal unit suggest that their officers had as much difficulty keeping men in the ranks as did their Confederate counterparts. In fact, the regiment was of little value as a Federal fighting force. In action at Plymouth, NC, in April 1864, "A considerable number of North Carolina soldiers (many of them deserters from the enemy) and all of them fearing bad treatment in the event of capture ... left in canoes."[42] "Cannot place the least dependence on them ... Second North Carolina much excited strictly demoralized and will not fight ... they look to swamps for protection."[43] "Your Second North Carolina are so demoralized that you had better send them up to Norfolk."[44] The regiment's shortcomings were placed squarely on the shoulders of recruiting officers. These officers were of an "utter incapacity and general uselessness." Their enrollments were "virtual impressment" and "fraudulent." They played on the fears of North Carolinians who had limited knowledge. They were enrolling the "weak, puny, scrofulous, eaten by disease old age and infirmity."[45] Men who were considering going over to the Federal side raised the question of their status, and their likely fate, if captured by Confederate forces. They were given assurance that the Federal government would punish anyone who outraged them or their families, neatly sidestepping what would happen to them if they were captured by the men they had betrayed.[46] Complicating the choice of allegiance was the threat to family and property if the wrong choice was made. The factors that cause a man to offer his life and to remain committed are starkly reduced when the bloodshed nears home and neighborhood. Word and commitment yield to the basic need for family survival. Some resolute men made only one decision, but others were swayed to reconsider their choice. In this second group were 27 North Carolinians, among some 50, that were captured by a Virginia regiment at Beech Grove, near Batchelder's Creek, NC, on February 2, 1864. They were among 70 men of the Second NCUV on outpost duty at a small, out-of-the-way fort located between Kinston and New Bern near the Neuse River. The presence of the fort was noted in a directive from General R. E. Lee to General Pickett prepared on January 20, 1864.[47] It forcefully suggested that General Pickett immediately move to capture New Bern and the Federal forces thereabouts. Capture of the small fort received specific mention in the opening phase of the plan. General Lee said that he had endeavored to think of everything in his order. General Pickett's troops arrived at the fort without difficulty and made a demand for surrender. Capitulation was negotiated without a shot being fired in defense of the position. As many as 20 men made their way along paths known to them to avoid capture, but 50 others who did not, or could not, flee were made prisoners. The service records of several of the men in the fort have comments that indicate there was a day of fighting before the fort surrendered. These comments are not supported by any other source, casualty lists or the like, and are directly contradicted by members of the attacking force, the Thirtieth Virginia Infantry.[48] Men with whom they had formerly served immediately recognized several of the prisoners. On continued questioning, these turncoats identified other men who had been enrolled in Confederate units, possibly hoping to gain leniency for themselves, or to make the group so large that drastic punishment would be unlikely.

The next day two of the men who were quickly identified as former Confederates were tried by a drumhead court. The order convening a general court-martial to try the captured traitors was issued by Major General G. E. Pickett. The President of the court was Lieutenant-Colonel James R. Branch, Confederate States Artillery. The findings of the court were published in General Order #6, February 3, 1864, Head Quarters Department of North Carolina, Camp on Dover Road. "Before a General Court Martial convened at or near the Headquarters of Major-General Pickett, on the 3rd of Feb'y 1864, were arraigned and tried the following named prisoners. The specifications being lengthy and exactly the same in all the cases, are omitted in this order, they representing that the prisoners after duly enlisting in the service of the Confederate States, deserted therefrom, and were taken in arms in the service of the United States: [The name, charge, specification and sentence for each of the twenty-seven prisoners then followed]."[49]

The first men to be tried were found guilty of desertion and taking up arms against their country, and they were hanged on February 5, 1864. These men were not in the Martin brigade and their records, along with those of 4 others, are included with their respective regiments. The execution of the first of the captured men brought forth this comment on February 5: "There were two men hung here to day and think they will hang 15 more, they belonged to the Confederate service, and deserted, and went to the Yankee's and joined them we captured them at or rather near Newburn."[50] On Sunday February 7, a diary entry: "On Friday after our return to K two men in Nethercutts battalion were hung they had deserted to enemy and were caught fighting against us. Two or three more were to have been hung on Sat but for some unknown reason the execution did not take place."[51] A few days later on February 9, a soldier wrote, "Among the prisoners taken were quite a number of buffaloes, two of whom who had deserted from our army quite recently & found with arms in their hands were hung in the presence of our Brigade on last Saturday [Friday] in town. It is quite probable that several more will share the same fate in a few days."[52]

The capture and execution of the first of the turncoats soon became known to Federal commanders in the area. This led to an exchange of letters between the senior area commanders, Major General John J. Peck, United States Army at New Bern, and Major General George E. Pickett. The Federal officer threatened retaliation and reprisal for the executions.[53]

Trials for 25 men went on over the next ten days. One man whose family was prominent in the area was turned over to civil authorities. Another was treated with leniency because of his extreme youth, some physical disability and mental imbecility; he was sentenced to hard labor for a year. Three men were to be branded with a letter "D" four inches high, and to wear a twelve-pound ball attached to their left ankle with a five-foot chain, while they were confined at hard labor for the rest of the war. The other 20 men who went to trial were all sentenced to be hanged. All were dead by the evening of February 22.

JOHN L. STANLY 66-F (February 4, 1864). Private Stanly enlisted in the Eighth Battalion Partisan Rangers on February 9, 1863. He did not report for duty when his company was transferred to the Sixty-Sixth in October 1863. On December 5, he agreed to serve in the Second NCUV, thereby becoming eligible for a $100 bounty to be paid in installments of $25, a wise enticement for continued service on the part of Federal authorities, considering that the men receiving the bounty had just departed the Confederate army. After Private Stanly was captured on February 2, 1864, he was tried two days later, found guilty, and hanged on February 12. Private Stanly was the third man listed in General Order #6. The findings of the court are similar for all of the men who were executed.

> Kinston Feby 4th, 1864 3-Private John L. Stanly, Nethercutt's Battalion. Charge Desertion, Finding of the Specification, Guilty. Of the charge Guilty. And the court do therefore, sentence the said private John L. Stanly, Nethercutt's Battalion, two thirds of the court concurring therein, to be hanged by the neck until he is dead, at such time and place as the General commanding may direct."[54]

LEWIS C. BRYAN 66-F (February 4, 1864). Although most were, not all of the men hanged at Kinston were middle-aged. Young men in their twenty-first year were also led up the scaffold steps. Private Lewis Bryan had enrolled in Company A of the Eighth Battalion in May of 1862 and was still on the rolls when the company was made part of the Sixty-Sixth Regiment. He did not report to his new command and was listed as a deserter on October 10, 1863. Six weeks later, on November 27, the young man enrolled in the Second NCUV and was mustered within a week. Private Bryan went before a court on February 4, was found guilty of desertion and of being captured in the uniform of the United States Army, and was sentenced to be "hanged by the neck until he is dead." The sentence was approved to be carried into effect twenty-four hours after publication of the order. A relative of Lewis did go to the execution but did not provide any detail when questioned as to the events.[55]

WILLIAM IRVIN 66-F (February 4, 1864). Private William Irvin went into Company A, Eighth Battalion, on January 21, 1863. A brother, Private Richard Irvin, enrolled along with him. Private William Irvin did not report to the Sixty-Sixth Regiment. On December 2, 1863, he did enroll in the Second NCUV. He was court-martialed on February 4 and hanged on February 12. After the execution of her son, his mother asked Isiah Wood, jailer at Kinston, for help in locating her son's body.[56] He said he was unable to do so because there were 3 men buried in a common grave and he could not distinguish her son's body. Compassion oftentimes yields to mean-spirited retribution, even toward those not directly engaged in a civil war.

MITCHELL BUSICK 66-F (February 4, 1864). Private Busick went into Federal service on December 9, 1863. According to his statement made on the gallows, he took that step under duress. Private Busick did not contest that he had voluntarily enrolled in Company A of the Eighth Battalion in June 1862 or that he had gone into enemy lines rather than report to the muster point of the Sixty-Sixth. But he did say: "I went to Newbern and they (the Yankees) told me if I did not go into their service I should be taken through the lines and shot. In this way I was frightened into it."[57] He then joined others in saying that they regretted that they had done wrong and wanted to "warn others not to follow our example." Private Busick was hanged moments later. The statement by Private Busick is at odds with that made by a Federal officer who said there was widespread loyalty to the Constitution and the Union throughout the area.[58]

After the first 2 deserters were hanged and just before the next 5 would mount the scaffold, Governor Vance was informed as to who was at least partially responsible for the sad affair and to the continuing bitterness.

> The subject of this letter is one in which I feel great interest Viz I am intimately acquainted with several young men of this (Craven) County who have absented themselves from their Regt (66th) without-leave — The reason they have thus acted they say is because they were enlisted under false pretences — Viz That when enlisted by Capt. Nethercutt (now Lt Col) as Rangers that he told them that they were intend only to operate from White Oak River to Neuse River and would in no case be carried out of the State, but if circumstance would ever require his removal from the State he would guarantee them a transfer. These men are of the best standing and I think never would have acted thus had they not been in some way deceived. They pray your intercession in their behalf, they most earnestly desire a transfer to Col Whitford but should it be impossible for you to secure them a transfer are willing to serve in any command but Col Nethercutt's. They do not consider themselves deserters and would never in any instance use force against their County. They also desire you to endeavor to have any punishment that might be the penalty of their offence omitted, and should you fail to secure their 1st or 2nd desires & the punishment be not to severe I guarantee their return to their command. I hope you'll intercede. Yours & R. A. Russell Member H.C. for Craven[59]

The Governor indicated the reply should say that he had no power to pardon or transfer but that he would use "every exertion" to secure some sort of resolution.

On February 11, General Hoke directed that a Chaplain visit the condemned men, which he did, and while there he wrote letters for 3 of them. The Chaplain noted that all of the men were penitent.[60]

WILLIAM D. JONES W&WRR GUARDS (February 6, 1864). Private William Jones enrolled in Captain John L. Cantwell's Company of Wilmington and Weldon Railroad Guards on January 11, 1862. He enrolled at Goldsboro, NC, and two weeks later was mustered for the first time at Wilmington. Private Jones was present then, as he was for all succeeding musters up to May 19, 1863, when his company became Company D, Wright's battalion. On January 19, 1864, he enrolled in the Second NCUV at New Bern. For this commitment he received the promise of a $300 bounty, the first installment to be paid on February 2. Federal Private Jones was mustered on January 21, and captured on February 2, the day that he was to receive his first bounty payment. Trial followed in four days and the noose nine days later; Private Jones was in the Federal army less than two weeks. After the war, Nancy Jones was asked, "What condition was your husband's body in when you received it"? In reply she said, "He had nothing on but his socks; I could not take my husband's body for want of a conveyance. I went home on Wednesday morning, and sent my son, aged 15, and nephew, aged 17, after the body. My son found the body a week after execution in an old loft, in charge of a guard placed over it by a doctor. The guard refused to let the body go until the doctor gave permission. Plenty would have been glad to have assisted me, but did not dare to for fear of being called Unionist."[61] The body may have been set aside for medical study; the condition when laid to rest is not known.

The company commander of Private Jones, Captain William H. Freeman, was drawn into the legal intricacies surrounding the men who had earlier enrolled in the consolidated battalions. That involvement began five months earlier in September 1863, following a decision by Judge William H. Battle, North Carolina Supreme Court. The Judge granted a writ of habeas corpus ordering the release from service of some 40 men of Captain Freeman's company, this action justified on the ground that the men had volunteered for local service as bridge guards and could not be transferred to Confederate or general service. Captain Freeman, when served, accepted the writ and told his men that he no longer had control over them, whereupon nearly all immediately left camp. Captain Freeman's acceptance of the writ and his remarks led to his arrest by order of Colonel Alexander D. Moore, Sixty-Sixth Regiment. Captain Freeman sought legal advice and assistance in obtaining a writ of habeas corpus to free him on the same grounds that had secured the release of the men in his company. His counsel, however, advised Captain Freeman that his reasoning was incorrect and that he had no authority to release the men. Captain Freeman continued to search for legal aid. Expense was of no concern. He instructed a legal counselor, "You will proceed regardless of any cost."[62] Captain Freeman and two other officers were court-martialed for their part in the handling of the writ issued by Judge Battle, but the defendants did not learn of the court decision until well into the next year. When the findings of the court were eventually released, it was found that General Lee had disapproved the entire proceedings, this after the court had found the officers guilty of the charge of aiding desertion. General Lee based his disapproval on the fact that the order convening the court did not appear in the record of the proceedings, which "vitiates and renders null and void" their effort.[63]

CALVIN J. HUFFMAN 66-F (February 6, 1864). Private Calvin Huffman enrolled in Company A of the Eighth Battalion on January 24, 1863, and was present for duty until the company was transferred to the Sixty-Sixth. He did not muster with his new company and was listed as a deserter on October 10. Two and a half months later, on December 22, he joined the Second NCUV, thereby becoming eligible for a $100 bounty. That act led to the scaffold on February 15, 1864.

STEPHEN H. JONES 66-D (February 6, 1864). Private Stephen Jones initially enrolled in Company D, Thirteenth Battalion but left the unit due to sickness and subsequently enrolled in Company C, Eighth Battalion. He was with his company when the unit was consolidated and was present for muster in September–October, but then had a change of heart and was absent without leave in November–December 1863. While absent, he enlisted in the Second NCUV on the day before Christmas and was mustered two days later. Capture, trial, and gallows followed in due course. Stephen's widow testified before congressional investigators. Her testimony did little to advance the Federal contention that the Kinston hangings violated the rules of war. She agreed that her husband had first volunteered, and was later conscripted into the service of the Confederate army, and that he had deserted that service. Elizabeth lived just a short distance from Kinston, which enabled her to frequently visit with her husband in the two weeks between his capture and his execution. On one visit she brought him a quilt.[64] She made no attempt to intercede on behalf of her husband after being told that it was "useless."[65] The day that he was hanged, her husband was returned to her for burial. Who, if anyone, helped her or where the body was laid to rest is not known. She owned no land for a grave.

LEWIS TAYLOR 66-F (February 6, 1864). Private Lewis Taylor began his military obligation on January 24, 1863, in Company B, Eighth Battalion, and was still on the rolls of the company when the transfer to the Sixty-Sixth was ordered. He did not report for duty with that regiment, instead enrolling in the Second NCUV on December 23. Apparently several men who enrolled around Christmas 1863 were not told that the enrollment bounty would be tripled in just a few days. Any delay that gave a Confederate time to reconsider would be deemed very risky by an officer anxious to enroll men changing their allegiance. Though some who volunteered at the end of December were given the larger bounty.

JOHN F. FREEMAN 66-F (February 6, 1864). Private John Freeman enrolled in Company A, Eighth Battalion in January 1863. After a half year of service, he was selected to go with a company officer, Lieutenant Franklin Foy, on a detached scouting assignment. Scouting duty occupied him for the rest of his time in the battalion. After the transfer to the Sixty-Sixth, he was listed as a deserter. The former Confederate scout enrolled in the Second NCUV on December 23, 1863.

JOHN J. BROCK 66-D (February 7, 1864). Private John Brock first enrolled in Company C of the Thirteenth Battalion in January 1862. At mid-year he transferred to the Eighth Battalion, first to Company A, and then in October to Company C. His service record shows that he was absent sick for the entire period after his company was transferred to the Sixty-Sixth. While still recorded as absent sick in Confederate records, he enrolled and mustered into the Federal army on the day after Christmas 1863. There he would serve until the events of February next. Private Brock was age forty when joining the Federal army. His wife had a brief visit with him on the morning of his execution. That same morning he was baptized in the Neuse River. During earlier visits she brought food to her husband and to others, because the jailers would only provide the prisoners "one cracker a day."[66] She buried her husband where she lived, about four miles below Kinston, on the Wilmington Road. The body was dressed in "cast off clothing" when turned over to her. She owned no property and relied on the kindness of others to offer a burial site. Hopefully, she selected a stand of pine where the remains would be undisturbed until nature completed the cycle of life for a turpentine worker. The widow was aided in her effort to provide a decent burial for her husband by Mr. John A. Parrott of Lenoir County. Mr. Parrott was a very wealthy man, having nearly $100,000 in assets in 1860. When testifying at the hearing, he mentioned that he had heard music at the time of John's execution.[67] This is the only reference to a band being present that has been found.

WILLIAM O. HADDOCK 8-A BATTALION (February 7, 1864). Private Haddock's service file is somewhat different from those of other men who swayed beside him on the scaffold. He had enrolled in Company A of the Eighth Battalion in July 1862, for which he received a $50 bounty. He transferred to Company C in October. In December of that same year, he was captured and later paroled by Federal troops. He rejoined his command, but then deserted after being paid on April 30, 1863. Private Haddock had not returned to his company at the time of the transfer to the Sixty-Sixth, and his name is not found on the rolls of the regiment. He remained a Confederate deserter for seven months. His next service decision was to volunteer for duty in the Second NCUV, which he did on November 27, 1863. A sister, Arsena, Mrs. Bryan McCullum of Kinston, desperately strove to intercede on his behalf by requesting to have counsel and witnesses at his court-martial. The thrust of her defense is not stated; her request was denied. Failing in her defense, the devoted sister then asked James B. Wells to obtain an order that she might take possession of and bury the body of her brother. At that point General R. F. Hoke reportedly queried if they intended to bury the young man in a Yankee uniform. The reply was that he would be buried as taken from the hangman's rope.[68] Even with an order giving them permission to take possession of the body, and with people present to do so, the hangman callously attempted to remove the shoes from the still warm corpse, which Wells resisted. Before going to the gallows, Private Haddock had told Catherine Summerlin that he wished her to take his clothes to his mother, who was a neighbor of the Summerlin family.[69] For his part, the hangman may have felt that he was, by custom or agreement, entitled to take the clothing from the dead as partial payment for his service. Younger and older brothers of Private Haddock also served in Federal units. Private Luke M. Haddock volunteered for service in the same company a week after his brother enrolled, this on December 5, 1863. Private Luke Haddock became eligible for a $100 bounty when he enrolled. His capture on February 2 did not lead to trial; he was a prisoner of war, and entitled to be so treated. He died at Richmond, VA, on April 10, 1864, likely still a prisoner of war. Private John A. Haddock joined the Federal service on the same day as his executed brother. He deserted the Federal army on June 5, 1864, and died while in confinement on October 10, 1864. The desertion charge was removed from Private John Haddock's record in 1883, perhaps to allow a claim for payment from the Federal government.

JESSE JAMES SUMMERLIN 66-D (February 7, 1864). Private Summerlin joined Company A, Eighth Battalion Partisan Rangers, on July 7, 1862. The recruit brought his own musket with him. A transfer to Company C of the battalion came in November. A year later, when his company was made part of the Sixty-Sixth, Private Summerlin decided not to muster with his new command, receiving his last Confederate pay on August 31, 1863. Some three months later he agreed to enlist in the Second NCUV on December 5, 1863. One Federal record indicates that he was a Sergeant in his unit. He was captured on February 2, tried on February 7, and hanged on February 15. Though not able to save the condemned man, the Sheriff of Lenoir County did aid the widow in moving his body some twenty miles for burial at her home.[70]

LEWIS FREEMAN 66-F (February 7, 1864). Private Lewis Freeman was present for duty with Company A, Eighth Battalion, from muster in January 1863 to the time of the transfer to the Sixty-Sixth in October 1863. Unwilling to report for muster with the Confederate regiment, he enlisted in the Second NCUV. There is no indication that John Freeman and Lewis Freeman were closely related. They did enlist at the same time and then drop below the same beam, but there was no testimony that there was any family relationship. In fact, some witnesses indicated that they knew only one or the other of the men. There is a reference that a Mrs. Freeman would be willing to testify at the inquiry, but no testimony or first name is given.

WILLIAM H. DOYETY 66-D (February 7, 1864). Private William Doyety was a substitute for Private Joel A. Heath in July 1862. He was enrolled in Captain J. H. Nethercutt's company of Partisan Rangers. The company was then active in and about Jones County. Private Doyety continued to serve with the same men when they were formed into the Eighth Battalion Partisan Rangers. When the battalion underwent further consolidation with the Thirteenth Battalion, Private Doyety did not appear for muster and was listed as absent without leave on company records. Having made the decision not to join the Sixty-Sixth, he was either coerced or willingly agreed to enroll in the Second NCUV on November 24, 1863. He was eligible for a $100 bounty. Private Heath, the soldier that Private Doyety replaced, was a wealthy young man, one with $26,000 in assets in 1860. For the substitute there was an opportunity for a significant financial gain while serving in a unit that was organized specifically for local duty. One must also reflect on the mind of Heath when he learned that his substitute went to the scaffold. What course would he have chosen given the same options?

ANDREW J. BRITTAIN 66-F (February 8, 1864). Private Brittain first enrolled for a year of service on June 12, 1861, with the Twenty-Seventh Regiment. For much of his term of duty he was either absent "sick," or his duty status was not stated. In that same indefinite light, his service in the regiment ends on an inconclusive note. Private Brittain next appears on service records as an enrollee in the Eighth Battalion, assigned to Company A, where in March 1862 he is classified as a musician. Along with the rest of the men in his company, he was reassigned to Company F of the Sixty-Sixth. Either he never reported to that unit or he immediately left after reporting, for he is listed as a deserter on October 10, 1863. Two months later, the reluctant Confederate volunteered for Federal service, agreeing to a three-year enlistment for which he was to be given a $100 bounty, the first payment due on February 2, 1864. He was promoted to Sergeant in the Second NCUV on January 24. Lieutenant Colonel Nethercutt, testifying in 1865, stated that in his opinion, Brittain was the "leading man in this business," likely referring to the exodus from the Sixty-Sixth rather than to the later enrollment in the Federal regiment.[71] Before he was led to the scaffold, Andrew sent word to his wife by the wife of another prisoner. He said to tell her "they would meet in heaven."[72]

One correspondent foretold the coming executions but said he did not want to attend.

> They are erecting additional gallows today upon which they will suspend 13 more of those criminals on Monday. I wish they had hung them all before my return, for however deserving they may be of this awful penalty I am not fond of seeing the execution of fellow men. While I believe they ought to be hung I would feel better & like the ceremony better, if they would exclude me from a seat.[73]

The executions were given little emphasis in letters home. "I have seen 7 deserters hung since I came to Kinston. They hung 2 last Friday was a week ago, 5 yesterday." In a subsequent letter: "Betty, I saw 13 men hung yesterday; there have been 20 hung since we got back from New Bern."[74] A carnivorous Confederate sailor, who was in Kinston on February 15, wrote rather tersely to a friend "I have not much news. There were five men hung last Friday and thirteen hung today. Our fare is nothing extra. We get one pound of meat for three days." On February 17, a letter home offered the view, "There has been twenty men hung here at Kinston since the fight Those who had deserted our army & gone over to the enemy & had taken up arms against us, I think such an example ought to learn our men better."[75] While not a witness to what was happening at Kinston, another man took the same stand of approval, and wanted to include one additional person: "My dear Pa I understand many traitors captured by our forces at New Bern are being executed by our authorities at Kinston. I hope this may be true as they richly deserve to die the death of a traitor. If Holden could only be shot or hung with them, I think there would be a great change in North Carolina."[76]

ELIJAH KELLUM ENROLLED CONSCRIPT (February 9, 1864). Enrolled Conscript Elijah Kellum first volunteered for service in the Eighth Battalion, Company B, as a teamster. From the day of his enrollment, July 1, 1862, to his discharge in May 1863, he was actually present only about half the time, due to a variety of illnesses which ultimately led to his discharge. In December, the discharged teamster, now an enrolled Confederate conscript, volunteered to serve in the Second NCUV and was promised the same bounty as given other volunteers. After he was captured on February 2, Conscript Kellum was tried on February 9, and hanged on February 22. The execution of Conscript Kellum presents an arguable case that his execution was a most flagrant violation of the "law and custom of war." Legally enrolled soldiers of the forces of one belligerent are to be treated as prisoners of war when captured. The military status of the alleged conscript was cloudy when he was taken at Beech Grove. His court-martial record identifies him as an "Enrolled Conscript," and the same designation is found in AIGO documents. Yet, Lieutenant Colonel Nethercutt could not swear whether or not the man was enrolled in his former battalion. He just did not know. The point was developed at the Federal investigation that Captain Reuben E. Wilson had fraudulently enrolled the conscript. The view was that some person who had wished to scare Kellum was instrumental in having him sent to a camp for conscripts. Perhaps he was treated as a "village idiot" by some people in the community, and perhaps the enrolling officer thought that Kellum would be immediately sent home upon reaching camp. This analysis is supported by a W. S. Huggins of Lenoir County who gave testimony that Kellum was so deformed and had so "little constitution" that no regiment would have him.[77] But that argument is weakened by the fact that Kellum was accepted for general service in the Federal army and given an enrollment bounty. The attending Chaplain recorded in his diary his impressions of the final two days of Kellum's life.

> Sunday 21 This morning I learned of the fate impending of two more deserters who are condemned to be hanged on to morrow. Visited them in prison, and heard the death sentence read to them. It fell with dreadful blight upon their feelings. They insisted they should not be hanged, as they had been persuaded to do so. Monday 22 Went to visit prisoners at nine Oclock. Prayed and talked with them. Kellum professed to be prepared for death. Hill was calm and declared he was not afraid to die. Tuesday 23 Nothing of interest today. Weather still very dry.[78]

The Chaplain who met with the condemned men in the Kinston jail observed that Kellum was "quite a young man."[79] What prompted the statement is not clear. Kellum's Confederate record indicates an age of twenty-five in 1862, his Federal record gives his age as thirty-four in late 1863. The 1850 census lists his age as eighteen. Perhaps a lack of maturity brought about the observation that he was a young man, rather than referencing his age.

On the last day of executions, one man who might have attended apparently had enough of the spectacle. "Dear Mack. Two more were hung today. I went down town, but did not go to the hang. I have seen five out of the 22 that has been hung."[80] A second man who witnessed a least some of the executions wrote: "Dear Wife I will tell you that there was 22 man hang at Kinston since we come here there 13 hang at one time and I can tell you it was an awful site to see. They had all run away and went to the Yanks and we got them prisoners."[81] In a more general comment, "We came back to Kinston and hanged twenty-five of those prisoners who were found to be deserters from our army."[82] More specific but partially inaccurate diary entries record, "February 5, 64 Two deserters hanged at Kinston; February 8, 64 Five deserters hanged at Kinston; February 12, 64 Thirteen deserters hanged; February 22, 64 Two deserters hanged being the last of 22 taken in the enemies ranks new Newbern."[83] Three weeks after the last men were hanged, a soldier wrote, "Dear Father I have sean a site since I left home I sean 13 men hung at one time Tha have been 22 hung hear since we cum to this place."[84] A less accurate account was written nearly thirty years after the war. "Our forces captured a number of deserters who had joined the enemy. They fought like tigers before they were captured. They were brought up to Kinston courtmartialed and hanged on a gallows four at a time. Their friends carried them off and buried them, all but one — he was buried near the gallows. They all lived in the country and belonged to Nethercutt's battalion before they deserted."[85] Another account of the events at Kinston does provide some additional information, but is obviously suspect on several counts.

> The jail was near the Neuse river, and back of it lay a flat country. On this plateau was erected a large scaffold of rude material, and around it was built a platform with triggers, with ropes attached. The fatal day arrived, the military was marched to the scaffold, and men detailed to pull the ropes and thus spring the triggers. Twenty-five men were placed on the platform at one time, the noose adjusted around their necks, their head covered with corn sacks in lieu of the black caps, which could not be obtained, the command given, the ropes were pulled, the triggers sprung, and twenty-five men launched into eternity. This was followed later by five other executions, and then two, the latter being brothers, of the same build and stature, about six feet tall and well-built. They were baptized in the Neuse river, taken to the jail to change their clothing, and from thence to the scaffold, where they paid the penalty of cruel war's demand.[86]

The error in the number and sequence of the executions suggests that the account was based on hearsay information. A soldier enrolled in a Virginia Regiment offered his recollection of the events at Kinston. "The guilt of twenty-two of them being fully established, they were sentenced to be hanged; the sentence being approved by the department commander, was carried into execution a few days thereafter in the vicinity of our camp: a gruesome piece of business, which duty did not require me to witness."[87]

A reflection on the moral rectitude of the 1860s is found in the comments of Confederate Chaplain John Paris who put great emphasis on the fact that the men who were hanged had committed the crime of perjury; they had broken their oath to the Confederate government. To his mind, this was the most serious of their sins and the Chaplain could not fully understand why the men mounting the scaffold would not accept the enormity of their crime and the justness of their sentence: "I urged upon them the importance of making a full and complete confession of all their sins, before both God and man, yet I am afraid these men were willing to look the great sin of perjury of which they were guilty, fully in the face."[88] Of course many of the men who were executed did not agree that they had violated their initial enrollment oath, convinced that they had volunteered only for local service. The attending Chaplain said:

> I told them they had sinned against their country, and their country would not forgive them but that they had also sinned against God, yet God would forgive if they approached him with penitent hearts filled with a Godly sorrow for sin and repose their trust in the atoning blood of Christ. They gave apparently marked attention to my ministrations of the word and of prayer.[89]

The Chaplain apparently felt it his responsibility to learn the names of those who had urged the condemned men to join the Federal army; he was given five names of citizens of Jones County which he turned over to a General, probably General Hoke, and commented, "They will no doubt be properly attended to."[90] No mention of the names is found in documents relating the events at Kinston. The opinion of an unidentified line officer in the Second NCUV was at great variance from that of Confederates. In a document headed "REBEL BARBARITIES," dated March 9, 1864, he presents the Federal view: "The unknown martyrs of this war are many." There was a wide-spread loyalty to the Constitution and the Union, "which neither scourging, starvation, bloodhounds, nor the gallows can ever eradicate.... Hiding for months in swamps and thickets, and enduring perils and hardships that are almost incredible these men, (or such of them as are not murdered by the guerrillas,) gaunt with hunger and clad in rags, at last reach our lines." After saying that these men could find profitable employment by the Federal government, he goes on, "but they are burning for the emancipation of their State and the rescue of their families from the horrors of the rebel despotism; and they enlist, without the lure of large bounties, in the service of the United States." The writer then explains that the "saddest fact of all" is that a large number of these men have families that are helpless without them, that they are poor and illiterate, and that there is no state aid to alleviate their suffering. The officer closes with a defense of the men in his regiment: "Rough in appearance, without banners or regimental music, partly drilled, and not thoroughly disciplined, as it is, the Kinston gallows testifies that it is still a regiment fearfully in earnest."[91] Federal officers may have felt that they were aiding the men they encouraged to enlist, even though their fate, if captured, was likely to be a hangman's hemp. Some support for this notion is found in Federal enlistment records that consistently show an older age for former Confederates. Federal officers were aiding older men who were not liable for Confederate service and not enrolling Confederate deserters. As earlier cited, the Second NCUV was not an effective regiment and enrollment virtually ended a month after February 1864. An astute, legally minded and politically oriented commentator offered the following: "A number of deserters from Neathercut's battallion, caught at New Berne in arms, were hanged last week all of them attributed their base conduct to the traitorous teachings of the Standard & Progress."[92] Once again, W. W. Holden and his fellow editors are singled out as responsible for a large portion of the unrest threatening the Confederacy. Major General Whiting had the opinion that much of the dissatisfaction among the members of Nethercutt's Battalion could be traced to a Mr. Roberson [Robinson]. As early as October 24, 1863, he explained to Governor Vance that the discontent in the battalion was greatly exaggerated and was spread by Mr. Roberson for his private ends. He went on to say that discipline in the unit was bad and that it was best for the men and the service that the change to the Sixty-Sixth Regiment be made.[93] The view of the General had not changed in December when he discussed the matter with Adjutant Cooper: "I have yet to learn what business this individual has with the organization referred to. He has perserveringly endeavored to break up the 66th & to prevent any organization of local companies ... his motive is to obtain either a separate command for his son—who is in one of the companies."[94] On the first day of the hangings at Kinston, General Whiting returned to the same theme in a letter to Judge French at Lumberton, NC. First explaining that Confederate authorities had the legal power to combine the battalions in question, he then stated that the trouble was traceable to Mr. Roberson, who wanted to keep the unit near home. He initially tried to have the order for consolidation revoked and failing that tried to create dissatisfaction among the men. In closing, "He has been at the bottom of a great many petitions for writs of habeas corpus."[95] In December of 1863 General Whiting made the same legal defense of the consolidation to Judge W. H. Battle of North Carolina when the judge was considering a petition for a similar writ. General Whiting sent along a muster roll of the company in question to show that it was not raised for local defense but as "Partizan [sic] Rangers" and could be organized into larger units to promote "efficiency and discipline."[96]

Of the several references to the affair at Kinston, none give much detail as to the actual executions. In the case of execution by musketry, witnesses frequently offer detail on the preceding ceremony, the last moments of the condemned, the numbers of balls that struck a man, the sagging on the cross, and the like. No references have been found that give any accurate detail on the events of each day at Kinston. What troops were present, how were the men taken to the gallows, what happened on the platform, was death merciful or prolonged and so on? One explanation for this might be that public hangings, perhaps including lynching, were not that unusual an occurrence in the lives of people living in the 1860s, and did not warrant detailed description in letters and diaries. For example, after a hanging in 1861, one witness gave this brief account: "There was a hanging about this time to which I went. The man was some what affected but took it coolly. He was quite an old man. He died very quickly."[97] The last comment suggests that strangulation was not uncommon at a botched hanging.

Those watching their neighbors go to the gallows may have remembered the many depredations committed by the same Federal army which these men were now willing to join. At Pollocksville in Jones County they had

> broken open the plastering and built a big fire between the walls ... killed all the stock on the farm and the house and yard were full of buzzards,—some of them regaling on a dead horse before the front door, and some of them puking in the parlor and on the piazza.... If every person in the South could witness the useless ruin that the Yankees have caused in Jones and the adjoining counties the name and sight of a Yankee soldier would be hated throughout all eternity.[98]

Fewer words were needed to describe the "nastiness," in the area, "if here stinkiness places in the world it is enough to make a ded man heave."[99] Comments of this nature give insight into the intense and conflicting emotions when men from Jones County were executed at Kinston.

The victors' privilege in warfare allows them to judge the legality of any acts their recent enemies may have perpetrated. A Federal investigation into the events at Kinston was ordered, and two Captains and one Lieutenant were assigned the task of determining the officers responsible.[100] They reported that General Pickett and General Hoke and the officers who served on the Kinston court should be among those to be tried. Judge Advocate Joseph Holt did not agree that the facts supported that conclusion and advised that a second investigation be made to gather more information. This was done and the report submitted that General Pickett was the responsible officer who should be tried for his alleged crimes. General U. S. Grant did not agree, his opinion was that no good would come from a trial of General Pickett and that it would open the whole question of amnesty offered to Confederate soldiers.[101] So closed, officially at least, the events at Kinston in February 1864. In his very detailed letter ordering the attack at New Bern, General Lee wrote, "I have endeavoured to anticipate everything." Surely he did not anticipate the tragic impact on many North Carolina families.

General Pickett may have had another Kinston-like spectacle in mind when he approved the execution of 13 men of Brigadier General Seth Barton's brigade of Virginians, a month after approving the Kinston executions.[102] President Davis did not give his approval although he was willing to accept a few executions if it would improve discipline in the brigade.[103] Service records do not show that any of the 13 were executed.

WILLIAM HOLDER 42-D (February 26, 1864). Two charges of violations of the Articles of War, each occurring in March 1863, were brought against Private Holder. The first, "misbehaviour in the face of the enemy," came about during an action near Tarboro, North Carolina, when the accused "did break the line to crawl behind a stump in the rear of the company." Direct orders by his Captain to return to the skirmish were ignored. Finally, on the third order, the Private left the shelter of the stump and rejoined his comrades. Three weeks after this incident, Private Holder deserted his company and remained a deserter for six months. He was finally arrested by the Home Guard in Davie County on September 30, 1863, and then taken to Wilmington. At trial on February 26, 1864, the defendant was found guilty, but only on the desertion charge. Still, that was sufficient to bring forth a death sentence; execution was set for March 7. Before that day the death sentence was commuted, and Private Holder eventually took the oath in June 1865. He enrolled on March 24, 1862.

JESSE LEE HEPLER 42-D (February 27, 1864). A conscript, Private Hepler deserted on August 8, 1863, after ten months with his regiment. This desertion ended after a relatively short absence of six weeks with arrest and return under guard. The next record for Private Hepler is that he was tried for desertion on February 27, 1864. At that time it was noted that this was his second attempt to flee from his company. The time lapse and comment indicated that Private Hepler was not tried for his first desertion in August 1863, so there may have been some punishment at a company or regimental level. Two charges of desertion were presented at trial. One charge was not supported in the opinion of the court, but a guilty finding was set forth on the other; Private Hepler was sentenced to be shot. General Whiting approved the findings and scheduled the execution for March 7, the same day set for the execution of Private Holder. Private Hepler was not given consideration under an amnesty announced to General Whiting's command in GO #16, Hdqs, Cape Fear, February 9. Privates Hepler and Holder were mentioned specifically in that order. It stated that they were to remain in custody awaiting trial. General Whiting then observed that some soldiers had already paid the extreme penalty for their crimes, which should serve as a warning that he would forbid leniency in the future.[104] The death sentences for Privates Hepler and Holder were commuted to imprisonment, and about a year later Private Hepler was restored to duty by virtue of General Order #2.

Private D. F. Barber enrolled as a substitute in Company B, Eighth Battalion Partisan Rangers, on February 1, 1863. He was present and paid in June and August of that year but thereafter was reported as absent without leave; this was later recorded as desertion. Assignment to Company H of the Sixty-Sixth followed on October 2, 1863; this led to a second absence in the November–December 1863 reporting period. The precise date of desertion is not known, nor are the specifics of the case against Private Barber that led General Whiting to advise Colonel Tansell on February 16, 1864, "Colonel will cause to be tried as soon as possible if found guilty the punishment should be ignominious that is death by hanging."[105] There is no record that Private Barber served in a Federal unit, though he may have otherwise taken up arms against the Confederacy or committed some other crime that warranted an "ignominious" death. The trial court did not follow the recommendation of General Whiting. Private Barber was found guilty but was sentenced to hard labor. Little information is found in a sparse service record for Private Barber, and no census record has been located. He was likely an older man, for the conscription laws covered men to age forty-five when he enrolled as a substitute.

WILLIAM F. CAMPBELL 42-D (Prior to March 1864). Another soldier with an inconclusive reference to a death sentence is Private William Campbell. The carded service file of Private Campbell from conscription in September 1863 to October 1864 does not reflect any infraction that would lead to an appearance before a court-martial. Other sources do indicate that he deserted in early 1864 and that he was tried and sentenced to be shot.[106] This sentence was suspended by General Whiting in March 1864, at which time the General asked for further direction from General Samuel Cooper. In November, the condemned man was in confinement and working on fortifications because in General Whiting's opinion, "It was hardly probable that the death sentence will be executed."[107] This assessment was apparently correct, for no additional reference to service or execution of Private Campbell has been found.

JOHN B. ELLIOTT 42-A (March 4, 1864). Private Elliott enrolled on May 5, 1862, and was tried by a court-martial convened on March 4, 1864. Found guilty of the charges brought against him, he was sentenced to be shot. GO #31, March 16, 1864, Department Cape Fear, issued by General Whiting, confirmed the sentence and set the day of execution as March 25. At the trial that led to the death sentence, it was brought out that Private Elliott had on a "previous occasion gone from a hospital in Raleigh without permission." In connection with his latest desertion he had also forged a furlough (authorization) to "secure a passport to Davidson [County]." The imaginative youngster, barely seventeen, left his command on September 8, 1863, and was able to elude arrest until February 15, 1864. On that date he was in custody in Davidson County. Again General Whiting quickly had a change of heart and commuted the death sentence for the private to twelve months on a chain gang. The reason that mercy was being shown was that the regiment had performed well in recent engagements, desertion had nearly ceased, and recent executions had set the needed example. General Whiting's turnabout led General Cooper to caution General Whiting on May 31, 1864, saying that the power to commute a death sentence rested solely with the President by authority of 65th and 89th Articles of War.[108] About a year after this exchange, Private Elliott's superiors were notified that General Order #2, issued in 1865, applied in his case, apparently bringing about his release though he was also near the end of his commuted sentence. In any event, Private Elliott tarried for only a few days before deserting to the enemy on March 15, 1865. He was released by them on the condition that he stay north of Philadelphia, PA, for the rest of the war. An older brother, Private Henry Harrison Elliott, also served in the same company as his younger brother. Private Henry Elliott deserted just over a week after Private John Elliott began his first desertion. How or when his desertion ended is not recorded, but Private Henry Elliott was captured by the enemy and paroled in May 1865. A second brother, Private Samuel C. Elliott, deserted from the Forty-Ninth after being present for three months. No record of further service has been located.

JAMES OAKLEY 42-D (March 5, 1864). Private Oakley earned a $50 bounty by enlisting in the Confederate army in March 1862. He was sick for a time and then deserted in the July–August period. This absence went on for the next six months until he rejoined the regiment in February. No record of punishment has been found. Three and a half months later, Private Oakley again deserted, on this occasion from camp near Greenville, NC. On this absence he avoided arrest for nine months but was then caught and delivered to Wilmington. Within two weeks he was standing before a court, and was found guilty of desertion. Apparently the Judge Advocate was unable to produce satisfactory evidence of the first desertion, and reference to it was deleted from the charges placed before the court. Still, the prolonged absence was sufficient to warrant a death sentence. This was duly announced in GO #32, March 16, 1864, Department of Cape Fear. General Whiting approved the sentence and ordered that the execution take place on March 25. Three days following publication of the general order, General Whiting, as he had in other recent cases, then announced that the death sentence was revoked for the same reasons earlier offered; desertions had virtually ceased and the regiment had performed well against the enemy. Private Oakley was ordered to work on fortifications for twelve months. The case of Private Oakley was included in the admonishing letter of General Cooper concerning the sentence of Private Elliott, but the issue was of no consequence to Private Oakley. He died of extreme diarrhea on June 1, while General Cooper's letter was on the way to General Whiting. The dead soldier left effects of a cap, jacket and pants valued at $17.

RICHARD IRVIN 66-F (June 13, 1864). Private Richard Irvin, likely the younger brother of Private William Irvin who was hanged at Kinston, had a similar service record. The men had enrolled in the Partisan Rangers on the same day and neither appeared for muster with the Sixty-Sixth at the time of consolidation. Again on the same day, the men enrolled in the Second NCUV. However, Private Richard Irvin apparently escaped capture at Beech Grove and made his way back to Federal lines. The next entry on his Federal record indicates that he is in confinement by decision of a Federal court-martial, having been convicted on some unknown charge. The prisoner was held at New Bern from June to year's end 1864. In the 1890 Census of Civil War Veterans of North Carolina, there is an entry by the name of the widow of Private Richard Irvin stating that he was "killed by execution."[109] There is no indication whether this was a formal execution after trial by Confederate or Federal authority, or an impromptu execution during a Civil War vendetta. No supporting document has been found.

One of the men in the Martin Brigade was critical of the manner in which their Brigadier approached his responsibility.

> If I had my way I would have the last one of them conscripted and placed in the army and then if they ever got away and went to the Yankees we would have a chance to try them as deserters, as we have 12 of the 17th Regt here now in jail, who deserted some time last year, and had joined the Yankee service, and on capturing this place we captured them, and as soon as we can get a Court Martial to set they will be hung as all traitors should be, I will tell you that this is a very rotten part of the state, and I am fretted at old Martins management.[110]

A soldier wrote that he had spent two days in Plymouth, NC, and that was two days too many. "Of all the mean places I have ever been about Plymouth beats them all. There is not one redeeming quality left. Just filth and corruption compose the main ingredients of the place occasionally relieved from the monotony by the sight of a dead Yankee or Negra. No one seems to care about taking the trouble to put into the ground."[111] In Washington County, citizen William Atchinson, son of a noted Buffalo, was accused of urging men of the Fiftieth Regiment to murder their officers and desert.[112]

The Seventeenth Regiment moved to the trenches around Petersburg, VA, in the summer of 1864. The shift from a neighborhood war in eastern North Carolina to the trench warfare in Virginia did not offer any physical or emotional relief for the men involved. After three weeks of misery in the foul mud of the trenches and the constant fear of instant death by the weapon of a concealed sharpshooter, a member of Company A wrote, "I was completely broken down in body & almost in spirit."[113] Death of a friend, losses to Federal sharpshooters, and the misery of the living conditions all combined to bring the young man to despair.

Kirkland Brigade

"Many of them will die the inglorious death of the deserter"[114]

Trials and executions continued at a steady pace after Brigadier William Wheedbee Kirkland assumed brigade command in August 1864. Thirteen executions were ordered by military courts and four were carried into effect. The brigade's reputation for being well disciplined did not suffer, and was perhaps even enhanced, while General Kirkland was in command.[115]

JAMES A. DANNER 42-F (August 10, 1864). Private James Danner went to trial on desertion charges a year after he deserted on August 30, 1863, and only weeks after his younger brother, Private Samuel Danner, had shown the way. Private Samuel Danner surrendered to the Home Guard after an absence of eleven weeks. His punishment after a court-martial was twelve months at hard labor, three months of which were to be served with a thirty-two-pound ball attached by a chain to his left ankle. Private James Danner did not follow the example set by his brother but chose to remain a deserter for nearly a full year. In custody and before a court on August 10, 1864, he was soon informed that he would be shot to death. Then began a series of special orders concerning the condemned prisoner. General Beauregard issued a rather convoluted SO #94 on September 22, 1864: "I The execution of sentence of James Danner 42-F suspended because communication on 9th instant constrained to rescind the order directing said suspension to order that the sentence be executed five days after reception of this order at Brig. Hd Qtrs."[116] Five days later, a more direct SO #99 came forth from the General, "II Pursuant to instructions from Army Hd Qrs the sentence in the case of Private James Danner Co. F 42NCT is hereby suspended one week from time originally appointed."[117] SO #236, October 4, SO # 242, October 11, and SO #249, October 18, all the Army of Northern Virginia, then continued the suspension of execution, each ordering a one-week delay. Private James Danner did not survive the war, but the time and manner of his death is not clearly established. One family recollection is that he was shot by Confederate authority for his willful stand that he would not fight for the Confederate cause. Another memory is that his body was returned to the family at Greensboro.[118] The second recollection would tend to discount the first; at least there is no known instance where the body of a soldier executed by musketry was returned to the family. The final special order delaying the execution of Private Danner was in effect until October 27. A letter from a soldier of the Seventeenth Regiment states that a man of the brigade, but not of his regiment, was executed during the week in which the suspension of execution was lifted, a fair indication that Private Danner of the Forty-Second was executed.[119]

BENJAMIN D. DILLON 17-H (August 27, 1864). Private Dillon volunteered for

Confederate duty about the time of the passage of the first conscription laws in April 1862 when he enrolled in Company H, Seventeenth Regiment, the Liberty Guards. Within a month he was absent from his company, and a month later he was officially dropped from company rolls, this decision made in July 1862. Some fifteen months later, the former Confederate decided to return to war, but this time he enrolled in the Second NCUV at New Bern. While engaged with this regiment at Plymouth, NC, on April 25, 1864, he was captured by more loyal Confederates. He was one of the men attributed to the Seventeenth Regiment captured at Plymouth who should be immediately taken to the scaffold, in the mind of a man in Martin's brigade.[120] Punishment for switching sides was not as immediate as hoped for, nor was death to be by hanging. Contrasted with the men captured at Beech Grove, trial for Private Dillon did not begin until August 27, 1864, a delay of four months before he was court-martialed for simple desertion and sentenced to be shot. In SO #24, September 24, 1864, General Beauregard delayed the execution of sentence while a petition for pardon for the condemned was being considered. The Secretary of War informed the General on October 11, "The case of Benj Dillon seems to present no mitigating circumstance which would justify being sent to the President. He was taken in arms against his country in the ranks of her enemies."[121] According to an entry in his Confederate service record, Private Dillon was executed on Saturday, October 29, 1864. The delay in the trial and punishment for a soldier who was captured while fighting with the enemy was unusual; turncoats were normally dispatched with little delay. His status in the Confederate service may have raised a legal question that resulted in a petition for a pardon. He had been dropped from the rolls of the Confederate company before enrolling in the Federal regiment, in which case he was entitled to be treated as a prisoner of war. Private Dillon's service records also show that he was given a $10 bounty for enrolling in the Seventeenth and the first $25 installment of a $100 bounty after joining the Federal regiment. Captain William Biggs of Company A, Seventeenth Regiment, wrote to his sister after witnessing the death of Private Dillon.

> I have just returned from witnessing one of the most awful & impressive scenes incident to war. The execution of a member of the regiment for the crime of desertion. This is the second from our Brigade during the past week and several more will soon follow. I truly hope it may be the means of checking that which is fast bringing the Brigade into bad repute. About a dozen have deserted to the enemy since we came to this side of the River & amongst the rest two of my company went night before last while on vedette duty in front of our works. They were Jno D. Groves from near Williamston and Wiley Hamilton from Jamesville neither of them any great loss to their country or their families.[122]

Service records note that the deserters did go into Federal lines and were then sent to Illinois. A soldier in the Forty-Second did not accept the need for executions and felt that someone would answer for them: "I also will state to you that there was two men shot to death for desertion last week out of our Brigade and there is two more to be shot. I tell you that its a sad and solemn thing to witness and I fear some man will have to answer for it for I never can think its right."[123]

JESSE DAVIS PRICE 17-F (September 21, 1864). Private Price joined the first organization of the Seventeenth and stayed with that unit when it was re-formed. Two years of loyal service ended when he chose to desert on August 4, 1864. Within a month he was arrested, and stood at trial on September 21. He was found guilty and sentenced to be shot, but the sentence was later commuted. While imprisoned, he died of disease on February 18, 1865. A record entry that he was released by General Order #2 is inaccurate.

MARTIN LAYTON 17-L (September 21, 1864). Private Layton enlisted in Company L, Seventeenth Regiment, on March 2, 1863, but remained at home for some time before presenting himself for duty. About a year later he deserted along with another man from his company. They were arrested together on August 26, 1864. Private Layton was tried on September 21, and sentenced to be shot. This sentence was commuted. Death came at Prison Hospital #13 at Richmond, on the last day of 1864, his worldly belongings amounting to $5. Records erroneously include his name on a list of men that were returned to duty by General Order #2.

WILLIAM H. JOHNSON 17-L (September 22, 1864). Private Johnson deserted on the same day as Private Layton; they enrolled in the summer of 1864 in the same company. They were arrested together on August 26. Private Johnson went to trial the day after Private Layton, on September 22. He was sentenced to death, but this was commuted. The next record for Private Johnson indicates that he was at Prison Hospital #13 for treatment before being sent back to Castle Thunder. In March 1865, the prisoner was released by virtue of General Order #2, which appears to be accurate in his case.

JOHN M. LAWING 42-K (September 22, 1864). Private Lawing served faithfully in the ranks for over two years before deserting in the summer of 1864. There were no periods of hospitalization or other absences, and there were no furloughs, which may in part explain his decision to desert. Whatever the reason, by August 28, the desertion was over and the deserter was in confinement at Petersburg, VA. A court held on September 22 determined that a death sentence was merited for the prisoner. The sentence was later commuted. Private Lawing died, very probably while still in confinement, in January 1865.

JULIUS VANDERBURG 17-L (September 22, 1864). As noted in the earlier cases of Privates Barnhart, Goodnight and Isenhour of Company L, Seventeenth Regiment, a fourth soldier of that company from Cabarrus County was mentioned in several records as involved with the others, but he was not given a death sentence. Private Vanderburg, decided to take advantage of his good luck following his first desertion and deserted once again on July 6, 1864. He was in arrest on August 28, court-martialed on September 22, and sentenced to be shot. Good fortune continued to bless, and his sentence was commuted. Full release was later brought about by General Order #2.

LLOYD TAYLOR 42-H (September 24, 1864). Private Taylor was 1 of 8 men who deserted from the camp of Company H, Forty-Second Regiment, on Saturday, August 9, 1862. He had been with the army less than five months. Of the 8, 5 of those men who deserted that day would again desert in the next two years. The first desertion for Private Taylor barely lasted for the weekend; he was back on duty in three days. The second desertion, which began on July 25, 1864, was a more serious affair. He was absent for a full month, for which he was brought before a court-martial on September 24. A guilty finding, a death sentence, and commutation to imprisonment all came in short order. A bout of colitis and confinement in the Prison Hospital #13 at Richmond were followed by return to Castle Thunder and then return to duty under authority of General Order #2.

ALEXANDER B. BATES 42-I (After September 28, 1864). Confederate service for Private Bates was largely a time of departure and detention. Four months after volunteering in March 1862 and accepting a $50 bounty, he was confined in a military prison at hard labor with a ball and chain fastened to his ankle. On returning to his company nearly a year later, he again deserted after a week or two at Fort Fisher. This attempt must have required considerable ingenuity on his part, as the fort is located at the end of a narrow peninsula of land teeming with soldiers. A year passed before Private Bates was in custody, at Petersburg, VA, awaiting a second military court. This court handed down a death sentence. While under sentence, he escaped from prison and avoided arrest until December 1864. How he escaped immediate execution when he was again securely in Confederate custody is not clear, but that he did. Capture by Federal troops and parole in April of 1865 then followed. Private Bates was a man with talents that might have been utilized, in some fashion, to better aid the Confederacy.

WILLIAM WALTERS 50-G (October 15, 1864). Private Walters first deserted on June 4, 1862, less than three months after enlisting in the Rutherford Farmers. Absences from the company were quite rare after an initial surge when a dozen or so men left in the summer of 1862. Private Walters was at large until October 16, when he was in arrest and remained so until year's end 1862. The finding of the court that heard his case was published on January 13, 1863. Either while undergoing the punishment set by this court or having satisfied the sentence, he had sufficient freedom to flee from his company, this on April 20. Private Walters was able to make his way back to Rutherford County in southwest North Carolina, traveling a distance of some 250 miles. Once safely in the county he avoided arrest until August 29, 1864, a period of sixteen months; when he was under guard at Goldsboro. No doubt well aware of the tendency of military courts to be rather stern with men who were absent for long periods of time, but also aware of the many commuted sentences affecting his brigade, Private Walters went before a court sitting on October 15, 1864. Two weeks later when the decision of the court was published in GO #64, October 31, 1864, Department of Northern Virginia, he learned that the foreseen death sentence had come to pass. Execution of sentence was to take place in seven days in the presence of troops of the post under direction of the commander of the Second Military District where the regiment was then assigned. At the end of the seven days, Colonel S. D. Pool requested of Colonel J. C. Van Hook, "Notify me of the day appointed for the execution of Waters [sic], and also of the final execution of sentence that I may communicate the same to the Gen'l Cmdg."[124] No other communication has been located and the tone of the order suggests that the sentence was to be executed with no further intervention by higher authority. As is occasionally the case with records of Confederate soldiers, it appears that at least one reference to a private with a similar name is mixed with that of Private Walters. One portion of that record indicates that Private Walters survived the death sentence. However, this record gives the height of the survivor as slightly over five feet four inches, while other records for Private Walters give his height as five feet ten inches. The shorter soldier served in Company B, Fiftieth Regiment. He was a resident of Robeson County.

WILLIAM C. PERRY ETCHISON 42-F (November 24, 1864). Private Etchison was below the legal age of service when he volunteered to join the Forty-Second in March 1862. He apparently rued that decision many times over. Private Etchison first deserted in December 1862, a second began in August 1863, a third in April 1864, and finally a forth in August 1864. After his arrest and imprisonment following the 1863 desertion, he was restored to duty without standing trial. But after the fourth desertion in August 1864, Private Etchison did go before a military court that found him guilty on all charges and sentenced him to death. General Lee approved this sentence. On December 6, General Hoke was directed to proceed with arrangements for the execution of Private Etchison and another soldier in Kirkland's brigade. The service record for Private Etchison has an entry that he was shot for desertion on December 15, 1864, and that his effects were released on December 18th. Though this seems quite definitive, particularly the note on the release of his effects, there is compelling evidence that Private Etchison did not go to the execution stake but returned to Davie County, married in 1866, and in 1908 submitted a soldier's pension application.¹²⁵

JOSEPH H. FULCHER 17-G (November 24, 1864). Another man who switched from Confederate gray to Federal blue and was captured at Plymouth, NC, went to trial in November 1864. Private Fulcher served from enrollment in April 1862 until September 10, 1863, when he deserted in the face of the enemy while engaged near Greenville. Unlike Private Dillon, Private Fulcher was on the rolls of his company when he deserted. After signing the Federal Oath, on October 28, 1863, he agreed to enlist in the Federal army, about a week after Private Dillon had done so. Capture at Plymouth in the ranks of the Second NCUV, led to a delayed court-martial, and the sentence that he was to be "hung by the neck until dead." On December 6, General Hoke was ordered to carry out the sentence:

> The execution of Privates Fulcher and Etchison will take place under your supervision. A notification of the day set for the execution and also of the execution itself will be sent up in accordance with Circular Letter Hd Qtrs Dept NV under date September 4, 1864. The prisoners have been placed in solitary confinement and will be sent to you on the morning of the day appointed for the execution. J. L. Washington¹²⁶

On December 15, Private Fulcher was executed. Nearly two months later a belated appeal reached General Cooper which led him to inquire of General Lee on February 4, "Petition on behalf of J. H. Fulcer, [sic] 17-G has been presented Records show he was to have been hung on November last. What has been done with him"? In reply Major Blackford addressed the issue: "Burton N. Harrison Esq. Pv Sec Re Pardon Joseph Fulcher referred on January 21, 1865 was shot to death under sentence of court-martial December 15, 1864. He having been taken with arms in his hands and in the uniform of the enemy at Plymouth. Honorable W. N. H. Smith also informed."¹²⁷ William Nathan Harrell Smith was a Confederate congressman with Unionist tendency. How he became involved in the case of Private Fulcher and the basis for his appeal is not yet known. In any event the matter was at rest, as was the subject of the appeal.

Private John Couch, Sixty-Sixth Regiment, writing foremost to soothe the feelings of a young lady who was irritated by a comment in a recent letter from him, perhaps to gain sympathy mentions, "Another horrible sight I witness yesterday one shot and one hung for deserting there countrys flag."¹²⁸ The soldier who was hanged was most certainly Private Fulcher. That was the sentence passed by the court and there would have been no authority for altering the method of execution. Unfortunately, Private Couch does not provide more detail on what he witnessed, as this is perhaps the only instance of a nearly simultaneous execution by hanging and by musketry. Relying on Private Couch's comment a day after the event, it is probable that the earlier quote that Private Fulcher had been shot was simply an inaccurate response made by a staff officer well after the event, when the manner of death was not the focus of the query. Years after the war, a son of a Confederate veteran who had been enrolled in the Forty-Second recalled his father relating events that took place in the winter or spring of 1863.

> But the actual horror was the trial and execution of a deserter, and of a traitor. It was his first sitting upon a court-martial, and as the youngest of all the officers his vote had to be given first. Well do I remember his vivid word picture of the scene that followed — the doomed man kneeling blind-folded, the regimental band playing a dreadful dirge, the semi-circle of comrades with six muskets loaded, six muskets with blank cartridges, the armed troops, the

watch in the officers hand telling a man's life in seconds, the word "Fire!" the soul into eternity. The traitor was hung.[129]

Although the secondhand reminiscence is displaced in time, the traitor reference must concern the execution of Private Fulcher. The Seventeenth and the Forty-Second were brigaded and there is no other record of a similar incident. This still leaves open the identity of the man who was shot when Private Fulcher was hanged. If not Private Etchison, then who? The most likely assumption would be that the man killed by musketry was Private Walters, Company G, Fiftieth Regiment, whose execution had been approved by General Lee. Privates Fulcher and Etchison were tried on the same day which may have led to a recording assumption that Private Etchison was executed.

JOHN B. TRIVETT 42-B (December 9, 1864). Private Trivett died while hospitalized at Raleigh; execution by musketry awaited him if he recovered sufficiently to be led to the stake. The events that brought about this double threat to his life began when the he deserted on August 30, 1863. A full year later he was returned under guard, on August 26, 1864. For prolonged absences of that length, military courts usually handed down death sentences, and that was their determination in his case. General Lee approved the sentence. On January 7, 1865, Brigadier Kirkland reported that there would be a delay in the execution of sentence. Private Trivett was hospitalized and then transferred from Wilmington to Goldsboro and then to Raleigh. During each transfer it was carefully noted that the patient was under sentence of death.[130] Death did come for Private Trivett on February 5; the cause was chronic diarrhea rather than lead musket balls. The record for Private Trivett erroneously indicates that he was freed by General Order #2.

Though the end was near, this was not known to a soldier in the Sixty-Sixth who wrote to his wife in on March 28, 1865.

> I hope that three more month will set this country all right as regard the tories and deserters of this State and others, it is a lamatable thing to see and know the amount of deserters from the Army but they will be attended to with in the next three months, and many of them will die the inglorious death of the deserter being shot in the woods, I think that I have seen the signs of the authorities being in earness in this matter, so I think they will be called to an rigid account before last of the next June.[131]

The writer seems to be of the view that local authorities and the Home Guard will be more diligent in searching out and killing "in the woods" the deserters in their neighborhoods, rather than a greater resolve on formal executions.

Summary

The number of men present at surrender of the Martin-Kirkland brigade is not known. About 6,050 were enrolled in the Brigade at one time or another. For the brigade 14 companies were sampled to find an average company enrollment of 151 non-commissioned men. Of these, 30 were absent at some point, 5 were court-martialed, 20 died of disease or unstated cause, and 6 died in combat or of resulting wounds.[132] From existing records, at least 61 men of the brigade faced death by execution during three years of service. From the Sixty-Sixth, 17 were hanged at Kinston, and another was so dispatched later in the war. Only 1 soldier in the Sixty-Sixth survived a court-imposed death sentence. For the rest of the brigade, 6 were executed, 1 by hanging and 5 by musketry. These 3 regiments experienced at least 134 high-level military courts with 7 trials ending in acquittal. After trial, 43 men were given death sentences, 37 survived their sentence. Just 3 companies in 3 regiments, the Sixty-Sixth excepted, accounted for 65 percent of their regiment's courts-martial and three-quarters of all death sentences, but just 2 men from the 9 companies were executed.

Of the 61 men condemned to death, 5 were conscripts; 1 was executed, as were 2 substitutes. At least two-thirds of the men who were given death sentences were married. Nearly half, 28, of those threatened with execution were from Jones, Stanly and Iredell counties. The other 33 were scattered over 15 counties. Men of the brigade received the most capital sentences of any North Carolina brigade. They fought their war closer to their homes than did men of other brigades. For some this increased the lure of a relatively risk-free opportunity to leave Confederate service, or at least to have an extended visit at home. For others, there was the enticement of a Federal bounty that in 1864 offered well over two years' pay to a Confederate private willing to switch sides and fulfill his commitment. Officers guiding the struggle in eastern North Carolina had to balance punishment of the disloyal against the compelling need to maintain support for the war in a vital and troubled area.

Part III. Army of Tennessee

16

History of North Carolina Troops in the Army of Tennessee

"Only the weak and timid need to be cheered by constant success."[1]

While a Major General, Braxton Bragg emphasized the absolute need for strict discipline and adherence to regulations for Confederates fighting in a section of deeply divided loyalty. General Order #9, March 16, 1862, Head Quarters, Second Grand Division, Army of Mississippi:

> With a degree of mortification and humiliation he has never before felt the Major General Commanding, has to denounce acts of pillage, plunder, and destruction of the private property of our own citizens, by a portion of the troops of this command, which bring disgrace upon our arms, and, if not checked, will assuredly entail disaster up on our cause.... The General will not hesitate to order the death penalty, where it may be necessary, and will approve its execution by subordinates, where milder measures fail.[2]

General Bragg repeated his determination in a letter to his wife: "It is my fixed purpose to execute the first one caught in such acts."[3]

The resolve of General Bragg to enforce his order was tested following the Battle of Corinth, MS, in late May. While the Confederate troops were moving from the area, a hungry soldier fired his musket at a chicken. The shot missed the mark and killed a bystander. General Bragg had the man seized and then shot within an hour or so.[4] When news of the execution reached the Confederate Congress, it touched off a long debate on that incident and two other alleged executions. Inflammatory words, "Murderer," "Tyrant," "Assassin," were used by those attacking the General; the absolute right of officers to enforce discipline was the rebuttal offered by his defenders.[5] Congressmen agreed to ask President Davis if he had any factual information on the matter. The President notified Congress that he had no information to guide their deliberations, and the matter was tabled.[6] A soldier offered his comments on June 10, 1862: "Gen. Bragg is trying to get the army under strict discipline. He is not like much by the boys, on account of having several men shot for being absent AWOL and deserters."[7]

Through the fall of 1862, General Bragg was effective in his efforts to discipline his army in the mind of one of those who served therein and wrote in September 1862: "Bragg is beyond doubt the best disciplinarian in the South. When he took Command at Corinth the Army was little better than a mob. The din of firearms could be heard at all hours of the day. Now a gun is never fired without orders from the Brigade Commanders. Bragg had one man shot for discharging his gun without orders on the march from Corinth to Saltello.

Since that time the discipline of the troops has improved so much. Men are not apt to disobey orders when they know death is the punishment."[8] Some six weeks later the same soldier again mentioned General Bragg.

> General Bragg arrived here today, he still commands this Army. Though everybody seems to have lost all confidence in him since his Ky raid. He is the man to drill and discipline an army. I am sorry to say that our army, or rather individuals in it act almost as badly as the Yankees that is they take forage and many other things with[out] either asking or paying for them, but these things are not done when Bragg is about, as death wold be the penalty if such acts were brot before his notice.[9]

Despite the indicated loss of confidence, General Bragg was made commander of the Army of Tennessee in November 1862. He addressed the growing problem of desertion by offering amnesty to those absent men who returned to their units, this in General Order #4 on December 1. A stern warning note emphasized that the formation of military courts would insure that "a vigorous and prompt administration of justice will be meted out to all delinquents."[10] No further excuses would be allowed and men who failed to take advantage of the amnesty must expect "full justice." General Bragg noted that seven months after passage of the conscription laws, not a single conscript had been added to his command.[11] In addition to the shortcomings of conscription, plundering continued to require attention. GO #11, December 12, 1862, Army of Tennessee restated that all supplies taken from the enemy were the property of the Confederacy as directed in the 58th Article of War. Infraction of the article "is alike destructive of personal honor and military discipline and an example will be made of those who violate it."[12] It was noted that "General Bragg is one of the strictest disciplinarians in the army, but is reported by all who know him to be scrupulously just."[13] And he had a more humane bent than some about him when he ordered that suitable medical attention be given to "all employees of this Army white and black."[14] In early 1862, General Bragg refused to accept a convicted murderer into his army. "The service in which we are engaged is of too high and holy a nature to allow our ranks to be made an asylum for convicted murderers."[15]

An amnesty offer in December 1862 did not fill the ranks as hoped. On July 25, 1863, officers of the Army of Tennessee joined in a rather unusual circular letter to General Cooper on the need for men.

> But we especially deplore that unfortunate provision of the exemption bill which has allowed more than 150,000 soldiers to employ substitutes, and we express our honest conviction that not one in a hundred of these substitutes is now in the service.... The friends of timid and effeminate young men are constantly besieging the War Department, through Congressional and other agents, to get soldiers in the Army placed upon details or transferred to safe places.[16]

It was estimated that a quarter of a million detailed and exempted men were not in the fighting force. The letter closed by saying that as more Confederate territory was lost to the enemy, problems of desertion and conscription correspondingly increased because a lesser number of conscripts was accessible to enrolling authorities, and the area where deserters might find haven was likewise increased.[17] General Bragg was one of eighteen officers, brigadiers, and higher ranks to sign the circular. It is unusual that an officer that placed such great emphasis on discipline and command structure as General Bragg did not insist that the subject matter of the circular be addressed by endorsement through the command chain. General Cooper responded: "General Braxton Bragg and other Officers." The War

Department had to follow the wishes of Congress. He would like to know the source of the numbers mentioned in the letter, and in any event the Confederacy could only arm the number of soldiers presently included in their planning as being available for duty.[18] While these upper-level events were going on, a soldier in the Army of Tennessee was tried for the crime of having a "slung shot" in his possession.[19] Possession of such a weapon — similar to a blackjack — indicated that the person was intent on robbing or harming someone.

As the General Commanding, General Bragg was resolute in the need for punishment for deserters, at one point remarking that arrested deserters were an "encumbrance" to his army and that they should be shot forthwith. He also felt that major generals were an "encumberance" but did not suggest that they be shot.[20] His failure to achieve complete and total victories, challenges to his competency, and his own personal concerns all led to the acceptance of his resignation."[21] A candid summation of the leadership of General Bragg was made by a fellow high ranking officer: "There was no man in either of the contending armies who was General Bragg's superior as an organizer and a disciplinarian, but when he was in the presence of the enemy he lost his head."[22]

Upon taking command, Lieutenant General William J. Hardee issued a circular order of intended encouragement. After noting the purpose, courage and patriotism of General Bragg, he went on: "The country is looking to you with painful interest. I feel that it can rely upon you. Only the weak and the timid need to cheered by constant success."[23] General Hardee did take an aggressive stand on executions when he directed that all suspended death sentences be executed in one week. He issued a similar order two weeks later, this time ordering that suspended executions be "carried into execution" on December 24, the day before Christmas.[24] General Hardee was replaced by Lieutenant General Leonidas Polk, who was in command for a week beginning on December 22. In his prior command, the Episcopal Bishop directed his subordinates to "execute penalties with firmness and prudence remembering that not in the severity of the punishment but in the certainty of their execution is the terror of the law."[25] "Prompt and certain punishment is the prevention of crime."[26] Men taking up deserters were ordered to "punish resistance with death on the spot."[27] The General also directed that any absence over seven days be treated as desertion, this five months before the first burst of executions in the eastern armies in their attempt to control the evil.[28] General Polk held the opinion that the several amnesty orders issued by various authorities were not effective in increasing the strength of the army.[29] Two months before General Bragg was relieved of his duties General Gideon J. Pillow notified the Secretary of War that he was forced to send Army of Tennessee deserters to the Army of Northern Virginia to get them further away from home, this being the only remedy available to him, for there were far too many to shoot.[30]

General Joseph E. Johnston was given command of the Army of Tennessee on December 27, 1863. The depleted Fifty-Eighth and Sixtieth North Carolina were placed in his care. They were led by a Captain and a Major respectively and fielded an effective strength of less than 400 in total.[31] When General Johnston was unable to check the advance of the Federal forces into Georgia, at least to the satisfaction of President Davis, General John Bell Hood was ordered to take command of the Army of Tennessee, this on July 18, 1864.

With his usual frankness General Longstreet addressed President Davis on February 2, 1865. He urged that General Johnston be restored as commander of the Army of Tennessee and took the opportunity to hurl a barb toward Richmond: "He has not been successful, but you can readily see that no general can be successful if he does not receive the support of the authorities above him."[32] General Johnston resumed command of the Army of

Tennessee on February 25, 1865, and would agree to surrender that command at Durham, NC, on April 26.

An unidentified source, possibly a staff officer, commenting on executions in the Army of Tennessee, stated that 16 executions took place in the year and a half that General Bragg was directing affairs. The same source notes that 31 were executed at Dalton, Georgia, while General Johnston was in command, for a brief seven months.[33] A measure of credibility is added to this comment by recollections of men in Alabama commands. One notes that 8 in the brigade of Brigadier General Zachariah C. Deas were executed that winter at Dalton.[34] These men died while sitting on their coffins unlike the executed men of the North Carolina regiments who were tied to stakes. A wounded man had to be placed on his coffin a second time, and then a third, before he was killed. Another recalls a single execution when "the whole top of his head was blown off."[35] This suffering soul, for a few seconds, thought that he was reprieved; then the balls shattered his bowed head. If accurately related these incidents, along with those of the Fifty-Eighth and Sixtieth North Carolina, account for virtually all of the executions while General Johnston was leading the Army of Tennessee. AIGO and service records are not definitive as to the number of men executed during the seven-month tenure of General Hood, but an estimate would be in the 6 to 8 range. Considering the likelihood that some executions were ordered during the retreat through Georgia and the Carolinas a reasonable estimate of the total number of men executed while the Army of Tennessee was in existence would be in the range of 60. One-quarter were North Carolina troops killed in one massive burst of musketry.

17

Fifty-Eighth and Sixtieth North Carolina Infantry Regiments

Fifty-Eighth Regiment

"Their cries was horrible in the extreme."[1]

The Fifty-Eighth and the Sixtieth were only briefly in the same brigade until November 1863, when they were assigned to the brigade of Alexander Welch Reynolds which included the Fifty-Fourth and Sixty-Third Virginia and the Fifth Kentucky. They served under a Brigadier and a Major General who were Virginians. A soldier from North Carolina voiced a concern to his father that was no doubt shared with the Virginians, "We North Carolinians and Virginians feel lost in this Army; there are so few of us."[2] At least 12 men in the Virginia regiments were given death sentences, about half the 21 death sentences meted out to the North Carolinians. Men of the Virginia regiments went before military courts as often as did the men of North Carolina, and they absented themselves more frequently.[3] Records show that 2 of the 12 condemned Virginians were executed. A diary entry indicates that an unnamed deserter was executed on February 11, 1864, "Deserter from the 54 Va executed at 10—A.M."[4] An officer in the Sixty-Third Virginia was executed later that same year.[5]

The core unit for the Fifty-Eighth was initially a company in a Partisan Ranger battalion; these men were augmented with volunteers and conscripts to form an infantry regiment. Governor Henry T. Clark had urged the Secretary of War to stop the formation of Partisan Rangers because such units placed a drain on state resources and allowed men to avoid conscription.[6] In January 1863, the number of men leaving the ranks and the stain on the reputation of the regiment were of concern for a man in the Fifty-Eighth. He wrote, "Conduct of conscripts should not be chargable to members of company," this after 11 conscripts had deserted the company a week earlier.[7] His dismay continued to year's end when he wondered what the newspapers in North Carolina were saying about his regiment.[8]

From AIGO records there were 61 courts affecting men of the Fifty-Eighth. After trial 15 were given death sentence, 14 received severe sentences, and 4 were acquitted. Company F, the McDowell Rangers; Company L, Ashe County; and Company G, Yancey County, led all companies with 12, 8 and 7 convictions, 44 percent of the regimental total. Company F enrolled 213 men, 72 incidents of absence occurred, 17 men were killed in combat, 33 died from disease or cause unknown. Company G enrolled 246 men, experienced 145 absences, suffered 8 dead in engagement with the enemy and 37 dead from disease or reason not given.

Sixtieth Regiment

"But it was an ignominious death."[9]

The Sixtieth was brigaded with 3 regiments of men from Florida and 1 from Tennessee when the time came to witness an execution. AIGO records indicate that 1 soldier from the 4 regiments was sentenced to be shot, whereas 6 men from the Sixtieth North Carolina were so sentenced. For the Sixtieth, 39 men appeared before the highest of military courts after December 1862; 3 were acquitted. Over half of the those convicted were from Company A, recruited as the Buncombe Light Artillery; Company D, the Henderson Rangers; and Company G, formed in Polk County. For the regiment, 4 of the 6 men who were sentenced to be shot were from Companies A and D. Company A experienced 43 incidents of unauthorized absence from 117 total enrollments. Of these absentees, only 19 were ever in custody to answer for their actions and only 5 went to trial. Desertion was not driven by deaths on the battlefield, just 7; disease killed 21. Absences may have been due to "terrori Yankeebus," at least for a member of the company.[10] Half of the 10 companies that made up the Sixtieth were enrolled in Buncombe County; they accounted for one-third of all courts attributed to the regiment. A company of the Sixtieth, Company H, was recruited in Cocke County, Tennessee, just across the border from North Carolina. No record of a court for any member of the company has been found. Company E, the Buncombe Farmers, also had no record of an enlisted man going to trial. This company experienced 19 unauthorized departures out of an enrollment of 115. Of the 19 absentees, 13 were present after absences averaging over five months, so the reason for the lack of a trial record is not readily apparent. The company lost 9 men in combat and 25 to disease, or cause unknown.

Toward the end of November 1862, four days before a life or death trial was to begin for a man enrolled in the Sixtieth, a full pardon was offered to deserters who returned to their place in the army. As was so often the case with amnesty orders, even at that early date, it was stated that this was to be the "last and most generous" appeal for the return of the absent men.[11] Equal generosity might well have been shown to a man who made a brief visit to his nearby home and then dutifully returned to his company.

Courts-Martial

WILLIAM LITTRELL 60-F (December 3, 1862). Private Littrell enrolled in a local defense unit that was later expanded to form the Sixtieth Regiment. While this expansion was in progress, Private Littrell, on October 2, 1862, deliberately left his company when they were near Greenville, TN, less than 20 miles from his home. Private James D. Littrell deserted at the same time; the men had enrolled on the same day in Buncombe County. Private James Littrell went into service as a substitute. His absence was limited to a few days and his punishment was a short time of confinement. Private William Littrell had a longer absence but voluntarily returned to his command. He was placed in arrest and taken before a court held on December 3, 1862. The charge, violation of the 20th Article of War, desertion after enlisting and having been paid for Confederate service, was deemed accurate and proven in fact, the prisoner was found guilty. Private Littrell had received a $50 bounty and had been paid $27.50 for his service prior to his desertion. The sentence of the court was that he be shot. After reviewing the sentence, on December 13, 1862, General Braxton Bragg ordered that the convicted man be held by the Provost Guard awaiting further orders.[12] On December 20, General Bragg directed that Private Littrell be shot on December 26, the Friday following Christmas.[13] An officer in the Sixtieth noted, "Military Execution — Christmas Day 1862 That morning, for the first time, we witnessed a military execution, a sad sight indeed, although the victim was not known."[14] A regimental surgeon had closer contact with Private Littrell.

> A few days before the great battle at Murfreesboro, I was made surgeon of the day to attend the execution of William Litteral [sic] of Madison Co. He lived near Warm Springs N.C. When the time came the regiment was ordered to form a hollow square and Litteral to kneel behind his coffin. I was placed about twenty steps to his right and ordered to watch the small piece of paper placed directly over his heart. Col. Henry Deaver was stationed about ten paces to my left, he was officer of the day. About five minutes before the time Litteral asked me to call the Colonel and handed me a cotton handkerchief and a small purse with money in it, which he asked me to hand to the Colonel, to send to his wife and write to her and say; "'I am dying for your sake. God Bless you and the children. Meet me in heaven." We took our former position and the order was given to fire. When I examined him a moment later I found that five bullets had struck through the paper into his heart. The facts about William Litteral I shall give here in justice to his memory. The evening before he left for home, he told me his wife was very sick and he felt he must go and see her. He had asked leave of absence, but Col D____ denied the request; he told me he intended to go that night and return as soon as his wife was better. I asked him not to tell me anything more about it. He did go home, but returned as he had said he would do, — but it was to an ignominious death. He was arrested, court martialed and condemned to die as a deserter. William Littrell was a good soldier, a true Christian and a praying member of the Baptist Church. My heart is grieved within me when I think of poor Wm Littrell, and his sad fate. His death was not justifiable.[15]

Lieutenant-Surgeon Robert V. Cooper Company A, had little, if any, medical training. He was told to watch the paper placed on Private Littrell's chest to verify that the prisoner was dead. Lieutenant Colonel William Harry Deaver of the Sixtieth was from Tennessee. The morning report for Company F, Sixtieth Regiment for December 27, states "1 shot by sentence of CM."[16]

Few instances of the execution of a soldier who voluntarily returned from an absence are found in Confederate records. Such rigid enforcement of the death sentence would do little toward encouraging absentees to return to camp. General Lee once remarked that he knew of no cases where this had happened, no doubt speaking with reference to his own commands.[17] In the case of Private Littrell, the execution order was issued over the signature of General Bragg, adding yet another line to his reputation as an unyielding disciplinarian. North Carolinians were not alone in their grieving; at least 2 others in the Army of Tennessee were executed on that day following Christmas 1862. They were Privates Edward P. Norman, Company C, and Zachariah Phillips, Company B, of the Twenty-Eighth Alabama.

JAMES SPAIN 60-D (December 4, 1862). Private Spain willingly entered the service of the Confederacy on July 10, 1862, at age twenty-two. He promptly deserted the Henderson Rangers on August 10, while in the area of Warm Springs, NC, not far from the home of Private Littrell. Private Spain seemed destined for a death decision when he was tried on December 4. He was found guilty and sentenced to be shot. The record did not prove that Private Spain had received pay or bounty while in Confederate service. This failure led to remission of the death sentence and restoration to duty. Over the next eighteen months, Private Spain was present for duty about one-third of the time and absent due to sickness about two-thirds. He was captured in May 1864, near Resaca, GA, and subsequently agreed to serve in the Federal army, still owing the Confederate government $5.00 for their bayonet that he had lost in early 1864.

WILLIAM R. TAYLOR 60-D (December 4, 1862). When Private-Musician Taylor deserted on October 7, 1862, he had not been paid as a Confederate soldier nor had he received a Confederate bounty, but he had accepted a $50 bounty from the State of North Carolina. As to his pay status, on which his life might depend, he was squarely between Privates Littrell and Spain. The court ruled that acceptance of a North Carolina bounty was sufficient to meet the "having received pay" requirement of the 20th Article of War. After deserting from near Greenville, TN, Private Taylor was absent for a month or six weeks. He went to trial on December 4, 1862. At trial he was found guilty, and the court put forth a death sentence. General Bragg approved the finding and then remitted the sentence, and the private was returned to duty. Following return to his company, Private Taylor was present for duty for nine months when he again deserted in September 1863. While carried on company rolls as a deserter he was captured by Federal forces at Franklin, TN, and took the oath at war's end. His Confederate service totaled less than a year actually present for duty. Private William Littrell might well have offered a better return on one of General Bragg's infrequent investments in compassion.

As the year of 1863 began, men continued to desert from the Sixtieth. For their crimes they were punished with head shaving, or wearing a barrel suspended from their shoulders and labeled "Runaway" or "Deserter," or sixty days of hard labor. These fairly light sentences led General Bragg to comment that while he had confirmed the several sentences — the word "approve" was initially written and then crossed out, and "confirmed" substituted — he went on to say, "but it is considered as totally inadequate to the offence and thereby calculated to [encourage] repetition." General Bragg made similar comments in a series of General Orders in February and March of 1863.[18]

Officers attributed to the Sixtieth were tried for misbehavior before the enemy. The first is identified as Captain F. S. H. Reynolds, Company C. The second, a Lieutenant J. B. Davis, offers something of a mystery. The service record for the Captain notes that he was tried by court-martial and acquitted, this announced in GO #25, February 8, 1863, Army of Tennessee; his resignation was accepted within the month.[19] The Captain was a physician with the middle name of Sarah; military leadership may have been a time of trial for a caring man. The service record of a Private Josiah B. Davis, Company E, also notes that he was tried by that same court and also acquitted. Company rolls do not list a Lieutenant Davis. In any event, the main interest centers on the remarks of General Bragg. The officers went to trial charged with misbehavior before the enemy, apparently on charges that originated with men in their company. Acquittal by the court caused General Bragg to comment: "Result should be a warning to commanders not to approve charges against officers preferred by soldiers without proper investigation and mature judgment. An officers reputation is too sacred to be made the sport of enlisted men."[20] This is a response to be expected of a professional soldier, a very strict disciplinarian vigorously affirming the sacred responsibility of command.

A letter written a few weeks later by a soldier in the Sixtieth to his wife back home in Buncombe County supports the wisdom of the General's comment.

I am still waiting for Ray to git back and then I am a cuming home if tha giv mee a furlow a not I say I will cum any how or not if you say for mee to cum I shal but I have studied it all over long a go I have got my pegs set tha hav bin shoo[t]ing severil hear latly for runing a way but I think when the woods better thair will be a many a man go home thair is a time to all things hear is this mutch I want to doo the best I can for my famley and my self to stay hear at a leven dollars a month you cant liv on that while stuf is so hy well to run a way and go home an hav to lay out I cant help you to any thing to liv an that seem to mee lik that will not doo I wood bee a draw back in stid of a help to you and the children well if cant up in this kind of a fix while under old Bragg he wood have mee put to deth well to stay hear and liv as I have to live and risk the horibilness of life an deth that is a hard part for mee bu tena I wood giv my life for you in any way if it becums nessary I hav thant I wood cum home any how if you think we can meck out.[21]

Though often absent due to sickness, there is no record that the writer ever deserted; he died in 1864. The writer expressed the dilemma faced by many; would he be able to help his family if he deserted? Would his presence be a burden? Would there be threats of physical harm to his family by the Home Guard, or from more firmly committed neighbors? After careful thought, this soldier was willing to accept the risk of execution if his wife agreed that they could survive.

ALFRED T. BALL 58-G (November 18, 1863). An eager volunteer, Private Ball was anxious to be off to the war, offering his services for duty in the Fifty-Third Regiment Company K, in April 1862. Within weeks, Private Ball was discharged as being underage. After remaining home for five months, the young man again volunteered, this time for service in the Fifty-Eighth. A short while after joining the regiment, Private Ball was promoted to Corporal Ball, Company M, indicating he had some aptitude for the service. Four months after promotion, Corporal Ball left his company on January 27, 1863. On March 20, he returned. If there was any punishment for this absence it was minimal, and the returnee was shortly promoted to 2nd Sergeant, Company G. But again, after four months duty, Sergeant Ball took leave of his comrades while stationed in the area of Charleston, TN, perhaps reasonably assuming that on this return he would be promoted to 1st Sergeant. He was not dropped from the rolls of the company after either departure; it was expected that he would return, and that may have been his intention. Sergeant Ball went before a military court held on November 18, 1863, under a charge of desertion. The court found that he was guilty and agreed on a death sentence, indicating that he was arrested and brought back to the army rather than returning voluntarily. Although as seen in the case of Private Littrell, a voluntary return was not always a guarantee that a deserter would be spared from a death sentence, or that it would even be considered a mitigating factor at that time in the Army of Tennessee. The Lieutenant General Commanding approved the decision of the court, and the execution was scheduled for December 18. Two days before the appointed time, a company officer wrote to the Adjutant General of the Army of Tennessee.

> Camp 58th & 60th Regts (Consolidated) Near Dalton Ga. December 16th 1863 Colonel I have the honor respectfully to state that Sergeant Alfred F. Ball of my Company condemned to death on Friday next 18th by sentence of Court Martial is only twenty one (21) years of age and has a widowed mother depending upon him for support. In view of these facts I respectfully and earnestly beg that his sentence be commuted to some severe punishment other than death. In case the commutation of his sentence be not within the province of the Lieut General Commanding I respectfully request that he be reprieved until this paper can be forwarded to the President of the Confederate State for his action in the case. Very Respectfully Your

Obt. Sevt John R. Norris 2nd Lieut Commanding Company G. 58th N.C. Regt. Vols. Col G. W. Brent A.A.G.[22]

The parenthetical reference to the Fifty-Eighth and Sixtieth as "consolidated" in December 1863 refers to a temporary consolidation that ended in April 1864; a second and final consolidation took place a year later. The execution of Sergeant Ball was delayed for nearly five months, but no record has been located that President Davis was directly involved. A note on the reverse side of the above request states, "Sgt Ball was shot with 12 others for desertion." No date is given, but the "12 others" indicates that he was among those shot at the mass execution at Dalton, GA.

JAMES N. JESTES 60-A (February 12, 1864). Private Jestes enrolled in Captain W. M. Hardy's Company at Asheville, Buncombe County, in April 1862, and there he stayed until the fall or winter of 1863 when he deserted. Private Jestes was in custody and at trial on February 12, 1864. Private Jestes was given a death sentence for his first and relatively short desertion. There his official service records come to an abrupt end. Possibly he escaped from confinement and avoided capture for the rest of the war. There is no morning report entry for his company that he was executed, as there are for the other men who were executed.

In GO #28, April 2, 1864, Dalton GA, Head-Quarters Army of Tennessee, 5 soldiers of the Twenty-Eighth Alabama were ordered to be executed for desertion. Their absences began on March 12, and they were in arrest on March 14. This regiment was not a stranger to the execution field; 2 of their men were executed on the day that Private William Littrell of the Sixtieth North Carolina was shot. But in GO #33, April 13, 1864, Head-Quarters Army of Tennessee, General Johnston suspended the execution of sentence until the pleasure of the President could be known. The General took that benevolent step, he said, not because of sympathy for the deserters but because brothers of the men had sent forward appeals on their behalf. Those appealing were "faithful soldiers," "exemplary soldiers"; therefore the lives of all of the condemned men would be saved. "No praise is too exalted, no earthly reward is too priceless for the soldier who is ever ready with his command to share the privations of the march, and is ever present to meet the enemy in battle."[23] The very short time of the absence no doubt contributed to the decision of General Johnston. Twelve days after publication of the magnanimous order suspending the death sentences, a more ominous general order over the signature of General Johnston was forthcoming. GO #41, April 25, 1864, Dalton GA, Head-Quarters Army of Tennessee, lists the names of 21 soldiers given death sentences by the military court attached to General Hood's Corps. If they knew of the earlier benevolence, these 21 condemned may well have expected that all, or at least a few, of them would receive the same consideration given the men from the Twenty-Eighth Alabama. The Fifty-Eighth and the Sixtieth surrendered 15 of the condemned, and 1 came from the Sixty-Third Virginia.[24] The Virginian was not executed, nor were any of the 5 soldiers from the Fifty-Eighth Alabama or the Thirty-Sixth, Fortieth, and Forty-Sixth Georgia regiments. A single life was spared in the North Carolina regiments. When General Order #41 was published, Sergeant Ball was still confined under sentence of death, awaiting a final disposition of his case. His agony of fearful waiting was now shared with men of the Fifty-Eighth and Sixtieth.

In contrast to other regiments, where soldiers who were sentenced to be shot or hanged were clustered within companies, the death sentences for the Fifty-Eighth affected 8 of 12 companies. Company F, McDowell Rangers, and Company G, Yancey County, each yielded

3 to the stake, but the other condemned men came from 6 companies. Seven North Carolina counties were home for 13 of the 15 condemned. One lived in South Carolina, another in Tennessee in 1860. This distribution strengthens the observation that most of the deserters from the Fifty-Eighth started home on their own decision, and that they intended to return. Of the 15 condemned, 6 had served since 1862, and only 2 had a record of an earlier attempt at desertion. The 9 other doomed men were recruited or conscripted in mid to late 1863 and were ordered to be shot after conviction of their first desertion. For these 9 the death decisions of the court were apparently driven by considerations beyond the facts of their individual cases. Their sparse service records give no indication of advance planning. None left at the same time, this in contrast to regiments where a significant number of soldiers joined in an attempt to leave the service, thereby warranting prompt and decisive punishment. Once the first death decision was on record, it may have been difficult for the court to find any clear line of compassion as each case followed in turn. The first soldier to appear before the court, and the first to be given a death sentence, was charged with persuading others to desert. The men that followed were all charged with desertion.

REUBEN A. DELLINGER 58-A (March 30, 1864). Privates Reuben, John and Henry Dellinger, brothers all, enlisted for Confederate duty in December 1861. Private Henry Dellinger was discharged soon thereafter as being underage. After being transferred to the Fifth Battalion of Cavalry, Privates Reuben and John returned to the Fifty-Eighth without benefit of official approval, such act in itself being a violation of the 22nd Article of War, and punishable as desertion, "and suffered accordingly." After returning to the Fifty-Eighth, the brothers were still restless and deserted while near Anderson County, TN, on August 20, 1863. They were not dropped from the rolls of the company. Service records do not state if their return was voluntary or in arrest. The record is clear that Private Reuben Dellinger was tried for desertion by a military court on March 30, 1864, he was found guilty as charged, and his sentence was to be shot to death. All indications are that said sentence was carried into effect on May 4. Private John Dellinger returned to duty in January and subsequently deserted in September 1864. No record of punishment has been found.

WILLIAM R. BYERS 58-G (April 2, 1864). The brief period that Private Byers was in the Confederate army provides little detail for his service record. After his conscription in late October 1863, it is next noted that he is in arrest in the March and April period of 1864. During that time he went before a military court on April 2, was found guilty of desertion and was sentenced to be shot. His service record simply shows that he died in the May–August reporting period. From the best available evidence, he was among those shot on May 4. He traveled from conscription to execution in just over six months. Six men went to trial on April 2; all were given death sentences.

IRA JESSUP 58-G (April 2, 1864). Private Ira Jessup was conscripted into the Fifty-Eighth in November 1863 and deserted from that regiment while his company was near Dalton, GA, on the first day of 1864. By April 2, he was in arrest to appear in court on charges of desertion. The court found that he was guilty and handed down a death sentence. Private Jessup had served less than two months in the Confederate army. On learning that he would be shot, Private Jessup suffered some severe trauma that led to his death. Ira's younger brother, Private Meshack Jessup, was conscripted for service in the Fifty-Third Regiment on October 16, 1862, along with three other Jessup men from Surry County. Within a month of their induction, three of the men, including Meshack, deserted from near Drewry's Bluff, VA. The fourth Jessup served a year before deserting to the enemy.

Meschack later joined a Federal unit but deserted from that command about five months later. The Jessup men of service age were not firmly committed to either side.

The service records for Privates Byers and Jessup each have the identical entry "died" to mark the end of their service. They served in the same company and had very similar service records. They were probably not known by the company clerk who entered "died" rather than "shot" for Private Byers. Other sources indicate that one of the condemned men in the Fifty-Eighth died after hearing that he was to be executed, but they do not give his name.[25]

JESSE HASE 58-A (April 2, 1864). Private Jesse Hase has a very concise service record. He was enrolled in Hamilton County, TN, on October 20, 1863, and deserted not long thereafter. Arrest and appearance before a court on April 2 then followed. The court agreed that he was guilty of desertion and a death sentence was their decision. He was shot on May 4, one of the older men executed that day; he was in his early forties.

WRIGHT HUTCHINS 58-F (April 2, 1864). Private Hutchins enlisted for three years of Confederate service in either McDowell County, NC, or Marion County TN, on October 6, 1863. Six weeks after agreeing to serve, he deserted his company and then remained absent until March 8, 1864, when he was in arrest. Within a month Private Hutchins went to trial, was convicted of desertion, and sentenced to be shot. The sentence was carried into effect on May 4, 1864.

HIRAM YOUNGBLOOD 58-F (April 2, 1864). Captain Pearson enrolled Private Youngblood for service in the McDowell Rangers for three years, or the duration of the war, on August 14, 1863, in Rutherford County. On February 12, 1864, Private Youngblood absented himself from his company to remain away for twenty-five days before he was placed in arrest and returned to his command. For this relatively short absence he was taken before a military court convened on Saturday, April 2. Private Youngblood was shot on May 4.

ASA DOVER 58-F (April 2, 1864). Private Dover volunteered to serve in a North Carolina regiment though he lived in South Carolina in the York District. Six months after agreeing to serve, he deserted on February 8, 1864. He was arrested exactly one month after leaving his regiment. He went to trial on April 2, was found guilty and sentenced to be shot to death for an absence that was often considered absent without leave. Two other men with the same family name, Privates John H. and Robert A. Dover, deserted on the same day as Private Asa Dover. They made the prudent decision to go directly to the enemy thus avoiding any further Confederate entanglement. Some records for Asa have the initials "S. A." rather than his name "Asa," an easy phonetic mistake, while in other documents the first name is spelled "Eza."

GEORGE W. MCFALLS 58-K (April 4, 1864). Private McFalls enlisted in the Fifth Battalion Partisan Rangers in June 1862 and was present for duty when the battalion went into the Fifty-Eighth Regiment on July 29. In December he was given a twenty-day furlough. When the allotted days came to an end, he chose not to return to his post and was absent until the March–April period of 1863. No record of punishment for this extended absence has been found. In the September–October period that same year, Private McFalls was not well and was granted a furlough to recover at home. Again he did not return at the end of the furlough. In March–April 1864, the soldier who had twice overstayed a leave was in arrest and awaiting trial for desertion. Private McFalls had received a $50 enrollment bounty and received two months pay, $22, just before leaving on his second furlough. A military court heard his case on April 4, determined his guilt, and issued a death sentence. Private McFalls was executed one month later.

GORDON MORROW 58-H (April 4, 1864). Private Morrow joined a company of men who were intent on forming the Fifth Battalion Partisan Rangers in March 1862. When this did not come about they were organized as Company I of the Twenty-Sixth Regiment; transfer to the Fifty-Eighth followed. He was among the first deserters from the newly formed company, an event that was duly noted in a letter home by a member of the same company. The letter was dated October 10, 1862. "Last night three deserters from Company H, first we have had, D & G Morrow and D. Matheson deserted."[26] No record has been found for D. Matheson. The other Morrow was Private Daniel Morrow; he and a second brother, Private Nathan Morrow, had earlier served with Private Gordon Morrow in the Twenty-Sixth, and then transferred to the Fifty-Eighth. Private Nathan Morrow died in August 1862, and Private Daniel Morrow followed in death in March 1863. The impact of these deaths on Private Gordon Morrow is not known, but for the fifteen months after leaving his company he accepted and endured life as a deserter. At the end of that time, he allegedly voluntarily surrendered to a local militia officer. After hearing the facts in his case, the court found that he was guilty of desertion and agreed that he should be executed. No mitigating factors were mentioned. The day before the scheduled mass execution, General Johnston issued an order that released Private Morrow. The basis for this decision is not recorded; no trial error was cited, but the voluntary return, as noted in the court record, was likely persuasive. Ironically, Private Morrow was absent from his company for a longer period, fifteen months, than were the other men who were shot. The next longest desertion was for eight months, and most were for three or four.

MICHAEL WARD 58-D (April 4, 1864). Private Ward enlisted while the Fifty-Eighth was forming but deserted after four months of duty. In June of 1863, he returned to his company without suffering severe punishment. Perhaps emboldened, three months later he again deserted, being absent from August 26, 1863, until March 15, 1864, when he was in arrest. During each absence, he was carried on the rolls of the company as if his return was expected. After his reappearance in March, he was at trial on April 4, and sentenced to death. He was executed on May 4. Private Duke B. Ward, a younger brother, enrolled in Company D some ten days after Private Michael Ward and deserted on March 1, 1863. He had no further service record.

E. F. YOUNTS 58-H (April 4, 1864). Private Younts enlisted in Company H of the Fifty-Eighth at Athens, McMinn County, TN, on December 16, 1863. Before March 15, 1864, he deserted from his company, for by that date he was in the guardhouse awaiting a court-martial, and there he would stand on April 4. When the decision of the court was published, Private Younts learned that he had been found guilty as charged and that he was to be shot to death by musketry. That was done on May 4. A fellow soldier noted in his diary: "Wed 4th clear and cool pleasant Fourteen men shot for desertion in the Brigade our E. F. Younts from Co. H."[27]

JAMES M. RANDAL 60-A (April 4, 1864). Drum Major Randal enlisted as a private in Captain Washington M. Hardy's company at Asheville in April 1862. The company was part of a battalion that was increased to regimental strength in October. When records for the Sixtieth were first compiled for the November–December 1862 period, Drum Major Randal mustered with the non-commissioned staff of the regiment. He continued in that position until May–June 1863, when he was assigned to Company A. Some time after his re-assignment, perhaps disgruntled, he deserted, this prior to October 1863. He was in arrest in March–April 1864. Private Randal went to court on April 4, was judged guilty of desertion, and sentenced to be shot. He was executed one month after his trial. Private John W. Randal, a brother, deserted on the same day as the executed soldier and had no further record of service.

CHRISTOPHER LEDFORD 60-C (April 5, 1864). Private Ledford enrolled in what was to eventually become the Sixtieth Regiment in the summer of 1862 and served until winter when he was hospitalized. While at the Military Hospital at Catiose Springs, TN, Private Ledford deserted, returned to duty for a spell, and then again departed on August 8, 1863. He continued his desertion until March 1864 when he was in arrest. During his second absence, the Confederate may have enrolled in the Second Mounted Infantry, North Carolina Union Troops, before changing his mind and leaving that regiment.[28] When Private Ledford appeared before a military court on April 5, he was charged with simple desertion; charges relating to traitorous behavior were not included. The single charge was sufficient for the court to find Private Ledford guilty and sentence him to death by musketry. Captain Thomas W. Patton, Private Ledford's company commander, relates the night before the executions.

> All of that fearful night I sat beside my man in what was called "The Bull Pen" and tried to comfort him as best I could and I never felt more sad than when Lieutenant Clayton, to whom the duty had by lot fallen, gave the command "Fire" and these Confederate soldiers fell by the hands of their brothers.[29]

Captain Patton continued his concern for his men and their loved ones when he wrote to Nancy Ledford, informing her that her husband had been executed and that he was resigned to his fate.[30] What more could be said under the circumstances? Whether Captain Patton wrote his letter as an official duty or simply as a measure of kindness is not known. No formal procedure for family notification of an execution has been found. Informal notification might be altered or embellished as needed to shelter family memories. Pension records do show that a few applications for a pension by a widow were denied because the husband was shot at the stake, leading one to wonder if the widow had ever been informed that her husband was executed. Nancy Ledford did not apply for a North Carolina widow's pension but did apply for a Federal pension on two occasions, apparently both based on her husband's putative service with Federal forces. The second claim was approved and payments made to Nancy, but a subsequent investigation determined that her claim was fraudulent. Nancy was not a party to the fraud, being an "illiterate woman, unable to write her name"; she had been misled by unscrupulous attorneys. Nancy's husband is identified as C. M. Ledford in Federal records and C. C. in other sources.[31]

JACOB A. AUSTIN 58-E (April 6, 1864). Private Austin was conscripted into service at Christmas time in 1863. Within weeks he deserted while his regiment was near Dalton, GA. A month later the conscript and deserter was in custody and awaiting trial, which took place on April 6. The accused was found guilty and sentenced to be shot. The finding of the court was published on April 25, and Private Austin was among those shot on May 4, not far from where he had started his desertion five months earlier.

JOSEPH A. GIBBS 58-C (April 12, 1864). Private Gibbs faithfully carried out his Confederate duties for fifteen months, from enlistment in June 1862 until September 27, 1863, whereupon he deserted while his regiment was in the area of Chattanooga, TN. As with several others, the absent Private was not removed from the company rolls. After an absence of at least three months, Private Gibbs was in arrest and confined in the guardhouse at Atlanta, GA. On April 12, he was court-martialed, found guilty of the charge and specification, and sentenced to be shot. Private Gibbs signed his enrollment papers and was given a $50 bounty. He was executed on May 4.

These 15 men of the Fifty-Eighth and the Sixtieth, along with 6 men enrolled in regiments formed in other states, had their cursory day in court. The results of the court's deliberations and the decision of the General Commanding were published on April 25, 1864 in GO #41, Army of Tennessee.

> The proceedings, findings and sentences in the forgoing cases are approved and will be carried into effect. The Officers Commanding the Divisions to which the accused respectively belong will give the necessary orders for the execution of the foregoing sentences, at such time and place as they may designate. By command of General Johnston.[32]

Convicted men normally were given a few days to prepare an appeal, notify their families and make their peace with the Almighty. No record of any such correspondence has been found, and events continued apace.

The day before the massive execution, General Johnston issued a rather cryptic order. "Dalton Ga, May 3, 1864 Col. B. J. Hill is requested to see that these sentences are promptly and *literally* carried into effect."[33] The reason why this order was thought necessary is not known. The intention of the order is clear; General Johnston wanted immediate punishment for convicted men in his command. Military leaders seem of one mind that effective punishment is prompt punishment. General Johnston may have wanted the sentences carried into effect before any other authority could intervene. He best understood the state of his army.

The day after the executions, a soldier summarized his thoughts.

> On yesterday, one of the most solemn scenes I ever witnessed, was seen in the valley near our camp. Fourteen deserters were shot at once in the presence of our whole division. They were, each one, tied to a stake a guard marched to within ten paces of the condemned prisoners, eight in front of each prisoner. The poor fellows were groaning terribly. The word of command was given and the guard fired. Only eight were killed at the first volley, though the other six were badly or mortally wounded. The Doctors immediately, after the first volley, examined the men, and those that were not instantly killed were again shot by the guard, who would step up within a few feet and fire. It was soon over and they were consigned to ignominious graves. Eleven from the 58th. N.C. 2 from our Regt. The impression created by thus summarily punishing men for this awful offence (desertion) was profound and I venture to say that the others of our Brigade will think better of it when a thought of desertion comes to their heads.[34]

The men surviving the first round of fire is overstated, and their final dispatch is less vivid when placed alongside other accounts. Another soldier in the Sixtieth apparently did not witness the executions but sent word of the occurrence to those at home. "I hear that Johnson had forteen men shot the other da out of the 58 and 60 North Carolinare Regmants But onley one or two out of my Regmant I hav not lernt any of thar names for dezerting."[35] An officer in the Sixty-Third Virginia offered his impressions:

> It was the worst sight I ever saw too horrible to think about. Yet some of them was not killed the first time & some of them not touched. Their cries was horrible in the extreme. Men were ordered up one at a time to put their guns close to their hearts or heads & fired. One poor fellow told them if they were going to kill him for God sake to do it and not shoot his flesh to pieces. They all seemed very much effected about their future except one who believed there was no God & died firm in his belief. That is old news but it is one of the scenes I shall never forget as long as life last.[36]

How the Virginia officer knew that one of the executed men was an atheist is not explained. From a soldier in the Forty-Fifth Tennessee:

> Several men were tried as traitors who had [gone home] ... to provide for the needs of their families and had returned to their commands, fourteen of these were condemned to be shot. Fourteen posts were prepared and a man was secured by a rope to each post. A platoon of soldiers were given guns loaded by the officer in charge with some blank cartridges. When the volley was fired all the men seemed to have been killed but two or three. The officer took several men with loaded guns and made a critical examination, with a surgeon, of every condemned man. When one was pronounced alive a soldier was ordered to place the gun to his heart and kill him. This was repeated until all were dead. Horrible, horrible to think about. The whole army was required to be present at every execution.[37]

Again from a diary account entered on the day of the executions.

> Today I witnessed a sight, sad indeed, I saw fourteen men shot for desertion. I visited them twice yesterday and attended them to the place of execution. Most of them met death manfully. Some, poor fellows, I fear were unprepared. I saw them wash and dress themselves for the grave. It was a solumn scene, they were tied to the stake, there was the coffin, there the open grave ready to receive them.... "Tell my wife," said one but a few minutes before the leaden messengers pierced his breast, "not to grieve for me, I have no doubt of reaching a better world"... I think they were objects of pity, they were ignorant, poor, and had families dependent upon them. War is a cruel thing, it heeds not the widow's tear, the orphan's moan or the lover's anguish.[38]

Captain T. W. Patton, Sixtieth Regiment, Company C, later wrote an impassioned description of the whole affair.

> There, by the dreadful order of the <u>dreadful General Bragg</u>, fourteen men of our Brigade were shot to death for what was called desertion. During the weary weeks of our stay at Dalton, these poor fellows, hearing bad news of the starving wives and children and knowing that no action was imminent, had gone home without leave, fully intending to report for duty, when any duty was to be done. At their poor cabins, they were arrested by some of those gallant "stay at home" soldiers, who had never smelt powder and never intended to see a fight, were brought back, tried and convicted, sentenced, and in spite of all that we could do, were shot <u>like wild beasts</u>. Twelve of these men belonged to the Fifty-Eighth N.C. which was in the same brigade with us, and two were our own. One was from Company A, and one from my Company.[39]

Although Captain Patton attributes approval of the death sentences to General Bragg, the execution order was issued by General Johnston. General Bragg had resigned as commander of the Army of Tennessee on December 1, 1863, and General Johnston took command on December 27. General Bragg's strict enforcement of discipline seared an indelible impression on many minds, then and to this day.

In a reminiscence prepared some years after the events, an attending doctor recalled the day.

> One other dreadful tragedy I will relate, and while it may reflect on our soldiers in some respects, it shows the hardships they were compelled to endure under the most discouraging circumstances. The great wonder is that so few comparatively, were not able to with stand overcome the difficulties in mind and body by which they were assailed. When we were near Dalton Ga. sixteen men were condemned to be shot by order of Braxton Bragg. One man was pardoned the day before the execution was to take place and one died in the hospital when he learned that he was to be shot. The next day these fourteen men were executed; Lt. Robert Clayton of Ashville was officer of the day and I was Surgeon for this dreadful occasion. All of the army there was ordered out; the infantry formed a hollow square with cannon in the rear, while the Cavalry just back of them made such a strong line it was impossible for any one to pass. A long ditch had been prepared, and the rude coffins placed in front of it,

with a stake by it, while the guard appointed to this duty marched each man to the stake & coffin prepared for him, and each man bound to his stake. The senior officer ordered all in position and to make ready, and Lt. Robert Clayton who always acted nobly, in command, gave the order to fire. All were killed but two, as I found when I advanced to examine them. One had been shot in the side,—the other in the arm. I reported that two were alive and the guard advanced and fired killing them immediately. Orders were then given to fall back to camp. Oh! what a Sunday was that! The private soldiers were all bitterly opposed to the execution of these men and that night several hundred of them left the army and never returned. I remained to attend the burial service of these fourteen men. Our Chaplain held service until about ten o'clock. I can never, never forget that sad scene; I was heart-sick. The Western Army never seemed to do much good after this most dreadful tragedy.[40]

To the mind of the doctor, as it was for Captain Patton, General Bragg was responsible for the executions at Dalton, GA.

As indicated, "The private soldiers were all bitterly opposed to the execution of these men," and well they might have been after looking at the record of the men for Company F, Fifty-Eighth for example. During the war there were 213 men enrolled in the company, there were 72 incidents of desertion or absence without leave, most of these in the fall and winter of 1863. The bulk of those involved had absences of two or three months and apparently received minimal punishment, if any, when they returned. A handful of men were tried and were sentenced to confinement for a month or two, with a ball attached to their leg, or pilloried and the like. The 3 men of Company F who were ordered to be executed had absences of one, four and five months as their only crime, and they were executed. Other men in the same company had absences of sixteen months, they were tried in that same period, and were given sentences of forty days at hard labor with a ball and chain fastened to a leg.[41] The justice, the fairness, the impartial consistency of court and officer, all must have been perplexing to those on the execution field on May 4. As the doctor observed, "The Western army never seemed to do much good after this most dreadful tragedy."

Returning to the events of May 4, another author described his recollection of the affair at Dalton, GA.

> But the scene above all that impressed me was the shooting of fifteen deserters from the army—two from Stewart's Division, eight from Stevenson's and five from other commands of infantry and cavalry. Early in the morning a detail from the provost guard marched to General Stewart's headquarters, stacked their arms and left. Staff officers were ordered to load the guns for the execution in their divisions, half with blank cartridges and other half with buck and ball. After this was done the guns were so changed that those who had loaded them could not tell the loaded from those with blank cartridges. The detail then returned and took them.... The doomed men were brought out, and to the tune of the "Dead March" were conducted around the square, an ambulance following with their coffins. When the provost guard filed to their places and the men were being blindfolded a courier came under whip and spur from General Johnston's headquarters with an order staying the execution of the old father's boy. The other poor fellows knelt at the foot of the graves dug for them, and the guards fired. To this day I thank my stars that those who loaded them and those who fired them were left in comforting ignorance as to which guns were loaded. A short time after this the half-witted soldier [the old father's boy] who so narrowly escaped is said to have again deserted to the enemy, showing persistent method in his madness. In some of the commands the guard made a "botch" of their work, and had to shoot the doomed men twice.[42]

Published some forty years after the end of the war, the above account appears to intermix detail on happenings in several different commands.

First explaining that the Southern soldier was at a great disadvantage to the Northern foe due to lack of arms, food, clothing and medicine, one author casts a far different emphasis on the executions at Dalton.

> Mention was made that sixteen Confederate soldiers were shot at Aults Mills, in Georgia, under the charge of desertion. Several of these soldiers had received letters from their wives stating that they and their children were starving and entreating them to come quickly to their relief. It was believed that these letters were exhibited to the commanding general and application was made for furloughs which were refused. They then risked life and disgrace by going home without leave. After providing for their families, they were voluntarily returning to their commands to report for duty when they were arrested, court-martialed, found guilty of desertion, and shot.[43]

Although one or two of the soldiers who were executed in May may well have gone home on the pleading of a suffering loved one, it is difficult to support that notion as typical, based on the length of desertion for most of the men. The average absence was four and a half months. Just 5 of the 16 are known to have been married before the beginning of war. Unauthorized absences are found on records of 5 of the executed; for the others it was their first venture in desertion.

WILLIAM B. BANKS 58-C (Prior to April 8, 1865). Private Banks served from the time of the expansion of the Fifth Partisan Ranger Battalion until the May–June period of 1863 when he was granted a furlough to recover from a sickness. Health improved, he returned to his company where he served until February 20, 1864, when he deserted. He was in desertion until the final days of the war. General Order #8, April 8, 1865, Army of Tennessee, announced the findings of a court that had convened at Asheville, NC. Private Banks was charged with "desertion and adhering to the enemy — aiding and abetting them to rob Dr. B. B. Whittington of two guns and ammunition" when taken before the court. Found guilty, he was sentenced to be shot. The findings of the court were approved and the day of execution set. "Approved officer cmdg district charged with execution of sentence Friday following receipt between ten and five at Asheville."[44] As the execution was scheduled some time after April 8, and the army surrendered on the 27, Private Banks escaped execution in the turmoil of those last confused days of strife.

Summary

When Private Littrell of Company F was shot in December 1862, the Sixtieth had an aggregate enrollment of 803 men, and Company F made up 84 of that number. When Privates Randal and Ledford were executed in May 1864 Company F had 20 men present for duty. The companies of the executed privates, Company A and Company C, were down to 24 and 12 men respectively, a pitiful band indeed, to watch the execution of 14 men.[45] These companies were not exceptional; the Fifty-Eighth and the Sixtieth, together made up less than half the strength of a full regiment. Company F of the Fifty-Eighth had just 1 recorded desertion in the two months preceding the killings at Dalton; 68 men had deserted the company prior to that time. In the remaining year of war 3 men departed the dwindling company. Court-martial records for the North Carolina men executed on May 4, were not posted by the AIGO until September 5, 1864. No information has been found as to when news of the events at Dalton reached authorities at Richmond.

The Fifty-Eighth was larger than the Sixtieth both in number of companies, 12 in the

Fifty-Eighth, and in enrolled men. In total, the regiments enrolled over 3,200 during two and a half years of service, slightly over one-third in the Sixtieth. A sampling of 4 companies of each regiment indicates the Fifty-Eighth enrolled 190 men in a company; 58 were absent at some point, 30 died of disease, and 9 died in battle. A Sixtieth Regiment company had an average enrollment of 117, with 32 absences, 26 deaths from disease or cause unknown and 6 battle-related casualties.[46] Nearly all of the companies of the regiments were formed on or close by the Tennessee border. Men of that state made up a full company and others were scattered through other companies. Just less than half of the 21 men who were threatened with execution are known to have been married. Three were conscripts. Just over half, 12 of the 21 enlisted in 1862, in mid-year on average; 7 were executed. The other 9 of the 21 went into service in late 1863, in October on average, and 8 of these men were executed eight months later. The executed 14 of the Fifty-Eighth and Sixtieth were allowed a few days of hope or resignation. They were officially informed of their fate nine or ten days before the appointed end of life and service.

18

Twenty-Ninth and Thirty-Ninth North Carolina Infantry Regiments

Twenty-Ninth Regiment

"He appeared to face death with as much boldness as a man could."[1]

Courts-martial in the Department of East Tennessee did not treat dishonorable or criminal conduct lightly in 1862. From the Twenty-Ninth, 9 men went to trial in mid-year; all were sentenced to be shot or to be flogged. The court did express a degree of compassion for Private W. A. Jones, Company A; his punishment was just ten lashes because of his "extreme youth."[2] The lad was likely of fifteen or sixteen years, the other boys who were to suffer the full penalty of thirty-nine lashes were eighteen years of age. The youthful offenders were thereafter to be drummed from the regiment to the tune of "Yankee Doodle." For the regiment, 5 of the 7 who were sentenced to be executed were between the ages of eighteen and twenty-one years.

Men enrolled in Company F received 3 death sentences; all were residents of Jackson County. Company F enrolled 127 men from organization to surrender. At least 20 deserted, but only half have specific dates of departure. In addition, 15 others have records of enrollment but no record of service or there is a notation that they failed to report after enrolling. Signing on for duty in the Twenty-Ninth was not looked on as an iron-clad commitment by many men of the troubled mountain area.

Company C, the Bold Mountain Tigers, Buncombe County; Company K, formed in Yancey County; and Company A, recruited as the Cherokee Guards, experienced the largest number of courts in the regiment. Company C led the others with 7 men at trial, this from the regimental total of 34; 1 was acquitted. As an aside for this company, of 32 desertions with known departure dates, 24 began in the month of September in the four successive years of war. Some of these men likely left to aid their families in harvesting and preparing for the winter. Others may have experienced the nostalgic remembrance of autumn in the mountains and simply wanted to go home. Company E, Haywood County; Company G, Yancey County; and Company D, Madison County, had the fewest number of men to be court-martialed. Company E had just 1 court of record, but of the 157 men that were enrolled in the company, 22 had charged absences, and 39 others had no service record after ostensibly enrolling in the company. In September 1864, 16 men left the company and had no further service record. There were very few Company E absentees ever in custody to be tried for their misdeeds.

Thirty-Ninth Regiment

"The evil has become so great"[3]

Major David Coleman's infantry battalion was authorized to expand to regimental strength and take its place in line as the Thirty-Ninth Infantry Regiment in May 1862. The Thirty-Ninth served with regiments from Arkansas, and at other times with men from Texas. The regiment may never have reached full strength. Company F, for example, had only 64 enrollees; 22 of them deserted. Court-martial records show that Companies A, B and C, formed with men from Cherokee and Macon counties, led the others in number of courts, but generally courts were proportionately distributed over all companies, considering that several companies were well under their authorized strength.

Over 100 men of Macon County were formed into Company B and led by Captain Alfred W. Bell, who had served in the Mexican War.[4] Frequent letters to his wife reveal an officer with a sincere concern for the well-being of soldiers in his care and a willingness to share their discomforts.[5] Captain Bell had little confidence in his commanding officer, "a fool who has no sense."[6] Throughout the war years, 140 men agreed to serve in his company. Only 9 are known to have lived outside of Macon County. For the company, 25 men were charged with desertion, 8 were absent without leave, and 2 failed to report after signing on. The enemy killed 5, 28 died from disease or with no stated cause. No death sentences resulted after 7 trials for those in the company. The experience of another company of Macon men was quite similar; 118 men enrolled in Company I, 14 absented themselves, 8 were killed in fighting, and 37 died of diseases or an unrecorded cause. The 3 men of the Thirty-Ninth who were sentenced to be executed were all residents of Cherokee County. Some men left the Thirty-Ninth and enrolled in the Thomas Legion. A company officer of the Thirty-Ninth wrote that he had no objection to this, which obviously did nothing to limit depletion of his already weakened company.[7] Enlisting in a unit while on the rolls of another is a serious violation of the 22nd Articles of War and carries a potential death penalty, whether agreeable to the company Captain or not. But war for the mountain men went more by local custom than army regulations. Considering the organization of the Thirty-Ninth, the frequent changes in assignment, the apparent laxity of company officers, the mountain men might easily have assumed a sense of freedom to serve where they wished, based on their own loyalty, whim, or grievance.

The conflict was nearly half over before a soldier of the regiment went before a court-martial, this occurring on March 2, 1863. The last recorded court of an enlisted man of the regiment was on January 2, 1864. In that ten-month span, 31 court appearances were ordered; 3 ended with acquittal. Officers of the regiment went before 11 courts; 5 were acquitted and 3 were cashiered or dismissed from the service. The remaining 3 were reprimanded or ordered to forfeit pay. Lieutenant Enoch Voyles, resigned his Confederate commission and went over to the Federal Army; under that banner, he was "prominent in committing depradations upon the people of Cherokee."[8] He resigned because he was "incompetent and physically unable" to continue in his duties; attacking citizens was no doubt considerably less demanding than leading men in mountain fighting.[9]

Courts-Martial

FRANCIS MARION JENKINS 29-F (July 1, 1862). Private Jenkins began his service on August 31, 1861. After ten months, primarily in East Tennessee, he deserted in June 1862.

Two others with the same surname deserted at the same time while in the vicinity of Cumberland Gap, TN. Private Jenkins was not long at large because he went before a court the next month. He was then informed that he would be executed. The sentence was set aside in February 1863. The reprieved young man returned to his regiment and was later transferred to Captain Levi's artillery battery in the Thomas Legion, this on April 1, 1864, and there he served until the fall of 1864, when his service record ends.

WILLIAM P. SHULER 29-F (July 1, 1862). Private Shuler's service record is nearly identical to that of Private Jenkins as to enlistment in August 1861, desertion in June 1862, trial in July 1862, a death sentence, reprieve, and release. Transfer to Captain Levi's artillery battery followed. After a short absence without leave he returned to duty and was present until August 29, 1864, when his record ends.

ANDREW C. WIGGINS 29-F (July 1, 1862). Private Wiggins was a third soldier from Jackson County to enlist in Company F in August 1861. He also deserted in June 1862, was arrested, court-martialed and sentenced to be shot. As in the other cases, his sentence was remitted on February 10, 1863. No service record for the time after his release has been located. There is no indication that he served in Captain Levi's command. A brother, Private Moses L. Wiggins, had a similar service record, including desertion in June 1862, but no arrest or statement of his duty status has been located. A third brother, Private Thomas Wiggins, served in the Thomas Legion.

BALIS NORTON 29-K (July 1, 1862). Private Norton first enrolled in Company B of the Twenty-Ninth in July 1861. Ten weeks later he was transferred to Company K. He deserted that company, likely in June 1862, for the next month he was in custody and at trial. He was given a death sentence which was set aside in February 1863, marking the end of company records for Private Norton. The reprieved Confederate soldier and a younger brother, Private James Norton, on September 1, 1863, enrolled in the Second Regiment Mounted Infantry, a Federal regiment.[10] A third brother, Private Josiah Norton, enrolled in the Third Regiment Mounted Infantry, also a Federal regiment.[11] There is some uncertainty as to whether the brothers were on leave from their Federal regiments, recruiting for them, or simply absent from their units, but they were at home in the fall of 1864. The Federal record for Private Balis Norton shows that he was absent without leave in February 1864, and classified as a deserter in June. Private James Norton and a fourth brother, Private George Norton, had deserted in October 1863. They had enrolled about two months before that date. On the morning of September 27, 1864, Balis, James and Josiah were at their home in Yancey County preparing to take their breakfast when their cabin was surrounded by armed men. The brothers attempted to flee, two were shot in their dooryard, and the third was killed a little distance away. They were buried in a common grave, and the cabin was burned. Josiah Norton was fifteen or sixteen when he was killed just outside the cabin door. One explanation for this outburst of hatred may be that 11 Norton men went into Federal service in the Second Mounted Infantry; Private Roderick Norton was allegedly killed by Confederates, while recruiting for Federal volunteers. When enrolled in the Sixty-Fourth Regiment he deserted three times before going into the Federal unit. No trial records for these offenses have been found.

Twenty years after the deaths of her sons, the mother applied for a pension from the Federal government. On first review the application was denied because it was not established that her sons were acting in line of duty at the time of their killing. A subsequent investigation determined that, as best known, the brothers were on furlough when they were killed and that the pension request should be approved. This seems to be a very generous interpretation of the facts by the investigator. Private Balis Norton, Bailes or Bayliss in various records, is listed as a deserter in Federal records after June 1, 1864. Of the 11 men bearing the Norton name that enrolled in the Second Mounted Infantry, 8 deserted. A casual view of military discipline was not confined to men of the Twenty-Ninth. It was said of the Federal regiment: "The men in this command came and went as they pleased. The Colonel allowed it ... strict discipline was unknown."[12]

The Twenty-Ninth was assembled to witness at least 1 execution. "Man in the 11th Tennessee shot for killing Lieutenant he appeared to face death with as much boldness as a man could."[13] The Eleventh Tennessee was brigaded with the Twenty-Ninth at the time. A court-martial record has not yet been located.

JACOB FRANKLIN 39-F (March 25, 1863). Sergeant Franklin reached that respected and responsible position only three months after enrolling in Company F. Three months after that recognition, he gave evidence that the trust may have been misplaced, as he deserted while near Loudon, TN, on July 27, 1862. At large for two months, the Sergeant was arrested and reduced in rank while at Harrodsburg, KY. The restless private was in camp for six weeks before again attempting to desert, this on November 15, near Lenoir Station, TN. This absence continued for the rest of the winter until he was returned under guard on March 1, 1863. The man who had made two attempts to desert was tried before a court held on March 25, found guilty of desertion, and was sentenced to be shot to death. General Bragg approved the sentence. The day of execution was set for June 5, between the hours of twelve and four P.M., under the command of Brigadier General J. K. Jackson.[14] Upon Presidential review, the sentence was either commuted or remitted, for at some point the private was returned to duty. In September the spared soldier was wounded at Chickamauga, TN. He survived the amputation of a leg, and the war.

BENJAMIN FRANKLIN 39-F (March 26, 1863). Private B. Franklin enrolled in the infantry battalion that was to become the Thirty-Ninth. On November 15, 1862, he was absent without leave from his company and stayed away until March 1, 1863. At his trial on March 26, Private Franklin was charged with desertion and was found guilty; a death sentence followed. This sentence was remitted around June 20. He either went back to his company or was hospitalized, but in any case he once again deserted while near Dalton, GA on September 22, 1863 and had no further record of service.

GILLUM B. WILES 39-G (November 3, 1863). Private Wiles served in his chosen regiment for a year before being hospitalized and then deserting. An earlier absence was treated as absent without leave in late 1862. After his second absence he was dropped from the rolls of the company by order of General Bragg. However, on November 3, 1863, Private Wiles appeared before a court charged with desertion, his record showing that he deserted and was arrested on the same day, June 30, 1863. The result of the court's deliberation was that Private Wiles should be shot. General Bragg approved the decision and GO #202, November 13, 1863, Army of Tennessee, set the day and time of execution as Friday, November 27, between the hours of 10 A.M. and 2 P.M. at Atlanta, GA, under the direction of the post commander.[15] Considering the record of Private Wiles, the record of General Bragg, and the lack of any other information, it is likely that he was executed, but verification has yet to be located. A soldier in the Sixty-Fifth Georgia who was also sentenced to be shot the same day as Private Wiles was freed from the sentence because the court did not properly state that two-thirds of the court concurred in the decision. Though it would seem reasonable that the court might make the same error in other sentences, no such indication appears in the record of Private Wiles.

Men still present for duty with the Thirty-Ninth in February 1864 may have witnessed the ritual of execution. Captain Bell, Company B, tersely wrote, "There is to be 3 men shot at town today for mutiny."[16] No supporting record has been found. It is unlikely that the men were enrolled in the Thirty-Ninth.

WILLIAM G. HANEY 29-H (July 15, 1864). Private William G. Haney enlisted on September 9, 1862, and deserted from his regiment on December 20, 1862. At the conclusion of his trial in July 1864, he was condemned to be shot, and the trial record went forward for review by the Secretary of War. No additional information has been located on the outcome of the review or on the service of Private Haney.

GEORGE C. HANEY 29-H (July 18, 1864). Private George C. Haney volunteered for Confederate service on September 9, 1862 and deserted from that service on December 20, 1862. On July 18, 1864, Private Haney was in arrest and standing before a court-martial. A guilty finding resulted from his trial and he was ordered to be shot to death. The proceedings were sent to the Secretary of War for his review. No further information concerning Private George Haney has been located.

JAMES W. HARRIS 29-B (Prior to April 8, 1865). Private Harris fought with the Twenty-Ninth for twenty-six months before deserting on September 6, 1863. A court-martial held in early 1864 resulted in Private Harris being imprisoned until December 1, 1864, when he was released by SO #285, AIGO. The same court tried two of his brothers. One was acquitted of the charge placed against him, and the other was given a light sentence. Private James Harris, who had previously served over two years without a mark on his record, went before a second court charged with robbery and desertion. A death sentence was handed down by this court, but on the day the sentence was published, April 8, 1865, the condemned man was apparently captured by Federal forces at the Spanish Fort, Mobile Bay, AL. The oldest of the 4 or 5 Harris brothers who served in Company B, Private Nathan M. Harris, deserted in March 1863 and had no further service record.

Summary

Men in the Twenty-Ninth and Thirty-Ninth had family ties to kin in North Carolina, Tennessee, South Carolina and Georgia, and in that sense, they were regional regiments. Federal and Confederate loyalty was about evenly divided in the mountain peaks and hollows, with a leaning toward the Federal side.[17] The loss of regimental loyalty was attributed to frequent command changes at the brigade and division levels.[18] The regiments were ordered to fight on widely dispersed battlefields under a variety of leaders when not fully prepared to do so. The struggle was intense, as was the inner, more personal conflict on where to place one's allegiance.[19] It was not a simple matter, nor was it a steadfast decision. Some men left and went home, some went to other regiments, others joined the enemy, and a few were faithful to the end. Record keeping was minimal. Service records for many men are very short, often not extending beyond the initial enrollment. Recorded activity for individual soldiers is concentrated in the year beginning in mid–1862.

Not unexpectedly, the number of men present for duty on the day of surrender at

Mobile, AL, is not known. Reference to remnants as being present is indicative of the strength of the regiments. Just under 2,500 men are found on regimental rolls, with the Twenty-Ninth half again as large as the Thirty-Ninth. Average enrollment for a company in the Twenty-Ninth was 142. In 4 sampled companies, 24 absented themselves, 25 died of disease or unknown cause, and 4 died in conflict with the enemy. Average company enrollment for the Thirty-Ninth was 106. A 5 company sampling indicates an average of 24 absences, 19 dead of disease and 4 killed in battle.[20] The service records of the 10 men sentenced to be executed indicate that 8 were last known to be alive. All 10 enrolled before March 1862; they had lived and worked an average of twenty-two and a half years before volunteering. None are known to have been married. All had volunteered before passage of conscription laws; none were substitutes. Men enrolled in the Twenty-Ninth and Thirty-Ninth apparently did not voice any objection to serving in brigades with troops from other states, and led by men from those states. As said, they were more regional in family ties and outlook than were most regiments of North Carolinians. After three years of leading a dwindling company of Confederates, Captain Bell dejectedly concluded, "We had as well then hang up the fiddle for I think the Confederacy will have danced its last gig,"[21] a soft phrase of resignation with no hint of vengeance to mark an end to four years of death and destruction.

19

Palmer Brigade

"The Toreys havnt got me yet."[1]

In the last December of the war the Sixty-Second and the Sixty-Fourth North Carolina were together in a command led by Colonel John B. Palmer. The situation in western North Carolina was so chaotic that winter that Governor Vance took the extreme step of asking the Secretary of War to appeal to Federal authorities for help in controlling the lawless area.[2] In Henderson County deserters and Tories were unchecked. Conditions were deplorable. Residents were either going into Federal service or fleeing to avoid Confederate duty. The enemy was arming people to further resist the Confederate forces. There was little sense in recruiting there: Colonel Palmer's forces were too small to be of any help, and Confederate authorities may as well withdraw and let the residents remain peacefully in their homes, as they would cause little trouble there on the South Carolina border.[3]

In their only recorded engagement with the enemy, nearly 600 men of the regiments were surrendered to a Federal force when about to be surrounded at Cumberland Gap, TN, in September 1863. That decision was controversial. The Brigadier who made the decision, John W. Frazer of Mississippi, said his troops were inexperienced, lacked discipline and were of questionable loyalty.[4]

Sixty-Second Regiment

The first recorded death sentence affecting an enrollee in the regiment was not made known until July 1864, two years after the regiment was formed. Death sentences for 3 others followed in 1865. Even with consideration that regimental records may have been lost in the defeat at Cumberland Gap, and that thereafter the Sixty-Second was a relatively small unit, the lack of records of severe punishment is not consistent with the indicated level of desertion, side switching, and random wandering about. The paucity of punishment likely reflects a general disorganization, men coming and going at will, and an overall lack of discipline. AIGO documents do offer that 28 men of the Sixty-Second were tried by military courts; none were acquitted, all but 3 of the trials occurred in 1864–1865. Company F, Rutherford County; Company B, Clay County; and Company K, Transylvania County, account for 60 percent of the total courts. Company F had 218 men enrolled during the war; service records list 65 unauthorized absences, 54 of these before the surrender at Cumberland Gap. No record of a court-martial for any of the 54 absentees has been found. Death in Federal prison camps came for 33 men of the company.

Sixty-Fourth Regiment

Originally formed as the Eleventh Infantry Battalion by Lieutenant Colonel Lawrence M. Allen, the unit was authorized to increase to full regimental strength in mid-1862. It then operated in the border area of Tennessee and North Carolina, an area where divided loyalty fostered violence and cruel passion, family to family, cabin to cabin. Military service for Colonel Allen was clouded by accusations of improper conduct centering on his use of his position for personal profit. In 1862, he was court-martialed for concealing the absence of an officer under direct questioning by a superior as to the facts surrounding the absence.[5] A second court-martial in August 1863 concerning the Colonel's acceptance of payments from men seeking substitutes led to his resignation in June 1864.[6] The Colonel was not alone, 18 officers of the regiment went before examination boards in 1863 and 1864; 17 were found to be incompetent to perform the duties of their rank.[7] One of the 17 was judged as "utterly incompetent."

Officers and men of the Sixty-Fourth were involved in the infamous Shelton Laurel, Madison County, massacre in January 1863. Regimental officers gave direct orders to shoot 12 men and boys and 1 woman in retribution for an earlier attack on the town of Marshall, Madison County. Shelton Laurel is less than 15 miles to the north of Marshall. Lieutenant Colonel James A. Keith of the Sixty-Fourth, ironically a physician there in Madison, was deemed accountable for the tragedy. He resigned from the service in April 1863. Among those killed were 4 deserters from his regiment, though this is not emphasized in accounts which focus more on the brutal nature of the mountain war.[8] Men with the Shelton family name made up 7 of the 13 dead; 3 others with that name were jailed in Madison following the confrontation.

Company officers of the Sixty-Fourth were not overly vigorous in bringing charges against their men. From March 1863 to March 1865, AIGO records reflect that just 25 men of the Sixty-Fourth were charged with military crimes and taken before military courts; 4 were acquitted. Half of these men were from Company B, Henderson County; Company E, Polk County; and Company D, Madison County. Company B, for example, had a wartime enrollment of 152 men. There were 55 recorded absences before the surrender at Cumberland Gap in September 1863, but the first man did not go before a military court until December 1864. All of those in the regiment who received death sentences were from the Madison County area. The first of these trials began in June 1864, the last in March 1865.

Courts-Martial

JAMES M. HANEY 64-D (June 29, 1864). Private Haney enrolled in Captain Dewees' Company D, Sixty-Fourth Regiment, in July 1862 and then deserted on April 12, 1863. He avoided arrest for a year but was taken before a court gathered on June 29, 1864. A death sentence by the court went to General Hood for review and approval, but only after an unexplained delay of three months. The next entry in the record of Private Haney reveals that he is at Salisbury Military Prison, NC. While confined there, the prisoner wrote to the Secretary of War.

> J. C. Breckinridge, Esqr. Salisbury March 24, 1865 Respected Sir. I have been a prisoner here for nearly 8 months and have not yet heard my sentence or whether there was nay against me.

The clerk at Head Quarters told me that there was no papers at this place saying anything about my case. The parties that were taken up with me and tried for the same offense (going home for the first time) have been released and went to their commands. By attending to this at your earliest convienence you will greatly oblige. Your with Respect J. M. Haney Co D. 64th NC Troops.[9]

Within a week of the plea to the Cabinet member the determination was made that General Order #2 applied to the imprisoned Private and he was returned to duty by authority of SO #78, April 1, 1865, AIGO.

HENRY RAMSEY 62-F (July 8, 1864). Private Ramsey enlisted in the Sixty-Second on July 21, 1862, and was captured by the enemy at Zollicoffer, TN, on December 30, 1862. After being officially exchanged, Private Ramsey did not return to duty and was considered a deserter. In mid-1864, on July 8, he was court-martialed for his long absence. The resulting death sentence was directed to General Hood on September 17. Apparently General Hood made a decision similar to that in the case of Private Haney, and this led to Private Ramsey being confined at the Salisbury Military Prison. While there he was admitted to the hospital on February 1, and there he died on Saint Valentine's Day 1865.

A member of the regiment describes an encounter with a small gang of apparent deserters: "The Toreys havnt got me yet. I havent any thing new to write to you at this time We killed one man yesterday he was in the wodes and started to run he was shot thru the head his name was Blackburn thare was 4 of them in a gang we got them all we still get a pen of them."[10] It is not stated that the man killed was a deserter, or that he was armed and resisted arrest, but by running he gave some legitimacy to his killing. No man with a Blackburn family name was enrolled in the Sixty-Second or the Sixty-Fourth, but families with that name are common in the area of Wilkes County.

JACKSON CODY 64-C (December 1864). Private Cody enlisted on the first day of 1863 and deserted on April Fools' Day the same year. His service records show that he was present for duty during the second half of 1863. That accepted, he then deserted a second time. The first desertion may have been treated rather lightly, as it occurred while Private Cody was in his home county of Madison. The second desertion resulted in a court-martial at the conclusion of which Private Cody was ordered to be executed. On review, it was decided that General Order #2 also applied in his case, and he was released to duty on issuance of SO #53, March 4, 1865, AIGO. A younger brother, Private Pierce Cody, enrolled in the same regiment and deserted on the same day as Private Jackson Cody and had no further record. Two other brothers, Privates Stephen and William Cody, also enrolled in the Sixty-Fourth; they had desertion attempts, but no court appearance, on their records.

JOSEPH JOLLY 62-F (January 10, 1865). Colonel Robert G. A. Love enrolled Private Jolly in the Sixty-Second in July 1862. Five months of service ended when he was captured in December 1862. The repatriated prisoner deserted on May 21, 1863, while near Greenville, TN. Nineteen months later Private Jolly appeared before a court-martial on January 10, 1865. The time and circumstance surrounding his return are not known, but the court sentence was that he should be shot. On March 4, 1865, SO #53, AIGO released Private Jolly from his death sentence and restored him to duty. Private Noah Jolly, an older brother, enrolled, was captured by the enemy, and deserted on the same dates as Private Joseph Jolly. Following his trial, Private Noah Jolly was sentenced to twelve months at hard labor with a ball and chain attached to his leg.

PERRY ROGERS 64-D (January 27, 1865). Private Rogers served a year after enrollment in July 1862 but then deserted. For his long absence he answered to a court on January 27, 1865, was convicted of desertion, and was given a death sentence. Release from this sentence was directed under authority of General Order #2. This was announced in SO #53, March 4, 1865, AIGO. Private William Rogers joined Company D at the same time as Private Perry Rogers and deserted on the same day. No punishment record for Private William Rogers has been found.

H. D. WHITMIRE 62-K (March 6, 1865). Private Whitmire served in the Sixty-Second for about four months before being granted a sickness furlough. He did not return when the furlough expired and was considered absent without leave after June 14, 1863. The absent man may have returned to duty in late 1863, or he may have prolonged his absence; the record is not clear, but seems to support the first view. It is clear that he was in serious trouble when he was court-martialed in March 1865. He was charged with desertion, harboring and protecting the enemy, and giving correspondence and intelligence to the enemy. The court found the prisoner guilty on the first and third charges, but guilt was not established for the second. On presidential review, the determination was made that the evidence on the third charge was not persuasive and that the amnesty offered in General Order #2 applied to the first charge. Cleared of all charges, he was released and restored to duty by SO #69, March 24, 1865, AIGO.[11] Private Whitmire survived the last few days of the conflict.

NATHANIEL ANDERSON 64-C (Prior to April 8, 1865). Private Anderson was absent without leave for a brief period around the Christmas season of 1862, five months after joining his regiment. The Private returned from this absence and stayed with his company until June 10, 1863, when he decided to desert while near Clinton, TN. It was not until the last weeks of the war that he was court-martialed on a charge of desertion, with three specifications. He was found guilty of the charge and on all three specifications and sentenced to death. The sentence was not officially published until April 8, 1865, and no further action was recorded in those chaotic days. Three brothers, Privates Robert, James and Green Anderson, enlisted in Company C along with Private Nathaniel Anderson. An entry in Private Robert Anderson's service record indicates that he ran away three times. Not unexpectedly, considering the turmoil in Virginia, the court-martial of Private Nathaniel Anderson was not recorded by the AIGO.

JOSHUA ORR 62-E (Prior to April 8, 1865). Private Orr survived capture by the enemy and an accidental wound before deserting the Sixty-Second toward year's end in 1863. He does not again appear in Confederate records until GO #8, April 8, 1865, Army of Tennessee, then at Smithfield, NC. The order informs that Private Orr has been found guilty of three specifications under a desertion charge and that he is to be "hanged by the neck with a rope, between the heaven and the earth, till he is dead."[12] The sentence was reviewed and approved by General Johnston, but no other information has been located in military or civil records. A sentence of death by hanging would normally be given for a traitorous act, perhaps captured while fighting with the enemy, or giving some form of aid and assistance to them. Such sentences were usually carried into effect rather promptly, within a matter of a day or two. But then, so close to the end, who can say what might have happened. The court record for Private Orr was not posted in AIGO records. There were 10 Orr men in the Sixty-Second, 8 enrolling within a few days of each other in July 1862. Private Joshua Orr and his brothers comprise the bulk of the lot. Death claimed 3 brothers and 3 others were captured in the debacle at Cumberland Gap in 1863.

Summary

The 8 men of Palmer's brigade who were sentenced to be executed were all volunteers. The oldest was thirty-four years on enrollment, the youngest eighteen. They were drawn from an enrollment of 3,000 in the two regiments, approximately 1,600 in the Sixty-Second and 1,400 in the Sixty-Fourth. Men left the regiments in large numbers beginning in November of 1862 and extending through the first half of 1863, with the departures culminating in a final burst in May and June of that year. A count of those present at the final surrender is not available. These regiments offer another example of the difficulty of maintaining a cohesive fighting force in an area of sharply divided loyalty. The service records for 8 companies show that on average a company experienced 55 absences from a total enrollment of 153 men, the bulk of these absences occurring before the surrender at Cumberland Gap in September 1863. The desire to leave the struggle was not driven by battle related deaths, less than 1 per company. Disease claimed 21 lives per company, two-thirds of them while confined in Federal prison camps far from the mountain hills and hollows.[13]

20

Jackson Brigade

"The mountains are fountains of men"[1]

Thomas Legion

The major portion of the brigade led by Brigadier Alfred Jackson consisted of the Thomas Legion which had a regiment of infantry, a battalion of infantry and a battery of artillery assigned at various times. Initially the legion included 2 companies of men of native Indian heritage, but they were later detached. Also 2 companies were made up of men from nearby counties in Tennessee. In all, there are 38 records of courts-martial concerning the Legion, 33 involving infantrymen and 5 concerning artillerymen; one trial ended in acquittal. Just 3 companies accounted for 21 of the 33 courts for infantrymen. Company E, Haywood County, was charged with 10; 6 to Company I, Cherokee County; and 5 for Company H, Cherokee County. All of these trials took place between March 1863 and November 1864. Trials for 5 resulted in 4 severe sentences of one or two years of hard labor; and one acquittal.

Courts-Martial

WILLIAM R. SILVEY T/L-K (November 10, 1863). Private Silvey enlisted at Winters Gap, TN, in February 1863. Less than six weeks later he deserted while still in that area. An entry in his service record dated a year later reads, "Deserted–Captured in arms with enemy–Shot." Nothing further is recorded, neither the date of the execution, nor the surrounding circumstances. He was afforded the perfunctory formality of a court-martial and not shot out of hand. The record of his trial was posted in AIGO ledgers. No mention is made as to why Private Silvey was shot rather than hanged, the usual punishment when deserters are captured bearing arms in the service of the enemy. Two other men with the Silvey name, Private James M. Silvey and Private Peter Silvey, served in the same company. They also deserted and one or both went over to the enemy around April 6, 1864, five months after the execution of Private William Silvey.[2] Comments made by a company officer in the legion may refer to his execution: "Around Blountsville A Painful example of discipline was made here one poor fellow of Co. K a Tennessean with 2 others of Tenn troops captured at Rogersville by Gen W. E. Jones in the uniform of the enemy were court-martialed and shot at stake."[3] Other references included with this statement would place the execution time as late 1863 or early 1864, which is consistent with the court-martial date of Private Silvey.

EZEKIEL B. CRISP T/L-H (May 23, 1864). Private Crisp was present from enlistment in July 1862 through the January–February period of 1863, when he was listed as a deserter. In May he was again identified as a deserter, along with the note that he deserted from Sevier County, TN, on April 6, 1863, apparently his second try at desertion. If so, it was also short-lived, for two weeks later Private Crisp went before a military court charged with desertion. He was found guilty as charged and sentenced to be shot. The day for his execution was set for the second Friday after receipt of the order by the officer directed to carry the sentence into effect, June 10, or June 17, the most likely dates. All this became moot, however, when Private Crisp escaped from his guard on June 8. From the record it seems that deserter and escapee avoided both Federal and Confederate captors until March 1865, when he became a Federal prisoner of war. Safe in their hands, he took the oath on the condition that he would stay north of the Ohio River for the remainder of the war. When taking the Federal Oath, Private Crisp said that he was conscripted into Confederate service.

MANSEL F. CRISP T/L-H (May 23, 1864). Private M. Crisp was absent without leave from his company in January and February 1863 but returned to duty on March 2. The short absence began six months after enrollment in July 1862. On April 6, he deserted while in Sevier County, TN, along with Private E. B. Crisp. Private Mansel Crisp was also given a death sentence following his court-martial. How he avoided execution is not known. One record states that he was captured by Federal troops in September and then exchanged in October 1864. It would seem that if he was still under sentence of the court at that time, he would not have agreed to repatriation. In any event, the returnee once again deserted the Confederate cause in December and was a Federal prisoner in March 1865 when he took the oath. When signing the form, he also made the point that he had been conscripted into service.

WILLIAM TIPTON WALKER'S BATTALION-E (May 23, 1864). Private Tipton enrolled in Walker's battalion, Thomas Legion, on September 25, 1862, and served therein until he was absent without leave in March or April 1863. There is no information in his service record on his return, but he went before a court on May 23, 1864, and was sentenced to be shot. The court relented and recommended clemency for the man they had just condemned. Their recommendation was accepted, and Private Tipton returned to duty. Within six months he again took his leave. Now experienced in the ways of a military court and having once received their blessing, he took the prudent path of going directly to the enemy, and there he took the oath.

Men enrolled in companies of the Thomas Legion died from disease or cause unknown far more often than they did in action. Company F, for example, had 1 man killed in fighting, and 15 dead from disease or cause unknown. Three other companies lost, on average, 7 men to disease and 1 in combat.[4] Company F listed 210 men on their rolls; over 50 were transferred to another company in September 1862. Approximately the same number absented themselves, virtually all doing so after the transfers.

Considering the Thomas Legion a regiment, there were 7 regiments of men from the North Carolina–Tennessee mountain area who fought their war not far from home. From these regiments, 43 men were sentenced to be executed for military crimes, 16 were executed. While the fate of 3 of the condemned is not clearly established, indications are that only 1 was executed, giving a total of 17 executions for the 7 regiments. From that same area, 2 regiments fought in the eastern armies of the Confederacy. They recorded 12 death sentences with 6 executions.[5] The mountains were fountains of men and blood.

Part IV. Attached Units and Local Defense

21

Cavalry

"Cannot a few men be shot"[1]

Not all Confederates held the cavalry in high esteem: "Our cavalry are a set of miserable disorganized thieves ... with few exceptions disgraced our army ... both by cowardice and promiscuous plundering committed on our own people."[2] Though the writer was referring to cavalry under the command of General Nathan Bedford Forrest, there is little reason to believe that his opinion was not reflective of many that lived in areas where the cavalry was active. Besides his woes with conscripts and deserters, the Governor of North Carolina also had to contend with "the plague" of the Confederate cavalry. In December 1863, the bedeviled executive appealed to Secretary James A. Sedden to do something to control their depredations: "Cannot a few men be shot for participating in these outrages, as an example."[3] Some held the opinion that a Confederate cavalry unit in the field was as great a threat to civilians as they were to the enemy. In June 1864, Major General Joseph Wheeler issued General Order #4 to his cavalrymen: "Demagogues have falsely told you that discipline meant harsh words, harsh treatment and haughty bearing on the part of your officers.... Discipline is the good soldier's greatest friend and protector.... Discipline requires the timid to march into action shoulder to shoulder with our brave men, who otherwise alone bear the brunt of the contest, while the timid skulker lags back to screen himself from danger.... Discipline prevents the straggling of a few bad men, who may commit outrages upon your families and other citizens, rendering your homes desolate and stigmatizing a thousand good soldiers by the bad conduct of a single man.... When crime, neglect, or misconduct, however slight is committed punishment must follow; its certainty alone can establish discipline."[4]

An estimated 8,500 men and boys were able to obtain mounts on which they would engage both the enemy and their fellow citizens while enrolled in one of 6 North Carolina cavalry regiments. Perhaps another 1,000 men and boys joined battalions and companies. Cavalry made up 7 percent of North Carolinians enrolled in Confederate forces. Existing AIGO records show that the North Carolina cavalry commands experienced at least 104 military trials; 17 resulted in a death sentence for a trooper, and 13 were acquitted. Seven troopers were executed. Courts for cavalrymen are 4 percent of those for all North Carolina troops. The percentage of death sentences for cavalrymen at trial, 16 percent, is approximately the same as for those "awaiding in the mud." More than 20 cavalrymen were killed by the accidental discharge of a weapon, in camp rows or while resisting arrest.

Ninth Regiment, First Cavalry

The first recorded court concerning the Ninth was held in December 1861, the last, three years later in December 1864. In the interval, 27 men of the regiment went before the highest level military tribunal, 3 received death sentences; 4 were acquitted. Company G, the Buncombe Rangers; Company A, Ashe County; and Company B, Northampton County, accounted for half of all courts. Every company of the regiment had men at trial. Trooper John Carver, was killed without trial while resisting arrest in North Carolina. Another was killed by "Tories" while at home to secure a horse. Justification for leaving the regiment surfaced as early as December 1862. First saying that the health of the regiment was good, Private Alfred Adams continued, "Notwithstanding they are half naked and barefooted there is some considerable grumbling about the way they are treated but my doctrine is submit to any [not legible] rather than to Lincoln."[5] Another trooper objected to "the rigid rules and harsh measures" they experienced.[6]

Confederate and Federal alike committed acts of barbarity on wounded defenseless soldiers, a prisoner who had put down his weapon, a person by chance there in the path of anger. A cavalryman in the Ninth related how civilians were assaulted and their property destroyed. A captured Confederate, apparently wounded and defenseless, was killed with his head battered beyond recognition by Federal troops. At the next opportunity, the cavalrymen retaliated by killing every retreating infantryman they could overtake.[7] One participant revealed an instance when he saved the life of a Federal prisoner who was but moments from being killed by a man of the Ninth.[8] Other incidents of fighting and killing among members of the regiment are described and the reflection made, "In the midst of arms, laws are silent."[9] But the laws of the Confederate military were not entirely silent for men of the Ninth.

Nineteenth Regiment, Second Cavalry

Court records for 26 men of the Nineteenth have been found. Company I, organized in Moore County; Company F, from Guilford County; and Company B, Iredell County, accounted for over half of them. Acquittal followed for 6 at trial. The number of courts would have grown by at least one if the Captain of Company H had his way. On July 31, 1864, Captain S. N. Buxton addressed the commanding officer at Plymouth, NC: "Henry O. Powell 2nd N.C. Cav captured and at Plymouth in hospital deserted last winter — has been serving Yankees ever since — inform of his where abouts."[10] No record has been found to show that the requested information was provided or that the deserter and turncoat was punished.

A regimental historian labeled the appointment of the regimental Colonel as political in nature. He continued, "Let me say in the beginning this regiment did not have the same thorough military training that the First Cavalry had, as well as other regiments commanded by old army officers."[11] Support for this expression is found in the comment of an enrolled soldier: "Our company and Capt is the best in camp and knows more than the Colonel himself and the Adjutant is an idiot."[12] The writer goes on to say that captured Federal soldiers are leading regimental drilling and then, "We don't like the Colonel." The regiment he led was formed in November 1861; the Colonel resigned in March 1862. Regimental shortcomings were not entirely his fault; four months after entering service they were still not equipped with Confederate manufactured sabers. This led Governor H. T. Clark to tell the Secretary of War that the state had gone to great expense to buy swords locally but they "proved worthless." The Governor concluded: "If you can let them have sabers they will be useful. They have been many months in your service without arms, and consequently are almost useless, though drawing pay and rations."[13] The remark is illustrated by an incident at a fortified house in Onslow County. In that minor engagement very few troopers heeded the command, "Charge." This caused Colonel R. B. Ransom to recommend that the officers involved be reduced and imprisoned and that the troopers be dismounted and disarmed. "To keep such troops in the presence of the enemy would be useless [and] criminal."[14] General Lee offered the reasoned response that the recommendation would require many courts-martial, thus it was better to maintain the regiment and give more training to officers and men.[15]

Forty-First Regiment, Third Cavalry

Few records of courts-martial have been located for the Third Cavalry, 5, and 1 is an acquittal. But one of the more forthright decisions put forth by a military court is found among that small number, this for Private Benjamin Patterson of Company K, who for some infraction was ordered to sit astride a pole while wearing a placard labeled, "Jackass."[16] A more serious crime is found for a trooper with the ironic family name Faithful. He deserted and was shot and killed while resisting those sent to arrest him in January 1864 in Edgecombe County.[17] A few days following this incident, charges were placed against a trooper of the Forty-First for committing one of the most serious of military offenses, joining and fighting in the ranks of the enemy.

Fifty-Ninth Regiment, Fourth Cavalry

Cavalrymen of the regiment went to trial at the highest level of military courts on 10 occasions. A death sentence, but no acquittals, resulted from these trials. The men who went to trial were evenly distributed over Companies A through E. A deserter from the regiment enrolled in a Federal command, the Eleventh Pennsylvania Cavalry, and was tried, convicted and executed after deserting their ranks.[18]

Sixty-Third Regiment, Fifth Cavalry

The Fifth Cavalry was organized as Partisan Rangers under an act of Congress enacted in April 1862. One attraction to the Rangers was that they were allowed to keep property seized from the enemy. The act was repealed in February 1864. General Lee offered his opinion that it was impossible to have discipline in such organizations.[19] The Fifth led all other North Carolina cavalry commands with 33 general courts-martial. An acquittal ended 1 trial, 1 court issued a death sentence, and 8 issued severe sentences. The toll might have been greater, a regimental historian recalled: "More men went to Company Q than were wounded or killed."[20] Company Q refers to men who were absent because of alleged sickness and those who absented themselves, some with the intention of joining the enemy.[21] A trooper in Company A wrote, "I am very well satisfied with company. The officers are brave and intelligent and the men are all well educated and gentlemanly."²² A trooper advised a friend: "Tell Newtons ... if he has to gon to get him a good horse and come to Captain Boos [Captain W. H. Booes, Company H, Sixty-Third] company for it is a heap better than to be afoot awaiding in the mud to his knees."²³ Others were demoralized by the horror of war: "There lay the dead of the previous day entirely naked and most of them partially eaten up by hogs. It was calculated to unnerve the stoutest heart."²⁴

Infantrymen of all rank had a poor opinion of the cavalry: "Footmen did not appreciate the man on horseback."²⁵ General D. H. Hill had an expressed dislike for the cavalry. He would like to see "a dead man with spurs on."²⁶ His verbal sword cut a wider swath: "In the whole brigade of cavalry there has been but one man killed in the war. I propose to have a magnificent monument erected in his memory."²⁷

Foretelling that a large measure of disciplinary action would be needed in the Fifth Cavalry, a trooper wrote home early in November 1862: "James I would rote to you some time ago but I have been trouble a little in camp our comp and the officers are A[t] war and are still yet and I do not no when it will be settled, we are too hard for them an allways will be our comp stick too gether an tha can do any thing."²⁸ Men of Company K vigorously objected to serving in a Partisan Ranger battalion that was led by a Virginian and included several companies of men from that state.²⁹ The company led all regimental companies with 16 appearances before a court-martial. Company D, the Rockingham Rangers, followed with 9. Company E, Chatham County, had 3 men court-martialed.

Sixty-Fifth Regiment, Sixth Cavalry

With a record of only 10 courts, it is surprising to find that 7 ended with death sentences. There was 1 acquittal. Company I, formed in Madison County; Company A, recruited in Johnson County, Tennessee; and Company D, Henderson County, were responsible for 6 of the 10 courts. It should be noted that despite the few courts, desertion was a problem. The Sixty-Fifth led all North Carolina cavalry regiments with 31 absences per company.³⁰ Of the 17 cavalrymen threatened with execution, 7 were from the Sixty-Fifth. The Fifth and Seventh battalions of North Carolina Cavalry were initially formed with men recruited in western North Carolina and in Tennessee. The battalions were consolidated into the Sixty-Fifth Regiment in August of 1863. Dissatisfaction with the consolidation was a factor in many desertions, based on the close proximity of the events in records of individual soldiers. Men who were absent did not report to their new command; men who were present soon departed. When volunteering for service, these men enrolled in North Carolina units of company size. They objected to being assigned to a regiment that included companies of Virginians and was led by a Virginian.³¹

An officer in the Sixty-Fifth, Captain Julius Gash of Company E, voiced his opinion of deserters in the fall of 1863. First explaining:

> My company has about "gave up" too! all deserted or at home without leave. Twenty five men of our Regt started home about a week ago but were nearly all aprehended! Two of my Company among them. Gen Buckner says he intends shooting every man of them and I do hope to God he will.... Should all thinxgs work to-gether for good and I live to see this difficulty adjusted there is a day when Ill get revenge from deserters Mark it ! You are probably tired of this subject and so am I for when I think of a deserter I get so mad it bothers me to keep

from saying <u>Cuss words</u> .... I have learned during this war that there is no Confidence to be placed in white men. I'll swear men have deserted my Company who I had the most implicit confidence in and men who had been for near twelve months good soldiers as I thought was in the Confederate Army. I naturally [not legible] for a deserter, and men who will at this particular time desert. I do candidly think aught to be shot. I think it is nothing more than what they justly merit. Why! Confound a man who is void enough principal to desert his Country in so perilous a time as now.[32]

The number of men who were "void enough principal to desert" the Sixty-Fifth was unabated a year later. The Captain of Company I resigned his commission because "my command has deserted to the enemy and to the mountains of western NC and after attempting I find it impossible to get them together."[33]

Desertion from the Sixty-Fifth reached such proportion in May 1864 that Colonel G. N. Folk wrote to Colonel J. B. Palmer, district commander at Asheville, NC, asking that 116 deserters from the Sixty-Fifth be arrested and returned to their proper command. Colonel Folk pointed out those men who were either at home or had enrolled in the Thomas Legion, a violation of the Articles of War, though apparently condoned by officers of the legion.[34] The ability of the Sixty-Fifth to maneuver about the mountain region was severely restricted due to the number of men leaving the regiment. The Colonel of the regiment offered a clear expression as to why. He said that his regiment "contains large elements of disloyalty. During service at least two-thirds of its number have been absent without leave and the disloyalty of the country from which they were raised has so increased ... could never move my regiment through that country without loosing half of its number."[35] The regiment was at that time at about one-third of its authorized strength. Despite their troubles, a trooper in Company D felt that he could "knock a bull down," and that he was going to "take care of number one." He went on that he was living like a "Yellow Dog," that he was "sound as a rock in a <u>shuck-pen</u>."[36]

Colonel Folk later had his own encounter with civil law when he was called to answer charges that he was responsible for the death of alleged bushwhackers when commanding the Sixty-Fifth. The claim was settled when Colonel Folk paid $800 dollars to the father of the man that was killed.[37]

Courts-Martial

DAVID CLIFTON 9-B (April 21, 1862). Private Clifton volunteered for duty on August 21, 1861, at Plymouth, NC. While at Camp Ransom near Kinston on April 13, 1862, he left his company and was absent for three days before being arrested. For this absence of seventy-two hours, usually treated as absent without leave, he was tried on desertion charges within a week of his return and sentenced to be shot. This was made known in GO #24, April 30, 1862, Department of North Carolina. No statement was inserted that two-thirds of the court concurred on the death sentence, and this oversight was pointed out in the published order.[38] The error negated the decision of the court and the youthful prisoner was released to return to his company. Nothing more is known of his war experience.

The reaction to military punishment varied widely from trooper to trooper. Some viewed an execution with relative disinterest. Others were deeply affected by a slight infliction of pain, and a substantial degree of humiliation. One such incident is described:

> Well Richard I saw one of the awfulest sights yesterday that I ever saw in my life a man mustered out of service he belong to 1st cavelry he had deserted was the crime that he had

comited they shaved one side of his head and marched him through every Regiment in the Brigade with his crime rote in large lettes on a peace of paper and tact to his back (Deserter) with ten or a dozen men on horse back after him with swoards and horns a making the ugliest noise that they cold make on their horns I dont think there will be any deserters from our Regiment it seemed to hurt the feelings of all that saw it I never want to to see such a sight again he bareheaded in the hot sun for half a day.[39]

The humiliated man was likely Private William Savage, Company G, who was court-martialed on May 6, 1862, and sentenced to the punishment that so impressed the young man.

MICHAEL BRYANT 63-D (December 10, 1862). Private Bryant enrolled in Company D on July 7, 1862. The recruit deserted just ten weeks later, on September 30, and was in arrest and at trial on December 10. Death was the court's decision. The sentence was carried into effect on January 14, 1863. One source states that the executed man was a substitute, which suggests that he had departed from other commands, thus accounting for execution following an absence of not much more than a month. However, an order issued by the brigade commander indicates that Private Bryant was executed for the one short-lived desertion.[40] The Brigadier may have wanted to use the occasion to forcefully impress that any desertion attempt might end in death for a convicted soldier. Brigadier General Beverly H. Robertson issued a general order on the day following the execution.

> HeadQtrs 2nd Cavalry Brigade, Jan 15, 1863 General Order No__ It becomes the painful duty of the Genl Comd to announce to his Brigade that on yesterday the 14th inst: in accordance with the sentence of a General Court Martial, Michael Bryant Co. "D," 63rd Regt C. Cavalry was shot to death for desertion. He did not desert to the enemy. He committed no greater offence than scores of this Brigade, now at their homes, are committing. Impressed with the sacredness of the cause we are defending, and the belief that success depends upon the individual exertion of every soldier engaged in its behalf, the Genl Comdg wishes it understood that he will spare no effort in bringing to trial all the base & cowardly traitors, who without the shadow of authority, or excuse have absented themselves from their Companies. All officer, and good citizens are requested to assist in arresting these men, so they can be punished as the law directs. By Order of Brig Genl B. H. Robertson.[41]

The execution made a significant impression on a private in the regiment.

> I have nothing of much importance to write you at present though I have witnessed one thing that I shall not forget the longest day I live and it was the death of a man by the name of Mr. Michael J. Bryant. He was a deserter of the Sixty-Third Regiment of Partisan Rangers. He was a private in Company D in Captain Galervery [Galloway] Company. He deserted the flag of his country twice before the last time. He was arrested and tried and was condemned to be shot. He was shot the 14th of this month at Camp White, two miles from Kinston. William M. Johnson, R. O. Brown, John Robertson, George Hughes, was the men detailed out of our company to shoot him. It seemed that he did not mind it the least in the world. He was a substitute and an Irishman in the Burgaw South Carolina.[42]

The letter was signed William M. Johnson, and is one of the few comments from a soldier who fired his musket at an execution. The writer has little emotion, does not directly refer to his participation, nor give any insight as to his feelings. There was no personal involvement; Private Bryant went to his death in a nonchalant and seemingly unconcerned manner. After all, he was an Irish substitute from South Carolina and well deserving punishment. It did not matter much to Private Bryant, so why should it trouble Private Johnson? The twenty-seven-year-old executioner from Guilford County was killed in battle in June 1864.

Fear of execution added to the prospect of no furloughs was a deterrent to at least one man of the regiment who was sure that he would return from any leave that he might be granted.

> I will get home in a few weeks I will come by [not legible] and bring that wool and you must try and get some of [not legible] fore to make me some socks and drores and try and have it wove if you can so tha will be ready Sarah I wod to stay at home with you but if I get home I will haft to come back gain fore tha are shooting men every few days fore running away and s[t]aying over there time and I dont want to be taken up if I can hep it fore if a man will do write he will fare a heap better the next time he want to gon home tha wont let pink Mabery gon home because he stad so long before.[43]

The letter was apparently written on one of the spoils of war. Stamped in bold letters is the name of the former owner, J. D. Hornbeck, Co. B. 120. N.Y. Another family member expressed similar sentiments: "They is deserters plenty and they are hunting them steady for some now and they are killing our men right smart I tell you I would rather stande my chance in the Army than in the bushes for they are going to have them now and they is some of them I want them to get."[44]

WILSON RAY 65-I (Prior March 1863). Private Ray mustered with Company A, Fifth Battalion Cavalry, on June 15, 1862. He was officially enrolled about a month before that date. Some time prior to March 1863 he deserted, was court-martialed and was executed on March 27, 1863. No court-martial record has been located but a statement in Private Ray's service record, "Died March 27 1863 under sentence of court-martial for desertion," is decisive.

THOMAS BUNCH 19-K (January 14, 1864). Private Bunch agreed to ride with the cavalry on November 11, 1861. Capture by the enemy and exchange followed in mid-1862. In October, he deserted his company and stayed in desertion for the next fourteen months — until December 21, 1863. Three weeks after his return he went to trial, was convicted on a desertion charge, and GO #9, January 27, 1864, Army of Northern Virginia, ordered that he be shot in seven days. A series of special orders delayed and then suspended execution. While confined, he volunteered to join Winder's Legion in the defense of Richmond in August 1864. This act of fidelity resulted in a full pardon for him and an end to his service record.

BENJAMIN L. MOSS 9-E (January 15, 1864). Private Moss enlisted on August 10, 1861. He was hospitalized in July 1862 when a forefinger was shot off; no mention is made that it was considered self-inflicted. Whatever the case, Private Moss was thereafter absent from his command. On November 17, 1862, he was officially classified as a deserter, but it was not until year's end 1863 that he was in confinement awaiting trial. The trial took place on January 15, 1864, and the result was a death sentence, as put forth in GO #9, January 27, 1864, Army of Northern Virginia. After some delay, SO #107, May 7, 1864, AIGO commuted the death sentence to one of hard labor for the remainder of the war. Three months after the commutation of sentence was announced, Private Moss was released from the service on a disability retirement.

ISAAC WOODARD 19-E (January 15, 1864). Private Woodard made his commitment to the Second Cavalry in June 1861. He violated his oath when he deserted while near Kinston on September 12, 1862. It was not until the following July that he was arrested and brought back to his regiment. Two days after his forced return he was able to elude his guard and once again set out for home or wood. He was unable to avoid detection as long on this second desertion; he was in arrest and under more watchful guard on August 25, 1863. For some reason he was not taken before a court for four months, until January 15, 1864. At trial, guilt was established and a death sentence followed. While the proceedings in his case were being reviewed, he was confined to Castle Thunder. There he volunteered to aid in the defense of Richmond in August 1864. Thereafter, he was pardoned of his crimes.

WILLIAM IRVING HILL 41-K (February 9, 1864). Private Hill volunteered for cavalry service on May 16, 1862. In late December 1863, he returned to his home to get clothing and while at home was either captured by the enemy or made the decision to join them. Soon thereafter, whether coerced or of his own free will, he enrolled in the Second NCUV and was captured by Confederate forces. As discussed, men from the Sixty-Sixth Regiment and a scattering of others were also involved in the change of allegiance that ended at Beech Grove, NC. Private Hill was hanged at Kinston on February 22, 1864. His case may have been one of the weaker prosecutions put to the court. A rather weak case was also presented for the man who fell from the trap along with him, conscript Elijah Kellum. A fellow cavalryman in the regiment gives some background information on the circumstances leading to the execution of Private Hill.

> Irvin Hill who rode the other horse of mine, had permission to go home in Chocowinity, to get some clothes & to report to the Regt at Kinston the Sunday night that I was home. He did not leave when his time was out and the Yankees came out and captured him & horse the same night (Sunday). It is quite a loss ... have already gone to look for another.[45]

The comment, with major emphasis on the loss of the horse, was made in mid–January, two weeks before Private Hill was captured and a month before he dropped beneath the gallows trap. The owner of the horse was killed in a skirmish some six months after the death of Private Hill. His letters were not without humor. When asked how an acquaintance "looked," he wrote, "He has got to be about as ugly as a white man aught ever to become."[46] In the congressional inquiry into the events at Kinston after the war, the comment was noted that Private Hill was very impenitent when he went to his death.[47]

JAMES C. BRADY 19-I (April 28, 1864). Private Brady enlisted in the Nineteenth on August 8, 1861. In 1862 he was assigned as a courier. The next year, in May or June Private Brady was detailed to secure a replacement mount. When he did not return from the detail, he was considered as being absent without leave. That status was maintained until March 6, 1864, when Captain N. B. Dunlop, Fifth North Carolina Militia, was paid $30 for delivering Private Brady to authorities at Camp Holmes, Raleigh. On April 28, the prisoner went before a court-martial where his guilt was established and he was sentenced to be shot. The decision of the court was announced in GO #45, May 24, 1864, Army of Northern Virginia, but it was not until July 18, that an order was issued to move the condemned man from Castle Thunder to Rufus Barringer's brigade for execution of sentence. Four days later, the sentence was carried into effect. A younger brother, Private Charles Brady, was discharged from the regiment before the execution took place. An older brother, Private Lucas Brady, enrolled in the Nineteenth two weeks after the executed man, and was present for duty through September 1864, two months after the execution of his brother. Comments that soldier-relatives of men who were to be executed were given any special consideration, such as time to visit the condemned or not attend the execution, have not been found.

ELI ROBERTS 19-A (May 2, 1864). Private Roberts signed on for duty in the Second Regiment of cavalry on June 18, 1861. Two years later while in Cherokee County, he deserted, possibly with the intention of going over to a Federal unit. He was charged with being a deserter on May 26, 1863, and continued in that condition until December 20, 1863. At that time he was arrested but was not finally returned to his command until March 13, 1864. On investigation it was noted that while a deserter, in August 1863, it was alleged that he joined other "Robbers, Bushwhackers and Tories under Goldman Bryson," who plundered and murdered loyal citizens of Cherokee County.[48] This particular charge was not sustained when Private Roberts went to trial on May 2, 1864, and it was dropped. But the related charges were sufficient to bring about a death penalty. He was transported under guard from the prison at Richmond, along with Private Brady, and they were executed side by side on July 22. Comments of cavalrymen were simply put: "There was two men shot in our Brigade last Friday of the 2nd regiment NC cavalry for deserting I did not see them as I was on pickett at the time."[49] Another wrote, "There was too men shot to death with musketry on the 22 day of this month for diserting and for staying over there time at home they belong to the 2nd N.C.C. in the same brigade that I do."[50] A staff officer who had a small role in the drama recalled a more moving memory of the executions.

> About this time, two North Carolinians (Tar Heels we called them) were tried by court-martial and ordered executed. Our whole Division apparently was ordered out to witness it. Garnett had to read the death warrant, and I went to help him by holding his horse. Troops were drawn up on three sides of a square, 2 graves were dug and posts set up by them. The deserters were marched around the entire dismounted line of Cavalry. A firing squad of 24 men faced the graves, the deserters were blindfolded and their arms tied behind them to the posts. Garnett read the death sentence. A squad Officer raised his sword and as it dropped, 24 men (half with unloaded muskets, but none knowing if his gun was blank or loaded) fired, and the two deserters hung dead to the posts. I had seen hangings, but this was my first sight of the Firing Squad in action. No doubt these things had to be, but it wasn't pleasant. One of the deserters was an unusually handsome young fellow, and carried his overcoat on his arm as if hoping yet to need it. He had on a pair of home knit gloves, and I couldn't help thinking that his mother had made them.[51]

The young cavalryman carrying his overcoat and wearing homemade gloves must certainly have been James Brady; he cherished his reminder of home and family to the very end.

WILLIAM PLEASANT CRAIG 65-I (July 6, 1864). Private Craig was a man for all branches of service. He first went into Confederate service in the Fourteenth Infantry on May 3, 1861. He was assigned to naval duty on board the CSS *Virginia* (*Merrimac*) on February 18, 1862, three weeks before that warship engaged the USS *Monitor*. Private Craig returned to duty on land when he joined the Seventh Cavalry Battalion, which was later merged into the Sixty-Fifth. On July 18, 1863, while at Sweetwater TN, Private Craig deserted the battalion and avoided return until April 26, 1864, when he was arrested and jailed at Asheville, NC. He went before a court-martial on July 6, 1864, charged with desertion, and a specification that he had aided and abetted the enemy on April 6, 1864, when he took a pistol and other items valued at $400 from a citizen of Asheville. A second specification involved a similar incident in which he took 5 muskets and 5 rifles valued at $250 from another citizen of that place. After a death sentence was published, an appeal was directed to Governor Vance on behalf of Private Craig. Dated August 29, it was prepared by J. L. Bailey at Asheville. He informed the Governor that the convicted private had been sent to Salisbury, that appeals had been directed to Confederate President Davis and that he, Bailey, submitted the matter in order that the Governor could "act in the premises as you may deem most proper."[52] The AIGO was asked for an opinion on the legality of the convicting court; they advised the convening officers that they had the authority to order a court to hear charges against a trooper of the Sixty-Fifth because the regiment was attached to the Army of Tennessee for "strategic Purposes." On September 12, Adjutant General Cooper contacted General Hood in reference to the case of Private Craig. He asked that General Hood review the proceedings as soon as possible and return his finding to the Richmond office. He added that should General Hood approve the execution of Private Craig, he should suspend any further action and that he should acknowledge receipt of the above information. Some portion of General Hood's reply must have rankled the venerable General Cooper, for he admonished, "The protest is harsh and intemperate and has a tendency to reflect upon the Executive through his aide-de-camp. Besides this is no time, when every effort should be devoted to the cause of the Confederacy to indulge in personalities between officers."[53] As can be inferred from these brief remarks, the writing was on the wall. The death sentence imposed on Private Craig was suspended and later remitted, and he was returned to duty.

EPHRAIM J. AMMONS 65-I (July 14, 1864). Private Ammons initially enrolled in Company A, Fifth Battalion Cavalry, on May 31, 1862, and was present when the unit was consolidated into the Sixty-Fifth. But within weeks of the consolidation, the disgruntled trooper decided to leave the new command by deserting on August 15, 1863. The record is not clear, but one possibility is that he returned from this absence, was captured and paroled by the enemy and then began a second desertion. The alternate interpretation is that he was a prisoner of the enemy for most of the absence. In any event, he was court-martialed on July 14, 1864, and given a death sentence. This sentence was forwarded to General Hood for his review, which eventually resulted in a commuted prison sentence of some unknown length. Private Ammons was sent to Salisbury Military Prison. While there he was hospitalized and there he died in December 1864. If the 1850 census record is correct, it was recorded within a few months of Ephraim's birth, he was barely fourteen years when spared the death sentence. His father, Allen Ammons, served as a soldier and as a Chaplain in another regiment of North Carolinians formed in the mountain area.

JAMES HOLLOMAN 59-D (July 18, 1864). Enrolled in July 1862, Private Holloman deserted after two months of duty and was arrested and held in the guardhouse at Franklin, VA. He escaped on October 3, 1862, and later agreed to serve in the New York Third Regiment. He was captured on June 9, 1864, in arms against his former comrades. After trial on July 18, 1864, he was ordered to be hanged in three days. An order was issued that he be moved from Castle Thunder in the custody of Major Bridgeford.[54] No further record has been located. A fair assessment would be that the sentence was carried into effect.

OBEDIAH B. JARRETT 65-I (September 1, 1864). Private Jarrett enrolled in the Fifth Battalion of Cavalry, this on May 14, 1862. He deserted on August 1, while at Concord, TN, just two days before he was officially transferred to the Sixty-Fifth on August 3. Arrest and return to that regiment took place on August 26. Four days later Private Jarrett went before a court-martial, after which appearance a death sentence was forthcoming. Execution of sentence was then suspended awaiting a decision of the President. H. H. Baird prepared a request for pardon directed to President Davis. The death sentence was remitted by SO #260, November 1, 1864, AIGO. A brother, Private Jacob P. Jarrett, also served in Company I of the Sixty-Fifth and was captured a day or two after Private Obediah Jarrett deserted. Another brother, Private Eli H. Jarrett, was an infantryman in the Fifty-Eighth and Sixty-Fourth regiments.

JOBE R. REDMON 65-I (September 6, 1864). Sergeant Redmon initially enrolled as a private in Company A, Fifth Battalion Cavalry, as did Private Jarret. They deserted on August 1, 1863, while at Concord, TN, before consolidation into the Sixty-Fifth was completed. On August 26, they were arrested and taken to the newly formed regiment. A court convened on September 6, heard the facts in the case of Trooper Redmon and agreed on a death sentence. After a delay, the sentence was made known to the prisoner. He began the last few days of his life by writing to tell wife and family of his fate.

> Kinston N C November the 2, 1864 My dear wife and children I seate myself this morning with a troubbeled harte and a destrest mind to try to rite a few line to let you no that I hird my sentens red yesterday and hit was very bad I am very sory to let you no for [one line not legible] all ready I hafte to bee shot the 9 of this month I am sory to in form you that I have but 7 days to live But I hope and trust in God when they have slane my body that God will take my sould to rest.[55]

The letter continues for several pages on raising the children and other family matters, and that he would like to see his wife one more time and hopes that she can come to see him and suggests a person that could accompany her, if she decides to make the trip. The signature on the letter is J. R. Redmond [sic]. A request for assistance from Governor Vance that was prepared by H. H. Baird, included pleas for each of the condemned men. The appeal pointed out that the men were misled when joining the Sixty-Fourth while enrolled in the Sixty-Fifth, and were promised fair treatment by a Captain in the Sixty-Fourth. The writer of the memorial to the Governor ended with the statement, "By complying with the above request by you will confer a great favor on your friend and Cousin." An added postscript "P.S. The day has not as yet been appointed for the execution of Private Obediah Jarrett."[56] The letter is interesting in several regards. First, the omission of Sergeant Redmon suggests that his day of execution was known. Second, the name of Private Jarrett is written over what appears to be the name "Redmond," verifying that the Sergeant was deliberately excluded from the statement. And lastly, Private Jarrett was court-martialed five days before Sergeant Redmon so the delay in his day of execution order suggests that he was given some special consideration not given the condemned Sergeant. The fact that Sergeant Redmon is not mentioned in the special order and is not with his family in subsequent census records, and the youngest child in his family in 1870 is five years old, all strongly indicate that he was executed.

GEORGE J. HANDLEY 9-H (December 16, 1864). Private Handley joined the Ninth while it was engaged in Virginia on July 7, 1862. He was present with his detachment until assigned to scouting duties on November 12, 1863. On April Fools' Day 1864, he was listed as a deserter. The record is not clear as to when he was scouting and when considered in desertion. On July 3, Private Handley was arrested as an alleged Federal spy. A court-martial on desertion and spying charges took place on December 16, 1864. The charges were proven to the satisfaction of the court and a death sentence was given to Private Handley. General Ewell did not approve and the sentence was set aside on the basis that Private Handley had been scouting for the entire period. He was released to return to his command on February 23, 1865, the final entry in his Confederate record.

J. BERRY DUCKETT 65-I (January 17, 1865). Private Duckett enrolled in Company A, Fifth Battalion, and then deserted well before consolidation. Enrollment on May 14, 1862, was followed by desertion on June 7, 1863, while at Winters Gap, TN. The next record is that of his trial on January 17, 1865, when it was ordered that he be shot. The sentence was remitted and he was returned to duty. Authority for this act was based on General Order #2, and announced in SO #53, March 4, 1865, AIGO. There is no record of how the trooper fared in the last month of war.

W. C. English 65-K (April 8, 1865). Private English first enrolled in an infantry regiment, the Fifty-Eighth, on June 10, 1862. Two weeks later he enrolled in the Fifth Battalion of cavalry and was promoted to Sergeant just a few days later, on June 27, 1862. Six months after making the switch, he was reduced in rank for being absent without leave on January 31, 1863. Record-wise, he was transferred to the Sixty-Fifth. The next we learn is that Private English was tried by a court-martial at Asheville on April 8, 1865, and that he was to be shot on the second Friday after receipt of the order by the responsible officer. No other record has been found.

Summary

If service records are accurate, cavalrymen had far fewer absences than did infantrymen. Sampled cavalry companies, 18, had an average enrollment of 143 men; 16 chose to absent themselves. A 12 company sample indicates average deaths of 12 from disease and 4 from battle.[57] Each may be understated due to the nature of cavalry record keeping. But cavalry officers and those they led were essentially early and healthy volunteers who could provide a horse. They were from the more affluent homes of North Carolinians and benefited thereby. All of the troopers who were threatened with execution volunteered between May 1861 and July 1862.

22

Artillery

"I dred them canons."[1]

Slightly fewer North Carolinians served their cannon than fed their horse; about 8,000 were in artillery units. Confederate records yield the names of at least 144 artillerymen that went before a military court. Death sentences resulted for 44; 13 were acquitted. At least 8 artillerymen were either hanged or shot to death by musketry. For those convicted, dates of service can be accurately established for 39, and it is found that over half, 21, deserted within five months of their service entry date. For the 17 cavalrymen who were sentenced to execution, just 2 deserted within five months of enrollment, and their median service time was thirteen months. Of the artillerymen who were given death sentences, 8 were conscripts; 25 others enrolled after passage of the conscription act and some were likely volunteers in name only. All of the condemned cavalrymen enrolled before the first conscription law was enacted. Life in either service was equally as dangerous on a day-by-day basis. As might be expected, 13 artillerymen were killed by the accidental bursting of a shell or a cannon, 2 were shot when caught up in an attempt at mutiny, 2 more died in personal affrays, and 5 drowned. In total, there were 22 such deaths for the men who wore the red of the artillery while those who wore the yellow of the cavalry lost 24 in a range of incidents.

Tenth Regiment, First Artillery

The month after formation in July 1861, 3 men of the Tenth Regiment were court-martialed. At least 49 men traced their steps for a total of 52 courts. Death sentences for 15 men followed these 52 courts; 3 men were acquitted. Of these, 2 were hanged as traitors, 2 died of disease and the rest escaped noose or stake. In the regiment, 5 companies, D, F, G, H and K were designated as heavy artillery, the other 5 were organized as field artillery. The heavy artillery companies accounted for 29 of the courts, and 14 of the 15 death sentences. Company H, the Topsail Rifles, with many recruits from Carteret and nearby counties, and Company G, the Beaufort Harbor Guards, also with men from the Carteret area, were the prime offenders, each with 8 courts. Company H men heard 6 death sentences, as did 5 men from Company G. Company B, formed as Guion's Battery in Craven County, had 2 men so sentenced. Nearly half of the men who were given death sentences were from a large contingent of replacements that had joined the regiment in February 1863. Company H, for example, needed recruits because 35 men did not return to the ranks after they were captured and exchanged in April 1862, and another 44 departed of their own will. Of 35 replacements in Company H on February 10, 1863, 22 deserted, half in the month of their enrollment. Company H had an exceptionally large enrollment of 264 men. The 2 men of the regiment who were executed were enrolled in Company B; 2 other men of that company were court-martialed and given lesser sentences. Companies A and B each enrolled slightly more than 190 men. The bulk of court-martial records for the Tenth Regiment concern Companies B, G and H. These companies were formed into Pool's Battalion of Pontooners in December 1862, hopefully to be kept in service while busy building and repairing pontoon and conventional bridges.

An "X" was the mark for 28 of 95 men who signed on for duty in Company A; 10 others signed their name with obvious labored difficulty.[2] But all served well, and no AIGO court records have been found for men of the company; service records show just one or two absences. Company A established an outstanding record of service, though one young man wrote home in December 1861 that his patriotism was "oozing" because he could not leave camp for more than fifteen minutes.[3] Contrast Company A with Company H, where desertion, once it infested the unit, fed on itself as an ever-larger number of replacements, often conscripts, were placed in the ranks.

When asked to recall noteworthy incidents of the war, a man enrolled in Company E remembered that he had once dug himself a protective trench. He was forced to leave his haven by the physical threats of a dominating man who wanted the shelter for his own safety. A shell burst immediately killed the intruder.[4] Another recollection of a man in Company C was that he remembered going back under fire to retrieve a fine horse left behind by a faster-running officer; they were heeding the order "save yourself."[5] The thrust of the memory is not evident — a reflection on the valor of the officer, or on the value of the horse, or was it affection for the animal? In the same company an artilleryman recounted that a cannon that was lost in battle was replaced by a howitzer cast from church bells donated by congregations in Charlotte, NC, from ringing to roaring affirmation of the values of the Confederacy.[6]

Thirty-Sixth Regiment, Second Artillery

The second regiment of artillery was organized in May 1862 and designated the Thirty-Sixth Regiment. Military court records for 31 men of the regiment have been located. Death sentences resulted after 4 trials and 1 defendant was acquitted. Company E, the Columbus Artillery, 174 total enrollment, led all others with 10 courts. These courts issued 2 death sentences and 1 severe prison sentence. Individual service records for the company show only a single instance of willful absence. There were also less dire crimes for courts to ponder, those of earthly trespass. An officer in Company K went before a court on charges of allowing a woman of lewd character into his quarters; he was acquitted when the evidence did not support the charge.[7] Whether his defense rested on erroneous characterization of his visitor, or he was unaware that she was a lewd person, is not stated.

Fortieth Regiment, Third Artillery

The Fortieth had 14 courts of record, with no acquittals; 6 issued a sentence of death. Company H, formerly known as the Branch Artillery, Craven County, and Company I, recruited in Beaufort County, but both with many men from across the state were the units with the most appearances before a military court.

Court-martial records, if any, for an abortive attempt at mutiny by men of the Fortieth on June 7, 1863, have not been located. Two days after the affair, General Whiting provided some detail to General Hill. General Whiting began by saying that there had been a most disgraceful and serious mutiny at Fort Jackson, Smithville [Southport], NC, in Captain Calvin Barnes' company. The men involved were almost exclusively Irishmen who were hard workers except when under the influence of liquor, which was the cause of the mutiny in the General's mind. The mutineers attempted to force the guard; the officer of the day ordered the guard to fire on them. The leader of the mutiny was killed and the others disarmed.[8] Service records indicate that Private James Stephens, Company I, Fortieth Regiment, was killed while participating in a mutiny on June 7, 1863. Referring to the incident in a letter dated June 16, a soldier in Company E, offered some additional background.

> They was a bad fray at Smithville They was a man kill their he got drunk and they put him in the guard house and he tred to run over the sentnal and he was order to shoot him and he dunn it he put a ball there in his head this war is a crwel thing to think of I am afraid that it want stop as long as they is so much meanness a going on I think they is a heap more meanness agoing on now thatn they was before the war commence.[9]

Records also show that the guard killed Private John Sweaney, Company I, while attempting to arrest him on August 7, 1863. What to do with the 30 mutineers now in custody was the immediate issue for General Whiting. He recommended that they be individually transferred to other commands and that they be replaced with conscripts. Captain Barnes was noted as being a very good officer who had held a turbulent set of men together for a long time. A main offender in supplying liquor to soldiers was identified. Two weeks later, General Whiting urged General Hill to act promptly on a decision to transfer the confined men to infantry units.[10] This was eventually done. Virtually all of the men involved had last names of their Irish forebears; six had the first name of Patrick.

A chronicler of the regiment from Carteret County, Sergeant T. C. Davis, Company G, gave a very sensible summary of his war, and equally so for far too many others.

> Permit me to say right here, that I realized during that Southern Campaign what I always believed; that the great popular heart was not then; and never had been, in the war. It was a revolution of the politicians; not the people; and was fought at first by the natural enthusiasm of young men; and kept going by the bitterness of feeling produced by the cruelties and brutalities of the enemy.[11]

Third Battalion Light Artillery

The Third Battalion was made up of just 3 companies. For the battalion 4 court-martial records have been found, and 1 is a death sentence. The Third Battalion had a considerable turnover in men, with an average enrollment of 215 per company. Transfers account for the large enrollment; casualties and absences were not major factors.

Tenth Battalion Heavy Artillery

The Tenth Battalion was formed in June 1863, with 4 companies, and 3 of them had men threatened with execution. Lesser offenses were also a concern of the battalion commander.

In late 1864, he issued a special order to control minor misdeeds: men must stop stealing sweet potatoes, stop gambling and stop selling their clothing. He closed by saying, "Good men should cooperate in reporting violations."[12] Overall, the battalion experienced 40 courts that resulted in 13 death sentences, 7 acquittals and 1 execution. Severe sentences were given to 4 men at trial. A death decision or a severe sentence resulted from 43 percent of battalion courts. Company A, formed with men who lived in Davidson and Randolph counties had 21 men go before a court, 10 of their trials ended with a death sentence. The company enrolled 183 men while in service and 26 absented themselves.

Thirteenth Battalion Artillery

A battalion of 6 companies was organized in November 1863; all of these companies were transferred from existing units, 1 from the Twelfth Battalion Virginia Artillery, 3 from the Thirty-Sixth North Carolina, and 2 from the Fortieth North Carolina. A company commander, Captain Lewis Webb, recorded some of his observations during the early days. Two days after Christmas in 1862, he assembled his company and read the Articles of War to them. He then announced how he would handle punishment in his company, "giving them a choice as to a cheerful willing submission to my sentence," or take their chances with a court-martial. He mentioned that a court-martial carried the risk of a death penalty and that he expected "genuine penitence" from the punished.[13] Some two months earlier, Captain Webb had noted: "Yesterday while drilling in the 'school of the Battery' outside of the works and near Camp Lee two men condemned by a court-martial for desertion were shot where we could see it all and the sickening tragedy made me feel with more than usual keeness the horrors of war."[14]

Courts-Martial

NOAH JACKSON BRANCH ARTILLERY (April 2, 1862). Private Noah Jackson signed on for service in Captain Latham's Branch Artillery on January 20, 1862, giving his age as thirty-five years. Private Jackson had a change of mind, or heart, and attempted to flee to the enemy while at New Bern, NC, this on March 15, 1862. Overtaken and arrested, he still refused to serve. Specifically it was charged that he "did bind and oblige to the enemy." For these acts and declarations he was court-martialed and given a sentence of death by musketry. There is little wonder that Private Jackson attempted to avoid further combat. His battery was in service less than three months and suffered severe loss in an engagement the day before he went to the enemy. It lost all of its weapons and horses, and 10 men were killed. From all causes, 43 men of the company were missing following the encounter.[15] As so often the case for military courts that were sitting in 1862, their record failed to show that two-thirds of the court concurred in the decision, and the prisoner was released. Captured by the enemy and then exchanged, Private Jackson was furloughed from a Confederate hospital in September 1862, ending his nine-month service record.

JAMES CAIN BRANCH ARTILLERY (September 10, 1862). Private Cain, while a member of the Branch Artillery, was court-martialed on September 10, 1862, and was then sentenced to be shot. The crime for which he was tried is not recorded, but it was possibly repetitive, for no leniency was forthcoming, and he was executed on November 4, 1862, along with a soldier from the Forty-Fourth Regiment. Nothing more is known of Private Cain's service, if that be his name; a variant spelling or an alias may hide his true identity. The record of his court was posted in AIGO ledgers. Details of his execution are found with that of Private John Bowers, Forty-Fourth Regiment, Company D.

JOHN J. MCNAIR BRANCH ARTILLERY (September 13, 1862). A second soldier from the Branch Artillery went before a court three days after Private Cain. Private John J. McNair was given a death sentence, but no further information has been located. The soldier in question enrolled on January 20, 1862. The death sentence for Private McNair was entered into the AIGO record on March 11, 1863. No notation was made as to whether or not the sentence was carried into effect. Suggesting that he was not executed, the execution of Private Cain was well publicized while no mention of Private McNair is made.

JOSIAH BYRD SUTTON'S COMPANY (October 6, 1862). Private Byrd began rather intermittent periods of service on August 1, 1861; the enemy captured him in the month that he enrolled in the Lenoir Braves in June 1861. Private Byrd was exchanged four months later. A soldier with the same name had earlier agreed to join the Fifth Regiment but "deserted day of his enlistment," this in June 1861. Having survived capture by the enemy and perhaps a desertion, Private Byrd attempted to desert sometime before July 17, 1862, for he was arrested and imprisoned at Fort Fisher, NC, on that day. A court-martial convened on October 6, 1862, to judge the charges against Private Byrd; they determined that he should be executed. But that was not to be; after a delay of eight months, General A. P. Hill released Private Byrd to duty on June 5, 1863. He was captured by the enemy on March 31, 1865, and died on May 22, 1865, while their prisoner. A brother, Private Nathan Byrd enrolled alongside Private Josiah Byrd in the same company, on the same day, and was present for duty through the end of 1864.

ALEXANDER HARGROVE 10-A BN ART (March 16, 1863). Private Hargrove enrolled on April 3, 1862. On March 16, 1863, while his company, then assigned as Company A, 10th Battalion of Artillery, was in the Wilmington area he went before a court-martial. The first charge, violation of the 7th Article of War, beginning, causing, exciting or joining a mutiny, was supported by the specification that he led an armed party to intimidate the guard and release prisoners they were holding. The second charge, violation of the 8th Article of War, failing to suppress a mutiny, had two specifications: one, "Not reporting to the commanding officer the fact known to him, that a mutiny was on foot, the object of which was to force the guard and release certain prisoners," and two, "Not using his utmost endeavors to suppress a mutiny at which he was present." The defendant was found guilty of all charges and all except the first specification of the second charge. Private Hargrove was sentenced to be shot. However, the court added an opinion, the gist of which was that company officers had shown such an utter disregard for their duties that Private Hargrove might have misunderstood the enormity of his actions, and that mercy should therefore be shown him "if compatible with the good of the service."[16] When General James Longstreet reviewed the findings and opinions of the court, he further discerned that evidence had not been presented that Private Hargrove was the prisoner before the court. Nor was it established that he was legally enrolled as a Confederate soldier. Both of these facts must be placed in evidence when a defendant enters a plea of not guilty. The verdict of the court was set aside and the prisoner held for a second trial. An order for a new trial was issued, and Private Hargrove was to be confined until that should take place. General W. H. C. Whiting weighed in on the matter of a second trial. He did not want to see such a grave crime go unpunished, which would likely happen with a second trial. Alleged facts could be put forth in a supplementary record of the court.¹⁷ Support of General Cooper on this point was mentioned by General Whiting, and further, a second trial would raise constitutional questions. No other trial record for Private Hargrove has been found, and after September 1864 there is no entry in his service record.

Men who were not willing to risk a flagrant attempt at desertion were still anxious to leave the service and return home. A thirty-three-year-old conscript in Company K, Tenth Regiment, wrote to his wife in May 1863:

> I want you to have a petition drawn that [cross out] stating the necessity of me at home and the the [sic] helpliness of my family stateing that the are all girls and cant do any toward work or making a living anyway that I have the helplesnest family of any body in the service.... I think if you have the facts stated in it and dont be too long about it that I will get off I will send you a little peace of paper containing the conscript law.¹⁸

The petition for Private Daniel W. Murph, if prepared, was not helpful for he was killed in the defense of Wilmington on Christmas 1864.

GEORGE L. BUCKMAN 36-G (August 1863). Sergeant Buckman joined his company on September 23, 1861. The enrollee, age thirty-six, was an artilleryman and a musician before being reduced in rank and then deserting on August 19, 1862. He was able to avoid return to his company until July or August 1863. For his extended absence he was tried by court-martial and then sentenced to be shot at such time and place as the commanding general might designate. The General Commanding directed that the execution take place at Fort Caswell on August 31, 1863, under the direction of Colonel T. M. Jones, the same officer who was president of the court that convicted Private Buckman.¹⁹ While this dual role in an execution is most likely to happen in a small command, it makes for interesting speculation as to the effect it might have on future courts. Would there have been far fewer death sentences if a court member knew that he might be ordered to carry a death decision into effect? Was there any real difference between voting for death or ordering an execution detail to aim and fire their weapons? Providently, Colonel Jones was not required to proceed with the execution. The prisoner was eventually released and later transferred to the Thirteenth Battalion Light Artillery and was there until February 22, 1865, when he was listed as absent without leave.

J. W. MILLER 10-A BN ART (October 25, 1863). Private Miller entered Confederate service at Camp Holmes, Raleigh, very likely as a conscript, on April 3, 1863. He was with the battalion until August 9; thereafter he was absent without leave. This absence continued until August 12, when he was under guard at Wilmington. His trial took place on October 25. Guilty was the sentence he heard, and he was to be shot for a three-day absence. The proceedings of the court were forwarded to Richmond for review and then to President Davis on December 18, 1863. After an agonizing six month delay, Private Miller learned that his death sentence had been remitted when SO #107, May 7, 1864, AIGO was issued. The remission of sentence was based on the facts in the case and the endorsement of Major General Whiting who sent the case forward for presidential consideration. Private Miller was restored to duty.

GASTON JACKSON 10-D BN ART (November 4, 1863). Private Jackson was a conscript assigned to Company C on March 24, 1863, and later transferred to Company D on May 23. He deserted on August 17, and was arrested in Union County and confined in the military prison at Wilmington. Company Captain W. Wheeler brought desertion charges against the prisoner and he was sent to trial on November 4. The judgment of the court was that he should be shot. After presidential review, the sentence was commuted to hard labor for six months by SO #199, August 23, 1864, AIGO. Private Jackson was present for duty through November 1864.

JAMES BANKS 3-C BN LT ART (November 12, 1863). A soldier giving the name of James Banks enlisted in Company C of the Third Battalion on March 26, 1863. The circumstances that led to his court-martial six months later are not mentioned in service records, but he was tried and sentenced to be shot. At trial, evidence was presented that the prisoner before the court was a deserter from the Lucas battalion, a South Carolina command. Whatever his name, he was to be shot on December 14. The General Commanding approved the sentence, but execution was suspended so that the case could be sent to the President to "enable him to form an opinion." While in the Lucas battalion the prisoner was known as Private James O'Donnell, apparently his given name. His battalion of record and name were verified by a statement made by a parish priest who knew both the defendant and his brother while they were enrolled in the Lucas battalion.[20] Service records support the statement. With this information in hand, it was agreed that Private Banks was actually Private O'Donnell, but despite the deception of the alias, he was still entitled to amnesty under a presidential proclamation, and this was granted on February 27, 1864. The pardoned man was still in confinement in March–April 1864, and there is no later service record.

ELISHA C. DODSON 10-A BN ART (December 3, 1863). Private Dodson enrolled in the battalion on April 20, 1862. On August 9, 1863, he deserted his company and went to Guilford County where he was arrested on October 5. The court that heard his case put forth a death sentence, but General Whiting did not approve their decision. The disapproval was based on the trial record which did not show that Private Dodson was properly identified as the prisoner before the court. Private Dodson was present through April–June 1864, but has no record after that date.

JOAB BOLTON 10-A BN ART (December 3, 1863). Private Bolton had a very similar experience to that of Private Dodson. The men enrolled on the same day, April 20, 1862, were arrested on the same day in Guilford County, October 5, 1863, and went to trial on the same day, December 3. Private Bolton also learned that he was sentenced to be shot, but that he had been freed upon General Whiting's finding that the court record did not show the plea, guilty or not guilty, of the accused and that he also had not been properly identified before the court. Private Bolton returned to duty by December 1864 and later suffered loss of an eye in battle in Georgia.

THOMAS R. WALTERS 10-A BN ART (December 3, 1863). Private Walters joined the battalion on October 1, 1862, and deserted on August 11, 1863. Brought back under guard on October 25, Private Walters was tried, convicted and sentenced to be shot. General Whiting did not approve his sentence, again because the court did not establish proper identification for the accused, and the relieved soldier returned to duty. He was paroled in May 1865.

JOHN DOBBINS 10-H (December 1863). Private Dobbins agreed to become an artilleryman in February 1863. He deserted his regiment on June 16, 1863, and was not back with it until November 1, 1863. It is not clear if he was returned in arrest or that he came back voluntarily. In any event he was free to move about, for six weeks after his return, on the night of December 12, Private Dobbins and a dozen others left Fort Branch near Hamilton, NC, and set out on the road to Plymouth. Before they had gone less than half a mile they were arrested. Adjutant General Samuel Cooper informed the Secretary of War of the incident. The men were arrested "at the place where certain suspected parties were to meet," in company with ten others, "all of whom were concealed under the trees and in some dog fennel."[21] A passion for precise detail no doubt caused the Adjutant General to note that the men were concealed in "dog fennel," rather than simply hiding in the bushes. The arrested men were tried by court-martial and Private Dobbins and several of his companions were sentenced to be shot. The death sentences were officially published in GO #4, January 22, 1864, Department of North Carolina, by the authority of Major General G. E. Pickett. In June 1864, a concerned Private Dobbins was still in prison awaiting a final decision as to his fate. The suspense continued into September while the case was under review, at issue was if a court comprised of seven officers was legally constituted. Courts with less than the required thirteen officers were legal, providing a decision was made by the convening officer that securing the full number of officers would cause manifest injury to the service and a statement to that effect was placed in the court record. The more complex question presented to legal authorities by this case: who had the authority to make a decision on the size of the court and when should such statement be entered in the court record? The Adjutant General gave his opinion that the decisions of this court were null and void, for the required statement was not entered in the court record. However, other legal authorities cited precedents that a statement on the smaller court was not needed and that the officer who appointed the court had the ability and authority to decide the issue. Their position was that the manifest injury statement was valid as long as it was entered on the record before final approval. On August 22, Judge John Archibald Campbell advised President Davis that it was proper to provide a reason why there were less than thirteen officers on a particular court after the court had finished their deliberations. The proceedings were not void because the statement was not made before trial, but submissions by the convening officer must at some point include a legal reason why the normal compliment of officers was not present.[22] An opinion of Judge Campbell carried considerable weight. He was a former Associate Justice of the United States Supreme Court and was then an Assistant Secretary of War. On September 12, SO #216, AIGO commuted the sentence of Private Dobbins, and he was moved to Salisbury Military Prison where he died on March 5, 1865. He had gained a year of life.

DAVID HENRY HOLMES 10-G (December 1863). Private Holmes enlisted on May 10, 1861, and was captured by the enemy on April 26, 1862, and again on October 31, 1864. He was exchanged after each capture. In between these events, he left his company in the band that hid in the dog fennel. He was sentenced to be shot. The printed order identifies the prisoner as Private Daniel H. Holmes in both the sentencing and approval sections. General Cooper advised the President that the case of Private Holmes was a plain case of desertion and that he had persuaded others to desert, "to quit the service and go to the enemy."[23] It is not clear if this is in reference to the incident on December 12, or to an earlier unrecorded desertion. Regardless, the Adjutant General still maintained that the action of the court was null and void because of not having the full complement of members. After the decision of the court was made known, Colonel S. D. Pool, Tenth Regiment, submitted a petition for clemency for Private Holmes, this to the President on June 24, 1864.[24] A telegram from General Cooper on September 19, 1864, also noted that Private Holmes had been in contact with the Honorable George Davis and indicated that the presidential direction for the suspension of sentence was in itself authority to delay further action.[25] The contact with the Honorable George Davis was deemed significant enough to warrant mention in the telegram from General Cooper. Davis was a member of an influential family living in New Hanover County, and was then Attorney General of the Confederacy. Private Holmes was jailed at Plymouth while the legal issue in his case was resolved. Once this resolution was made, he was transferred to the prison at Salisbury, NC, lived through the confinement, and was paroled in May 1865.

JOSEPH C. DOUB 10-H (December 1863). Private Doub enrolled on February 16, 1863. He was in jail at Plymouth along with 5 men of the regiment in May 1864. He was among the men who left camp on the night of December 12, 1863, and was likewise tried and sentenced to be executed. SO #107, May 7, 1864, AIGO commuted his sentence to one of hard labor for the rest of the war, or for the term of his enlistment. This favorable action was taken in "consideration of families of the accused."[26] The prisoner was sent to Salisbury Military Prison and there is no record of his return to active service. A brother, Private John F. Doub, enrolled within days of Private Joseph Doub. There is one reference that he deserted and was given a death sentence, but this is not substantiated in any other records.

WILLIAM H. LONG 10-H (December 1863). Private Long joined the Tenth Regiment on February 16, 1863, and deserted four months later on June 16. He was in custody on November 25, and went before a court-martial in December. He was sentenced to be shot. This sentence was commuted to hard labor for the remainder of the war and he was still confined at Salisbury Military Prison in February 1865. As in the case of Private Doub, the commutation order included the note that the action was taken in consideration for the families of the threatened man; the families were not wealthy, but they were substantial members of their community.

WILLIAM M. WILLIS 10-G (December 1863). Private Willis was an early volunteer for the fray, going into the Tenth Regiment on June 4, 1861. He was captured at Fort Monroe, NC, on April 2, 1862, and again at Plymouth in October 1864. Between these events he joined the half-mile desertion effort that ended in the dog fennel. That was his only recorded violation of the Articles of War. Still, he was sentenced to be shot, and the decision was approved by the General Commanding but was remitted by SO #199, August 23, 1864, AIGO. The relieved man was restored to duty. Capture by the enemy and taking of the oath followed in 1865.

JAMES M. PIPKIN 10-G (December 1863). Private Pipkin enlisted October 3, 1862. In the November–December 1862 reporting period, he was absent without leave for a time and in the March–April 1863 period, he deserted. No punishment for either incident is recorded. His next escapade was his involvement with Private Dobbins, the subsequent trial and a like judgment. While imprisoned at Plymouth, Private Pipkin composed a letter to Governor Vance in which he asked for aid in getting a reprieve. He mentioned the names of several men who were confined with him, some who were too young to vote in the past election but would certainly vote in the future, he pointedly explained. A second reference to voting came later in the letter when Private Pipkin suggested that he had supported Governor Vance when exercising his voting right in Johnson County. He goes on to mention his poor and feeble mother, that his wife and child have been deprived of his soldier's pay, and that he has made no attempt at escape.

> We have bored our punishment with as much patients as any set of men in the world and our officers are Aware of the fact that we never have made the least attempt in the world to get Away sins we have been under arrest and it does not seem that our officers is trying to do anything for us.... If you will seek into this matter as soon as possible and as much as possible and let me know what you think the result will be you will oblidge [not legible] very much."[27]

This was the second letter to the Governor by Private Pipkin.[28] In August the AAG advised that in regard to Private Pipkins it was a simple case of desertion, and the Secretary of War respectfully submitted to the President that "there are no circumstances of special extenuation and I see no ground to recommend executive interposition which would not apply to most cases of desertion."[29] Despite the lack of extenuating circumstances, the death sentence for Private Pipkin was commuted to imprisonment with the issuance of SO #216, September 12, 1864, AIGO.[30] Private Pipkin was paroled in May 1865.

JOSEPH HUDSON 10-H (December 1863). An enlistment date into Company H on February 10, 1863, is shown for Private Hudson. Next recorded is a desertion in the January–February period with the note that he deserted and either returned, or was returned, on the same day and that he was then in arrest at Weldon. Service records then state that he enlisted on November 1, 1863, at Fort Branch and deserted after a few weeks of service, on December 14. He was tried by the same court that heard the charges against the men who left on the night of December 12. The court agreed that a death sentence was warranted. The General Commanding approved this decision, but no further record has been found on execution of sentence, remission or commutation.

ANDERSON SHORES 10-H (December 1863). Private Shores enlisted on February 10, 1863, but left his newfound companions before the month had elapsed. No information on his return is found in his service record. Private Martin Shores enlisted and deserted on the same days as did Private Anderson Shores. No record of arrest or punishment has been found. Private Anderson Shores began a second desertion in December 1863. He was arrested, convicted and given a death sentence. The soldier identified as Anderson Shores in Confederate records is most likely Henderson Shores of Yadkin County. He survived the war.

RANSOM GALIMORE 10-A BN ART (December 14, 1863). Private Galimore went into service on March 30, 1863, and was absent without leave on August 4. He was present for duty for four months and then absent for about three months. The deserter was in arrest by December 11, and a court-martial quickly followed. A death sentence was handed down by the court and approved by the General Commanding as published in GO #7, January 23, 1864, Department of North Carolina. Private Galimore was executed on January 29, 1864.

A soldier had promised to tell his folks what had happened on the day of execution, and he did so in an emotional and explicit recounting. A portion of the letter was written at a right angle directly over horizontal writing, a common practice when there was so much to tell those at home.

> The day appointed for the execution was Friday the 29th inst. At day break a very heavy fog overspread the land and obscured the sun from view but at 10 o'clock they sun was shining and the fog had almost disappeared. The Regiment formed in the usual order upon the Parade ground and by a series of very awkward involutions was formed into a <u>hollow square</u> with one side open and awaited the hour for the execution. The detachment of executioners eighteen in number who had been previously chosen by Col and armed with Springfield Rifles ten loaded with ball cartridges and eight with blank cartridges then took position inside the square fronting the open side. They were pale and seemed loth to perform the painful duty which was assigned them. The Col then ordered a stake to be brought and driven into the earth ten paces in front of the detachment. At 11 o'clock the prisoner accompanied by the Rev. Mr. Andrews of the Methodist Church and followed by [not legible] made their appearance and with a slow measured tread passed inside the Square and directed their course to a point in rear of the [not legible] The prisoner and the minister placing themselves beside the stake facing the detachment. After reading the proceedings the Court

Martial and the order for the execution the Adjutant motioned the Reverend Andrews that he might address the troops then in a few pointed remarks for the solemnity of the occasion and exhorted the spectators to prepare for death which was no less certain to them than to the prisoner and with his hand upon the stake he knelt upon the earth and prayed earnestly for the prisoner. After speaking a few words of encouragement to him. His eyes were then blindfolded and he was made to get upon his knees and with his back resting against the stake he awaited his doom with commendable fortitude. It was a melancholy and impressive scene — a man upon the verge of eternity who was to die by the hands of his comrades in arms. God grant that I may never witness another scene like that. A flourish of the sword and a roll of the drum announced that the moment had arrived when followed in quick succession in the commands Ready, Aim <u>Fire</u> and the prisoner with a bound fell forward upon his face a cor[p]se pierced through the breast by two balls one passing through his heart. Thus died a man who was branded with the infamous epithet <u>Deserter</u> and richly deserved his fate. He was apparently about thirty five years of age and leaves a Wife and six small children with no inheritance. But the infamy which attaches itself to the epithet deserter. He appeared calm and met his fate with fortitude that was worthy of a better man. You must not think me hard hearted, for a man who has the smallest amount of love for his country will hate a Deserter though he may at the same time sympathize with him in his untimely end. Who would not rather die a thousand times upon the field of battle than to be shot down like a dog for cowardice![31]

A year later the writer was killed in battle close by the execution site.

These expressive comments bring to light the largest known detail to execute a single soldier. Ten loaded muskets, nearly double that normally found, to kill a deserter a few paces away. But from the account, the Colonel of the regiment may have accurately foreseen the marksmanship of his men, or of their will, in aiming at the kneeling man, if in fact, only two balls hit close to the fatal mark. In an ironic aside, considering all the attention to legal proceedings: Private Galimore was never paid for his time in the Confederate army, but no mention is made that the point was raised in court. A document notes that the sentence for Private Galimore was commuted, again underscoring that Confederate records must be treated with diligence.

CALVIN C. COLE 10-A BN ART (December 1863). Private Cole enrolled on April 3, 1863, a few days after Private Ransom Galimore. The two deserted on the same day, August 4, 1863, and were in arrest at the same time. When the court's decision in the case of Private Cole was published on January 23, 1864, he learned that he was to be shot. A month after the death sentence was made known, General Whiting wrote to Private Coal's [sic] brigade commander to inform him that the prisoner was "not regarded as a fit subject for such extreme punishment ... the sentence of death must not be carried into effect ... will be put to 12 months hard labor and then to duty."[32] What led General Whiting to conclude that Private Galimore was a fit subject for execution and that Private Cole was not is not obvious from the records of the men. Whatever the circumstance, the General's directive was obeyed and Private Cole went to Fort Caswell, NC, to serve his sentence. There he died of disease in April 1864, having outlived Private Galimore by three months. A third soldier of the battalion, charged along with Privates Galimore and Cole, Private Samuel J. Burton, in some fashion gained sufficient freedom to desert to a Federal gunboat in February 1864, thus avoiding stake or hard labor.

EDWARD J. LITTLETON 10-G (December 28, 1863). Six months after signing on for duty on July 1, 1863, Private Littleton was tried for a serious infraction of military law and was sentenced to be shot to death. The sentence was not approved, and he returned to duty. In July 1864, he was transferred to the Third Battalion of Artillery and served with that unit until he deserted in February 1865. He later took the oath, ending his allegiance to the Confederacy.

SILAS HOLLOWAY 10-G (December 29, 1863). Private Holloway enlisted in August 1862 and was absent without leave toward year's end. A year later he was in arrest at Weldon for desertion. The court that heard his case concurred that a death sentence was proper. The decision of the court was not approved by the responsible officer, and Private Holloway went back to his duties where he stayed through February 1865, the last entry on his service record.

SAMUEL HAMMOND 10-H (December 31, 1863). After enrolling on February 10, 1863, likely as a conscript, Private Hammond was present for duty until he was in arrest at Weldon in the November–December period. When tried on the last day of the year, the evidence was such that he was given a death sentence. Said sentence was not approved, and Private Hammond returned to duty where he continued to serve for the remainder of the war.

JOSEPH HASKETT 10-B (February 3, 1864). Private Haskett volunteered for duty on June 12, 1861. He was captured on April 26, 1862, and exchanged in August. On November 15, 1863, he deserted and within two weeks agreed to serve in the Second NCUV. He was mustered into Federal service on December 4, and was among the men captured at Beech Grove on February 2, 1864. Court-martialed the next day, he was hanged at Kinston on February 5.

DAVID JONES 10-B (February 3, 1864). Private Jones enlisted in the Tenth Regiment on November 15, 1862, and deserted exactly a year later, on the same day as Private Haskett, November 15, 1863. Enrollment in the Second NCUV came a few days after Private Haskett, on December 10, 1863. Capture on February 2, court on February 3, and noose on February 5, then followed.

On the day set for execution a Chaplain wrote in his diary:

> February 5 Requested by Gen. Hoke to visit two deserters who are to be hanged at 12 Oclock, named Jones and Haskett. They were found in the enemys line in arms against us. They were the most hardened and unfeeling men I ever encountered, [not legible] and met their fate with apparent indifference.[33]

The body of Private Haskett dropped beneath the scaffold beam about two weeks before the first anniversary of his wife's death, perhaps explaining his "apparent indifference" to his own death. "Thursday Feb. 26th [1863] ... Private Joseph Haskett left the camp to go to his home in Craven County, his wife having died a few days previous.... March 8th (Sun.) ... Joseph Hasket [sic] returned to the camp having had a furlough for 10 days." In 1864, "Sunday Nov. 15th ... Serg't Lawrence Miller of Co. B, 10th Reg. came to our Hd. Qrs. in search of three deserters from that Co. (viz) Joseph Hasket [sic], R. T. [L] Paul & David Jones.... Sat. Feb. 6th Two men, deserters from Co. B 10 Reg't who were captured at Bachelor's Creek were hung at Kinston Joe Haskett and David Jones."[34] No further record following his desertion, has been found for Private Raymond Paul, age twenty, of Craven County. He deserted from Company B, Tenth Regiment, on November 15, 1863, and joined the Second NCUV in early December 1863. While detailed as a Federal hospital steward, he was absent without leave in December 1864 and had no further record in that service.

Also on the day of the execution:

> Friday Feb 5th 1864 This morning men hung at Kinston. Jos. Haskett and D. Jones, two privates of my old company B who were men taken in arms at the Beech Grove Chapel, among

the Yankee prisoners. They deserted their Company about three months ago and were no doubt forced into the Yankee service, they were readily discovered and identified by their own comrades who were among the attacking party and informed upon immediately, a drum head Court martial held upon the side of the road found them guilty and they were sentenced to be hung at noon the next day. The execution was witnessed by nearly the whole Company together with a large portion of the army and they were swung off without [not legible] the sympathy of a single individual. I did not witness it but hear they died a sullen death not speaking a word with their former companions in arms.[35]

Directly after the hangings a soldier stationed at Kinston wrote home to tell: "There were two men hung here today and think they will hang 15 more. They belonged in the Confederate service and deserted and went to the Yankees and joined them we captured them at or rather near Newburn."[36] Another soldier also wrote home on February 5. "Some of the men that was captured was some of our men that deserted and takend arms against us two of them was hung here to day."[37] Later the attending Chaplain expanded on his remarks in regard to the men. They were "raised up in ignorance and vice. They had little concern about eternity. Private Jones was quite young and never shed a tear though he was guilty of perjury."[38] Perjury was a great sin to the Chaplain and frequently drew his condemnation when referring to the crimes of other men. To his mind they had forsaken their Confederate oath, their bond, and well-merited their fate. Private Jones apparently had a confrontation with General Pickett and told him that he did not care a damn whether they shot him then or what they did with him, according to the Chaplain.[39]

CHARLES CUTHRELL 40-H (February 7, 1864). A third North Carolina artilleryman followed the privates from the Tenth Regiment to the gallows at Kinston. Private Cuthrell had volunteered on January 30, 1862, enrolling in Captain Alexander C. Latham's company. The company was transferred to the Fortieth Regiment in November 1863. Private Cuthrell apparently deserted his company at that time, though no desertion date is recorded. On December 22, 1863, while absent from the Fortieth, he volunteered for the Second NCUV and was with the men captured at Beech Grove on February 2, 1864. He was among the 13 who were hanged on February 15, 1864.

ALAN BLANTON 10-I (March 3, 1864). Private Blanton first enrolled in Company A, Thirty-Sixth Regiment on March 18, 1863, and was transferred to Company I, Tenth Regiment in November 1863. Less than a month after going into the Thirty-Sixth, Private Blanton deserted while near Kinston, this on April 14, 1863. The Provost Guard at Goldsboro arrested him the day after he deserted. Two weeks after this brief escapade, Private Blanton broke from his guard and departed for parts more to his liking. This time he was partially successful and avoided arrest until November 31, 1863, when he was delivered under guard to the military. He went before a court-martial on March 3, 1864, and was found guilty and sentenced to be shot. The day of execution was set for March 18, 1864. The order for the execution was revoked. Private Blanton died on May 16, 1864, of typhoid fever. Two months of life were exchanged for further erosion in the will of Confederate leaders to execute.

MCRUFFIN SMITH 10-B BN ART (April 5, 1864). Private Smith enrolled on March 11, 1863, and deserted four weeks later. Sometime before August 1863, he went to trial and was given a death sentence. This was commuted to confinement of 150 days hard labor with a twenty-four-pound ball and chain attached to a leg, a diet of bread and water for seven days in every thirty, to have his head shaved, and to stand on a barrel with hat off every alternate two hours for two days from reveille to retreat. How much of this complex sentence was inflicted is not recorded. Possibly not much, for two months later Private Smith was able to again desert, this time on October 15, 1863, and to avoid arrest until March 8, 1864. A second court-martial gathered on April 5, 1864, heard his case and handed down a death sentence; he was to be shot on April 19, 1864. But again there was a suspension of sentence and Private Smith was last known to be in confinement in October 1864. An undated entry in AIGO records indicates that the sentence was commuted but gives no further information.[40] Private Smith had the rare experience of two death sentence commutations.

GUILFORD COLEMAN 36-E (April 20, 1864). Enrolled at Fort Caswell on May 3, 1862, Private Coleman was with his regiment until early 1864, when he left without permission to return to his home; there he stayed for about a month. When he was taken back in arrest, he was court-martialed and sentenced to be shot. This sentence was commuted to twelve months of hard labor at Fort Holmes. While a prisoner there, Private Coleman wrote to Governor Vance asking for his aid in gaining his release and return to duty.

> Fort Holmes Smiths Island NC July 21st 1864 To your Excelency Z. B. Vance Dear Sir I as a prisoner apply to you for a recommendation to the head war department to be released from the following sentence that is to work on Smiths Island twelve months my offense was that I left my company without permision and went home about one month and was sick while their & was arrested and tried by a court martial and sentanced to be shot and then released from that sentance to work 12 months on this Island and I have bin here for the period of two month and twenty days to this date I belong to the 36th Regiment NC Co E. Capt O H. Powell commanding troops I remain very Resptectfully your obedient servant Guilford Coleman.[41]

No further service record is found for Private Coleman after August 1864. There were 10 men in Company E with the family name of Coleman; among them were brothers Guilford, Bryant, Travis, and John Q. Coleman. Private John Coleman died a Federal prisoner; the others either took the oath or had no record after August 1864.

The month after Private Coleman was sentenced for desertion, a Federal deserter came into Confederate lines. It was noted that one ear was "cropped," indicating that he had been so marked after conviction for an earlier desertion attempt. No record of Confederate ear-cropping has been found. Such obvious marking may have been appropriate for flagrant offenders or men who had no established place in society, bad characters not wanted in any respectable community.

JOHN W. CLIFTON 36-I (July 20, 1864). Private Clifton was conscripted into the Thirty-Sixth on October 28, 1863. After a month or so he deserted along with his brother, Private Wade H. Clifton. Private John Clifton was tried by court-martial on July 20, 1864, convicted, and ordered to be shot. The death sentence was commuted to hard labor for the rest of the conflict. A sentence of hard labor for the war was given to Private Wade Clifton. He had returned to service in February. While in the Military Prison at Wilmington on August 15, the brothers and a third prisoner, Private J. W. Ritter, prepared a common appeal to Governor Vance asking his help in having them returned to duty.

> We privates in Companies D and I of N. C. T. have been in the military prison for six months for <u>nothing</u> but going home one time.... We are brothers & never heard the Army Regulations read: We were ignorant of what was our duty....We done no <u>harm</u> at home.... Hoping you will look over our cases carefully Do all in you power for us we most cordially solicit you aid in releasing us in case you approve of our petion [sic].[42]

An earlier appeal for an expedited trial had been directed to President Davis.⁴³ A sister of the brothers also submitted a petition for their release.⁴⁴ The several appeals and petitions may have been of help to Private John Clifton, for he was returned to duty on March 5, 1865. A third brother, Private Watson Clifton enrolled in November 1861 and took the oath in June 1865. No trial record for Private Ritter has been located.

DEMPSEY WATTS 36-E (July 28, 1864). Private Dempsey Watts went into the Thirty-Sixth on February 26, 1863. Enrolling on the same day, Private Meredith Watts indicated his age was forty-three years; he was discharged in September 1863. For some earlier transgression or for a breach of discipline while in the regiment, no mention of the violation is found in service records, Private Dempsey Watts was court-martialed on July 28, 1864, and sentenced to be shot to death. General Whiting approved the sentence of the court, but it was not carried into effect forthwith. He was confined for an unexplained three months and then suffered two volleys before dying.⁴⁵

PLEASANT A. HASKET 10-A BN ART (August 8, 1864). Private Hasket enlisted to fire Confederate cannon on March 23, 1863. Desertion from Wilmington began on August 4, 1863. The length of his absence is not stated. Private Hasket went to trial nearly a year later. When the result of the trial was published in GO #62, October 21, 1864, Department of North Carolina, the prisoner was informed that he would be shot. During the review that followed, it was noted that he had experienced an exceptionally long confinement and that no reason for the delay was offered.⁴⁶ It was acknowledged that little was known of the case by those reviewing the matter. All this resulted in a suspension of further activity, awaiting a decision by the President. Private Hasket was eventually released on March 5, 1865, by GO #2.

G. W. WORKMAN 40-I (September 6, 1864). Private George Workman was a conscript sent to the Fortieth Regiment on September 30, 1862. Six weeks later he departed on November 18, 1862, and after an absence of a week was caught and confined in jail. Still anxious to avoid army duty, he broke from the jail at Asheboro, Randolph County. Sixteen months elapsed before he was confined at Wilmington. For this long absence, he was court-martialed on September 6, 1864, and, not unexpectedly, given a death sentence. But a mitigating factor was placed on record when the decision of the court was published in GO #62, November 1, 1864, Army of Northern Virginia. Private Workman apparently had a change of heart and had returned voluntarily to his regiment, and this was sufficient to suspend execution of sentence until the President could review the case. The review resulted in Private Workman being restored to duty by SO #260, November 1, 1864, AIGO. The freed soldier survived the remaining months of war. Private Berry Workman, the father of the condemned man, served in the regiment for a brief time in 1862. He was a substitute and his age, fifty-five years, was a factor in his early discharge. Private W. H. Workman, a younger brother, also served in the regiment, father and sons all joining on the same day.

VINCENT H. ALLEN 13-D BN LT ART (September 7, 1864). Forty days after Private Dempsey Watts went to his trial and subsequent death sentence, Private Allen faced the same ordeal. Private Allen began his service in the battalion sometime prior to May 13, 1863, for on that date he decided to end his commitment. While at Camp Pettigrew, Topsail Sound, NC, he deserted and remained absent until taken up on April 13, 1864. He went to trial on September 7, 1864, under charges and specifications that were referred to a Lieutenant Reid for review and preparation for trial. Apparently all was in order, for Private Allen was tried and found guilty as charged and was sentenced to be shot when the decision of the court was made known in GO #62 October 21, 1864, Department of North Carolina.

Private Allen was executed on October 24, alongside Private Watts of the Thirty-Sixth. Colonel Walter H. Taylor, on the staff of General Lee, was so informed two days after the executions. General Whiting reported on October 26, 1864: "I have the honor to report that the sentence of death against Private Dempsey Watts 36-C [E] & Private Vincent H. Allen 13-D NC Battalion were duly executed between the hours of 11 am and 12 n on Thursday the 24th instant."[47] Private Watts was executed some three months after publication of his death sentence. Private Allen was put to death three days after publication of his sentence. No explanation for such haste has been found, though it would suggest some involvement with the enemy or perhaps it was merely convenient.

Colonel William Lamb of the Thirty-Sixth kept a detailed diary of his wartime experience. On the day of execution, the prisoners were brought to a holding office for an hour and a half. Accompanied by a Chaplain, they were then taken to the place of execution where a prayer was offered. "They declined making any remarks & requested not to be tied." One half of the guard nervously fired prematurely at the command of "Aim," and the other fired erratically thereafter. "Allen who was at the old stake was instantly killed." Private Watts was only wounded:

> He groaned distressingly "Lord have mercy on me," when I immediately ordered up the reserve of four to within two paces of him & he rec'd two shots through the head, and died.... Both men were cool, Watts as calm as if he had been on parade, the last thing he did before being bandaged, was to turn & look at Allen and adjust his arms & hands like his. Allen stood during the Chaplain's prayer & seemed a little effected but as if in prayer, he was praying while shot.... Allen received seven shots. Watts rec'd seven shots, three first time & four the last.[48]

The regimental surgeon made a postmortem examination of the bodies. In a very unusual happening, perhaps only at an artillery post, a gold bracelet was donated to aid the families of the executed men. Also noteworthy is the comment that "Allen was at the old stake," apparently a reference to the stake left in place after the execution of Private Ransom Galimore, 10-A Battalion Artillery. A standing execution stake was a daily reminder of death for desertion and a stark warning for every passing artilleryman. The prisoners had asked that they not be tied to their stakes, so Private Watts was likely conscious and on the ground when killed by the musket balls fired into his head. Nearly thirty years after the fall of Fort Fisher, Colonel William Lamb recalled the execution in a slightly different tone.

> Among the saddest events which occurred previous to the battles were the execution of deserters. On one occasion one soldier was shot, and on another two were executed at the same time. It is a solemn sight to see a command draw up to witness the death of fellow soldiers, and it is made as impressive as possible as a warning against desertion. The condemned ride to the stake upon their coffins, the band playing the dead march, are blindfolded when shot, and are usually tied to the stake unless they request otherwise. The weapons are loaded by the ordnance sergeant, one with a blank cartridge so that no soldier detailed is positive that his gun is loaded with a ball when he fires. All three shot at Fort Fisher had been farmers, and were married, and doubtless the condition of their families at home had much to do with their crime. They had not deserted from my command but when captured their companies were stationed at Fort Fisher, and it was my painful duty to see the sentences of the courtmartial enforced. They all died fearlessly.[49]

THOMAS S. HANSLEY 40-H (September 8, 1864). Another unwilling conscript was put in the Fortieth Regiment on March 23, 1864. Private Hansley remained at his post five months, until August 24, 1864, when he was found on board a blockade runner appropriately named *Will of the Wisp*. Once discovered, he was immediately arrested, taken back to shore, and confined awaiting trial. In a hand with the beauty of calligraphy, Private Hansley composed a letter to Governor Vance on September 3.

> In your proclamation to deserters now before the good people of North Carolina dated August 27th 1864 in the name of the State North Carolina and also in the name of the Confederate States a promise of forgiveness to all who will repent and become good soldiers. It is with deep regret and mortification that I am compelled to call on you for the same leniency." [He goes on to outline the facts in his case and then explains why he did what he did.] "My Capt is a man of strong prejudices and although a good soldier took a dislike to me & treated me very severely. I tried to get out of his Company by exchange (he refusing) I failed to do so. He made me work very hard in the hot sun whilst I have a disease in my head and feared it would kill me. Solely for this I tried to escape to some neutral place.... Will you not extend the same mercy to me who have never in my whole life been charged with any crime of misdemeanor before.[50]

The Captain that Private Hansley referred to is the same officer that led Company H, when the men of Irish lineage were involved in the mutiny attempt a little over a year past. Following that incident, General Whiting noted that Captain Calvin Barnes was a good officer, suggesting he was an officer that would not accept any excuse for shirking of duty, nor transfer of a recalcitrant soldier, with a "disease" in his head, for others to bring into line. Private Hansley's regret and mortification were well founded, for the court upon hearing the facts in his case handed down a sentence of death. The finding of the court was published on November 21, 1864. Governor Vance directed an appeal on behalf of the threatened man to authorities at Richmond on the day after the sentence was published.[51] The sentence was remitted, and Private Hansley was captured in February 1865 and took the oath.

PLEASANT SIMPSON 10-D BN ART (September 19, 1864). Private Simpson was a conscript when he went into Company C on April 1, 1863. Transfer to Company D was ordered for the unwilling soldier on May 23. Private Simpson deserted on August 16, 1863, and was then absent over a year, until September 13, 1864, when he voluntarily returned, supposedly under provision of an amnesty proclamation by Governor Vance put forth on August 24, 1864. The Governor became involved in the case through a number of telegrams to officials in the War Department asking to delay several executions, including that of Private Simpson. Further contact was made with General Bragg who directed a reply that summarized the current status of Private Simpson's case.[52] It noted that Private Simpson was tried by a general court-martial, and their decision was announced in GO #62, October 21, 1864, Department of North Carolina. General Lee ordered that the sentence be suspended until the decision of the President could be known, and there the matter rested on January 24, 1865. In March, Private Pleasant Simpson returned to duty, under authority of General Order #2.

JOHN M. MCKEEL 40-I (September 26, 1864). Private McKeel went into the Fortieth on January 25, 1862. Within two months, on March 15, he left his company and was not again present until March or April 1863. No record of punishment for this yearlong absence has been located. After a few more months of army life, Private McKeel deserted, this time on July 28, 1863. He was not arrested and brought back until May 15, 1864, an absence of ten months. With a record of lengthy desertions, he may well have had some trepidation when he went before a court-martial held on September 26, 1864. Any such feelings by Private McKeel were well founded, for he was found guilty and was to be shot.

An AIGO record indicates that he was executed on November 19; in contradiction, his service record has an entry that he was absent in arrest in February 1865.[53] A gloss alongside the posting of his court-martial offers that the court record was returned to General Lee at the General's request, but the entry was made after the stated day of execution. A few records for this soldier have the name as McNeil.

Private John W. Mozingo deserted from Company K, Tenth Regiment, on August 5, 1864. The protection of a pardon from Governor Vance was secured, and he was on a train going back to duty when he heard he was going to be imprisoned. On hearing this revelation, he jumped from the train, but once again, after reflection, wrote to Governor Vance for another pardon to return to the ranks. The Governor noted on the second appeal, "If he could not trust my first pardon the second would he use better."[54] No further record has been found for Private Mozingo.

LAWRENCE LATHAM 10-D BN ART (October 19, 1864). Private Latham initially joined his artillery battalion in Company C on April 3, 1863, and then was transferred to Company D on May 23, 1863. A period of hospitalization offered an opportunity for Private Latham to desert, which he seized on August 17, 1863. Arrest did not come about for a full year, occurring on September 1, 1864. While in custody, Private Latham required hospitalization on September 17. A court-martial held on October 19, issued a death decision, but General Lee did not approve their decision. There the record ends.

BARNABAS POWELL 13-A BN ART (Prior to October 21, 1864). Private Powell was conscripted into service in May 1862. Hospitalized at Weldon, he deserted on June 17, 1863, and was arrested in Cumberland County on July 15. After his arrest, he went back to a hospital and again found an opportunity to desert, this time on July 27. Nearly a year later he was returned under guard to face a court whose decision in the case was made known in GO #62, October 21, 1864, Department of North Carolina. The decision was that Private Powell should be shot, but the court did not place on the record the number of officers that were on the court. That omission vitiated the proceedings. The court had made a unanimous recommendation for clemency.

AARON SEARCY 10-B BN ART (November 5, 1864). Private Searcy enrolled on March 22, 1862, and was absent without leave for much of the year. Service records indicate that he was absent without "lief" in the July–August reporting period. The absent without "lief" became full-blown desertion on May 9, 1863. On June 8, the absent soldier wrote to Governor Vance:

> I have been absent from my company a short time without leave and being anxious to go back to my co if I knew I would not be shot or whiped and knowing no way to get back without a pass I have this propose [sic] to address you asking you if it is in your power to send me a pass by which I can get back to my company ... the cause of my coming home was I had a son lying at the point of death with dropsy [not legible] and derangement of the liver and I could not get a furlough.[55]

Private Searcy may have returned from this absence and then left his command again. A note in his record shows that he was "taken in the morning," around March 12, 1864. On April 13, 1864, the Brigadier General of his brigade was told to suspend his execution, which had been announced in GO #47, April 12, 1864, Head Quarters Department Cape Fear, and was set for April 19. The General was asked to "investigate character of and forward any matters bearing on case." The investigation into the character of Private Searcy was starkly summarized a week later, "The character of this man Cearcey [sic] as a soldier is bad he has deserted three times." The letter then goes on to say that the unit in which he is enrolled is now in another command.[56] Despite the damning character comment and alleged desertions, the execution of Private Searcy was suspended. The sentence was later commuted, and he was at Smith's Island in the last entry in his service record.

WILLIAM R. QUICK 13-A BN ART (December 1864). Private Quick enlisted in Company D, Twelfth Virginia Light Artillery Battalion, and then deserted from that unit in July 1863. Shelter in South Carolina was found until October when he was arrested by a company officer of the newly formed Thirteenth Battalion. Private Quick was tried and sentenced to be shot to death. The court-martial record was posted by the AIGO under the designation of the Virginia battalion. There was a flurry of correspondence with Governor Vance and the officer who arrested Private Quick. An embittered Captain L. H. Webb mentioned that Private Quick was on his second desertion and that he wanted to capture him. Colonel James T. Roper, commander of the Richmond County Home Guard, was asked to aid in the arrest.[57] While imprisoned, Private Quick was officially transferred to the Thirteenth Battalion. His company Captain writing in his diary on March 30th, [1864] states: "Today I was officially informed that private Wm R. Quick of my company who deserted last July & who was arrested by me last Octr & tried by Genl Court Martial at Petersburg last Decr had been by the Court sentenced to be shot & that Friday the 1st of April was the day appointed for the execution."[58] No other entry concerning the execution has been found.

Twenty-year-old Sergeant Michael H. Turrentine of the Thirty-Sixth wrote of incidents during the defense of Savannah, this within a month of his death at Fort Fisher. A plan for a mutiny was devised by a "young Sergeant" from Delaware. It was revealed to authorities by a "gigantic Irish Corporal," one devoted to his officers.

> A riot occurred during the night and Co F of the 36th N.C.T. was ordered down to suppress it. Captain White of Baker's staff took command of the Company and [not legible] suppressed it, but not until he had shot several of Wheeler's Cavalry. They are the meanest set of men that ever lived have stolen and destroyed more than the enemy have been guilty of acts that a decent Yankee would be ashamed to commit.[59]

In the melee, 7 men were allegedly shot by Captain White or men of Company F; though there may have been some organized executions at the conclusion of the affair. Sergeant Turrentine wrote on December 22, and a day or two later he described a similar tragic killing.

> A member of Col Jackson's Regt of Mississippians was shot by his Adj of the Regt for simply firing his gun off without orders. The ball entered his head on the left side and passed out below the ear on the other scattering his brains out on the ground. Not content with shooting him through the head he fired a second time the ball passing entirely through his body. Strange to say none of his comrades resented it.[60]

The Adjutant was arrested awaiting a civil trial. The Sergeant continues, "If an officer ever shoots a man in my Company for any offense but mutiny I shall certainly try my rifle at him."[61] In the same tenor he mentions that the spirits of the men have been crushed by the "rod of discipline," that less is now required of officers than he would require of "one of my slaves," incidents and comments not unexpected in the final months of a civil war.

Summary

Service records for North Carolinians serving in artillery companies are not as detailed as are those for infantry commands. Such basic information as age of the enrollee and county of residence, if known, is frequently missing. On average, a company of artillery enrolled 204 men and experienced 14 unauthorized absences.[62] Battle related deaths were 4 per company, while non-battle deaths were 24 per company.[63] Courts-martial sentenced to death 31 percent of the 144 artillerymen appearing before them; about 15 percent of cavalrymen and infantrymen were so sentenced. The percentage turns when comparing those executed after a death sentence—18 percent for the artillery, 36 percent for the cavalry and infantry. Death in battle was not as common for the cannoneers, nor would they as often die of various deadly maladies that befell infantry regiments. Whether the 8 conscripts chose to absent themselves to avoid any form of service or simply did not want to serve in the artillery, is not clear. It would seem if they had to serve, the artillery was the most desirable service that they could hope for. Enrolling in an artillery unit was one way to avoid conscription into the infantry. It was reported that "men were volunteering in the heavy batteries at Wilmington and in cavalry companies upon the coast to escape conscription and filling existing units."[64] Men in South Carolina made that same decision.[65]

In overview, courts hearing cases concerning North Carolina artillerymen were frequently not legally precise; when they did manage that hurdle they were not consistently and firmly supported by officers of higher rank. Unrest, even outright mutiny, finds more frequent expression in the records of North Carolina's artillery units than is found for infantry commands. Courts and responsible commanders might have reduced this tendency had they been more attentive to their responsibilities. Artillerymen often served within the borders of North Carolina and were not hesitant to appeal to Governor Vance when threatened with punishment by the military. Others placed their faith elsewhere: "We must put our trust in god and if it is his will for us to be Killed we must not murmer."[66]

23

North Carolina Local Defense Force

"We will cherish, protect and defend her."[1]

Sixty-Seventh Regiment

Captain John N. Whitford of Craven County organized a local defense force in March 1862 at New Bern. At first, the small command was called to active duty when the need arose; later it became a permanent battalion engaged in repulsing enemy raids, doing scouting activity, and guarding railroads and bridges. An increase in strength was authorized, and the Sixty-Seventh Regiment came into official existence on January 18, 1864. Within a month a soldier who deserted from the original battalion was court-martialed and then executed. Four other court records for the regiment have been found. All trials ended in severe punishment for the accused.

Second Battalion Local Defense

Men of the Battalion went before 5 military courts as recorded by the AIGO. Three men were sentenced to be shot and 2 were given severe sentences.

Courts-Martial

SOLOMON B. SLADE BUIE'S COMPANY (Prior to August 15, 1863). Private Slade enlisted in Captain Duncan M. Buie's company at Wilmington on March 12, 1863. In company records he is listed as Sol B. Slade. This unit later became Captain W. J. McDugald's company. Sometime after three months of service, Private Slade left his company, was arrested, imprisoned and then court-martialed for the desertion attempt. The sentence of the court was death for Private Slade. General Whiting notified President Davis that Private Slade was guilty of the crime of desertion, that there were no mitigating circumstances and therefore "with great reluctance he was compelled to sign their death warrants."[2] Along with Private Slade, 3 deserters were sentenced to the same fate. The condemned soldier was imprisoned awaiting death until fall of the year when, rather surprisingly, he was released and detailed as a detective at Wilmington. His death sentence had been ordered to be carried into effect on August 15, under command of Major W. H. Gibbs, "in the presence of the command forming the city and river defense" of Wilmington.[3] The other 3 men, their fate sealed with "reluctance," were in the Fiftieth Regiment; they were also released from their sentences. It bears speculation whether the death sentence was a ruse to place a detective where he might ferret out information from other prisoners, or if it was intended to coerce a deserter into service as a detective.

AMOS AMYETT WHITFORD'S BATTN (February 5, 1864). Private Amyett did not volunteer for duty until the war was well into the third year. At that point, he agreed to enroll in Captain C. D. Foy's company of Partisan Rangers, doing so on August 20, 1863. Private Amyett had no record of service with the company after early September 1863. On November 24, Private Amyett again volunteered, this time in the Second NCUV. He was among those captured by Confederate forces in February 1864. Along with the other former Confederate soldiers who were captured while in the uniform of the enemy, he was tried, convicted and hanged. On the day before Private Amyett was to be executed, a Chaplain visited with him.

> Requested by Gen. Hoke to visit five more men in prison who are to be hanged tomorrow. Found these men in great distress apparently. The oldest one among them [Private Amyett] professed to be a Christian, whilst practicing his perjury and treason. I wrote letters for three of them to their friends.[4]

On the day of execution, the Chaplain noted in his diary that he baptized two of the men. It is not likely that Private Amyett was one of the two. The Chaplain recalled that Private Amyett said that he was a member of the Methodist church during their conversation. Events proceeded: "These prisoners five in number all made some confession of penitence at the gallows for their crimes, but said nothing about their perjury. They all went upon the scaffold together and paid the forfeit of their lives for their crimes of treason."[5] According to the attending Chaplain, one condemned man made a statement from the gallows. "I believe my peace is made with God. I did wrong in volunteering after I got to Newbern. I would rather have laid in jail all my life than have done it. I have rendered prayer unto God to forgive my sin. I trust in him, and in him only." The other 4 men who were hanged on the same scaffold all said that they felt the same way.[6] An officer of the Second NCUV described the last agony of Private Amyett: "Another, a robust man, Amos Amyett, was tortured for fifteen minutes before the ill-adjusted rope could strangle him to death."[7] No mention is made that anyone came forth to claim the body for family internment.

D. J. MORLEY 2-B BATTN LD (August 16, 1864); and J. C. MORLEY 2-B BATTN LD (August 16, 1864). Privates Daniel and John Morley joined the local defense unit on January 22, 1864. They served without incident until August 2, when they deserted. Their company had just returned from detached duty to the north; the youngsters were understandably anxious for a little time at home. After eight days at large, they were in confinement and awaiting court-martial. On August 16, they were sentenced to be shot. General R. E. Lee did not approve the death sentences, and the young men returned to duty.[8] They were with the battalion in December 1864.

CALTON W. AUTRY 2-B BATTN LD (September 1, 1864). Private Autry enrolled in the Armory Guards on August 3, 1863. While the unit was assigned to Fort Lamb near Wilmington Private Autry deserted on July 26, 1864. Three weeks later he was caught and brought back to stand trial on September 1. At the conclusion of his trial, Private Autry was sentenced to be shot. When the decision was published in GO #62, October 21, 1864, Department of North Carolina, it was noted that the sentence was suspended awaiting review by the President, this being done on the basis of the youthfulness and good character of Private Autry. The President's decision was made known to General Lee by letter on March 5, 1865.[9] The prisoner was pardoned by virtue of General Order #2, and restored to duty. A month later Private Autry was captured by Federal troops; he lived through imprisonment and finally took the oath.

Snippets of reference to men who may have been executed, or were so threatened, occasionally come to light. Usually not enough detail is included to support a definitive search, or to preclude any of the various recording errors that often occur.

JAMES L. KEELER SECOND NCUV (No record). Second Lieutenant Keeler was allegedly captured by Confederate troops at Plymouth on April 25, 1864, while serving in the Federal regiment. An entry in his Federal service record dated July–August 1864, "executed by the enemy—date unknown," would indicate that he was either a deserter from a Confederate unit or engaged in spying; otherwise, he would have presumably been treated as a prisoner of war.[10] No court-martial record has been found. A note in his service record states that he was appointed by Federal General Benjamin Butler, which suggests that he was engaged in some form of clandestine activity.

JOHN BUCK SECOND NCUV (No record). Federal records for the Second NCUV have an entry that a Private John Buck was hanged at Kinston. The record date was September–October 1864.[11] This soldier enrolled for Federal service on December 7, 1863, at age forty-five, and is listed as present through August 1864. Another entry states that the soldier was transferred to another Federal command in 1865, and that he was later denied a Federal pension. One of the entries may be a simple posting error, perhaps due to the similarity in names with Private John Brock, who was hanged at Kinston in February 1864. The only North Carolina record for a Private John Buck is for a man who enlisted at age twenty-five in an artillery unit but never reported for duty.

KELLY FOURTH REGIMENT (USA No record); and SPEER FOURTH REGIMENT USA (No record). The jurisdiction of military courts was increased to include more military departments and the states within the Confederacy in February 1864. Comment on a decision of one court is found following reference to the poor farming weather: "I was surprised to learn of the shooting of Speer and Kelly for desertion by order of a Court Martial. I was not aware that the Government organized a roving Court before. I suppose we will have them in our Circuit soon."[12] More detailed identification of Speer or Kelly has not been found. Apparently they were known to the letter writer, A. C. Cowles, and the addressee, Isaac Jarratt of Yadkin County. There are Speer and Kelly families in the Yadkin area. The most likely lead is that two Speer men, both of Yadkin County, enrolled in Company F of the Twenty-Eighth Regiment, deserted and reportedly enrolled in Company E of the Fourth Infantry, USA, in October 1864.[13] Neither is found by name on the rolls of Federal army units for men enrolled in the months around that time. However, men often enrolled under an alias; there are an uncommon number of John Smiths.[14]

PINZE (No record). General Whiting, on October 13, 1864, wrote Colonel W. H. Taylor, aide to General Lee, for permission to shoot a conscript named Pinze. The General went on to say that the man had been exempted from service but had then met with the enemy, was arrested and imprisoned. In some unexplained circumstance, he had escaped from confinement and then continued to meet with the enemy. General Whiting gave his opinion that the man should have been shot immediately by the arresting officer.[15] No other material has come to hand concerning Pinze, nor is any likely candidate found in North

Carolina census records, or in court-martial records. Whether Pinze was actually conscripted or General Whiting was simply saying that he should be considered as such is not evident. In any event, General Whiting certainly realized that such permission was highly unlikely without the formality of a trial of some sort.

S. BLEVINS (No record). On April 13, 1864, Brigadier General John H. Winder notified Major Isaac H. Carrington that Captain Bates should receive and be responsible for the movement of a prisoner identified as S. Blevins, of a North Carolina command shown as 2-B.[16] The prisoner was under sentence of death and was to be taken to his command for execution. No other identification for this soldier or a court-martial record has been located. Men with that name and initial enrolled in North Carolina commands are accounted for.

JAMES FLYNT (No record). The struggle to force men into service continued to the very end. "The first Battalion has been here sometime hunting deserters they have caught several and have taken up several that wer at home who I suppose did not have the proper proper [sic] papers to let them off they taken up Dewit & James Flynt and after James had his papers fixed up all wright they shot him for what cause no one knows they shot four ball in him and they have shot several others who I suppose refuse to go to the army. It is hard times here and geting no better fast."[17] The man shot was James M. Flynt. The Flynt family was a lingering source of contention throughout the war years. In 1862, a writer mentioned: "They have had another battle at ole Allen Flynts latela old nancy got slitela wounded."[18] A newspaper article adds a bit more to the Flynt saga. The First Battalion of North Carolina Sharp Shooters was in the area for a visit home and to provide for the safety of citizens. While so doing 5 or 7 men were shot by the battalion commanded by Captain Reuben Everett Wilson.[19] Some were killed in an attempt to free prisoners. Captain R. E. Wilson is mentioned as the officer in command of the Provost Guard at the time of the executions at Kinston in February 1864. His reputation was that of a strict disciplinarian.

In the final days of war, a futile execution of Confederate soldiers is referenced as having occurred at Raleigh: "They shot some 7 or 8 men here in at [sic] Raleigh for deserting but I didn't see it."[20] The letter was written on March 26, 1865, from Babtist [sic] Grove. No supporting evidence has come to light.

While these last bits of information suggest execution of North Carolinians, there is little doubt that other executions left only the bloody ground to mark the man and his fate.

Epilogue

March Off, Straggle Home

> *"A farmer ... may be a good soldier if you take care to have him properly disciplined."*[1]

Rare indeed was a full-strength company of North Carolina infantrymen after the first year of campaigning.[2] Disease led the first assault; absences followed in a second wave. Companies established distinctive patterns of loss. Company B, Fifth Regiment, buried 51 dead by the end of 1862. Company H, Twenty-Seventh Regiment, had 27 men leave for five days in the spring of 1862.[3] For other companies there was a less dramatic attrition as day by day soldiers drifted away. Company A of the Forty-Ninth experienced a consistent loss of men over three years, and there were no executions to check the exodus. Beginning in January 1862, Company H, Forty-Fourth Regiment, had 60 incidents of absence from a total enrollment of 128.

Nearly one-quarter of the total, 13, departed camp and company on August 14, 1863. A sudden burst, perhaps a second, is characteristic of many companies. Companies with an urgent need for replacements had to be vigilant, lest the newly enrolled depart within hours of arrival. In Company E, Fifty-Fourth Regiment, 15 replacements deserted on the day of their enrollment, and 2 more followed after a night in camp. Comparison of companies with extreme absences to those with a minimal number emphasizes the disparity from company to company within a regiment, and from regiment to regiment. The absent column (Abs) includes those absent without leave (Awol).

Half of the 16 high absence companies, 8, are from just 3 regiments. Companies that were lax in keeping men in the ranks were identifiable for corrective action. Not included in the low absence list are 67 companies that reported fewer than 15 absences; that cut-off point was chosen as best reflective of accurate company record keeping. Low absence companies experienced departures in the 10 percent range while high absence companies approached 46 percent. Nearly 36 percent of absences went on the offender's record as absent without leave in the high absence companies; that fell to 31 percent for the low absence companies.

Service records are often not specific as to dates of departure and return for absentees, but a scan indicates that less than 15 percent of men absent without leave returned within three months of their departure. Men in some high absence companies made multiple departures; 71 men accumulated 93 absence incidents in Company D of the Thirty-Third. Likewise, 64 men were charged with the 87 incidents for Company B, Thirty-Seventh, as were 50 men responsible for 87 absences from Company F of the same regiment. The tendency toward repetitive absences is not apparent in other companies: in Company H, Forty-Fourth,

Company Absences [4]

		High						Low			
Reg	Co	Enr	Abs	Awol	Ex	Reg	Co	Enr	Abs	Awol	Ex
33	D	172	93	40	2	53	A	142	15	9	0
37	B	177	87	41	1	11	D	128	15	1	1
37	F	191	87	24	1	6	D	196	15	3	1
38	B	163	84	30	2	46	K	155	15	1	0
37	A	190	83	37	2	51	D	156	15	11	0
34	A	139	80	44	1	23	F	169	16	8	0
53	E	136	80	31	0	38	H	136	16	2	0
38	E	150	76	28	1	53	B	134	17	15	0
26	C	185	74	17	2	26	E	200	17	2	0
49	A	143	73	11	0	21	G	186	17	7	1
4	E	193	71	3	4	7	F	149	17	3	0
37	K	171	71	33	0	27	C	124	17	1	0
56	B	133	69	13	0	17	H	163	17	4	1
22	I	184	65	40	2	8	G	120	17	0	0
33	G	157	62	44	0	2	E	180	17	9	0
44	H	128	60	5	1	14	D	149	17	5	0

57 men accounted for 60 absences; the same count is found for Company D of the Forty-Eighth, while 69 men were responsible for the 71 absences in Company E of the Fourth. Of the 16 high absence companies, 11 marched 19 men to the execution field; 4 low absence companies each sacrificed a single soldier. Three regiments have companies on both the high and low absence list. Just 3 regiments with a regimental numeric designation lower than 30 are found among the high absence companies. The low absence listing has 11 such regiments.

North Carolina infantrymen who faced execution were enrolled in one of approximately 560 infantry companies in 11 brigades from the state, or in a near dozen regiments that were brigaded with troops from other states. Of these companies, men of 186 heard that their ranks would be reduced by execution, and for just less than half, 89 companies, that reality occurred. On the other side of the ledger, 105 companies had no record of men at trial before a general court-martial or military court. Obviously these apparently exemplary companies were not entirely free of malefactors; some had rather high desertion rates but were formed in areas where arrest of deserters varied from difficult to impossible. For other companies, records were lost or never started on the way to Richmond to be entered in AIGO ledgers.

Companies with no court-martial record were selected to offer a cross section by regiment. These 39 companies had 5,373 men enrolled, and there were 691 recorded absences, an absence rate of 13 percent. For companies that experienced 7 or more courts, 60 were studied, 8,551 men were enrolled in these companies and they accounted for 2,089 absences, a rate of 25 percent. With one absence rate half that of the other, court-martial records are a sound indicator of absence activity. In some instances they are more accurate than service records, for it is not unusual to find that an absence, trial and punishment are not entered on a soldier's service record, but are listed in AIGO records.

The effectiveness of executions in limiting desertion is most evident at the company level. Witnessing the execution of a company member gave greater pause to a soldier mulling desertion than did the execution of a soldier in another company. Effectiveness was increased if the execution was accepted as just and necessary. It cast a different pall if it was known that the man at the stake left to aid a sick or starving family or that he was a good soldier swept into an impulsive act. How men of a company balanced fact, feeling and fancy about the sacrifice they were witnessing influenced their absence decision.

Service records for 24 companies that had men executed were searched for absences the half-year prior to and following an execution. For these companies, incidents of men departing were halved, 263 incidents before the execution, 133 after. Brother companies in the same regiments saw little change in absence activity; 32 companies recorded 142 absences six months before an execution and 136 in the six months thereafter. Also noted, the absence tendency following an execution was nearly the same for all 56 companies that were examined. Executions lowered absences from the wayward companies to an average level, but did not further reduce the evil.

As to the effectiveness of executing 2 deserters with one volley compared to a single execution and then another a few days later: 9 companies in 7 regiments had 2 men shot to death at the same time. Absences for these companies fell from 71 six months before the executions to 17 in the six months thereafter, a 76 percent reduction. Absences from 15 companies that witnessed a single execution went from 192 six months prior to the event to 116 in the following six months, a reduction of 40 percent. With an absence improvement about double, side by side executions were more effective than single executions.

While executions tended to keep men with their companies, the handmaiden of war, death, took her toll from others.

Company Deaths

	Killed			Died			Total Dead	
Reg Co	#	Brigade	Reg Co	#	Brigade	Reg Co	#	Brigade
26 F	41	Kirkland	5 G	63	Garland	4 H	88	Cox
37 A	40	Lane	5 H	63	Garland	5 B	85	Garland
20 B	40	Garland	52 F	60	Kirkland	37 A	84	Lane
23 B	38	Scales	4 H	56	Cox	5 G	82	Garland
4 A	34	Cox	2 C	56	Cox	4 C	81	Cox
26 B	33	Kirkland	5 B	53	Garland	28 C	81	Lane
12 D	33	Garland	4 C	53	Cox	2 E	80	Cox
4 H	32	Cox	44 E	52	Kirkland	5 H	80	Garland
28 C	32	Lane	6 K	50	Hoke	26 F	78	Kirkland
5 B	32	Garland	28 C	49	Lane	37 B	75	Lane

Over half of the above companies are in either the Cox or Garland brigades. These brigades had just 5 men executed though suffering grievous loss in early engagements. The companies with the highest casualties are concentrated in 6 of the 11 North Carolina infantry brigades. Company A of the Thirty-Seventh Regiment is the only company found in the above Killed column and the High Absence column in the absence listing. There is little connection between battle deaths and absences.

Approximately half of all North Carolina infantry companies were searched for men who were absent, who died while in service, or who were killed in battle or died of wounds. For those killed in battle there is a near normal company distribution with a slight skew toward a company high of 41 killed with a company median of 17 killed. Command decisions tended to maintain a degree of balance in company casualties. Still, placement on the battlefield, company leadership, an unexpected volley, a rain of shells, all led to devastation in some companies. Non-battle deaths also have a slight drift toward a company high of 63 and a company median of 30 deaths. Companies with men who had little prior exposure to infectious disease were not prepared for the maladies of camp life. When deadly disease infected, it easily passed to nearby companion and concerned comforter. Absences reveal a deviation far greater than that found for died or killed. Company absences range from 3, or fewer, to a high of 93, with a median of 23 absentees per company.[5] Regimental court-martial distribution closely follows that of company absences with a median of 35 courts per regiment and a high of 106 courts. The crux of the absence dilemma for North Carolinians rested with these deviant companies. Men were recruited, lived, died and deserted in clusters.

A man departing his company most often did so with at least one accomplice, frequently a relative. Fear, faith, malcontents, messmates or relatives: all contributed to the natural tendency of soldiers to form small groups. That clustering then eased the way to an absence decision.[6] Clustering also had a positive side; for many it strengthened their loyalty and kept them in the ranks, a contributing factor to the wide variance found in company absences. Other considerations added to the company to company absence imbalance: ease of departing, minimal punishment for earlier deserters, diligence of the local militia and the likelihood of finding sanctuary at home. The effectiveness of those attempting to dissuade or arrest deserters in North Carolina influenced the decision of those considering desertion.

Service records of men enrolled in 229 infantry companies show that one-third of North Carolina deaths are clearly identified as killed in combat or died of wounds. Two-thirds died of disease, including those in Federal prison camps, or an unknown cause.[7] However, there is a definite indication that deaths in each group increased at the same rate. The generally weakened condition of men in a company, and their inability to fight off either wound or disease was a contributing factor. Nine companies lost more than 40 percent of their enrolled men. On average, they recorded 54 deaths due to disease or cause unknown, and 28 were killed in combat or died of wounds.[8] Company level officers lost their lives in the exact opposite relationship. A search of 234 deaths shows that 163 — 70 percent — were combat connected, while 30 percent were due to disease or cause unknown. The same record is found for company officers from Georgia, South Carolina and Virginia: 73 percent of officer deaths were combat related. Also consistent across 3 of the states, 1 officer died for every 24 or 25 who died in the ranks. Virginia lost 1 officer for every 22 of the men they led.[9] Few companies had an equal balance of combat and non-combat deaths. Company A, Thirty-Seventh Regiment, with 40 men killed and 44 dead from illness or disease, was one of the few.

Infantry companies of North Carolinians were organized into regiments and sent to fight in Virginia. Once there, men soon began to appear before a general court-martial. For the war, regiments in the Third Corps, Army of Northern Virginia, account for 9 of the 14 most highly court-martialed North Carolina regiments. For these regiments, 1 of 7 men appearing before a court was given a death sentence; 1 in 20 was executed. For the least active regiments, the same death judgment is found —1 in 7 of those at trial — but just 1 in 50 was executed. Pender-Scales and Branch-Lane-Barry brigades have 7 of the 14 high-court regiments. The Clingman and Garland brigades have 6 of the 14 low-court regiments. Courts-martial are convictions only; acquittals are not included.

Courts-Martial by Regiment[10]

	High				Low		
Reg	CM	TBE	Ex	Reg	CM	TBE	Ex
16	106	7	4	24	8	2	0
22	88	11	3	56	11	1	0
37	81	14	6	8	12	4	0
44	74	9	4	23	13	1	0
53	73	11	3	61	13	7	2
46	70	5	4	12	15	1	0
38	66	17	5	57	16	3	1
42	63	24	3	14	16	0	0
28	62	6	1	5	17	1	0
45	57	2	1	52	17	9	4
21	55	7	1	31	18	1	0
7	54	7	4	64	21	4	0
4	51	8	4	11	22	2	2
34	50	7	3	30	22	1	0

Little difference is found in the wartime deaths suffered by regiments with frequent appearances before a military court and those with fewer trials. The regiments that sent the most men before a court averaged 31 natural deaths and 17 killed. The regiments with few court appearances averaged 28 natural deaths and 16 killed.

Regiments that were formed at the onset of conflict experienced fewer courts than did those that were organized a year later.

Infantry Regiments[11]

Regiment #	1–9	10–19	20–29	30–39	40–49	50–59	60–69
Average CM	35.8	36.4	43.6	42.3	50.0	30.3	23.0

Regiments 1 through 9 were formed in May and June of 1861, 40 through 49 were organized in April and May of 1862. Regiments formed at the beginning of conscription had more court-martial activity in a year less service. Several regiments in the far right columns had companies with little or no court activity due to successful desertions, wholesale capture by the enemy or a lack of will to take men to trial.

In the second year of war, Confederate leaders determined that a more effective fighting force would result if regiments were brigaded by their home state. The majority of North Carolina infantry regiments were thus brigaded, and were led by a native of the state or by an officer that had some connection therein. Others were led by officers from other states, notably Virginia. Over the course of the war, 33 officers who were appointed to the rank of Brigadier, or higher, were attributed to North Carolina, 8 percent of the Confederate total of 423. General officers from Virginia, 79, comprised 19 percent of the total. Yet war deaths were dramatically reversed; 40,000 North Carolinians—30 percent of Confederate casualties; compared to 15,000 Virginians—11 percent, lending some substance to the bewilderment of North Carolinians as to who was leading the war and who was fighting the fight.

Men in 11 North Carolina infantry brigades went before 1,892 military courts, 1,141 of these, 60 percent, were attributed to the 3 most court-martialed companies of their regiment. Of nearly 1,900 courts, 948 were charged to men in the 14 most often court-martialed regiments. The evil of desertion might better have been immediately confronted on a company and a regimental basis rather than awaiting the capture and trial of guilty individuals. The months or years that elapsed between the departure and punishment of a deserter negated the beneficial effect of prompt corrective action. Those considering departure may, in fact, have been encouraged by a deserters' initial success. In the few court-martial summaries available, the court sometime asked if the accused was a good soldier. The follow-on question, "Is he from a desertion-prone company or regiment?" was not presented to the court.

Adding that factor to the decision to execute a deserter from a troubled company would not have met great resistance. There are instances where condemned men accepted that they were to be sacrificed because many others had deserted. They were aware that in a different circumstance they might have gone unpunished or received relatively light sentences. But at that time and place they were to serve as a deadly warning for the assembled troops.

North Carolina Infantry Brigades

	Company Average				Brigade Total[12]		
Brigade	Enr	Abs	Died	Killed	CM	TBE	EX
Scales	148	30	25	15	352	50	18
Lane	172	38	39	23	254	36	20
Cooke	145	22	29	17	223	32	13
Grimes	142	31	27	11	216	14	6
Kirkland	170	33	32	16	204	32	17
Martin	151	21	9	5	143	43	6
Cox	162	17	40	26	127	11	5
Ransom	150	30	23	12	111	28	6
Hoke	152	16	35	13	107	22	5
Garland	152	12	30	23	83	16	0
Clingman	130	29	20	10	72	15	2
					1,892	299	98[13]

The first 4 brigades listed above fought in the Third Corps of General Lee's army. Each brigade was made up of 5 regiments. These 20 regiments had 150 men given death sentences by military courts and at least 68 were executed. The remaining 7 brigades of North Carolinians carried the flags of 29 regiments. These regiments had 142 men given death sentences and 30 were executed. The 4 brigades in the Third Corps suffered 70 percent of the executions of men in North Carolina infantry brigades.

Infantry Brigades
To Be Executed and Executed

	1862	1863			1864	1865	ND	
TBE	1	6	48	79	69 53 28	15	299	
Executed		1	6	21	42 18 6	4	98[14]	

Executions went forward with determination in September 1863, slacked off later in the year, and renewed with vengeance in January and February 1864, long after the surge of absences in 1862.

North Carolina Troops
Month of Execution

J	F	M	A	M	J	J	A	S	O	N	D	
23	33	9	11	18	2	1	4	30	8	8	4	151

Summer months were for campaigning and deserting, others were for trial and stake.

Executed
By County of Residence or Enrollment

Wilkes	14	Rutherford	5	Lenoir	4		
Jones	12	Stanly	5	New Hanover	4		
Randolph	8	Union	5	Stokes	4		
Burke	7	Yadkin	5	Wake	4		
Catawba	6	Craven	4	Ashe	3		

Of 89 North Carolina counties, 15 were either the home county or the point of enrollment for 60 percent of the North Carolinians who were executed. Following Ashe, 17 counties had 2 or 3 of their men executed, and 17 others had only one. For the State, 49 counties had at least one soldier executed; 34 of the counties were west of Wake County. But for the mass executions at Kinston in 1864 and in the Third Regiment in September 1863, all of eastern North Carolinians, the imbalance — east to west — would have been larger.

To gain full meaning, the record of troops from North Carolina must be compared to that of troops from nearby states.

Sampled Infantry Regiments[15]
Eastern Armies

State	Regs	Records	Absent	%	Dead	%
NC	23	3,140	426	14	839	27
VA	23	3,085	670	22	412	13
GA	26	2,912	254	9	820	28[16]
	8	1,054	121	12	285	27[17]
	10	1,469	200	14	331	22[18]
SC	21	3,568	387	11	675	19

Non-commissioned men whose last name began with the same letter, "B" or "S" for instance, within a given regiment, were searched for the above information. Searching by name rather than by sample or by company reveals a mournful sequence as men die, or absent themselves, in deadly iambic cluster: one survives, two die, two desert, four die.

Percent of Total Absences
by Half-Year[19]

	1861	1862		1863		1864		1865
NC	2	8	19	18	13	7	15	17
VA	11	25	27	9	10	9	6	3
GA	4	5	5	3	12	18	20	34
SC	2	6	14	13	21	17	17	11

Nearly half of all absences of troops from North Carolina began before the last half of 1863, and nearly three-fourths of the absences charged to Virginia infantrymen were recorded during that same time. Men of the Palmetto State were quite consistent in their rate of departure, peaking in late 1863, when absences by their northern neighbors were in decline. Infantrymen from Georgia assigned to the Army of Northern Virginia had consistently fewer absences through the first two years of fighting. Absences increased when they were sent to aid the Army of Tennessee in the defense of Georgia.

Well over 6,000 absentees were returned to the struggle by North Carolina and neighboring states in late 1863 and early 1864. Nearly the same number of conscripts were bundled off to the service during that time. North Carolina accounted for 24 percent of the men sent to the army; slightly less than its 28 percent share of the total enrollment from the 4 states. Georgia and Virginia returned more deserters than did North Carolina but their soldiers made far fewer marches to the execution field.

Men Sent to the Army[20]
December 1863–March 1864

		Dec	Jan	Feb	Mar	Total
NC	Deserters	404	322	363	253	1,342
	Conscripts	386	204	198	856	
VA	Deserters	503	575	492	590	2,160
	Conscripts	223	361	859	595	
GA	Deserters	354	438	507	621	1,920
	Conscripts	376	192	335	637	
SC	Deserters	256	270	190	189	905
	Conscripts	193	373	143	197	
	Volunteers	46	286	545	312	

Disciplinary record for all branches of Confederate service offer another perspective on North Carolina troops and those of her neighbors to the north and south.

Eastern Confederate States[21]

State	Enroll	Conscripts	Military Dead	Courts-Martial	Death Sentence	Executed
NC	127,000	21,000	40,000	3,200	450	160–170
VA	155,000	13,000	15,000	5,600	380	70–80
GA	130,000	9,000	11,000	2,100	140	15–20
SC	60,000	9,000	18,000	2,000	140	15–20

Infantry Courts-martial[22]

State	Regs	CM/ Reg	Inf %/ All CM	High 10% Inf. CM	Reg Most CM Reg	Most CM
NC	56	46	81	23	16	106
VA	57	50	51	27	57	252
GA	67	22	69	23	10	84
SC	31	38	60	26	15	168

The percentage of infantry courts-martial to the total courts of troops from a state advances neatly, 50 percent for Virginia, 60 percent for South Carolina, 70 percent for Georgia, 80 percent for North Carolina [column 3]. Military deaths advanced in not far different cadence. One-quarter of all infantry courts-martial were charged to just one-tenth of the infantry regiments in each of the states [column 4]. Within these highly court-martialed regiments, 3 companies accounted for from 50 percent to 60 percent of courts affecting their regiment. In that light, it might be expected that orders and correspondence relating to these troublesome companies would be found. There are few references that something was awry in Company D, or Company E, and that regiment or brigade officers should take some action. Comments are directed toward the performance or competence of a particular officer, but there is little focus on a company as a unit.

North Carolina recorded nearly as many service deaths, and more executions, than did Georgia, South Carolina and Virginia combined. For all combatant states, North and South, only New York lost more men to death. The Empire State had about one-fifth more dead from a total enrollment over three times as large. North Carolina was essentially an infantry-producing state; she suffered accordingly in deaths and executions. Eighty-four percent of her men that went into service were enrolled in infantry units. Death by execution decisions were closely aligned; over 80 percent of those concerning North Carolina's troops went to infantrymen. Of all the North Carolinians that were executed, 90 percent were infantrymen. The percentage of infantry deaths was twice that of absences.[23]

Virginia infantrymen had the opposite experience; for them the percentage of absences was nearly twice that of deaths.[24] It is worth noting that Virginia enrolled on the order of one-fifth more men than did North Carolina, yet recorded fewer than one-half the deaths. Many more cavalry and artillery units were formed in Virginia, just 59 of 100 Virginians fought in infantry units, one factor leading to the fewer deaths.[25] There were 60 or more artillery batteries in the Army of Northern Virginia in mid-1862; two-thirds, 39, were formed in Virginia, 5 in North Carolina. Absences for Virginians reached serious levels in 1862, an experience similar to that of North Carolina. However, many of the Virginia absences were later entered as "absent sick" on service records, with no explanation provided. At least three factors support the notion that Virginia's absent sick records are suspect. One, in that time frame, it was necessary to issue orders to securely lock doors on trains taking men to hospitals and to post sentinels to arrest deserters on all trains.[26] Two, troops from other states fighting alongside the Virginians had lower rates of absence with presumably an equal, or greater, exposure to sickness.[27] Three, death records do not suggest that Virginia's troops suffered an undue amount of sickness.[28] Absent-sick records may also partially explain why Virginia enrolled about 20 percent more men than did North Carolina and experienced 40 percent more courts but far fewer executions. Considering the frequency of courts-martial death decisions for troops from Virginia, more executions might have been expected. Half of the death decisions to Virginians went to infantrymen. Service records for troops from Virginia are generally very consistent in bimonthly entries. The Thirty-Third Regiment, for example, was meticulous in recording absent without leave violations. The same attention was not evident in placing charges against absentees. The regiment experienced approximately 700 incidents of absence but courts-martial were in the range of 80. The regiment lost 2 men by execution.[29]

Georgia had a comparable level of deaths to North Carolina, and men from Georgia who were assigned to the Army of Northern Virginia had a much better absence record. Based on infantry service records, the total military dead of 11,000 in the table of Eastern Confederate States understates Georgia deaths; something akin to that of South Carolina is likely more accurate. Records for Georgia regiments serving in the Army of Northern Virginia are very brief, often just a clothing or pay record, and have little or no detail on the soldier. As noted, the Georgians resisted the urge to depart until the fall of 1863, when they were temporarily assigned to the Army of Tennessee and were closer to the attraction of home. A final surge of absences began in February 1865. Georgia enrolled approximately as many men as did North Carolina but had fewer than one-fourth the men sentenced to be executed.

South Carolina infantrymen had an absence record equally as good as that of Georgia. Proportionate to men enrolled, as many South Carolinians were buried by war's end as were men from North Carolina. As listed above, the range given for South Carolina dead is based solely on service records and is understated, something in the range given for North Carolina being more representative. Unlike the other states, nearly half of all death sentences given to South Carolinians went to artillerymen or cavalrymen.

Was there was a tendency toward severe punishment for North Carolinians that was not evident for other states? Consider that 12 percent of Tar Heels going to trial were acquitted, while 14 percent were given death sentences by military courts. For all Confederate states, 16 percent of men at trial were acquitted, and 6 percent were given a death sentence.[30] True, there may have been an immediate and pressing military necessity that caused some of the imbalance. Over 50 men of North Carolina were killed in 4 massive executions at precarious times in the war. No other Confederate state suffered similar slaughter. Death decisions were approved by senior officers from Virginia. These officers might well have directed that proven instigators or more egregious offenders be executed. Their judgments were otherwise, and their reasoning — on the crime, the point in the war, the condition of the army, the reaction of soldier and citizen — remains forever with them. But beyond need and effectiveness, the wisdom of military leaders in ordering these spectacles begs scrutiny. Particularly if the primary purpose of a military execution was to dissuade others from committing a similar crime. Toward the end of deterrence, grouping men for killing did not provide an example of balanced, reasoned, military justice. Surely those at the stake or on the trap had varying degrees of guilt. Might not the most guilty have been determined and their death accepted as a well-deserved warning? Courts and generals were then judging man and crime on an individual basis, not conveniently grouping men for hasty killing. The spared men would certainly attest to the value that Confederate leaders placed on the life of every soldier. Those marching by the executed men would be equally impressed; every death decision was carefully weighed at all levels of command. Those spared might have been positioned near the condemned, during or after the ritual, to heighten the awareness of select and reasoned execution. The military benefit of a just execution was realized. A soldier's life was not seen as a trifle to be casually placed on a balance, even at a critical moment in a war with thousands already dead.

Some 300 North Carolinians were in some fashion released from court-imposed death sentences. The President, the Secretary of War and General Lee were involved in 60 percent of these cases. Nearly 10 percent of those condemned escaped from confinement while under a death sentence and the same number were found to have returned under an amnesty offer. About 5 percent of condemned Confederates died while awaiting execution and a slightly larger number were returned to duty because of an error in court records or proceedings. For the remainder, the record is not clear. Would the number of released men been lower had field commanders followed the admonition of General Cooper and accepted their responsibility in regard to the death sentence? With the exception of one or two field commanders that would certainly have been the case. And if this resolve had been present in 1862 there would have been a significant benefit to the Confederacy.

Early on, men of North Carolina were marked as frequent deserters, often cited as being at the very center of that curse on the Confederacy. What led to the damning condemnation of so many who gave so much? Lacking more persuasive evidence, consideration centers in four areas. Most North Carolinians fought defending the soil of their northern neighbor, one not greatly admired, rather than directly in defense of their own state. This while their own homes were in the path of the enemy and their families were threatened by inflamed neighbors, lawless bands, and opportunistic criminals. Of every 100 men in Confederate service 12 were North Carolinians, well within the range of men furnished by the other states. However, a larger proportion of the North Carolinians were conscripts or hesitant volunteers. Of every 100 Confederate conscripts, 26 were North Carolinians. Men who were forced into service, were more likely to take an early opportunity to absent themselves, though the line between an unwilling conscript and a reluctant volunteer is wavy at best. Governor Vance led a determined effort to take up conscripts, and with that went the risk of increasing the number of men willing, even eager, to chance the path of desertion. And the decision to allow conscripts to choose their regiment of service had the unintended consequence of placing wavering men alongside others of the same mind.[31] Of every 100 Confederate men who died while in the service, 30 were North Carolinians. The obvious disparity in deaths must have caused North Carolinians to question why they bore so great a share of the deadly burden and to seek relief as best they might. Another unintended consequence may have resulted from the desire of North Carolinians to be led by Brigadier Generals from their state. As an AIGO officer pointed out in his comments on a lack of discipline in the army: "The Brigade Commander, more than anyone else, is at fault ... he has the power to control and correct the evils."[32] That accepted, North Carolina brigades may have fared better if state considerations had not entered into the selection of the Brigadier that led them. The best brigade in the Army of Northern Virginia was one of North Carolina troops led by a brigadier from another state, Brigadier J. R. Cooke.[33]

Absences peaked in the second half of 1862, executions in the first half of 1864. Would earlier and firmer execution decisions have led to ending the war? Greater resolve in 1862 certainly offered that prospect. Soldiers would have been kept in the ranks by executing deserters from 15 or 20 selected companies. The men thus kept in the field would have had a significant impact in winning more decisive victories in the summer and fall of the year. With that success, a negotiated settlement and a functioning Confederacy might well have come to pass. General Lee recognized that possibility and suggested to President Davis that he open negotiations with the North to recognize Confederate independence.[34] A stronger army, a few decisive battles, would have strengthened Confederate determination and weakened that of the enemy. But time and technology would have soon forced a change in the Confederate course and led to some form of reunion. So the sacrifice of a few, 20 or 25 North Carolinians — and a like number of Virginians — may well have ended the terrible toll of civil war and preserved the lives of many hundreds of thousands, Federal and Confederate. This is not to say that a random selection of men be shot in a Roman style decimation, or that guilt-free men be forced to draw straws or black beans before being sacrificed. But rather than drumming convicted deserters from the ranks, or sending them off to prison for the war, drum the most egregious offenders to the stake. Replace the reliance on humiliation with the decisive crack of a well-aimed volley. Little empathy is found for a deserter facing a deserved and warranted execution, though the poor marksmanship at executions does suggest that men were not eager to take part in the killing. Soldiers wrote of their horror while watching an execution, particularly when bungled, and they often said they did not want to witness another such affair. But by and large, they recognized that men not willing to stand with them in battle placed their lives, and the safety of their family and of their state, in greater jeopardy.

How the people at home would have reacted to early executions is more difficult to judge. Considering the general acceptance of the task to be done and the creeping pace of news, it would not have been a deterrent in 1862. In the eastern counties a stringent application of death for deserters would have had little effect on the citizenry. Patterns of absence were studied for 110 companies; 15 gave evidence that early absences foretold a looming threat to the Confederacy. Just 2 of the 15 companies were from counties east of Wake. The eastern section that remained in Confederate control was generally loyal and their men would not have experienced any marked increase in executions. The counties that were west of Wake were polarized in support of the war, and the fissure would most certainly have deepened but not greatly altered in balance. Confederate families in western North Carolina who had men dead of disease, maimed, or killed, while they themselves were beset by deserters and Tories would have accepted the need for executions. It is not likely that a widespread adverse response would have developed or matured before the benefit of the decisive use of military execution was realized by the armies in the field. There was no means for any such general awareness to be formed or to be made known. When mentioned at all, newspaper accounts were published weeks or months after an execution, and generally lacked specific detail. They did sermonize that the event described was sad, but necessary. In sum, death for desertion decisions eighteen months earlier than when belatedly begun would not have met serious opposition at home or in the service.

The need and benefit of more frequent marches to the execution field was recognized in the ranks, and in the command tent, by the fall of 1862. Moments before being bound to his execution stake in September 1862, a soldier allegedly testified that if the Confederacy had been as strict in executing deserters a year earlier the army would be much larger, and he would still be in it.[35] This same point was emphasized after the war by a staff officer: "It has been the opinion of many good men, both during and since the war, that if such a just and salutary example had been offered both earlier and oftener it would have been far better for the cause and for the men who supported it.... Such examples are always painful; but it is necessary for discipline and safety that cowards and traitors should die in the cold blood of felons as that brave men should be sacrificed for honor in the warm blood of glory."[36] These comments emphasize that a small number of early executions would have more effectively controlled desertion than did a much larger toll later on. A similar observation was made by a Confederate officer: "There can be no question that a person becomes hardened and indifferent to the sufferings of others, and this will increase, in spite of every exertion to the contrary."[37] A few lines before he gave the view "that this life was calculated to drive away and destroy all finer feelings a soldier ever possessed." Soldiers became disciplined to be indifferent to death as their time in service increased.[38] Witnessing an execution before that indifference was deeply ingrained increased the effectiveness of the ritual.

What would be a final amnesty was urged in a letter to President Davis from General Lee written on February 9, 1865, three days after he was ordered to the post of General in Chief of the Confederate Armies.[39] He said that he must have the authority to remove field officers who failed in their responsibility, rather pointedly telling the President that political considerations must not influence military decisions or appointments. A year earlier a lower-grade officer sounded a warning: "I am afraid our cause is in imminent peril. The folly that characterizes the conduct of the President in military affairs, the great reverses that have resulted recently from his direct interference."[40] A thirty-day amnesty period for absent men not previously convicted of desertion was also recommended by General Lee. Any convicted deserter after this period would receive his full sentence without suspension, remission or delay; there could be no appeal for clemency. General Lee closed by saying that this was the only method he could propose to return those in desertion to their place in the ranks. His hope was that public sentiment would then force these men from their shelters and back to service. The President promptly agreed, and two days later a general order was issued to the Confederate armies.[41] Unfortunately, General Lee was two and a half years late with his suggestions, though it is unlikely they would have been given serious consideration at some earlier point. At that late date the writing was on the wall, or the fiddle hung on the nail; as foretold by the astute General Longstreet, there is "but three months left us for this work."[42]

Assistant Secretary of War John A. Campbell made a brutally objective analysis of Confederate capacity to wage war on March 5, 1865.[43] Essentially the Confederacy had no remaining resource to continue the struggle. They were destitute of food, finance, men and weapons. Desertion was not controllable, some states were near revolt, others were falling to the enemy. Under such desperate conditions it is difficult to understand why General Lee voiced any hope that public sentiment would accept harsh punishment for deserters or shame men into returning to their companies, especially following a winter of discouragement, for these same men had forsaken their companies when battles were won and victory was within reach in 1862. Greater resolve to execute at that pivotal juncture would have strengthened the one resource — a disciplined Confederate army — that could bring about a negotiated end to the war, the many lives thus saved thereby forging a living monument to honor the men and boys who were sacrificed on the execution field. For who dare say the honor is not due, or that the body sagging on the execution cross was not of greater benefit to the Confederacy than a mangled corpse on a battlefield.

Chapter Notes

Introduction

1. National Archives and Records Administration, RG 109, Chapter 1, Vol. 42, Letters and Telegrams Endorsements, September 21, 1864. Hereafter cited as NARA.
2. James Anson Farrer, *Military Manners and Customs* (Piccadilly, London: Chatto & Windus, 1885), p. 244.
3. Manuscript Department, Perkins Library, Duke University, Confederate States Army, Box 2, Military Court 1st Corps, January 15, 1864. Hereafter cited as Perkins.
4. Lt. Col. John Gurwood, *Selections from the Despatches and General Orders of Field Marshall the Duke of Wellington* (London: Murray, 1851), p. 921.
5. Ibid.
6. Ibid., p. 769.
7. Theodore Ayrault Dodge, *Napoleon* (Boston: Houghton Mifflin, 1904), p. 38, 208, 244, 246, 320, 380, 694.
8. Jay Luvaas, ed., *Frederick the Great on the Art of War* (New York: The Free Press, 1966), p. 77.
9. Ibid., p. 114.
10. George Macaulay Trevelyan, *Garibaldi's Defence of the Roman Republic 1848–1849* (London: Phoenix Press, 1920), fn p. 247.
11. G. Putney Beers, *Guide to Federal Archives Related to the Civil War* (Washington: Government Printing Office, 1968), p. 141.
12. Don Higgenbotham, *George Washington and the American Military Tradition* (Athens: University of Georgia Press, 1985), p. 19.
13. Appleton P.C. Griffin, ed., *Orderly Book of General George Washington, Commander in Chief of the American Armies; Kept at Valley Forge, 18 May–11 June, 1778* (Rpt. New York: New York Times, 1971).
14. Rudolf Cronau, *The Army of the Revolution* (New York: N.p., 1923), passim.
15. Perkins, V. V. Anderson Papers, May 2, 1862.
16. Perkins, Henry Toole Clark Papers, July 17, 1862.
17. NARA, RG 109, Chapter 2, Vol. 13, Letters Sent, Lt. General Polk, February 26, 1863.
18. NARA, RG 109, E 98, Circular Order, Army of Tennessee, April 5, 1863.
19. NARA, RG 109, Chapter 8, Vol. 346, GO #5, Letters and Circulars, 54 Va., January 23, 1863; E 85, Box 83, GO #5, Goldsboro, January 23, 1863.
20. North Carolina State Archives, Governor Zebulon Baird Vance Letter Book, 50.1, p. 226, May 13, 1863.
21. Brigadier General Fred G. Ainsworth, and Joseph W. Kirklin, *The War of the Rebellion: A Compilation of the Official Records of the Union and Confederate Armies* (Washington: Government Printing Office, 1880–1901), Ser. 4, Vol. 2, p. 788, September 3, 1863. Hereafter cited as OR.
22. Southern Historical Collection, Wilcon Library, University of North Carolina, Chapel Hill, Charles S. Venable Papers, October 4, 1863 (hereafter cited as SHC); April 26, 1864; see also North Carolina State Archives, Richard W. Obst Collection, October 1863; also OR, Ser. 1, Vol. 42, Pt. 3, p. 961, December 11, 1864.
23. OR, Ser. 1, Vol. 33, p. 441, December 9, 1864; Ser. 1 Vol. 36, pt. 3, p. 175, May 24, 1864.
24. OR, Ser. 1, Vol. 33, p. 1266, May 7, 1864.
25. Wilson Library, University of North Carolina, Chapel Hill, SHC, Boykin Family Papers, GO #3, Department of Northern Virginia, April 21, 1862. Hereafter cited as Wilson.
26. NARA, RG 109, Chapter 8, Vol. 346, Entry 38, Letters and Circulars, 54 Va., January 20, 1863.
27. NARA, RG 109, Chapter 2, Vol. 182, General Orders South Carolina, Georgia, Florida, March 6, 1863.
28. NARA, M269, Roll 10, SR Private O. F. Jarman.
29. NARA, M324, Roll 652, SR Private Robert W. McCutchen.
30. North Carolina State Archives, Thomas Merritt Pittman Collection, GO #139, AIGO, October 28, 1863.
31. Perkins, Flowers Collection, Circular, Army Northern Virginia, August 14, 1863; NARA, RG 109, E 175, Box 2, Army of Tennessee, August 16, 1864.
32. C.H. Lee, *The Judge Advocates VADE MECUM Embracing a General View of Military Law and Practice Before Courts Martial with an Epitome of the Laws of Evidence as Applicable to Military Trials* (Richmond: West and Johnson, 1863), passim.
33. NARA, RG 109, Chapter 1, Vol. 221, Records of the Distribution of Blank Forms and General Orders, p. 102.
34. *Records of the 1st Congress of the Confederate States of America*, p. 157–193.
35. OR, Ser. 4, Vol. 2, p. 1003, November 26, 1863.
36. Wilson, SHC, David M. Carter Papers, August 26, 1863.
37. Ibid.
38. OR, Ser. 4, Vol. 3, p. 1080, February 11, 1865.
39. NARA, RG 109, Chapter 2, Vol. 84, Entry 33, Letters Sent, Army of Northern Virginia, April 24, 1863.
40. Lee, *The Judge Advocates VADE MECUM*, Sections 154–58, 165–7, 252.
41. Southern Historical Society Papers, Vol. 47, p. 203.
42. Lee, *Vade Mecum*, Sections 235, 338.
43. NARA, RG 109, Chapter 2, Vol. 113, GO #8, District of Texas, February 27, 1865.

44. Henry Kyd Douglas, *I Rode with Stonewall* (Chapel Hill: University of North Carolina Press, 1940), p. 213.
45. NARA, RG 109, Chapter 1, Vol. 42, Letters and Telegrams Endorsements, August 16, 1864, October 7, 1864.
46. J. A. Simpson, and E. S. C. Weiner, eds., *Oxford English Dictionary* (Oxford, UK: Oxford University Press, 1989), entry for court-martial.
47. NARA, RG 109, Chapter 2, Vol. 84, Entry 56, Letters Sent, Army of Northern Virginia, May 22, 1863.
48. NARA, RG 109, Chapter 2, Vol. 83, Entry 395, Letters Sent, Army of Northern Virginia, February 14, 1863.
49. OR, Ser. 4, Vol. 3, April 28, 1864, p. 331.
50. Lee, *Vade Mecum*, p. 170.
51. *Confederate Veteran*, Vol. 15, p. 353.
52. Ibid., Vol. 15, Note 84, p. 2; OR, Ser. 4, Vol. 2, p. 401.
53. *Confederate Veteran*, Vol. 15, p. 376; OR, Ser. 4, Vol. 2, p. 511.
54. NARA, M324, Roll 547, SR Thomas Dunphy.
55. NARA, RG 109, Chapter 1, Vol. 42, Letters, Telegrams and Endorsements, August 16, 1864.
56. Ransom Brigade, fn 5.
57. *List of U. S. Soldiers Executed by United States Military Authorities During the Late War* (Washington, DC: Adjutant General Office, 1885).
58. Thomas P. Lowry, *Don't Shoot That Boy!* (Mason City, IA: Savas, 1999), p. 88.
59. James C. Neagles, *Summer Soldier* (Salt Lake City: Ancestry, 1986), p. 34.
60. Donald S. Frazier, ed., *The United States and Mexico at War* (New York: Macmillan Reference USA, 1998), p. 372.
61. Dennis Winter, *Death's Men: Soldiers in the Great War* (London: Harmondsworth, 1979).
62. Cathryn Corns and John Hughes Wilson, *Blindfolded and Alone: Executions of British Soldiers in the Great War* (London: Cassell, 2001), p. 103.
63. Ibid.
64. Ibid.
65. Robert M. Bohm, *Deathquest* (Cincinnati: Anderson, 1999).
66. Robert M. Citino, *The German Way of War* (Lawrence: University Press of Kansas, 2005), p. 273.
67. David Stone, *Fighting for the Fatherland* (Washington, DC: Potomac Books, 2006), p. 363.
68. Alan Axelrod, *The Real History of World War II* (New York: Sterling, 2008), p. 532.
69. Chris Bellamy, *Absolute War: Soviet Russia in the 2nd World War* (New York: Knopf, 2007), p. 37.
70. Herbert R. Lottman, *The People's Anger* (London: Hutchinson, 1986), p. 272.

Chapter 1

1. OR, Ser. 1, Vol. 19, pt. 2, p. 597, September 7, 1862.
2. Ibid.
3. Ibid.
4. Ibid.
5. OR, Ser. 1, Vol. 19, pt. 2, p. 618, September 22, 1862.
6. OR, Ser. 1, Vol. 29, pt. 2, p. 650, August 17, 1863.
7. NARA, RG 109, Chapter 2, Vol. 83, Entry 408, Letters Sent, Army of Northern Virginia, February 24, 1863.
8. OR, Ser. 1, Vol. 29, pt. 2, p. 806, October 30, 1863.
9. OR, Ser. 1, Vol. 29, pt. 2, p. 820, November 4, 1863.
10. Douglas Southall Freeman, *Lee's Dispatches* (New York: Putnam, 1957), p. 154–155.
11. Ibid.
12. Ibid.
13. Ibid., p. 149.
14. North Carolina State Archives, PC, Thomas Merritt Pittman Collections, GO #54 Hd Qtrs Army of Northern Virginia, August 10, 1864.
15. OR, Ser. 1, Vol. 42, pt. 3, p. 1213, November 18, 1864.
16. OR, Ser. 1, Vol. 42, pt. 3, p. 1213, November 29, 1864.
17. OR, Ser. 1, Vol. 46, pt. 2, p. 1229, GO #2, Hd Qtrs Army of Confederate States, February 11, 1865.
18. OR, Ser. 1, Vol. 46, pt. 2, p. 1249, GO #4, Hd Qtrs Army of Confederate States, February 22, 1865.
19. OR, Ser. 1, Vol. 46, pt. 2, p. 1258, February 25, 1865.
20. OR, Ser. 1, Vol. 46, pt. 2, p. 1247, February 22, 1865.
21. OR, Ser. 1, Vol. 46, pt. 2, p. 1270, February 24, 1865.
22. NARA, M921, GO # 8, Headquarters Armies of Confederate States, March 27, 1865.

Chapter 2

1. Perkins, Patterson-Cavin Family Papers, September 21, 1863.
2. LC, Cadmus M. Wilcox Collection, C. M. Wilcox to John, September 26, 1862.
3. Perkins, Mary Margaret McNeil Papers, T. J. Love to Franklin McNeil, n.d.
4. Perkins, Scarborough Family Papers, November 20, 1861.
5. Perkins, Hugh MacRae Papers, November 13, 1861.
6. Louis H. Manarin and Weymouth T. Jordan, *North Carolina Troops 1861–1865, A Roster*, Vol. 4 (Raleigh, NC: Department of Archives and History, 1966–2008), p. 442.
7. Perkins, Scarborough Family Papers, September 13, 1861.
8. Perkins, Patterson-Cavin Family Papers, [loose slip, no date].
9. NARA, RG 109, Chapter 2, Vol. 84, Letters Sent Army of Northern Virginia, November 6, 1863.
10. NARA, M270, Roll 402, SR Phillip C. Griffin.
11. Perkins, Thornton Sexton Papers, March 24, 1863.
12. Ibid., October 5, 1863.
13. OR, Ser. 1, Vol. 25, pt. 2, p. 814, May 21, 1863.
14. Vance Papers, GP 165, May 21, 1863.
15. NARA, RG 109, Chapter 2, Vol. 84, Letters Sent Army of Northern Virginia, May 20, 1863.
16. *Special Orders of the AIGO Confederate States*, Vol. 2 (Washington: Government Printing Office, 1918), p. 427, SO #222, September 20, 1862.
17. Wilson, SHC, Francis Milton Kennedy Diary, June 1, 1863.
18. Ibid., June 2, 1863.
19. Perkins, Rare Book Room, GO #87, Department of Northern Virginia, August 21, 1863.
20. Wilson, SHC, Kennedy Diary, September 18, 1863.
21. Perkins, Patterson-Cavin Family Papers, September 19, 1863.
22. Ibid., September 21, 1863.
23. Wilson, SHC, Kennedy Diary, September 19, 1863.

24. J. S. Harris, *Historical Sketches of the Seventh Regiment North Carolina Troops* (Mooresville, NC: Mooresville, 1893), p. 41.
25. NARA, M921, GO #88, Army of Northern Virginia, September 17, 1863.
26. Perkins, Confederate States of America, Box 1, Roll of Company D, n.d.
27. NARA, M921, GO #88, Army of Northern Virginia, September 17, 1863.
28. NARA, M921, GO #136, Department of Northern Virginia, December 27, 1862.
29. Wilson, SHC, Kennedy Diary, September 28, 29, 1863.
30. Ibid., November 12, 1863.
31. C. J. Preslar, *A History of Catawba County* (Salisbury, NC: Rowan, 1893), p. 273–274.
32. Wilson, SHC, Clingman-Puryear Family Papers, September 20, 1863.
33. Preslar, *A History of Catawba County*, p. 273–274.
34. NARA, M921, GO #88, Army of Northern Virginia, September 17, 1863.
35. Wilson, SHC, Kennedy Diary, September 25, 1863.
36. Ibid., September 26, 1863.
37. Wilson, SHC, William D. Alexander Diary, September 26, 1863.
38. North Carolina State Archives, Newspaper Collection, Microfilm FYOW, Roll 12, *Fayetteville Observer*, October 3, 1863.
39. Wilson, SHC, George Sidney Thompson, Confederate Quartermaster, Articles Expended in the Quarter Ended 30th September 1863.
40. Ibid.
41. Jerald H. Markham, comp., *The Diuguid Records, 1861–1865* (Westminster, MD: Heritage Books, 2007), p. 35–36.
42. North Carolina State Archives, Elisa Ellis Robeson Collection, April 24, 1865.
43. See also, Third Regiment, Early Division, 2nd Corps, Army of Northern Virginia.
44. Manarin and Jordan, *North Carolina Troops*, Vol. 9, p. 559.
45. Pen-Lile Pittard, *Alexander County's Confederates* (Taylorsville, NC: N.p. 1960), Private Joshua Bowman and Boon Little.
46. NARA, M921, GO #90, Army of Northern Virginia, September 25, 1863.
47. Wilson, SHC, Kennedy Diary, November 5, 1863.
48. NARA, M921, GO #97, Department of Northern Virginia, November 4, 1863.
49. Wilson, SHC, Kennedy Diary, November 14, 1863.
50. Wilson, SHC, William D. Alexander Diary, November 14, 1863.
51. Wilson, SHC, Proffit Family Papers, November 16, 1863.
52. Ibid., November 17, 1863.
53. Michel W. Taylor, ed., *Cry is War, War, War* (Dayton, OH: Morningside House, 1994), p. 161.
54. Wilson, SHC, Proffit Family Papers, November 15, 1863.
55. NARA, RG 109, E 86, Box 83, GO #11, District of Cape Fear, December 23, 1861.
56. Perkins, Thornton Sexton Papers, January 11, 1864.
57. Perkins, Mary A. (Horton) Councill Papers, January 17, 1864.
58. Jordan, *North Carolina Troops*, Vol. 9, p. 468.
59. NARA, RG 109, Chapter 1, Vol. 42, Letters Sent, Entry 133, March 3, 1865; Entry 134, March 5, 1865.
60. Perkins, Hugh MacRae Papers, January 22, 1864.
61. Perkins, Kennedy Diary, March 18, 1864.
62. Perkins, William D. Alexander Diary, March 18, 1864.
63. Perkins, Charles Rothrock Papers, March 18, 1864.
64. Perkins, Jane Peterson Papers, March 21, 1864.
65. Ibid., March 12, 1864.
66. Perkins, William A. Tesh Papers, March 13, 1864.
67. Perkins, Charles Rothrock Papers, February 27, 1864.
68. Perkins, Jonas A. Bradshaw Papers, April 14, 1864.
69. Vance, GP 175, March 27, 1864.
70. Harris, *Historical Sketches*, p. 44.
71. Wilson, SHC, John McKee Sharpe Papers, April 29, 1864.
72. Manarin and Jordan, *North Carolina Troops*, Vol. 9, p. 133, Peter C. Stewart.
73. Private collection, Augustus Evander Floyd, Eighteenth Regiment, Company D, courtesy of Robert B. Floyd and Robert Krick.
74. Vance, GP 179, August 22, 1864.
75. Private collection, Augustus Evander Floyd.
76. Perkins, Thomas Nixon Papers, February 21, 1865.
77. North Carolina State Archives, Military Collection Box 77, Folder 21, *Newton Enterprise*, clipping.
78. Ivey L. Sharpe, *Stanly County, USA: The Story of an Area and an Era* (Greensboro, NC: Media Press, 1990), p. 214–215.
79. Manarin and Jordan, *North Carolina Troops*, 7 Reg Co B-G, 18 Reg Co A-B-D-E-F-H, 28 Reg Co C-E-G, 33 Reg Co D, 37 Reg Co A-B-C-H.

Chapter 3

1. M. W. Taylor, ed., *The Cry is War, War, War* (Dayton, Ohio: Morningside House, 1994), p. 186.
2. William W. Hassler, ed., *The General to His Lady: The Civil War Letters of William Dorsey Pender* (Chapel Hill: University of North Carolina Press, 1965), p. 79.
3. North Carolina State Archives, P. H. Warlick Letters, October 4, 1863.
4. North Carolina State Archives, Alfred Moore Scales Papers, October 1, 1863.
5. Ibid., April 20, 1864.
6. Jordan, *North Carolina Troops*, 16 Reg Co D-F, 22 Reg Co I-L, 38 Reg Co B-F.
7. Perkins, A. J. Dula Papers, Typescript p. 14, September 22, 1908.
8. NARA, E 69 GO #6, Orders and Circulars Department of North Carolina, February 10, 1862.
9. Taylor, *The Cry is War*, p. 148.
10. NARA, M270 Roll 848, SR William A. Tomlin.
11. Jordan, *North Carolina Troops*, Vol. 10, p. 29.
12. Wilson, SHC, Proffit Family Papers, February 26, 1863.
13. Taylor, *The Cry is War*, p. 131.
14. North Carolina State Archives, Sanders M. Ingram Letters, March 30, 1863.
15. North Carolina State Archives, Military Collection Box 70, File 22, John H. C. Burch, 24 Reg Co H.
16. Jordan, *North Carolina Troops*, Vol. 10, p. 58, Captain A. Deal.
17. North Carolina State Archives, Oliver C. and Calier G. Hamilton Letters May, 30, 1863.
18. Wilson SHC, William J. Hoke Books, September 29, 1862.
19. North Carolina State Archives, Sanders M. Ingram Letters, March 30, 1863.
20. Perkins, J. F. Coghill Papers, March 29, 1863.

21. NARA, RG 109, Chapter 1, Vol. 194, AIGO Court Martial, p. 218, Entry 40.
22. NARA, RG 109, Chapter 2, Vol. 84, Letters Sent, Army of Northern Virginia, Entry 77.
23. Perkins, Alexander Keever Papers, June 5, 1863.
24. Vance, GP 166, June 6, 1863.
25. OR, Ser. 1, Vol. 18, p. 860, May 21, 1863.
26. Vance, GP 164, April 18, 1863.
27. Taylor, *The Cry is War*, p. 155.
28. NARA, RG 109, Chapter 1, Vol. 195, Entry 392.
29. SHSP, Vol. 26, p. 18.
30. NARA, M921, GO #90, Army of Northern Virginia, September 25, 1863.
31. North Carolina State Archives, Thomas Merritt Pittman Collection, GO #88, Department of Northern Virginia, September 10, 1863.
32. NARA, RG 109, Chapter 2, Volume 84, Letters Sent Army of Northern Virginia, Entry 170, October 2, 1863.
33. Vance, GP 169, September 24, 1863.
34. Ibid., September 29, 1863.
35. NARA, Microfilm M347, Roll 156, Unfiled Correspondence, G. L. Greeson.
36. Taylor, *Cry is War*, p. 136.
37. North Carolina State Archives, P. H. Warlick Letters, October 4, 1863.
38. North Carolina State Archives, Sanders M. Ingram Letters, March 30, 1863.
39. North Carolina State Archives, Eban Ingram Collection, October 4, 1863.
40. Vance, GP 169, September 19, 1863.
41. NARA, M921, GO #92, Department of Northern Virginia, October 7, 1863.
42. NARA, M921, GO #93, Department Northern Virginia, October 24, 1863.
43. Vance, GP 169, September 16, 1863.
44. Vance, GP 182, December 30, 1864.
45. NARA, M270 Roll 285, SR Samuel C. Allred.
46. Vance, GP 171, November 4, 1863.
47. North Carolina State Archives, Military Collection, Box 65, File 30, Deserters 10th Congressional District.
48. NARA, RG 109, Chapter 2, Vol. 84, Letters Sent Army of Northern Virginia, December 7, 1863.
49. Vance, GP 171, November 7, 1863.
50. Wilson, SHC, John McKee Sharpe Papers, November 11, 1863.
51. NARA, RG 109, Chapter 2, Vol. 100, Letters Sent, November 27, 1863.
52. NARA, M270, Roll 286, SR Wiley Bare.
53. NARA, RG 109, Chapter 1, Vol. 196, Court-martial Records, January 9, 1864.
54. NARA, M270, Roll 286, SR Wiley Bare.
55. Ibid.
56. Ibid.
57. NARA, RG 109, E 126, Correspondence General R. E. Lee, January 4, 1864.
58. Perkins, Josiah S. Roberson Papers, January 3, 1864.
59. NARA, RG 109, E 126, Correspondence General R. E. Lee, January 10, 1864.
60. Wilson, SHC, Perkins Family Papers, February 1, 1864.
61. NARA, M270 Roll 286, SR Wiley Bare.
62. Perkins, Alfred W. Bell Papers, March 14, 1864.
63. Perkins, Josiah S. Roberson Papers, March [torn], 1864.
64. Ibid., March 13, 1864.
65. Taylor, *Cry is War*, p. 172.
66. *The Heritage of Wilkes County*, Vol. 2 (Winston-Salem, NC: Wilkes Genealogical Society, 1982–1990), Section 302, Entry 7.
67. NARA, RG 109, E 183, Box 6, April 13, 1864.
68. *Special Orders of the AIGO Confederate States* (Washington: Government Printing Office, 1918), Vol. 4, SO #206–7, p. 568.
69. NARA, RG 109, Chapter 1, Volume 201, R-10, Endorsements Court-martial Correspondence, July 4, 1864.
70. NARA, M270, Roll 220, SR Alexander Westmoreland.
71. North Carolina State Archives, Newspaper Collection, *Greensboro Patriot*, August 1, 1864; Jordan, *North Carolina Troops*, Vol. 9, p. 329.
72. Vance, GP 173, July 12, 1864.
73. NARA, RG 109, Chapter 1, Vol. 42, p. 65, Letters Sent, September 15, 1864.
74. Vance, GP 163, March 3, 1863.
75. Vance, GP 178, June 6, 1864.
76. NARA, RG 94 and RG 407, M594, Roll 139, SR Abner Brooks, 2nd Mtd Inf, North Carolina; North Carolina State Archives, Military Collection, Box 65, Folder 30.
77. Jordan, *North Carolina Troops*, Vol. 9, p. 173; Vol. 10, p. 13.
78. Library of Congress, Newspaper Collection, *Philadelphia Weekly Times*, January 26, 1878.
79. Taylor, *Cry is War*, p. 186.
80. Jordan, *North Carolina Troops*, Vol. 5 p. 380, SR John Mansfield.
81. Perkins, Alexander Keever Papers, March 3, 1865.
82. Jordan, *North Carolina Troops*, 16 Reg Co F, 22 Reg Co I-F, 34 Reg Co A, 38 Reg Co B-E-F.
83. Ibid., 13 Reg Co C-H, 16 Reg Co C-H, 34 Reg Co C-K, 38 Reg Co A-C-H.

Chapter 4

1. OR, Ser. 1, Vol. 51, pt. 2, p. 712, May 22, 1863.
2. OR, Ser. 1, Vol. 52, pt. 2, p. 584, June 9, 1862.
3. James L. Morrison Jr., ed., *The Memoirs of Henry Heth* (Westport, CT: Greenwood Press, 1974).
4. Perkins, John A. McDade Papers, December 22, 1862.
5. NARA, RG 109, E 97, Box 75, GO # 64, July 12, 1864, Army of the Mississippi.
6. Perkins, John A. McDade Papers, January 14, 1863.
7. Perkins, Elizabeth F. Glen Papers, February 18, 1862.
8. Ibid., July 18, 1862.
9. Perkins, Sion Hart Rogers Papers, August 7, 1862.
10. Ibid., November 8, 1862.
11. Jordan, *North Carolina Troops*, Vol. 11, p. 262.
12. Ibid., Vol. 12, p. 459, John Kelly.
13. NARA, RG 109, E 69, GO #24, April 30, 1862, Department of North Carolina.
14. Perkins, Scarborough Family Papers, August 10, 1862.
15. North Carolina State Archives, Newspaper File, *Hillsborough Recorder*, HiHR Roll 6, November 12, 1862.
16. Wilson, SHC, Kennedy Diary, January 26, 1863.
17. Perkins, John A. McDade Papers, December 7, 1863.
18. North Carolina State Archives, Military Collection, Box 70, Folder 17, D. H. Brantly, 38 Regiment, Co G.
19. George C. Underwood, *History of the 26th Regiment of North Carolina Troops in the Great War* (Wendell, NC: Broadfoot's Bookmark, 1978), p. 98.

20. Wilson, SHC, Laura Cornelia McGimsey Papers, January 25, 1863.
21. Perkins, Confederate States of America—Army, Box 2, John R. Marley 26-G, April 13, 1863.
22. North Carolina State Archives, Thomas Merritt Pittman Collection, GO #32, June 18, 1863, Department of North Carolina.
23. Ibid.
24. Perkins, Elias Gordon Hall Boyles Papers, March 11, 1863.
25. Wilson, North Carolina Collection, Order Book Forty-Fifth Regiment, May 2, 1863. Hereafter cited as NCC.
26. Perkins, John Hendricks Kinyoun Papers, May 13, 1863.
27. Perkins, Elias Gordon Hall Boyles Papers, May 11, 1863.
28. Wilson, SHC, James E. Green Diary, May 11, 1863.
29. North Carolina State Archives, Leonidas L. Polk Papers, May 12, 1863.
30. North Carolina State Archives, A. C. Meyers Papers, April 8, 1863.
31. Wilson, SHC, Fife Family Papers, May 12, 1863.
32. Louis Leon, *Diary of a Confederate Soldier* (Charlotte: Stone, 1913), p. 27.
33. Jordan, *North Carolina Troops*, Vol. 12, Fifty-Third Regiment, Companies G and K.
34. OR, Ser. 1, Vol. 51, pt. 2, p. 712, May 22, 1863; New Revised Standard Version Oxford Bible, Matthew 3:10.
35. Vance, GP 166, June 2, 1863.
36. OR, Ser. 1, Vol. 51, pt. 2, p. 709.
37. Vance, GP 167, July 5, 1863.
38. NARA, RG 109, Ch 1, Vol. 195, Court Martial Records, p. 466, Entry 2986, April 25, 1863.
39. North Carolina State Archives, Richard A. Cole Papers, May 9, 1863.
40. Vance, GP 167, July 21, 1863.
41. Stuart T. Wright, ed., *The Confederate Letters of Benjamin H. Freeman* (Hicksville, NY: Exposition Press, 1974), p. 29.
42. Wilson, SHC, Julius A. Linebeck Collection, September 20, 1863.
43. Ibid., November 1, 1863.
44. North Carolina State Archives, Henry Clay Albright Papers, August 21, 1863.
45. Wright, *Confederate Letters*, p. 29.
46. Perkins, William Lafayette Scott Papers, April 3, 1863.
47. North Carolina State Archives, State Auditor, Confederate Pensions, 1885, 1901.
48. Wilson, SHC, Julius A. Linebeck Collection, November 1, 1863.
49. Wilson, SHC, Steed and Phipps Family Papers, February 1, 1864.
50. North Carolina State Archives, John Wright Family Papers, February 1, 1864.
51. Ibid., April 10, 1864.
52. Wright, *Confederate Letters*, p. 33.
53. Vance, GP 178, January 7, 1864.
54. Manarin and Jordan, *North Carolina Troops*, Vol. 4, p. 133.
55. Wilson, SHC, Webb Family Papers, February 13, 1864.
56. North Carolina State Archives, John Wright Family Papers, February 18, 1864.
57. Wilson, SHC, Webb Family Papers, February 2, 22, 1864.
58. Wright, *Confederate Letters*, p. 34.
59. North Carolina State Archives, John Wright Family Papers, March 24, 1864.
60. Ibid., March 24, 1864, Dear Fanny.
61. Wright, *Confederate Letters*, p. 36.
62. Wilson, SHC, Julius A. Linebeck, March 24, 1864.
63. Perkins, J. L. Henry Papers, April [7], 1864.
64. Wright, *Confederate Letters*, p. 36.
65. Wilson, SHC, Kenneth Rayner Jones Papers, March 8, 1864.
66. NARA, M270, Roll 499, SR Elias Robbins.
67. Perkins, John C. Warlick Papers, December 1, 1901.
68. OR, Ser. 1, Vol. 42, pt. 2, p. 1274, September 23, 1864.
69. Perkins, Nevin Ray Papers, July 29, 1864.
70. *Home Front*, August–September 1989, courtesy of editor Greg Mast.
71. Wright, *Confederate Letters*, p. 53.
72. NARA, RG 109, Chapter 1, Vol. 42, Letters and Telegrams Endorsements, Entry 68, September 20, 1864.
73. Ibid., Entry 134, February 5, 1865.
74. Perkins, John C. Warlick Papers, December 1, 1901.
75. Ibid., February 27, 1865.
76. Ibid., March 22, 1865.
77. Ibid., March 27, 1865.
78. Wilson, SHC, Alexander Carey McAlister Papers, March n.d.
79. Ibid.
80. Ibid., GO #3, Cooke's and Lane's Brigade, March 30, 1865.
81. North Carolina State Archives, A. C. Meyers Papers, October 6, 1862.
82. Jordan, *North Carolina Troops*, 11 Reg Co B-G, 26 Reg Co C-F-H, 44 Reg Co E-H, 47 Reg Co F-D, 52 Reg Co F-B.
83. Ibid., 11 Reg Co D-E, 26 Reg Co B-E-K, 44 Reg Co A-D, 47 Reg Co B-H, 52 Reg Co A-D.
84. L. Barron Mills Jr., *Randolph County: A Brief History* (Raleigh: Office of Archives and History, Department of Cultural Resources, 2008), p. 62.

Chapter 5

1. Wilson, SHC, James Augustus Graham Papers, February 1, 1864.
2. Vance, GP 162, February 10, 1863.
3. Vance, GP 163, March 14, 1863.
4. Private Collection, Powhatan B. Whittle, February 15, 1864, Courtesy Robert B. Krick.
5. Jordan, *North Carolina Troops*, Vol. 5, p. 536.
6. Perkins, Hugh MacRae Papers, March 15, 1862.
7. Jordan, *North Carolina Troops*, Vol. 8, p. 13.
8. Henry McGilbert Wagstaff, ed., "Letters of Thomas Jackson Strayhorn," *North Carolina Historical Review* 4 (1936): 315, 322.
9. Wilson, SHC, Samuel Hoey Walkup paper January 30, 1864
10. Wilson, SHC, E. F. Satterfield and Merritt Family Papers, March 21, 1862.
11. Perkins, Patterson-Cavin Family Papers, August 28, 1862.
12. NC State Genealogy, Vertical File, George Washington Woodard, Typescript, December 27, 1863.
13. Perkins, James King Wilkerson Papers, December 16, 1862.
14. Vance, GP 162, February 11, 1863.
15. North Carolina State Archives, Thomas Merritt Pittman Collection, GO #21, Department of North Carolina, May 27, 1863.
16. Ibid.

17. Perkins, Obed William Carr Papers, p. 22, (June 7, 1863).
18. Ibid., p. 23.
19. Vance, GP 161, January 6, 1863.
20. NARA, M921, GO #105, Department of Northern Virginia, December 7, 1863.
21. Perkins, Riley Luther Papers, May 20, 1862.
22. Perkins, Daniel Setzer Papers, September 25, 1863.
23. Ibid., Decemer [December] 19, 1863.
24. Ibid., February 12, 1864.
25. Ibid., August 8, 1863.
26. Ibid., March 9, 1865.
27. Vance, GP 161, January 5, 1863.
28. Vance, GP 170, October 29, 1863.
29. Vance, GP 171, November 15, 1863.
30. Vance, GP 172, December 16, 1863.
31. NARA, RG 109, E 126, Correspondence of General R. E. Lee, January 29, 1864.
32. Wilson, SHC, James Augustus Graham Papers, February 1, 1864.
33. Henry C. Clegg, *War Record from 1862–1865 as Published in the Chatham Record* (Pittsboro: Chatham Record, 1925), p. 18.
34. Wilson, SHC, Kenneth Rayner Jones Papers, January 30, 1864.
35. Perkins, Hugh Conway Browning Papers, January 31, 1864.
36. Wilson, SHC, Steed and Phipps Family Papers, February 1, 1864.
37. NARA, RG 109, E 126, Correspondence of General R. E. Lee, January 30, 1864.
38. Vance, GP 171, November 11, 1863.
39. Wilson, SHC, James Augustus Graham Papers, January 24, 1864.
40. Ibid., March 8, 1865.
41. Wilson, SHC, Kenneth Rayner Jones Papers, January 26, 1864.
42. Perkins, Alexander Frank Papers, January 27, 1864. Wilson, SHC, Frank Family Papers, (January 27, 1864).
43. Perkins, Riley Luther Papers, January 27, 1864.
44. Wilson, SHC, Samuel Hoey Walkup Papers, January 25, 1864.
45. Ibid., January 27, 1864.
46. Wilson, SHC, Samuel Hoey Walkup Papers, January 28, 1864.
47. Ibid., January 30, 1864.
48. Perkins, David Frank Caldwell Papers, January 13, 1864.
49. NARA, RG 109, Chapter 1, Vols. 186–189, Examination Boards.
50. Perkins, Shadrach Ward Papers, April 25, 1863.
51. Ibid., October, 13, 1862.
52. Wagstaff, "Letters of Thomas Jackson Strayhorn," p. 319.
53. Ibid., p. 325.
54. Ibid.
55. Ibid., p. 328.
56. Ibid., p. 332.
57. Perkins, Hugh Conway Browning Papers, July 27, 1862.
58. Ibid., May 11, 1862.
59. Ibid., September 28, 1863.
60. Wilson, SHC, Kenneth Rayner Jones Papers, March 13, 1864.
61. Perkins, Alexander Frank Papers, April 26, 1864.
62. Ibid., February 19, 1865.
63. North Carolina State Archives, Newspaper Collection, *Greensboro Patriot*, GbPA Roll 9, March 10, 1864.
64. Wilson, SHC, Samuel Hoey Walkup Papers, March 17, 1864.
65. Ibid., March 24, 1864.
66. Perkins, Alexander Frank Papers, March 24, 1864.
67. Ibid., April 3, 1865.
68. Wilson, SHC, Kenneth Rayner Jones Papers, March 25, 1864.
69. Wilson, SHC, Samuel Hoey Walkup Papers, March 30, 1864.
70. Ibid., April 20, 1864.
71. Ibid., March 25, 1864.
72. OR, Ser. 1, Vol. 29, pt. 2, p. 820, November 4, 1863.
73. Wilson, SHC, Samuel Hoey Walkup Papers, March 24, 1864.
74. Ibid., April 14, 1864.
75. NARA, M270, Roll 233, SR Thomas N. Faulkner.
76. Ibid.
77. Ibid.
78. Ibid.
79. NARA, RG 109, Chapter 1, Vol. 42, Entry 71, Letters and Telegrams Endorsements, September 23, 1864.
80. NARA, RG 109, Chapter 1, Vol. 201, Entry F-5, Endorsements on Court Martial Correspondence, n.d.
81. NARA, M270, Roll 233, SR Thomas N. Faulkner.
82. Perkins, Hugh Conway Browning Papers, May 30, 1864; July 9, 1864.
83. Perkins, Alexander Frank Papers, April 26, 1864.
84. Perkins, James King Wilkerson Papers, August 23, 1864.
85. North Carolina State Archives, Peter M. Mull Papers, n.d.
86. NARA, RG 109, Chapter 1, Vol. 197, Entry 1924, p. 208, Court-Martial Records.
87. NARA, RG 109, M270, Roll 472, SR William B. Smith.
88. Ibid.
89. NARA, RG 109, Chapter 1, Vol. 42, Entry 70, Letters and Telegrams Endorsements, September 22, 1864.
90. Perkins, James King Wilkerson Papers, December 29, 1864.
91. NARA, M270, Roll 239, SR John Strother.
92. Ibid.
93. Stuart T. Wright, ed., *The Confederate Letters of Benjamin H. Freeman* (Hicksville, NY: Exposition Press, 1974), p. 59.
94. Jordan, *North Carolina Troops*, 15 Reg Co E, 27 Reg Co C-I-K, 46 Reg Co H-I, 48 Reg Co H-I-K, 55 Reg Co B-F, sampled companies, 17 to 60 absences.
95. Ibid., 15 Reg Co B-G, 27 Reg Co B-G-H, 46 Reg Co G-K, 48 Reg Co C-G, sampled companies, 6 to 13 absences.

Chapter 6

1. Perkins, James O. Coghill Papers, January 12, 1864.
2. Percy Gatling Hamlin, ed., *The Making of a Soldier* (Richmond, VA: Whittet & Shepperson, 1935), p. 97.
3. Ibid., p. 113.
4. Jordan, *North Carolina Troops*, Vol. 9, p. 60.
5. Wilson, SHC, Leonidas Lafayette Polk Papers, November 20, 1863.
6. Ibid., November 20, 1863.
7. Jordan, *North Carolina Troops*, Vol. 11, p. 56.
8. Perkins, James H. C. Leach Papers, January 31, 1864.
9. Perkins, John Hendricks Kinyoun Papers, May 13, 1863.
10. North Carolina State Archives, L. L. Polk Papers, March 25, 1863.

11. Wilson, SHC, James E. Green Diary, p. 14.
12. Wilson, SHC, George Whitaker Wills Letter, n.d.
13. North Carolina State Archives, Thomas Merritt Pittman Collection, GO #6, Goldsboro, Department of North Carolina, March 19, 1863.
14. North Carolina State Archives, Thomas Merritt Pittman Collection, GO #29, Department of North Carolina, April 13, 1863, Private J. H. Cox.
15. Jordan, *North Carolina Troops*, Vol. 10, Forty-Third Regiment Company D, Private Alexander Hill, Private Jonathan Hill, Private Thomas Nixon.
16. North Carolina State Archives, Thomas Merritt Pittman Collection, GO #6, Head Quarters Kinston NC, May 19, 1863.
17. North Carolina State Archives, Henry Brantingham and W. H. S. Burgwyn Diary, May 18, 20, 1863.
18. Wilson, NCC, 45th Regiment Order Book, June 22, 1863.
19. NARA, RG 109, Chapter 1, Vol. 195, Court Martial Records, Entry 340, May 6, 1863, GO #18, Army of Northern Virginia, May 18, 1863.
20. Perkins, John C. Hackett Papers, August 16, 1863.
21. Vance, GP 171, November 16, 1863.
22. Ibid., November 12, 1863.
23. North Carolina State Archives, Shaffner Diary and Papers, January 8, 1864.
24. Wilson, SHC, David M. Carter Papers, January 15, 1864.
25. Perkins, James O. Coghill Papers, January 12, 1864.
26. Louis Leon, *Diary of a Tarheel Confederate Soldier* (Charlotte: Stone, 1913), p. 56.
27. Perkins, Stephen Frazier Papers, January 11, 1864.
28. Perkins, John C. Hackett Papers, March 26, 1864.
29. NARA, M921, GO #3–3, Department of Northern Virginia, January 8, 1864.
30. Perkins, John C. Hackett Papers, April 22, 1864.
31. Pulaski Cowper, comp., *Extract of Letters of Major-General Bryan Grimes* (Raleigh, NC: Williams, 1884), p. 76.
32. Perkins, Bryan Grimes Papers, April 25, 1864.
33. William S. Powell, *Dictionary of North Carolina Biography* (Chapel Hill: University of North Carolina Press, 1979–1996), Vol. 2, p. 9; North Carolina State Archives, John G. Young Papers, n.d.
34. Perkins, John C. Hackett Papers, April 22, 1864.
35. North Carolina State Archives, Adjutant General Letter Book, Vol. 44, p. 303, December 27, 1862.
36. Jordan, *North Carolina Troops*, Vol. 13, p. 163.
37. Max R. Williams, and J. G. de Roulhac Hamilton, eds., *The Papers of William Alexander Graham, 1857–1863*, Vol. 5 (Raleigh: State Department of Archives and History: Raleigh, 1973), p. 540.
38. Vance, GP 182, November 19, 1864.
39. North Carolina State Archives, Shaffner Diary and Papers, December 13, 1864.
40. Wilson, SHC, Shaffner Papers, December 18, 1864.
41. Jordan, *North Carolina Troops*, 2nd Battalion Co F-H, 32 Reg Co F-I, 45 Reg Co A, 53 Reg Co C-E-F.
42. Ibid., 2nd Battalion Co B, 32 Reg Co B, 43 Reg Co G-I, 45 Reg Co E-H, 53 Reg Co A-B-D-I.

Chapter 7

1. Vance, GP 176, April 21, 1864.
2. William S. Powell, *Dictionary of North Carolina Biography* (Chapel Hill: University of North Carolina Press, 1979–1996), Vol. 1, p. 33.
3. P. L. Ledford, *Reminiscences of the Civil War* (Thomasville, NC: News Printing House, 1909), p. 78.
4. Perkins, Sion Hart Rogers Papers, June 18, 1861.
5. Ibid., October 3, 1861.
6. Ledford, *Reminiscences of the Civil War*, p. 73.
7. North Carolina State Archives, Francis M. Parker Papers, April 5, 1862.
8. NARA, RG 109, Chapter 2, Vol. 84, Letters Sent Army of Northern Virginia, Entry 139, August 17, 1863.
9. Wilson, NCC, Logbook of General and Special Orders, GO #40, Rodes Division, September 12, 1863.
10. Louis Leon, *Diary of a Confederate Soldier* (Charlotte, NC: Stone, 1913), p. 47.
11. North Carolina State Archives, J. E. Green Diary, September 16, 1863.
12. Wilson, SHC, Leonidas Lafayette Polk Papers, September 16, 1863.
13. SHSP, "Civil War Diary of Captain Robert Emory Park," Vol. 26, p. 18.
14. North Carolina State Archives, Leonidas Polk Denmark Diary, September 16, 1863.
15. Perkins, James A. Burrows Papers, September 17, 1863. See also First and Third Regiments.
16. Wilson, SHC, William Gaston Lewis Papers, September 17, 1863.
17. Perkins, John C. Hackett Papers, September 21, 1863.
18. Gary W. Gallagher, *Stephen Dodson Ramseur, Lee's Gallant General* (Chapel Hill: University of North Carolina Press, 1985), p. 84; Jesse D. Hardy, ed., *The Civil War Letters of Thomas W. Gaither* (Raleigh, NC: Hardy, 1983), p. 52, April 1, 1863.
19. NARA, RG 109, Chapter 2, Vol. 226 1/2, Letters, Orders and Circulars, p. 38, August 27, 1863; Wilson, SHC, Charles K. Gallagher Papers, August 14, 1863.
20. Wilson, SHC, Charles K. Gallagher Papers, Prisoners at Chancellorsville, May 31, 1863, to October 31, 1863.
21. NARA, M921, GO #5, Army of Northern Virginia, January 19, 1864.
22. Wilson, SHC, McClelland Family Papers, n.d.
23. Hardy, *Civil War Letters*, p. 69.
24. NARA, M270, Roll 139, SR James King.
25. Vance, GP 174, February 9, 1864.
26. Ibid.
27. Wilson, SHC, Charles K. Gallagher Papers, October 4, 1883.
28. Ibid., Prisoners at Chancellorsville, May 31, 1863, to October 31, 1863.
29. North Carolina State Archives, Military Collection, Box 72, Folder 12, Chaplain S. D. Betts.
30. See Martin-Kirkland Brigade, Private James A. Danner.
31. NARA, RG 109, Chapter 8, Vol. 232, Letters Received Virginia Forces, p. 85, February 3, 1864.
32. NARA, M921, GO #71, Army of Northern Virginia, June 8, 1863.
33. North Carolina State Archives, Vance Papers, PC 15.5, September 14, 1864.
34. North Carolina State Archives, John J. Armfield Letters, January 31, 1864.
35. North Carolina State Archives, Bryan Grimes Papers, October 3, 1863.
36. Ibid.
37. NARA, M270, Roll 138, SR James F. Honeycutt.
38. Vance, GP 179, August 29, 1864.
39. Vance, GP 176, April 21, 1864.
40. Perkins, Robert O. Linster Papers, April 2, 1864.
41. Perkins, J. F. Newsome Papers, Camp of 14 North Carolina Troops, n.d.

42. Gallagher, *Stephen Dodson Ramseur*, p. 91.
43. W. A. Betts, ed., *Experience of a Confederate Chaplain 1861–1864* (Greenville, SC: c1900), p. 58.
44. Wilson, NCC, Shaffner Diary, April 28, 1864.
45. North Carolina State Archives, Shaffner Diary and Papers, April 30, 1864.
46. William R. Trotter, *The Civil War in North Carolina* (Winston-Salem, NC: Blair, 1991), p. 142.
47. Perkins, J. B. Goodin Papers, April 30, 1864.
48. Wilson, SHC, Charles K. Gallagher Papers, October 4, 1883.
49. NARA, RG 109, Chapter 1, Vol. 42, Letters and Telegrams Endorsements, p. 67, September 20, 1864.
50. Wilson, SHC, Charles K. Gallagher Papers, Enlistment Records, 4 Reg Co E.
51. Perkins, J. F. Newsome Papers, December 24, 1864.
52. Manarin and Jordan, *North Carolina Troops*, 2 Reg Co E, 4 Reg Co A-H, 14 Reg Co D-F, 30 Reg Co I.
53. Ibid., 2 Reg Co G, 4 Reg Co C-G, 14 Reg Co A, 30 Reg Co E-F.

Chapter 8

1. LC, Confederate Papers, Jedediah Hotchkiss Papers, Draw 114, Roll 4, March 1, 1863.
2. North Carolina State Archives, Richard W. Iobst Collection, May 1864.
3. Wilson, SHC, Laura Cornelia McGimsey Papers, October 10, 1864.
4. OR, Ser. 2 Vol. 7, p. 459, July 11, 1864.
5. Jordan, *North Carolina Troops*, Vol. 4, p. 278.
6. Perkins, Obed W. Carr Papers, September 5, 1863.
7. Perkins, James C. Zimmerman Papers, August 14, 1862.
8. Ibid., November 16, 1862.
9. Joe M. Hatley, ed., *Letters of William F. Wagner, Confederate Soldier* (Wendell, NC: Broadfoot's Bookmark, 1983), p. 63.
10. Perkins, James C. Zimmerman Papers, April 13, 1863.
11. Ibid., May 23, 1863.
12. NARA, M921, GO #13, Army of Northern Virginia, February 2, 1863, p. 18.
13. Ibid., p. 19.
14. Perkins, James C. Zimmerman Papers, February 28, 1863.
15. Perkins, Patrick H. Cain Papers, February 28, 1863.
16. Perkins, Joseph Overcash Papers, February 29, 1863.
17. William Whitley Pierson, ed., *The Diary of Bartlett Yancey Malone* (Chapel Hill: University of North Carolina Press, 1919), p. 73.
18. LC, Hotchkiss Papers, March 1, 1863.
19. C. L. Shaffner, trans. *Diary of Dr. J. F. Shaffner Jr.* (Winston-Salem, NC: N.p., 1936), March 6, 1863.
20. LC, Hotchkiss Papers, March 1, 1863.
21. Perkins, James C. Zimmerman Papers, February 26, 1863.
22. Ibid., September 17, 1863.
23. NARA, M 921, GO #19, February 14, 1863.
24. Richard W. Iobst, *The Bloody Sixth: The Sixth North Carolina Regiment* (Raleigh: North Carolina Confederate Centennial Commission, 1965), p. 113.
25. Pierson, *The Diary of Bartlett Yancey Malone*, p. 74.
26. Vance, GP 165, May 25, 1863.
27. Perkins, Joseph Overcash Papers, May 31, 1863.
28. Wilson, SHC, Confederate Papers, (miscellaneous) December 5, 1863.
29. Vance, GP 166, August 15, 1863.
30. Vance, GP 179, August 17, 1864.
31. Vance, GP 171, November 17, 1863.
32. Vance, GP 180, September 3, 1864.
33. Vance, GP 165, May 29, 1863.
34. Max R. Williams, ed., *The Papers of William Alexander Graham* (Raleigh, NC: State Department of Archives and History: Raleigh, 1973), Vol. 5, 1857–1863, p. 539.
35. North Carolina State Archives, Capus M. Wayne Collection, August 29, 1864.
36. Jordan, *North Carolina Troops*, Vol. 14, p. 135.
37. Perkins, Editor, *Greensboro Patriot*, September, 1862.
38. Jordan, *North Carolina Troops*, Vol. 6, p. 643, Elmore W. Dobson.
39. Wilson, SHC, George Whitaker Wills Letters, n.d.
40. Jubal A. Early, *A Memoir of the Last Year of the War for Independence in the Confederate States of America* (Lynchburg, VA: Button, 1867), fn p. 73.
41. Perkins, William Lafayette Scott Papers, September 5, 1863.
42. North Carolina State Archives, Marcus Hefner Papers, June 29, 1863.
43. Perkins, John F. Poindexter Papers, April 2, 1863.
44. Jordan, *North Carolina Troops*, Vol. 4, p. 278, R. M. Morgan.
45. Perkins, John A. Smith Papers, April 16, 1864.
46. Shaffner, *Diary of Dr. J. F. Shaffner*, February 17, 1865.
47. NARA, M921, GO #1, Army of Northern Virginia, January 17, 1865.
48. NARA, M270, Roll 779, SR Nathan Yancey Crutchfield.
49. North Carolina State Archives, Riley W. Leonard Papers, January 4, 1865.
50. NARA, RG 109, Chapter 1, Vol. 42, Letters and Telegrams Endorsements Sent, Entry 119, February 2, 1865.
51. NARA, RG 109, Chapter 1, Vol. 200, Miscellaneous Correspondence, February 3, 1865.
52. North Carolina State Archives, Riley W. Leonard Papers, January 30, 1865.
53. NARA, RG 109, Chapter 1, Vol. 42, Letters and Telegrams Endorsements Sent, Entry 123, February 17, 1865.
54. Ibid., Entry 124, February 20, 1865.
55. North Carolina State Archives, Richard W. Iobst Collection, February 16, 1863.
56. Perkins, Wade H. Hubbard Papers, June 13, 1862.
57. James Anson Farrer, *Military Manners and Customs* (Piccadilly, London, UK: Chatto & Windus, 1885), p. 232.
58. NARA, RG 109, Chapter 1, Vol. 200, Courts-martial Cases Referred to the President and Secretary of War, February 2, 1865.
59. NARA, RG 109, Chapter 1, Vol. 42, Letters and Telegrams Endorsements Sent, March 5, 1865.
60. NARA, RG 109, Chapter 1, Vol. 198, Entry 463, January 25, 1865.
61. C. H. Lee, *The Judge Advocates VADE MECUM Embracing a General View of Military Law and Practice Before Courts Martial with an Epitome of the Laws of Evidence as Applicable to Military Trials* (Richmond, VA: West and Johnson, 1863), Section 258, p. 160.
62. Perkins, Obed W. Carr Papers, August 16, 1863.
63. Ibid., August 31, 1863.
64. Perkins, James C. Zimmerman Papers, August 30, 1863.
65. Wilson, SHC, John Paris Papers, Diary February 16–21, 1865.

66. Jordan, *North Carolina Troops*, 6 Reg Co A-D-K-F, 21 Reg Co F-G-M.
67. Ibid., 54 Reg Co C-E-G-I, 57 Reg Co A-B-K.
68. Ibid., 6 Reg Co A-E, 21 Reg Co A-F, 54 Reg Co E-G-I, 57 Reg Co B-K.
69. Ibid., 6 Reg Co D-K-F, 21 Reg G-M, 54 Reg Co C, 57 Reg Co A.

Chapter 9

1. Wilson, SHC, Leonidas Chalmers Glenn Collection, March 28, 1863.
2. Walter Clark, *Histories of the Several Regiments and Battalions from North Carolina in the Great War*, Vol. 1 (Wendell, NC: Broadfoot's Bookmark, 1982), p. 605.
3. Ibid., p. 649.
4. North Carolina State Archives, Elizabeth M. Montgomery Collection, p. 43.
5. Wilson, SHC, Leonidas Chalmers Glenn Collection, March 28, 1863.
6. Perkins, James O. Coghill Papers, March 29, 1863.
7. Wilson, SHC, Leonidas Chalmers Glenn Collection, May 25, 1864.
8. Perkins, Archibald Erskine Henderson Papers, May 26, 1863.
9. NARA, M921, Roll 2, SO #173.5, July 10, 1863.
10. NARA, M921, GO #71, Army of Northern Virginia, June 14, 1863, p. 19.
11. Ibid., p. 20.
12. NARA, RG 109, Ch 2, Vol. 84, Letters Sent, Army of Northern Virginia, Entry 90, June 12, 1863.
13. Perkins, William H. Brotherton Papers, September 21, 1863.
14. Vance, GP 171, November 6, 1863.
15. Perkins, William H. Brotherton Papers, September 21, 1863.
16. Ibid., August 31, 1863.
17. Ibid., August 28, 1863.
18. Ibid., September 21, 1863.
19. Ibid., August 30, 1863.
20. Ibid., Camps Near Orange, n.d.
21. North Carolina State Archives, Henry C. Wall Diary, n.d., p. 211.
22. NARA, RG 109, Ch 1, Vol. 196, Court-martial Records, Entry 361, December 11, 1863.
23. NARA, RG 109, Ch 1, Vol. 197, Court-martial Records, Entry 381, February 23, 1865; Jordan, *North Carolina Troops*, Vol. 5, p. 182.
24. Perkins, William H. Brotherton Papers, April 24, 1864.
25. Jordan, *North Carolina Troops*, Vol. 5, p. 137, William W. Neal.
26. Ibid., Vol. 5, p. 171.
27. Vance, GP 181, October 2, 1864.
28. Vance, GP 182, December 10, 1864.
29. Ibid., December 9, 1864.
30. Jordan, *North Carolina Troops*, 5 Reg Co B-E-G-H-K, 12 Reg Co A-B-C-D-G, 20 Reg Co B-D-G-K, 23 Reg Co A-B-F-I.
31. Ibid., 12 Reg Co A-B-C-D-G, 20 Reg Co G-K, 23 Reg Co B.

Chapter 10

1. Wilson, SHC, John S. R. Miller Papers, August 14, 1861.
2. Ibid.
3. North Carolina State Archives, Futch Papers, September 1, 1861.
4. NARA, RG 109, E 450, Box 4, Telegrams General Beauregard, December 11, 1864.
5. Jordan, *North Carolina Troops*, Vol. 3, p. 351, J. W. Stokes.
6. NARA, RG 109, E 69, GO #23, Department of North Carolina and Southern Virginia, April 29, 1862.
7. Vance, GP 168, August 29, 1863.
8. Vance, GP 171, November 22, 1863.
9. J. A. Simpson and E. S. C. Weiner, *Oxford English Dictionary*, Vol. 4 (Oxford, England: Clarendon Press, 1989), p. 1132, durance, Entry 8.
10. Vance, GP 171, clipping, *Wilmington Daily Journal*, November 14, 1863, Filed with November 22, 1863.
11. Ibid., November 27, 1863.
12. NARA, M921, Roll 2, SO #172-9, Army of Northern Virginia, August 4, 1862.
13. Wilson, SHC, Calvin Leach Diary, July 3, and July 12, 1862.
14. Edgar Allen Jackson, *Letters of Edgar Allen Jackson* (Franklin, VA: N.p., 1939).
15. Walter Clark, *Histories of the Several Regiments and Battalions from North Carolina in the Great War*, Vol. 1 (Wendell, NC: Broadfoot's Bookmark, 1982), p. 222.
16. North Carolina State Archives, Military Papers, Adjutant General Letter Book, Vol. 44, p 217.
17. NARA, M921, GO #88, p. 23, Army of Northern Virginia, September 10, 1863.
18. North Carolina State Archives, Futch Papers, February 5, 1863.
19. E. B. Long, *The Civil War Day by Day: An Almanac, 1861–1865* (Garden City, NY: Doubleday, 1971), p. 394, August 1, 1863.
20. Ibid., p. 394.
21. Clifford Dowdey, and Louis H. Manarin, eds., *The Wartime Papers of R. E. Lee* (Boston: Little, Brown, 1961), p. 589.
22. Ibid., p. 593.
23. OR, Ser. 1, Vol. 29, pt. 2, p. 640, August 8, 1863.
24. Ibid., p. 649, August 11, 1863.
25. NARA, RG 109, Chapter 2, Vol. 84, Letters Sent Army of Northern Virginia, Entry 142, August 20, 1863.
26. Perkins, Rare Book Library, GO #83, Army Northern Virginia, August 13, 1863.
27. Wilson, SHC, Proffit Family Papers, August 10, 1863.
28. North Carolina State Archives, Newspaper File, *Fayetteville Observer*, FyOsw, Roll 12, "The Last Words of a Christian Soldier," September 9, 1863.
29. North Carolina State Archives, Isaac Lefevers Papers, August 30, 1863.
30. Wilson, SHC, William Robert Gwaltney Papers, August 25, 1863.
31. Dowdey and Manarin, *The Wartime Papers of R. E. Lee*, September 4, 1863, p. 302.
32. John O. Casler, *Four Years in the Stonewall Brigade* (Marietta, GA: Continental, 1951), p. 188.
33. Ibid., p. 188.
34. Wilson, SHC, Richard Woolfolk Waldrop Papers, September 5, 1863.
35. Wilson, SHC, William Robert Gwaltney Papers, Vol. 4, p. 20.
36. Perkins, letter misfiled.
37. Perkins, Henry Kagy Papers, September 7, 1863.
38. Wilson, SHC, Thomas Frederick Boatwright Letters, September 5, 1863.
39. Perkins, Irby H. Scott Papers, August 27, 1863.

40. Wilson, SHC, Edward Hall Armstrong Papers, September 8, 1863.
41. Perkins, James A. Burrows Papers, September 18, 1863.
42. Perkins, John C. Hackett Papers, September 21, 1863.
43. North Carolina State Archives, Newspaper File, *Spirit of the Age*, RaSA, Roll 4, September 17, 1863.
44. North Carolina State Archives, Newspaper File, *Fayetteville Observer*, FyOsw, Roll 12, September 10, 1863.
45. G. Moxley Sorrel, *Recollections of a Confederate Staff Officer* (New York: Neal, 1905), p. 222.
46. Casler, *Four Years*, p. 190.
47. Perkins, Henry Kagy Papers, September 7, 1863.
48. North Carolina State Archives, Futch Papers, July 12, 1863.
49. Benjamin La Bree, *The Confederate Soldier in the Civil War 1861–1865* (Louisville, KY: Courier-Journal, 1895).
50. Perkins, John Hendricks Kinyoun Papers, October 29, 1863.
51. North Carolina State Archives, Futch Papers, October 16, 1861.
52. Ibid., August 20, 1863.
53. Ibid., August 18, 1863.
54. Ibid., March 26, 1863.
55. Ibid., August 19, 1863.
56. See Private Jesse M. Luther, Branch-Lane-Barry Brigade.
57. NARA, M474, AIGO Letters Received, William Preston Johnson, September 28, 1863.
58. NARA, RG 109, Chapter 2, Vol. 84, Letters Sent Army of Northern Virginia, Entry 166, September 28, 1863.
59. NARA, RG 109, E 183, Box 9, File 2668, September 25, 1863.
60. North Carolina State Archives, Adjutant General's Department, Roll of Honor, S:1.79P, Vol. 1 & 2, William Barefoot.
61. North Carolina State Archives, Robert H. Hutspeth Letters, November 30, 1864.
62. OR, Ser. 1, Vol. 29, pt. 2, p. 806.
63. NARA, RG 109, E 126, Correspondence of General R. E. Lee, January 23, 1864.
64. Wilson, SHC, William Robert Gwaltney Papers, January 21, 23, 24, 25, 30, 1864.
65. Government Printing Office, *Special Orders of the AIGO Confederate States* (Washington: Government Printing Office, 1918), SO #116, May 19, 1864.
66. Wilson, SHC, William Calder Papers, March 17, 1864.
67. Manarin, *North Carolina Troops*, 1 Reg Co B-C-D-I.
68. Ibid., 3 Reg Co B-D-H-K.
69. Ibid., 1 Reg B-C-D-E-H-I-K, 3 Reg all companies.

Chapter 12

1. Daniel Harvey Hill, *An Address by Major General D. H. Hill: The Confederate Soldier in the Ranks* (Richmond, VA: Jones, 1885), p. 5.
2. OR, Ser. 1, Vol. 9, p. 445, March 15, 1862.
3. Perkins, V. V. Anderson Papers, n.d.
4. NARA, RG 109, Chapter 2, Vol. 358, T. H. Holmes Correspondence, May 28, 1861.
5. Ibid., November 10, 1862.
6. OR, Ser. 1, Vol. 9, p. 452, March 27, 1862.
7. Ibid., p. 453, March 28, 1862.
8. Ibid., p. 456, April 6, 1862.
9. Ibid., p. 459, April 15, 1862.
10. OR, Ser. 1, Vol. 19, pt. 1, p. 1026, n.d., Report #293.
11. OR, Ser. 1, Vol. 51, pt. 2, p. 601, July 29, 1862.
12. Joe E. Mobley, *The Papers of Zebulon Baird Vance* (Raleigh: Archives and History, 1995), p. 126, April 21, 1863.
13. Vance, GP 165, May 9, 1863.
14. North Carolina State Archives, Thomas Merritt Pittman Collection, GO #13, Department of North Carolina, May 11, 1863.
15. Ibid., GO #18, Department of North Carolina, May 18, 1863.
16. Hill, *An Address by Major General D. H. Hill*, p. 5.
17. NARA, RG 109, Chapter 2, Vol. 335, Letters Sent, District of Cape Fear, May 12, 1863.
18. Ibid., May 16, 1863.
19. NARA, RG 109, Chapter 2, Vol. 337, Letters and Telegrams Sent W. H. C. Whiting's Command, June 2, 1864.
20. North Carolina State Archives, Thomas Merritt Pittman Collection, GO #7, Headquarters Wilmington, January 23, 1864.
21. NARA, RG 109, Chapter 2, Vol. 335, Letters Sent Military District of the Cape Fear, May 4, 1863.
22. NARA, RG 109, E 97, Box 75, GO #13, Army of the Mississippi, March 25, 1862.
23. NARA, RG 109, Chapter 2, Vol. 182, General Orders Department of South Carolina, Georgia and Florida, GO #9, January 17, 1863.
24. Ibid., GO #34, February 27, 1863; GO #75, June 1, 1863.
25. NARA, RG 109, Chapter 2, Vol. 182, General Orders Department of South Carolina, Georgia and Florida, GO #44, March 21, 1863.
26. Ibid., GO #34, February 27, 1863.
27. NARA, RG109, E 97, Box 75, Orders Army of Mississippi, GO #33, May 3, 1862.
28. Ibid., GO #25, April 26, 1862.
29. Ibid., GO #21, April 24, 1862.

Chapter 13

1. Perkins, Edward Alston Thorne Papers, July 11, 1862.
2. Ibid., November 7, 1862.
3. North Carolina State Archives, John R. Hood Diary, February 10, 1863.
4. OR, Ser. 1, Vol. 25, pt. 2, p. 746, April 23, 1863; North Carolina State Archives, Governor Vance Letter Book, 50.1, p. 221.
5. Vance, GP 168, August 14, 1863.
6. NARA, RG109, Chapter 1, Vol. 70, AIGO Register of Letters Received, Entry 59, December 14, 1864.
7. North Carolina State Archives, Thomas Merritt Pittman Collection, GO #13, Department of North Carolina, May 11, 1863.
8. Ibid.
9. Perkins, Nevin Ray Papers, December 28, 1861.
10. Perkins, John Lane Stuart Papers, April 4, 1863.
11. Wilson, SHC, Phifer Family Papers, April 13, 1863.
12. Jordan, *North Carolina Troops*, Vol. 12, p. 90, Rufus Roberts.
13. W. A. Day, *A True History of Company I, 49th Regiment North Carolina Troops in the Great Civil War Between the North and the South* (Newton, NC: Enterprise Job Office, 1893), p. 15.

14. Ibid., p. 43.
15. NARA, RG 109, Chapter 1, Vol. 195, Court Martial Records, Entry 454.
16. NARA, RG 109, Chapter 1, Vol. 197, Court Martial Records, Entries 228, 229, 230.
17. Vance, GP 162, February 3, 1863.
18. Vance, GP 164, April 25, 1863.
19. North Carolina State Archives, Thomas Merritt Pittman Collection, GO #27, Department of North Carolina, June 7, 1863.
20. North Carolina State Archives, Thomas Merritt Pittman Collection, GO #19, Department of North Carolina, May 26, 1863.
21. NARA, RG 109, E 183, General Orders Army of Tennessee, GO #115, August 20, 1863, Lieutenant W. H. White; GO #174, August 30, 1863, Captain J. R. Rhodes; E 99, General Orders Army of Mississippi, GO #18, n.d., Lieutenant T. Lyon.
22. North Carolina State Archives, Thomas Merritt Pittman Collection, GO #27, Petersburg, June 7, 1863.
23. North Carolina State Archives, Henry A. Chambers Papers, p. 177.
24. James Carson Elliott, *The Southern Soldier Boy: A Thousand Shots for the Confederacy* (Raleigh, NC: Edwards and Broughton, 1907), p. 11.
25. Wilson, SHC, John McKee Sharpe Papers, October 21, 1863.
26. Perkins, Wright Family Papers, November 27, 1863.
27. North Carolina State Archives, Governor's Letter Book, 50.2, p. 320, August 26, 1863.
28. Perkins, Wright Family Papers, November 27, 1863.
29. Home Guard Letter Book, Vol. 3, Entry 690, July 2, 1864.
30. Perkins, Patterson-Cavin Papers, March 2, 1865.
31. Elliott, *Southern Soldier Boy*, p. 39.
32. North Carolina State Archives, Thomas Merritt Pittman Collection, GO #24, Department North Carolina and Southern Virginia, September 24, 1864.
33. NARA, M270, Roll 477, SR Craton Manors.
34. Perkins, Charles S. Powell Papers, Typescript, p. 29.
35. Perkins, Edward Alston Thorne Papers, Box 2, July 21, 1862, July 23, 1862.
36. Jordan, *North Carolina Troops*, Vol. 7, p. 293.
37. See Scales Brigade, 38th Regiment, Company F.
38. Vance, GP 174, February 17, 1864.
39. Vance, GP 170, October, 17, 1863; Vance, GP 177, May 3, 1864.
40. Wilson, SHC, Phifer Family Papers, October 13, 1863.
41. Ibid., December 2, 1863.
42. Hugh Douglas Pitts, ed., *Letters of a Gaston Ranger: 2nd Lt. James Wellington Lineberger* (Richmond, VA: privately printed, 1991), p. 78.
43. Perkins, Matthew N. Love Papers, December 7, 1863.
44. Wilson, SHC, Henry Alexander Chambers Papers, December 9, 1863.
45. Pitts, *Letters*, October 19, 1863, addenda, n.p.
46. Ibid., February 20, 1864, p. 85.
47. NARA, M347, Roll 337, Miscellaneous Papers, J. M. Roberts, February 27, 1864.
48. Pitts, *Letters*, April 28, 1864, p. 97.
49. North Carolina State Archives, Henry A. Chambers Papers, Typescript, May 2, 1864, p. 199.
50. Ibid., May 2, 1864.
51. Day, *A True History*, p. 60.
52. North Carolina State Archives, Military Collection, Box 64, Folder 3, Role of Confederate Veterans of Gaston County.
53. North Carolina State Archives, Henry A. Chamber Papers, February 18, 1864, p. 177.
54. Perkins, John Lane Stuart Papers, February 23, 1864.
55. Pitts, *Letters*, February 20, 1864, p. 85.
56. Perkins, Wright Family Papers, February 19, 1864.
57. Day, *A True History*, p. 47.
58. Vance, GP 174, February 5, 1864.
59. NARA, RG 109, Chapter 1, Volume 201, Endorsements on Court Martial Correspondence, Entry F-6.
60. NARA, M270, Roll 393, SR Thomas Carver.
61. Vance, GP 163, March 27, 1863.
62. Vance, GP 181, October 6, 1864.
63. NARA, M270, Roll 393, SR Thomas Carver.
64. NARA, RG 109, Chapter 1, Volume 42, Letters and Telegrams Endorsements AIGO, Entry 78, October 11, 1864.
65. Perkins, John Lane Stuart Papers, September 22, 1864.
66. Ibid., October 11, 1864.
67. Wilson, SHC, James Augustus Graham Papers, November 27, 1864.
68. NARA, RG 109, Chapter 1, Vol. 200, Court Martial Correspondence to the President and the Secretary of War, January 19, 1865.
69. Jordan, *North Carolina Troops*, Vol. 13, p. 583.
70. North Carolina State Archives, Military Collection, Box 65, Folder 30; *North Carolina Troops*, Jordan, Vol. 9, p. 420, p. 427.
71. Vance, GP 183, January 21, 1865.
72. Perkins, John Lane Stuart Papers, February 14, 1865.
73. Perkins, Wright Family Papers, February 23, 1865.
74. Day, *A True History*, p. 41.
75. Jordan, *North Carolina Troops*, 24 Reg Co A-B-E, 25 Reg Co B-C-F-G-H-K, 35 Reg Co B-D-K, 49 Reg Co A-F, 56 Reg Co B-K.

Chapter 14

1. Perkins, Edgar Smithwick Papers, January 14, 1864.
2. Perkins, Hugh MacRae Papers, August 16, 1861.
3. Ibid., September 3, 1861.
4. Perkins, John A. McDade Papers, December 22, 1862.
5. NARA, RG 109, Chapter 2, Volume 182, GO #73, Department of South Carolina, Georgia and Florida, May 28, 1863.
6. Walter Clark, *Histories of the Several Regiments and Battalions from North Carolina in the Great War* Vol. 3 (Wendell, NC: Broadfoot's Bookmark, 1982), p. 512.
7. Wilson, SHC, Thomas Lanier Clingman Papers, January 25, 1863.
8. Ibid., February 18, 1863.
9. North Carolina State Archives, Thomas Merritt Pittman Collection, GO #11, Department of North Carolina, August 17, 1863.
10. Ibid.
11. Perkins, John A. McDade Papers, August 21, 1863.
12. Vance, GP 171, November 25, 1863.
13. NARA, RG 109, Chapter 2, Volume 182, GO #123, Department of South Carolina, Georgia and Florida, September 26, 1863.
14. Perkins, Edgar Smithwick Papers, January 14, 1864.
15. NARA, M270, Roll 182, SR Monroe Clayton.
16. Ibid.
17. Perkins, Thomas Lanier Clingman Papers, January 13, 1864.
18. Ibid., January 20, 1864.
19. Ibid., March 21, 1864.

20. NARA M474, Letters Received AIGO, January–March 1864, 967T.
21. NARA, RG 109, Chapter 1, Volume 42, Letters and Telegrams Endorsements, Entry 54, June 17, 1864.
22. NARA, M270, Roll 547, SR Amos Neal.
23. North Carolina State Archives, Adjutant General's Department Roll of Honor, Vol. 9, Roll S.1.82 P, 61 Regiment, Co B, Entry 38, Amos Neal.
24. Frank Moore, ed., *The Rebellion Record* (NY: Van Nostrand, 1863–1868), Vol. 8, p. 379.
25. NARA, M270, Roll 138, SR Calvin Forrest.
26. North Carolina State Archives, Thomas Merritt Pittman Collection, GO #20, Department North Carolina and Southern Virginia, July 27, 1864.
27. NARA, RG 109, Chapter 2, Volume 216, General Beauregard Order Book, Entry 78, August 3, 1864.
28. NARA, RG 109, Chapter 1, Volume 42, Letters and Telegrams Endorsements, Entry 52, August 16, 1864.
29. Ibid., Entry 134, March 5, 1865.
30. North Carolina State Archives, Thomas Merritt Pittman Collection, GO #20, Department North Carolina and Southern Virginia, July 27, 1864.
31. Vance, GP 181, October 22, 1864.
32. Vance, GP 180, September 22, 1864.
33. Wilson, SHC, Thomas Lanier Clingman Papers, November 23, 1864.
34. Perkins, Thomas Lanier Clingman Papers, January 8, 1865.
35. North Carolina State Archives, Robert F. Hoke Papers, January 10, 1865.
36. North Carolina State Archives, Major Uzzle Letters, January [not legible] 1865.
37. Perkins, Thomas Lanier Clingman Papers, December 3, 1864.
38. Wilson, SHC, Thomas Lanier Clingman Papers, November 25, 1864.
39. Ibid., n.d., 1864.
40. Perkins, Confederate States of America, Box 2, Camp Dudley, May 1st, 1863.
41. Jordan, *North Carolina Troops*, 61 Reg Co B-G.
42. Ibid., 8 Reg Co D-G, 31 Reg Co A, 51 Reg Co F-K, 61 Reg Co D-H.
43. Ibid., 8 Reg Co B-F, 31 Reg Co D-H-K, 51 Reg Co D, 61 Reg Co A.
44. Ibid., 8 Reg Co B-D-F, 31 Reg Co A-D-K, 51 Reg Co D-F-K, 61 Reg Co A-D-H.

Chapter 15

1. Perkins, Caleb Hampton Papers, January 31, 1864.
2. William S. Powell, *Dictionary of North Carolina Biography*, Vol. 4 (Chapel Hill: University of North Carolina Press, 1979–1996), p. 226.
3. Walter Clark, *Histories of the Several Regiments and Battalions from North Carolina in the Great War*, Vol. 3 (Wendell, NC: Broadfoot's Bookmark, 1982), p. 162.
4. Perkins, Henry Toole Clark Papers, June 16, 1862.
5. Jordan, *North Carolina Troops*, Vol. 12, p. 202.
6. SHSP, Vol. 47, p. 203.
7. Vance, GP 170, October 24, 1863.
8. Perkins, John Hendricks Kinyoun Papers, January 9, 1864.
9. Vance, GP 170, October 28, 1863.
10. Vance, GP 165, May 17, 1863.
11. Perkins, Caleb Hampton Papers, May 31, 1863.
12. North Carolina State Archives, Thomas Merritt Pittman Collection, GO #34, Department of North Carolina, June 27, 1863.
13. NARA, M270, Roll 481, SR W. H. Barnes.
14. NARA, RG 109, Chapter 2, Vol. 344, District of the Cape Fear, Endorsements Sent, Entry 12, July 25, 1863.
15. Ibid., July 25, 1863.
16. NARA, M347, Roll 316, Miscellaneous Records, J. T. Pike.
17. North Carolina State Archives, Thomas Merritt Pittman Collection, GO # 6, Department of North Carolina, July 30, 1863.
18. NARA, RG 109, Chapter 2, Vol. 337, Letters and Telegrams Sent W. H. C. Whiting's Command, Entry 5, July 31, 1863.
19. North Carolina State Archives, Thomas Merritt Pittman Collection, GO #6, Department of North Carolina, July 30, 1863.
20. NARA, RG 109, Chapter 2, Vol. 337, August 3, 1863.
21. North Carolina State Archives, Thomas Merritt Pittman Collection, SO #24, Department of North Carolina, August 15, 1863.
22. NARA, RG 109, Chapter 2, Vol. 346, Military Department Endorsement W.H.C. Whiting, Entry 211, December 26, 1863.
23. Perkins, John Hendricks Kinyoun Papers, January 23, 1864.
24. Government Printing Office, *Special Orders of the Adjutant and Inspector Generals Office* (Washington: Government Printing Office, 1918), SO #107, May 7, 1864, Vol. 4, p. 287.
25. North Carolina State Archives, Thomas Merritt Pittman Collection, GO #7, Hdqtrs Wilmington, January 23, 1864.
26. NARA, RG 109, Chapter 1, Volume 201, Endorsements on Court-martial Correspondence, Entry B-10, n.d.
27. NARA, RG 109, Chapter 1, Vol. 42, Letters and Telegrams Endorsements, Entry 11, February 16, 1864.
28. NARA, RG 109, Chapter 2, Vol. 337, Letters and Telegrams Sent W. H. C. Whiting's Command, Entry 298, May 5, 1864.
29. Perkins, Caleb Hampton Papers, January 31, 1864.
30. Perkins, William James Papers, February 9, 1864.
31. North Carolina State Archives, Thomas Merritt Pittman Collection, GO #58, Headquarters Wilmington, December 21, 1863.
32. Ibid., GO #7, Headquarters Wilmington, January 23, 1864.
33. NARA, M270, Roll 420, SR Wilson A. Carter.
34. Ibid.
35. NARA, RG 109, E 183, Box 6, Miscellaneous Manuscripts, Entry 1873, January 25, 1864.
36. NARA, M270, Roll 251, SR Jesse M. Barnhart.
37. NARA, RG 109, Chapter 2, Vol. 337, Letters and Telegrams Sent W. H. C. Whiting's Command, Entry 192, February 14, 1864.
38. NARA, RG 109, Chapter 2, Vol. 347, Military Department Endorsements, Entry 39, February 19, 1864.
39. NARA, RG 109, E 183, Box 8, Miscellaneous Manuscripts, Entry 2546, November 31, 1864.
40. NARA, M401, Union Volunteer Soldiers, Rolls 10–11, Surname letters B and H.
41. OR, Ser. 1, Vol. 29, pt. 1, p. 979, December 18, 1863, p. 989, December 26, 1863.
42. OR, Ser. 1, Vol. 33, p. 297, August 18, 1864.
43. Ibid., p. 948, April 22, 1864.
44. OR, Ser. 1, Vol. 51, pt. 2, p. 1289, May 2, 1864.
45. OR, Ser. 1, Vol. 33, p. 870, April 14, 1864.
46. Rush C. Hawkins, *An Account of the Assassination of Loyal Citizen of North Carolina* (New York: Fulan, 1897), p. 9.

47. OR, Ser. 1, Vol. 33, p. 1102, January 20, 1864.
48. SHSP, Vol. 25, p. 295.
49. Wake Forest University, Rare Book Collection, GO #6, Department of North Carolina, February 3, 1864.
50. Wilson, SHC, Phifer Family Papers, February 5, 1864.
51. T. H. Pearce, ed., *Henry A. Chambers Diary* (Wendell, NC: Broadfoot's Bookmark, 1983), February 7, 1864.
52. Wilson, SHC, M3008, Francis Milton Kennedy Diary, February 9, 1864.
53. Wilson, NCC, 30th Congress, 1st Session, House of Representatives, *Murder of Union Soldiers in North Carolina*, Executive Document 98, p. 5.
54. Wake Forest University, Rare Book Collection, GO #6, Department of North Carolina, February 3, 1864.
55. 30th Congress, 1st Session, House of Representatives, *Murder of Union Soldiers in North Carolina*, Executive Document 98, p. 23.
56. Ibid., p. 33.
57. Ibid., p. 13.
58. Frank Moore, ed., *The Rebellion Record*, Vol. 8 (New York: Putnam, 1861–1868), p. 379.
59. Vance, GP 174, February 11, 1864.
60. Executive Document 98, p. 13.
61. Ibid., p. 31.
62. Wilson, SHC, Bryan Family Papers, September 20, 1863.
63. NARA, M270, Roll 560, SR William H. Freeman; Jordan, *North Carolina Troops*, Vol. 15, p. 392.
64. Executive Document 98, p. 19.
65. Ibid., p. 31.
66. Ibid., p. 30.
67. Ibid., p. 46.
68. Ibid., p. 46.
69. Ibid., p. 19.
70. Ibid., p. 18.
71. Ibid., p. 23.
72. Ibid., p. 19.
73. Wilson, SHC, Leonidas Lafayette Polk Papers, February 13, 1864.
74. Wilson, NCC, Confederate Letters of J. R. P. Ellis, Typescript, February 14, 1864.
75. North Carolina State Archives, Richard W. Iobst Collection, February 17, 1864.
76. Perkins, Samuel Sampson Biddle Papers, February 16, 1864.
77. Executive Document 98, p. 40.
78. Wilson, SHC, John Paris Papers, Diary, February 22, and 23, 1864.
79. Ibid., p. 14.
80. Perkins, Obed William Carr Papers, February 22, 1864.
81. Perkins, Caleb Hampton Papers, February 26, 1864.
82. James Carson Elliott, *The Southern Soldier Boy: A Thousand Shots for the Confederacy* (Raleigh: Edwards and Broughton, 1907), p. 12.
83. North Carolina State Archives, John Willis Councill Diary, February 5, 8, 12, 22, 1864.
84. Perkins, Mary Ann Boyles Papers, March 12, 1864.
85. W. A. Day, *A True History of Company I, 49th Regiment North Carolina Troops in the Great Civil War Between the North and the South* (Newton, NC: Enterprise Job Office, 1893), p. 51.
86. SHSP, Vol. 25, p. 296.
87. David E. Johnston, *The Story of a Confederate Boy in the Civil War* (Portland, OR: Glass and Prudhomme, 1914), p. 238.
88. Executive Document 98, p. 13.
89. Ibid.
90. Ibid.
91. Moore, *Rebellion Record*, Vol. 8, p. 379.
92. Wilson, SHC, David M. Carter Papers, February 23, 1864.
93. NARA, RG 109, Chapter 2, Vol. 337, Letters and Telegrams Sent W. H. C. Whiting's Command, Entry 72, October 24, 1863.
94. NARA, RG 109, Chapter 2, Vol. 346, Military Department Endorsements, Entry 93, December 1, 1863.
95. NARA, RG 109, Chapter 2, Vol. 337, Letters and Telegrams Sent W. H. C. Whiting's Command, Entry 183, February 5, 1864.
96. NARA, RG 109, Chapter 2, Vol. 346, Military Department Endorsements, Entry 139, December 20, 1863.
97. Perkins, Hinsdale Family Papers, p. 82, n.d.
98. Perkins, Hugh MacRae Papers, August 4, 1862.
99. Perkins, James C. Zimmerman Papers, July 12, 1862.
100. Executive Document 98, p. 17.
101. Hawkins, *An Account of the Assassination*, p. 39.
102. North Carolina State Archives, Thomas Merritt Pittman Collection, GO #11, Headquarters Wilmington, March 3, 1864.
103. NARA, M627, Letters and Telegrams Sent AIGO, March 24, 1864.
104. North Carolina State Archives, Thomas Merritt Pittman Collection GO #16, February 12, 1864, [handwritten].
105. NARA, Chapter 2, Vol. 347, Military Department Endorsements, Entry 30, February 16, 1864.
106. NARA, M270, Roll 420, SR William F. Campbell.
107. NARA, RG 109, E 183, Box 8, Miscellaneous Manuscripts, Entry 2546, November 31, 1864.
108. NARA, RG 109, Chapter 1, Vol. 42, Letters and Telegrams Endorsements, Entry 29, May 31, 1864
109. Sandra L. Almasy, comp., *North Carolina 1890 Civil War Veterans Census* (Joliet, IL: Kensington Glen, IL, 1990).
110. Perkins, John Hendricks Kinyoun Papers, May [n.d.] 1864.
111. Perkins, Asa Biggs Papers, May 3, 1864.
112. North Carolina State Archives, PC 123.16, Thomas Merritt Pittman Collection, n.d.
113. Perkins, Asa Biggs Papers, June 12, 1864.
114. Perkins, John Hendricks Kinyoun Papers, March 28, 1865.
115. Powell, *Dictionary of North Carolina Biography*, Vol. 3, p. 371.
116. NARA, RG 109, Chapter 2, Vol. 216, Beauregard Order Book, Entry 113, September 22, 1864.
117. Ibid., Entry 117, September 27, 1864.
118. Correspondence to author, J. L. Danner, March 10, 1994.
119. Perkins, Asa Biggs Papers, October 29, 1864.
120. Perkins, John Hendricks Kinyoun Papers, May [n.d.] 1864.
121. NARA, RG 109, Chapter 1, Vol. 42, Letters and Telegrams Endorsements, Entry 78, October 11, 1864.
122. Perkins, Asa Biggs Papers, October 29, 1864.
123. Perkins, Caleb Hampton Papers, November 2, 1864.
124. North Carolina State Archives, PC 123.16, Thomas Merritt Pittman Collection, November 8, 1864.
125. North Carolina State Archives, State Auditor, Pension Records, 1885, 1901.
126. North Carolina State Archives, Robert F. Hoke Papers, Letterbook, December 12, 1864.

127. NARA, RG 109, Chapter 1, Vol. 42, Entry 120, Letters and Telegrams Endorsements, February 4, 1865.
128. Perkins, John Couch Papers, December 12, 1864.
129. North Carolina State Archives, Military Collection, Box 71, Folder 18, August G. Leazar, Forty-Second Regiment, Co G.
130. NARA, M270, Roll 246, SR John B. Trivett.
131. Perkins, John Hendricks Kinyoun Papers, March 28, 1865.
132. Jordan, *North Carolina Troops*, 17 Reg Co F-G-H, 42 Reg Co B-D-H, 50 Reg Co A-B-D-G, 66 Reg Co A-D-H-K.

Chapter 16

1. NARA, RG 109, E 97, Box 75, Army of the Mississippi December 2, 1863.
2. NARA, RG 109, E 97, Box 75, GO #9, Army of the Mississippi, March 16, 1862.
3. Perkins, Braxton Bragg Papers, March 20, 1862.
4. Perkins, John Buie Papers, September 30, 1862.
5. SHSP, Vol. 46, p. 61, p. 113–131.
6. Ibid., p. 142.
7. Perkins, John Euclid Magee Diary, June 10, 1862.
8. Perkins, John Buie Papers, September 30, 1862.
9. Ibid., November 14, 1862.
10. NARA, RG 109, Chapter 8, Vol. 347, Miscellaneous Orders, GO #4, Army of Tennessee, November 29, 1862; NARA, RG 109, Chapter 2, Vol. 308, November 29, 1862.
11. Walter Clark, *Histories of the Several Regiments and Battalions from North Carolina in the Great War*, Vol. 3 (Wendell, NC: Broadfoot's Bookmark, 1982), p. 738.
12. Perkins, George William Brent Papers, GO #11, Army of Tennessee, December 12, 1863.
13. North Carolina State Archives, Military Collection Box 70, Folder 16, Typescript p. 2.
14. NARA, RG 109, E 97, Box 75, GO #39, Army of Tennessee, February 20, 1863.
15. Ibid., E 90, Box 16, GO #41, Dept. of Alabama and W. Florida, February 1, 1863.
16. OR, Ser. 4, Vol. 2, p. 670, July 25, 1863.
17. Ibid.
18. Ibid., p. 695, August 6, 1863.
19. NARA, RG 109, E 86, Box 83, GO #93, May 1, 1863.
20. Shelby Foote, *The Civil War*, Vol. 2 (New York: Random House, 1958), p. 115.
21. NARA, RG 109, E 86, Box 83, GO #214, Army of Tennessee, December 2, 1863.
22. James L. Morrison Jr., ed., *The Memoirs of Henry Heth* (Westport, CT: Greenwood Press, 1974), p. 168.
23. NARA, RG 109, E 97, Box 75, To the Soldiers of the Army of Tennessee, December 2, 1863.
24. LC, Confederate Records, Container 112, Reel 64, Army of Tennessee, Circular, December 4, 19, 1863.
25. NARA, RG 109, Chapter 2, Vol. 13, Letters Sent Lt General Leonidas Polk, September 4, 1863.
26. NARA, RG 109, Chapter 8, Vol. 98, Order Book Mississippi 24 and 29 Volunteers, March 23, 1863.
27. OR, Ser. 1, Vol. 32, pt. 3, p. 820, April 25, 1864.
28. NARA, RG 109, Chapter 8, Vol. 98, Order Book Mississippi 24 and 29 Volunteers, April 5, 1863.
29. OR, Ser. 1, Vol. 32, pt. 3, p. 824, April 16, 1864.
30. OR, Ser. 4, Vol. 2, p. 853, October 5, 1863.
31. OR, Ser. 1, Vol. 31, pt. 3, p. 823, December 1863.
32. OR, Ser. 1, Vol. 47, pt. 2, p. 1078, February 2, 1865.
33. North Carolina State Archives, Manuscript box with Ridley handwritten ledger.
34. *Confederate Veteran* (Nashville, TN: S. A. Cunningham, 1893–1932), Vol. 11, p. 113.
35. Ibid., Vol. 2, p. 235.

Chapter 17

1. Jordan, *North Carolina Troops*, Vol. 14, p. 237.
2. Wilson, SHC, George Phifer Erwin Papers, March 13, 1864.
3. NARA, M324, Roll 954, Enrolled men letter "B"; Roll 958, Enrolled men letter "W"; Roll 1041, Enrolled men letter "S."
4. Wilson, SHC, George Washington Finley Harper Papers, February 11, 1864.
5. Jack A. Bunch, *Roster of the Courts-Martial in the Confederate States Armies* (Shippensburg, PA: White Mane Books, 2001), Lieutenant T. H. Spencer, p. 325.
6. OR, Ser. 4, Vol. 2, p. 4, July 13, 1862, p. 71, August 28, 1862.
7. Wilson, SHC, George Washington Finley Harper Papers, January 24, 1863.
8. Ibid., December 3, 1863.
9. North Carolina State Archives, Military Collection, Box 70, Folder 37, Some Experiences of Dr. V. W. Cooper in the Confederate Army.
10. Jordan, *North Carolina Troops*, Vol. 14, p. 511.
11. NARA, RG 109, E 86, Box 82, GO #19, Headquarters Army of Tennessee, GO #4, Army of Tennessee, December 1, 1862.
12. Ibid., GO #14, Army of Tennessee, December 13, 1862.
13. NARA, RG 109, Chapter 8, Vol. 347, Miscellaneous Orders AIGO Western Department and Army of Tennessee, December 22, 1862; NARA M270, Roll 541, SR William F. Littrell.
14. North Carolina State Archives, Military Collection, Box 74, Folder 6, Captain Thomas W. Patton, Personal Reminiscences, p. 7.
15. North Carolina State Archives, Military Collection, Box 70, Folder 37, Some Experiences of Dr. V. W. Cooper in the Confederate Army, p. 2.
16. NARA, RG 109, Chapter 8, Vol. 107, Morning Reports, 60th Regiment, December 27, 1862.
17. OR, Ser. 1, Vol. 29, pt. 2, p. 870, November 11, 1863.
18. NARA, RG 109, E 86, Box 82, GO #19, Headquarters Army of Tennessee, February 3, 1863; GO #42, March 1, 1863; GO #50, March 9, 1863.
19. NARA, RG 109, Chapter 2, Vol. 306, Orders Received 1st Kentucky Brigade.
20. NARA, RG 109, E 86, Box 82, Headquarters Department and Army of Tennessee, GO #25, Army of Tennessee, February 8, 1863.
21. Perkins, John W. Reese Papers, March 26, 1863.
22. Wilson, SHC, George Washington Finley Harper Papers, December 16, 1863.
23. NARA, E 86, Box 82, GO #28, Army of Tennessee, April 2, 1864.
24. LC, Confederate Records, Container 112, Reel 64, GO #41, Army of Tennessee, April 25, 1864.
25. North Carolina State Archives, Military Collection, Cooper, p. 8.
26. Wilson, SHC, George Washington Finley Harper Papers, October 10, 1862.
27. Ibid., Wednesday 4th, [1864].
28. Wilson, NCC, Congressional Reports Relating to North Carolina, Forty-First Congress Session 2, Report 205, p. 29.

29. North Carolina State Archives, Military Collection, Patton, p. 11.
30. Wilson, NCC, Congressional Reports Relating to North Carolina, Report #13.
31. Ibid.
32. LC, Confederate Records, Container 112, Reel 64, GO #41, Army of Tennessee, April 25, 1864.
33. NARA, RG 109, Chapter 2, Vol. 15 1/2, Army of Tennessee, Endorsements on Letters Received, May 3, 1864.
34. Wilson, George Phifer Erwin Papers, May 5, 1864.
35. Perkins, John W. Reese Papers, n.d., after May 4, 1864.
36. Jordan, *North Carolina Troops*, Vol. 14, p. 237.
37. Ibid., p. 347, fn 80.
38. Ibid., p. 463, fn111.
39. North Carolina State Archives, Military Collection, Patton, p. 10.
40. North Carolina State Archives, Military Collection, Cooper, p. 8.
41. NARA, RG 109, Chapter 1, Vol. 198, AIGO, Court Martial Records, Private Pinkney Shehan, Private Albert Shehan, p. 147; Jordan, *North Carolina Troops*, Vol. 15, p. 355.
42. *Confederate Veteran* 11, p. 113.
43. Ibid., Vol. 18, p. 517.
44. NARA, E 85, Box 81, GO #8, Headquarters Department and Army of Tennessee, April 8, 1865.
45. Jordan, *North Carolina Troops*, Vol. 14, p. 263, p. 500.
46. Ibid., 58 Reg Co F-G-H-I, 60 Reg Co A-D-E-F.

Chapter 18

1. Wilson, SHC, Joseph Sams Papers, July 19, 1862.
2. NARA, RG 109, Chapter 1, Vol. 195, Court Martial Records, p. 87, May [n.d.], 1862.
3. OR, Ser. 1, Vol. 18, p. 821, January 5, 1863.
4. Perkins, Alfred W. Bell Papers, March 20, 1848.
5. Ibid., March 6, 1862.
6. Ibid., April 10, 1862.
7. North Carolina State Archives, Stephen Whitaker Papers, October [n.d.], 1863.
8. Jordan, *North Carolina Troops*, Vol. 10, p. 163.
9. Ibid., p. 140.
10. NARA, M401, Roll16, SR Balis Norten [sic].
11. Ibid., Roll 22, SR Josiah Norten [sic].
12. Wilson, NCC, 49th Congress, 1st Session, Reports Relating to North Carolina, Report 1065.
13. Wilson, SHC, Joseph Sams Papers, July 19, 1862.
14. NARA, M270, Roll 416, SR Jacob Franklin.
15. NARA, RG 109, E 85, Box 83, GO #202, Army of Tennessee, November 13, 1863.
16. Perkins, Alfred W. Bell Papers, February 26, 1864.
17. Walter Clark, *Histories of the Several Regiments and Battalions from North Carolina in the Great War*, Vol. 2 (Wendell, NC: Broadfoot's Bookmark, 1982), p. 708.
18. Ibid., p. 701.
19. Ibid., p. 702.
20. Jordan, *North Carolina Troops*, 29 Reg Co C-E-F-H, 39 Reg Co B-F-G-H-I.
21. Perkins, Alfred W. Bell Papers, March 30, 1865.

Chapter 19

1. Perkins, Matthew N. Love Papers, October 13, 1862.
2. OR, Ser. 1, Vol. 42, pt. 3, p. 1183, October 29, 1864.
3. NARA, RG 109, Chapter 1, Vol. 25, Inspection Reports of Units and Commands, June 6, 1864.
4. Jordan, *North Carolina Troops*, Vol. 15, p. 11.
5. NARA, RG 109, E 83, Box 82, GO #35, Department of East Tennessee, January 30, 1864.
6. Jordan, *North Carolina Troops*, Vol. 15, p. 169.
7. NARA, RG 109, Chapter 1, Vols. 186–189, Officer Examinations.
8. Phillip Shaw Paludan, *Victims* (Knoxville: University of Tennessee Press, 1981), passim; Clark, *Histories of the Several Regiments*, Vol. 3, p. 661.
9. NARA, M270, Roll 556, SR James M. Haney.
10. Perkins, Matthew N. Love Papers, November 26, 1863.
11. Government Printing Office, *Special Orders of the AIGO Confederate States*, Vol. 5 (Washington: Government Printing Office, 1918), p. 209.
12. NARA, RG 109, E 83, Box 81, GO #8, Department and Army of Tennessee, April 8, 1865.
13. Jordan, *North Carolina Troops*, 62 Reg Co B-D-F-K, 64 Reg Co A-C-D-G.

Chapter 20

1. John Bartlett, ed., *Familiar Quotations* (Boston: Little, Brown, 1982), John Muir, p. 637.
2. NARA, M270, Roll 573, SR William Silvey.
3. North Carolina State Archives, William Williams Stringfield Papers, n.d.
4. Brown and Coffey, *North Carolina Troops*, Thomas Legion, Vol. 16, Co C-E-H.
5. See Sixteenth Regiment, Pender-Scales Brigade, and Twenty-Fifth Regiment, Ransom Brigade.

Chapter 21

1. North Carolina State Archives, Governors Letter Book, 50.2, p. 381, December 21, 1863.
2. Wilson, SHC, Thomas Butler King Papers, August 8, 1864.
3. North Carolina State Archives, Governors Letter Book, 50.2, p. 381, December 21, 1863.
4. NARA, RG 109, E 450, Box 3, GO #4, Head Q'trs Wheeler's Cavalry Command, Item 2524, June 10, 1864.
5. Perkins, Alfred Adams Papers, December 10, 1862.
6. Walter Clark, *Histories of the Several Regiments and Battalions from North Carolina in the Great War*, Vol. 1 (Wendell, NC: Broadfoot's Bookmark, 1982), p. 417.
7. North Carolina State Archives, Fred C. Foard Papers, Typescript p. 10, n.d.
8. Ibid., p. 11.
9. Ibid., p. 4.
10. North Carolina State Archives, PC 123.16, Thomas Merritt Pittman Collection, July 31, 1864.
11. Clark, *Histories of the Several Regiments*, Vol. 2, p. 79.
12. Perkins, V. V. Anderson Papers, August 20, 1861.
13. OR, Ser. 4, Vol. 1, p. 987, March 11, 1862.
14. OR, Ser. 1, Vol. 9, p. 303, April 20, 1862.
15. Ibid., p. 303.
16. NARA, RG 109, Chapter 1, Vol. 198, Court Martial Records, p. 175, December 2, 1864.
17. Manarin, *North Carolina Troops*, Vol. 2, p. 256, December 5, 1864.
18. Ibid., p. 300; John T. Barnett, *List of United States Soldiers Executed by United States Military Authority During the Late War* (Washington, DC: Adjutant General's Office, 1885).

19. OR, Ser. 1, Vol. 33, p. 1252, April 1, 1864.
20. Clark, *Histories of the Several Regiments*, Vol. 3, p. 534.
21. Webb Garrison, *The Encyclopedia of Civil War Usage* (Nashville: Cumberland House, 2001), p. 54.
22. Perkins, Hugh MacRae Papers, August 18, 1862.
23. North Carolina State Archives, William S. Powell Collection, n.d.
24. Clark, *Histories of the Several Regiments*, Vol. 3, p. 541.
25. Ibid., p. 554.
26. Ibid.
27. Ibid., p. 555.
28. Perkins, J. T. Robinson Papers, November [n.d.], 1862.
29. Manarin, *North Carolina Troops*, Vol. 2, p. 444.
30. Ibid., 9 Reg Co A-C-E-G, 19 Reg Co A-B-H, 41 Reg Co B-K, 59 Reg Co D-G, 63 Reg Co D-H-K, 65 Reg Co C-E-F-I.
31. Ibid., Vol. 2, p. 444.
32. Ibid., September 5, 1863.
33. Manarin, *North Carolina Troops*, Vol. 2, p. 505.
34. Wilson, SHC, J. B. Palmer Papers, May 12, 1864.
35. Manarin, *North Carolina Troops*, Vol. 2, p. 456.
36. Perkins, Matthew N. Love Papers, June 17, 1864.
37. Wilson, SHC, George Nathanial Folk Papers, October 24, 1866; Clark, *Histories of the Several Regiments*, Vol. 3, p. 677; Manarin, *North Carolina Troops*, Vol. 2, p. 575.
38. NARA, RG 109, E 69, GO #24, Department of North Carolina, April 30, 1862.
39. North Carolina State Archives, Richard A. Cole Papers, May [not legible], 1862.
40. Wilson, SHC, Perkins Family Papers, Headquarters 2nd Cavalry Brigade, January 15, 1863.
41. Wilson, SHC, Perkins Family Papers, January 15, 1863.
42. Wilson, SHC, Martin Moser Papers, June 29, 1863.
43. North Carolina State Archives, William S. Powell Collection, M. A. Riddick, October 19, 1863.
44. Ibid., September 1, 1864.
45. North Carolina State Archives, Henry Machen Patrick Papers, January 9, 1864.
46. Ibid., July 18, 1863.
47. Executive Document 98, p. 14.
48. NARA, M921, GO #37, Army of Northern Virginia, May 2, 1864, p. 11.
49. Perkins, John A. Smith Papers, July 25, 1864.
50. Perkins, William D. Smith Letters and Papers, July [n.d.], 1864.
51. Frank S. Robinson, "Memoir," Washington County, Virginia, Bulletin, p. 31, n.d.
52. Vance, GP 179, August 29, 1864.
53. NARA, RG 109, Chapter 1, Vol. 201, Endorsements on Court Martial Correspondence, Entry C17, September 9, 1864; NARA, RG 109, Chapter 1, Vol. 42, Letters and Telegrams Endorsements, Entry 64, September 12, 1864.
54. NARA, RG 109 Chapter 9, Vol. 250, Special Orders Department of Henrico, Entry 46.
55. North Carolina State Archives, Military Collection, Box 85, Folder 7, J. R. Redmon Letter, November 2, 1864.
56. Vance, GP 182, November 1, 1864.
57. Manarin, *North Carolina Troops*, Vol. 2, 9 Reg Co D-H, 19 Reg Co C-G, 41 Reg Co B-F, 59 Reg Co A-E, 63 Reg Co B-I, 65 Reg Co C-K.

Chapter 22

1. Perkins, John Lane Stuart Papers, April 4, 1863.
2. North Carolina State Archives, Thomas S. Kenan Papers, May 5, 1862.
3. North Carolina State Archives, Mrs. Lucretia West Parsons Scrapbook, MFp. 66, December 11, 1861.
4. North Carolina State Archives, Military Collection, Box 72, Folder 29, M. B. Wilford, 10-E.
5. North Carolina State Archives, Military Collection, Box 73, Folder 48, K. G. Nantz, 10-C.
6. North Carolina State Archives, Military Collection, Box 76, Folder 59, R. E. Nantz, 10-C.
7. NARA, RG 109, E 69, GO #29, Department of North Carolina, April 13, 1863.
8. NARA, RG 109, Chapter 2, Vol. 335, Letters Sent Military District Cape Fear, Entry 78, June 9, 1863.
9. North Carolina State Archives, Lyman Henry Webb Papers, June 16, 1863.
10. NARA, RG 109, Chapter 2, Vol. 335, Letters Sent Military District Cape Fear, Entry 98, June 22, 1863.
11. Walter Clark, *Histories of the Several Regiments and Battalions from North Carolina in the Great War*, Vol. 2 (Wendell, NC: Broadfoot's Bookmark, 1982), p. 759.
12. North Carolina State Archives, Cape Fear Chapter United Daughters of the Confederacy Papers, Order Book 10 Battalion, November 19, 1864.
13. Wilson, SHC, Lewis Henry Webb Papers, December 27, 1862.
14. Ibid., between October 6, 1862, and October 16, 1862.
15. OR, Ser. 1, Vol. 9, p. 246, March 14, 1862.
16. NARA, RG 109, E 69, GO #27, Department Virginia and North Carolina, April 9, 1863.
17. NARA, RG 109, Chapter 2, Vol. 335, Military District of Cape Fear, Entry 5, April 28, 1863, Entry 20, May 4, 1863.
18. Perkins, Daniel W. Murph Papers, May 24, 1863.
19. North Carolina State Archives, Thomas Merritt Pittman Collection, GO #11, Headquarters Wilmington, August 17, 1863.
20. NARA, RG 109, Chapter 2, Vol. 346, Military Department Endorsements, Entry 51, November 5, 1863; Entry 111, December 8, 1863; Chapter 2, Vol. 337, Letters and Telegrams Sent W. H. C. Whiting's Command, Entry 141, December 18, 1863.
21. NARA, RG 109, Chapter 1, Vol. 42, Letters and Telegrams Endorsements, Entry 55, June 23, 1864.
22. Ibid., Entry 58, June 26, 1864.
23. Ibid., Entry 55, June 23, 1864.
24. NARA, RG 109, Chapter 1, Vol. 201, Endorsements on Court Martial Correspondence, p. 13, June 24, 1864.
25. NARA, RG 109, Chapter 1, Vol. 42, Letters and Telegrams Endorsements, September 19, 1864.
26. Government Printing Office, *Special Orders of the AIGO Confederate States* (Washington: Government Printing Office, 1918), SO #107, Vol. 4, p. 287, May 7, 1864.
27. Vance, GP 177, May 15, 1864. Vance, GP 183, January 24, 1865.
28. Vance, GP 174, February 12, 1864.
29. NARA, RG 109, Chapter 1, Vol. 42, Letters and Telegrams Endorsements, Entry 56, August 25, 1864.
30. Government Printing Office, *Special Orders*, SO #216, Vol. 4, p. 599, September 12, 1864.
31. Perkins, Michael H. Turrentine Papers, February 7, 1864.
32. NARA, RG 109, Chapter 2, Vol. 337, Letters and Telegrams W. H. C. Whiting's Command, Entry 204, February 25, 1864.

33. Wilson, NCC, Executive Document 98, p. 12–13.
34. Wilson, SHC, William Alexander Hoke Papers, February 5, 1864.
35. Ibid., February 5, 1864.
36. Wilson, SHC, Phifer Family Papers, February 5, 1864.
37. Perkins, John Lane Stuart Papers, February 5, 1864.
38. Wilson, NCC, Executive Document 98, p. 12–13.
39. Ibid.
40. North Carolina State Archives, Thomas Merritt Pittman Collection, GO #8, Wilmington, August 17, 1863; GO #47, Department of Cape Fear, April 12, 1864.
41. Vance, GP 178, July 21, 1864.
42. Vance, GP 179, August 15, 1864.
43. NARA, RG 109, M270, Roll 62, SR John W. Clifton.
44. NARA, RG 109, Chapter 1, Vol. 201, Endorsements on Court Martial Correspondence, Entry C-14.
45. NC Historic Sites, Fort Fisher, Diary of Colonel William Lamb, Typescript, November 24, 1864.
46. North Carolina State Archives, Thomas Merritt Pittman Collection, GO #62, Department of North Carolina, October 21, 1864.
47. NARA, RG 109, Chapter 2, Vol. 338, Letters Sent Whiting Command, October 26, 1864.
48. NC Historic Sites, Fort Fisher, Diary of Colonel William Lamb, Typescript, November 24, 1864.
49. William Lamb, *Colonel Lamb's Story* (Carolina Beach, NC: Blockade Runner Museum, 1966), p. 8–9; SHSP, Vol. 21, p. 265.
50. Vance, GP 180, September 3, 1864.
51. NARA, RG 109, Chapter 2, Vol. 348, Military Department Endorsements, September 9, 1864.
52. Vance, GP 183, January 24, 1865.
53. NARA, RG 109, Chapter 1, Vol. 197, p. 230, Entry 2101, September 26, 1864.
54. Vance, GP 181, October 3, 1864.
55. Vance, GP 166, June 8, 1863.
56. NARA, RG 109, Chapter 2, Vol. 347, Military Department Endorsements, Entry 200, May 19, 1864.
57. Vance GP 170, October 10, 1863.
58. Wilson SHC, Lewis Henry Webb Papers, Diary, March 30, 1864.
59. Perkins, Michael H. Turrentine Papers, December 22, 1864.
60. Ibid., December 29, 1864.
61. Ibid.
62. Manarin, *North Carolina Troops*, 1 Battalion Co A-B, 3 Battalion Co B-D, 10 Battalion Co C-A, 13 Battalion Co B, 10 Reg Co A-C-F-G-K, 36 Reg Co A-C-E-F-H, 40 Reg Co B-C-E-H-I.
63. Ibid., 1 Battalion Co A-B, 3 Battalion Co B, 10 Battalion Co B-C, 13 Battalion Co B, 10 Reg Co C-F-K, 36 Reg Co A2-F-H, 40 Reg Co B-E-I.
64. OR, Ser. 1, Vol. 33, p. 1087, January 13, 1864.
65. Ibid., p. 1097, January 19, 1864.
66. Perkins, John Lane Stuart Papers, April 4, 1865.

Chapter 23

1. "The Old North State," William Gaston, official state song of North Carolina, 1927.
2. NARA, RG 109, Chapter 2, Vol. 337, Letters and Telegrams Sent W. H. C. Whiting's Command, Entry 5, August 3, 1863.
3. North Carolina State Archives, Thomas Merritt Pittman Collection, GO #7, Department of North Carolina, July 30, 1863.
4. Wilson, NCC, 30th Congress, 1st Session, House of Representatives, Murder of Union Soldiers in North Carolina, Executive Document 98, p. 13.
5. Ibid.
6. Ibid.
7. Frank Moore, ed., *The Rebellion Record*, Vol. 8 (New York: Putnam, 1861–1868), Document 78, p. 379.
8. NARA, RG 109, Chapter 1, Vol. 198, AIGO Court Martial Records, Entry 3054, p. 322; Entry 3057, p. 323.
9. NARA, RG 109, Chapter 1, Vol. 42, Letters and Telegrams Endorsements, Entry 134, March 4, 1865.
10. NARA, M401, Roll 12, SR James L. Keeler.
11. NARA, M401, Roll 10, SR John Buck.
12. Perkins, Jarratt-Puryear Family Papers, March 5, 1865.
13. NARA, M270, Rolls 346, 350, SR Lewis H. and William A. Speer.
14. NARA, M94, Rolls 29, 30, Register of Enlistments United States Army 1864–1865.
15. NARA, RG 109, Chapter 2, Vol. 338, Letters Sent General Whiting, October 13, 1864.
16. NARA, RG 109, Chapter 2, Vol. 100, Miscellaneous Records, April 13, 1864, S. Blevin.
17. Ibid., March 27, 1865.
18. Ibid., December 19, 1862.
19. North Carolina State Archives, Newspaper file, *Peoples Press*, WsPP, Roll 5, March 23, 1865; *Western Sentinel*, March 16, 1865.
20. Perkins, Wright Family Papers, March 26, 1865.

Epilogue

1. J. H. Simpson, and E. S. C. Weiner, *The Oxford English Dictionary*, Vol. 4 (Oxford: Clarendon Press, 1989), Entry for discipline, p. 735.
2. OR, Ser. 4, Vol. 2, November 22, 1862, p. 204.
3. NARA, RG 109, E 69, GO #28, Department of North Carolina, May 18, 1862.
4. Manarin and Jordan, *North Carolina Troops*, Vols. 3–15, 285 sampled companies.
5. Ibid.
6. Peter S. Bearman, "Desertion As Localism: Army Unit Solidarity and Group Norms in the U.S. Civil War," *Social Forces*, December 1991, p. 321–342; Robert C. Kinzer, *Kinship and Neighborhood in a Southern Community* (Knoxville: University of Tennessee Press, 1997), passim.
7. Manarin and Jordan, *North Carolina Troops*, Vols. 3–15.
8. Ibid., 2 Reg Co E, 4 Reg Co C-H, 5 Reg Co B-G-H, 28 Reg Co C, 37 Reg Co A-B.
9. Ibid., Vol. 3–15, 140 Companies, 1,191 enrolled officers.
10. NARA, RG 109, Chapter 1, Vols. 195–201, Court-Martial Records.
11. Manarin and Jordan, *North Carolina Troops*, Vols. 3–15, 57 Infantry Regiments.
12. Ibid., Vols. 3–15, Col 1–4; NARA, RG 109, Chapter 1, Vols. 194–200, Col. 5–7.
13. Executions in Third, Fifty-Eighth, Sixtieth and Sixty-Sixth Regiments not included.
14. Author's compilation from all sources.
15. North Carolina—Manarin and Jordan, *North Carolina Troops*, Vols. 3–15; Virginia—NARA, RG 109, M324, Compiled Service Records; Georgia—Lillian Henderson, *Roster of the Confederate Soldiers of Georgia 1861–1865* (Hapville, GA: Longino & Porter, 1964); South Carolina—NARA, RG 109, M627, Compiled Service Records.

16. Henderson, *Roster*, Vols. 2–6, names beginning with B, H, S or W.
17. Ibid., names beginning with B.
18. Georgia — NARA, RG 109, M266, Compiled Service Records, enrolled men, names beginning with B.
19. As source 15 above.
20. OR, Ser. 4, Vol. 3, p. 359, April 30, 1864.
21. North Carolina State Archives, Newspaper File, *Raleigh Standard*, RaStDew, Roll 13, March 7, 1865, Col 2; Jack A. Bunch, *Military Justice in the Confederate States Armies* (Shippensburg, PA: White Mane Books, 2000), p. 117, Col. 4; Author's compilation, Cols. 5–6.
22. Bunch, *Military Justice*, passim.
23. See chart "Eastern Armies."
24. Ibid.
25. Aaron Sheehan-Dean, *Why Confederates Fought Family and Nation in Civil War Virginia* (Chapel Hill: University of North Carolina Press, 2007), p. 198.
26. Douglas Southall Freeman, *A Calender of Confederate Papers* (Richmond: Confederate Museum, 1908), p. 19, 20.
27. Chart "Percent of Total Absences by Half-Year."
28. Chart "Eastern Confederate States."
29. Sheehan-Dean, *Why Confederates Fought*, p. 95.
30. Author's compilation, eleven infantry brigades; Bunch, *Military Justice*, p. 130.
31. North Carolina State Archives, Governor's Letter Book, 50.1, p. 245, May 22, 1863.
32. OR. Ser. 1 Vol. 42, pt. 2, p. 1276, September 23, 1864
33. John A. Sloan, *Reminiscences of the Guilford Grays Co B 27th Regiment North Carolina Troops* (Washington: Polkinhorn, 1883), p. 52.
34. OR, Ser. 1, Vol. 19, pt. 2, p. 600, September 8, 1862.
35. See Pettigrew-Kirkland-McRae Brigade, Private John Bowers.
36. Walter Harrison, *Pickett's Men: A Fragment of War History* (New York: Van Nostrand, 1870), p. 119.
37. Perkins, Fries and Shaffner Family Papers, December 30, 1863.
38. James Anson Farrer, *Military Manners and Customs* (Piccadilly, London, England: Chatto & Windus, 1885), p. 230.
39. Clifford Dowdey, and Louis H. Manarin, *The Wartime Papers of R. E. Lee* (New York: Bramhall House, 1961), p. 892.
40. Perkins, Confederate States Army, Box 2, Military Court 1st Corps, January 15, 1864.
41. OR, Ser. 1, Vol. 46, pt. 2, p. 1229, February 11, 1865.
42. OR, Ser. 1, Vol. 51, pt. 3, p. 1056, January 1, 1865.
43. Ibid., p. 1064, March 5, 1865.

Bibliography

Absher, W. O., and Nancy Williams Simpson. *The Heritage of Wilkes County*. Winston-Salem: Wilkes Genealogical Society, 1982–1990.

Ainsworth, Brigadier General Fred G., and Joseph W. Kirklin. *The War of the Rebellion: A Compilation of the Official Records of the Union and Confederate Armies*. Washington: Government Printing Office, 1880–1901.

Allota, Robert I. *Stop the Evil*. San Rafael, CA: Presidio Press, 1978.

Almasy, Sandra L., ed. *North Carolina 1890 Civil War Veterans Census*. Joliet, IL: Kensington Glen, 1990.

Auslander, Fietje. *Verrater oder Vorbilder*. Germany: Temmen, 1989.

Axelrod, Alan. *The Real History of World War II*. New York: Sterling, 2008.

Babington, Anthony. *For the Sake of Example: Capital Courts-martial 1914–1920*. London: Leo Cooper with Secker & Warburg, 1983.

Bardolph, Richard. "Confederate Dilemma: North Carolina Troops and the Deserter Problem." *North Carolina Historical Review* 66–67, (1989).

Bearman, Peter S. "Desertion as Localism: Army Unit Solidarity and Group Norms in the U.S. Civil War." *Social Forces* 70, no. 2 (December 1991).

Beaumont, Roger. *War, Chaos, and History*. Westport, CT: Praeger, 1997.

Beers, G. Putney. *Guide to Federal Archives Related to the Civil War*. Washington: Government Printing Office, 1968.

Bellamy, Chris. *Absolute War: Soviet Russia in the 2nd World War*. New York: Knopf, 2007.

Berry, Mary E. Strayhorn. "Letters of Thomas Jackson Strayhorn." *North Carolina Historical Review* 4 (1936).

Betts, W. A., ed. *Experience of a Confederate Chaplain 1861–1864*. Greenville, NC: n.p., c1900.

Bohm, Robert M. *Deathquest*. Cincinnati: Anderson, 1999.

Bond, Brian, and Nigel Cave, eds. *Haig: A Reappraisal 70 Years On*. London: Leo Cooper, 1999.

Boykin, James H. *North Carolina in 1861*. New York: Bookman Associates, 1961.

Bradley, Stephen E. Jr. *North Carolina Confederate Militia and Home Guard Records*. Virginia Beach, VA: privately printed, 1995.

Bridges, Hal. *Lee's Maverick General: Daniel Harvey Hill*. New York: McGraw-Hill, 1961.

Brown, Matthew M., and Michael W. Coffey. *North Carolina Troops 1861–1865: A Roster*. Vol. 16. Raleigh: Department of Archives and History, 1966–2008.

Brooks, R. P. "Conscription in the Confederate States of America, 1862–1865." *Bulletin of the University of Georgia* 17, no. 4 (1917).

Bunch, Jack A. *Military Justice in the Confederate States Armies*. Shippensburg, PA: White Mane Books, 2000.

_____. *Roster of the Courts-Martial in the Confederate States Armies*. Shippensburg, PA: White Mane Books, 2001.

Caldwell, J. F. J. *The History of a Brigade of South Carolina*. Columbia: Baird, 1866.

Carmichael, Peter S. "So Far from God and so Close to Stonewall." *Civil War Times*, June, 2005.

Casler, John O. *Four Years in the Stonewall Brigade*. Marietta, GA: Continental Book, 1951.

Citino, Robert M. *The German Way of War*. Lawrence: University Press of Kansas, 2005.

Clark, Walter. *Histories of the Several Regiments and Battalions from North Carolina in the Great War*. Vols. 1–5. (Reprinted) Wendell, NC: Broadfoot's Bookmark, 1982.

Clegg, Henry C. *War Record from 1862–1865 as Published in the Chatham Record*. Pittsboro, NC: Chatham Record, 1925.

Clodfelter, Micheal. *Warfare and Armed Conflicts*. Jefferson, NC: McFarland, 1993.

Confederate Veteran 11, p. 113.

Corns, Cathryn, and John Hughes-Wilson. *Blindfold and Alone: Executions of British Soldiers in the Great War*. London: Cassell, 2001.

Cronau, Rudolf. *The Army of the Revolution*. New York: Cranau, 1923.

Day, W. A. *A True History of Company I, 49th Regiment North Carolina Troops in the Great Civil War Between the North and the South*. Newton, NC: Enterprise Job Office, 1893.

Dodge, Theodore Ayrault. *Napoleon*. Boston: Houghton Mifflin, 1904.

Douglas, Henry Kyd. *I Rode with Stonewall*. Chapel Hill: University of North Carolina Press, 1940.

Dowdey, Clifford, and Louis H. Manarin, eds. *The War Time Papers of R. E. Lee*. Boston: Little, Brown, 1961.

Early, Jubal A. *A Memoir of the Last Year of the War for*

Independence in the Confederate States of America. Lynchburg, VA: Button, 1867.

Elliott, James Carson. *The Southern Soldier Boy: A Thousand Shots for the Confederacy.* Raleigh: Edwards and Broughton, 1907.

Farrer, James Anson. *Military Manners and Customs.* London: Chatto & Windus, 1885.

Faust, Drew Gilpin. *The Republic of Suffering.* New York: Knopf, 2008.

Firth, Charles Harding. *The Parallel Between the English and the American Civil Wars.* Cambridge, England: University of Cambridge Press, 1910.

Fite, David Emerson. *Social and Industrial Conditions in the North During the Civil War.* New York: Macmillan, 1910.

Foote, Henry S. *Casket of Reminiscences.* Washington: Chronicle, 1874.

Foote, Shelby. *The Civil War.* New York: Random House, 1958.

Fortescue, Hon. J. W. *A History of the British Army.* London: Macmillan, 1910.

Frazier, Donal S., ed. *The United States and Mexico at War.* New York: Macmillan Reference USA, 1998.

Freeman, Douglas Southall, ed. *Lee's Dispatches.* New York: Putnam, 1957.

_____. *A Calendar of Confederate Papers.* Richmond: Confederate Museum, 1908.

Frey, Sylvia R. *British Soldier in America.* Austin: University of Texas Press, 1981.

Gallagher, Gary W. *Stephen Dodson Ramseur: Lee's Gallant General.* Chapel Hill: University of North Carolina Press, 1985.

Garrison, Webb. *The Encyclopedia of Civil War Usage.* Nashville, TN: Cumberland House, 2001.

Gordon, Lesley J. *General George E. Pickett in Life and Legend.* Chapel Hill: University of North Carolina Press, 1998.

Government Printing Office. *Special Orders of the AIGO Confederate States.* Washington: Government Printing Office, 1918.

Griffin, Appleton P.C., ed. *Orderly Book of General George Washington, Commander in Chief of the American Armies; Kept at Valley Forge, 18 May–11 June, 1778.* Rpt. New York: New York Times, 1971.

Gurwood, Lt. Col. John, ed. *Selections from the Despatches and General Orders of Field Marshal the Duke of Wellington.* London: Murray, 1851.

Hall, Harry T. *A Johnny Reb Band from Salem: The Pride of Tarheelia.* Raleigh: North Carolina Confederate Centennial Commission, 1963.

Hamlin, Captain Percy Gatling, ed. *The Making of a Soldier.* Richmond: Whittet & Shepperson, 1935.

Hardy, Jesse D., ed. *The Civil War Letters of Thomas W. Gaither.* Raleigh: Hardy, 1983.

Harris, J. S. *Historical Sketches of the Seventh Regiment North Carolina Troops.* Mooresville, NC: Mooresville, 1893.

Harrison, Walter. *Pickett's Men: A Fragment of War History.* New York: Van Nostrand, 1870.

Hassler, William W., ed. *The General to His Lady: The Civil War Letters of William Dorsey Pender.* Chapel Hill: University of North Carolina Press, 1965.

Hatley, Joe M., ed. *Letters of William F. Wagner: Confederate Soldier.* Wendell, NC: Broadfoot's Bookmark, 1983.

Hawkins, Rush C. *An Account of the Assassination of Loyal Citizens of North Carolina.* New York: Fulan, 1897.

Heidler, David S. *Encyclopedia of American Civil War.* Santa Barbara, CA: ABC Clio, 2000.

Henderson, Lillian. *Roster of the Confederate Soldiers of Georgia 1861–1865.* Hapville, GA: Longino & Porter, 1964.

Hewett, Janet B. *The Roster of Confederate Soldiers, 1861–1865.* Wilmington, NC: Broadfoot, 1995.

Higgenbotham, Don. *George Washington and the American Military Tradition.* Athens: University of Georgia Press, 1985.

Hill, D. H. *An Address by Major General D. H. Hill: The Confederate Soldier in the Ranks.* Richmond: Association of the Army of Northern Virginia: Jones, 1885.

Holden, W. W. *Memoirs of W. W. Holden.* Durham, NC: Seeman, 1911.

Huffman, James. *Ups and Downs of a Confederate Soldier.* New York: William E. Rudge's Sons, 1940.

Iobst, Richard W. *The Bloody Sixth: The Sixth North Carolina Regiment.* Raleigh: NC Confederate Centennial Commission, 1965.

Jackson, Edgar Allen. *Letters of Edgar Allan Jackson.* Franklin, VA: N.p., 1939.

Johnston, David E. *The Story of a Confederate Boy in the Civil War.* Portland, OR: Glass and Prudhomme, 1914.

Jones, Rev. J. William. *Christ in the Camp, or Religion in Lee's Army.* Richmond: Johnson, 1887.

Jordan, Weymouth T. Jr. *North Carolina Troops 1861–1865: A Roster.* Vols. 4–15. Raleigh: Department of Archives and History, 1966–2008.

Kinzer, Robert C. *Kinship and Neighborhood in a Southern Community.* Knoxville: University of Tennessee Press, 1997.

Kirkland, Ralph W. Jr. *Broken Fortunes.* Charleston: South Carolina Historical Society, 1995.

Krick, Robert E. L. *Staff Officers in Gray.* Chapel Hill: University of North Carolina Press, 2003.

La Bree, Benjamin. *The Confederate Soldier in the Civil War, 1861–1865.* Louisville, KY: Courier-Journal, 1895.

Lamb, William. *Colonel Lamb's Story.* Carolina Beach, NC: Blockade Runner Museum, 1966.

Ledford, P. L. *Reminiscences of the Civil War.* Thomasville, NC: News Printing House, 1909.

Lee, C. H. *The Judge Advocates VADE MECUM Embracing a General View of Military Law and Practice Before Courts Martial with an Epitome of the Laws of Evidence as Applicable to Military Trials.* Richmond, VA: West and Johnson, 1863.

Leon, Louis. *Diary of a Confederate Soldier.* Charlotte, NC: Stone, 1913.

Long, E. B. *The Civil War Day by Day: An Almanac, 1861–1865.* Garden City, NY: Doubleday, 1971.

Lonn, Ella. *Desertion During the Civil War.* NY, London: Century, 1928.

Lottman, Herbert R. *The People's Anger.* London: Hutchinson, 1986.

Lowry, Thomas P. *Don't Shoot That Boy!* Mason City, IA: Savas, 1999.

Luvaas, Jay, ed. *Frederick the Great on the Art of War.* New York: The Free Press, 1966.

Manarin, Louis H. *Richmond at War: The Minutes of the City Council, 1861–1865.* Chapel Hill: University of North Carolina Press, 1966.

Manarain, Louis H. *North Carolina Troops 1861–1865: A Roster.* Vols. 1–3. Raleigh: Department of Archives and History, 1966–2008.

Markham, Jerald H., comp. *The Diuguid Records.* Westminster, MD: Heritage Books, 2007.

Martin, Bessie. *Desertion of Alabama Troops from the Confederate Army: A Study in Sectionalism.* New York: Columbia University Press, 1932.

Martin, Edgar W. *The Standard of Living in 1860.* Chicago: University of Chicago Press, 1942.

Mast, Greg, ed. *Home Front.* August-September 1989.

McCarthy, Carlton. *Soldier Life in the Army of Northern Virginia, 1861–1865.* Richmond: Johnson, 1882.

McCaslin, Richard B. *Tainted Breeze: The Great Hanging at Gainsville, Texas, 1862.* Baton Rouge: Louisiana State University Press, 1994.

Mills, L. Barron Jr. *Randolph County: A Brief History.* Raleigh: Office of Archives and History, 2008.

Mitchell, Memory F. *Legal Aspects of Conscription and Exemption in North Carolina 1861–1865.* Chapel Hill: University of North Carolina Press, 1965.

Mobley, Joe E. *The Papers of Zebulon Baird Vance.* Raleigh: Archives and History, 1995.

Moore, Albert Burton. *Conscription and Conflict in the Confederacy.* New York: Hillary House, 1963.

Moore, Frank. *The Rebellion Record.* New York: Putnam, Van Nostrand, 1864.

Moore, William. *The Thin Yellow Line.* London: Leo Cooper, 1974.

Morrison, James L. Jr., ed., *The Memoirs of Henry Heth.* Westport, CT: Greenwood Press, 1974.

Neagles, James C. *Summer Soldiers.* Salt Lake City: Ancestry, 1986.

Parrish, T. Michael, and Robert M. Willingham Jr. *Confederate Imprints: A Bibliography of Southern Publications from Secession to Surrender.* Katonah, NY: Foster, 1984.

Paludan, Phillip Shaw. *Victims.* Knoxville: University of Tennessee Press, 1981.

Pearce, T. H., ed. *Henry A. Chambers Diary.* Wendell, NC: Broadfoot's Bookmark, 1983.

Pierson, William Whitley. *The Diary of Bartlett Yancey Malone.* Chapel Hill: University of North Carolina Press, 1919.

Pittard, Pen-Lile. *Alexander County's Confederates.* Taylorsville, NC: N.p., 1960.

Pitts, Hugh Douglas, ed. *Letters of a Gaston Ranger.* Richmond: Privately printed, 1991.

Polk, William M. *Leonidas Polk: Bishop and General.* New York: Longmans, Green, 1893.

Pollock, Sam. *Mutiny for the Cause.* London: Leo Cooper, 1969.

Powell, William S. *Dictionary of North Carolina Biography.* Chapel Hill: University of North Carolina Press, 1979–1996.

_____. *The North Carolina Gazetteer: A Dictionary of Tar Heel Places.* Chapel Hill: University of North Carolina Press, 1968.

Preslar, C. J. *A History of Catawba County.* Salisbury, NC: Rowan, 1893.

Radley, Kenneth. *Rebel Watchdog: The Confederate States Army Provost Guard.* Baton Rouge: Louisiana State University Press, 1989.

Ridley, Louis Bromfield. *Battles and Sketches of the Army of Tennessee.* Mexico, MO: Missouri, 1906.

Robertson, James I. Jr. *Stonewall Jackson.* New York: Macmillan, 1997.

_____. *General A. P. Hill: The Story of a Confederate Warrior.* New York: Random House, 1987.

Robinson, William M. Jr. *Justice in Grey: A History of the Judicial System of the Confederate States.* Cambridge, MA: Harvard University Press, 1941.

Roman, Alfred. *The Military Operations of General Beauregard.* New York: Harper & Brothers, 1884.

Sellers, Leonard. *For God's Sake, Shoot Straight.* London: Leo Cooper, 1996.

Shaffner, C. L. *Diary of Dr. J. F. Shaffner, Jr.* Winston-Salem, NC: N.p., 1936.

Sharpe, Ivey L. *Stanly County, USA: The Story of an Area and an Era.* Greensboro, NC: Media Press, 1990.

Sheehan-Dean, Aaron. *Why Confederates Fought: Family and Nation in Civil War Virginia.* Chapel Hill: University of North Carolina Press, 2007.

Sifakis, Steuart. *Compendium of the Confederate States: North Carolina.* New York: Facts on File, 1992.

Silver, James W. *Confederate Morale and Church Propaganda.* New York: Norton, 1967.

Simpson, J. A., and E. S. C. Weiner, eds. *Oxford English Dictionary.* Oxford, England: Clarendon Press, 1989.

Sloan, John A. *Reminiscences of the Guilford Grays Co. B 27th Regiment North Carolina Troops.* Washington: Polkinhorn, 1883.

Sorrel, General G. Moxley. *Recollections of a Confederate Staff Officer.* New York: Neal, 1905.

Stone, David. *Fighting for the Fatherland.* Washington: Potomac Books, 2006.

Tatum, Georgia Lee. *Disloyalty in the Confederacy.* Chapel Hill: University of North Carolina Press, 1934.

Taylor, Michael W. *Cry is War, War, War.* Dayton, OH: Morningside House, 1994.

Taylor, Walter. *Four Years with General Lee.* New York: Bonanza Books, 1962.

30th Congress, 1st Session, House of Representatives. "Murder of Union Soldiers in North Carolina." Executive Document 98.

Trevelyan, George Macauley. *Garibaldi's Defence of the Roman Republic.* London: Phoenix Press, 1920.

Trotter, William R. *The Civil War in North Carolina.* Winston-Salem, NC: Blair, 1991.

Underwood, George C. *History of the 26th Regiment of North Carolina Troops in the Great War.* Wendell, NC: Broadfoot's Bookmark, 1978.

War Department. *Revised Regulations for the Army of the United States 1861.* Philadelphia: Lippincott, 1861.

Weitz, Mark A. *A Higher Duty.* Lincoln: University of Nebraska Press, 2000.

Wiley, Bell Irvin. *The Life of Johnny Reb: The Common Soldier of the Confederacy*. Baton Rouge: Louisiana State University Press, 1943.
Wilkinson, David. *Deadly Quarrels: Lewis F. Richardson and the Statistical Study of War*. Berkeley: University of California Press, 1980.
Williams, Max R., ed. *Papers of William Alexander Graham*. Vol. 6. Raleigh, NC: Department of Archives and History, 1976.
_____, and J. G. de Roulhac Hamilton, eds. *Papers of William Alexander Graham*. Vol. 5. Raleigh, NC: Office of Archives and History, 1973.
Williams, T. Harry. *P. G. T. Beauregard: Napoleon in Gray*. Baton Rouge: Louisiana State University Press, 1955.
Winter, Dennis. *Death's Men: Soldiers in the Great War*. London: Hardmondsworth, 1979.
Wright, Stuart L., ed. *The Confederate Letters of Benjamin H. Freeman*. Hicksville, NY: Exposition Press, 1974.
Wyckoff, Mack. *History of Kershaw's Brigade*. Wilmington, NC: Broadfoot, 1990.
Yearns, Wilfred Buck. *The Confederate Congress*. Athens: University of Georgia Press, 1960.
Yearns, W. Buck, and John G. Barrett. *North Carolina Civil War Documentary*. Chapel Hill: University of North Carolina Press, 1980.

Manuscripts

Duke University, William R. Perkins Library, Manuscript Department

Alfred Adams Papers
V. V. Anderson Papers
Doctor Warren Bagley Diary
James H. Baker Papers
Alfred W. Bell Papers
Samuel Sampson Biddle Papers
Asa Biggs Papers
Eliza Gordon Hall Boyles Papers
Mary Ann Boyles Papers
Jonas A. Bradshaw Papers
Braxton Bragg Papers
George William Brent Papers
William H. Brotherton Papers
Hugh Conway Browning Papers
John Buie Papers
James A. Burrows Papers
Patrick H. Cain Papers
David Frank Caldwell Papers
Obed William Carr Papers
Lunceford R. Cherry Papers
Henry Toole Clark Papers
Thomas Lanier Clingman Papers
James O. Coghill Papers
Corpening Family Papers
John Couch Papers
Mary A. (Horton) Council Papers
Leonidas Polk Denmark Papers
A. J. Dula Papers
John B. Evans Papers
C. [William] Fackler Papers
Frank Family Papers
Alexander Frank Papers
Stephen Frazier Papers
Gill Family Papers
Elizabeth F. Glen Papers
J. B. Goodin Papers
James E. Green Diary
Bryan Grimes Papers
John C. Hackett Papers
Caleb Hampton Papers
Cornelious R. Hanleiter Papers
Archibald Erskine Henderson Papers
J. L. Henry Papers
Hinsdale Family Papers
Thomas Hinshaw Papers
Wade H. Hubbard Papers
William James Papers
Jarratt-Puryear Family Papers
J. E. Johnston Papers
Charles Colcock Jones Papers
Henry Kagy Papers
Alexander Keever Papers
John N. Kelly Papers
John Hendricks Kinyoun Papers
James H. C. Leach Papers
Julius A. Linebeck Collection
Robert O. Linster Papers
Matthew N. Love Papers
Riley Luther Papers
Hugh MacRae Papers
John Euclid Magee Diary
Alexander Carey McAlister Papers
John A. McDade Papers
Duncan McLaurin Papers
Alexander McMillan Papers
Mary Margaret McNeil Papers
Daniel W. Murph Papers
J. F. Newsome Papers
Joseph Overcash Papers
Patterson-Cavin Family Papers
Jane Peterson Papers
John F. Poindexter Papers
Charles S. Powell Papers
D. F. Ramsaur Letters
Nevin Ray Papers
John W. Reese Papers
Roberson Papers
Josiah S. Roberson Papers
J. T. Robinson Papers
Sion Hart Rogers Papers
Charles Rothrock Papers
Scarborough Family Papers
Irby H. Scott Papers
William Lafayette Scott Papers
Daniel Setzer Papers
Thornton Sexton Papers
John A. Smith Papers
William D. Smith Letters and Papers
Edgar Smithwick Papers
John W. Staley Papers
John Lane Stuart Papers
Lewis Sugg Papers
William A. Tesh Papers
Edward Alston Thorne Papers
A. S. Townes Diary
Michael H. Turrentine Papers
Isham Sims Upchurch Papers
Eugene Verdery, Jr. Papers
John Wesley Walker Papers
Shadrach Ward Papers
John C. Warlick Papers
James King Wilkerson Papers
Wright Family Papers
James M. Wright Papers
James C. Zimmerman Papers

• **RARE BOOK ROOM**
Confederate General Orders

University of North Carolina–Chapel Hill

• **WILSON LIBRARY, SOUTHERN HISTORICAL COLLECTION**

William D. Alexander Diary
Edward Hall Armstrong Papers
Thomas Frederick Boatwright Letters
Boykin Family Papers
Bryan Family Papers
William Calder Papers
David Carter Papers
David M. Carter Papers
Henry Alexander Chambers Papers
William John Clarke Papers
Clingman-Puryear Family Papers
Thomas Lanier Clingman Papers
Raleigh Edward Colston Papers
Confederate Papers
CSA Conscript Department
George Phifer Erwin Papers
George Nathanial Folk Papers
Charles K. Gallagher Papers
Leonidas Chalmers Glenn Collection
James Augustus Graham Papers
James E. Green Diary
William Robert Gwaltney Papers
George Washington Finley Harper Papers
William Alexander Hoke Papers
William J. Hoke Books
Edward Vernon Howell Papers
Robert Phillip Howell Memoirs
Kenneth Rayner Jones Papers
Francis Milton Kennedy Diary
Thomas Butler King Papers
Joseph Overcash Papers
Calvin Leach Diary

William Gaston Lewis Papers
Alexander Carey McAlister Papers
McClelland Family Papers
Laura Cornelia McGimsey Papers
John S. R. Miller Papers
Martin Moser Papers
J. B. Palmer Papers
John Paris Papers
Perkins Family Papers
Phifer Family Papers
Leonidas Lafayette Polk Papers
Proffit Family Papers
E. F. Satterfield and Merritt Family Papers
Joseph Sams Papers
Shaffner Papers
John McKee Sharpe Papers
Steed and Phipps Family Papers
George Sidney Thompson Papers
Richard Woolfolk Waldrop Papers
Samuel Hoey Walkup Papers
Webb Family Papers
Lewis Henry Webb Papers
George Whitaker Wills Letter

- **WILSON LIBRARY, NORTH CAROLINA COLLECTION**

Confederate Letters of J. R. P. Ellis
Lawson Harrill Reminiscences
Forty-Fifth Regiment Order Book
Rodes Division Logbook of General and Special Orders
Shaffner Diary

North Carolina State Archives

- **PRIVATE MANUSCRIPT COLLECTIONS**

Henry Clay Albright Papers
John J. Armfield Letters
R. T. Barnes Diary
Henry Brantingham and W. H. S. Burgwyn Diary
Henry A. Chambers Papers
Richard A. Cole Papers
John Willis Councill Diary
Leonidas Polk Denmark Diary
Alexander England Family Papers
Fred C. Foard Papers
Futch Papers
Mary A. Gash Papers
Bryan Grimes Papers
Oliver C. and Calier G. Hamilton Letters
Robert F. Hoke Papers
John R. Hood Diary
Vernon Howell Collection
Robert H. Hutspeth Letters
Eban Ingram Collection
Sanders M. Ingram Letters
Richard W. Iobst Collection
Thomas S. Kenan Papers
James H. Lane Papers
Isaac Lefevers Papers
Riley W. Leonard Papers
A. C. Meyers Papers
Elizabeth M. Montgomery Collection
Peter M. Mull Papers
Thomas Newby Letters
Mrs. Lucretia West Parsons Scrapbook

Henry Machen Patrick Papers
George W. Pearsall Letters
Thomas Merritt Pittman Collection
Leonidas L. Polk Papers
L. L. Polk Papers
William S. Powell Collection
Alfred M. Scales Papers
Shaffner Diary and Papers
Edmund Smithwick and Family Papers
Major Uzzle Letters
Zebulon Baird Vance Papers
Governor Zebulon B. Vance Letterbook
Governor Z. B. Vance Correspondence
Henry C. Wall Diary
P. H. Warlick Letters
Lyman Henry Webb Papers
Stephen Whitaker Papers
John Wright Family Papers
John G. Young Papers

- **GENEALOGY DEPARTMENT**

Vertical File
George Washington Woodard

Library of Congress

Jedediah Hotchkiss Papers
C. M. Wilcox Papers
Microfilm, Civil War Records
Microfilm, Confederate Records

Wake Forest University

Rare Book Collection: General Orders

Index

Abernathy, John W. M. 53
absence: defined 5; pattern of 311, 322; statistics 40, 312
Abshear, William H. 58
Absher, Allen 27
Adams, Alfred 276
Adams, Asa 74–5
Adams, S. 189
Adcock, Henry C. 91
AIGO 9, 11, 260; Judge Advocate section 11
Alabama troops: 5th Infantry 122, 125; 28th Infantry 249, 252; 58th Infantry 252; Battles Brigade 123; Deas Brigade 246; executions 249; infantry 192
Alamance County, NC 74, 139
Albright, Henry Clay 76–7
Alexander, J. C. 164
Alexander, William D. 31, 33, 35–6
Alexander County, NC 31, 33, 54, 95, 106, 186
Alleghany County, NC 26
Allen, Lawrence M. 269
Allen, Vincent H. 301
Allison, Julius F. 200
Allred, Samuel C. 52–3
Alred, John W. 60–1
Ammons, Allen 284
Ammons, Ephraim J. 284
amnesty 15, 47, 110, 178, 245; granted by B. Bragg 244, 248; granted by J. Davis 25–7, 49, 75, 118, 126, 162, 184, 188, 201, 293; granted by R. F. Hoke 129; granted by R. E. Lee 18, 322; granted by J. G. Martin 39, 63; granted by G. W. Smith 5; granted by Z. B. Vance 47, 74, 128, 144, 205, 303
Amyett, Amos 308
Anderson, George Burgwyn 120
Anderson, Green 271
Anderson, James 271
Anderson, Joseph R. 33
Anderson, Nathaniel 271
Anderson, Robert 271
Anderson County, TN 253
Anderson-Ramseur-Cox Brigade 120, 124, 131–3, 313
Angell, James S. 60

Anson County, NC 49, 109, 113
appeals 10; to AIGO 101, 192; to commanding officer 101, 251; to S. Cooper 192, 239; to J. Davis 29, 48, 62, 78, 80, 94–5, 101, 105, 128, 143, 171, 217–8, 283–4, 294, 301; to R. E. Lee 29, 173; to Secretary of War 59, 203, 216, 218, 239, 269, 303
appeals to Z. B Vance by: deserter 46, 50, 54, 73, 94, 193, 304, 306; influential person 38, 76, 127, 202, 223, 283, 285; mother 113, 139; officer 48–9, 128, 157; prisoner 51, 129, 155, 161, 184, 189, 192–3, 295, 300, 303; wife 37, 93–4, 113, 139
Appomattox Court House 119
Arkansas troops 263
Armistead, Lewis A. 176
Army of Mississippi 243
Army of Northern Virginia 15, 321; brigaded by state 315; executions 31; service in 34
Army of Northern Virginia Corps: 1st 176; 2nd 108, 134, 149, 176; 3rd 18, 20, 42, 56, 65, 88, 176, 179, 314, 316
Army of Northern Virginia Divisions: Anderson 20; Early 134; Heth 65, 88, 94; Johnson 162, 165; Pickett 176; Rodes 108, 120, 149; Wilcox 20–1, 42
Army of Tennessee 243–6, 252, 259, 265 318; Reynolds Brigade 247
army regulations 300
Articles of War 5, 6, 290; 7th 291; 8th 291; 9th 12; 20th 29, 248, 250; 21st 28; 22nd 24, 29, 71, 253, 263; 23rd 18, 76; 46th 39, 93; 52nd 25–6, 29, 212; 55th 8; 58th 244; 64th 203; 65th 16, 233; 79th 6; 82nd 6; 89th 7, 16, 60, 233
Ashe County, NC 24, 34, 55, 69
Asheboro, NC 56, 186, 301
Asheville, NC 63, 252, 255, 260, 283, 286
assault 182
Atchinson, William 234
Athens, TN 255

Atlanta, GA 256, 265
Aults Mills, GA 260
Austin, Jacob A. 256
Autry, Calton W. 308
Avery, I. E. 144

Bailey, J. L. 283
Bailey, Portland 137
Bailey, Sidney J. 137
Bailey, William A. 137
Baird, H. H. 285
Baker, Allen 215
Baker, Jonathan 215
Baker, Matthew 215
Ball, Alford T. 251–2
Banks, James 293
Banks, William B. 260
Baptist Grove, NC 310
Barber, D. F. 232
Barbour, William M. 24, 34
Bare, Wiley 55, 57
Barefoot, William 172
Barker, William A. 216
Barnes, Calvin 289, 303
Barnes, Canada 213
Barnes, Joshua 127
Barnes, Willis P. 212–3
Barnhart, Jesse M. 219
Barringer, Rufus Clay 282
Barringer, Victor C. 219
Barringer Brigade see Gordon-Barringer Brigade
Barry, John Decatur 21
Barry Brigade see Branch-Lane-Barry Brigade
Barton, Seth M. 179, 232
Bass, Frederick 204
Batchelders Creek, NC 221, 298
Batchelor, John A. 153, 155
Bates, Alexander B. 237
Battle, William H. 224, 231
Beale, George W. 161
Beam, David L. 26
Beam, Henry Simpson 26
Bear Creek, NC 85
Beasley, A. T. 61
Beasley, Ephraim 213
Beasley, John 159
Beaufort County, NC 129, 131, 201, 203–4
Beauregard, Pierre G. T. 73, 179, 186, 193, 200, 205, 235–6

350   INDEX

Bedsole, John R. 171
Beech Grove, NC 221, 234, 298–9
Bell, Alfred W. 263, 266–7
Bell, James W. 57–8
Bells Grove, VA 143
Benefield, Philo 130
Benfield, Marcus 151
Benneck, David J. 46
Benson, Archibald 169
Benson, Francis 169
Benson, Thomas 169
Benson, William W. 169
Bentley, Benjamin E. 99
Bentley, Esquire 100
Bentley, Fannie 100
Bentley, William F. 106–7
Bentonville, NC 218
Berry, Edmond M. 53
Bertie County, NC 173
better class 150
Biggs, John D. 207
Biggs, William 236
Billings, Calvin 117–8
Bird, Thomas 111
Black Creek Church, VA 212
Black, George 35–7
Blackburn, ___ 270
Blackburn, Jeremiah 35–7
Blackford, Charles M. 54, 57, 60, 103, 192, 194–5, 239
Blackmon, Ashley 213
Blacknall, Charles 156
Blackwater River, VA 83
Bladen County, NC 168–9, 178
Blanton, Allen 299
Blevins, S. 310
Blountsville, TN 273
Bolton, Joab 293
Bonaparte, Napoleon 3
Booes, William H. 278
Boone, Thomas D. 173
Boonsboro, MD 137
Boswell, Eli 152
Bowers, Giles 185
Bowers, John 69, 291
Bowman, Noah 155
Boyles, Ivan 71–2
boys 22, 57, 80, 171
Bradshaw, William A. 59
Brady, Charles 282
Brady, James C. 282
Brady, Lucas 282
Bragg, Braxton 243–6; and confidence 244; comment concerning 258; on court decision 250, 303; on discipline 243, 245; on medical treatment 244; orders execution 249, 265; on substitute 244
Branch, James R. 221
Branch, Lawrence O'Bryan 21
Branch-Lane-Barry Brigade 20, 40, 63–4, 314
Brandy Station, VA 54, 94
Brawley, William Johnson 128
Breckenridge, John C. 18, 269
Brent, G. W. 252
Brewer, Joseph 79
Bridgeford, D. B. 284

Briggs, George 70
Bristoe Station, VA 76, 78, 97
British military: courts-martial 13; executions 13
Britt, Alexander S. 205
Britt, Giles 205
Britt, Henry C. 205
Britt, Joseph 102
Brittain, Andrew J. 227
Brock, Celia Jane 226
Brock, John J. 225
Brock, Joseph 98–9
Brooks, Abner 61
Brooks, Robert 49
Brotherton, William H. 155–6
Brown, Jasper 63
Brown, John Edmunds 215–6
Brown, Jonathan 62
Brown, R. O. 280
Brown, Reuben 63
Browning, Ellen 95
Brunswick County, NC 155
Bryan, Lewis C. 222
Bryant, Michael J. 280
Bryson, Goldman 283
Buck, John 308
bucket stealer 47
Buckman, George L. 292
Buckner, Simon B. 278
Buff, James 104
buffalo 222, 234
Buie, Duncan M. 307
bull pen 256
Bunch, Thomas 281
Buncombe County, NC 51, 157, 181, 248, 250, 252
Bunfield see Benefield
Bunker Hill, VA 49, 53
Bunn, Dallas 169
Bunn, George A. 170
Bunn, James Dawson 170
Bunn, Wesley 170
Burgaw, SC 280
Burgwyn, H. K. 70
Burgwyn, W. H. S. 70, 112
Burke County, NC 48, 84, 128
Burnette, John A. 86
Burton, Samuel J. 297
Bush, Jacob Alexander 70
Busick, Mitchell 223
Butler, Benjamin J. 308
Buxton, Ralph P. 161
Buxton, Samuel N. 276
Byers, William R. 253
Byrd, Josiah 291
Byrd, Nathan 291

Cabarrus County, NC 209, 219, 237
Cagle, Riley 61
Cain, James 68, 290
Caldwell County, NC 76, 81
Camp Campbell, VA 71
Camp French, VA 71
Camp Gregg, VA 29, 35, 54, 63
Camp Holmes, NC 21, 27, 39–40, 45, 48, 52, 59, 61–2, 74, 127, 129, 190, 203, 214, 282, 292
Camp Inspection, VA 166

Camp Lamb, NC 160
Camp Lee, NC 290
Camp Lookout, MD (F) 196
Camp Mangum, NC 83, 91–2
Camp Pettigrew, NC 301
Camp Ransom, NC 279
Camp Vance, NC 54
Camp White, NC 280
Camp Winder, VA 36
Campbell, J. F. 215
Campbell, James B. 157
Campbell, John Archibald 294, 323
Campbell, W. F. 233
Cannon, Sampson K. 48
Cantwell, John Lucas 223
Captain Bush 39
Caroline County, VA 131
Carpenter, Joseph 157
Carpenter, W. R. 126
Carr, Obed William 92
Carrington, Isaac H. 310
Carter, David H. 7–8
Carter, David M. 114
Carter, William B. 152
Carter, Wilson M. 218
Carver, Aden 194
Carver, John 276
Carver, Thomas 194, 197
Cash, William F. 217
Castle Thunder 27, 52, 54, 57, 59, 82, 99, 102, 105, 128, 140, 155, 164, 171, 188–9, 205, 237, 282, 284
Catawba County, NC 35, 44, 51–2, 64
Catiose Spring, TN 256
Cearcey, Aaron see Searcey
Cearley see Kerly
Chambers, George W. 191
Chambers, Henry A. 191
Chancellorsville, VA 28, 32, 47, 50, 53, 61, 152, 154–5, 168–70
Charles, H. E. 47
Charleston, TN 251
Charlotte, NC 93, 288
Charlotte Court House, VA 114
Charlottesville, VA 122, 164
Chatham County, NC 66, 70, 74, 76, 85, 201
Chattanooga, TN 256
Cherokee County, NC 263, 283
Chickahominy Swamp, VA 161
Chickamauga, TN 265
Chilton, Robert H. 55, 126, 173
Chocowinity, NC 282
Church, Anderson M. 116–7
Church, Harrison 117
Church, Jackson 38
Church, James 74
Church, James 117
Church, Jesse 117
City Point, VA 71
civil: legal 79; trial 161, 222, 279
Civil War, end of 72
Clapp, William 48–9
Clark, Detroit L. 84
Clark, Henry T. 177, 210, 247, 277

Index

Clarke, Duncan R. 169
class 4, 49, 98, 140, 146, 150, 187, 289; comment on 36; in military 150
Clayton, Monroe 203
Clayton, Robert 256, 259
Clegg, Henry C. 95
Cleveland County, NC 184
Clifton, David 279
Clifton, John W. 300
Clifton, Wade 300
Clifton, Watson T. 301
Clingman, Thomas L. 179, 199, 207
Clingman Brigade 179, 204, 207–8, 314
Clinton, TN 271
Clontz, Isham 188
Cloud, Abel Sidney 48
clustering 314
Cocke, TN 248
Cody, Jackson 270
Cody, Pierce 270
Cody, Stephen 270
Cody, William 270
Coghill, J. F. 114
Cold Harbor, VA 28, 83, 204–5
Cole, Calvin C. 297
Coleman, Bryant 300
Coleman, David 263
Coleman, Guilford 300
Coleman, John Q. 300
Coleman, Travis 300
Collins, Sampson 28
Colquitt, Alfred H. 152
Columbus County, NC 30, 155, 168
Company Q 277
Concord, TN 284–5
Confederacy 105, 321
Confederate Congress 20, 151, 211, 243
confinement: escape from 35, 73, 92, 126, 131, 140 143, 207, 281, 299, 301; guard prisoners 207; reaction to 93, 139
Congressional Districts 4th 213
Connecticut troops 12
Conner, Zebedee F. 94
Conrad, Tim 27
conscription 4, 20, 23, 50, 68, 150–1, 211, 244, 287, 321; legal opinion 74, 180
conscripts 58, 64, 111–2, 141, 148, 151, 195, 247; attitude toward 46, 49, 57; confrontation with 86; desertion of 124; execution of 21, 40, 43, 60, 64, 87, 107, 119, 132, 175, 198, 228, 241
Cook, Columbus L. 60
Cooke, John Rogers 88, 90, 321
Cooke Brigade 88, 99, 107, 321
Cooper, Robert V. 249
Cooper, Samuel 8, 16, 17, 155, 192, 220, 230, 244, 294; on court-martial 10, 196, 203, 233, 284; on death sentence 7, 48, 104, 239; on GO2 (1865) 144; suspends execution 62, 84, 105, 132, 143, 171, 294
Corinth, MS 243
Corzine, James C. 146
Costner, Zimri 190–1, 197
Couch, John 239
Councill, Jordan S. 34
coup de grace 80
courts-martial: *in absentia* 5; charges and specifications 6, 47, 71, 76, 88, 92–3, 101–2, 174, 185, 212, 221, 232, 271, 291; comment on 57, 97–8, 122, 181, 185, 200, 212; convened 6; decision not approved 4, 26, 213, 298; drumhead 85, 186, 221, 299; error 7, 68, 93, 97, 151, 159, 162, 178–9, 186, 203, 205, 217–8, 224, 249, 265, 279, 290–1, 293, 304; evidence 54; of impaired 126, 128, 212, 222; inquiry concerning 212; Judge Advocate 7; legal issues 7, 54, 60, 162, 226, 283, 291–2, 297; leniency of 3, 8, 9, 28, 32–3, 51, 97, 128, 154, 214–5, 222, 250, 262; manifest injury 203, 294; mitigate decision 10, 17; of officers 263, 269; procedure 6; reconsider decision 34, 146; records 9, 11, 97, 312; recommendation of 137, 154, 179, 184, 192, 274; sentence of 8, 74, 201, 202; serve on 178–9, 239; statistics 315, 320; strain of 42; testify at 39; *see also* death sentence; Military Courts; *Vade Mecum*
Cowles, Andrew C. 309
Cox, Sarah 139
Cox, William 139
Cox, William Ruffin 120
Cox Brigade *see* Anderson-Ramseur-Cox Brigade
Craig, William Pleasant 283
Craven County, NC 200, 223, 298, 307
Crisco, David S. 212
Crisco, Jacob A. 212
Crisp, Ezekiel B. 274
Crisp, Mansel F. 274
croakers 111
cross the branch 115
Crouch, Augustin W. 96
Crouch, John 96
Crouse, Hampton 85
Crowson, Elisha J. 61
Crumpler, Bennet 127
Crutchfield, Nathan Yancey 141–3
Culpeper, VA 52, 81, 144, 156
Culpeper Court House, VA 52
Cumbee, Armiza F. 153
Cumberland County, NC 304
Cumberland County, VA 92
Cumberland Gap, TN 264, 268, 272
Currituck County, NC 199
Curtner, Zeno 113
Cuthrell, Charles 299
Cutts, Addison D. 103

Dalton, GA 246, 251–3, 256, 258
Daniel, Junius 108, 111, 115
Daniel, Thomas 63
Daniel, Thomas B. 91
Daniel, Zachariah G. 91
Daniel-Grimes Brigade 72–3, 108, 111, 115, 119, 125, 152
Danner, David 81
Danner, James A. 235
Danner, Samuel 235
Danner, William 195
Danville, VA 39
Darden, James P. 161
Davidson County, NC 97, 186, 233
Davie County, NC 54, 232, 239
Davis, ___ 79
Davis, George 294
Davis, Jefferson 15, 74, 157, 215, 219, 232, 243, 245, 294, 296, 307, 321; on deserters 17, on troops 163
Davis, Joseph R. 65, 90, 94
Davis, Josiah B. 250
Davis, Syl D. 23, 27
Davis, Thaddeus C. 289
Davis, W. L. 71
Davis, William L. 144
dead march 28, 259
Deal, Sylvanus 188
Deas, Zachariah C. 246
death: accidental 133, 199, 287; assassinated 116; described 168; in Federal prison 268, 272; indifference to 322; murder 134, 140, 149; reaction to 132; statistics 41, 313; by suicide 149, 199
death sentence: approve of 179, 214; approved 39, 60, 63, 84, 107, 117–8, 137, 142, 145, 147, 193, 257, 265, 271, 301, 307; commuted 29, 59, 91, 101–2, 105, 115, 174, 188, 194, 196, 220, 232–3, 281, 284, 293–7, 299, 305; confirmed 46; declined to interfere 55–6, 94, 104; defer to president 7, 24–5, 28–9, 35, 50, 52–3, 58–9, 75, 83, 128, 141–2, 145, 154, 188, 205, 214–5, 218–9, 252, 265, 271, 284, 292–3, 301, 303, 309; died while under 82–3, 99, 101, 185, 240, 253; empathy for condemned 81–2; escaped while under 33–4, 53, 55, 83, 92, 127, 132, 138, 152, 154, 186, 190, 195, 202, 205, 238, 274; for impaired 80; inform of 97, 165, 261; inquiry concerning 57, 91, 103–4; mandatory 8; not approved 111, 218, 232, 297, 304, 308; released from 24, 59, 62, 84, 106, 107, 132, 147, 152, 154, 173, 174, 188, 204, 206, 212, 213–5, 218, 250, 260, 269, 291–2, 295, 307, 320; suicide while under 99, 135; *see also* appeals; courts-martial; execution

Deaver, William Harry 249
debts 30, 31, 39
Delaware 305
Dellinger, Henry 253
Dellinger, John 253
Dellinger, Reuben A. 253
Department of East Tennessee 262
Department of North Carolina 177, 180
Department of Western North Carolina 39
deserters: advertised 219; arrest of 17, 24, 29, 32, 36, 74, 85, 124, 126, 139, 169, 185–6, 203, 245, 279; attitude toward 67, 73, 130, 297; comment on 28, 50, 58, 84, 110, 183, 240, drowned 159, 217; escape of 35; kill pursuer 71, 74, 191; killed 23, 31, 61, 68, 79, 89, 107, 110–11, 133, 149, 156, 196, 201, 210, 276, 277; letter from home 94–5; numbers of 140; persuaded 54, 94, 184–5, 204; reason deserted 249; take weapon 25, 34, 46, 52, 60–2, 83, 102, 137, 140, 152–3, 163, 169–72, 214; threaten arrestors 127–8; transfer of 245; urged to return 53, 76, 94, 139, 205; voluntary return 16, 24, 39, 101, 142, 184, 249, 255, 301; warning to 190; will shoot 37–8, 65; *see also* desertion
desertion: cause of 18, 48, 96, 111, 123, 142, 172, 184, 258, 260; comment on 5, 58, 73, 96, 163, 178, 196, 259, 279, 321; considered 63, 75, 76, 83–4, 93, 115, 127, 156, 251; discouraged 24, 58, 91, 94; encouraged 76, 93, 131, 138, 234; to enemy 5, 25, 34, 39, 43, 50, 55, 62, 83, 94, 96, 103, 115, 126, 151, 154–5, 159, 161, 205–7, 214–5, 233, 236, 274, 290; in groups 25, 36, 44, 58, 70, 111, 135, 139–40, 143, 146, 151, 163, 172, 180, 211, 214–5, 218, 237, 247, 279, 311; from hospital 35–6, 39, 46, 80, 82, 92, 142, 191, 206, 232, 256, 304, 319; with kin 29, 46, 51–2, 58, 60, 75, 92, 114–5, 125, 144, 153, 186, 194, 202, 205, 212, 235, 248, 253, 255, 264, 270, 271, 274, 296, 300, 308; pattern of 68, 311; pledge to stop 48; repetitive 23, 265; *see also* deserters; NC Militia
Dial, Thomas W. 100
Dillon, Benjamin D. 235
discipline 66, 77, 83, 122, 138, 166–7, 244, 265, 276; and confidence 150; need for 3, 4, 18, 20, 30, 116, 177–9, 199, 201, 243, 275; lack of 116, 211, 268, 278
disobedience 27
Dobbins, John 293
Dobson, Elmore Watson 140

Dodson, Charles Carrol 95
Dodson, Elisha C. 293
Dogwood Grove, NC 170
Doles, George P. 123
Doub, John F. 295
Doub, Joseph C. 295
Dover, Asa 254
Dover, John H. 254
Dover, Robert A. 254
Doyety, William Hardy 227
Drewry's Bluff, VA 92, 117, 201, 213, 215, 253
drill 104, 150, 158, 178, 199, 276
Drum, Cyrus 50
Drum, Nancy E. 50
drunkenness 9, 12, 44, 71, 98, 116, 289
Duckett, J. Berry 285
Dudley, Guilford E. 162
Dudley's Depot, NC 131
Dula, Seth T. 78
Dunlop, Noah B. 282
Dunphy, Thomas 12
Duplin County, NC 44, 69, 78, 159, 217
Durham, Thomas L. 82–3

Earle, Martin J. 46
Earle, William 46
Early, Jubal Anderson 115, 118, 132, 134, 140
Earnhart, William 146
Edgecombe County, NC 59, 76, 199, 277
Edwards, Devreau A. 205
Edwards, Eliall 201
Edwards, Emanuel 201
Edwards, Lucius 205
Edwards, Thomas 201
elba dritches 8
Elixson, R. B. 91
Elkins, Jonathan 153
Elkins, Stephen 153, 155
Elliot, John B. 233
Elliott, Henry Harrison 233
Elliott, Samuel C. 233
Ellis, Alferd 58
Ellis, James 168
Elmira, NY 83, 128, 203–4
Engelhard, Joseph A. 55
English, W. C. 286
enrollment: with brother 132; illegal 18; legal 66, 132
escape from confinement 35, 73, 92, 126, 131, 140 143, 207, 281, 299, 301; reaction to 93, 139
Etchison, William C. P. 238, 240
Evans, Davidson 201
Evans, Michael 201
Everhart, Hamilton 195
evil 5, 9, 13, 16–7, 25, 62, 73, 86, 163, 178, 321
Evitt, Andrew J. 57–8
Ewell, Richard S. 108, 122, 285
execution 31, 37, 72, 79, 81, 84–5, 88, 167, 243, 290; approve of 38, 46, 236, 279, 297; bungled 32–3, 49, 78, 80, 112, 166–7, 217, 246, 259, 301–2; burial of

deceased 31, 125–6, 166, 235; carried into effect 174; choice of 61; comment on 69–70, 121, 196; conduct of 11; day of execution 62, 73, 80, 92, 116, 138–9, 143, 196, 202, 217, 249, 266, 304; demeanor of executed 33, 69, 72, 81, 100, 114, 137–8, 191, 249, 257–8, 265, 280, 297; dual 28, 62, 65, 87, 313; as example 30, 129; family aided 302; family informed 33, 77, 256, 285; immediate 6, 65; of impaired 55; last words 125, 249, 258; march past 11; name of executed 33, 37, 57, 60, 72, 82, 96, 104, 125, 138, 161, 190, 252, 255, 309–10; need for 18, 122, 219, 275, 322; official notification 56, 94–5, 280, 302; prisoners at 114; reaction to 79, 82, 123; reserve detail 49, 167; staged 69; on statistics 20, 108, 246, 274, 312, 316–7; Sunday 65, 76–7, 84, 197; at sunrise 191; suspended 46, 48, 53, 75; threat of 46, 49, 66, 78, 93, 138–9, 204, 223, 281; unit of executed 27, 35, 49, 58, 76, 95, 96, 101, 114, 123, 166, 191, 257, 273
execution by hanging 11, 99, 271, 284, 298–9; approve of 227, 299; band at 225; burial 223, 224–6; chaplain visit 223, 228, 308; comment on 221, 230; demeanor of executed 223, 228, 282, 298–9; described 229, 231, 299, 308; family visit 225; last words 227; mentioned 99, 228–9, 282; order for 239; 307; pending 227; witnessed 227–8, 239
execution by musketry 236
execution described by: chaplain 32, 80, 166; doctor 130–1, 249; enlisted soldier 72–3, 77, 79, 95, 123–4, 131, 137, 161, 166, 190–1, 197, 217, 258, 296; in memoir 62, 259; newspaper 31, 68–9, 167; officer 28, 57, 78, 112, 123, 130, 138, 166–7, 187, 191, 239, 257–8, 283, 302; witness 27, 30, 32–3, 35, 39, 45, 80–1, 95–6, 112, 123, 130, 155, 236, 239, 246, 257–8, 280, 283
execution effectiveness 16, 22–3, 25, 28, 37, 40, 42, 52, 70, 73, 87, 107, 112, 139, 166, 168, 215, 243, 259, 322; within company 77, 78–9, 81–2, 92, 94, 102, 114, 216, 312; of dual 25, 87, 215–6, 313; of multiple 64; *see also* death sentence
execution, preparation for 165; assigned to detail 84, 91, 96, 104, 190, 296; chaplain visit 25, 27, 30, 32, 35, 80, 130, 147, 173; empathy for condemned 70, 81–2; guard condemned 81; inform

condemned 97, 165, 261; inquiry concerning 214, 216; letter home 30, 39, 285; mother visit 173; orders for 72, 112, 122, 126, 139, 155, 165, 203, 206–7, 232, 235, 238–9, 245, 249, 257, 265; pending 46–7, 56, 58, 69, 76, 81, 91, 96, 99, 101, 112, 130, 137, 139, 147, 164, 189, 190, 207, 286; supplies for 31; suspended 18, 26, 62, 65, 84, 105, 115, 132, 141, 143–4, 146, 161, 171, 173, 189, 203, 205, 213–4, 216, 218, 233, 235, 252, 281, 284, 294, 304
Exum, William D. 214

Faison, Paul F. 185
Faithful, Joseph J. 277
fasting, day of 82, 163
Faulkner, Thomas N. 102
Federal army 4, 6, 108, 222, 231; bounty 99, 220, 222, 236, 241; court-martial 234; depredations 231; desertion 43, 226, enrollment in 117, 220, 223, 228, 239, 250, 254, 256, 263; executions 12, 140, 156, 277; kill prisoners 276; pension claim 256, 264; prison deaths 272
Federal loyalty 266
Federal troops: 1st NCUV 207; 1st USV Inf 83; 2nd Mtd Inf 256, 264; 2nd NCUV 99, 203, 220–31, 234, 236, 239, 265, 308; 3rd Mtd Inf 264; 4th Inf USA 309
Fiddler, Milton 23
file closers 18
Fincannon *see* Cannon
finger of scorn 47
Fisher, T. Joseph 191
Fleming, Robert E. 84
Florida troops 248
Floyd, Augustus Evander 39
fluttering 211
Flynt, Allen 310
Flynt, Dewit 310
Flynt, James 310
Folk, George N. 279
Ford, Francis W. 145
Ford, Green W. 28, 191
foreign-born 12, 21, 108, 129
Forrest, Bedford 275
Forrest, Calvin 204
Forsyth County, NC 23, 96, 138
Fort Branch, NC 293, 296
Fort Caswell, NC 91, 153, 181–2, 218, 292, 297, 300
Fort Fisher, NC 184, 207, 212, 237, 291, 302
Fort Holmes, NC 300
Fort Jackson, NC 289
Fort Lamb 308
Fort Monroe, VA 295
Foulkes, James 122, 124
Fowler, James C. 192
Fowler, Zachariah 58–9
Foy, Christopher Dudley 308

Foy, Franklin 225
Frank, Theophilus 96, 100
Franklin, Benjamin 265
Franklin, Isaac 59
Franklin, Jacob 265
Franklin, TN 250
Franklin County, NC 67, 105
Franklin County, VA 32
Frazer, John W. 268
Frazier, Stephen 114
Frederick the Great 4
Fredericksburg, VA 24–5, 29, 32, 39, 46, 54, 92, 99, 125–6, 131, 138, 143, 156
Freeman, Benjamin H. 79–80, 84
Freeman, John F. 225–6
Freeman, Lewis 226
Freeman, William H. 224
Freeman, William K. 77
French military: executions 13
French, Samuel G. 70
Front Royal, VA 32
Fugit, Esom 27
Fulcher, Joseph H. 239
furlough 70, 73–4, 140, 155; denied 206–7; forge 202, 233; harvest 90; recruiting 115; stop 196, 281
Furr, Daniel M. 40
Futch, Charles 169
Futch, Hanson M. 167, 169, 171
Futch, John 167, 169
Futch, Martha 169
Futch, Wily 169

Gaines, Henry C. 187–8
Gaines Mill, VA 153
Gaines, Reuben K. 188
Gaines, Simon 188
Gaither, Burgess Sidney 128, 143
Galimore, Ransom 296–7, 302
Gallagher, Charles 124
Gallahorn, Aaron 85
Gallahorn, Alpheus 85, 87
Gallahorn, Milton 85
Gallahorn, Zebedee 85
Galloway, John Marion 280
gambling 98, 290
Gamewell, Jacob 109
Garabaldi, Guiseppe 4
Gardner, Daniel 184–5
Gardner, William N. 200
Garland, Samuel Jr. 149, 157
Garland-Iverson-Johnston-Toon Brigade 149, 151, 155, 157, 313, 314
Garysburg, NC 69
Gash, Julius 278
Gaston County, NC 26, 190
Gatlin, Richard C. 177
General Green 39, 70
Georgia troops: 22nd Infantry Regiment 18; 36th Infantry Regiment 252; 39th Infantry Regiment 57; 40th Infantry Regiment 252; 46th Infantry Regiment 252; 65th Infantry Regiment 265; brigades 176; Colquitt Brigade 152; Doles Brigade 123; infantry regiments 134, 192, 318; statistics 314, 317; Thomas Brigade 21
German military executions 13
Germanna Ford, VA 173–4
Gettysburg, PA 28, 70, 78, 105, 156, 168
Gibbs, Joseph A. 256
Gibbs, W. H. 307
Gibson, Benjamin C. 206–7
Glenn, William H. 66
Goble, Lawson 194
Goble, William 194
Godwin, Archibald Campbell 141
Godwin Brigade *see* Hoke-Godwin-Lewis Brigade
Goff, J. H. 122, 125
Goings, George W. 116
Goldsboro, NC 71, 75, 92, 102, 160, 169, 206, 212, 223, 238, 240, 299
Goodnight, John H. 219
Gordon-Barringer Brigade 282
Gordonsville, VA 33, 75
Gore, Edward 153
Gore, Wesley P. 153
Gore, William 153
Graham, Hezekiah C. 24
Graham, James Augustus 94–6
Grant, Ulysses S. 231
Grason, Gideon L. 49
Green, D. E. 85
Green, James E. 72
Greene, Maston 84
Greene County, NC 78, 204
Greensboro, NC 156, 213
Greenville, NC 74, 190, 212, 216, 234, 239
Greenville, TN 248, 250, 270
Greer, James S. 29
Greer, Madison 29
Greer, Newton 29
Greer, Vincent 29
Greeson *see* Grason
Gregory, Archibald H. 203
Gregory, George A. 105
Gregory, John 105
Gregory, Thomas 105
Griffin, Phillip C. 24
Grimes, Bryan 115–6, 125
Grimes Brigade *see* Daniel-Grimes Brigade
Griswold, Elias 164
Groff *see* Goff
Groves, John D. 236
grub worm set 111
Guilford County, NC 48, 53, 147, 280
Guinea Station, VA 56
Gullet, Andrew J. 137
Gwaltney, William R. 173

habeas corpus 224, 231
Hackett, Christopher 124
Haddock, Benjamin F. 78
Haddock, John A. 226
Haddock, Luke M. 226
Haddock, Thomas W. 78
Haddock, William O. 225

Hafner, George 189
Hagaman, Hamilton D. 34
Hagerstown, MD 50
halberd 210
Haley, Joseph H. 71
Halifax County, NC 112
Hall, Barney 39
Hall, Edward Dudley 164
Hall, Richmond 36
Hamilton, NC 293
Hamilton County, TN 254
Hamilton, Wiley S. 236
Hamilton's Crossing, VA 26, 29
Hammond, Samuel 298
Hanchy, James 159
Hanchy, Obed 159
Handel, George Friderick 11
Handley, George J. 285
Haney, George C. 266
Haney, James M. 269
Haney, William G. 266
hang up the fiddle 267
Hanover Junction, VA 52, 75
Hansley, Thomas S. 302
hard eggs 199
Hardee, William J. 245
Hardee, William Loftin 152
Hardy, Washington M. 252, 255
Hargove, Alexander 291
Harnett County, NC 187
Harpers Ferry, WV 153
Harrell see Horrell
Harris, Elisha R. 46, 73
Harris, James S. 28, 37
Harris, James W. 266
Harris, Jordan 77
Harris, Nathan M. 266
Harrison, Burton H. 239
Harrison, John M. 76
Harrodsburg, KY 265
Hart, Benjamin T. 85
Hart, William C. 106
Hartsell, Jackson M. 215, 217
Hartsell, Jacob M. 215
Harvell, Govan 112
Harvell, Isham 131–2
Hase, Jesse 254
Hasket, Joseph L. 298
Hasket, Pleasant A. 301
Hatcher, Hardy 118
Hatchett, William 216
Hatley, Ephraim 216–7
Hatley, Israel 218
Havner, J. Franklin 94
Hawkins, Harris B. 142–3
Hays County, VA 59
Haywood County, NC 191, 193
Hefner, Marcus 140
Henderson County, NC 196, 249, 268
Hepler, Jesse Lee 232
Hertford County, NC 173
Heth, Henry 40, 65
Hewett, John 153
Hiatt, George W. 25
Hickman, Samuel 154
Hicks, James 84
Hicks, Leonard 141
Hicks, Milton John 56

Hicks, Peter 141
High Point, NC 174
Hill, Ambrose Powell 20, 46, 84, 97, 100, 105, 108, 111, 291; approve sentence 38–9, 60, 92, 107; on court decision 26, 97, 111
Hill, Benjamin J. 257
Hill, Daniel Harvey 72, 289; on cavalry 278; on court decision 111, 178, 185, 213; on discipline 178
Hill, James M. 58
Hill, Robert C. 88, 101
Hill, William Irving 228, 282
Hinchey, John 91
Hinkle, Alexander 92
Hinkle, Christian 92
Hinkle, Emanuel 92
Hinkle, Ransom 92
Hinson, George W. 212, 217
Hinson, Goodin 217
Hobbs, W. C. 128
Hobgood, Simpson 99
Hoey, Samuel A. 57
Hogan, Alexander 74
Hogan, Martha J. 74
Hogan, Martin 161
Hogan, William 193, 197
Hoke, Robert Frederick 134, 207, 226, 230–1, 239, 308
Hoke-Godwin-Lewis Brigade 134, 141, 147–8
Holden, William Woods 57, 114, 125, 195, 202, 228, 230
Holder, William 232
Hollar, David 51
Holloman, James 284
Holloway, James 35
Holloway, Silas 298
Holly Shelter, NC 92, 167
Holman, James 32
Holmes, Braswell 214–5
Holmes, David Henry 294
Holmes, John W. 214–5
Holmes, Theophilus Hunter 68, 159, 177–8
Holt, Joseph 231
Honeycutt, James F. 127
Honeycutt, Joseph 39
Honeycutt, Nancy 39
Honeycutt, Phillip Henry 92
honor 4, 37, 83
Hood, John Bell 7, 245, 269, 284
Hood, Samuel H. 214
Hood, Sidney 76
Hooker, Joseph 4
Hookerton, NC 78
Hooperas, Litel 84
horizontal refreshment 202
Hornbeck, J. D. 281
Horrell, Americus V. 167, 172
Hotchkiss, Jedediah 138
house-burner 102
Howington, Elbert J. 118
Hoyle, Lemuel J. 84
Hudson, Joseph 296
Huff, Wilson 59
Huffman, Allen 51–2
Huffman, Calvin J. 224

Huffman, David 51–2
Huffman, Miles 188
Huggins, W. S. 228
Hughes, Frank 12
Hughes, George 280
Humphrey, Henry W. 112
Hunter, R. W. 165
Hurley, Willis 44
Hutchings, Wright 254
Hyman, Joseph H. 59

Illinois 128, 236
Indiana troops: 3rd Cavalry 86
Ingram, John B. 49
Iredell County, NC 37, 58, 73, 90, 127–8, 132, 136, 216, 241
Ireland 21, 161
Ireland, Jackson 53
Irish 289, 305
Irvin, Richard 222, 234
Irvin, William 222, 234
Isbell, Arrister 182
Isbell, Richard 182
Isenhour, D. M. 219
Italian military executions 13
Iverson, Alfred Jr. 149
Iverson Brigade see Garland-Iverson-Johnston-Toon Brigade

Jackson, Alfred Eugene 273
Jackson, Edgar Allen 161
Jackson, Gaston 292
Jackson, John A. 75
Jackson, John K. 265
Jackson, Noah 290
Jackson, Thomas J. 7, 9, 108, 136
Jackson Brigade 273
Jackson County, NC 262, 264
Jacobs, John W. 203
James, Lawson 58
James River, VA 117, 127, 130, 164, 213, 215
Jamesville, NC 236
Jamision, Samuel 157
Jarrett, Eli H. 284
Jarrett, Isaac Augustus 82, 309
Jarrett, Jacob P. 284
Jarrett, Obediah B. 284, 285
Jenkins, A. L. 194
Jenkins, Francis M. 263
Jessup, Ira 253
Jessup, Meshack 253
Jestes, James N. 252
Johnson, Edward 8, 162, 165
Johnson, George A. [W.] 159–61
Johnson, William H. 237
Johnson, William M. 280
Johnson, William Preston 171, 187
Johnston, Joseph E. 73, 245, 255, 257, 271
Johnston, Robert Daniel 155
Johnston Brigade see Garland-Iverson-Johnston-Toon Brigade
Johnston County, NC 110, 116, 180, 214, 295
Jolly, Joseph 270
Jolly, Noah 270
Jones, David 298
Jones, Elizabeth 225

Index

Jones, John 174
Jones, John N. 50–1
Jones, Kenneth Rayner 96, 99, 101
Jones, Montraville M. 51
Jones, Nancy 224
Jones, Stephen H. 224
Jones, T. M. 292
Jones, William 147
Jones, William A. 262
Jones, William D. 223
Jones, William E. 273
Jones County, NC 227, 230, 241
Jordan, John V. 193, 200
Jordan, Sampson 185
Joyce, J. J. 116
Joyner, Hillory Harvey 174
Joyner, John E. 174

Keeler, James L. 308
Keiley, John D. 192–5
Keith, James A. 269
Kerley, Richard 107
Kellum, Elijah 228, 282
Kelly, ___ 309
Kelly, Noah R. 49–50
Kelly, Richmond Y. 50
Kelly, William H. 169
Kenansville, NC 217
Kennedy, Milton F. 29, 30, 32–3, 35
Kenney, Michael L. 151
Kentucky troops: 5th Regiment 277
Kilby, Benjamin H. 32
Kilby, John H. 32
King, Howell 124–5
King, James 124–5
King, Johnson Jr. 125
Kinston, NC 72, 79, 92, 99, 140, 143, 146, 203, 211, 213, 215, 217–8, 222–3, 229, 279, 280–2, 285, 298–9, 308, 310
Kirkland, William W. 76–7, 235, 240
Kirkland Brigade *see* Martin-Kirkland Brigade
Kirkland Brigade *see* Pettigrew-Kirkland-MacRae Brigade
Kittrell, NC 204
Knight, Bart B. 218
Kuykendall, Ezekiel 196–7
Kuykendall, George W. 196

Lael, Elias 52
Lael, Lawson 52
Lafevers, Catherine 76, 164
Lafevers, J. Harvey 76, 164
Lamb, Elkanah H. 56
Lamb, Milton 53, 56
Lamb, William 302
Lambert, Franklin 58
Lane, James Henry 21, 31
Lane Brigade *see* Branch-Lane-Barry Brigade
Lanier, Elkana 29–30
Lanier, Jacob E. 29–30
Lankford, William 58
Latham, Alexander C. 299
Latham, Lawrence 304

Lawing, John M. 237
Lawrence, Lewis C. 161
Laws, Braxton 82
Layton, Martin 237
Leach, Calvin 161
Leach, James Thomas 116, 144
Ledford, Christopher C. 256, 260
Ledford, Nancy 256
Ledford, Preston Lafayette 121
Lee, Charles H. 7
Lee, Charles W. 82
Lee, Robert Edward 7, 15–7, 21–6, 32, 101, 104, 124–5, 128, 177, 205, 221, 239, 304, 308; on amnesty 18, 322; confirms sentence 46, 145, 161; on court decisions 15, 93, 154, 162, 224; on death sentence 16; on desertion 15, 17, 24, 75, 122, 153, 163, 249; on discipline 15, 17, 277; on execution 16, 122, 125, 163; on independence 321; on leniency 16, 154, 172; orders issued 221, 231; on Partisan Rangers 277; on prisoners of war 6; promotion 17–8; on punishment 10, 15, 142, 151; resignation 163; on straggling 15; suspends execution 48, 161, 173; on troops 15
Lee, Wayne Gallington 82
Lee, William P. 30
Leggett, William 214
Leggett, Wright 214
Lenoir County, NC 146, 225–6, 228
Lenoir Station, TN 265
Leon, Louis 73
Lewis, Andrew Jackson 31
Lewis, William Gaston 141
Lewis Brigade *see* Hoke-Godwin-Lewis Brigade
Liberty, VA 153
Liberty Mills, VA 31, 34, 38
Lincoln, Abraham 22, 202, 276; suspends executions 12
Lindsey, William 101
Lineberger, James Wellington 189–90
Linster, Robert Osborne 130
literacy 132, 170
Littleton, Edward J. 297
Littrell, James D. 248
Littrell, William 248, 252
Long, John C. 93
Long, William H. 295
Longstreet, James 6, 7, 17, 176, 207, 245, 291, 322
Looper, John W. 37
Looper, Nancy 37
Looper, Oliver H. 54
Loudon, TN 265
Louisa County, VA 27
Louisiana 211; troops 134, 162
Love, Henry D. 47
Lowrance, William Lee 56
Luck, Elizah 96
Lumberton, NC 214, 230
Lury, William 113

Luther, Godfrey 29
Luther, Jesse M. 28–9, 171
lynching 116

Mabery, James Pinkney 281
Macon County, NC 263
MacRae Brigade *see* Pettigrew-Kirkland-MacRae Brigade
Madison, James 165
Madison County, NC 43, 63, 139, 193, 196, 249, 269–0
Magnolia, NC 69, 78, 92
maiming 63, 89, 91, 136, 145, 156, 159, 172, 281
Mallett, Peter 49
Mallett, Richardson Jr. 164, 171
Malvern Hill, VA 170–1
Manassas, VA 32, 144
Manley, James M. 53–4
Manning, Lorenzo D. 204–5
Manning, William A. 205
Manors, Craton 186
Manors, James B. 186
Mansfield, John 63
Marion County, TN 254
Marshall, NC 269
Martin, James Green 39, 63, 67, 212, 216
Martin County, NC 206
Martin-Kirkland Brigade 179, 234, 235
Martinsburg, VA 113
Maryland troops: 3rd Cavalry
Massachusetts troops: executions 12
Matheson, D. 255
Matheson, Dilla 35
Mayberry *see* Maberry
McAllister, Alexander C. 85–6
McCullum, Arsena 226
McDaniel, Alexander 201
McDaniel, David 184
McDaniel, Nathan 126
McDowell County, NC 182, 252, 254
McDugald, W. J. 307
McEntire, Felix 57
McFalls, George 254
McGown, Samuel 21
McIntire, David M. 44
McKaskill, W. R. 60
McKeel, John M. 303
McKethan, Hector 206–7
McKinney, Joseph Tarpley 194
McKinney, Robert M. 88
McMinn County, TN 255
McNair, John J. 291
McRae, Duncan K. 97
McRae, William 83
McRorie, William F. 128
McSwain, Charles J. 29–30
McSwain, George 56, 57
McSwain, M. A. 29
McSween, M. J. 189
Mecklenburg County, NC 21, 185
Medlin, Joseph 102
Meeks, A. L. 24
Melton, Zachariah 36

Mexican War 263; military executions 12
Michaels, John M. 48
Michaels, William D. 188
Military Commision 15, 20
Military Court 7–8, 11, 15, 34, 38, 86, 294, 309
Military District 2nd 238
Miller, J. W. 292
Miller, John Fullwinder 55
Miller, Lawrence 298
Miller, William 35
Minnierode, Charles 29
Mississippi troops: 2nd Infantry Regiment 90; 11th Infantry Regiment 90; 26th Infantry Regiment 90; 42nd Infantry Regiment 90; Davis Brigade 65; infantry regiments 268, 305
Mobile, AL 266–7
Montgomery, William V. 74
Montgomery County, NC 44, 47, 61, 67, 77, 85
Montgomery County, VA 59
Moore, Alexander Duncan 224
Moore, Alexander S. 106
Moore, Edwin L. 165
Moore, Robert 106
Moore County, NC 61, 79, 83, 85, 90, 174, 183
Morley, Daniel J. 308
Morley, John C. 308
Morris, A. W. 32
Morris, Green Richardson 26–7
Morrow, Daniel 255
Morrow, Gordon 255
Morrow, Nathan 255
Moss, Benjamin L. 281
Mozingo, John W. 304
Mull, Peter M. 104
Murfreesboro, NC 173
Murph, Daniel W. 292
Murphy, George W. 35
Murphy, John 151
Murray, Patrick 134
mutiny 88, 135, 143, 305–6; charges of 60, 76; joined 105, 287, 289; not suppressed 43, 291; punishment for 289
Myers, Anderson C. 72

Nance, Shadrack 137
Nanny, James 112
Nanny, Joseph 112
Nash County, NC 127
Neal, Amos 203
Nethercutt, John H. 211, 223, 227
Neuse River, NC 221, 223, 225, 229
New Bern, NC 68, 75, 81, 103, 221, 223, 234, 290, 307
New Hanover County, NC 32, 168-0
New Market, VA 117
New Orleans, LA 195
New York infantry regiments 319; 3rd 284; 120th 281
Newman, Madison Thomas 31
Newsom, James W. 132

Newsom, Jesse 132
newspaper 178; list deserters 219
newspaper articles: *Fayetteville Observer* 31; *Greensboro Patriot* 99, 140; *Hillsborough Recorder* 69; *Petersburg Express* 69; *Raleigh Standard* 125, 230; *Raleigh Progress* 230; *Richmond Enquirer* 99; *State Journal* (NC) 230
Nichols, Jefferson N. 146
Norman, Edward P. 249
Norris, John R. 252
North Carolina: Adjutant General 162; defense of 121; pension applications 77, 99–101, 239; Roll of Honor 71, 105, 116, 160, 172, 203
North Carolina artillery 287, 306; Branch 290; 3rd Battalion 289; 10th Battalion 289; 13th Battalion 290, 292, 305; Pool's Battalion 288; 10th Regiment 287, 292, 298–9, 304; 36th Regiment 288, 299–300, 302, 305; 40th Regiment 288, 290, 299
North Carolina brigades: Anderson-Ramseur-Cox 120, 124, 131–3, 313; Branch-Lane-Barry 20, 40, 63–4, 314; Clingman 179, 204, 207–8, 314; Cooke 88, 99, 107, 321; Daniel-Grimes 72–3, 108, 111, 115, 119, 125, 152; Garland-Iverson-Johnston-Toon 149, 151, 155, 157, 313, 314; Gordon-Barringer 282; Hoke-Godwin-Lewis 134, 141, 147–8; Jackson 273; Martin-Kirkland 179, 234, 235; Palmer 268, 272; Pender-Scales 42, 62, 63–4, 314; Pettigrew-Kirkland-MacRae 65, 73, 76–7, 111; Ransom 179, 180, 185, 197
North Carolina cavalry 275, 287, 306; statistics 286; 5th Battalion 278, 284–5; 7th Battalion 278, 283; 9th Regiment 276; 19th Regiment 276; 41st Regiment 277; 59th Regiment 277; 63rd Regiment 277; 65th Regiment 278
North Carolina counties *see* Alamance County; Alexander County; Alleghany County; Anson County; Ashe County; Beaufort County; Bertie County; Bladen County; Brunswick County; Buncombe County; Burke County; Cabarrus County; Caldwell County; Catawba County; Chatham County; Cherokee County; Cleveland County; Columbus County; Craven County; Cumberland County; Currituck County; Davidson County; Davie County; Duplin County; Edgecombe County; Forsyth County; Franklin County; Gas-

ton County; Greene County; Guilford County; Halifax County; Harnett County; Haywood County; Henderson County; Hertford County; Iredell County; Jackson County; Johnston County; Jones County; Lenoir County; Macon County; Madison County; Martin County; McDowell County; Mecklenburg County; Montgomery County; Moore County; Nash County; New Hanover County; Onslow County; Orange County; Pitt County; Randolph County; Richmond County; Robeson County; Rowan County; Rutherford County; Sampson County; Stanly County; Stokes County; Surry County; Tyrrell County; Union County; Wake County; Washington County; Watauga County; Wilkes County; Wilson County; Yadkin County; Yancey County
North Carolina Home Guard/Militia 32, 37, 79, 82, 94–5, 212, 219, 240; killed arresting deserters 74, 196, 203, 213, 232; kill deserters 139, 149, 156, 210
North Carolina infantry battalions: 1st SS 137, 310; 2nd 110; 2nd LD 308; 5th 255; 8th 211, 222, 232; 11th 269; 13th 211
North Carolina infantry regiments: 1st 158, 161, 174–5; 2nd 120, 310; 3rd 158–9, 163, 168, 172, 174–5; 4th 54, 116, 120–1, 124–5, 128–9, 131–2; 5th 75, 79, 149, 151, 157, 291, 311; 6th 134, 138, 140, 147–8; 7th 21, 28, 35; 8th 199, 276; 11th 66, 81, 84; 12th 150–1, 152, 156–7; 13th 43, 58, 64; 14th 32, 86, 121; 15th 83, 88, 103, 105, 115, 195; 16th 43, 48, 51, 57, 64; 17th 209, 234; 18th 22; 20th 150, 155, 157; 21st 135, 138–40, 142, 147–8; 22nd 43, 53, 56; 23rd 150–1, 155–6; 24th 180–1; 25th 181; 26th 66, 70, 73, 76, 82–3, 86, 255; 27th 89, 95, 96, 98, 101, 162, 227, 311; 28th 22, 30, 35, 41, 171, 309; 29th 262, 267; 30th 99, 122; 31st 200, 207, 32nd 109, 111; 33rd 23, 28, 36, 41, 61, 311; 34th 43, 49, 55–6, 63; 35th 71, 181, 196; 37th 23–5, 29, 31, 34, 71, 191, 311, 313–4; 38th 44–5, 49, 55; 39th 263, 267; 41st 169; 42nd 195, 209, 217, 239; 43rd 72, 109, 111; 44th 67, 74, 77, 79–81, 291, 311; 45th 109; 46th 89, 93–5, 164; 47th 67–8, 78, 99; 48th 88–90, 94, 96, 100, 102, 311; 49th 115, 182–

3, 185, 233, 311; 50th 9, 210, 308; 51st 200, 202, 206, 234, 238; 52nd 68, 72, 78–9; 53rd 73, 110, 116, 146, 251; 54th 135–6, 139–40, 147–8, 311; 55th 79, 90, 101; 56th 183–5; 57th 136, 139, 146, 143, 147–8; 58th 245, 247, 252, 259–60; 60th 211, 245, 248–50, 252, 260; 61st 200–1, 207; 62nd 268, 272; 64th 269, 272; 66th 179, 223–4, 239–40; 67th 307; Thomas Legion 263–4, 273–4, 279
North Carolina regiments/battalions: 5th 282; 32nd 127; 41st 214; 48th 74; 63rd 61; 68th 48, 53; 54th 186; 79th 127–8; 80th 49; 93rd 116
North Carolina troops 97–8, 176, 211; desertion 16, 28; executions 15; statistics 489–92
Northcutt, ___ 186
Norton, Bailes 264
Norton, George 264
Norton, James 264
Norton, Josiah 264
Norton, Roderick 264

Oakley, James 233
O'Donnell, James *see* Banks, James
officers: in arrest 151, 224; attitude of 108; comment on 77, 88, 93–4, 97–8, 111, 178, 234, 303, 305; competence 15, 18, 20, 49, 74, 88, 150, 158, 177, 183, 187, 263, 269, 276, 278, 291; confidence in 4, 21, 177; court-martial of 88, 97, 180, 185, 250, 263, 269, 288; deaths 314; death sentence 12; demeanor 46, 239; on detailed men 244; and discipline 21, 150, 178, 180, 278; drunkenness 44; examination of 97; execution of 12, 140, 156, 185, 247; killed 196, 265; leadership of 49, 263; need for 210, 315; respect for 200, 278; training of 121, 277; warn deserter 190
Onslow County, NC 159, 277
Orange County, NC 96, 162
Orange Court House, VA 30, 49, 56, 58–9, 76–7, 81–2, 84, 113, 141, 164, 166, 169
orders 10; Circular Orders 6, 7, 71, 164, 239, 245; General Orders 10; GO 2 (1865) 17, 34, 38, 55, 101, 105, 142, 144–7, 187, 196, 205, 207, 223, 236, 240, 270–1, 285, 301, 303, 309; GO 3 (1865) 18, GO 4 (1865) 18; Special Orders 10
Orr, Joshua 271
Orrant, Jacob 25
Orrant, Lewis 25
Osborne, Ephraim 34
Osborne, James 218
Osbourn, Joshua 218
Overcash, James Wilson 137

Overcash, Joseph 139
Overman, Emanual 147
Owens, George Washington 81
Owens, J. F. 129
Owens, Murphy 61

Palmer, John B. 268, 279
Palmer, Napolean 40
Palmer, Pierson 40
Palmer, Winchester C. 40
Palmer Brigade 268, 272
Paris, John 147, 229
Parrish, Elizah 118
Parrish, B. D. 118
Parrish, Stephenson 118
Parrott, John A. 225
Partin, J. P. 146
Partin, John H. 68
Partisan Rangers 231, 247, 277, 308
Pate, Daniel 38–9
Patterson, Benjamin 277
Patton, Thomas Walton 256, 258
Paul, Raymond L. 298
Peck, J. J. 222
Pender, William Dorsey 42
Pender-Scales Brigade 42, 62, 63–4, 314
Pendergrass, John H. 35
Pendry, Daniel C. F. 60
Pendry, John 60
Pennsylvania troops: cavalry, 11th 277
Peoples, Albert 36
perjury 229
Perkins, John 211
Petersburg, VA 25, 59, 69, 71, 91–2, 104, 118, 142, 195, 203, 219, 234, 237–8
Peterson, Peter 35
Pettey, Charles Q. 190
Pettigrew, J. Johnston 73, 77, 111
Pettigrew-Kirkland-MacRae Brigade 65, 73, 76–7, 111
Philadelphia, PA 33, 55, 215, 233
Phillips, J. 43
Phillips, James R. 174
Phillips, Zachariah 249
Pickard, Alvis 115
Pickard, John 115
Pickett, George E. 17, 188, 204, 221–2, 231, 294, 299
Pike, John 70
Pike, Johnathan S. 214
pillage *see* plunder
Pillow, Gideon J. 245
Pinze, — 309
Pitkin, James M. 295
Pitt County, NC 67, 89, 116, 204, 209
Pittman, George D. 118
Pittsylvania County, VA 113
Plowman, Henry 36
plunder 20, 139, 179, 181, 243–4, 263, 275, 277
Plymouth, NC 207, 214, 220, 234, 236, 239, 276, 279, 293, 295, 308
Point Lookout, MD 101

Polk, Leonidas 245
Polk, Leonidas L. 72, 123
Pollocksville, NC 231
Pool, Felix 146
Pool, Stephen Decatur 238, 294
Poolsville, MD 92
Pope, Elkanah 193, 197
Powell, Barnabas 304
Powell, Henry O. 276
Powell, James R. 173–4
Powell, Oliver Hazard 300
Price, Jesse Davis 236
Price, Needham 196
Prime, Louis 38
Prison Hospital 13 26, 35, 52, 100–1, 116, 155, 237
Prisoners of War 3, 6, 134, 276
Privett, Kearney 170
Proffit, Andrew J. 33
Provost Guard 310
Provost Marshal 11, 15, 30, 122, 125, 299
Pruitt, Isham 114
Pruitt, Joshua 113–4
Pryor, Roger A. 6
Puckett, Stephen Randolph 91
punishment 3, 8–9, 116, 141–2, 180, 250; ball and chain 5, 33; branding 9, 23, 189, 215, 222; castration 111; company 290; drum out 160, 262; effectiveness 43; ear cropping 300; flogging 43, 102, 151, 193, 210; gauntlet 23, 151; humiliation 21, 50, 128, 156, 217, 277; moderate 109; by peers 22, 124; prompt 10, 201, 245; reaction to 34, 93, 139, 279; severe 21, 74, 96, 112, 134, 210, 235; as warning 16, 103; wooden horse 124

Quick, William R. 305

Racoon Ford, VA 123
Rainer, John N. 167, 170
Rainer, Stephen D. 170
Rains, James 59
Raleigh, NC 57, 82–3, 111, 233, 240
Ramseur, Stephen Dodson 120, 124, 130
Ramseur Brigade *see* Anderson-Ramseur-Cox Brigade
Ramsey, Henry 270
Ramsey, Nathan Alexander 207
Randal, James M. 255, 260
Randal, John W. 255
Randolph, George W. 5
Randolph County, NC 43, 62, 78, 85, 94, 186, 301
Ransom, Matthew Whitaker 180
Ransom, Robert B. 180, 187, 277
Ransom Brigade 179, 180, 185, 197
Rapidan River, VA 173, 174
Rappahannock Academy, VA 151
rations 166, 170
Ray, Thomas L. 136–7
Ray, Wilson 281
Raymond, William M. 152, 154

reconstruction 35
Redmon, Jobe R. 284
Reece, William L. 191, 197
Reeves, John E. 45
religion: atheist 257; Baptist 98, 249; baptized 30, 95, 123, 225, 229, 308; Christian 150, 249, 308; Episcopal 166, 245; faith 79; Jewish 211; Methodist 109, 296, 308; Lutheran 32; prayer 92, 98, 141, 195, 308; preaching 104; revival 123
Resaca, GA 250
Revolutionary War: courts-martial 12; executions 12
Reynolds Alexander Welch 247
Reynolds, Fletcher Sarah H. 250
Rich, Josiah 94
Rich, Robert 94
Richmond, VA 24, 26, 61, 102, 117, 126, 160, 164, 170, 207, 283; defense of 173, 188–9, 281
Richmond County, NC 44, 46, 305
Riddick, Sarah 281
Riddick, M. A. 281
Riley, James 151–2
Ritter, John W. 300
Roanoke River, NC 69
Robbins, Clarkson 83
Robbins, Elias 83
Roberson see Robinson
Roberts, A. 184
Roberts, Eli 282
Robertson, Beverly H. 280
Robertson, John 280
Robeson County, NC 38, 201, 213, 238
Robinson, James 56, 58, 230
Rockett, John A. 194–5
Rocky Point, NC 167
rod of discipline 305
Rodes, Robert Emmett 108, 122, 126
Rodman, William B. 7
Rogers, Perry 271
Rogers, William 271
Rogersville, TN 273
Roper, James T. 305
Rosser, Thomas L. 8
Rowan County, NC 135–6, 139, 146
Rowland, John 134
Ruffin, Thomas 7
Russell, R. A. 223
Rutherford, Andrew 26
Rutherford, Thomas 26
Rutherford County, NC 53, 57, 112, 182, 238, 254

sabers 277
Salisbury Prison 59, 130, 136, 209, 212, 269, 283–4, 294–5
Sampson County, NC 92, 206
Sanders, Hilton 160
Sanders, Thomas 160
Saul 11; see also dead march
Saunders, David E.
Savage, William 280

Savannah, GA 305
Scales, Alfred Moore 21, 42, 55–6
Scales Brigade see Pender-Scales Brigade
Scarborough, Franklin 68
Scarce, John 113
Scott, Winfield 12
Scottsville, VA 164, 166, 171–2
Searcey, Aaron 304
Secretary of War 16, 59, 172–3, 178, 188, 247, 268, 277, 294; on appeals 10, 236, 296; suspends execution 26, 115, 188, 212–3
Sedden, James A. 8, 25, 186–7, 275
see the monkey 134
Setser, Thomas W. 84
Setzer, Daniel 93
Seven Pines, VA 53, 137
Sevier County, TN 274
Sexton, Marion 24
Sexton, Thornton 24
Seymour, Leonidas B. 210
shade officers 98
Shaffner, John F. 114, 117, 130–1, 138
Shannon, William Jasper 101
Sharp Shooters 62
Sharpsburg, MD 25, 53, 137, 150, 168, 170, 174, 178
Shaw, Augustus 54
Shaw, Henry M. 199
Shaw, William 54
Shenandoah Valley, VA 54, 115
Shelton Laurel, NC 269
Shelton, William 58
Sheridan, P. H. 188
Sherrill, Milas 142–4
Shipwash, George W. 33
shoes 20
Shook, John 32
Shores, Anderson 296
Shores, Henderson see Shores, Anderson
Shores, Martin 296
Shorter, Jack 106
Shuler, William P. 264
Shull, Charles Washington 189
Shumate, Esley 39
Shumate, Samuel 39
Sides, John M. 48
Sigman, M. D. 32
Sills, Henry W. 206
Silvey, James M. 273
Silvey, Peter 273
Silvey, William R. 273
Simmons, James 206–7
Simmons, Moses 153
Simmons, Pleasant 61
Simmons, Powell 58
Simmons, William 153
Simpson, Pleasant 303
Singletary, George B. 69, 75
Slade, Solomon B. 307
slave 178; whip 130
slung shot 245
Smith, Alfred 80
Smith, Austin A. 203
Smith, Gustavous W. 5, 7

Smith, Isaac 93
Smith, James A. 99
Smith, John 79, 95
Smith, Lemuel M. 79–80
Smith, McRuffin 299
Smith, Noah 38
Smith, Robert F. 95–6
Smith, Samuel 190
Smith, William B. 104
Smith, William Nathan Harrell 239
Smithfield, NC 271
Smith's Island 305
Smithville, NC see Southport
Snyder, John W. 59
South Carolina 305–6
South Carolina troops 184, 253, 280; Lucas Battalion 293; McGowan Brigade 21; infantry 192; statistics 314, 317–9
South Mountain, MD 172
Southport, NC 289
Soviet military executions 13
Spain, James 249
Spanish Fort, AL 266
Sparks, Robert 129
Sparrow, Thomas 160
Spaugh, Alexander 23
Speaks, A. L. 132
Spease, Augustin J. 137
Speer, ___ 309
spicey 27
spider 47
spider wagon 47
spying 178, 285
Spottsylvania, VA 141
Spottsylvania Court House, VA 115, 153
Sprilley, Temple 61
Springfield, IL 103, 106
squad 25
Stamey, Joshua 84
Stanley, John L. 222
Stanly County, NC 30, 217–8, 241
Stark, Rufus H. 80
Starnes, Dulin 71
Starney see Stamey
Staunton, VA 49, 143
stealing 21, 32, 47, 124, 160, 172, 180, 283, 290, 305
Steiner, William U. 97
Stephens, James 289
Stephensburg, VA 52
Steuart, George H. 162, 165
Stewart, Peter C. 37
Stewart, William H. 147
Stokes, Mumford Sidney 158
Stokes County, NC 116
Stone, Samuel 138–9
straggling 20, 178
Strayhorn, Thomas Jackson 98
Strickland, Nick 106
Strickland, Rufus G. 50
Strickland, Wiley 213
Strother, John P. 106
Stuart, John L. 196
Stutts, Benjamin W. 75
Stutts, William 78
Styers, John A. 145

substitutes 70, 74, 82, 99, 105, 107, 111, 113, 151, 157, 159, 216, 227, 232, 244, 248, 280, 301; execution of 69, 87, 107, 119, 210, 241; desire for 98, 124
Sullivan's Island, SC 203
Summerlin, Catherin 226
Summerlin, Jesse 226
Summers, James Albert 37
Summerville Ford, VA 123
Surry County, NC 25, 45, 60, 114, 116, 253
Swain, William 204
Sweaney, John 289
swearing 95, 98
Sweetwater, TN 283
Swindell, Isaac S. 132
Swing, Alfred 96, 100–1
Swing, John D. 100
swords 277

Talton, John W. 118
Tansell, Robert 232
Tarboro, NC 206, 232
Tar Heels 283
Taylor, Lewis 225
Taylor, Lloyd 237
Taylor, Thomas W.
Taylor, Walter H. 302, 309
Taylor, William R. 250
Taylorsville, VA 94, 164
Teague, John A. 33–4
Teague, W. Robert 37
teamster 105
Tennessee troops 248, 253, 273; 11th Infantry Regiment 265; 45th Infantry Regiment 257
terrori Yankeebus 248
Tew, Lewis 92
Tew, Richard 92
Texas troops 263
Tharrington, A. P. 203
Tharrington, Willis 106
theft *see* stealing
Thomas, Edward 21
Thomas, John 46–7
Thomas, Washington H. 104
Thompson, Catherine 93
Thompson, George Sidney 31
Thompson, Isaac 93
Threat, Benjamin 71–2
Thruston, S. D. 159
Tilly, Drummond 160
Tippett, Thomas H. 140–1
Tipton, William 274
Tomlin, William A. 45
Toon, Thomas F. 149, 157
Toon Brigade *see* Garland-Iverson-Johnston-Toon Brigade
Topsail, NC 92
Topsail Sound, NC 301
Tories 57, 94, 117, 196–7, 240, 268, 270, 276, 283
Torrence, L. 151
Tory *see* Tories
Traffenstedt, Peter 51
Trafinstead, Joseph H. 189
treason 11
Tripp, Edward 125, 131

Trivett, John B. 240
Tucker, John O. 218
Tucker, Leonard G. 218
Turner, Talton R. 181–2
Turrentine, Michael H. 305
Tyrrell County, NC 204

Union: loyalty to 223, 230; return to 30, 47, 130, 146, 186, 202
Union County, NC 66, 71, 73, 110, 186
Ussery, Martin Alford 62
Uzzle, Major 207

Vade Mecum 7, 179
Vance, Zebulon Baird 5, 18, 25, 57, 73, 85–6, 121, 125, 139, 178, 205, 211, 223, 230, 268 303; on cavalry 275; on charges 212; and conscription 321; on desertion 5, 61; request for troops 117; *see also* appeals
Vanderburgh, Julius 237
Vanderford, John 86
VanHook, J. C. 238
Vaughn, Joseph H. 190
Vernon, John 113
Vinson, John 70
CSS *Virginia* 283
Virginia: attitude toward 5, 88, 90, 278; executions 20, 162, 247; officers 97, 141, 149, 314–5; service in 121, 151
Virginia troops 97, 134, 192; 2nd Infantry Regiment 165; 5th Infantry Regiment 8; 10th Infantry Regiment 162; 12th Artillery Battalion 290, 305; 14th Infantry Regiment 12; 23rd Infantry Regiment 162; 30th Infantry Regiment 162, 221; 33rd Infantry Regiment 319; 37th Infantry Regiment 162; 41st Infantry Regiment 16; 49th Infantry Regiment 209; 52nd Infantry Regiment 16; 54th Infantry Regiment 247; 63rd Infantry Regiment 247, 252, 257; Armistead-Barton Brigade 176, 179, 232; desertion 16; records 319; Robertson Brigade 280; statistics 317–9; Steuart Brigade 162; H. H. Walker Brigade 65
Von Steuben, Wihelm L. 4
Voyles, Enoch 263

Wadesboro, NC 49
Waggoner, Henry 75
Waggoner, James H. 75
Waggoner, Moses 75
Waggoner, William 75
Wake County, NC 39, 67, 87, 127, 129, 144, 168
Walker, Alfred 183
Walker, H. H. 65
Walker, John 183
Walker, Jonathn 183
Walker, W. 199

Walkup, Samuel Hoey 90, 97, 100–2
Walsh, Phillip 33
Walters, John H. A. 62
Walters, Thomas R. 293
Walters, William 238
Walters, William F. 85–6
Ward, Duke B. 255
Ward, Lemul B. 98
Ward, Michael 255
Warlick, John C. 84–5
Warlick, Kenneth H. 143–4
Warlick, Pinckney H. 49
Warm Springs, NC 196, 249–50
Warren, Dennis P. 215
Warren's Ferry, VA 129
Washington, George 4, 12
Washington, J. L. 239–40
Washington, NC 72, 204, 212, 214
Washington County, NC 159, 234
Watauga County, NC 25, 29, 34
Watson, Wesley F. 162
Watts, A. W. 145
Watts, Dempsey 301
Watts, Hosea 79–80, 85
Watts, James B. 154
Watts, Meredith 301
Watts, William D. 145
Way, Alford A. 70
Way, Anderson M. 70
Webb, John 98
Webb, Lewis H. 290, 305
Webb, William Pressley 80, 91
Weldon, NC 102, 188, 190, 192, 212, 298
Wellesley, Arthur 3
Wells, David W. 84
Wells, James B. 226
West, Charles H. 156
West, Cyrus 139
West, Elisha B. 156
West, George Spencer 104
Western District of North Carolina 63
Westmoreland, Alexander 59
Wheeler, Joseph 275, 305
Wheeler, Woodbury 293
white badge 155
White, David N. 105
white feather 156
White, Mason M. 99
Whitford, John N. 223, 307
Whiting, William H. C. 161, 178–9, 211, 216–9, 230, 232, 292, 309; on court decision 178–9, 291, 293; on execution 214–5, 220, 232–3, 297, 301–2, 307; on mutiny 289
Whitley, Stephen B. 125
Whitley, William P. 212
Whitmire, H. D. 271
Whittington, B. B. 260
Whittle, Powhatan B. 88
Wiggins, Andrew C. 264
Wiggins, Moses L. 264
Wiggins, Thomas 264
Wilcox, Cadmus M. 20
Wilcox, John Alexander 20

Wilderness, battle of 58, 154
Wiles, Gillum B. 265
Wilkerson, James 104
Wilkerson, Robert D. 91, 104
Wilkes County, NC 30, 32, 40, 58, 66, 68, 87, 99, 110, 116–7, 129, 130, 136, 139, 175, 185–6, 270
Will of the Wisp 303
Willard, M. F. 62
Williams, Melvin E. 58
Williams, Offa G. 58
Williams, Oliver 152
Williams, S. B. 58
Williams, Washington A. 58
Williamsburg, VA 151
Williamston, NC 236
Willis, Martin V. 38
Willis, William M. 295
Wilmington, NC 172, 179, 206, 217–9, 232, 234, 291–2, 306; military prison 159, 161, 292, 300–1, 308

Wilson, Reuben Everett 228, 310
Wilson County, NC 127
Winchester, VA 144
Winder, John H. 24, 310
Winder Legion 126, 128, 281
Wineberger, Daniel 52
Wineberger, Noah 52
Winston Salem, NC 138
Winters Gap, TN 273, 285
Wolf, John A. 144–5
Wolf, Gaston B. 144–5
Wood, Isiah 223
Woodal, Duncan 61
Woodard, Bunyan 91
Woodard, George W. 91
Woodard, Isaac 281
Woodstock, VA 142, 147
Woody, Calvin 55
Workman, Berry 301
Workman, George W. 301
Workman, W. H. 301
World War I executions 12–3

World War II executions 13
Wrenn, John 100
Wright, Clement G. 211, 223
Wright, John L. 80, 81
Wyatt, Andrew 69–70
Wyatt, William W. 129

Yadkin County, NC 33, 44, 74, 76, 296, 309
Yancey County, NC 252, 264
Yankee 231, 234
Yarbrough, William H. 106
yallow dog 279
York District, SC 254
Young, H. E. 103
Young, Peter Wesley 55
Youngblood, Hiram 254
Younts, E. F. 255

Zimmerman, James C. 136, 138
Zollicoffer, TN 270

www.ingramcontent.com/pod-product-compliance
Lightning Source LLC
Chambersburg PA
CBHW081535300426
44116CB00015B/2643